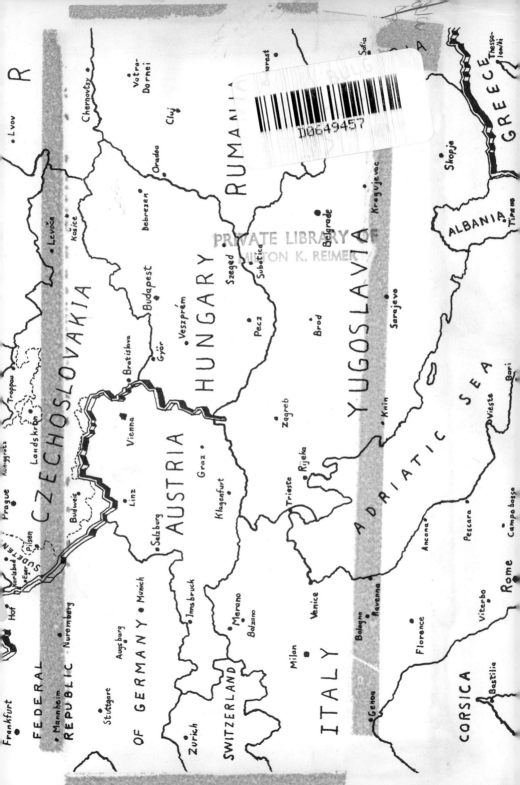

PRIVATE LIBRARY OF
MILTON K. REIMER

13649457

BEHIND THE IRON CURTAIN

From

THE MONUMENT OF PETER THE GREAT

His charger's reins Czar Peter has released;
He has been flying down the road, perchance,
And here the precipice checks his advance.
With hoofs aloft now stands the maddened beast,
Champing its bit unchecked, with slackened rein:
You judge that it will fall and be destroyed.
Thus it has galloped long, with tossing mane,
Like a cascade, leaping into the void,
That, fettered by the frost, hangs dizzily.
But soon will shine the sun of liberty,
And from the West a wind will warm this land—
Will that cascade of tyranny then stand?

—Adam Mickiewicz (1798-1855)
(Translator Unknown)

BEHIND THE IRON CURTAIN

The Soviet Satellite States—East European Nationalisms
and Education

By

JOSEPH S. ROUCEK, University of Bridgeport

KENNETH V. LOTTICH, Montana State University

With a special section devoted to
MAINLAND CHINA by DR. THEODORE H. E. CHEN,
Professor of Comparative Education and Asian Studies,
Director, Soviet-Asian Studies Center,
University of Southern California

THE CAXTON PRINTERS, LTD.
CALDWELL, IDAHO
1964

© 1964 BY
THE CAXTON PRINTERS, LTD.
CALDWELL, IDAHO

Library of Congress Catalog Card No. 64-15390

Printed and bound in the United States of America by
The CAXTON PRINTERS, Ltd.
Caldwell, Idaho
97580

TO
DR. ARTHUR W. SAMUELSON
and His Polity
AND
PROFESSOR TIBOR KEREKES
Freedom Fighter

Milton Keimer-Gift

⊔⊓⊔⊓⊔⊓⊔⊓⊔⊓⊔⊓⊔⊓⊔⊓⊔⊓⊔⊓⊔⊓⊔⊓⊔⊓⊔⊓⊔⊓

ACKNOWLEDGMENTS

THE AUTHORS wish to express their deep indebtedness to the following friends and institutions, whose support or early encouragement crystallized the decision to present, in book form, this analysis of the historical nationalisms and agencies of education within the satellite states of East Central Europe—ten countries, each of which played a significant role in World War II, yet currently (and unfortunately) are now situated beyond the Communist Iron Curtain.

Dr. Norman P. Auburn, President, University of Akron, Akron, Ohio

Dr. Peter Berger, Editor, *Der Donauraum*, Vienna

Dr. Helmut L. Demel, Secretary, International Institute of Arts and Letters, Geneva

Dr. Lev E. Dobriansky, Chairman, Ukrainian Congress Committee of America, New York

Dr. Alfred Domes, Director, Deutsche Stiftung fur europaische Friedensfragen, Bonn

Dr. Walter Dushnyck, Editor, *The Ukrainian Quarterly*, New York

Professor John Eppstein, Chairman, *The British Survey*, London

Dr. Uriah J. Fields, Director, American Christian Freedom Society, Los Angeles

Dr. Edmund Gaspar, Deputy Secretary General, Assembly of Captive European Nations, New York

Mr. Werner Guillamine, Director, Berliner Buro, Bund der Vertriebenen, Berlin

Dr. Santiago Gutierrez, Secretary General, Movement for American Federation, Bogatá

Dr. Walter Hahn, University of Utah

Professor G. C. Hallen, Editor, *Indian Journal of Social Research*, Baraut, India

Dr. Tibor Kerekes, former Director, Institute of Ethnic Studies, Georgetown University

Dr. Stephen D. Kertesz, Slavic Institute, Notre Dame University

Dr. Bruno Leoni, *Il Politico*, Institute for Political Science, Pavia University

Dean Clarence Manion, former head, Notre Dame University Law School

Dr. Kewal Motwani, Head, Department of Sociology, Annamalai University

Dr. D. P. Rastogi, Department of Political Science, University of Ghaziabad

Mr. Dinkar Sakrikar, Editor, *United Asia*, Bombay

Dr. Lew Shankowsky, Chairman, *Prologue Quarterly*, New York

Dr. Roman Smal-Stocki, Director, Slavic Institute, Marquette University

Dr. Ralph T. Templin, Editor, *Journal of Human Relations*, and Professor Anne O'Hare Williams, former editor, Wilberforce, Ohio

Dr. Juris Veidemanis, University of Wisconsin-Milwaukee

Professor Anton F. Wuschek and Mrs. Mary Campion Wuschek, Sudeten German Archive, Munich

Dr. Jorge Xifra, Director, *Instituto de Ciencias Sociales*, Barcelona

Dr. Waclaw Zajackowski, Director, Catholic Library Association, Lancaster, Penna.

To the editors of *Current History*, *Science* (American Association for the Advancement of Science), *The China Quarterly*, *The Social Studies*, and *Newsweek* special appreciation likewise is given.

The map of the East Central European satellite countries was drawn by Mr. Bryce E. Meyer, Montana State University.

J.S.R.

K.L.V.

TABLE OF CONTENTS

CHAPTER I

NATIONALISM AND EDUCATION

THE ASTONISHING SUCCESSES of the architects of the contemporary Soviet propaganda-educational system have produced definite international political repercussions. Their achievements—or rather what the Free World has considered their achievements—have quickly served to strengthen the initial suspicion that the masters of the Kremlin, in their practical insistence on education as a branch of politics, have cleverly refurbished an old principle; indeed that they have so strengthened thereby their whole educational front as to make it an integral part of the persistent drive of the USSR and a strong supporting pillar of Marxist strategy; thus to reap the aid of education in their realization of that final goal of all Soviet efforts—to make the rest of the world an adjunct of the universal Communist Empire.

Much has been written lately on the political changes behind the Iron Curtain. Yet little systematic information is as yet available on the educational and cultural revisionism demanded by Moscow. Nor has the still continuing impact of nationalism in the ten satellite countries of Central Eastern Europe received the attention it adequately deserves — the force of East European nationalisms being one of the last best hopes for the eventual return of this area, whose population comprises more than a tenth of a billion people, to the historic conventions of Western civilization.

Already in the USSR and in Soviet Russia's satellites the state-owned and state-administered school systems have become virtually parts of the Communist political system, their assigned role that of playing the key in-

strument in the "building of Socialism." In complete
agreement with the Soviet theory of education as proposed by Nicolai Lenin himself, "the school outside of
life, outside of politics, is falsehood and hypocrisy," basic
changes in line with Marxism-Leninism are now reshaping the entire educational fabric of ten captive countries;
new generations of fanatical Communist youth are now
being reared, whose standards, values, and very thought
processes stand 180 degrees from those of the Atlantic
community or Western man and his Free World.

In the Eastern satellites this educational revolution
(now complicated by the advent of the "polytechnicalization" concept) has had to take on the imperialistic
technique, since not one of the half score of states (with
the possible exception of Hungary, whose brief Bela
Kun episode following World War I can hardly be considered representative) currently under Soviet bondage
had any educational traditions which would favor the
Marxist blueprint. Unhappily the Western world has
long paid little attention to—and thus actually knows
very little of—the long educational heritage of these
formerly free and proud countries of Central Eastern
Europe; even less as to the methods whereby their pro-
Soviet masters have been able to manipulate this birth-
right in behalf of Red global strategies.

The present volume is an attempt to brush the cob-
webs from the eyes of those not yet acquainted with the
national histories and educational achievements of the
countries of East Central Europe. It represents a synthesis of whatever educational knowledge of these countries is available and the national history of their peoples.
Much information is based upon Professor Roucek's first-
hand experience as a student and teacher in Central
Europe and his repeated visits to these countries both
prior to and after World War II. The junior author is
a historian and professor of the history and philosophy
of education; he toured East Europe in the spring of
1963.

The treatment selected will show the national historical trends in the educational processes and thought of
the ten occupied countries—with a special chapter for

Yugoslavia, which has been identified as "a satellite in revolt." It will survey the transformation presently taking place under Russian direction. In this analysis, a definite effort has been made to clearly separate the Marxist theoretical claims from actual educational practices in the Soviet-controlled area. Here, perhaps, the Red regime in China offers some exception to Russian practice, and this will be subject to a special attention.

Numerous excellent studies are already available which deal with Soviet Russia's educational experiments and changes, and it is not the purpose of this book to repeat them; but the picture of what is evolving in education within the Soviet orbit in Central-Eastern-Balkan Europe is nebulous indeed and is nowhere treated in a systematic and synthesized manner. Yet there has long been a need for such an endeavor, since, once having analyzed the techniques and processes of Red pedagogy as it exists within the area of East Central Europe, one can the more easily expect to determine the means whereby Soviet commissars hope to capture and transform the culture and politics of other free nations. For — as remarked above — none of the captive nations in East Central Europe, prior to their conquest by Marxism, had anything remotely resembling sovietism, their educational roots springing from the soil of the ancient Latin culture, the Holy Roman Empire of the German Nation, or from Greek antecedents of Byzantium.

A systematic survey of events behind the Iron Curtain is likewise of definite value to all students of comparative education as well as of international relations, since an awareness of Russian successes (and an analysis of their failures) is of inestimable value in predicting the course of pedagogical and social change, as well as serving as an object lesson in the effectiveness of imperialistic impositions in the case of these (temporarily) subjugated nations.

If this process of producing pro-Russian and pro-Soviet adherents continues unchecked, the results are obvious: masses of people, like Pavlov's dogs, conditioned only to the Marxist-Leninist-Khrushchev framework, utterly ignorant of much of the world heritage and especially contemporary history and the cultural crosscurrents that exist beyond the Iron Curtain, present an ominous threat to the stability and perpetuation of the whole Free World; with the passing of a few years—or the rearing under the conditions described above of a new generation or so—the culmination of this trend will apparently fix the fate of the West as one not too full of hope. Thus both the Free World and the Soviet slave empire alike are vitally interested in the workings of the Great Design of the Politburo as it affects their lives and fortunes today; yet more sinister and significant are the implications of these efforts for the not too distant future should the Soviet schemers—either by strength or guile —be able to extend their peripheries further into Western Europe or elsewhere within the Western orbit, whether it may be within the Atlantic Community or those parts of the Free World now identified as neutralist or noncommitted.

For it is a painful but true fact that the USSR has gradually—and persistently—sought to obtain the leadership of the world's latecomers to the national and industrial scene. The recent eclipse of colonialism, let it be said immediately, aided, encouraged, and abetted by the West, not Red Russia or Red China, has proved to be an opportunity of incalculable advantage to the Marxist Empire. Indeed—and unfortunately—in many cases untutored and naïve members of the new national statehood have apparently fallen like ripe plums square into the lap of Soviet imperialism. That such a lamentable circumstance has been allowed to develop may be laid directly at the door of the West—for its failure to produce and maintain an aggressive (yet democratic) political leadership in the years during and subsequent to the second World War. With a realistic appraisal of this unprecedented opportunity for Marxist advance, Stalin and his successors were only too eager to move into this entirely unparalleled power vacuum. Specifically true in Eastern Europe, this clear tendency toward Soviet imperialistic expansion is hardly to be confined there; Asia, Africa, and Latin America, likewise offered—and are still presenting—some of the most fertile fields for the advancing Communist ideology spurred on indeed by Marxist ideological and technical "success" all the way from Sputnik in 1957 through Gagarin and Titov on April 12 and August 6-7, 1961. That the recent space achievements of the United States of America will counteract and possibly reverse this swing to the East may be devoutly hoped for; on the other hand, the arising of this Favonian drift (West Wind) may be just a trifle late, auspicious though the recovery of the initiative for the Free World may appear to be.

Even a review of statistics sounds a somber note. Within the Russian Motherland live two hundred million people, including that parcel of humanity whose birthrate is among the highest on earth; for without further territorial expansion (a pious expectation) the aims and tactics of Communism must govern the lives of a constantly growing proportion of mankind. Moreover, and terrible to relate, this prediction does not, of course, include the astronomic totals of mainland Red China—an even greater threat to the world's security.

The population of the East European captive nations is approximately one hundred million — equivalent to the combined total of France and West Germany—enough easily to play a significant role in the coexistential balance between the East and West. Notwithstanding this, even more important is the geopolitical significance of Eastern Europe—one of the most strategically situated regions of the world. Furthermore the direct importance of East Central Europe to the Soviet Empire has been consistently augmented during the past decade, due particularly to the operation of the Marxist economic league —the *Komekon*—as it has been developed by the Kremlin's trade planners into a most necessary adjunct to the Motherland. Indeed while considerations of the quality and quantity of production in the East European states have frequently been raised, Moscow now needs the internal and external trade of the satellites to balance her own.

Always to be remembered is the fact that Central Eastern Europe—eternally a battleground, it seems—

lost more than twice as many lives and suffered more than twice as much damage as Western Europe did during the course of World War II; yet, as a region, the area passed—under Soviet organization and hence no Marshall Plan aid—in the postwar years, pre-1939 figures even before this plateau was achieved in Western Europe. While the present population of Western Europe is indeed rising (and frequently beyond that region's previous local subsistence level), that of East Central Europe is skyrocketing—with a leveling off nowhere in sight. The meaning of this is quite clear: manpower and urgency, to be mobilized against the Western world at whatever time the signal for finalizing the argument is decreed from Moscow. East Europe is a treasure-trove of natural resources—this area has only scraped the surface of its true potential. There is no current limit here for industrial expansion; Moscow directs the whole enormous complex which stretches from the Elbe-Werra, two-thirds of the distance across the European continent, all the way to the eastern littoral of the Pacific Ocean. Of course, without the human cooperation of Central Eastern Europe *Komekon* goals cannot be achieved; yet in this case possession is considerably more than the usual nine points of law and here again the role of education is utilized to soften resistance; moreover, time favors the East.

The recent rift between the East European satellite Albania and the Soviet Union and Albania's adherence to the Chinese sector of the Sino-Soviet Axis prompts the inclusion of an additional chapter dealing with mainland China and its propaganda education system. As an example of the extremes to which Marxists have gone in their drive to indoctrinate politically almost one-half of the world's population, plus the threat to the Free World through Red China's undeclared war against India and the blustering attitude of Mao Tse-tung toward the West in general, this section becomes a virtual necessity if one is to be able to apprehend correctly the greater danger now facing the Western democracies. Mao's plans for the "re-education" of 660,000,000 Chinese offer a sobering shock to those who may have, with typical complacency, regarded the fortunes of the East European sector of the Communist Empire as insignificant.

Before it is already too late, Western man must learn not only how to "hold the line" (containment) but also how to advance it in behalf of his own cause—individualism, democracy, and representative government. In order to be able to achieve this, he must become intimately acquainted with the standard Soviet ideological technique—educational as well as economic and political, the pedagogical being, in the long run, perhaps that of the greater significance.

In addition to this (and here is his greatest weakness), he must learn and use the great traditions of the ten satellite countries—those unfortunate victims of Communism whom, at this very moment, the Soviet viceroys are twisting to the service of their own ends. Western appeal should come through its knowledge of the indigenous forces and strong underlying national urges of these captive peoples; only in this way can they be prepared to assist naturally in their own necessary liberation; furthermore, this must be accomplished soon indeed—if ever the currently successful drive of the USSR toward world economic supremacy and a full political hegemony is to be reversed.

CHAPTER II

THE COMMUNIST IDEOLOGY

Communism as a Universal Movement

COMMUNISM[1] HAS, from its very inception, catholicity (universality); that has been one of the basic dogmas driving the Communist machinery to its conquest of the world. Without delving into the theories of Marxism and Leninism, let us note that the charter of the Third (Communist) International, shaped by its first Congress in March, 1919, stated that: "The Communist International has for its purpose the struggle by all available means, including armed force, for the overthrow of the international *bourgeoisie* and the creation of an international Soviet republic as a transition stage to the complete abolition of the state." The second Congress of the International elaborated in 1920 upon the above statement by adding that: "The international proletariat will not lay down its sword until Soviet Russia has become a link in the federation of the Soviet republics of the world."

The Third International dissolved itself in May, 1943, mainly to facilitate the flow of Lend-Lease (eleven billion dollars). But the dissolution act contained nothing to justify the almost unanimous opinion of many Western statesmen, journalists, and the so-called "experts on the USSR," that the Kremlin had given up its revolutionary eccentricities and had returned to the fold of "normalcy." World revolution was not, and could not

---

[1] The basis for this chapter originates in a paper published by Joseph S. Roucek and Kenneth V. Lottich, "Cracks in the Communist Ideology," in *Il Politico* (Pavia, Italy), December, 1961, and is used through the permission of the editors.

be, repudiated by Marxism-Leninism; and hence one of
its expressions was the Cominform creation in 1947.
The initial stage in the onward march of Soviet Communism was ushered in by the Soviet-German pact of
1939, which unleashed World War II. This allowed the
Red forces to invade eastern Poland, Latvia, Estonia,
and Lithuania. Poland was partitioned and the Soviet
Union annexed the eastern provinces, which for centuries had been a bone of contention between Russia
and Poland. Under the Soviet pressure, governments
subservient to Moscow were soon founded in the Baltic
States and obediently voted themselves into the USSR.
In June, 1940, the Kremlin turned the heat on Romania;
and, again partly by virtue of the Soviet-German agreement and partly by extending its terms, annexed Bessarabia and northern Bukovina.

At the end of World War II, the Soviet Union, by agreement with the leaders of the Western powers, not only
retained its 1939-40 gains but added to them the Ukrainian districts of Czechoslovakia (Carpathian Ruthenia),
East Prussia (with Königsberg), the southern portion
of Sakhalin, and the Kurile Islands. The fact that these
territories (with the exception of Bukovina, the Ukrainian districts of Czechoslovakia, and East Prussia) were
once parts of the Russian Empire, tended to create the
impression that Soviet expansion was but the revival of
Russian imperialism of the prerevolutionary vintage.

The Soviet invasion of Central-Eastern-Balkan Europe
unfolded against the background of the collapse of Hitler's
empire and of acute divergencies between British and
American policies, Churchill showing most of the time
a far greater awareness of the danger of Soviet expansion
than did President Roosevelt. In January, 1944, the Red
Army crossed into Polish, and in April, into Romanian
territory. A Soviet-Romanian Armistice of September
12, 1944, sanctioned Russia's "temporary" occupation
of that country. Three days later (September 15, following a Soviet-Bulgarian war that lasted twenty-four
hours) Soviet tanks rolled into Sofia. On September 6,
the Red Army entered Yugoslavia, and, on September
23, Hungary. By the end of April, 1945, the Soviet

armies had reached the outskirts of Berlin and on May 9 marched into Prague. (It was by agreement with the Allied Command that the Russians occupied both Prague and Berlin.)

The basic factor in establishing Soviet domination over Central-Eastern-Balkan Europe was military occupation. Here the process of implanting "People's Democracies" followed broadly the same pattern. A small core of local Communists trained in Moscow formed the nucleus of the new governments. Under the shadow of the Russian bayonets the non-Communist elements were speedily disposed of, and the elaborate arrangements in the agreements of Teheran, Yalta, and Potsdam collapsed. Between 1945 and 1948, the once sovereign nations of Central-Eastern-Balkan Europe were forced into the mold of Soviet Communism.[2]

We must deal with the backgrounds and independent experiments of education in these "satellite" countries, as well as with their educational changes under Soviet impact. We should remember that the main object of Soviet policies in these countries is the integration of the political, social, economic, and cultural activities with those of the USSR—especially Russia. Strict adherence to the Moscow-determined party line has become the prerequisite for remaining in the good graces of the Kremlin.

The objectives and methods of Soviet expansion are basically different from those of the imperial government of the Czars. Czarist imperialism, harsh as it was at times, did not involve the wholesale destruction of the social and economic institutions in the annexed ter-

---

[2] There have been numerous works covering this period; a good summary is: E. Day Carman, *Soviet Imperialism* (Washington, D.C.: Public Affairs Press, 1950). For a general survey of the main tendencies affecting Central-Eastern-Balkan Europe under the pro-Soviet regimes, see: Joseph S. Roucek (ed.), "Moscow's European Satellites," *The Annals of the American Academy of Political and Social Science*, CCLXXI (September, 1950); Roucek, "Central-Eastern Europe," chap. VIII, pp. 138-55, in the National Council for the Social Studies, *Twenty-Fifth Yearbook*; "Approaches to an Understanding of World Affairs," edited by Howard R. Anderson (Washington, D.C., 1954). Historical articles from Russia and satellites' language journals are listed in the monthly issues of the Library of Congress publications, *East European Accessions List* and *Monthly List of Russian Accessions*.

ritories.[3] But Soviet expansion is but a step in the grand strategy of Communism aimed at the destruction of the capitalistic system and the establishment of world Communism. This means, for the countries we have dealt with here, the extermination of their traditional institutions, beliefs, customs, and indeed the replacement of their entire way of life through the superimposition of an alien ideology.

Yet this imperialistic march has not been without difficulties for the masters of the Kremlin. There has been resistance, both token and real (as we have noted), not only among the satellites but among the 175 odd differing nationalities which currently live under Soviet rule—to say nothing of the frictions developed from religious groups and other discontented elements. Glaringly, the seeds of national feeling remain to plague the Soviets within their own borders as well as those of the satrapies.[4]

That there are divergencies within the Soviet Empire (with the exception of Albania and mainland China) is a myth. This item of belief is foisted on the unsuspecting by the so-called "autonomy" of Soviet minorities and by the even more crass "sovereign independence" of the satellite states.[5] Yet the Bolsheviks have always been

---

[3] Michael T. Florinsky, "Soviet Expansion," *Current History*, XXVI, 154 (June, 1954), pp. 321-26; Kenneth V. Lottich, "Plight of the Baltic States," *Sudeten Bulletin*, IX, No. 2 (February, 1961), 28-36.

[4] The massive hostility of the Ukraine to Soviet rule revealed itself openly during World War II, when Ukrainians welcomed their Nazi invaders; furthermore, Ukrainians formed the overwhelming majority of General Vlasov's army composed of Soviet defectors. Caucasian and Trans-Caucasian discontent with—and resistance to—Moscow's rule are similarly attested to by well-known facts. See Olaf Caroe, *The Soviet Empire: The Turks of Central Asia and Stalinism* (New York: St. Martin's Press, 1953); Firuz Kazemzadeh, *The Struggle for Transcaucasia* (1917-1921) (New York: The Philosophical Library, 1951); John S. Reshetar, Jr., *The Ukrainian Revolution* (Princeton University Press, 1952); Kenneth V. Lottich, "Soviet Russia's First Victim," *Sudeten Bulletin*, VIII, No. 10 (October, 1960), 243-49.

[5] Corliss Lamont, *Soviet Civilization* (New York: Philosophical Library, 1955), in a bitterly criticized work, supports the Soviet minorities' policies and claims that "The advanced Soviet theory and practice of friendly race relations is important for international ethics and peace . . . the Soviet Union, in establishing full ethnic

centralistic by conviction, and today native officials have only the most limited and chimerical scope for independent action within the overall Soviet framework. No diversity of spiritual or educational values—among them the deeper manifestations of inner life—is tolerated by Soviet Russia. Everywhere the languages of the peoples of the Soviet Union and of the rimland countries behind the Iron Curtain are compelled to sing exclusively the praises of Lenin and Marx (soon perhaps those of Nikita S. Khrushchev), not only in their own vernaculars but also in Russian. At the same time Great Russians have been in the process of moving into the strategetically important parts of the Empire and occupying the key positions.

Let us now consider the imperialistic efforts through pedagogy that aim to solidify, educationally, the Red Empire under the aegis of Mother Russia.

The Machinery of Domination

Although, in the window dressing of face-saving international relations the satellite countries are treated as "independent" states, actually these satrapies located on the rimland of Western Community states are even less than satellites: they are but colonial outposts of the Central-Eastern-Balkan section of the Soviet Empire. Without at this time—to avoid duplication—going into specific details of this imperial framework, for our purpose it is only necessary to notice that in all of these states the position of the Communist parties is such that it is impossible to take a decision in opposition to their policies; in fact, a representative of the secret branch of the Department of the Interior was put into power, in every Ministry, as Deputy Minister; this secret agency later became the independent Ministry of State Security — obviously, the most consequential Ministry of all. These Deputy Ministers maintain direct contact with the personnel branch of the Communist party—that is,

democracy among its multitude of minorities, has taken genuine leadership and made a profound contribution of global significance" (chap. III, "Soviet Ethnic Democracy," p. 120).

with the Cadre Commission; each supports a number of secret observers and informers in his own Ministry, and is responsible only to the General Secretariat of the Party and to the Ministry of State Security. All Ministries in the ten satellite states are constructed on these same lines, with relationships as suggested.[6]

This Red network is buttressed by a system whereby each Communist party of a satellite has its representative in Moscow—usually unknown to the official diplomatic representative of that country and identifiable only by the Ministry for State Security. To cement the system further, the Communist party of the Soviet Union has its representatives in the capitals of the satellite states; the party representative makes the final decision in all matters. Should the Kremlin desire a satellite government to take certain steps, the Politburo (Moscow) —or its appropriate agency—instructs their man in the Secretariat of the Communist party in the Soviet Union in charge of relations with Eastern bloc countries to follow the policies decided upon; he then instructs the representative, the General Secretariat of the Party; the official diplomatic representatives are informed at the last stage of the proceedings, just before it is necessary to inform the public.

This system implements, therefore, a most efficient method of insuring the absolute domination of the satellite countries, as the policies and details are initiated and controlled by the organization of party representatives in the Soviet Union and in satellite countries, which in turn control all respective state machinery. Such an arrangement also explains the operation of the educational and cultural machinery of the satellite states, which has been operating, especially since 1948, more and more on behalf of the Russian-Soviet cause.

The Soviet regime is a convenient instrument for broadening Russian Church imperialism, bringing under its sway the entire Orthodox Church throughout Russia and its satellite countries, destroying Catholicism of the Eastern Rite in western- and Carpatho-Ukraine and Ro-

---

[6] Bedrich Bruegel, "Methods of Soviet Domination in Satellite States," *International Affairs*, XXVII, No. 1 (January, 1951), 32-44.

mania, and finally making the Russian Church supreme in the entire Orthodox world, be it within or outside of the Russian sphere of influence. Realizing the moral power of Catholicism, Moscow fears that if the Russian Empire should collapse, thereby depriving the Moscow Patriarch of a defender, the Catholic Church would quickly extend its sway over the formerly Russian-dominated lands, especially those which traditionally have gravitated toward the West: the Ukraine, White Ruthenia. This is the basic reason underlying the destruction of the Ukrainian Catholic Church of the Eastern Rite in western- and Carpatho-Ukraine and the Ukrainian Autocephalous Orthodox Church in eastern Ukraine, also the Autocephalous Church in Romania and the Balkans.

The Free World forces need to continue extending help to the non-Orthodox forces in Russia and elsewhere. In this respect, it must be stressed, too, that the support of such religious forces is also the support of nationalism, since these two elements are frequently identical —Catholicism with Poland's history, John Hus's and Comenius' Protestantism with Czech history.

All in all, the cleavage between the men in the Kremlin and the vast numbers of the Soviet and satellite citizens is clear and definite. The Russian and satellite people, in spite of the well-organized terror and the planned educational "reconditioning" system, are the allies of the Free World. The problem is how to make them conscious of that fact. And this has to be done soon, since no individual, no group can resist indefinitely the persistent social control devices of the Soviet society. On our part, the starting point is the need to get better acquainted with the history of each country and how, today, Russia is twisting its satellites to its long-range plans.

Hardly anything is said in the Senate reports about the usefulness of recent political refugees from behind the Iron Curtain. Political immigration of World War II played a prominent role in these countries. Men like Mikolajczyk of Poland, Benes and Jan Masaryk of Czechoslovakia, and many others, returned to their native countries and took important, though often tragic, roles. Those who preferred political emigration retained their influence mostly among their compatriots, and continued to exercise a good deal of influence on public opinion of those who were of Central Eastern European background both in the United States and Latin America, as well as in Europe (mainly France and Great Britain).

Since 1948, following Communist manipulations and *coup d'état*, another wave of political *émigrés* has come here from Central Eastern Europe, statesmen, politicians, writers, professors, intellectuals. This group, as a whole, represents an important factor, both politically and culturally. Education and culture are Communist-controlled behind the Iron Curtain and can develop only within the limits permitted by the Party.   There is thus no variety, no chance for opposition or difference. Abroad, however, on the free soil of America, both politics and culture of those countries develop in liberty of choice. Political emigration becomes a real miniature of the political life of those countries. At the same time, while the cultural life of the satellite countries is being forcibly Russianized, these "Titoists" have been trying to preserve, symbolically at least, the pre-Sovietized cultures of their countries; the work of the Mid-European Studies Center of the National Committee for a Free Europe, the accomplishments of the Voice of America, have been especially commended in this connection.

Further than this, we need stress here only the assistance which must be extended to the religious forces still existing in the Soviet slave empire—especially the Roman Catholic bodies. The Marxists, of course—openly anti-Christian in theory and practice and militantly atheistic —are opposed to any form of religion whatsoever (although this aversion does not extend to their own peculiar ideology or to religious fronts established for the purpose of the subversion of the recognized religious agencies in order that Communism may be inculcated through these nominally respectable means). The Kremlin despises the dogma of the Moscow Patriarch, regardless of the fact that their own ideology is more than willing to accept the implications of the "Third Rome." Nonetheless, pragmatically, this same Patriarch has recently given his frequent approval to Marxist practices and goals, and this can, perhaps, be most realistically attributed to the subtlety of the Communist subversion, which has already reached into the upper echelons of the Orthodox hierarchy.

The United States Senate reports, especially those sections covering youth, the intelligentsia, the mislabeled "national minorities," the army and other military forces, women, farmers, industrial workers, management, the Party, and conscript or slave labor are highly informative and exceptionally useful—many citations, indeed, are to be found in evidence here and there throughout this book. The greatest credit for the editing and organization of these Senate reports—to say nothing of the source of impetus behind their production—is due Professor Tibor Kerekes, Executive Director of the Institute of Ethnic Studies, Georgetown University, Washington, D.C. A Hungarian by birth with experience on many educational levels both in Europe and America, Dr. Kerekes produced a monument to the cause of the Communist-dominated countries of East Europe.

What Hopes for the West?

In 1951, at the request of Senator Alexander Wiley, the Legislative Reference Service of the Library of Congress prepared a study of conditions in the Soviet Union that were leading the Russian people to oppose more and more strongly Communist oppression. That study, *Tensions Within the Soviet Union,* was published as a Senate document (1951). Given widespread distribution both in the United States and abroad, it was translated into several languages and has been used frequently to document our understanding of events in the Soviet Union. On April 10, 1953, the Committee on Foreign Relations of the U.S. Senate voted to publish studies probing similar areas of tension in the satellite countries —Bulgaria, Albania, Eastern Germany, Romania, Czechoslovakia, and Hungary—as noted above.

These are valuable, since outside the Iron Curtain there

are relatively few publications showing the tactics of the
Communists in the several Communist-controlled areas.
As a result, there has been a tendency to lump all Communist governments into a single category, on the theory
that their tactics are the same everywhere. This is a
vastly erroneous assumption, since Communists are adept
at suiting their deeds to the needs of a particular country. For that reason, we have treated, in more detail,
the differences in the cultural background of each satellite country and noticed the differences, as well as the
similarities in the ways and means used by the pro-
satellite rulers to accomplish the sovietization process.

Yet, the informed observer of the workings of the
Communist system cannot avoid being wary of the
Senatorial reports. Despite their merits, these Senate
documents contain certain illusions which, if not pointed
out, can influence unfavorable short perspective, which
can lead to a variety of unfortunate consequences of
misjudgment and miscalculation in America's political,
psychological, and possibly military campaigns against
the multiform aggressions of Soviet Russian imperialism.[7]

Above all, we must guard ourselves against the generally prevailing tone of optimism that characterized these
surveys. There are tensions in Soviet Russia's empire;
but there are tensions in every country in the world.
Of importance to us must be, however, only those tensions which would directly weaken the Communist hold
on the governmental machinery of Soviet Russia and
the satellites, and those tensions which might eventually lead to the liberation of Central-Eastern-Balkan
Europe from the Soviet yoke.

In this respect, some American reports seem relatively
uninterested in one of the most significant sources of
unrest and disorders in the Soviet Empire—namely, the
so-called "national minorities," which as a matter of
fact, have come to form the majority in the population
complex of that area since World War II. From the
point of view of the American people, here is a most

---

[7] Lev. E. Dobriansky, "Tensions Within the Soviet Union,"
Ukrainian Quarterly, VII, 3 (Summer, 1951), pp. 259-66, is a valuable critical evaluation of the initial report on Russia.

explosive and useful concept of immense value to the American cause—as well as to the nations concerned. On the idealistic plane, Wilson's "self-determination" principle and Roosevelt's expression of the respect of the right of all peoples to self-realization (the Atlantic Charter of August, 1941) are also extremely realistic policies, denoting the realization that the "united" blocs of states under a hostile power can be extremely dangerous to our welfare; contrariwise, the world composed of free, independent states is a more safe place for the United States—and hence the United States is actually defending itself when creating the world of freedom-seeking nations which, as in the more recent case of the so-called satellite countries—Poland, Hungary, Czechoslovakia, Romania, Albania, and Bulgaria —has been ruthlessly seduced and enslaved by Soviet Russia's imperialism.

In this respect, we must remember the thesis of Sir Halford J. Mackinder is more than just a hypothesis:

> Who rules East Europe commands the Heartland;
> Who rules the Heartland commands the World Island;
> Who rules the World Island commands the World.[8]

Between 1945 and 1948, the Soviet Union extended its direct and masked frontiers into Central-Eastern-Balkan Europe; adding to this conquest the Asiatic expansion, we can only shudder when realizing that Soviet Russia now commands more than the "Heartland."

But Soviet Russia has been unable to rule the world island and command the world. In this respect, the course of unforeseen historical events has saved the United States. Although Soviet Russia controls most of the European-Asian continent, yet its power has ebbed from its fullest tide and it hesitates to launch an all-out bid for power. The answer to the malfunctioning of traditional axioms of geopolitics lies in the rise of a new kind of power created out of man's conquest of the air. No longer can navies and merchant marines rule the waves without the permission of land-based air power.

---

[8] Sir Halford J. Mackinder, *Democratic Ideals and Reality* (New York: Holt, Rinehart and Winston, Inc., 1942), p. 150.

No longer can the possessor of the largest land army count his Heartland inviolable. Air power has entered the equation. The B-47 or the B-36, armed with the atomic bomb, can wreck a substantial portion of the over-strained Soviet industrial system. The modern bomber's speed and its range have reduced to an uncomfortable minimum the protection always previously afforded by the vast reaches of Russian land mass. The Soviet leaders are well aware that the distance between New York and Moscow over the Great Circle route is only 4,600 miles and that the distance between any major city in the United States and any in the Soviet Union scarcely exceeds 6,000 miles. Since the range of missiles has become almost limitless, here is a weapon which has become a major factor in preventing the Politburo from using Eurasia as the jumping-off base for its world conquest. For the first time in history, the "Heartland" can be directly and devastatingly attacked. Hence, geo-politically speaking, Soviet Russia has been trying to conquer the "rimlands" by indirect tactics, either by guerrilla warfare or by fifth-column strategies, while strengthening its stronghold on the satellites by all the modern weapons of education and propaganda.[9]

Underground Operations

The first task of American foreign policy planners is obvious—to prevent the disruption of the "rimlands" and to promote all the forces operating among the satellites against the Russian rule. The knowledge of techniques used educationally—in the widest possible sense—is one of the most important elements involved.

The second outstanding weakness of the Committee on Foreign Relations reports springs logically from the first in that, although they are intended to present the broadest possible information as foundational ground-work for intelligent psychological warfare, they are gravely deficient in their coverage of the known under-ground operations and other forms of resistance found

---

[9] Joseph S. Roucek, "Geopolitics and Air Power," U.S. Air Force, *Air University Quarterly Review*, V, 3 (Fall, 1952), pp. 52-73.

in the spacious non-Russian areas of the Soviet Union, and having the nationalistic beliefs as their dynamos. Here we must recognize that among more than a hundred million non-Russians in the Soviet Empire, whose profound hatred of traditional Russian imperialism has been proverbial, we enjoy actual, dependable, and certain allies, not simply potential ones which may never be actualized.[10] It can be safely said that none of the satellites enjoy being subservient members of the Soviet house and that the nationalistic memories of each of the formerly free nations burn in the hearts of old generations.[11]

It has been becoming increasingly evident that scores of active American anti-Communists, both official and nonofficial, have been displaying a keen and lively interest in subversive underground action as a major and crucial weapon for the eventual defeat of Soviet Russian imperialism. Undoubtedly one of the most salutary features is a sincere desire to inspire and encourage this mode of operation behind the Iron Curtain among all the peoples enslaved by the Soviet regime. This hope rightly extends not only to the numerous non-Russian peoples who have been subjugated by the imperialistic yoke of the Kremlin, and whose courageous resistance

---

[10] Joseph Tenenbaum, *Underground, The Story of a People* (New York: Philosophical Library, 1952), gives a vivid account of the amazing underground existence of Polish Jewry during World War II; Nicholas D. Czubatyj, "The Ukrainian Underground," *Ukrainian Quarterly*, II, 2 (Winter, 1946), pp. 154-66; United Committee of the Ukrainian-American Organizations of New York, *The Ukrainian Insurgent Army in Fight for Freedom* (New York, 1954), describes the desperate character of the Ukrainian struggle for liberty during and after World War II; D. Karov, *The Partisan Movement in the USSR* (Munich: Institute for the Study of the History and Culture of the USSR, 1954), deals with the work of the Soviet Central of Diversion, which aimed to organize and control the partisan movement in World War II. For the broader aspects of the underground techniques, see: William J. Donovan and Joseph S. Roucek, *Secret Movements, Espionage and Treachery*, chap. 17, pp. 308-30, T. V. Kalijarvi, *Modern World Politics* (New York: Thomas Y. Crowell, 1953), Jan Karski, *The Story of a Secret State* (Boston: Houghton Mifflin Company, 1944).

[11] For the nationalistic ideologies of the satellite states, see: Joseph S. Roucek (ed.), "A Challenge to Peacemakers," *The Annals of the American Academy of Political and Social Science*, CCXXXII (March, 1944).

to this terrorist force is becoming widely appreciated, but also to the oppressed Russian masses. Guerrilla operations have been taking on increasing importance for the United States in the nuclear-warfare era—particularly with reference to possible perimeter conflicts.

There has been much discussion in American military circles about the desirability of incorporating basic doctrines and practices of guerrilla fighting into all army training programs.[12]

The Communist military campaigns of the past few years are in part responsible for the widespread new interest in guerrilla tactics. During the civil war in China, the Korean fighting, and more recently in Indochina, the Reds demonstrated that the cumulative effect of many guerrilla raids directed and coordinated from the top of a command chain can often be devastating —even against forces having air superiority and motorized transport. During World War II, the Soviet Union successfully used guerrillas to harass German panzers on the Eastern front. Generalissimo Chiang Kai-shek's Nationalists—who saw their American-trained motorized units ambushed by the Communists in Manchuria several years ago—recently have been giving the Communists considerable trouble with guerrilla raids of their own from the mountains of Yunnan and Kwangsi and the offshore islands. Atomic war would put the highest premium on dispersal and concealment, as well as on the ability to make accurate ground reconnaissance and rapid offensive strikes. It is likely that under such circumstances guerrilla operations would really come into their own. Army tactical experts presently are study-

---

[12] Wilhelm Hoettl, *The Secret Front* (New York: Praeger, 1954), covers the Nazi security service, by an official of the Sicherheitsdienst, who was responsible for central and southeastern Europe; Irwin R. Blacker (ed.), *Irregulars, Partisans, Guerrillas* (New York: Simon & Schuster, 1954), has chapters on all regions of the globe; Ronald Seth, *Spies at Work* (New York: Philosophical Library, 1955), a history of espionage; C. Aubrey Dixon and Otto Hoibrunn, *Communist Guerrilla Warfare* (New York: F. A. Praeger, 1954), analyzes guerrilla warfare, as developed by Mao Tse-tung and perfected by Stalin during the Nazi campaign. See also, "GI Trains for Guerrilla Warfare," *Life* (October 27, 1961), 51, No. 17, 44-52.

ing ways of coordinating the activities of guerrilla bands, whenever necessary, with those of airborne and armored units in both offensive and defensive operations. There are many thousands of Iron Curtain refugees available and willing to form such bands in an emergency.

Communist successes with guerrillas appear to cause many Americans to forget that their own nation has a long and distinguished tradition in the same field. General Francis Marion, the "Swamp Fox" of the American Revolution, for example, won lasting fame by cutting British lines of communication and ambushing patrols and reconnaissance parties. Colonel Davy Crockett and other Indian fighters of the early 1800's were able to best a wily adversary at his own game. The Confederate Ranger leader, Colonel John S. Mosby, rode through the Union lines with a few picked men in 1863 to bag Major General Edwin H. Stoughton and his staff in their beds at Fairfax Courthouse, Virginia. In a later raid, he just missed capturing General Ulysses S. Grant on his way to assume command of the Northern armies.

American and Filipino guerrillas were responsible for reviving the art against the Japanese. Army chiefs now feel that the partisans of a Free World could bring it to a high degree of perfection in any future military contest. While it is true that one arm of the United States Central Intelligence Agency is devoted to subterranean and even surreptitious revolutionary activities, apparently its development in no way matches that of the equivalent agency of the USSR. Recent events (1961) in Cuba and Laos indicate certain weaknesses in the American system—that is, if it is to be used in direct counterrevolutionary action against the Soviet or in the interests of the Soviet-controlled or dominated satellites.

An Irony of History

There is yet another aspect of the Communist drive for world supremacy which has only recently reached fruition, although—strange to say—motif and method were advanced in the primeval days of the Soviet bid for and seizure of political power. Over forty years ago, an obscure Kazanite, Mir Sayid Sultan Oglu (called in Russian, Sultan Galiev), conceived and outlined the strategy for a "colonial international"—an idea vastly unpopular in 1919, when it first originated. Beginning as a member of the Social Revolutionaries, Sultan Galiev later became a Menshevik, then, in 1917, a Bolshevik. Named as editor of *Zhizn Natsionalnostei*, the organ of the Commissariat of Nationalities, Galiev possessed an unparalleled opportunity for the dissemination of his views. Fortunately for the Western world, his ideas then proved unacceptable to the Marxist-Leninists; soon Galiev was being charged with "nationalist deviations"; incarcerated for a time, he appears to have been purged during the hecatomb of the thirties directed by Joseph V. Stalin.[13]

The irony of Galiev's disgrace and death may be added to the other errors of Stalin. Yet, with the advent of World War II, the Georgian soon pursued a rather similar policy. On the other hand, however, the Galiev approach was not without a certain danger to the vested interests in Russian Communism. And Mao Tse-tung, during postwar years was to adopt just such techniques, much to the discomfiture of Stalin's successor Nikita S. Khrushchev (although this is not to say that Khrushchev was above using them himself when ways could be found to protect the Russian national interest).

How close to political realities political unknown Sultan Galiev had come is revealed by Walter Z. La queur in a summation[14] of the Kazanite's basic thesis.

(1) Classical Marxists are making a mistake by concentrating their attention and hopes on the industrially developed West. The backward countries of the East provide a far more fertile territory for Communism;

(2) The backward nations of the East are more truly

---

[13] Walter Z. La queur, *The Soviet Union and the Middle East* (New York: Frederick A. Praeger, Inc., 1959), p. 308. (No. 81 in the series of Praeger Publications in Russian History and World Communism). See also the Bibliography on Sultan Galiev as listed on pp. 314-15.

[14] *Ibid.*, pp. 308-9.

progressive than the working class in the West; they are the real proletarian nations. It is extremely doubtful whether any community of interest exists between the Eastern countries and the Western working class;

(3) The establishment of a dictatorship of the proletariat in the West would not be tantamount to world revolution; it would only mean the perpetuation of Western rule over the rest of the world; true change could only be brought about by a dictatorship of the colonial peoples over the metropolitan nations;

(4) Since all classes in the Eastern countries have been subjected to Western rule and exploitation, there is no room for a class struggle. Communist policy should be based on an alliance between all classes, including the upper and middle classes;

(5) A new International of colonial peoples should be created. It should be independent of the Comintern, though Russia should participate in it. The leading roles in this new International must be taken by the ex-colonial peoples themselves; above all by Moslem representatives.

The seriousness of such an ideological program to the non-Communist world is readily apparent.[15] Nevertheless, as far as Moscow goes, complete subscription to Sultan Galiev's theses would wreck the Russian ship, although portions of the program might be (and actually are now) pursued with profit. In other words, while Galiev offered a recipe for the possible triumph of world Communism, adherence to his program might well prevent the present masters of the Kremlin from executing the testament of Peter the Great—the task which contemporary Bolshevism has set as its goal.

Summary: Cracks in the Communist Ideology

Communism's basic dogma springs from its inherent conception of universality; the self-revealing charter of the First Congress in March, 1919, as well as numerous other pronouncements and manifestos confirms the

---

[15] See also Joseph S. Roucek, "Ideology as an Aspect of the Sociology of Knowledge," *Sociologia* (São Paulo), XXII, No. 4 (December, 1960), 385-96.

Marxist goal as a drive to federate the Soviet republics
of the world. The enormous expansion of the Red Empire following World War II suggests that the Kremlin
wishes only to implement the dreams of Czarist Russia;
this observation is faulty in two respects: (1) the methods
of control of minority groups are vastly dissimilar; and
(2) the stated goal of Marxism-Leninism as practiced
in the USSR is fomenting world revolution and the creation of the Communist world state.

The Communist drive, especially in East Central
Europe and the Balkans, has been extremely well conceived—if not completely successful; all the agencies
of social and political control have been bent to the aim
of creating a Marxist society—Marxism, as interpreted
by Moscow, that is. Because of this apparent victory
the Western world has tended to discount the possibilities of reversing the Red wave which currently threatens
the whole of Western Europe. The internal minorities
and subjugated peoples must be considered as allies in
any move to forestall and limit Communist aggression.
The public in Western Europe and the United States
need to be better informed so that their appraisal of
the situation—and their will to resist further encroach-
ment—can be strengthened.

The various propaganda devices and guerrilla counter-
activities (since these have been used efficiently in Asiatic, African, and American settings by the Communists)
should be expanded and utilized by the nations of the
Free World. The advance of Russian (and Chinese)
Communism must be viewed as a species of ideological
colonialism, and evidence from the writings of early
Marxists clearly indicates both goals and methods. These
writings should be studied and made the basis for action.
One hope for the West lies in a correct appraisal of the
contemporary scene and consequent positive activity; the
other in possible dissention and failure, based most
fortuitously for the West on those very ideological principles which have brought the movement to its present
pinnacle—triggered from within the Communist blocs in
East Europe and Asia—the net result of which would
most certainly be the practical disruption of the massive Marxist crusade for world hegemony.

CHAPTER III

NATIONALISM AND THE EAST CENTRAL EUROPEAN SATELLITES OF THE USSR

Myth vs. Reality

THERE IS general agreement[1] that recent advances of our knowledge present ideology as a relative conception of human thought as well as the most powerful weapon in the determination of human behavior. This being accepted, it follows that all intellectuals engaged in the development and dissemination of secular knowledge must assume full responsibility for the presentation, in their proper perspective, of such doctrines as those of nationalism or the state.

It is not even necessary to hide behind the traditional cliché that the primary task of each scientist—and most certainly every social scientist—is the search for "truth." For we cannot debate here whether the various historical myths are actually more effective as the dynamic elements of historical movements than the true historical ideologies which gain recognition by the power of cold hard facts.

Without denying the immediate effectiveness of the "big lie" principle of Adolf Hitler, or the whole conceptual structure of fairy tales raised by the contemporary prophets of Marx, we can also point out that the whole course of human development demonstrates that such historical appeals have eventually led to violent social explosions when their mythological claims have been confronted by the factual test of history.

Witness the passing of the "Holy Roman Empire"; the dilemma of French and English monarchs who, de-

---

[1] The foundation for this chapter rests on a recent address by Professor Roucek at the Institute of Ethnic Studies, Georgetown University, Washington, D.C.

spite their protestations of the "divine right of kings," felt the executioner's blade; Hitler's suicide (regardless of his claims to the invincibility of the German "race") ; or—most recently—the bloody revolts of the Polish and Hungarian peoples against the myth of their proclaimed "happiness" under Soviet masters.

Happily there is no special volume that would support the hypothesis that human history is also a story of the wreckage of human aspirations, coupled with the most criminal record of human misery, produced by the ideologies built on the quicksands of falsehood.

The problem is being discussed at the capital of the most powerful state in the world today, a state whose decisions have influenced the course of history in East Central Europe[2] in two World Wars; thus, let us note the pertinence of our thesis relating to an adequate definition of "nationalism" to the general welfare of the United States.

In spite of the recent breakthrough of the American public in awareness of the existence of the USSR, the Iron Curtain, and the captive nations behind that Iron Curtain, together with the persistent efforts of such organizations as the Institute of Ethnic Studies, Georgetown University, the Mid-European Studies Center or the Russian Center at Harvard, or the Slavonic Departments at Marquette, Columbia, or the University of California, an overall examination of the importance attached to East European affairs by Americans is rather disappointing!

We are made well aware of this by the snap judgments presented by the American press, radio, and television, and reflected in popular discussions, the periodicals, and other media of modern mass communication; by the difficulty in securing a large acceptance of specialized studies on East Europe—most American institutions of higher learning preferring the standard approach to

---

[2] The expression "East Central Europe" used throughout this volume is defined by Dr. Oscar Halecki in *The Limits and Divisions of European History* (New York: Sheed and Ward, 1950), p. 137, as the borderlands between Germany and the eastern Slavic state, the power of which is presently held by the Communists.

world history in limiting it to Western European civilization, and—above all—by official decisions made, on the summit level, by American statesmen—as at Yalta or Potsdam—in which, it seems, the true significance of the "borderlands of Western civilization" was lost sight of.[3]

In spite of official pronouncements of the State Department and some American officials favoring the "independence" of the captive countries, and regardless of the systematic efforts to re-create the atmosphere which would allow potential Masaryks and Paderewskis to bring some order out of the embarrassment of American policy-makers, not much has been achieved. For example, consider the official inability to act more constructively during the 1956 Hungarian revolt or the bowing to demands of the Marxist regimes to abandon the policy of releasing "Free World" balloons from Munich to be carried by the westerly winds beyond the Iron Curtain.

Perhaps in defense of what appears to be American apathy, the political influences are too closely integrated with the domestic and international situation to offer any clear-cut understanding of the relation of the nationalisms of East Central Europe to the identification of American welfare. In that respect, too, academic minds have apparently not helped much. Basically, American thinking rejects what it considers to be the concepts of geopolitics; yet the fact remains that the United States (as did indeed the British Commonwealth) went into two World Wars in order to prevent the domination of the Eurasian continent by an alien hostile power.

In other words, it is clearly shown that America's safety lies in the restoration and survival of the independence of those small nations inhabiting the area which

---

[3] Nevertheless, there is some evidence suggesting that both Roosevelt and Churchill were victims of a unique combination of circumstances which prevailed at Yalta; that each pushed as hard as the current military situation would allow for democratic and independent organization of the countries of the borderland, especially Poland and Yugoslavia. See John L. Snell and Others, *The Meaning of Yalta* (Baton Rouge: Louisiana State University Press, 1956); Winston Churchill, *Triumph and Tragedy* (Boston: Houghton Mifflin, 1953); and Robert E. Sherwood, *Roosevelt and Hopkins* (New York: Harper & Brothers, 1950).

has been—ironically—denominated "the shatter zone of Europe."[4]

Despite idealistic proclamations by certain East Central European intellectuals and their American counterparts, it is difficult to concede that any possible federation or confederation of states in that region will help their cause; one can well say that this same idea — refurbished for propaganda purposes — is actually the gravest danger to the true life of this region. Does not the *Komekon* organization—the Marxist alter ego of the Atlantic Community—work on that principle? Is not the whole region—in Soviet theory—working on that principle? It may be remonstrated that the "new" federation of the Eastern European community will be without the domination of the Politburo or Moscow Presidium; but there are also many historical lessons which could teach the habitants of this very region that "confederation" has a way of degenerating into imperialism. What leads us to believe that it will be too different this time?

It follows thus that the future of Central Eastern Europe—and indeed the future of the whole Western world—lies in the re-establishment, protection, and preservation of the so-called "small nations" of these "borderlands" which, unhappily, at this very moment—with no exception save Finland, Greece, and perhaps Yugoslavia —rest uncomfortably behind the Iron Curtain.

Yet victory for the West in World War II implied that the democratic idea (and education in democratic principles) had prevailed. With the cessation of hostilities in 1945, the totalitarian governments of Germany, Italy, and Japan were overthrown and democratic regimes instituted. The educational systems likewise were revised in accordance with democratic principles; although in each case the organization was somewhat more

---

[4] R. Hartshorne, "The United States and the 'Shatter Zone' of Europe," H. W. Weigert and Victor Stefansson (eds.), *Compass of the World* (New York: The Macmillan Company, 1944), pp. 74-88. This work, on the whole, questions some of the general concepts of "Geopolitics"; nevertheless, based on the evidence that it presents in attempting to destroy Geopolitics as a science, a real justification for thinking "geopolitically" appears to emerge.

class-oriented than that in the United States of America. However, the danger from totalitarianism was far from vanquished. By the end of the European phase of the war, Marshal Stalin had moved the army and institutions of the USSR into ten countries of East Central Europe and (although under the terms agreed upon by the Grand Alliance) occupied the central section of Germany; here another "People's Democracy" —the German Democratic Republic, a carbon copy of the Soviet system—was established. Eastern Germany, including Danzig and East Prussia, was put under Polish and Russian administration—a procedure that is interpreted as tantamount to outright cession by the Marxists. The Communist brand of totalitarian education was imposed in each of these settings.[5]

Politically the situation steadily worsened, and by as early as 1947 a cold war was said to obtain between the Soviet-controlled bloc and the Western democracies. When the former Republic of China (the island of Formosa excepted) became Communist—adopting Marxist collectivism—the peril became increasingly greater.

Is Nationalism New?

In recent years the disposition has been to look upon nationalism as a comparatively new phenomenon.[6] Actu-

---

[5] See Winston S. Churchill, *Triumph and Tragedy* (Boston: Houghton Mifflin Company, 1953) ; also early volumes of *East Europe and Soviet Russia* (London) and *The Sudeten Bulletin, A Central European Review* (Munich).

[6] Carleton J. H. Hayes, for example, considers that "nationalism —the paramount devotion of human beings to fairly large nationalities and the conscious founding of a political 'nation' on linguistic and cultural nationality—was not widely preached or seriously acted upon until the eighteenth century." *The Historical Evolution of Modern Nationalism* (New York: Richard R. Smith, 1931), p. 6. Hans Kohn in *The Idea of Nationalism: A Study in Its Origins and Background* (New York: The Macmillan Company, 1951) offers a brilliant survey of nationalism in Israel and Hellas ("From Tribalism to Universalism," pp. 27-62), Rome and the Middle Ages ("The Universal Tradition," pp. 63-118), Renaissance and Reformation ("The Emergence of Nationalism," pp. 119-86), and so on up to contemporary times. But Kohn also follows the lead established by Hayes when he states in his latest work, *Nationalism: Its Meaning and History* (Princeton, N.J., D. Van Nostrand Co., 1955),

ally, this contemporary interpretation hinges upon the matter of definition; while it is generally accepted that a "rise of nationalism" accompanied the development of the greater centralized modern state—in fact, accounts for its existence—it need not necessarily follow that nationalism was born at the time of Renaissance, Reformation, or Enlightenment. If indeed this were proved to be true in the case of Britain, France, Spain, or others of the "new" monarchies, then a great priority in the invocation of the idea would rest with the kingdoms of the borderlands in East Central Europe.

In terms of the latest definition, nationalism reached its culmination in the full sense with the eighteenth century and the French Revolution. This is quite true. But modern concepts of nationalism and "nation" can actually be traced to certain institutions and ideas from the very origins of what we call "civilization." More specifically, "sentiments akin to nationalism are possibly as old and as prevalent as man and society."[7]

Ethnocentrism characterizes not only tribes but also modern nationalities. In the fifth century B.C., the citizens of Athens and Sparta were devoted to their city-states as were indeed the men of Corinth and Aegina. The members of ancient Israel or the men of the Middle Ages had a common faith in a creed or religious leader;

"Nationalism is a state of mind, in which the supreme loyalty of the individuality is felt to be due the nation-state. A deep attachment to one's native soil, to local traditions and to established territorial authority has existed in varying strength throughout history. But it was not until the end of the 18th century that nationalism in the modern state of the word became a generally recognized sentiment increasingly molding all public and private life. *Only very recently* has it been demanded that each nationality should form a state, its own state, and that the state should include the whole nationality (p. 9). . . ." (Italics added.) And further, "even before the age of nationalism, we find individuals who profess sentiments akin to nationalism. But these are confined to individuals. The masses never feel their own life—culturally, politically, or economically—to depend upon the fate of the national body. Danger from outside may arouse a passing feeling of national cohesion. . . . But, as a rule, wars before the French Revolution did not arouse deep national emotions (p. 10). . . ."

[7] B. C. Shafer, *Nationalism: Myth and Reality* (New York: Harcourt, Brace and Co., 1955); E. Westermarck, *The Origin and Development of Moral Ideas* (New York: The Macmillan Company, 1912), II, 167ff.

likewise to emperor, monarchy, feudal class, and race. Otherwise, for example, how could we explain—or understand—such phenomena as the concerted effort of the Bulgarians under their first empire in the tenth century, the saga of Alexander Nevsky and his famous defeat of the German Knights of the Sword at Lake Peipus; or the Hussite Wars of Bohemia. This last—as indeed in amity with the other two instances—was the expression of a mass movement showing more than reaction to danger from outside the national community—the arousal of deep "national" emotions including attachment to the use of the Czech language, Czech melodies and legends, and consequent resentment against the intruding Germanization process.

It may be argued that these loyalties can be distinguished from "modern" nationalism by the object of the loyalty. But modern means of communication have simply extended the object of loyalty to a mass phenomenon— the nation-state. Since this is a mass movement, the transfer of loyalty and allegiance to the mass concept has to be conceived as an object meaning a different thing, varying with time, place, and the individual.

Nationalism then, in today's meaning—and this does not really differ from those earlier circumstances related above—connotes (1) a definite state; (2) a definite territory; and (3) a special group of people distinguished from other nations by their common culture (language, literature, history, and a common hope to live together). A survey of the "rise" of modern nationalism indicates that the advent of the nationalistic spirit came without particular planning or design; it was slow; "it was not a continuous but an intermittent and sporadic process," and "it still goes on."[8]

The forces shaping the nation cannot always be precisely isolated and evaluated, since the process may be halting and, more frequently than not, met by rebuffs and retreats. Nor has the rise of nationalism always been a democratic process, since monarchies do not frequently have democratic goals in view.

---

[8] Shafer, *op. cit.*, p. 62.

But, in all fairness, the monarchial and dynastic institutions utilized for this upbuilding have eventually become national agencies and institutions; at the same time there are evidences that national political and social institutions initiated their growth in opposition to the royal power. Thus, the processes—often antagonistic in their immediate aims—have created resultants which are the bases for modern nationalism.

That the processes referred to above have been instrumental in shaping the nationalisms of East Central Europe has already been suggested. Geography, too, has been a highly instrumental factor. There are few natural boundaries here, the saucer of Bohemia, the ring of the Carpathians, and the crests of the Balkans being the most easily recognizable. Otherwise, plainland and interrelated valley formations identify the landscape. That the geography has been conducive to the development of the national spirit finds a parallel in the history of the Greek peninsula.

East Central Europe occupies the area between the great inland seas of Eurasia, the Baltic and the Black —a circumstance which, if for no other reason than the necessity for east-west migration across their precariously drawn frontiers, would result in either assimilation or the development of strong local allegiances to protect their own interests. In the course of history at least eleven political entities have survived (or were in existence just prior to the advent of World War II). Beginning at the north these include Finland (currently the only independent country remaining in East Central Europe), Estonia, Latvia, Lithuania, Poland, Czechoslovakia, Hungary, Romania, Bulgaria, Albania, and Yugoslavia—of somewhat uncertain political status.

Generally speaking, the history of East Central Europe dates from the tenth century. Most of the states were in existence at that time, and boundaries (which may never be settled in this area of ebb and flow of nationalities) were roughly defined. Several states, especially Poland, Czechoslovakia (Bohemia is meant), and Hungary already were kingdoms or virtual monarchies; Bulgaria had been, for a brief space, an "empire." Regardless of the impermanence of their boundaries and the changing dynasties or ultra-national allegiances forced upon these and others of the East Central block, tradition had been made and nationalisms born.

Indeed the peoples of East Central Europe have long been considered as among the most nationalistic of all such groups, for these tendencies were forced upon them by geopolitical factors and their own historical development. As we traced above, these tenacious middle-European countries had to assume an intense nationalistic spirit in order to survive culturally, economically, and politically, surrounded as they have always been by much more powerful Teutonic and Slavic neighbors. It was—and is—this group solidarity and concept of mission that has allowed them to exist when resistance in the face of prolonged foreign domination and occupation —Habsburg, Muscovy, Hohenzollern, and Nazi—and now the Soviet—meant individual death and always entailed the grim prospect of national ruin as well. It may well be said that "It is that spirit of nationalism in East Central Europe which is today providing the Communists with their greatest problems as they try to strengthen their control over the captive countries."[9]

Although the countries of East Central Europe have chapters in their history replete with individual and national achievement as well as the darker phase of subjugation and satrapy, their present situation is undoubtedly the most severe that they have been called to experience in the thousand or so years of their existence.

A Unified Region

Many features have led to the creation in East Central Europe of one of the unique sections of the world. This is especially to be noted in the Danubian region.

First in these categories is the Danube itself. This great river is not a boundary, not a natural frontier;

---

[9] Alvin M. Bentley, "Post-Liberation Problems," chap. 18, pp. 425-47, Stephen D. Kertesz (ed.), *The Fate of East Central Europe* (Notre Dame, Indiana: University of Notre Dame Press, 1956), p. 444.

it invites rather than discourages invasion; and so it has been for the past three thousand years. The Danubian region is a third avenue of access through and across East Central Europe; the Baltic rimland and the Polish lowland representing the others. Each has been —and still is—of the greatest significance to Europe.

Secondly, one must mention the diversity of peoples. This, of course, devolves from the geography and from millennia of history with subordinate and superordinate "races" sometimes changing positions with confusing rapidity; and then too the minorities significant for their number; religious complexions likewise, again due to geography and history, set beside each other in unique fashion.

Third in the series of complications, the general absence of a middle class (regardless of Soviet slander concerning the bourgeois tendencies to be uprooted and so forth). A few great families, lords, boyars, magnates, at the top and a pitifully large majority of peasants and unskilled workers far below them. A lack of common educational opportunities was a natural concomitant and served to maintain the gap established in medieval and feudal times.

Another item in this strange compound stems from the proximity to Byzantium of much of this region. In addition to religious orientations must be mentioned Byzantine imperialism, the autocracy of the Byzantine state, its famed intrigue, and the East-West schism of almost one thousand years' standing. Then the Turks, their conquests and subjugations, glorious and even inglorious national chapters obtain here; some Balkan national states reckon their independence in fractions of a century rather than a millennium.

To sum up, possibly the fiercest nationalisms of the civilized world have arisen in this Balkan-Danubian setting. This plus the ever-present minorities problem, the irredentas, and colonial enclaves, make the southern half of East Central Europe perhaps the world's most difficult political perplexity. Economically too, and socially, the problems demand a regional solution, and yet there is an equity due southern East Central Europe's nationalities that cannot be disregarded.

Theory suggests abridgment of nationality in terms of confederation or union; practice demands the security nationalism sometimes offers. The Russian "solution" for East Central Europe has been little more advanced than that of Cyrus the Great, the satellites representing the satrapies, Moscow taking the place of Susa. Nationality problems wrecked the Persian Empire. One invokes this analogy as the antidote for Soviet imperialism.

These fierce nationalisms—based on the geography as well as the desire for solidarity against invasion—can be felt in the folk music and especially in the patriotic anthems or hymns of the peoples. Thus the Romanians[10] voice their national aspirations:

> Awaken, Romanian, from thy deadly sleep
> Into which thou wert forced by barbarous tyrants!
> Now or never: create another fate for thyself
> To which even thy cruel enemies should bow!

In comparison with the imperial Austrian (Habsburg) hymn, a colorless dirge, the Magyar faith burst forth:

> Unshaken to thy Fatherland
> Be loyal, O Magyar!
> It is thy cradle, it is thy grave
> Which nourishes thee and covers. . . .

as did the heartbeat of the Croat:

> Flow Sava, flow Drava,
> Neither thou Danube lose thy strength!
> Whenever thou roarest, tell to the World
> That the Croat loves his nation

---

[10] For an excellent treatment of national and dynastic patriotism see: Oscar Jászi, *The Dissolution of the Habsburg Monarchy* (Chicago: University of Chicago Press, 1929), pp. 447-50. Dr. Jászi, who served as Minister of Racial Minorities in the Habsburg Empire, construes the royal dilemma as follows: "The dynastic patriotism of the Habsburgs became more and more pale, losing its real driving force . . . [while] the various national hymns too, this real emanation of the popular souls, symbolized even more strikingly that Habsburg patriotism was incapable of checking the national patriotism."

Until his soil is not lit up by the sun,
Until his oak forests are struck by the lightning,
Until his body is covered by the grave,
Until his heart no longer beats.

This near-perfect welding of emotion and word is reproduced in only slightly less exalted form by the Czech singing:

Where is my Fatherland?
The waters rumble in the fields,
The pinewoods roar on the rocks,
In the gardens bloom spring flowers.
'Tis a Paradise on earth,
And this is the beautiful country,
The country of the Czechs, my Fatherland. . . .

And the less abstract Slovak spirit:

Up, ye Slovaks, still is living our true Slovak language,
While our loyal hearts are beating truly for our nation.
Living, living, yea and deathless is the Slovak spirit:
Hell and lightning, Hell and lightning rage in vain against us.

That the Slovak spirit may eventually overcome the "Hell and lightning" of Marxism is the fond hope of idealists, but perhaps more pressure than that still resident in these conquered people is essential.

In all of the East Central European countries we have considered, and particularly in Danubia, the prime weapon has always been physical division of the peoples —and nations—through a reshuffling of the lands. Byzantine, Habsburg, and Czarist Russia, each followed this strategem. Therefore it may be not unexpected that the Soviets, inheritors of the Czarist expansion policies, in Romania, Bulgaria, and the other satellites should follow this device, already so clearly indicated in Poland. A Central European writer points up the fact that "Rumania is an example to the world that Soviet Russia even abuses Communist ideology in its own imperialistic and colonial interest. . . . Marxism-Leninism is important only when it helps Soviet ambitions."[11] The

---

[11] Rudolf Wagner, "Partition—A Soviet Weapon," *Sudeten Bulletin* VII, No. 7-8 (July-August, 1959), 151-55.

same point was made previously in the chapter; here it refers to Soviet juggling of the Romanian lands along the Black Sea: Bessarabia, Moldavia, the controversial Dobrudja, and of course Transylvania.

In any discussion of the satellites' position, two expressions are frequently employed. They are "sovietization" and "Russification." The first needs no clarification, and the second has come to be the mode. The Soviet attempt to superimpose the Russian language on the satellite states wherever possible is a clear indication of the power which the Kremlin attaches to "national" languages.

Language as a Factor

Yet, interestingly enough, the potential significance of the emergence of national languages (and their relationship to national consciousness and unity) was not generally apparent to contemporaries in the days of their popularization. For example, consider the arguments of John Hus regarding the use of Czech and German languages at Charles University.

A similar point could be made in regard to the emergence of national religions and churches; in some countries national sentiment helped the rise of national churches, and favored the nationalization of religion; in turn, these national churches helped to strengthen the national consciousness.

It is difficult to ascertain what the common people thought in the early days since they were universally illiterate and there were no public opinion polls. But considerable light is thrown on their mental states when we note a general tendency toward love of the commonwealth and native country. Is not the same principle involved in Petrarch's (1304-74) sonnets:

> Is not this my own nest
> Where I was nourished and was given life?
> Is not this the dear land in which we trust,
> Mother loving and kind
> Who shelters parents, brothers, sisters, wife?

Or in Shakespeare's:

> This other Eden, demi-paradise,
> This fortress built by Nature for herself
> Against infection and the hand of war,
> This happy breed of men, this little world,
> This precious stone set in the silver sea . . .
> This blessed plot, this earth, this realm, this England.[12]

Or in the "Testament" of Jan Amos Comenius?

Thee, my Bohemian and Moravian nation, my precious fatherland,
I cannot forget in this my last farewell, yet turning to thee in the
first place I bequeath the treasures entrusted to me by God.

And are not the chronicles, annals, and histories written
in East Central Europe before modern times but the
expression—as we have already found it revealed in
their folk music and anthems—in more than one sense,
national histories?

In East Central Europe the concept of nationality is
frequently defined in ethnic and cultural terms—adherence to a people characterized by common ancestry,
language, religion, or culture—that denote homogeneity.[13]
Sometimes even the terms "nation" and "nationality"
have different connotations. In Hungary there was the
Magyar "nation"; the others were "nationalities"—here
equivalent to minorities.

The literature of this field is truly enormous. At the
same time much debate has been occasioned in attempting to define both nationalism and "minorities." For the
purposes of discussion let us cite President Wilson's
commentary[14] on his famous Fourteen Points:

---

[12] *King Richard the Second,* Act II, scene 1, ll. 42-50.

[13] Wilhelm Winkler, *Statistisches Handbuch der Europaischen
Nationalitaten* (Vienna, 1931); L. Eisemann, "Rights of Minorities
in Central Europe," *International Conciliation,* September, 1926,
pp. 320-21; C. J. H. Hayes, *Essays in Nationalism* (New York:
The Macmillan Company, 1926), pp. 3-4; *Encyclopedia of the
Social Sciences,* II, 231ff.; Oscar Jászi, *The Dissolution of the Habsburg Monarchy* (Chicago: University of Chicago Press, 1929), p.
29, n. 1.

[14] Woodrow Wilson, "Address to the Congress on the Addresses
of the German Chancellor and the Austro-Hungarian Minister for
Foreign Affairs," February 11, 1918. *President Wilson's Foreign
Policy,* J. B. Scott (ed.) (New York, 1918), pp. 364-73.

An evident principle runs through the whole programme I have outlined. It is the principle of justice to all people and nationalities, and their right to live on equal terms of liberty and safety with one another, whether they be strong or weak. Unless this principle can be made its foundation, no part of the structure of international justice can stand.

What a far cry is the idealism of President Wilson (regardless of the sure difficulties in producing viable definitions for implementing his "evident principle" and the denigration of the father of the League of Nations by Communist-inspired writers) from that better-to-be-forgotten statement of Prime Minister Chamberlain during the Czechoslovak crisis of 1938: "How terrible, fantastic, incredible, it is that we should be digging trenches and trying on gas masks here because of a quarrel in a faraway country between people of whom we know nothing."

An American Error

Yet in the United States at this very moment the conclusions of the Congressional Immigration Commission (created by Act of Congress of February 20, 1907, and whose findings appeared in 1911)[15] is of more pertinence to the immigrant from East Central Europe than the glowing words of Woodrow Wilson.

The conclusions of the commission, although obviously based on prejudice and ignorance, have molded the thinking of generations of Americans toward East Central Europe and its peoples. Let us quote a few of these generalizations: "The old immigration movement [Western Europe is meant] was essentially one of permanent settlers [p. 24]. . . . As a class the new immigrants (Central and East Central Europe) are largely unskilled laborers coming from countries where their highest wage is small compared to the lowest wage in the United States [p. 24] . . . an immigration of diseased aliens [p. 26] . . . an immigration of criminals [p. 27] . . . the coming of criminals and persons of criminal tendencies

[15] Reports of the Immigration Commission, *Abstracts of Reports of the Immigration Commission* (2 vols.: Washington, 1911).

constitutes one of the serious social effects of the immigration movement [p. 27] . . . the commission's investigation of the importation of women for immoral purposes, commonly known as the 'white slave traffic,' disclosed the fact that this business is regularly carried on between some European countries and the United States [p. 30]. . . . The proportion of the more serious crimes of homicide, blackmail, and robbery, as well as the least serious offenses, is greater among the foreign-born [p. 33] . . . [of Central Eastern Europe]."

The innuendo of this report is still felt in terms of the limited quotas for immigrants from the countries of East Central Europe, whose histories (had they been known) in many cases antedate that of the British Isles. The resulting inferiority complex has had more effects on the attitude of native-born Americans and the descendants of East Central European immigrants than is commonly realized. The resulting "marginal culture" aspects of many children of immigrants is a phenomenon well known to contemporary sociologists.[16]

The cause, however, of East Central European peoples received sudden attention during World War I because of President Wilson's interest. This undoubtedly was stimulated by the influence of Thomas G. Masaryk of Bohemia-Moravia, Jan Ignace Paderewski from Poland, and others. George Creel, of World War I propaganda fame, utilized his powerful Committee of Public Information to organize an assembly of the "Oppressed Nationalities of Central Europe" in New York City, and newspapers throughout the country hailed "nationalism" as the topic of the day.

---

[16] George Seward, *Psychotherapy and Culture Conflict* (New York: Ronald Press, 1956); Francis J. Brown and Joseph S. Roucek, *One America* (New York: Prentice-Hall, 1952); E. T. Glueck, "Culture, Conflict and Delinquency," *Mental Hygiene*, XL, 46-68; L. Saunders, *Cultural Differences and Medical Care* (New York: Russell Sage Foundation, 1954); W. I. Thomas and Florian Znaniecki, *The Polish Peasant in Europe and America* (New York: Alfred A. Knopf, 1927); William L. Warner and Leo Srole, *The Social Systems of American Ethnic Groups* (New Haven, Conn.: Yale University Press, 1945).

Self-Determination

It is easily recognized that when Woodrow Wilson hurled the slogan "self-determination" into the world arena, he used a phrase capable of many interpretations. So far as the meaning of self-determination itself is concerned, it is indeed clear enough. But when the Versailles Conference met, it had a difficult time drafting the so-called "Minorities Treaties," which were designed to protect the subnational groups for whom creation of states or principalities was deemed unviable. What is a minority? This is the problem with which Wilson and his colleagues wrestled.

After many disagreements, proposals, and counterproposals, such treaties (signed by Poland, Yugoslavia, Czechoslovakia, Romania, Greece, Austria, Bulgaria, Hungary, Turkey, Albania, Estonia, Finland—for the Aland Islands—Latvia, Lithuania, and Iraq) were designed to protect the minorities of "race, language, or religion."[17]

Historically, wherever the conception of nationality arises, the idea of racial unity and solidarity arises with it and becomes a fundamental factor in the driving force of that nationalism. So Pan-Germanism and Pan-Slavism became important political weapons; Pan-Slavism is presently being used by the clique in the Kremlin to present Communism in a more palatable fashion to the Czechs and Slovaks or Romanians and Bulgarians. Nevertheless, race, nationality, and nation are difficult to identify.[18] The territories of the historical nations may have been—at one time or another—the home of nearly pure races.

But in consequence of migration and conquest their populations have become heterogeneous. Regardless of this, in each of them, through the development of common customs and traditions, and especially as a result

---

[17] Jacob Robinson, *Were the Minorities Treaties a Failure?* (New York: Institute of Jewish Affairs, 1943); Joseph S. Roucek, *The Working of the Minorities System Under the League of Nations* (Prague: Orbis, 1928), *passim.*

[18] Frank H. Hankins, *The Racial Basis of Civilization* (New York: A. A. Knopf, 1926), pp. 9-10. The literature covering "racism" is much too enormous to be cited here.

of "racial" amalgamation, all elements of the population acquired first a consciousness of a common group
destiny, and thence a realization of common blood. Nevertheless, race both precedes and follows nationality, and
yet there is never an instance where race and nationality are more than roughly identifiable. The interaction
of racial qualities with national customs and traditions
produces a joint product of cultural evolution in which
it becomes impossible to distinguish that which may be
due to specific racial traits from that which is indebted
to the milieu operating in human qualities diffused generally throughout mankind. The expression "race" must
be eliminated from serious intellectual discussion (although talk like this willingly becomes a potent weapon
in the contemporary "Russification" process operated
under the new imperialism of the USSR).

Language, on the other hand, is a matter of prime
importance. Speech is a fundamental element in creating consciousness of kind; the man in the street certainly knows whether he can understand the discourse
of his neighbor; he may always have opprobrious epithets
for those who speak an alien tongue. The very sound of
the *lingua matris* creates comfort or a near sense of kin-
ship. Confidence and empathy are at once established.
Yet it is notorious that the language spoken in a given
area has often not been that of a minority, and thus
language can be as little as race the chief criterion of
nationality.

Language may be the expression of a common spirit
and of intellectual intercourse, and as such it may be
used powerfully to aid nationalism. Language unity, however, is not indispensable to the growth of real nationality—nor it is sufficient to create it. It can be learned
or unlearned by a new generation, especially when the
resources of universal education are controlled by the
totalitarian state. It can be safely stated that the Russian-
speaking groups in the satellites today still are nationalists, or that the Russian-speaking captives in the slave-
labor camps are even more nationalist because they have
been compelled to abandon their mother tongue.

Unity of religion has sometimes been regarded as a

factor in nation-making and there are numerous cases in which a common faith has proved itself a potent nation-maker. Men usually prefer to associate with those who share their beliefs or convictions and worship in the same manner; although religion has played and still plays an important role in confirming nationality in East Central Europe, it has no indispensable connection with nationality. At the same time, we must remember that —although there are nations in which nationality and a common religion are inseparable—calculated efforts to erect a national unity solely—and compulsively—on the basis of religious unity have usually tended toward failure.

What Is Nationalism?

Obviously, there is no infallible test of what constitutes a nation—unless we take as valid the conclusion that the most important and indispensable factor in the nation-molding process is the mosaic of historical memories, the record of sufferings endured and victories won, their reflections in folk song, anthem, and legend, in the venerated names of great personalities which somehow symbolize the character and ideals of the nation, and of the sites and shrines where the national remembrances are immortalized.[19]

Manifestly, nationalism cannot be an artificial invention, deliberately contrived, or inculcated overnight by Nazi or Communist-dominated regimes. In this respect our concept of the nationalism behind the Iron Curtain today is closest to that suggested by Herder and his disciples. Herder stressed the importance of national language and showed his preference for folklore and the poetry of the people; he emphasized the advantage of village communities over an industrial society; he praised folk culture (myth, ballad, adages, dances, folkways), indigenous art, religion, legal systems, political and economic institutions as true representations of the national

---

[19] Ramsey Muir, *Nationalism and Internationalism* (London: Constable and Company, 1916), pp. 48, 56.

individualism; as a *Volksgeist*—"people's spirit."[20] According to Herder's philosophy, the individual could attain his highest self-development only in the life of the group as a whole.[21]

Yet it would be an error to fall completely under the spell of Herder's theories, especially since he wrote during a period (1744-1803) antecedent to the arrival of the agencies of mass communication. Important to note also is the extent to which totalitarian regimes have realized the tricks of twisting the "popular culture" for their own sinister purposes.[22] For example, by identifying Pan-Slavism with Pan-Russian policies, the men in the Kremlin have turned the edge of the antagonism of their satellites in pointing out how the Russians and the other Slavs are blood brothers and how together they represent the greatest people on earth. Thus, everything done in the past by Russia and especially all efforts in the direction of the satellite have been done for, and have reflected, their mutual glory.[23]

Moreover, the process of unifying the traditional symbols with the local symbols, along with the "glorious past," is used constantly to remind the satellite peoples of the ten countries behind the Iron Curtain of the old symbols of the Russian nation. Writers, poets, actors, party notables, statesmen, scientists—they are always playing the leading role in world history or pioneering in invention, and all of this is cleverly worked into the local history.

---

[20] John P. Sydoruk, "Herder and the Slavs," *Ukrainian Quarterly*, XXII, No. 1 (Winter, 1956), 58-62; Hans Kohn, *Prophets and Peoples, Studies in Nineteenth Century Nationalism* (New York: The Macmillan Company, 1946), *passim;* Hans Kohn, *The Idea of Nationalism, passim;* Robert T. Clark, Jr., *Herder, His Life and Thought* (Berkeley, Calif.: University of California Press, 1955); John P. Sydoruk, "Ideology of Cyrillo-Methodians and its Origins" (Winnipeg-Chicago: *Slavistica*, Vol. XIX, 1954).

[21] F. H. Adler, *Herder and Klopstock* (Urbana: University of Illinois, 1913), Doctoral dissertation, pp. 248-50.

[22] Joseph S. Roucek, "Soviet and Russian Educational Imperialism," *The Journal of Human Relations*, Vol. IV, Nos. 1 and 2 (Winter, 1956).

[23] The fallacy of Pan-Slavism is exposed in Joseph S. Roucek, "Pan-Slavism, an Ideological Myth," *Prologue*, III, No. 1 (Spring, 1959), 18-25.

Local folk dances are encouraged but by recasting them into the proletarian framework the party line is served. Music, too, is bent to this end. For example, *East Europe and Soviet Russia* (London) reports: "On February 12, Bucharest Radio said that Rumanian music was based on the life of the people and dedicated to the construction of Communism. The symphonies, 'The Road of the Danube Towards the Sea' and 'A Summer Day on a Collective Farm' represent music of an advanced kind."[24]

Conversely, the "anti-proletarian" symbols, such as Masaryk, Benes, Horthy, and lately Imre Nagy, are degraded, or others such as Mickiewicz and Kossuth are reinterpreted with the Marxist ideological twist. Even such religious figures as St. Cyril and Methodius are now being depicted as "proletarian precursors," whose early work "played a beneficient, preserving, and stimulating role in keeping alive the flame of democratic culture, ties with the Slav peoples and with the great Soviet Union."[25] History, too, is being rewritten under the orders of the Kremlin[26] to induce moral subservience of the masses in the captive countries to the pro-Communist regimes by perpetually reminding them how grateful they must be to the Russians for their "liberation."

---

[24] Vol. VIII, No. 368 (February 28, 1952), p. 22.

[25] Quoted in Roucek, "Soviet and Russian Educational Imperialism," p. 40.

[26] This "1984"-like gem is reported in *East Europe and Soviet Russia:* "On February 13, Gusztav Heckenast broadcast a lecture on the strikes of the Beszrecebánya miners in 1525 and 1526. As a result of this, 'the serfs and the small but resolute workers' force refused to support the King in his battle against the Turks at Mohács, where Hungary lost her independence.' The battle of Mohács might have been altered had János Zápolya, who stood with 20,000 men between the Danube and the Tisza, thrown in his men. He did not; most historians believe because he had a secret agreement with the Turks that in case the King—who had no son—were killed, he should receive the throne. The handful of miners in northern Hungary could not possibly have affected the battle in any way, even if these strikes had taken place." VIII, No. 368 (February 28, 1952), 21.

America's Role

What then are the hopes of the survival of the pre-Communist nationalities in East Central Europe? Let us return, first, to the point raised at the outset of this discussion. Every effort must be made, by the anti-Communist regimes and by the spokesmen of these captive peoples abroad, in order to keep alive the historical memories of the nation that are not tainted by the myths and lies injected into them by the Marxists. Secondly—and this is history—the concept of *nationalism*, which we equate with the true spirit of these unhappy people, must not be given up, or—and this is most important—looked upon merely as a modern manifestation; a new idea in antique dress. The deeper the roots can be shown to be (and this is the basic purpose of this chapter), the stronger this nationalism must persist. The more clearly it can be shown that the nationalisms of these ten conquered states is but a persistent, steady, and underlying theme rather than an artificial, intellectual, and recent invention, the more potent and compelling such a nationalistic appeal will be.

The demand of these nations for freedom is related to the support which these movements secure from the Free World in general, its governments, and—above all —the descendants of the immigrants from these countries and from their friends. If these lose interest, most surely the people of East Central Europe will lose hope. Strive to keep alive the spirit of pride among the descendants of these peoples in the United States. Encourage the closer integration of the sons and daughters of the emigrants with the higher cultural and political levels of American society, for they have much to offer and the American people have much to give.

Now, finally, it cannot be stressed positively enough— to both the American people (and to those of the Free World wherever disposed) as well as to the nationalistic remnants (in the captive countries or in exile *ubique*) —that the cause of the satellite peoples is not different from their cause, that freedom is never to be restricted to this hemisphere, that valley, or to any other geographical subdivision.

That only so long as this so-called "shatter zone"— East Central Europe—retains the nation-spirit of pre-Communist days will it be impossible to mount the power for a new war of conquest—"civilization itself hanging in the balance." "Who rules East Europe . . . commands the World." If, however, nationalisms flourish behind the curtain (as recently in Poland and Hungary) there is hope that—either through their own efforts or by concert—the situation may be changed. Nor can East Central Europe become the springboard of plans for aggressive conquest of the remainder of Eurasia—and the world—if the satellite countries are encouraged and inspired to maintain their natural nationalisms.[27]

There is yet another reason for the preservation of the ancient nationalisms of East Central Europe. We now speak in the name of humanity and of Christ. Ten countries are forced to live in brutal darkness, a gloom which the greatest triumph of economics could never dissolve. The darkness is political, social, and atheistic. It negates the human spirit and will. It crushes individuality, hope, and the soul's desire that man should be guided by that which is above him—not below.

---

[27] See Kenneth V. Lottich, "Stalin's Greatest Blunder," *Sudeten Bulletin*, VIII, No. 3 (March, 1960), 63-69; Hans Speier, *The Soviet Threat to Berlin* (Santa Monica, Calif.: The Rand Corporation, April 15, 1960), pp. 40-48, 61-67.

CHAPTER IV

POLAND: ONE THOUSAND YEARS OF WESTERN CIVILIZATION

Poland's Messianic Complex
The Bastion of Catholic Christianity
The Communist Attack
Education in Poland
Education between World Wars I and II
The Educational Structure under the Satellite Regime
The Political Check on School Admissions
Youth Organizations
Planned Employment
Stakhanovite Schools
Regimentation of Vacations
The Use of Sports
The Army Training
Church and State Relations
Press, Radio, Film
Higher Education
The Russification Process
Developments in Elementary Education
Indoctrination in Higher Education
The School Program
Teacher Training
A Report from Disneyland
Another Political Note

Poland's Messianic Complex

SINCE WE ARE concerned with the significance of East Central Europe, its relationship to Communist hegemony, and the nationalism[1] of this region which may —we hopefully suggest—eventually play its role in the liberation of ten unfortunate countries, it is appropriate to consider the roots of this ethnocentrism in the various states (although in their present circumstances, the use of the term "state" for the European satellites of the USSR is a perversion of political science as well as semantics).

In our consideration of those East Central European nations which still possess nominal statehood, it is best to begin with Poland. Poland represents one of the oldest of the East European entities and possibly the firmest in its devotion to what in the West are called democratic and national principles. Moreover, the Poles are, among all the East European peoples, the best known in both England and the United States.

In order to understand the Poles and their civilization, one must realize (1) that they are Slavs; (2) that they have been—for almost one thousand years—linked closely with Latin Christianity and the culture of Western Europe (Christianity came to Poland in 966, just three years subsequent to the founding of the Polish state) ; and (3) that, until our own time, they have been overwhelmingly an agricultural people. Coupled with

---

[1] Permission has been granted to republish parts of the ensuing chapter by the Institute of Arts and Letters, Zurich, Switzerland, under whose auspices this survey of Polish nationalism and education first appeared.

this trio of distinctives is the fact that—contrary to the social and political development of the whole of Western Europe—until a very late modern period, a middle class or *bourgeoisie* failed to arise in Poland.

Although undoubtedly of mixed racial origins—the inevitable result of living in an open plainland at the crossroads of Europe—their speech, a cousin language of Russian, Czech, and Slovak, and their folklore and folkways Slavonic, the Poles face both east and west. In both of the respects mentioned, a sharp line of cleavage divides them from the German world immediately to the west; no less clear is the cultro-ethnographic line which severs them from their fellow Slavs to the east —first the Kievan Russi and the Muscovy—the result of these having accepted the faith of the Eastern Church, and that, after the fall of Byzantium, they came to regard Moscow as the rival of Rome. It is well known that Moscow affected the style, after 1453, "Third Rome."

This frontier between Catholicism and Orthodoxy has played a dominant role in the historical antagonism between Poland and Russia; it is perhaps more important in European affairs than any other national or political "boundary."

At the west, although Poles and Germans both belonged to the "Western" tradition, a life and death struggle between these two peoples for control of the lower Vistula dates from the coming of the Knights of the Cross in 1229. Unpleasant to relate, the Teutonic Knights were invited by Conrad of Mazovia to make Poland their headquarters in the drive against the pagan Prussians. This lack of foresight proved to be a cause for grief among Poles from that time forward.

Three centuries later when northern Germany became almost solidly Lutheran this rivalry became even more bitter, and the Poles firmly rejected the idea of a national church in favor of their ties with Latin Christendom, as they thought, a wider and more influential allegiance. Thus the Poles, midway between Protestant Germany and Orthodox Russia—glorying in their adherence to Roman Catholicism—utilized this "championship" of Latin Christianity as a focus for their ethnic spirit; as one significant part of their national-cultural heritage following the first two dynasties of Polish rule (Piast and Jagellonian) ; and as a reinforcement to their claim to independence through their time of troubles in the partitions of the late eighteenth century.

There is a Messianic compulsion in the Polish will to recollect this magnificent period in the development of their country. By the fifteenth century, Poland had become the largest state in Europe; in 1569 complete union with Lithuania was achieved and the commonwealth arose. During the fifteenth, sixteenth, and seventeenth centuries, Poland played a powerful role in East Central Europe—not only through recourse to its armed strength, but also by virtue of its democratic internal policies and the liberal spirit pervading its government institutions.

As an elective monarchy Poland—in the face of an absolutism that dominated the remainder of Europe in the seventeenth and the eighteenth centuries—offered the example of the only constitutional kingdom of that day having a practical form of parliamentary system. As early as 1431 Poland had promulgated a law guaranteeing personal liberty (*neminem captivabimus*) ; and, regardless of their attachment to Roman Catholicism, the Poles—eschewing the horrors of the Thirty Years' War—offered almost complete religious toleration, and many, fleeing persecution in Western lands, found asylum here. In fact, it was at Leszno, in western Poland, that Jan Amos Comenius—the great Moravian bishop and educator—found refuge, and it was in Poland that he wrote the most comprehensive treatise on education of all time: the *Didactica Magna*.

Nevertheless, growing disunity, enmity between Catholic and Orthodox churches within the kingdom, and the intransigence of the nobility undermined the foundations of the Polish state. The monarchy could no longer defend itself; and, in 1772, 1793, and 1795, Poland suffered partition among Austria, Prussia, and Russia and ceased to exist as a sovereign political entity.[2]

---

[2] For cultural histories of Poland, see Sigmund Uminiski, *Poland's Contribution to the World's Civilization* (New York: Polish Ameri-

Although the state had vanished from the map of Europe, Polish nationalism was anything but dead. Following the first partition, a new champion in the person of Tadeusz Kosciuszko had arisen. It was he along with Casmir Pulaski who had assisted General George Washington in the American Revolution. In 1791, a veritable revolution had swept Poland. "The outcome was the adoption of a constitution not unlike that which emanated in the same year from the National Assembly at Paris; what remained of the old Polish state was converted into an hereditary limited monarchy, with biennial parliaments and ministerial responsibility; the 'liberum veto' (a device while excessively democratic could—and did—stalemate previous Polish assemblies) was abolished; class distinctions were swept away; serfdom was mitigated; and absolute religious toleration was sanctioned."[3]

Unhappily a few Polish nobles had appealed to Catherine, the Czarina, who was pleased to come to their assistance and to share in the second partition. Kosciuszko continued the fight, assumed the post of dictator, and led a desperate national revolt, but in vain. The third partition followed, and Kosciuszko spent the remainder of his life in France.

Now Polish nationalism and liberalism were more alive than ever. The religious and intellectual currents arising from Roman Christianity saved the Poles from the isolation imposed upon Russia and Balkan Slavs through their acceptance of the Byzantine rite with its medieval Greek culture. Poland continued to regard herself as the remote bastion of Western Latin civilization in Eastern Europe. It is true that Poland lost contact with Europe during the nineteenth century, an age of tremendous social, political, economic, and ideological evolution in Western Europe. The three partitioning powers did their utmost to make the outside world forget Poland,

can Press, 1942); Roman Dyboski, *Poland in World Civilization* (New York: J. M. Barrett Corp., 1950).

[3] Carleton J. H. Hayes, *A Political and Cultural History of Modern Europe* (New York: The Macmillan Company, 1932), pp. 700-702.

or else they grossly misrepresented her. The bloody revolutions of 1830 and 1863 were evidence that the Polish spirit of independence was not dead.

In the Russian sector Poland was treated as a conquered province, and the Russification process was imposed on the Polish people just as it is today, under the guise of Communism, an excellent ideological device for rationalizing the drive for power by the Russian state. All Polish institutions were abolished, and the language itself was prohibited in administration and education. A similar situation existed in the Austrian and Prussian sectors but, while Polish national and cultural life was repressed in Russian and Prussian schools, Galicia built a complete network of Polish schools, including two universities. Cracow became the center of Polish nationalism, taking over the position formerly held by Warsaw.

The rebirth of Polish independence was one of the most significant historical and moral results of World War I. The new Polish state came into the world, as Joseph Conrad said, "morally free, not in virtue of the nation's suffering, but in virtue of its miraculous rebirth and of its ancient claim for services rendered to Europe."[4] This is, of course, evidence of the self-imposed Messianic complex of the Poles.

The two following decades of newfound independence were stormy. A would-be great power after World War I (again the complex), Poland essayed the role of leader of the *cordon sanitaire* between Germany and Russia. From the close of 1918 to 1923 she was engaged in continuous warfare. (Is this evidence of the "traditional Slavonic friendship" emphasized so much by the USSR today?) The "minorities" population in her midst and the traditional individuality of the Poles led to the creation of a complicated pattern in the political and social life of the nation. The domestic policies reflected the extreme poverties and the cleavages of class and nationality; between the resignation of the first President, the pianist Paderewski, in 1919, and the coup of Marshal

---

[4] Joseph Conrad, *Notes on Life and Letters* (London: J. M. Dent and Sons, 1921), p. 170.

Joseph Pilsudski in 1926, thirteen premiers had held office. Unfortunately, the Polish workingman had neither the education nor the tradition of organization to stand up for his own inherent right. The agrarian reform of 1920 remained largely a paper reformation, and the great historic — and legendary — estates were left untouched; in 1931, three-quarters of the agricultural holdings in Poland were still less than the subsistence minimum of twelve acres. Pilsudski, as the dictator, was determined that the old constitution which had collapsed in 1926 had to be revised or scrapped altogether. When he died in 1935, the country suffered from the severe disabilities of history, economics, and geography, and its population was heterogeneous and backward. The agrarian problem was not solved.

A third of the population of the new Poland was non-Polish and, after Czechoslovakia, no other state in the new Europe contained so large a percentage of aliens. Indeed, when one seeks reasons for the internal difficulties experienced by the Poles in their twenty years of twentieth-century independence, minority problems are among the most prominent.

Certainly the Poles, themselves harassed and oppressed minorities for almost a century and a half, might have realized how indestructible a minority can be and that large numbers of unassimilables are sources of weakness to any state. The earliest Polish dynasties had attempted for centuries to assimilate Cossacks, Germans, Lithuanians, and "old" Ruthenians—even in an age when the masses were without a voice—without success. Yet Polish leaders, in the postwar period, extended their borders—no doubt in the thrill of their wonderful renaissance and its implications in terms of Polish history—frequently by force of arms—and rapidly annexed units of non-Polish peoples with basic differences in religion, language, and cultural backgrounds.[5]

Specifically, the Russo-Polish Treaty of Riga (1921) transferred to Poland, roughly speaking, the boundary of 1793 and approximately 1,500,000 White Russians,

---

[5] Roman Dyboski, *Poland* (London: Benn, 1933), pp. 155-57.

which meant that three-quarters of the population of the three eastern provinces (Norvogrödek, Wilno, and Plesie) were neither Poles nor Roman Catholics. Although these White Russians formed one of the least disturbing minorities, their lower economic and cultural status was a hindrance to Poland's development. Moreover, this acquisition was to spell doom to the Poles when, in 1939, the USSR took occasion to extend her boundaries.[6]

The German minority was not so numerous as it was influential. The Teutons—of whom there were about one million—were scattered throughout the country—as were, of course, the Jews. There were, however, areas where the Germans tended to concentrate, especially in industrial and mining centers such as Polish Silesia; the city of Lódz, although situated in the sector previously held by Russia, was chiefly German and Jewish; it contained almost one-fifth of all the people of German extraction in Poland and most of the Protestants. Since a high proportion of the Germans were large property owners—and exempt from agrarian reform—they added to the economic burden of the state. They were eventually to form a fifth column for the fatherland.

Pilsudski's death made little difference in the Polish government, and his dictatorship continued under General Smigly-Rydz, Inspector General of the Polish Army. But the death of the state was already on the way, engineered by the Hitler clique. Although Poland tried to save herself by the German-Polish Non-Aggression Pact of 1934, a painful hesitancy began to govern the country's foreign policy. After the elimination of Austria and Czechoslovakia, Hitler turned on Poland at the end of 1938. Early in the morning of September 1, 1939, without declaration of war, German forces attacked Poland. World War II had begun.

The Bastion of Catholic Christianity

Historically, Poland is usually considered—along with

---

[6] For the Polish view, see S. J. Paprocki, *Minority Affairs and Poland* (Warsaw: Nationality Research Institute, 1935).

Ireland—as the stronghold and bastion of Roman Catholicism; Poland, according to the dominant schools of Polish historiography, was the spearhead of Catholicism in the Danubian area.[7] There are, however, valid grounds for alleging that—between the two World Wars—Catholicism was not only a religious, but in several aspects a political and a "minority" problem.

It may be noted with some surprise that, although throughout the history of the Polish people the Catholic Church has played a prominent part in the cultural, educational, and political life of the nation, Poland was not, after 1918, a predominantly Catholic state. While 95 percent of the Poles were, it is true, Catholics, Roman Catholicism was the religion of only 65 percent of the total population; and with the exception of a small group of Lithuanians, the ethnic minorities were almost always religious minorities as well.

After World War I, with atheistic Communism rampant in the East and the rising ideology of Nazism (semi-pagan National Socialism) in the West, Poland rightly conceived herself to be a stronghold of Christian belief and tradition. But this very position weakened the excessive claim of the Church that it was—in its official form—the legatee for the administration of a monopoly of the Faith over all Christians; the results in regard to policies toward the minorities—especially the Orthodox and Uniate communities—brought on bitter repercussions.

But in all fairness it must be admitted that in postwar Poland Catholics faced persistent opposition in several areas of the country. Although Catholicism had come to be identified with patriotism and its role in the culture pattern of the Polish peasantry one of guidance and comfort, its importance—at the same time—

---

[7] Anthony F. Dzajkowsky, "Twentieth Century Tendencies — Poland and the Baltic Countries," in Matthew A. Fitzsimons, Alfred G. Pundt, and Charles E. Nowell (eds.), *The Development of Historiography* (Harrisburg, Pa.: The Stackpole Co., 1945), chap. 21, pp. 286-89; for other interesting background information see Clifford R. Barnett and Others, *Poland: Its People, Its Society, Its Culture* (New York: Grove Press, 1958), chap. 5, "Religions," pp. 63-83; Oscar Halecki (ed.), *Poland* (New York: Praeger, 1958).

was not as great in the cities as in the countryside. This was especially true among circles favoring the imported ideology of Socialism that criticized the Church as being mainly interested in promoting the *status quo* rather than supporting measures directed toward social justice.

When the peculiar position of the Roman Catholic Church in Poland—a majority with minority status—is compared to the nearly 90 percent Roman Catholic majority in Austria, it is easily seen that governmental control and the perpetuation of Catholic ideology could be achieved by only the slenderest of margins, the vested rights of the Latin Church to the contrary.

Probably the lack of a Polish middle class was the basic reason why a viable bloc was difficult to maintain; the Pilsudski dictatorship following World War I and the ancient spirit of Polish individualism so evidenced during the Commonwealth seem to suggest this. The poverty of the peasants and lack of industrialism provide other clews; it is difficult to secure concerted action without strong centers. In recent times, the gentry were not able—or willing—to provide this.

A fundamental problem of the Roman Catholic Church in Poland was the establishment of a cultural homogeneity out of materials that were basically individualistic, welded to their geography, and already obsessed by the danger from Teutons in the West and from a monolithic giant—Slavic to be sure, but also under a regimentation never to be condoned in the Polish plainland—in the East; that the Church succeeded more generally in the cultural and spiritual sphere than in the political may be readily understood.

By a strange combination of circumstances the second World War relieved the Roman Catholic Church in Poland of the greater part of its minority problems, although it did not, by this token, assure it of greater political strength—at least after the Russian resurgence following the Nazi defeat in the East. When Hitler attacked Poland, Catholic worshipers (including the Uniate Rite) formed approximately three-fourths of the population, a tenth belonged to the Orthodox faith, and another tenth had Jewish affiliations, while the Protestants accounted for the remainder.

Before the end of the war the Jewish minority had been deported or executed by the Nazis. Even the most rabid Polish opponents of the Jews were horrified at the German methods of ending the Jewish problem by applying with progressively inhuman efficiency the formula of scientific extermination.[8]

Population shifts, too, helped change the minorities picture. By Russian order, the Greek Catholic Church had been liquidated by 1946. In 1959, less than 5 percent of the population belonged to other faiths than Roman Catholicism. There were about 100,000 Orthodox, approximately the same number of Uniates (mostly Ukrainians), 330,000 Protestants (chiefly Lutheran—around Warsaw, in the Mazury region, and in Silesia), and the remnant of Jewry, thirty to seventy thousand, remained in the cities of Lódz, Warsaw, Wroclaw, and Walbrzych.

Yet, following the devastation of war, Poland faced an even greater peril in the Russian occupation and in the setting up of the satellite state. It remains to be seen whether the Catholic Church will be able to assert much more than moral suasion in this latest travail of the Polish state.

The Communist Attack

The complete eradication of religion in Poland is the long-range objective of the Communist master plan, and this in the face of the fact that Poland, both historically and ideologically, is wedded to Roman Catholicism. Naturally the Marxists are aware of the deep-rooted religious sentiments of the Polish people; also of the rela-

---

[8] The Jews throughout those horrible years proved their traditional heroism in such ways as the battle of the Ghetto (May, 1943) and ultimately won from Poles at home and abroad a respect unlike anything in previous history. In 1945, however, only a handful of the former more than three million Jews remained alive. Jan Karski, *The Story of a Secret State* (Boston: Houghton Mifflin, 1944), offers a terrifying picture of this extermination of the Warsaw Jews. See pp. 320-52.

tionship of the Polish nationalistic ideology to the anti-Greek Orthodox historical experiences vis-à-vis Russia; and the anti-Protestant historical reactions in the direction of Germany.

So—at the beginning—the Marxist leadership tended to tread rather softly in religious matters. Steps soon were taken, however, for the Greek Catholic Church to join the pale of Russian Orthodoxy; a number of the Uniate priests were arrested and tried, especially those favoring the "Nazi policies" of separatism for the Ukraine.

The Communists also realized that if the Roman Catholic Church could be so denigrated as "international" and "unpatriotic," over half their battle for complete supremacy would have been won. In Poland, Roman religion and nationalism had been, for centuries, only different sides of the same shield.

Denouncing the Pope as a "warmonger" and a servant of American imperialism, the Reds sought to create doubt in the minds of faithful Catholics so that their seizure of the Church itself through infiltration and a gradual shift in policies might go unobserved. This indeed was the astute process in progress in the Soviet Union and a maneuver that was highly successful.

Another thesis suggests that the Communists have in mind the creation of an independent church, subservient to the Party, on the Romanian model based on the *Status Catholicus*, or as in Albania, where existing organizations were merely taken over.

Poland's strength — sometimes literally, but always ideologically — has been her attachment to the West; indeed the realization of her Messianic role in history depends upon this fact. Her history, position, the Roman Church, and her Western connections especially those *ultra* Prussia, coincide to demonstrate this as a first postulate.

To destroy Polish nationalism, then, this orientation must be shaken loose. The campaign of vilification instigated by the Marxists in the early fifties had this aim. Premier Cyrankiewicz addressed a conference of teachers: "We must know how to create men who are conscious of the dangers threatening us from the American-Nazi imperialists and yet are not afraid of those dangers." Minister Ochab reveals his plot against the Catholic Church, reviling "the American genocides and the reactionaries in the Vatican" who are trying to corrupt the youth "by Goebbels lies and Jesuit hypocrisy."

The eventual strategy is to turn Poland from West to East and, of course, to destroy her as a national entity at the same time. As we shall see, this maneuver has virtually succeeded in Czechoslovakia. The plan for Poland has been cleverly contrived. First there is the boundary question. Poles cannot afford a revision of the Oder-Neisse western border because they have lost too much in the east. Only the USSR can guarantee it. Secondly, the Russians and their stooges have, together with the backbreaking labor of the Poles themselves, rejuvenated and even transplanted industry. They have "rebuilt" Warsaw and placed one of their "Palaces of Culture" there.

Pressure, too, is being exerted from the western side, which intensifies Poland's problem. For example, a recent pro-German source prints that "Professor Count Stefen Lubienski recently expressed in a lecture in West Berlin" what it calls a "Polish Appeal for Fair Treatment." The Count is said to have "emphasized the necessity of a just solution of the Oder-Neisse question and stated that the majority of the Polish nation consider the mass expulsion of the East German population from their homeland as an act of bitter injustice."[9]

In order to keep the water muddy, "Communists lost no time in sharply attacking Count Lubienski for his views. . . ." But the journal continued: "It is vital indeed that the nations of Europe finally get together and join efforts on behalf of a better future. The shaping of German-French relations already indicates those great changes which have taken place between so-called 'hereditary' enemies."[10]

---

[9] "Polish Appeal for Fair Treatment Seen a Step Toward United Europe," *Sudeten Bulletin* (Munich), VII, No. 9 (September, 1959), 183-84.

[10] *Idem;* also, see "Robbing Germany to Pay Poland," *Ibid.*, pp. 185-86.

During the latest stage of Communist attack on the Church (beginning in 1950) the new Constitution of July 22, 1952, was enacted. This did not, however, completely clarify the status of the Church in Poland, and on February 9, 1953, a "Decree on the Appointment of Clergymen to Ecclesiastical Office" was promulgated; at all times the hiatus between this law and its application was marked.

In this second attack the real blows began to be felt. On March 20, all religious properties were nationalized, the state becoming the "trustee" of church property. Caritas, the central organization of Catholic welfare agencies, which maintained kindergartens, nurseries, recreation rooms, homes for the aged, dispensaries, and gave support to many kinds of other welfare agencies (and financed largely by the American Poles) was accused— quite typically—of being a stooge of "American imperialism."

At the same time sovietization was proceeding along other national sectors: Marshal Rokossowski ran the army, while the Polish civil service administration was reorganized according to the Russian model. On April 14, the Marxists forced the Church-State Agreement mentioned above upon the hierarchy. Worded in such a manner that it, in theory, violated no Catholic principles, it recognized the Pope as the supreme authority in matters of faith and morals. It guaranteed what remained of freedom of worship and religious education. But it also implied a recognition by the Church of the Communist regime and a condemnation of resistance against the Marxists. A pledge to support the movement for "international peace" was immediately used to take steps against those priests unwilling to subscribe to the Communist-sponsored Stockholm appeal.

Yet the riots in Poznan (June, 1956) showed that dissatisfaction was not limited to ecclesiastical or academic circles alone. The results were far-reaching. While the "National Communist" regime of Wladyslaw Gomulka did not intend to jettison Marxist ideology and its system of governance, it did dissociate itself from Titoism and has kept its reformist supporters within bounds, Hungary's fate serving as a warning.

However, Polish-born Soviet Marshal Konstantin Rokossowski, who headed Poland's armed forces during the Stalinist years and was eased out after the October Days, received an official visit from the Polish ambassador to Moscow on November 18, 1958, and he was presented a medal in celebration of the fifteenth anniversary of Polish armed forces.

The history of Poland is entirely unique; the close relationship between Church and nation—in contradistinction to Church and state—is the key to this anomoly. Nor have Church and state always appeared on the same side of national issues; Polish cardinals have crusaded against the Crown as well as loaned it support.

Until as late as 1945, the minorities problem constituted the second most important nonunifying factor. The habit of thinking in terms of minority status has placed its mortgage on the post-1945 potential of church leadership.

Indisputably, Poland's geographical situation—at the mercy of her terrain (and neighbors)—is the salient factor. That this number one problem has contributed powerfully to the development of the chauvinistically national spirit attributed to her people is hardly to be denied, although her geography is her weakness as well.

The Slavic heritage with its mood of intense individualism is a third, but nevertheless thoroughly significant, element. It has directed historically and culturally (and still controls) many of the actions involving Poland's fortunes.

Poland, under Communist government since 1944, has had few free choices. The Marxist regimes, backed by Russian bayonets, precluded any revision of their status whether instigated by the Polish government-in-exile in London—or at Yalta and Potsdam. The Communist authority has varied in intensity of control—but not in purpose. Their stated objective is to destroy that which does not match the Marxist-Leninist ideology founded in materialism, based on a concept of world domination.

The hostility of the Roman Catholic Church has only driven the Marxist oligarchy to more subtle maneuvers. Thus, flushed by their economic rehabilitation—in terms of utility to the USSR, that is—of the Polish state and emboldened by the practical necessity faced by the Poles to maintain their postwar frontiers (especially the Oder-Neisse line, Communist-derived), the Party's position has developed so that a positive program of opposition to the regime has become increasingly difficult.

With Byzantive artfulness the Party plans to so infiltrate and subvert the Roman Catholic Church that, while its physical body may remain, its spirit will be dissipated and its utility to the Marxist cause will become that of a semi-official front or party mouthpiece. The process of denigration begun in full violence about 1950 continues regardless of the so-called Gomulka reform movement after 1956. Indeed, it is not at all difficult to suspect that Gomulka's "objective" in playing up Polish nationalism—at least his special brand of Communism for Poland—is partially to satisfy the Polish people, especially the younger generation, with the seeming "progress" achieved under his regime in order to weaken the true national spirit and attachment to the "national" Catholic Church.[11]

If this can be accomplished, it will be a simple matter to reconstruct the Church—along with other institutions of national control—and utilize their prestige and sanction for political purposes.

In April, 1961, the uneasy "coexistence" between the Polish Communist leadership and the Roman Catholic Church was ruptured as the Party began its campaign

---

[11] See Joseph S. Roucek and Kenneth V. Lottich, "Church and State Relationships in Poland," *Il Politico*, (Pavia), XXV, No. 3 (September, 1960), 512-39, especially the "Gomulka Coup," pp. 522-24. Wladyslaw Gomulka, very recently, in an American publication dealing with international affairs had this to say: "I do not exclude the possibility that there may be Polish priests who would like to play the part of political fighters against Communism, *but they are unable to find support either among the larger circles of the clergy or among the population.*" ("The Policy of the Polish People's Republic," *Foreign Affairs*, XXXVIII, No. 3 [April, 1960], 407. Italics added.) Here, of course, the facts are too well known to admit such a bald-faced distortion.

toward national elections. Denouncing Communism, Cardinal Wyszynski declared that it "can build streets and factories but it cannot administer the human conscience. . . . I tell you . . . serve only your God, because man is too noble to serve anyone but God. Man was created not just to be a consuming animal; man is called to something higher."[12] As of the moment, at least, the Red strategem to subvert religion in the Polish state had met a stiffening resistance.

Education in Poland

Polish culture, as a whole, is (or rather was) a Western culture with a Latin base, Poland being the easternmost area of Roman culture in Europe; its development has been uneven and frequently checked by such factors as internal dissention and the effects of partition; then the peak of its development in all fields—literature, art, and science—came at a time where there was no independent Poland. Cracow University was founded in 1364. Reorganized in 1400, it was subsequently called the Jagellonian University. The famous astronomers, Adalbertus of Brudzew and Nicolaus Copernicus, were alumni of this institution. Thanks to the high development of Polish culture, the sixteenth century has been called Poland's "Golden Age."

Although Polish schools, notably Cracow University, lagged behind this splendid intellectual development, many prominent scientists lived in Poland and worked in the fields of medicine, classical philology, and law; the best known has been Copernicus. In his renowned footsteps followed other Polish scientists—David Gabriel Fahrenheit, the inventor of the thermometer, who became a member of the London Royal Society. No less known abroad, and above all in England, was Samuel Hartlib (1610-70), at whose request Milton wrote his *Tractate of Education*. The Poles claim that they established the first Ministry of Education in the world. Just after the first partition of Poland, on October 14, 1773,

---

[12] *Newsweek* (New York), April 3, 1961, p. 61.

Poland's parliament voted the formation of the Commission of National Education. Deriving its funds from the property and holdings of the Jesuits (whose order had been dissolved), it made the Polish tongue the language of instruction in all schools.[13]

Education Between World Wars I and II

In spite of severe domestic and foreign problems, World War I Poland achieved a considerable amount of success in the educational field. One of the first bills passed by the government in 1920 was to establish universal compulsory education. This was most urgently needed in the territories regained from Russia, where the educational conditions were appalling. In 1921, 64 percent of the people over ten years of age, that is, born and raised in Russia's Poland, were illiterate, and among children of school age illiteracy was as high as 71 percent. By 1931, illiteracy was brought down to 41 percent in the first group and 17 percent in the second. Between 1918 and 1937, 23,604 new primary schools were opened, and in the last year preceding the outbreak of World War II, 5,402,300 children or 91 percent attended school.

Just before World War II, Poland had 27 institutions of higher learning, 74 teacher training colleges, 2,230 high schools, 103 technical training schools, 28,772 primary schools, and 1,651 kindergartens.[14]

---

[13] See Nellie Aspanasewicz, "The National Education Commission of Poland, 1773-1794," *Education Around the World* (Washington, D.C.), April 8, 1960, pp. 1-5; Frank J. Drobka, *Education in Poland, Past and Present* (Washington, D.C.: The Faculty of Philosophy of the Catholic University of America, 1927).

[14] See Wojciech Swietoslawski, "Education," chap. XVII, in B. E. Schmitt, *Poland* (Berkeley, Calif.: University of California Press, 1945), pp. 257-73; see Bibliography, p. 472. See also: Severin K. Turosienski, *Poland's Institutions of Higher Education* (Washington, D.C.: Office of Education, 1937); Maria Danielewicz, *The Libraries of Poland* (St. Andrews: W. W. Henderson & Son, 1943); R. Dyboski, *Literature, Art and Learning in Poland 1863*, in *The Cambridge History of Poland from August II to Pilsudski* (Cambridge, 1941); R. Dyboski & K. Abierski, "Poland," *Educational Yearbook of the International Institute of Teachers Colleges* (New York: Columbia University Press, 1926), pp. 321-50;

There were also the minority schools forced upon Poland by the Minorities Treaties of 1919; and there were bilingual schools and private schools—Ukrainian, Polish, German, Russian, Jewish, Lithuanian, and Czech.[15]

But as the international situation became more difficult for Poland, Poland's government restricted the minorities' rights. After 1934, when Russia became a member of the League of Nations and Poland, remembering Catherine II's intervention on behalf of her Orthodox minorities in the eighteenth century, feared that the Soviets might attempt a repeat performance of this act —which indeed they did in 1939!

Poland's educational system was divided into nine school circuits, each controlled by a "curator." Poland's nursery and primary schools were divided into 124 districts, each in charge of a school inspector subordinated to the curator who was directly responsible to the Minister of Education. The District School Councils and City Schools cooperated with the school inspector. The schools were classified as follows: (1) nursery schools for children from three to seven years of age; (2) elementary schools which are begun when the child turns eight years old with compulsory attendance of seven years; (3) secondary schools which correspond to the American high school. The organization was changed in 1932; the two lowest grades were transferred to the elementary school and the two upper schools were transformed into a separate unit called a lyceum, still attached to the gymnasium and forming with it a common combined unit. Students were not obliged to go through

---

Education in Poland (Warsaw: Ministry of Education, 1929); Stanislaw Kot, *Five Centuries of Polish Learning* (Oxford: Basil Blackwell, 1941); The Association of Polish University Professors and Lecturers in Great Britain, *Polish Science and Learning* (London, Oxford University Press, 1942); Polish Facts and Figures, No. 4, *Public Education in Poland* (New York: Polish Government Information Center, April 25, 1944); Seweryn Szczepanski, *Education in Poland* (London: Scottish-Polish Society, 1943); Joseph S. Roucek, "The Problems of Adult Education in Poland," *School and Society*, XXXXII, 1085 (October 12, 1935), pp. 512-13; Roucek, "The Results of the School Reform in Poland," *ibid.*, L, 1289 (Sept. 9, 1939), pp. 344-45; Drobka, *op. cit.*

[15] For details see Joseph S. Roucek, "Minorities," chap. X, in B. E. Schmitt, *op. cit.*, pp. 148-66.

the lyceum, but could be graduated from the gymnasium only, receiving after four years of study in the gymnasium the so-called "little *matura.*" They could then be enrolled in any kind of vocational school. But those wishing to enter a university had to graduate from the lyceum. In principle, the two-year lyceum corresponded to a junior college in the United States. (4) The professional schools, for training people for industry and trade, had two- or three-year courses in the lower grades, two- or four-year courses in the secondary school's grade after graduation from the primary school, and two- or three-year courses of lyceum's grade after graduation from a grammar school. The course in the teachers' lyceum lasted three years, and the pupils were admitted upon graduation from the third-year class of the secondary school. In the teachers college (*pedagogia*), the course lasted two years for the lyceum graduates. All teachers in the secondary school system had to be university graduates. (5) To the thirteen institutions of higher education within Poland's boundaries when the republic was formed, there were added more than twenty-two other institutions after 1918; they included four universities, an academy of mines, eight schools specializing in commerce, several for various kinds of teacher training, a school of dentistry, and a number for national defense. Applicants for admission to degree or diploma courses had to hold a maturity certificate from a former eight-year gymnasial curriculum or the two-year lyceum of general education (*liceum ogólnoksztalace*), or evidence of equivalent training. There were lower and higher degrees, the former being the *sine qua non* for admission to the latter. Lower degrees marked the completion of university studies and were essential to the practice of any profession; they were: master (*magister*) for law and philosophy; engineer (*inzynier*) for the various types of engineering; and physical (*ledarz*) for the various types of medicine—general and veterinary, and for dentistry. The doctorate was the higher scientific degree. It was conferred only on capable research workers and was not a requirement for professional standing. It could be attained in philosophy, general medicine, veterinary medicine, dentistry, and technical sciences.

In contrast to the American system, the Polish schools emphasized religion; it is interesting to note that Poland's Minister of Education was officially titled "Minster of Religious Denominations and Public Education." There was also a strong emphasis on nationalism, whether in the Polish or in Poland's minorities schools. Although the organization and curricula for the gymnasia resembled those of the American "high school," there were more required subjects in the Polish secondary school than in the American counterparts. While the Polish "high school" furnished a general education, the lyceum prepared pupils for university studies. But the insistence of Poland's masses on acquiring higher education eventually increased the attendance of the secondary schools to the bursting point; and the fold was not reduced in strength when it reached the universities. The Polish higher institutions of learning had so many graduates that the unemployed and bitter intellectual "Proletariat" became an important factor in glaring anti-Semitism and in politics. The Student Brotherhood (*Bratnia Pomoc*), the largest and strongest university student association, was dominated by chauvinistic influences and anti-Semitism.[16]

The Educational Structure under the Satellite Regime

Administration of the present educational system is essentially the same as that which existed before World War II. It is unified under the authority of the Minister of Education.[17] For administrative purposes Poland

---

[16] We shall not deal here with the standard system of continuation and vocational schools of prewar Poland. More details can be found in the references already cited.

[17] UNESCO, *World Handbook of Educational Organization and Statistics* (Paris: UNESCO, 1952), pp. 303-5, contains only some meager statistics, and no bibliography; we have summarized here the information provided by the Polish Research and Information Service (205 West 57 St., New York): *Education in Poland* (November, 1947); *Higher Education* (April, 1948); *Vocational Education* (April, 1949); *Cultural Life in Poland* (January, 1949); *Poland of Today* ("Plonia" Foreign Languages Publishing House,

is divided into fourteen school districts, supervised by a curator appointed by the President upon the recommendation of the Minister of Education and approved by the Council of Ministers. The curators have wide powers in the field of public school and preschool administration. The fourteen districts are further divided into 283 smaller units, each headed by an inspector.

Preschool training for children between the ages of four and seven is organized and maintained by state and local governments. Parents may send their children to private kindergartens, operated by social agencies, trade unions, or religious organizations and many municipalities have made attendance compulsory for those children whose mothers work or are unable to devote their full time to their children. But the system has not caught up with the needs of the country due to the high number of orphans, the large percentage of women employed in industry and in the professions, and to the inadequate housing prevailing in Poland.

The elementary school forms the basis of the entire Polish educational system; it is compulsory and free. In contrast to the prewar seven-year school, the present elementary school consists of eight consecutive year classes.

There are two types of lyceums, one for general academic education and the other for technical courses, both of which present four-year programs. The entrance requirements for lyceums is graduation from primary school. These lyceums are products of the new reform. In addition, there still remain four-year gymnasia based on the six-year elementary schools, remnants from the prewar system; efforts have been made to eliminate them entirely.

Education "of the working people" has been greatly developed. In particular, the network of primary schools for the employed was expanded in close relationship

1954), pp. 112-43. Exaggerated appraisals of Poland's educational reconstruction can be found in: Irving Brant, *The New Poland* (New York: International Universities Press, 1946); and William Cary, *Poland Struggles Forward* (New York: Greenberg, 1949), pp. 167-74.

with work establishments, Homes of the Young Worker, Workers' Hotels, and cooperative farms. There are also special institutions in which various forms of educational work are being developed outside of school hours: Pioneer Homes, Houses of Culture for the Youth, and Youth Palaces (in Stalinogrod and Szczecin). The network of vocational schools was especially expanded. The system of vocational training embraces three types of schools: basic vocational schools, technical colleges, and preparatory trade schools. The most important of these, best suited to training on a mass scale, are the basic vocational schools, preparing skilled workers for specialized work of various kinds. Students in these basic schools spend two years studying general educational and vocational subjects, as well as practical vocational tasks in school workshops. Technical colleges train personnel for average technical supervisory work, as well as for general and industrial administrative work in all branches of national economy. The courses run from three to five years. Graduates of outstanding abilities are directed to higher studies. Preparatory trade schools afford practical training in special skills which require less than a two-year training period. They are designed for adolescents over sixteen years of age, graduates from primary school, or those who, for any reason, did not finish a seven-grade school. Training lasts from three to six and one-half months. The most promising pupils are sent to technical colleges. In addition, Poland has numerous evening technical schools in all the larger industrial centers for those who are employed.

Primary school teachers must be graduates of a two-year teachers college, with two years of practice teaching and who have passed a government examination. (But a great shortage of teachers has forced the government to be lenient in enforcing these qualifications.) Pedagogic courses of six weeks to six months are offered to the graduates of secondary schools who wish to enter the teaching profession, and such teachers are appointed only on a temporary basis. Those wishing to qualify for permanent appointments attend evening educational and college classes and also study correspondence and summer courses.

Qualified teachers of secondary schools must possess a Master's degree, complete a period of practice teaching, and take a special teachers' examination. Because of the teacher shortage, those who do not meet the requirements may still be appointed if they pass a specific examination. For all teachers, the Ministry of Education provides special courses in pedagogy and in the various fields of specialization.

The new regime has brought changes in the school curricula. Stronger emphasis is placed on perceptual aids in learning. Mathematics and the natural sciences are studied more systematically. The curriculum usually includes the Polish language (grammar, writing, literature); history of Poland and Europe; geography, sciences, art, foreign languages, and religion. Recently compulsory instruction in one foreign language (English, French, Russian, or German) was introduced into the upper classes of the primary school; in addition, Latin is taught in the academic lyceum. Theoretically, religious instruction is provided by priests in each school, and while participation is not compulsory, "Most students avail themselves of this instruction."

The Political Check on School Admissions

The Polish Communist party has developed its own system of recruiting its most promising members. Recruitment officers are attached to regular schools, pass on their opinion about the graduates, and make them fill out individual forms of application. District (urban and borough) recruitment commissions accept the formal applications from June 22 to July 7, and express their opinion. The final decision depends upon the opinion of the school and district recruitment commission and upon the preliminary examination; this final examination is taken from a school recruitment commission (*komisja uczelniana*) headed by the president of the faculty. The central revocation (*Oswolawcza*) commission of the Ministry of Superior Education considers the case of stu-

dents who have been refused admission, in spite of their
having passed the preliminary examination. The political background of the candidate is a major consideration for admission, and each candidate must submit to
the recruitment commission a special certificate or a
letter of recommendation either from the Union of Polish
Youth (ZMP), from the Society for the Polish Soviet
Friendship (TPPR), or from a Communist organization.

Youth Organizations

By 1950, a complete monopolization of the school system by the ZMP (Union of Polish Youth, the Polish vari-
ant of the *Komsomol*) had been completed. This applied
equally to teen-agers of both the lower and higher classes
and the schools of higher learning. Without serving
in the ZMP, which officially controls the teaching of
Marxist dialectics, it is impossible to finish a secondary
school and it is impossible to enroll in a university or
later obtain a position. A student expelled from the
ZMP is automatically expelled from school. The fourteen to twenty-five age grouping drawn upon by ZMP
numbers approximately 4,500,000, and ZMP membership
is probably 1,200,000. But entry into the ZMP is not
truly voluntary, as indicated by the fact that ZMP
members, education once completed, do not join the
Communist party as expected. Bierut in March, 1954,
complained that the number of party members and candidates up to twenty-five years of age was still too low,
since it amounted to only 14.2 percent, while the number of those over fifty years of age was 16.6 percent.[18]
In May, 1949, 50 percent of all school youth of the ZMP
age were members, and at the end of 1951 about 70
percent.[19] Most resistance appears to come from the
young industrial worker, although he can be checked
on by the factory management,[20] and the young peasant
who openly reflects the hostility shown by his elders. In

---

[18] *Radio Warsaw* (March 12, 1954).
[19] *Kultura* (Paris), Issue Devoted to Poland, No. 5 (1953), p. 59.
[20] *Nowe Drogi* (September-October, 1951), p. 76.

May, 1949, when 50 percent of the student body were ZMP members, only 30 percent of the youth employed in industry and 15 percent of peasant youth had joined.[21]

The Youth Service, or "Service to Poland," was introduced by a law passed on February 25, 1948. The program aims: (1) To organize youth participation in the rebuilding and development of Poland; (2) to promote the acquisition of skills by young workers; (3) to improve their physical development and cultural attainments; and (4) to prepare them for the defense of the integrity and independence of Poland.

The Chief Council for Youth and Physical Culture Affairs, which is directly responsible to the President of the Council of Ministers of Poland, is responsible for determining policy of the "Service to Poland." The principal goal is the mobilization of promising boys for training as brigade and unit leaders. These are recruited mostly from overpopulated rural areas, for training and work rebuilding factories, highways, railways, draining land, and improving waterways. The brigades are organized on a military pattern, with battalions, companies, platoons, and squads. On the basis of their ability, experience, and training, the boys are eligible to advance in rank within the brigade. Manual labor in the camps is, theoretically, limited to five hours per day, six days a week. A daily three-hour period of training includes indoctrination (which is to "acquaint youth with the fundamental deep changes which are taking place in Poland"), military training (emphasizing marksmanship), and physical training. There are several reading rooms in each camp.

The vocational training part of the organization has now been organized. Special courses in wireless telegraphy, teletyping, and aeronautics have been inaugurated, but facilities are extremely limited for training in these lines, and the majority of youth has no chance, at the present, to enroll for special courses.

Scouts in Poland are Scouts in name only; step by

---

[21] Committee on Foreign Relations, *Tensions Within the Soviet Captive Countries: Poland* (Washington, D.C.: Government Printing Office, 1954), Part 5, p. 144.

step, they have been taken over by the regime until now
they are completely controlled by the Union of Polish
Youth, which the so-called Scouts are expected to join
when they reach the age of sixteen. Politically trained
activists are appointed leaders and instructors for all
the Scout troops. The Scout traditions and program have
been long since discarded as wholly capitalistic and therefore not for a "People's Democracy." Many troops bear
the name of "Paval Morozov," a Soviet Pioneer who
denounced his parents and other Russian peasants as
"kulaks" during the time when collectivization was being forced upon the rural population of the USSR. For
this act, surviving peasants killed him. The authorities
have ever since glorified the boy's action as an example
of patriotism and true devotion to the country; statues
have been erected to him and books written about him.
Now he is the model for satellite children of "Pioneer"
age, whatever their organization may be called.

The law provides that persons of both sexes between
the ages of sixteen to twenty-one inclusive, and men
twenty-one to thirty years of age who have not served
a basic two-year military duty, are subject "to the universal duty of preliminary military training." The period
of service is, theoretically, limited to six months for
youth under twenty-one, or two years for those men
between twenty-one and thirty. Exempted from training are the physically handicapped, married women,
sole supporters of families, the clergy, and certain other
groups. Rural and municipal authorities draw up lists
of those beyond the age of fifteen and deliver these rolls
to the proper county or municipal "Service to Poland"
officials.

The first day of June, officially designated Children's
Day, is handled in Poland's cities, towns, and villages
all over the country by specially appointed committees
arranging programs with unique appeal to children. In
Warsaw, for instance, the preparations for the 1952 day
were most elaborate, the city being divided into twenty
districts, with an entertainment center for each. Sports
events, games, and attractive stage shows were accompanied by the sale of Communist literature, the bulk of

which consisted of books about the Soviet Union. In Lódz, the great Polish textile center, the best pupils received prizes, and all children were given an opportunity to meet the authors of Polish children's books. The movie houses showed films for children (mostly Soviet), and entertainment was provided in the parks for both the little folks and their older brothers and sisters. Here, as everywhere, propaganda was the dominant feature of the celebration. The Polish Scouts held a great meeting on that day in Moscow. Ten thousand of then assembled in Victory Square and used a sport field in a more open part of the city for their events. This was not, however, the day celebrated as The Scout Day; that came several days earlier on the occasion of the thirtieth anniversary of the founding of the Soviet "Pioneers," the organization for children from eight to fifteen years of age to which the Polish Scouts now correspond.

Planned Employment

On March 7, 1950, a law was passed about the planned employment of graduates of vocational schools as well as high schools. Among its provisions is one which states that "Graduates of vocational schools as well as high schools can be obliged to work in their specialized fields in a given state of autonomous institutions or in some other prescribed socialized place of work." The President of the Central Bureau of Schools will "define the place of work to which the graduate is directed, also the duration of his employment, according to the needs of the given trade or specialized occupation." This can be regarded as a complement to the law relating to "Socialist discipline of work" (which was of the same date) ; together they create one system of slave labor, one of the educated class, and the second of the laborers. In 1950, and thereafter, the regime took advantage of this law to organize a mass shipment of graduates of technical high schools to Russia. Groups of graduates and students have been sent to Soviet industrial plants for "apprenticeship," but few of them have returned.

The Stakhanovite Schools

The opening of Stakhanovite schools, hitherto called "schools for work leaders," was announced from Warsaw in 1952. These schools are primarily organized near industrial establishments which have failed to fill their production plans for each year.

Regimentation of Vacations

The school vacations, under the pro-Soviet government, have become another weapon of Communism. Vacation time in Poland's schools since 1949 has been taken over and used for further indoctrination. Nationalization of resort hotels, rest homes, and boarding houses has been completed since the early spring of 1952. All the larger and better known places had been taken over by the regime in earlier years. In many instances, Communists have been put in charge who are also members of the secret police. The fortunate ones who are allowed to spend their vacations in such places cannot enjoy themselves without surveillance; they are not supposed to spend their time in doing nothing or playing without an objective. A meeting of several thousand "cultural-educational instructors" in preparation for their work in summer camps and resorts was held April, 1952, and from their number came the "instructors" assigned to work with adults. They are expected to see that adult vacationers use their week or two for more "ideological training" and less idling.

All teachers must spend their vacations being "indoctrinated." Indoctrination in the spirit of Marxism takes place at summer courses, sixty-seven of which had 4,500 participants in 1951, and in mass ideological self-education. In 1951, about thirty thousand teachers of secondary schools and employees of school administration passed an examination for "ideological self-education."

The Use of Sports

Following the example set by Soviet Russia, Poland

has a mass interest in sports. The enormously increased sport activities led to the creation of a Central Committee for Physical Culture, attached to the Office of the Prime Minister. In 1950, Poland trained 3,360 physical culture leaders and 730 athletic instructors; the Ministry of Education gave thirty-seven physical training courses to 2,500 teachers. Soccer is the most popular sport.

The Army Training

As all pro-Soviet regimes, Poland has also utilized army training for her reconditioning process of Polish citizens. Poland's army, the largest army of any of the satellites, and with a long and glorious military tradition, is being rapidly sovietized. While President Bolesaw Bierut was technically commander in chief of Poland's armed forces, Rokossovsky became the actual leader. The head of his General Staff was General Korzcyz, a Soviet officer who has been working on reorganization of the Polish Army since 1945.

Without going into details, it is obvious that not a single item in military instruction is without Soviet taint. On the higher levels, it is indicative that in June, 1952, the commencement of the Evening University of Marxism-Leninism was held in the relatively new Felix Dzerzhynski Military Political Academy at Warsaw. The occasion was the graduation of a group of soldiers and officers who had finished a two-year course in Stalin-revised Communist ideology. These men were scheduled to form a still higher army political control strata than the regular company *politruks* (political instructors).

Church and State Relations

The complete eradication of religion in Poland is a long-range objective of the Communist master plan. But, due to the well-known Polish piety, the regime has hesitated to start immediately with a direct frontal attack on religion. For a short time there was an uneasy peace which the Communist leaders attempted to wrap up in the cloak of sanctity. Some observers were even lulled into thinking that the Soviet masters had reconciled themselves to the fact that Poland is a Catholic country.

Actually, the state was elaborating a policy which, when finally revealed, was far more subtle and effective than the use of crude force. The regime's plan was to push the church hierarchy out of the national life, to isolate it by making it somehow "non-Polish" and "foreign." To this end all governmental information sources have been pouring out a continual stream of vituperation against the Papal See. When the Pope is mentioned, it is usually with the addition of the phrases "enemy of the people" or "agent of American imperialism."[22] All the theological institutions are now fully controlled by the state. The struggle between Church and state reached a climax in 1953, when the Communist government arrested the highest Roman Catholic official in Poland, Stefan, Cardinal Wyszynski, Archbishop of Gniezno and Warsaw. Many lesser clergy had been arrested early in the year. The Pope protested vigorously but in vain. The conflict was owing in part to a difference in interpretation of an agreement, never approved by the Pope, between the Polish clergy and the Polish government in 1950.

After 1949, the preparatory period of the Communists' actions against the Catholic Church resulted in the period of repressive tactics, utilizing such forms as the introduction of divorce, the breaking of the Concordat, the secularization of schools, the destruction of the Catholic press and Catholic Action, the suppression of Caritas (a clerical welfare organization), and the persecution of the Episcopate and the clergy. The state took over church properties guaranteeing to parish priests the ownership of their lands and creating a church fund. A special Office for Religious Matters, headed by a Communist, was created and made directly responsible to Premier Cyrankiewicz.

---

[22] Committee on Foreign Relations, *Tensions Within the Soviet Captive Countries: Poland* (Washington, D.C.: Government Printing Office, 1954), Part 5, p. 132. See also Roucek and Lottich, *op. cit.*

Officially Polish schools have classes in religion both in basic and secondary schools. There is of course an anti-religious trend and a tendency to suppress religious instruction by various means. Anti-religious schools have been set up since 1947. These institutions are organized and conducted by the Society of Children's Friends, the Towarzystwo Przyjaciol Dzieci (TPD), headed by Dorota Kluszynska, an old Communist party member. In 1952-53, there were 463 such schools (93 public schools, 36 secondary, 45 pedagogical lycea, and 42 training schools, and 9 lyceums for nursery teachers). The TPD also handles some 300,000 children in the field of recreational, cultural, and summer camp activities.

Press, Radio, Film

With the typical Soviet enthusiasm for using all media for propaganda purposes, the Polish government has forced a considerable development of the Polish press since World War II. The press is almost entirely Communistic, with the exception of a few religious publications. The circulation of the thirty-two dailies, with six to eight pages per copy, shows an increase of 28 percent over 1935. The seventy-six weeklies reveal an even greater increase. In addition, 550 magazines and official publications are issued. The Warsaw University School of Journalism is attended by some five hundred students; tuition fees are free and courses last four years; one year of actual training on newspapers is also required. Interestingly enough, the paper with the largest circulation is *Przyjaciolka* ("Girl Friend"), a publication for women with a circulation of 2,000,000. It need not be stressed that the country is flooded with Russian dailies and magazines.

The Polish Radio is one of the most important elements of Communist propaganda. All broadcasting stations are directed by its headquarters in Warsaw. Local and foreign communiqués are broadcast only by the Warsaw station, and are retransmitted to other provincial stations. The same rule applies to political commentaries, which are edited and worked out by a single team and used by all stations. The Sunday programs were reorganized long ago, and all religious services and sermons eliminated, thus depriving the clergy of a potent tool in its work. All concerts and shows are interrupted time and time again by propaganda slogans or by appeals. The Polish Radio also has a program for Poles "abroad," mostly for those living in France, and has until recently carried anti-Titoist broadcasts directed to Yugoslavia. The radio system derives its funds from a tax on sets, and a state subsidy. Advertising is not prohibited, but it is given limited air time, and is broadcast only by small regional stations. Shortwave programs for abroad are sent out daily by a 7.5-kw. transmitter in thirteen languages. About three hundred centers transmit programs by wire to 4,600 villages and over 200,000 loudspeakers. Some 10,000 schools are equipped with radio sets. A television transmitter is now in operation in Warsaw; the Warsaw School of Journalism has a course in radio journalism. One of the most interesting programs introduced by the Communists has been the University of the Air. A basic feature is the discussion group; each group has a leader who keeps in touch with the radio university and consults it on questions raised by his group. Members of the Polish Teachers' Union visit and assist discussions; the lectures appear in the monthly, *Radio University*. Those passing the examinations at the end of the course, which "take the form of discussion," receive a University of the Air Certificate and a prize.

The state is also directly interested in all the aspects of film production and distribution. Since 1947, Poland has produced numerous feature films, newsreels, cartoons, and marionette films. Educational films are the responsibility of the Polish Film Institute, a section of *Film Polski;* its studio produced over twenty films annually. The Institute also manages a film library and loans 16-mm. projectors to schools. Approximately 80,000 screenings are given in 3,000 schools annually, as well as in youth and workers' clubs. (Projection facilities include 574 permanent motion picture houses and 160 mobile cinemas, all publicly owned.) *Film Polski* conducts a "High School of Cinematography" for film workers.

Higher Education

Poland has had a long and noteworthy record in the field of higher learning.[23] When freedom was regained following World War I, her policy was to build more schools and to resume the old tradition of academic freedom in university life. This was accomplished, but Poland's institutions lacked a popular base, the majority of students being recruited from the middle classes.

War operations were still in progress when the Polish Committee of National Liberation (Communist) issued its first Manifesto (1944). It included as a prime objective the "reconstruction" of higher education. In the first six months of 1945, all universities that had existed in prewar Poland were again in operation, although functioning under heavy difficulties. In most situations there was a dire shortage of classrooms, facilities, and textbooks.

Cracow—least touched by the war of all Polish cities—has continued its role as one of the most active cultural centers. The new regime added other institutions to the famous university in this city as well as elsewhere in Poland. Since the most imperative demand created by World War II was the immediate functioning of the universities, no great changes were made immediately in their organization. In this the Communists played a waiting game; but repression came later.

The 1946 reform set up preparatory university sources for those who, due to war conditions, had not completed secondary courses, or who had graduated so long ago that they could no longer pass the current entrance ex-

---

[23] The following section is based on Joseph S. Roucek, "Recent University Trends in Sovietized Poland," *College and University*, XXIX, No. 1 (October, 1953), 53-64; see also G. L. Seidler, "The Universities in Poland," *Universities Review*, XX (January, 1948), 98-103; Janina Wojcicka, *Higher Education in Poland* (New York: Mid-European Studies Center, January 18, 1954), mimeographed series; and contemporary issues of *East Europe*, the publication of the Free Europe Committee, New York City.

aminations. All institutions of higher learning were made tuition free, although a registration fee is still levied. The required examination is of a general nature and covers the subjects taught in secondary schools including foreign languages, history, and civics. The institutions still maintain the divisions "academic" and "nonacademic" which had existed before the war. Over half of these schools in Poland are of the "academic" type. Polish schools are classified further, according to the sources of their funds, into government and private. The academic institutions aim to: (1) organize and pursue research; (2) prepare students for professional status in the theoretical branches of knowledge; and (3) prepare students for high technical skill.[24]

The task of the nonacademic schools, on the other hand, is limited to training persons for simple technical skills; they grant certificates or professional diplomas but do not confer degrees. Normal schools and most higher agricultural colleges fall into this category.

The lowest degree conferred by Polish universities is the master's degree. A university course leading to this degree continues for four years in every field except that of medicine, which lasts six. In all areas, a certain minimum number of hours per week of lecture attendance is required; each student must also complete a given amount of seminar or laboratory credits. Examinations are held twice a year. Before receiving the M.S., the student must pass a final examination and also present a thesis in the subject of his specialization.

A special department in the Ministry of Education administers the system of higher education, assisted by the Chief Council for Higher Education (formed in September, 1946) consisting of fifteen persons appointed by the President on the recommendation of the Minister

---

[24] Poland's engineering and physician's degrees are equivalent to master's degrees; as in France, there are Polish "physicians" and "doctors of medicine." The first title applies to the general practitioners. The B.A. corresponds to the diploma issued, for example, to a two-year graduate in mechanical engineering. See M. M. Chambers (ed.), *Universities of the World Outside U.S.A.* (Washington, D.C.: American Council on Education, 1950), pp. 751-65, for further details.

of Education. The president, or Rector, of the nonacademic institution is its director and is appointed for
five years by the Minister of Education; the president
is assisted by the School Senate, composed of the entire
teaching staff. The president of an academic institution is recommended by the staff council which elects
three members from among the staff of professors; these
three are recommended for the university presidency,
and the names are submitted to the President of the Republic of Poland, who appoints the individual for a term
of three years. The president represents the institution;
he is the executor of decisions of the Senate; he is responsible for the proper functioning of the schools, and
for its publications. Twice during the year he must
report to the Senate concerning the state of the university.

The academic Senate is composed of chairmen and
vice-chairmen of the departments, representatives of professors and instructors (one for ten). The Senate determines the budget and the needs of the institution,
and checks details of the administration. In addition
to the Senate there is also the newly created Staff Conference, which consists of the entire teaching and administrative staff and student representatives; it is an advisory and opinion-giving organ.

Departmental chairmen are elected for two years by
a majority vote of the entire teaching staff of a given
department, and the election is confirmed by the Minister of Education; the chairman represents his department and carries out the decisions of departmental
meetings. He is assisted by a vice-chairman elected in
the same manner. A recent addition to the university
structure is the post of the administrative director, filled
by nomination of the Minister of Education and directly
responsible to the president or Rector of the University.

Faculty members are appointed from a list of docents,
selected by a process known as habilitation by a council of professors of the faculty in which a docent wishes
to teach. Habilitation is conducted also by the Chief
Council of Higher Education. Normally the candidate
must possess a doctor's degree, but this requirement
may be waived by the Chief Council when the appli-

cants are outstanding scientists or educators. The applicant for habilitation must first submit an habilitation
thesis in his specialty of teaching, must satisfy the council of professors on his knowledge of the theme of his
thesis in a public discussion, and must deliver an habilitation lecture.

The majority decision of the Faculty Council must
be confirmed by the Chief Council. Professorships may
be filled by the individuals who have made outstanding
contributions to learning; they are nominated by the
President of the Republic at the recommendation of the
Minister of Education, but the Minister must consult
the faculty of the school where a vacancy exists before
making his recommendation.

Between 1945, at the time of the "revolution," and
1948, the Communist regime showed hesitation in tampering with the universities for fear of alienating certain elements of the Polish intelligentsia; thus they did
not then force the issue of Marxist instruction.

However, in 1949 all this was ended and government
protagonists—whether politicos or professors—were proclaiming "Marxism-Leninism" as the foundation of Polish
education. The universities, stigmatized as "nurseries
of reaction," were made spearheads of activity. Student
and professional groups of young natural scientists were
organized to propagate Communist doctrines in their particular fields. Radical changes had been taking place
quietly for some time in university appointment, and
the government now felt strong enough to act.[25]

It is true that the Nazi campaign for physical extermination of the Polish intellectual greatly weakened
this social class. For all practical purposes the Polish
intelligentsia has disappeared as a distinct group standing somewhat above and apart from the others. But
those who have remained thus become a weak link in
the Communist system. In the artist-intellectual the problem of preservation of his artistic integrity under Communism creates tensions. For the technician there is

---

[25] "Poland: Education Tailored to Marxist Line," *Christian Science Monitor* (August 2, 1949).

the tension rising from contact with irrational, arbitrarily exercised power and the resentment of the mechanical political conformity of a Communist garrison state. While the Polish intelligentsia can no longer be considered as a source of tension in itself, the individual Polish intellectual contributes to the stresses in Party and bureaucracy, and can become dangerous with his ideological "deviationism."

Furthermore, the Communist masters are aware that not only the old intellectuals but also the young intelligentsia hate Communism. Both groups have shown their resentment by many spectacular escapes.[26] Contrary to the periodic reports from the Communist press about the joyous life of the Polish students, it appears that there is not much enthusiasm among the university students for the new regime. To conform with the regime's demands for loyalty, this group has had to give up more than any other class. Yet the regime—rightly —mistrusts them. It hits them by limiting their scope in every direction; the students must join the Communist youth organizations. To enter a university a young man must have completed eleven years of primary and secondary school—and, above all, must be in good standing with the Party. In the Departments of Natural Sciences, entrance examinations subjects are: Soviet Agrobiology, Science of Miczurin, Reactionary Western Biology, Materialistic Genetics, and Darwinism in Soviet form. In addition, there is a separate examination on the problems of Marxism and Leninism (Stalinism). Students of "higher studies," comparable to postgraduate work in the United States, have two periods of study: (1) The first period lasts three years and the graduates receive a professional degree, such as that of foundry engineer, lawyer, etc.; (2) the second period of study, the higher "Master's course," lasts one or two years and is intended for scientific research.

The teaching program in the universities is constantly changing. At the Law Department of the University

[26] Dr. Marek S. Korowicz, "If I Were a Diplomat for the West. . . ," *Life*, XXXVI, 10 (March 8, 1954), 129ff., describes harsh life of worker, teacher, lawyer, and doctor under Soviet master plan.

of Cracow, the curriculum varies to respond to the change in Communist juridical concepts; those who have to "repeat" the course must start learning everything anew. Former lecturers are replaced by new ones with Soviet diplomas, chiefly "reactived" Poles; this term is applied to Soviet citizens of allegedly Polish descent (such as Rokossowski, the recent Commander in Chief of the Polish Army and formerly a Soviet general).

Every course, even postal laws, starts with instructions on the base and superstructure of Marxist philosophy. This basic preamble includes Russian contributions to Marxism, quotations of the classics of Marxism, and a constant repetition of the superiority of Soviet science.

The purge of professors is never absent, and includes even the cadres called Marxist scientists. (Among the promising Marxists who have recently disappeared were Professor Piwarski, of Ancient History, and Professor Sieradzki, of Contemporary Problems.) If an eminent scientist falls under suspicion, he continues to teach, but he is often isolated by a team of assistants over whom he has no influence. Sometimes, visiting Soviet scientists directly supervise the education of Polish intellectuals.

Every teacher in Poland must be a convinced Communist, who is at the mercy of the Communist school inspector. At the close of each school year, a conference of teachers is held in the capital of the district. Pictures of Lenin (now probably of Khrushchev), Bierut, and Cyrankiewicz adorn the walls of the meeting room. The head of the tuition section of the district, the school inspector, some party secretaries, and a delegate from the district administration are in attendance. After the teachers' reports are read, they are criticized on a number of counts; if the teacher has failed a pupil, if he did not participate actively in political lectures, if there is an unfavorable report on him from a pupil —all these "shortcomings" are subject to severe upbraiding.

Before the regular school year, the principal, instructed by school inspectors, who in turn depend on the Commissariat of Education for their directives, holds work meetings twice a week with teachers and outlines instructions to them. These are then incorporated by the teacher into a highly detailed "plan of operation," which is submitted to the principal for signature at the following meeting. The plan must cover the subject of instruction for each class hour, tie-in the topic with contemporary political events in the village or district, describe visual aids to be used, and utilize all special occasions (birthday anniversaries of Communist leaders and heroes). The system of the "observation visit" requires each teacher to enter his colleagues' classrooms without warning, listen for teachers' "mistakes," and report the findings "critically" at the next work meeting.

Even this apparently airtight system has not been working too satisfactorily. In 1949, the government decided to substitute for the old independent class a new "so-called People's Intelligentsia," to consist of men whose spiritual functions have been standardized and are perfectly controllable from the outside. The Polish universities were deprived of the right to select their heads or their professors, to determine the curriculum and methods of teaching, to select the textbooks, or even to decide on the admission of students.[27] The "planless and undisciplined" organization of the old universities had to give way to "the modern Socialist system of the planned production of cadres, which so brilliantly passed and is passing the test in the Soviet Union."[28] Then, with Lysenko genetics *de rigeuer* up to the Oder and Neisse boundary (if not beyond), Polish natural science was being smartly stepped up to the party line.[29]

The newly formed Polish Society of Marxist Scientists was directly affiliated to the *New Roads,* Communist party organ, then ideological Stalinism exponent in Poland, for the purpose of facilitating supervision and seeing that the ideas of the natural scientist and Politburo coincide. At the same time, a congress of teachers for

---

[27] T. Sulimirski, *The Pattern of Life in Poland: The Universities, Professional Education and Science* (New York: Mid-European Research and Planning Center, April, 1952).

[28] *Trybuna Ludu* (October 2, 1950).

[29] "Poland: Education Tailored to Marxist Line," *Christian Science Monitor* (August 2, 1949).

the Warsaw area was used by government speakers to
warn them that Marxism must be given its due place
in the school curriculum. Vacation time in Polish schools
in 1949 was already used for further purging of teachers
suspected of lack of proper political loyalty. An Institute of Education of Scientific Cadres was set up in
1950 as an agency of the Communist party to insure
ideological conformity. Polish scientists started to receive the unasked advice of their Soviet colleagues, and
in Warsaw a thirty-story skyscraper has been built as
a gift from the USSR to house the Polish learned societies. Thus the Poles are also reminded of the Orthodox church which the Czars built to tower above the
city of Warsaw.

In October, 1952, the Polish Academy of Sciences was
established by parliamentary decree; it is closely pat-
terned on the Soviet model (which is controlled directly
by the Council of Ministers). All important blueprints
for scientific projects relating to Poland's economy and
culture are worked out under government guidance and
implemented by the Academy, which exercises comprehensive powers under constant government supervision.

The Russification Process

In another chapter, we describe how the Russification
process is being imposed on the cultural base of all
satellites. The importance of this weapon is glaring in
the case of Poland, Czechoslovakia and Bulgaria, too,
since these nations are considered as being Slavs by
reason of their origins, and hence also receptive to the
Pan Slav propaganda which now identifies this concept
with the "great" Russian people, their history, and contemporary world-wide contributions.[30] It is sufficient to

[30] For more details, see Joseph S. Roucek, "Soviet Nationality
Policy: Pan-Slavism as an Ideological Weapon," *Problems of
Communism*, IV, 3 (July-August, 1954), pp. 20-28; Jindrich Kucera,
"Soviet Nationality Policy: The Linguistic Controversy," *ibid.*,
II, 3 (March-April, 1954), pp. 24-29; Solomon M. Schwarz, "The
Soviet Concept and Conquest of National Cultures," *ibid.*, II, 6
(1953), pp. 41-46; Uriel Weinreich, "The Russification of Soviet
Minority Languages," *ibid.*, II, 6 (1953), pp. 46-56; Richard E.

state here that, apart from the Russification of the school textbooks, and forcing the youth to read the Russian classics, efforts have been made to spread Moscow's language to the level of "the world language of the Socialist era"; the "Circles of Polish-Soviet Friendship," existing in all schools, are now enforcing the knowledge of the Russian language and culture.

The pro-Kremlin line on education adopted in Poland twists history by leaving out chunks of it that today are unpalatable politically. It glorifies the Soviet Union and pretends that Soviet-Polish "friendship" is essential to the interests of peace. The songs that the Polish sing today have been taking on the Communist tinge. Masurs are still coming down from the mountains, the rain keeps on falling, and old father Virgil has lost none of his 123 children. But other songs are about the Communist "pioneers" from the Soviet land and about the joy of work for the "Socialist fatherland." Some of the words commonly used by children are new—adaptations of words from foreign lands, usually with Soviet influence. A trollybus is called a *trailus,* an office building a *bluroweic,* a skyscraper a *weisowiec.*

In 1949, in order to rewrite and expunge the dismal record of Polish-Russian history, the pro-Soviet authorities inaugurated "Friendship with the USSR Month" in Poland. During this drive, which started on October 9, no phase of propaganda appeared to have been overlooked. The drive included mass meetings all over the country, performances of Russian plays and films, exhibitions, lectures, concerts, and the sale of 500,000 books at drastically cut prices. During the "friendship month," all theaters in Poland showed Russian modern and classical plays; most cinemas are restricted to Russian films. A troupe of well-muscled and often handsome boys and girls of the *Komsomol* are always touring the country telling of "their happy lives" under the Soviet system.

Pipes, "Bolshevik National Theory Before 1917," *ibid.,* II, 5 (1953), pp. 22-27; Solomon M. Schwarz, "Self-Determination Under the Communist Regime," *ibid.,* II, 5 (1953), pp. 28-34; Nicholas Vakar, "Soviet Nationality Policy: The Case History of Velorussia," *ibid.,* III, 5 (September-October, 1954), pp. 25-32.

Russian musicians are imported to do the same with cellos and oboes. The Polish radio gives time every evening to Russian "subjects" and also Russian music, with which even the world-publicized Chopin Centennial had to compete for place.

Similarly, schoolteachers are briefed to include in their daily program talks informing Polish children of the Soviet Union's might, of its struggle for the happiness of humanity, and of the great care it devotes to its children. Huge posters are displayed in the streets and meeting halls. The biggest and brightest was in 1949: "Russia's Help, Russia's Example—These Are the Basis of Our Victory." And the controlled press always plays its part with monotonous fidelity of phrase.

But how little sympathy the Poles have for the Russians is seen in the fact that, although the Association for the Friendship with Russia was founded in 1945, in 1949 it had only five thousand members out of a population of 25,000,000. There are many Poles whose memory goes back to Czarist days. And their grandchildren need only recall the Molotov-Ribbentrop Pact of 1939, followed by the invasion of Poland by the German Wehrmacht, with the Red Army not far behind (in fact, only three days).

Special treatment has been reserved for Poland's historians. This springs from the Polish nationalistic attitude rooted in the terrible days of the Four Partitions and their consequences; Polish feeling runs contrary to the pro-Soviet ideology sponsored by the Marxist regime. So prior to the Seventh Congress of Polish Historians, held at Wroclaw in September, 1948, Polish historiography was allowed to develop quite freely.[31] Up to that time, Polish scholars continued to avail themselves of the traditional approach, so firmly grounded in the Polish nation's whole history. But as the Communist govern-

---

[31] Elizabeth Valkenier, "Soviet Impact on Polish Post-war Historiography, 1946-1950," Journal of *Central European Affairs*, XI, No. 4 (January, 1952), 372-96; O. Forst de Battaglia, "Polish Post-War Historiography," *Eastern Review* (Klagenfurt-Wien), I, Nos. 3-4 (October-December, 1948), 22-43. See also M. A. Zinoviev, "Soviet Methods of Teaching History (Ann Arbor, Mich.: J. W. Edwards, 1952).

ment increasingly consolidated its forces and Poland was being drawn ever more closely into the Soviet economic orbit, Polish historiography came under heavy criticism.

The regime insisted that written history should support it and withdraw from its nationalistic and neo-Marxian approach. Indeed, the Wroclaw Congress had been organized by the Ministry of Education with these ends in view. The methods of dialectical and historical materialism were to be introduced into Polish historiography. Standards for such a change had already been set by Soviet historians, who had been occupied for some time rewriting Polish history according to the basic tenets of Soviet internationalism and dialectical materialism.

Out of this Congress emerged the newly formed "Association of Marxist Historians," a pivotal element within the body of Polish historians, a small group of self-styled Marxist historiographers who responded to the official demand for a "progressive" science; this group assumed leadership with Soviet briefing under governmental prodding; it began the transformation of Polish historiography from a bourgeois into a Marxian "science." Three leading Soviet historians attended: P. Tretiakov, A. Sidorov, and I. Udaltsov.

At the same time, the government sponsored the joint meeting of secondary history teachers with the Association. However, a lukewarm response—only eight having joined the A.M.H.—induced the Ministry of Education to allow only the members of the Association to report to the meeting of history teachers. Historical journals were reorganized, scholars began to be carefully supervised, and new textbooks for schools and universities were published. The emphasis of Polish historiography was shifted from West to East in the journals, and their pages were devoted to a critical revision of Polish history.

The former objectivity of Polish historical schools was ridiculed, and it was stressed that Polish historical writing would gain from the study of Soviet historical methods—with Stalin as the greatest theoretician in history! Marxist historiography of the Soviet Union provided the basis and produced a new periodization and evaluation of the past. No allowance was made for an

honest difference of opinion or for a reconciliation of the
old with the new; every discussion was based on the
polarization of all historical writing into "antiquated"
bourgeois, and "progressive" scientific Marxist works.
Having great difficulty in securing enough articles and
studies of this type, the Ministry invoked the use of
pressure to secure it. In order to facilitate supervision
and to see that the ideas of the historians and the Politburo coincided, the Association was directly affiliated to
New Roads, the Communist party organ in Poland and
ideological exponents of the now discredited Stalinism.

An all-out drive by Poland's government to revamp
education along Marxist lines was even more visibly
under way following a visit to Moscow by Stanislaw
Skezeszewski, Minister of Education, in 1949. In an
address at a conference of school superintendents, he
commended teachers for spreading Communist doctrines,
but emphasized that still more was to be done; there
was need for "reform" in certain places. Among these
was the ancient (1364) Jagellonian University at Cracow, which received special attention for "not progress-
ing with the tempo of revolutionary changes." (Only
23 percent of the students belonged to Communist organizations.) The Communist party of the Cracow district sent several groups of young Communists to the
USSR for training, so that their activities in proselyt-
izing might prove more fruitful. A special decree of
the Ministry of Education provided for "School Youth
Teams" in Polish professional, vocational, normal, and
general education schools; these teams, consisting of the
director of the school, with two other school officials
and several students, were to keep watch over the political attitudes of both teachers and students. Regional
youth conferences soon were taking place all over Poland.

Members of the Union of Polish Youth—the Polish
counterpart of *Komsomol,* the Soviet Youth agency—were
leaders in this drive. Present also were the so-called "Political Instructors," whose job it is to whip up and support
enthusiasm for the regime and its Moscow-inspired line.
Medical and engineering courses were shortened because
the government was eager to replace officials and em-

ployees of the older prewar generation with its newly indoctrinated younger men and women. To tighten its grip
on an even more immature group, the state took over the
Polish Boy Scout organization; a new eight-point scout
law was adopted, emphasizing that Polish children are expected to become solidly integrated into the "front of
builders of Socialism."

In addition to submitting historians and others to official supervision, the Marxists made substantial changes
in the teaching of history. Schools on all levels had their
programs and textbooks changed; all were to present historical development in the light of the class struggle;
carefully left unmentioned were the points of friction in
the history of Polish-Russian relations. The Polish Marx-
ian-historians visited Moscow in October, 1950, and con-
sulted the members of the Soviet Institute of Slavic Studies on how to handle problems in teaching the history of
Poland.

General directives for the future tasks of Polish historians were promulgated in 1952 by Edward Ochab, Secretary General of the Central Committee of the Polish United Workers' (Communist) party.[32] Speaking to a year-
end Warsaw Congress of historians, he told them that they
should take as the text for their work a declaration of Karl
Marx's disciple, Friedrich Engels, that "Poland will be
revolutionary, or there will be no Poland."

Polish history, reiterated Ochab, must be written in
such a way that "it helps President Bierut, the Polish
United Workers' party, and the nation as a whole to build
Socialism in the country." He complained that prewar
history in Poland had been "to a great extent falsified to
serve the ruling bourgeois clique." But, he added happily,
if they studied the research work of Soviet historians carefully, Polish historiographers would "find it easy to unmask the anti-Polish rule of the Vatican and English-
American imperialism."

Ochab also said that the return of the Western territories, Silesia and Pomerania, had placed a huge task in

---

[32] "Polish History Due for Kremlin Slant," *Christian Science
Monitor* (February 9, 1952).

the lap of the historians. They must rewrite the history of these lands in the light of their struggle against German imperialism. The Polish peasant must be pictured in his struggle against landlords and foreign invaders; of course, this fight ended in victory under the leadership of the working class and their friends of the Soviet revolution. But the historian must not stop even at this; he must look beyond the borders, toward the brotherly nations of the Ukraine and Byelorussia, which for centuries had been oppressed by the Polish gentry. The modern Polish historian must seek inspiration in the wars of the old Polish kings, for, said Ochab: "The party and a large part of the nation are aware that they cannot properly fight to bring socialism to Poland without a right knowledge of the country's past. The historian must prove that patriotism and internationalism can join forces. . . . He must expose cosmopolitan traitors and agents of the imperialists, and must stress the leading part played by the Soviet Union in its fight for peace against the gangsters under the sign of the dollar and the atom bomb."

Indeed the historian who was to follow this program had no easy task. Three times in the eighteenth century, and once in the nineteenth, Poland had been partitioned among Prussia, Russia, and Austria. One hundred years after the Congress of Vienna, Poland again gained her independence at the insistence of American President Woodrow Wilson. She maintained it for twenty years, but then, in 1939, after a short-lived resistance to Hitler's blitzkrieg, division again occurred, Germany and the Soviet Union operating under the secret provisions of the Molotov-Ribbentrop Pact. Five years of brutal occupation followed, until Poland experienced "liberation" by the Soviet Army, which conveniently brought a Russian-made government in their baggage train. The Poles never had a chance. This is straight history which the Polish historian must slant to justify the policies of the Marxist regime; according to the so-called Stalinist dialectic of history, the old "error" must be completely cleaned up for the new history textbook.

"History" in today's Poland is the "study of mankind." First one encounters a simplified version of Darwinism.

Then, in the subsequent struggle for life, the Polish nation is shown as having one powerful and dangerous neighbor—the Prussian state. The new textbooks gloss over—or simply ignore—Poland's difficulties with the Russian state, a conflict extending over approximately one thousand years. Finally—according to the "new history"—blessings uncounted came via the USSR signaled by the Bolshevik revolution and culminated by the granting of "independence" to Poland. It is conceded that, in the early days, Christianity proved a boon; lately, however, its consequences have been disastrous (This is because of the "unholy alliance" between the Vatican and the warmongering democracies). Except for the Nazi persecution, there is no word about the Jews. Generals Kosciuszko and Pulaski are mentioned, but in the "study of mankind" Kosciuszko is the hero.

The Communist party is the all-pervading influence in the whole system; it has its own social-educational commission which controls all admissions to higher education. Recruitment officers are attached to each school; they pass on the qualifications of graduates and require them to submit individual forms of application; they are supervised by district (urban and borough) recruitment commissions. (The central revocation commission *(Odwolawcza)* of the Ministry of Superior Education considers the cases of students who have been refused admission, and each candidate must produce for the recruitment commission a special certificate or a letter of recommendation either from the Union of Polish Youth (ZMP), from the Society for the Polish-Soviet Friendship (TPPR), or from another Communist organization.

With the introduction of the "aspirancy" system in academic studies, Poland's government in 1952 took another step toward making Polish educational policy identical with that of the USSR. When a Pole obtains a master's degree, he starts to work not for a "doctorate" but for an "aspirancy." The decree of the regime states: "To prepare for the degree [master's] or the equivalent of those studies, those who have shown a love and aptitude for scientific work, may be accepted for aspirancy studies." This indicates that such applicants must have the degree of Master of Arts, Doctor of Medicine, or Master of Engineering.

However, the mere possession of such a degree does not mean that the applicant has to be accepted. The final decision rests with the executive committee of the Polish Academy of Sciences, or the Minister under whose authority the educational department concerned happens to be. If he is accepted, the student has two years of study with a stipend of 700 slotys (about $175 at the official rate of exchange) per month, but he is not allowed to carry on any outside work except by permission of the appropriate Minister.

After acceptance, the student is assigned to a special Department or Institute, to which he is attached throughout the two years. The rector of the University or the director of the Institute then appoints one of the independent workers in that body as the student's responsible supervisor. The tutor maps out the course, which must be likewise approved by the Dean or Director. The plan is similar to that required for the doctorate in Western universities, but the contents of the course work differ. The "aspirant" must pass three examinations; the first in dialectical materialsm, another in his special field, and a third on the basic discipline in the branch he has chosen. In addition, he must demonstrate his proficiency in two foreign languages. On the satisfactory completion of his studies, he is granted the degree of "Candidate of Sciences" and is sent to work in a post assigned to him.

Moreover, the Communists have tightened the standards since 1951, which of course gives them an even better leverage. All students must attend classes and pass examinations. An absence of one day without justification results in a reprimand; two days' absence merits the same plus the placing of the student's name on the blackboard; three days missed incur a reprimand, notation in the personal record, name placed on the blackboard and—for those on scholarships—withholding of one month's pay; unexcused absence of four days results in the previous punishments plus the loss of four months' stipend—or expulsion from the university.

Another pro-Soviet innovation is a system known as

"transfer of credits" *(dwustopniowsosc)*, whereby graduates of nonacademic institutions may enter a university without loss of the credit earned in their previous schools and then work toward an academic degree.

As indicated above, discipline and punishments are severe. Fines and penalties are decided by the disciplinary commission, consisting of the Dean and two delegates of the respective departments chosen from among professors or assistant professors. The Commission arranges a hearing and, having listened to the student's explanation, considers the opinion of the delegate of that branch of the Union of Polish Students before making a final decision.[33]

As in all satellite countries, Poland's spokesmen for the pro-Soviet regime have claimed considerable accomplishments for the educational system tailored to the Marxist line. There is no question that, since World War II, Poland's education has been undergoing a tremendous expansion and overhauling. In relation to the total pattern of the social transformation of Poland into a Soviet satellite, Poland offers an illuminating example of how education can be used to transform the Christian and Catholic nation, formerly antagonistic to everything Russian and insistent on retaining all its cultural links with the West, to an inferior and servile state tied up to the Soviet chariot, whose Communist and Asiatic dominant characteristics have only one relationship to the people of Poland—that the Russians are also of Slavic origin. Education has been the main weapon of the followers of the Kremlin in this forcible process of transformation. Russian is taught in all schools and universities. Translations from Russian loom large among manuals, scholarly books, and popular scientific literature. All Polish history, not only political but cultural and literary history as well, is being rewritten. This is calculated to demonstrate that, in all Russian-Polish historical relations, Russia seemed always to have been the leader and giver. At the same time, many historical facts are conveniently forgotten. (For instance, during the seventeenth century,

---

[33] For further details, see National Committee for a Free Europe, *Poland in the Year 1951* (New York, 1952), pp. 103-8.

Polish cultural influences were fairly strong in Russia; the Polish language was spoken at the Kremlin, Polish books were translated, Polish manners imitated by the boyars. But there is no mention of these influences today in Polish history.)

But, next to Hungary, the Soviet masters have been confronted in Poland with the most persistent opposition to Soviet imperialism. The peasantry has opposed the Soviet collective farm system; the industrial workers have been groaning beneath the burden of intolerable workloads and an ever-lowering standard of living; the clergy has led the forces against godless persecution; and some six million Americans of Polish descent have been helping the aspiration of Poland's young people, many of whom have been refusing to abandon the proud heritage of pre-Soviet Poland.[34]

Even the early Communist ranks of Poland produced their "Titos"—as shown by the charges against Wladyslaw Gomulka, the first postwar Communist party leader, who was guilty (among other things) of having appealed to nationalist sentiments by evoking the traditions of the old Socialist party. Although he fell from favor, Gomulka was reinstated following the October demonstration in 1956. While not a Titoist, he is a nationalist.

In its own social composition, for example, the Communist party has not been able to attain that representation of the peasant-worker alliance demanded in Leninist theory. Party membership among the workers and the peasants, all evidence shows, has decreased, particularly among the latter (probably because the organizational pressures used against the factory worker cannot be applied in the countryside).

As noted above, Poland's intellectual class, as a result of the Nazi terror, hardly exists any longer. Those who remain have their memories of the past glory of Poland and are resentful of the tactics of a Communist garrison state. "While the intelligentsia can no longer be consid-

---

[34] Committee on Foreign Relations, *Tensions Within the Soviet Captive Countries*, Part 5: *Poland* (Washington, D.C.: Government Printing Office, 1954), is the best available systematic survey of the nationalistic forces opposing Poland's pro-Soviet regime.

ered as a source of tension in itself, the individual Polish intellectual may well contribute to the stresses in Party and bureaucracy.[35]

The Marxists have tried to substitute a new so-called "People's Intelligentsia" for the old independent intellectual class. But the regime has had difficulties in creating this class, and the authorities have complained about the inability of the history teachers to grasp the intricacies of the Marxist dialectic and the failure of the universities to denounce teachers who reject Marxism, and the scientists who are still enticed by "the myth of the predominance of Western science." It is apparent that youth in the universities are hand-picked (as described in previous pages) for political orthodoxy and social origin. But the system is learning that it has the same old human nature to contend with, and there is evidence that many young Poles still entertain "capitalistic" ideas and habits derived from their homes or from listening to the Voice of America. Furthermore, those who read Polish must sooner or later reach Mickiewicz or Slowacki, and the amount of "Catholicism and anti-Russianism to be found there will require much Orwellian 'newspeaking.' "[36]

Developments in Elementary Education

Probably most successful have been the Communist educational efforts in the primary school, where the Church has been forced to teach. In this respect, the Western world should realize that "It is later than you think," and that in the more than 300,000 children who yearly begin primary school in Poland, the Kremlin has manpower which in a few years will contribute strongly to the Polish armed forces.

After 1944, the new Communist regime in Poland declared its policies in education to consist of (1) the broadening of the social composition of youth in schools and (2) the "democratization" of higher education. A "nationwide" educational conference was held in Lódz in June,

---

[35] *Ibid.*, p. 142.
[36] *Ibid.*, p. 144.

1945, at which the first plans for school reform were elaborated; the changes were formalized by a decree on November 23, 1945.[37]

The educational policy of the post-1945 Polish government (Communist) contemplated a gradual replacement of the old Polish system by one based on the educational principles followed by the USSR. Although the new regime expanded the size of the school system, it—at the same time—narrowed the range and scope of studies. Everything was controlled by central ministerial bodies. The goal was to (1) indoctrinate along Marxist Socialist lines and (2) to produce quickly and maintain a skilled labor force in order to carry out the government's economic plans for a new industrial expansion tied to the Soviet Union.

On February 25, 1948, a decree was passed on the "universal duty of preparing the youth in vocational, physical education, and military fields." Every boy and girl between sixteen and twenty-one was obliged to serve for six months with troops of the "Service for Poland," a para-military-type organization. Youth had to work for six hours a day and spend the remaining time on education, recreation, and ideological indoctrination."[38]

After 1948, new textbooks on biology, history, and geography, rewritten as described above, were ready for use by the fall of 1949. Russian language instruction and Russian literary classics likewise became a part of the revised curricula. The chief purpose of the educational system was to emphasize industrialization and close ties with the USSR. Through its territorial reduction, mentioned earlier, Poland became more homogeneous, and the acquisition of the former German-held sections in Silesia served to emphasize industrialization.

Children between the ages of three and seven may attend nursery schools, where emphasis is on play and games so that the child may gain a feeling for cooperative liv-

---

[37] For a more complete analysis of Polish education, see *Educational Systems in Poland*, by Nellie Apanasewicz and William K. Medlin (Washington, D.C.: U.S. Department of Health, Education and Welfare, 1959), No. 12 (March), 32 pp.

[38] *Educational Systems, op. cit.*, p. 19.

ing. The child learns to count, measure, and help with home duties. Subjects including drawing, music, and the Polish language are taught. These schools are maintained by the government but are operated by the local school authorities, factories, or other places of employment, and even by social organizations. If there are no facilities for regular nursery schools, centers are organized for a few hours, once or twice per week.

The seven-year elementary school (reduced from eight years and begun in 1948-49 offers basic education; it is compulsory between the ages of seven to fourteen. However, if a student has not completed the prescribed courses, he must remain in school until he becomes sixteen. This is another safeguard in the drive to establish a young and basically educated work force, educated both in the rudiments and in Communist ideology. (The youth organization "Service for Poland" was disbanded in late 1956, apparently having fulfilled its purpose.)

Indoctrination in Higher Education

In the field of higher education the decree of October 28, 1947, abolished the traditional forms of academic organization and nationalized all private higher schools, with the exception of the Catholic University of Lublin. As noted above, in 1950 control passed from the Ministry of Education to the Ministry of Higher Education. In 1951, a new Polish Academy of Sciences—modeled on the Soviet organization—superseded the Polish Academy of Sciences and Letters.

Regardless of all these controls, the government was still unhappy with the cooperation gained and, after the political reorganization effected in October, 1956, with the reinstatement of Wladyslaw Gomulka, it granted a certain degree of autonomy to universities by allowing them to elect members of the Commission on Higher Education. They were also given some authority to develop their own courses of study although—in such a situation —this freedom may be reduced as rapidly as it has been gained. Moreover, Communist motives are not always clear.

Institutions for higher education operate under a law of December 15, 1951 (*Dziennik Ustaw*, No. 6, Item 38). It is clearly stated in Article I that higher schools "are responsible for the development of cadres of the people's intelligensia devoted to sacrificial service to the country to fight for Socialism and peace, and to spreading the scientific outlook throughout the world." This law transplanted the Russian system, called *aspirantura*, for the education of scientific specialists and the provision of cadres for scientific teaching. A graduate of this system receives the title Candidate of Science *(kandydat nauk)*, which replaces the Doctor of Philosophy of Western higher education.

Between 1950 and 1956, the faculties of theology were abolished; Pavlovian psychology was instituted, and—under the Soviet influence—the teaching of philosophy, political science, and economics was reorganized within the Marxist context.[39] Research was separated from the universities and transferred to centrally controlled institutes. Required subjects were Marxism-Leninism, dialectical and historical materialism, political economy, and the Russian language. Curricular offerings involving the study of the Soviet Union were expanded, many students being sent to the USSR to continue their study.

Since 1956 (as noted elsewhere), the above requirements have been somewhat relaxed. Chairs in philosophy have been reestablished, and social science teaching again includes the study of all major points. Nevertheless, speaking of economics only (although this may be considered typical), the dilemma in Soviet education becomes apparent. "It is clear that the student who follows the course up to this point will obtain a thorough grounding in the economic ideas of Marx, Engels, and Lenin, together with some knowledge of current Soviet criticisms of 'bourgeois' economic theory. It is not so clear—although naturally a great deal depends upon the way in which the subject is taught—that he will obtain anything like a really ob-

---

[39] See "The Teaching of Economics in the USSR and Poland" by Ronald L. Meek, *Soviet Studies*, X, No. 4 (April, 1959), 339-59.

jective view of economic conditions in the contemporary capitalist world."[40]

Summing up the Polish program it can be said that: "it clearly bears the marks of compromise. On the one hand, it reflects a certain revulsion against the dogmatism, apolegetics, and uniformity which seem to have been characteristic of the teaching of political economy in Poland in the years prior to 1956, and also a feeling (on the part of at least a substantial minority) that Marxist economists have unduly neglected some of the more positive achievements of 'bourgeois' economics. On the other hand, it reflects the view that a political economy course in a country like Poland should remain basically Marxist in character, and that the freedom of the lecturer to put forward his own views should exist only within this Marxist framework. It seems fair to say, however, on the basis of a comparison of the Soviet and Polish programs, that the boundaries of the Marxist framework are much more elastic in the case of the Polish course than they are in that of the Soviet course."[41]

There are at present eighty-three institutions of higher education. Under the Ministry of Higher Education and Science there are eight universities; twenty technical universities including nine evening schools of engineering; ten higher schools of economics and two higher schools of agriculture. The Ministry of Culture and Art has eighteen higher art schools under its control. Six state universities are under the Ministry of Education, ten academies of medicine under the Ministry of Health, and one higher school of law under the Ministry of Justice. Under the Chief Commission for Physical Culture are four academies of education, three military academies, and an institute for training scientific manpower. Faculty appointments are made by a political committee which requires teachers to be ideologically and politically dependable—from the Marxist point of view, that is.

Historically and culturally, Poland is one of the best known, to the average American, of the East Central Eur-

[40] Meek, *op. cit.*, p. 347.
[41] *Ibid.*, p. 357.

opean countries. Polish assistance at the time of the Revolution, sympathy directed toward the Poles in their own struggles against the partitioning powers upon numerous occasions, the influence of Wilsonian self-determinism in the creation of the new Polish state in 1919, and the contributions of the Poles to the world of science, literature, and the creative arts, all served to produce strong attachment to the Polish people and their state. Jan Wepsiec, in *Polish Institutions of Higher Learning*,[42] says:

"Expanding relations between Poland and the Western countries in recent years [and this in spite of Communist restriction and control) have encouraged intensified research on Poland . . . (and her institutions for cultural advance)." Wepsiec lists, in addition to universities and colleges, learned societies, libraries, art galleries and museums, observatories and botanical gardens, and institutes in the various specialized fields.

Because it is pertinent to our study, his list (both in Polish and in English) of colleges and universities, together with the dates of their founding, is included here.

Katolilicki Uniwersytet Lubelski (Catholic University in Lublin), 1918.

Uniwersytet im. Mikolaja Kopernika w Toruniu (Nicolaus Copernicus University in Toruń), 1945.

Uniwersytet im. Adama Mickiewicza w Poznaniu (Adam Mickiewicz University, Poznań), 1919.

Uniwersytet Jagielloński w Krakowie (Jagellonian University in Kraków), 1364.

Uniwersytet Lódzki (University of Lódz), 1945. Absorbed Syzsza Szkola Pedagogiczna in 1956.

Uniwersytet Marii Curie-Sklodowskiej w Lublinie (Marie Curie-Sklodowska University, Lublin), 1944.

Uniwersytet Warszawski (University of Warsaw), 1818. Absorbed Wyzsza Szkola Pedagogiczna in 1956.

Uniwersytet Wroclawski im. Bieruta (The Boleslaw Bierut University of Wroclaw, founded in Lwów (Lemberg) in 1661, transferred to Wroclaw (Breslau) after World War II.[43]

Under the Communist regime schooling has been great-

---

[42] (New York: Polish Institute of Arts and Sciences in America, 1959), 110 pp.

[43] Wepsiec, *op. cit.*, pp. 11-13.

ly extended to citizens of all ages in the form of primary, secondary, and higher education. There are elementary schools for adults as well as the regular four-year adult secondary schools. In the latter, one foreign language is compulsory, and the usual requirements in physical education, art, and singing are waived. Examinations in the Polish language and mathematics are given at the year-end in grades VIII, IX, and X. On the completion of Grade XI, a matriculation certificate—corresponding to that awarded at the completion of the general secondary school —is given.

But so-called "Popular Universities" and "People's Universities" are not really institutions of higher education. The first were begun in 1957-58 by industry and by various social and educational organizations and institutions. The two-year program, in the form of lectures and seminars, is based on three or four hours twice a week; seven months in urban areas and five months in rural areas are required.

"People's Universities," although financed by the government, were set up by young people's unions and other cultural and educational organizations and institutions. All candidates for admission to the "People's Universities" must be eighteen years old and must have had at least an elementary school education. This course continues for five months and is based on lectures, seminars, administrative and social work of a practical nature, and participation in sports. The significance of these last two programs in the building of the Socialist state can hardly be overemphasized.

Two goals motivate the Soviet educational planning in East Central Europe; first, their objective is to replace the old middle-class intelligentsia—too strong in its allegiance to Western culture, or so the Communist mind runs—with a new "intelligentsia" whose support of the Communist system is to be insured by its own self-interest as well as by indoctrination in Leninism-Marxism; secondly, the avowed function of higher education under Communism is to train specialists for science, industry, and professional duties in the expanding Socialist empire. Indeed, the objective is to prepare "not only specialists, not only class-conscious citizens, but class-conscious fighting Communists who will take an active part in political life after graduation."[44]

Today, Poland's place in the higher education picture of the Soviet bloc is somewhat of an anomaly. Following the October, 1956, crisis, the Gomulka regime lightened the requirements in university education in one Communist country. "Perhaps the most profound, if least tangible, change unique to Poland was the official espousal of the principle of intellectual freedom, however hedged by qualifications and conditions. Marxism-Leninism was still the official ideology, but intellectual practice was far less doctrinaire."[45]

The question of political prestige in connection with matriculation was discussed in *Zycie Szkoly Wyzszy* (Warsaw) in June, 1958:[46]

"The opinion is common that in order to be admitted to a university one has to 'pay,' one has to find 'somebody' who will fix up the matter for a certain remuneration (bribe). . . . This creates an unwholesome atmosphere, which threatens the good name of the universities and of the teaching staff. . . . This kind of intervention no doubt has its roots in the errors of the past years, when unwritten privileges or reservations were in force regarding admittance to universities. It was no secret to anybody that during those years the pupils of the 11th [final high school] classes joined the ZMP [Communist Youth League] in droves in order to get into the university."

The best Communist defense is an offense, and here we see the admission of past "error" used as a shield to suggest purity in the present. The Western world would do well to learn to understand the Communist double-talk, although indeed no special codebook is needed.

Thus in September, 1958, less than a week after Khrushchev's announcement of educational reforms in the Soviet Union, Gomulka revealed that Poland should follow the lead of the USSR in measures to tighten the

---

[44] *Pravda* (Bratislava), May 19, 1958, quoted in *East Europe*, VII, No. 10 (October, 1958), 14.

[45] *East Europe*, IX, No. 5 (May, 1959), 16.

[46] Quoted in *ibid.*, p. 19.

link between education and work. Gomulka said that the new program would be a means of integrating university students with the "actualities" of Socialism, politically as well as economically; thus, in effect, diminishing their leverage as a separate element in society.

According to *Polityka* (October 4, 1958),[47] the proportion of worker-peasant students in the universities in Poland has fallen; during the past academic year 29.7 percent of the university students were of working-class origin, 22.9 percent peasant, and 42.4 percent intelligentsia. Yet one reads in *Trybuna Ludu (The People's Tribune*, Communist party organ) that the principle of ability-selection would be maintained, and it is suggested that the decline (in peasant-class admissions) was due to a lack of interest on the part of the worker-peasant parents and the inferior showing of the worker-peasant students on entrance tests because of the lower academic level of provincial schools. There was not, however, any suggestion that the state revert to class origin as qualification for preferred admission to higher education.[48] One is tempted to suspect that what really is at stake here is efficiency. The peasants could as well be used in the work force, and the middle-class students could be used for both indoctrination and work; in other words, much more was at stake in neutralizing the intelligentsia if this could be achieved; the peasants were probably more adaptable anyway.

Nevertheless, Communist control of higher education in East Central Europe is plagued with dilemmas (and Poland, for all its seeming advance, is no exception); with the introduction of the work program—"polytechnicism—academic life is taking a definite anti-scholastic and anti-intellectual turn. The new plan will not only reduce the number seeking access to the professions but it will also reduce the concentration of youth in universities and other higher education institutions. This reduces their force as a special—and, from the standpoint of the government, unreliable—power bloc.

Meanwhile (says *East Europe*) the question of how to

---

[47] Quoted in *ibid.*, p. 21.
[48] May 3, 1958, as quoted in *loc. cit.*,

reconcile academic and scientific achievement with ideological thought control continues to fascinate the Polish "liberals," but has been carefully laid aside throughout the rest of the East European bloc in the interest of conformism. The record of three years—1956 to 1959—thus indicates that the problems of higher learning in the Soviet-controlled area will continue to be profound—and disturbing.

The School Program

A shortened seven-year primary school is compulsory for all children from ages seven to fourteen with the proviso that, if the student has not completed the work prescribed in all elementary school classes, his schooling must continue until he has reached sixteen. This general education study plan[49] for grades I through VII is as follows:

Subjects	I	II	III	IV	V	VI	VII
			Number of Class Hours Per Week				
Polish	9	10	9	8	7	6	6
Foreign language	....	....	....	....	3	3	3
History	....	....	....	2	2	3	2/3*
Biology	....	....	3	2	3/2*	2	2
Geography	....	....	....	2	2/3*	2	2/3*
Mathematics	4	5	5	6	6	6	4
Physics	....	....	....	....	....	3	3
Chemistry	....	....	....	....	....	....	2
Drawing	1	1	1	1	1	1	1
Handicraft	1	1	1	1	1	1	1
Singing	1	1	1	1	1	1	1
Physical education	2	2	2	2	3	3	3
Total class hours	18	20	22	25	29	31	31

*The first figure represents the number of hours per week for the first half of the school year; the second figure, for the second half.

Upon completion of the elementary schooling, the student receives the primary school certificate (*Swiadectwo ukończenia szkoly. podstawowej*), provided that he passes written and oral examinations in Polish and mathematics and an oral examination in history.

It is normal practice to offer seven years of education with a teaching staff of four or more teachers, a six-year program with three teachers, and a four-year program with only one teacher.

Religious instruction is optional in post-war Poland.

---

[49] Apanasewicz and Medlin, *op. cit.*, pp. 20-21.

There are two types of secondary schools: (1) the general high school (lyceum), and the vocational or technical school. The lyceum—grades VIII-IX—represents a fusion of the former gymnasium (lower secondary) and the traditional lyceum (upper secondary) programs, which have reduced the years of study from twelve to eleven. The basic study plan[50] follows:

	Number of Class Hours Per Week			
Subjects	VIII	IX	X	XI
Polish	5	5	5	5
Russian	3	3/2*	3	3
Another foreign language or Latin	3	3	3	3
History	3	3	3	3
Contemporary Poland and the World	....	....	....	2
Biology	....	2/3*	3	2
Geography	2	3	2	....
Astronomy	....	....	....	1
Mathematics	5	4	4	4
Logic	....	....	....	1
Physics	4	3	3	3
Chemistry	2	2	2	....
Drawing	2	1	....	....
Physical education	3	2	2	2
Military training	....	2	2	2
Total class hours	32	33	32	31

*The first figure represents the number of hours per week for the first half of the school year; the second figure, for the second half.

Religious instruction is optional.

In the 1957-58 school year a basic course in genetics was introduced at grade XI. Prior to the 1957-58 school year, the subject "Contemporary Poland and the World" was referred to as "Study about the Constitution."

Upon completion of secondary school, students must pass written examinations in the Polish language and mathematics and oral examinations in Polish, mathematics, history, and one other subject selected from the following: physics, chemistry, biology, geography, English, French, German, or Russian.

In addition to the regular school program specified above, there are vocational schools and technical schools (based on the Russian *technicums*).

Elementary trade schools admit students of fourteen to fifteen years of age and offer a program lasting for three years. Preparation is made for skilled work in industry, agriculture, and commerce. The program of studies includes practical work; general subjects, including

[50] *Ibid.*, p. 22.

the Polish and Russian languages, history of Marxist Poland, physical education; vocational subjects (includes technology, study of materials and machines, technical drawing, electro-technique, administration; and auxiliary subjects: either mathematics, physics, and hygiene or chemistry, domestic science, and bookkeeping). During the 1957-58 school year, 131,326 students received training in such schools.

The following distribution indicates the arrangement of courses in an elementary trade school[51] over a period of three years:

A. Practical work:
I—12 hours per week
II—18 hours
III—21 hours

B. General subjects:
I—9 hours
II—9 hours
III—6 hours

C. Vocational:
I— 8 hours
II— 6 hours
III—10 hours

D. Auxiliary subjects:
I—7 hours
II—5 hours
III—2 hours

Technicums for the unemployed are usually five-year programs based on a seven-year elementary school. Variation exists, however; some are based on a nine-year general education and run for three years. The program of studies for the former is as follows: 33 hours per week are allotted for workshop or laboratory practice—or field work; 39-115 hours for vocational subjects, depending on the specialization; 29-37 hours for the auxiliary subjects —usually mathematics, physics, chemistry, and hygiene) ; and 50-56 hours for general subjects—history, Polish and Russian languages, information concerning Poland, economic geography, and physical education.

These schools provide a general scientific and technical training but also prepare administrative and supervisory personnel. Graduates receive both certification as technicians in a specialized field and a Certificate of Maturity, which qualifies them for admission to institutions of higher education.

---

[51] Apanasewicz and Medlin, *op. cit.*, p. 23.

Special schools are provided for handicapped children (blind, deaf, crippled, mentally retarded, and those ill with polio and tuberculosis).

Students unable to attend classes in technical schools may continue their education through correspondence schools or "non-attendance *technicums.*" These schools— five years in length—follow the program of the regular technical school and are based on the conventional seven-year elementary school. Students are required to do practical field work, must participate in conferences, and take semester and matriculation examinations. It is reported that "during the 1957-58 school year, correspondence schools received an enrollment of 60,781 students."[52]

Teacher Training

Primary school teachers receive their education in teacher-training secondary schools. The course of study is four years, based on the seven years' foundation. The curriculum consists of general education subjects: Polish and Russian languages, civics, logic, history, geography, and geology, mathematics, physics and astronomy, chemistry and biology; professional subjects: education and history of education, general and special psychology, methods of primary teaching; and special subjects: physical culture, drawing, handicrafts, music, singing, choral singing, and premilitary instruction. In the larger training schools, subjects of specialization are combined as follows: Polish language; Russian language; history and civics; geography and geology; biology, physics, chemistry, and astronomy; mathematics and logic; education and psychology, methods of teaching; drawing and handicrafts; singing, music, and choral singing; physical culture; and premilitary instruction.

Primary school teachers may also be trained in teachers' colleges *(Studjum Nauczycielskie).* The course of study is two years, based on the completion of secondary studies. The curriculum includes foreign language, economics, education, history of education, psychology, meth-

---

[52] *Loc cit.; Educational Trends* (Geneva: International, 1962), p. 52.

ods of primary teaching, school health, and physical culture. In addition to these general subjects, each student selects from the following pairs of subjects in which he will specialize: mathematics and physics; geography and biology; Polish language and history; drawing and handicrafts; singing and music. Nursery school teachers prepare for five years at institutions on the secondary level, based on seven years of elementary education.

General and specialized secondary school teachers receive their training in teachers' colleges or in humanistic, mathematics, and science faculties of universities. They must first have completed a regular secondary school education. Courses of study are offered in Polish and Russian philology, history, geography, biology, mathematics, physics, and chemistry. Teachers of technical subjects and those in agricultural schools are trained in institutes conducted by the Central Office for Vocational Training and the Ministry of Agriculture and Land Reform. Instruction is within the limits of a selected field of science; and social and civic training, pedagogical practice, and teaching practice are included. These colleges also offer a five-year "external" or extension program, which qualifies an applicant for the same teaching degree. Such programs are organized on an extension basis, including seminars and the passing of written and oral examinations.

Teachers in teacher-training secondary schools must have completed five years of higher studies at a university or four years in a higher school of education and must have the licentiate degree. Their training is the same as that of other secondary school teachers, but usually the candidates who have had at least three years' teaching experience are selected for the teacher-training secondary schools and, of course, they must be "reliable."

Teachers in these various schools are recruited from higher schools, teacher-training secondary schools, or general secondary schools. They must have a university master's degree, *magisterjum,* or, when possible, a doctorate. Those appointed to teach professional subjects and methods of teaching must have a thorough knowledge of the whole field of primary education.

Special teachers for all types of atypical schools are trained for two years at the College of Special Pedagogy. Public schoolteachers with three years' teaching experience are admitted to the college. The curriculum includes lectures on the subject of vocational rehabilitation, so that teachers may familiarize themselves with the problems involved in preparing the handicapped for professional work. At the same time, a three-year correspondence course is offered to those unable to attend the regular courses.[53]

Throughout the Soviet educational system (and this applies no less rigorously in the satellites) education is used as a political weapon as well as a socializing and culturalizing device.[54] The strategy and the overt methods of this are revealed in Soviet pedagogical publications as follows.

In the September-October, 1952, issue of the Soviet pedagogical bimonthly, *The Teaching of History in Schools,* M. A. Ershova published an article on "The Use of Newspapers and Periodicals in Lessons on the Constitution of the USSR." Mrs. Ershova teaches Soviet Constitution in No. 649 Secondary School in Moscow. Before quoting some remarkable passages from her articles, we wish to point out that Mrs. Ershova's "true and basic material" for the study of Western life is restricted to Soviet newspapers and periodicals. She says

the children whom we now train and teach were born in the Stalin epoch. They do not know the horrors of capitalist slavery. On May 1, 1919, in the Red Square of Moscow, V. I. Lenin referred to them when he said, "Our grandchildren will examine the documents and monuments of the epoch of the capitalist system like a curiosity. They will be able to imagine only with difficulty how trade in primary consumer goods could be in private hands, how factories and plants could belong to individual persons, how one man could exploit another, how people could exist who are not engaged in work."[55]

So that pupils may better understand, value and feel the im-

---

[53] Generally speaking, the material on teacher education is taken from Apanasewicz and Medlin, *op. cit.,* pp. 25-26.

[54] See Roucek and Lottich, *op. cit.,* pp. 518-19, 521-22.

[55] "Skyscraper of Lies," by "Pachydermus," *East Europe and Soviet Russia* (London), VIII, No. 403 (November 27, 1952), 13-15.

measurable advantages of the Soviet social and state structure, it is essential to study this structure in concrete contrast to the capitalist structure. That is why the necessary concrete material from the history of our country, and from the history of the modern capitalist countries, must, without fail, be included in the course on the Constitution of the USSR. Newspaper and periodical articles, and also individual pamphlets, are a notable source of vivid and easily memorized examples both of the joyous, happy life of the peoples of the USSR, and the gloomy reality of the capitalist countries. . . . Thus, for example, reading *Pravda* of January 3, 1951, I made an excerpt from the article, *International Review*, to the effect that on the walls of American universities announcements like the following can be read ever more frequently: "I am ready to quit my town, my country, and even my planet to obtain permanent work." This announcement typifies the difficult situation of American youth, and may be successfully read while going over the theme of "The Right to Work."

In *Pravda* of February 1, 1951, in a leading article entitled "Triumph of Bolshevik Policy," data are quoted on the striking changes in Kirghizia, which before the revolution was one of the most backward outlying regions of Czarist Russia. . . . In the same article it is pointed out that India—one of the largest countries of the world with tremendous natural wealth—has, as a result of the domination of the British, been turned into a bankrupt pauper country, where millions of working people die annually from starvation.

When dealing with the theme, "The Right to Work," I tell the pupils that there is no unemployment in the USSR which is the threatening scourge of the laboring masses of capitalist countries. Every Soviet citizen is guaranteed the right to work with a wage in accordance with its amount and quality. In one of the Ford motor works the management gave a nickel-plating worker, Philip Caruso, a gilt button in view of his 30 years' service at the works. Within a fortnight Caruso was thrown onto the street. The old man, who had given all his strength to working for a capitalist, was fired without a pension and without the right to receive any unemployment assistance. (Agitator's Notebook, No. 36, pp. 23 and 24, 1948).

Medical treatment for a poor man in a capitalist country is a luxury beyond his means. The son of a small employee injured his eyes while he was playing a game. The doctor examined him and said, "He must go at once to the hospital." "I haven't got the money," replied the distracted father. "His eyes can be removed," the doctor proposed, "that will be cheaper." The child lost his eyes because this was cheaper than the treatment which the father could not afford to pay. (Agitator's Notebook, No. 8, p. 21, 1950).

Soviet leaders use the line that in capitalist countries children of the working people often die because they cannot obtain medical treatment. They say that in Britain (reported by the *Literary Gazette* of February 16, 1948), a sick child died because fourteen hospitals had refused its parents' application on account of being full up. But let Mrs. Ershova continue:

> My pupils listened with great emotion to the following tale which I took from the *Literary Gazette*; the three-year-old daughter of Anna Shulyak, an inhabitant of the small Ukrainian town of Krolevets, was dangerously ill. The child's condition was serious and there were no specialists in the town. Anna Shulyak decided to turn to Comrade Stalin for aid. "Dear Comrade Stalin," she telegraphed the Kremlin, "an ear specialist is needed for my dying child. Help me to save my child." Within three hours Anna Shulyak received a wire from Moscow: "A specialist has been sent you. Notify me of the state of health of the child." Within a few hours a second telegram arrived, this time from Kiev: "On the instructions of Stalin a doctor is flying to you." On arrival the doctor immediately performed an operation. The child's life was saved. (*Literary Gazette*, May 26, 1948.)

But is its hardly possible that the name of Stalin would be invoked today!

Such quotations show that the Soviet press has published some shocking lies about the Western world. Soviet teachers select among these the most sensational ones, and use them as "illustrations" of life in the Western world. Soviet children assimilate these distorted pictures and build on them their image of the West. No wonder that, when before the war an English editor visited a school near Moscow, she was asked the following questions: "Is it true that in Britain the tramways are reserved for the rich bourgeois?" "Why are old workers thrown into the streets by the capitalists and why must they live by begging?" "Can workers' children attend school in Britain?" "Is it right that whites [in the United States] should continually beat up and lynch Negroes?" and so on. Even more distressing was the fact that the children did not believe her answers. In Russia there is a saying among the common people that identifies a "three-story-high lie"—*Tryokhetajinaya lozh*. Education by the contrast method of Marxist pedagogues surely is a skyscraper of lies.[56]

---

[56] *Ibid.*

A Report from Disneyland

The monthly journal *Foreign Affairs,* is one of the first among United States periodical publications. Subtitled "An American Quarterly Review" with the mythic *Ubique* at its masthead, it welcomes contributions from almost every segment of the world political scene. Nikita S. Khrushchev spoke in the October, 1960, issue, and the April issue had carried comments from Chester Bowles, V. S. Yemelyanov, Nelson Rockefeller, and Wladyslaw Gomulka—among others.

Disneyland is a famous American fun park, whose special attraction relies on its opportunities for escapism through the invocation of various types of romantic adventure, scientific fantasy, and fairyland.

The tens of thousands who visit Disneyland annually presumably know just when they are being fooled. On the other hand, perchance many Americans who read "The Policy of the Polish People's Republic," by W. Gomulka, in the April issue of *Foreign Affairs* may not have achieved such discernment. Let's see what tall tales the Wizard of the Vistula was able to produce to substantiate his claim that the Polish people "never had it so good."

"There are no differences of opinion among the overwhelming majority of Poles as to the fundamental principles of our People's Republic," he said. "Socialism in Poland is growing out of Polish soil and has struck deep roots in it."[57]

"Polish agriculture—though still based mainly on small holdings, insufficiently equipped technically—has increased the yield per acre by 50 percent over the prewar period. . . ."[58] This is most difficult to believe; the December (1959) issue of the *Sudeten Bulletin* (Munich) reported the failure of agricultural production and the threat of famine in the most fertile of the Polish-controlled lands—the former Oder-Neisse territories. The Polish radio (Stettin) itself is quoted as admitting:

---

[57] Vol. 38, No. 3 (April, 1960), pp. 405-6.
[58] *Idem.,* p. 406.

"There have been enormous shortages of foodstuffs. The western areas are starved for meat and fats; the queues are growing daily! the militia is powerless; we are threatened with general chaos."[59]

Yet, let the Red boss continue: "Another subject in which Western observers take a special *though less sympathetic interest* is the relationship between the state (Polish People's Republic) and the Roman Catholic Church."[60] Here, however, the truth is at variance with the Marxist's contention. The facts are that the West is particularly sympathetic to the struggle of the Roman Catholic Church in Poland to preserve its autonomy. American weekly publications, especially *Newsweek, United States News and World Report, Time*—and *Look*, a bi-weekly—have carried many items relative to Polish Church-state relations in recent months.

"Poland's new position as a socialist country means that for the first time in her one-thousand-year-old history her frontiers are lasting frontiers of peace and friendship."[61] Perhaps Gomulka is right; her neighbors are the Soviet Union, the CSR, and the "German Democratic Republic"! Nevertheless, the desirability of such a "peace" may be open to serious question. As to "friendship," the dictionary has been so emasculated in recent years that one is reminded of a famous passage from "Alice in Wonderland."

"But you can't use the word that way," cried Alice in amazement. "Indeed I can," replied the Red Queen. "When I use a word it means exactly what I propose it to mean. Nothing more, nothing less. It depends on who is master, I or the word."

"It is only natural that Poland should concentrate on the main problem of European security, i.e., the conclusion of a peace treaty with Germany. . . ." Here the Communist satrap reveals his real purpose in writing such an essay: hatred and fear of West Germany and the West. "The latest fascist and anti-Semitic excesses in

---

[59] Vol. VII, No. 12 (December, 1959), p. 256.
[60] Gomulka, *op. cit.*, p. 407. Italics added.
[61] *Ibid.*, p. 408.

Western Germany have revealed to all what is hidden
behind the screen of the ruling regime. . . . It is the
natural fruit of the German Federal Republic's policy, a
continuation of the age-long traditions of the Prussian
invaders, the *Drang nach Osten*."[62]

Even though this is hardly rational, Gomulka does
make sense (although, of course, when he hardly pretends to) in the following truth: "That this is not an
imaginary danger is best proved by the whole policy pursued by the West German government, *which is today
playing the role of the main bastion* of the cold war. . . .
Herr Adenauer even went so far as to say that he regards peaceful co-existence as an illusion. One cannot
deny that he is consistent in his attitude."[63]

It is indeed doubtful whether anyone from the West
could have expressed this as clearly—and as truthfully.

One could quite cheerfully stop on this note. However,
the Red leader continues with the addition of a Section
IV—the orthodox party line concerning peace and coexistence. This is nothing but a polemic, composed of
Communist double-talk, dissimulation and political clap-
trap. Gomulka is even bold enough to use former Secretary Herter's speech to the National Foreign Trade
Council as a propaganda device, and his peroration here
is worthy of inclusion as a copybook maxim for students
of all countries—were it only sincere!

The world is entering a new era greatly influenced by the universal desire to remove the threat of extermination and to utilize
the splendid achievements of the human mind for the good of man.
. . . Fifteen years ago the nations which had bathed in the blood
of the World War raised the cry: "No more wars." Today we are
convinced that the realization of this universal demand is nearer
than even before.[64]

The honesty of such protestations coming from the
Marxist-Leninist camp is debated in the same issue of
Foreign Affairs by Dr. Leonard Schapiro. This author,
a professor at the London School of Economics and crea-

---

[62]*Ibid.*, pp. 410-11.
[63] *Ibid.*, p. 412. Italics added.
[64] *Ibid.*, p. 418. Mr. Herter has been named to *Polonia Restituta*.

tor of *The Origin of Communist Autocracy,* asks the
question, "Has Russia Changed?"[65] His answer can be
stated simply. It is "No."

Communist ideology—and mentality—is designed for
nothing but conquest. It moves openly or stealthily—
but always eventually forward, seeking new positions of
strength. Any Western weakness, or inclination to seek
security through diplomatic or conventional maneuvers,
will most certainly be fatal. Thus, propaganda that it is,
Gomulka's statement deserved a careful reading. For it
is a peculiar weakness of the Communist propaganda
vehicle that each phrase reveals its hidden motive; such
a flaw should be of inestimable value to the West.

The Overstreets[66] demonstrate a danger to the Communist empire in its inability to completely control university
life and student reaction. He writes:

Within the Soviet Union itself, university students have started
discussion groups without asking anyone's leave; and in these have
shown a startling lack of respect for the regime. . . . In Poland,
they show themselves tenaciously curious about the West, hungry
for uncensored facts, and prone to exercise civil liberties whether
or not these are officially granted.

Thus, the professor's task is a particularly unhappy
one. Overstreet tells the following story (as related by
Sir Robert Boothby) :

A friend of mine the other day was in Warsaw. . . . He was
talking to a student . . . and one of the Professors was there and
introduced him. There were two or three students. Suddenly
the students began to make a violent attack upon Marxism. The
Professor looked a little disconcerted—rather surprised—and my
friend turned to the Professor and said, "Surely, Professor, these
are rather strong sentiments coming from your students." The
Professor thought a moment and said: "Yes. We have not succeeded in mis-educating them."

The Kremlin seems committed to the task of trying to
make two incompatible policies look alike. It encourages
artists, writers, and students to express themselves more

---

[65] Vol. 38, No. 3 (April, 1960), pp. 391-401.

[66] Harry and Bonaro Overstreet, *What We Must Know About
Communism* (New York: W. W. Norton and Company, Inc., 1958),
pp. 130-31.

freely; but warns that such expression must not lead toward "rotten bourgeois liberalism." A (recent) article
in *Kommunist* has attempted to present this policy as
both generous and firm, but has succeeded only in presenting it as the nonsensical end product of an untenable
relationship between the Party and the human intellect.
Kommunist editorialized[67] as follows:

> . . . the clash of opinion, on a foundation of Marxist-Leninist
> principles, must be thoroughly encouraged and developed. . . . Of
> course, there can be no compromise with views and pronounce-
> ments hostile to Marxism. . . . It must be remembered firmly that
> we are for peaceful co-existence of states with diverse social sys-
> tems, but against peaceful co-existence of ideologies, since that
> would mean ideological disarmament. But this, we repeat, does
> not exclude the clash of opinion—of course within the framework
> of allegiance to the Party and Marxism—a clash in the course
> of which incorrect tenets and conclusions are rejected.

Another Political Note

In the light of Poland's current position as a satellite
and vis-à-vis the Soviet Union, one may well ask wherein
lies any hope at all of her final emergence as a sovereign
nation or for any realization of her assumed splendid
destiny—this seemingly sanctified by more than a millennium of Western-oriented history and by heroic achievements in fields as diverse as science, politics, and the arts.

A recent writer in *Corriere della Sera* (Milan, Italy)
sees as Poland's last best hope the assumption of a neutralist role in the continuing conflict through cold war
between East and West—that is, if such a part is still
available in the contemporary masque of power strategy.
This commentator, Enrico Altavilla, sees an upsurge of
great Polish consternation at the very thought (particularly in the light of twenty years' experience, first with
Nazi Germany and now with the Communists) of any
definitive arrangements in regionalizing Europe into accepted Communist and (Western) democratic blocs.
Altavilla says that Poles are terrified at the thought of

---

[67] Overstreet, *op. cit.*, pp. 131-32.

making the present situation internationally agreeable[68] (although, unfortunately the various World War II concords, Yalta, Teheran, Potsdam, etc., do appear to approach this dreary conclusion).

Such a viewpoint, apparently held by non-Communists and Communists alike, is predicated upon the idea that Poland's present regime is not truly "Communist" (in the Russian sense) and that a large freedom of choice still remains to the Polish people. This, of course, would be totally wiped out if finalization of the contemporary "spheres of influence" were effected. In the words of Altavilla: "But talking here in Warsaw with several members of Parliament, I heard that the 'Polish road to socialism' would be a dead-end street if the United States and the USSR should come to an agreement about their respective zones of influence. *On that day Poland would really become a Communist country.*"[69]

What is really wanted, according to Altavilla, is the implementation of the Rapacki Plan (or some variation of this neutralization scheme). Originally suggested by the Polish Foreign Minister, Adam Rapacki, at United Nations on October 3, 1957, this "plan" calls for the setting up of a large "atom-free belt" in East Central Europe extending both west and east of the Iron Curtain. It would include Poland, Czechoslovakia, and East and West Germany.

Obviously, there are two ways to interpret such a proposal. First, and immediately discernible, is the Western thought that the Rapacki Plan is merely just another Marxist device for immobilizing the most strategic sector of Europe—indeed, the very zone in which a third World War might focus. In this view the West has everything to lose by the maneuver; Soviet troops (held at the ready all along the periphery) would be in a position to strike fast if Kremlin policy directed it; in fact many Westerners doubt the good faith of any Soviet withdrawal which the proposal most certainly should entail. And in

---

[68] *Corriere della Sera*, October 18, 1961. As translated and reprinted in *Atlas* (New York), 2, No. 6 (December, 1961), 465-66.

[69] *Ibid*. Italics added.

the West no such opportunity would be given. Washington, London, and Paris are leagues from the border of the Germanies; even the Soviet fear of a NATO concentration in Scandinavia and Benelux appears to be a mirage; such a buildup would run into immense practical difficulties.

On the other hand, given an honest administration of the idea, or even a modified plan with stringent policing, with a control organ in the hands of Warsaw, NATO, and United Nations, including free access by both East and West, the Rapacki concept has real merit. Honorably supported, it could give status and dignity once more to the political entities of this borderland (although, to be consistent, Hungary, Austria, Romania, and Bulgaria should then be entitled to membership also); sufficiently policed, this "solution" would place a bar on further Soviet westward expansion, although the economics of an area in which both Common Market and *Komekon* competed might, of course, raise supplementary problems.

However, even in its present scope, the Rapacki Plan has gained firm support in Norway and Denmark, themselves small countries which might eventually seek inclusion. This is not to say that they are lukewarm on NATO, but actually favor any solution which may conceivably give them a stronger grasp on the elements of a more permanent and durable peace.

From the Polish standpoint, their position—between the East German satrapy and the Soviet Union herself, is certainly unenviable. When added to this is the gnawing fear of a possible *détente* between Moscow and the West based on some one of the old pre-World Wars sanctions of influence zones in Central Eastern Europe, the suspense becomes almost unbearable.[70] An apocryphal story recently going the rounds in Poland stresses a natural desire to endure as a people and as a nation:

Let us imagine that Nikita S. Khrushchev, John F. Kennedy and a good average Polish citizen have passed on and are now at the

---

[70] For good background material see George F. Kennan, *Russia and the West Under Lenin and Stalin* (Boston: Little, Brown and Company, 1961), and John Gunther, *Inside Europe Today* (New York: Harper and Brothers, 1961).

pearly gates of St. Peter. As a portion of their reward each is granted his innermost wish.

The Russian, seizing the initiative, blurts out, "Destroy the United States of America," and *pouf*, it is done.

President Kennedy, as an exhibition of massive retaliation, demands the destruction of the Soviet Union. This immediately follows.

Turning to the Pole, the gatekeeper asks, "And what do you desire, citizen of Lublin?"

"Just my pipe and slippers, Most Reverend Sir," he delightedly answers.

In a more serious vein Altavilla reports his conversation with a Polish political leader: "We need a fluid, a dynamic situation. . . . This will let us follow, within the limits imposed by geography and by our relations with the Soviet Union, an active policy, something like the policy aspired to within the limits of the Atlantic Pact."[71] Well-wishers of Poland everywhere perhaps hope for much more than this.

---

[71] *Corriere della Sera, op cit.* In a desperate effort to assert over their sometimes recalcitrant citizens the power that control of the agencies of education conventionally allows, the Gomulka regime has implemented educational statutes in the following manner: "A law just placed before the Warsaw Parliament would require graduates to pay for their state-financed education if they refused to accept jobs assigned to them by the government. The average (return) . . . would run to about $5,000, almost seven years' wages for a Polish worker." *Newsweek* (New York), February 17, 1964, p. 89. (Special permission to reprint granted.)

CHAPTER V

EAST GERMANY: EDUCATION
AS A BRANCH OF POLITICS

Victory Without Peace

IT IS WELL KNOWN that the occupation of Germany following her defeat in World War II, with three zones of control (one each for the United States, the USSR, and the United Kingdom plus a possible fourth for France), was confirmed at Yalta on February 4-11, 1945, by Churchill, Roosevelt, and Stalin. It is true likewise that Berlin was settled upon as the seat of the Central Control Commission, consisting of the supreme commanders of the three great powers.[1]

However, unfortunately, neither Roosevelt nor Churchill correctly conceived what Russian occupation meant; nor did they at Yalta see that Russian trusteeship was tantamount to Soviet possession. The arrangements, moreover, ratified at Potsdam in 1945, never worked as planned. The Central Control Commission (Kommandatura) proved to be an ineffectual device, and soon each of the wartime allies began to follow its own counsel; yet it is a significant exception that the Western powers showed a much greater degree of cooperativeness than did the Soviets, who quickly converted their Eastern Zone into another Red satrapy.

As indicated above, the effort to govern Germany as an entity may be said to have been unsuccessful. Conferences held in Moscow in March and April, and in London in November and December, 1947, were unable to harmonize the difficulties that had arisen between Britain, France, and the United States—the Western occupy-

---

[1] Yet, see Kenneth V. Lottich, "Berlin, Stalin's Greatest Blunder," *Sudeten Bulletin*, VIII, No. 3 (March, 1960), 63-69, for another interpretation of the Berlin involvement.

ing powers—and the Soviet Union. Consequently, on March 20, 1948, the Soviet seceded from the Kommandatura; on November 30 of the same year the four-power Berlin Allied Control Council abandoned operation.

Following this impasse, Britain, France, and the United States agreed to an Occupation Statute (May 12, 1949), a preliminary to the creation of the German Federal Republic on May 23. In October the Marxists organized the German Democratic Republic out of the territory allocated to them as the Eastern Zone; this was controlled through the fiction of the independence of action of the Socialist Unity party (SED)—a Red front.

Using the 1937 boundaries and the 1939 census as a yardstick, the division of the German Reich, through the split mentioned above and by the award of the "Eastern Territories" including Königsberg (former German territory beyond the Oder) to Russian and Polish authority, the following distribution of land and population[2] resulted:

Territory	Prewar Percent of Population	Prewar Percent of Area	Density per Sq. Mi.
Federal Republic including West Berlin	62.0	52.8	450
Soviet Zone and East Berlin (D.D.R.)	24.1	22.9	403
Eastern Territories under Polish and Russian Administration	13.9	24.3	220
Totals	100	100	378

Indeed the area of Germany had been reduced, following World War II, to 143,200 square miles, of which 94,723 square miles currently are held by West Germany and 42,112 square miles comprise the Soviet sector. Berlin, omitted from these figures, is split between the Soviet and the West, and covers three hundred square miles. Recent figures indicate a population of Western Germany of approximately fifty-five million, of "East Germany" around seventeen million, although the Eastern sector— regardless of resettlement from Sudetenland—has been

---

[2] See *Germany in a Nutshell* (Bonn: Press and Information Office of the Federal German Government, 1958), p. 6.

decreasing steadily through flight to the West (voting,
as the Germans say, by foot) regardless of the wall.

The city of Berlin itself has a population of between
four and five millions. (Germany's prewar area comprised 182,471 square miles and contained a population
of approximately seventy million.

Continuous flight from East Germany is having its
effect on labor, resulting in a "marked bottleneck" in the
growth of the "German Democratic Republic's" economy.
The aims of a seven-year plan, now developed for the
Eastern Zone, say the Research Council, are the completion of collectivization, additional reinforcement of the
power of the central planning agencies, and the closer
dovetailing of the D.D.R. with the total economy of the
East Block. To attain such goals, pressures bearing a
growing semblance to those of Nazi totalitarianism are
being put on the people of East Germany.

Yet the Council has already designated the agricultural
production goals of the seven-year plan as "unrealistic
and unjustified by developments within the past years."
Their incapability of fulfillment has been revealed
through the debates in the last session of the SED (Socialist Unity party) Central Committee.

Although the drought and the lack of party and state
"leadership activity" were made responsible for the inadequate supply situation, it is clear that the real cause
is to be found in the rigorous forced collectivization and
the new system of centrally planned forced economy.
Furthermore, the Council raised some doubt as to whether
the goal set by the seven-year plan of 100,000 new dwellings annually can be met. Official communications have
even spoken of being "completely unsatisfied with building totals" thus far, which tallied only 40,000.[3]

The Educational Pattern

The arbitrary division of Germany between the East
Zone of the occupation under Soviet control—now the

---

[3] See "Soviet Zone of Germany," *Sudeten Bulletin,* VIII, No. 3
(March, 1960), 76.

German Democratic Republic—and the three Western Zones under Great Britain, France, and the United States which had been fused into the German Federal Republic, imposes immediately special conditions which limit the study of the educational system. Indeed, there are two school systems just—to be realistic—as there are two different and competing governments. As would be expected, the Soviet Union has reorganized the school in the Eastern Zone so that it currently is completely Communist-oriented and has very little in common with the school system of West Germany—essentially a humanist-Reformation development.

Education and cultural affairs within Germany have traditionally been the responsibility of the separate *Länder* (states) rather than the national government. Nevertheless, both in the Second Reich and under the Weimer Republic, education in all of the states shared quite a high degree of conformity both in structure and in the curriculum. That system consisted basically of a thirteen-year elementary-secondary school program, reinforced by an intensive network of vocational, technical, and teacher-education institutions, and was succeeded by the universities and other agencies of higher education. Although, to be sure, this principle of individual State responsibility was abrogated during the Nazi interlude (1933-45) with the establishment of a National Ministry of Science, Education, and Public Instruction, which maintained jurisdiction over all education until the end of the second World War, this period does not really reflect the German mentality in regard to education.[4]

With minor variations—considering that eleven *Länder* are involved—the educational pattern in West Germany is essentially that of the pre-Nazi period, with, of course, a slightly more democratic orientation, especially in North Germany and Berlin. While this program does not represent a "Single Track" by any means (the history of the German people traditionally following an entirely differ-

---

[4] See *Education in the Soviet Zone of Germany,* Office of Education Bulletin No. 26 (Washington, D.C.: U.S. Department of Health, Education, and Welfare, 1959).

ent path), there is a great deal of uniformity, and two
or three easily marked curricula may be discerned, as (1)
elementary-technical; (2) general elementary; and (3)
university preparatory.

Within the Eastern Sector, the German Democratic
Republic, a Soviet-type regime, a "Single Track" is in
operation. That such a revision, under Soviet auspices,
has been made is significant to the perpetuation of the
Communist ideology (although it is readily apparent that
the "Single Track" idea is partially "window dressing").
Moreover, in the last few years, an emphasis on work
education, quite in harmony with the master Marxist
pattern, has been achieved. That the "Single Track"
principle is not necessarily a democratic reality is revealed by its special purpose in a Marxist society.

Perhaps a reference to the purpose of East German
education and the ideology within which it functions is
appropriate here. In the phraseology of Education Minister Lange (of the D.D.R.), this is the type of education
that is generated and fostered[5] within the Eastern school
milieu:

> Education for patriotism, for unlimited devotion and unshak-
> able fidelity to our Republic, to the cause of Socialism, to the
> working classes and their Party must be the central task of all
> education. We are training in our schools that generation which
> one day will utilize its experience and knowledge, obtained through
> the developments in our Republic, in the service of all Germany.
> Such youth must be filled with hate for the enemies of our peace-
> ful, constructive work. It must be trained in such a way that it
> will rise against everyone who desires to rob us of our great po-
> litical and social achievements and to threaten our peaceful fu-
> ture....

As an element of contrast between the Zones, the following excerpt suggests a more truly "democratic" approach to the broad education of children; it indicates a
tolerant solution to an educational problem that arose in
the German Federal Republic.

---

[5] See Gerhard Moebus, *Erziehung zum Hass* ("Education for
Hate") (Berlin: Morus Verlag, 1956), p. 110.

West German Tolerance

"While much ado is being made about the alleged anti-Semitic defacement of public edifices in West Germany, with alarmists and witch-hunters seeing the country at the brink of a new 'Nazi' era, the *Bundesrepublic* [German Federal Republic] is quietly and efficiently going about solving a critical race problem that is hardly entirely of its own making.

"The Easter season will see 400,000 young German lads and lasses leaving the elementary school and entering apprenticeship for various trades. Among this number are 1,500 half Negro children, so-called "children of the occupation," sired by fathers who were stationed in Germany with the armies of the occupation.

"Conferences lasting many hours have taken place in the Römer in Frankfurt am Main, to find ways and means of integrating these young folks into positions of apprenticeship as mechanics, machinists, bakers, printers, lathe-operators and the like.

"Dr. Klaus Eyferth of the Psychological Institute of the University of Hamburg, working with Dr. Curt Bondy, has tested 200 half-Negro children in West Germany and found that the colored children are not behind the white children in either intelligence or achievement; nor are they further ahead in physical development.

"Most of the mothers of these children, it has been shown, are good mothers to them and want to keep the children, shunning the idea of farming them out to others. Participants in the Frankfurt conferences have held exhaustive discussion as to the possibilities for giving these first 1,500 *Mischlinge*—children of Negro-white blood—a quick start as apprentices which will include good treatment." (All told there are some 6,000 colored and 72,000 other occupation children in West Germany).[6]

---

[6] "Integration of German Negro Youth Disproves Claims of Rising Nazism," *Sudeten Bulletin*, VIII, No. 3 (March, 1960), 75.

Another East-West Contrast

Although progessive school reform had marked the educational climate of the early Weimer Republic (1919), the older forces of Prussian authoritarianism—the *Junkers,* the military, and the higher social classes—had, by the 1930's and the advent of Adolf Hitler, restored much of the former practice of a traditional separation of the elite and common schooling. Moreover, under National Socialism, while a retreat from the intellectualism of the pre-World War I era became a cardinal principle in the training of an ideologically correct population, regimentation in terms of "scientific" theory (biology and race "hygiene" is meant) and through the creation of paramilitary organizations for both boys and girls merely changed the emphasis and authority of educational practice but did not disturb its rigors.[7]

Nevertheless, the *Einheitsschule* or "common track" idea which had flowered during the days of the Republic was not completely dead. Following the surrender of Germany, the Allied educational missions in each of the Western Zones—British, American, and French—advocated a pattern designed to encourage equal educational opportunity. That the "Single Track" contemplated was not accomplished need not be considered an absolute failure of the democratic idea. The autonomy of each of the *Länder* plus the continuing strong class tradition provided a situation radically dissimilar from that which obtained east of the Elbe (in the "German Democratic Republic"), where class lines as well as provincial boundaries were to be erased by government ukase under the cloak of the Russian version of "democracy." It was indeed clear also that such a procedure is a basic item of strategy in the establishment of a Communist state.

But more recent developments in the German Federal Republic (West Germany) suggest that some modification is in the offing, and that the old solidly elite system has lost some ground, at least, to the common track. Ur-

---

[7] See Gregor Ziemer, *Education for Death* (New York: Oxford University Press, 1941), for a shattering picture of party control of education in Nazi Germany.

sula Kirkpatrick recently has pointed out that a *Rahmenplan* ("master plan") can be designed to cause schools "to adjust to the revolutionary social and political changes [which have occurred] during the last fifty years."[8] No less than two new schools are contemplated: the *Förderstufe* (for grades V and VI) and the *Hauptschule* (for grades VII-X), although, of course, transition from the *Grundschule* (grades I-IV) may lead as well to a higher type of secondary school training, as heretofore, in one of the Gymnasia.

Developments in Satellite East Germany

Superficially, education in the German Democratic Republic bears a strong resemblance to that of the Single Track 8-4 system of the United States of America. The elementary schools (grades I-VIII) are coeducational, utilize the self-contained classroom principle, and operate on the basis of class standards or goals rather than on individual achievement; departmentalization, however, begins with grade V (a practice usually reserved for the seventh and eighth grades in America). The secondary schools comprise grades IX-XII as is typically the case in the United States. Yet there is a "Middle School," a holdover from the earlier class-oriented German system of education; technically including classes IV-X, the Middle School was designed to furnish a slightly more advanced program than that of the conventional elementry school—although not as specialized as that of the high school. It leads to the Certificate of Middle Maturity,

In practice, grades IX and X are sometimes attached to an eight-year elementary school, although again, theoretically, when this is done the goals of the institution likewise are presumed to change. Otherwise, the secondary school program may provide classes IX and X of a type appropriate to the demands of a ten-year terminal program. While, naturally, the Middle School is sometimes found within its own organization as a separate

---

[8] Ursula Kirkpatrick, "The *Rahmenplan* for West German School Reform," *Comparative Education Review*, 4, No. 1 (June, 1960), 18-25.

institution, most frequently developments have not reached this anticipated stage.

The Battle for Youth

The formal education program in East Germany, like that of the Nazi Third Reich, is buttressed by extracurricular activities; calculated to develop allegiance and loyalty to Marxism and also to provide a full day for the sometimes at loose ends adolescent student, this group activity is beginning in many areas to supplant the work of the home and church.

In the German Democratic Republic the "Youth Consecration" Festival is rapidly becoming an integral part of adolescent education. This secular ceremony, the *Jugendweihe*, is designed to replace the ancient Christian "Confirmation," and it has recently been reported that "the number of young people undergoing Confirmation dropped from 90 percent to about 20 percent."[9]

The success of this movement—in the light of its recent development and the generally strong religious ties of the central area Germans—may be indicated by the above percentages. No longer ago than November 24, 1954, the Central Committee for Youth Consecration issued its first general invitation urging German young people to participate in this dedication of their lives to the state. The proclamation[10] read as follows:

Every year many young people, upon completion of their school program, begin a new period in their lives. It is their wish, and the wish of their parents, to celebrate this pleasant step into [adult] life with a festival. . . . All young people, regardless of their world-view, should be able to participate. . . . The consecration festival will be prepared through youth hours in which the questions of life, of nature, and of society will be discussed. . . .

In the conference preceding the formal dedicatory rites ten major topics have been selected for review by

---

[9] Johannes Lilje, "A Mighty Fortress Is Their God," *Presbyterian Life* (Philadelphia), XIII, No. 15 (August 1, 1960), 5-8.

[10] Quoted from Paul S. Bodenman, *Education in the Soviet Zone of Germany* (Washington, D.C.: United States Department of Health, Education and Welfare, 1959), p. 24.

the young initiates. These are further subdivided to provide for twenty-four group meetings. Such items as the
ensuing serve to condition young minds to the taking of
their vows of fealty to the East German[11] Communist
state:

> The greatest sons of our people, Karl Marx and Friedrich Engels,
> founded the doctrine of scientific socialism and Lenin developed it.
> We shall create a socialistic culture.
> Soviet man—conqueror of space—the best friend of the German
> people.
> The German Democratic Republic is the example for the future
> United, peace-loving and democratic Germany!

But perhaps a German youth is not impressed (or indoctrinated) in the conference sessions. Maybe he is too
firm in his religious convictions to take the secular oath.
He may say, "No, I won't accept the Youth Dedication.
I'll go to Confirmation." Then he may suddenly realize
that, by avoiding the state's rite, he has forfeited his
chance for a higher education—the university—a hard
choice indeed, especially for an alert adolescent. And, in
addition to his religious problem, there is the strong prob-
ability of ostracism and ridicule from his peer group.[12]

For the smaller fry of East German youth there is the
Pioneer Organization, "Ernst Thaelmann," which, under
the constitution of the FDJ (Free German Youth), undertakes the ideological training of young children between the ages of six and fourteen. The motive of this
society, originally founded as the "Young Pioneers" on
March 10, 1949, is revealed in the *Freien Deutschen Jugend* constitution mentioned above. Children are to be
developed "according to the example set by Ernst Thaelmann, in the spirit of patriotism, of love and loyalty to
the German Democratic Republic, the working class and
its party, the Socialist Unity Party of Germany, in the
spirit of firm friendship with the Soviet Union and friendship among nations."[13]

---

[11] *Ibid.*, p. 25.

[12] Lilje, *op. cit.*, p. 7.

[13] See *Die Pionierorganisation "Ernst Thaelmann" in der Sowjetzone* (Bonn: Bundesministerium fuer gesamtdeutsch Fragen,
1957), p. 14.

Red boss Walter Ulbricht, East German would-be strong man, has identified the primary purpose of this far-reaching organization, as its duty to "assist the school in patriotic education and to work toward that end that the entire life of the children—their behavior in the family, their play, and their recreation—are filled with thoughts and feelings of unlimited loyalty to the Workers-and-Peasants' State, of respect for the workers' party, of brotherly solidarity with the patriots of Western Germany, of friendship and love for the Soviet Union and the Glorious Soviet Army."[14]

The current membership of "Ernst Thaelmann" is perhaps two million children. On the surface, affiliation is simple, being like that of the Boy or Girl Scouts in Western countries. Actually—as reported above in connection with the Youth Consecration Festivals—membership is not quite voluntary. To illustrate, when a child applies for admission to high school after the completion of the eighth grade, he is required to submit a testimonial from his "Ernst Thaelmann" leader in addition to the statement from his elementary school head regarding his scholarship.

Nevertheless, there is some evidence to suggest that, rigid though the program appears to be in terms of its compulsive features, it is not actually holding the upper age group. The FDJ organ, founded March 7, 1946, was designed to make Communism palatable to the adolescent and young adult between the ages of fourteen and twenty-six. Dr. Peter Paul Nahm, State Secretary in the German Federal Ministry of Expellee and Refugee Affairs, Bonn, insists that Walter Ulbricht has failed miserably in attracting youth to his banner. This, too, in the face of constant degradation and/or reprisals. So whether the parent or the offspring has rebelled at the overt Red pressure, the end is the same—flight. Figures concerning those fleeing from the Zone (including East Berlin), 200,000 in 1960 alone, show that one-half of the escapees are under twenty-five years of age. It is readily apparent that the FDJ has been found seriously ineffectual in its

---

[14] As quoted in Bodenman, *op. cit.*, p. 112.

attempt to capture East German youth for the movement and to infect them with the Communist "ideals" set
up twenty years ago.

Nahm elaborates: "Decent youth never reacts to this
tactic with hypocrisy, but by rebellion or—since it is impossible for those living in the midst of Soviet troops to
rebel—by flight. That is why young folks are always
among those escaping, youths who were not only well off
materially, but were excellently situated and had a free
foot toward a rapid rise to success (that is, on Communism's terms). They turn their backs on that chance and
enter the Western world. They do not enter an unknown,
neither do they go where there is enticing bait; they leave
because something oppresses them. The flight of youth
is the most perceptible and visible defeat of a political
regime that is striving to create the global impression
that it would, if possible, mould the world of tomorrow."[15]

Thus, regardless of the much-touted Marxist educational planning and obligatory Marxist-Leninist indoctrination, one of the most conspicuous failures of the Red
regime in East Germany could be inability to entice the
youth. Although unwillingness to affiliate with the SED
holds grave penalties for parents as well as their children
seeking advancement or preferment in the schools or in
industry, for those who will not knuckle under, escape is
the only alternative. Moreover, the son or daughter of a
father with non-Communist leanings will surely be denied admission to high school and higher education. Consequently, flight from the Russian Zone continues to be
the outstanding phenomenon of life in the "German
Democratic Republic."

It is reported further by a German Lutheran official
that not all youth have been lost. He tells of a student
demonstration at the University Church of Leipzig (the
university there, famous for many centuries, has been
renamed "Karl Marx" and now offers the standard Soviet
program) of perhaps two thousand members, who pa-
raded into the street following a religious revival, all

---

[15] Peter Paul Nahm, "Youth Challenges Walter Ulbricht," *Sudeten Bulletin* (Munich), IX, No. 3 (March, 1961), 60-62.

singing Martin Luther's old hymn, *Ein feste Burg ist Unser Gott* ("A Mighty Fortress is Our God") !

"Tomorrow we shall have to pay for this," explained one student, "but today we sing."[16]

Understandably then the SED-controlled press accuses East German youth of "decadent Western leanings." It also berates them for a "lack of respect" for Socialist leaders and of preferring "hot music" and the attempt to imitate the clothing of degenerate Western young people. Recently SED cadre chief Neumann is reported as admitting that the Marxist youth programs have failed, saying, "Much can be forgiven or made good if here and there [only] short-comings crop up, but it is unforgivable if the masses of youth are not firmly on our side."[17]

Other SED higher-ups have alleged "negligence" in the educating of East German youth. The state has invested much time and money in trying to persuade young people to the Communist ideology. Indeed, paralleling efforts to indoctrinate the young with the uptopian dreams of becoming "active builders of a new world," the Marxists have attempted to wean them away from home and Church as well, and thus to bring all youth under the total superintendence of the Party and its subsidiary organizations.

Yet "balloting by foot" indicates that the vast program of "enlightenment" promised by Walter Ulbricht as part of the FDJ jubilee year has little chance for success. Generally reliable observers maintain that the Communist regime in East Germany is despised by young and old alike (no less after the brutal crushing of the 1953 rebellion by Russian tanks and armed might) and, from all present appearances, will stay hated so long as the Reds are able to remain in the saddle.

The Formal Education Program

In the state-supported schools themselves all textbooks

---

[16] Lilje, *op. cit.*, p. 8.

[17] As quoted in the *Sudeten Bulletin*, IX, No. 3 (March, 1961), 71-72.

and other materials are closely supervised. Books are published by the state-owned publishing establishment. No other works besides the approved textbooks are permitted. Teaching aids, including charts, pictures, and films are also provided by an agency of the Ministry of Public Education. At the beginning of the occupation in the Eastern Sector, Soviet texts translated into German were utilized in the secondary schools. Today's tone is still pro-Soviet and, in social studies, is heavily burdened with references to the "class struggle."

For example, the topical headings for the twelfth-grade course, as developed by the Ministry of Public Education in 1956, leave no doubt about this type of indoctrination. Note the following[18] headings:

1. The Great Socialist October Revolution and the Development of Socialism in the USSR.
2. The November, 1918, Revolution in Germany.
3. The Revolutionary Post-War Crises of 1919 to 1923.
4. The Period of Relative Stabilization of Capitalism and the Struggle of the German Communist Party and the Resurging German Imperialism.
5. The Economic Crisis of the Imperialistic World, 1929-32; the Consistent Struggle of the German Communist Party Against Imperialism and Fascism.
6. The Fascist Dictatorship in Germany; the Preparation for World War II.
7. The Second World War, an Anti-Fascist War of Liberation.
8. The Establishing and Development of the Democratic Peace Camp. . . . The Founding of the German Democratic Republic.

Fifth-grade students of geography and history in the German Democratic Republic are treated to a cunning piece of propaganda which is at once more subtle and yet revealing of the motives of their Soviet masters than any amount of political double-talk. That the same technique exists in the various East Central European satellite

---

[18] Martin Dietrich and Frederick Blage, *Das Schulbuch in der Sowjetzone,* as quoted in Bodenman, *op. cit.,* p. 46.

countries is not to be doubted (history courses of study originating in the Russian homeland invariably tell as much and usually more). As an example of the use to which education in East Germany is put, however, the following excerpt is damning enough.

The city of Berlin is the subject, and the poison offered[19] is stronger than hemlock:

At the lower course of the Spree River lies Berlin, the capital of our German Democratic Republic. Berlin is the largest German city and one of the largest cities in the world. . . . As you know, Berlin is presently a divided city. Just as there are two different states within Germany, there are in Berlin two different city sectors, our democratic sector and West Berlin.

The partition of the city is the fault of the imperialists who divided all of Germany as well. They cut off the portions of Berlin that were occupied by the American, British, and French troops from the democratic sector. Thus the section West Berlin was formed.

Whereas the administration of our democratic sector is in the hands of the workers and farmers, in West Berlin the capitalists, militarists and their deputies are in charge. They are enemies of the working class and constantly agitate against our German Democratic Republic, the State of workers and farmers.

To this end they employ the West Berlin radio transmitter. Particularly in the American sector they incite—by means of the Radio RIAS[20]—against our workers' and farmers' government and against the Soviet Union. From West Berlin they send criminal elements, agents, into our republic. These are supposed to sabotage and cause unrest by damaging machinery and railroad networks, blowing up bridges and igniting barns.

Other agents are told to spread lies or ferret out economic and military secrets. In West Berlin there are roughly 100 spy centers. Our People's Police and our population are, however, on the alert. Many agents have already been caught and given the severe punishment they deserve. Berlin was divided by the imperialists. West Berlin is being misused by them as a spy base. The attempts to interfere with our progress are frustrated by the alertness of our People's Police and the general population.

In order to achieve the peaceful reunification of Germany, all the peaceful elements in West Germany ought to be united under the leadership of the workers. They must break the power of the warmongers and the atom-politicians. This will bring about co-

---

[19] *Sudeten Bulletin* (Munich), VIII, No. 2 (February, 1960), 48-49. Quoted from East German state syllabus.

[20] Perhaps here Soviet thought is to damn all radio broadcasts that emanate from this side of the Iron Curtain, especially Radio Free Europe (RFE), which originates in Munich and is beamed especially at the East Central European satellite capitals.

operation between our republic and the peaceful forces in West Germany. The boundary now dividing us, that runs through Germany's very heart, will be done away with and both German States can unite in a uniform, peace-loving, and democratic Germany.

The criminality of exposing young minds to such fodder is readily apparent; the falsities and innuendo are visible enough, but under the composition of the whole runs a clear thread of information about the methods of the police state of East Germany itself. Spies, sabotage, barn burning, radio propaganda, the constant presence of the police, and the epithets—imperialists, warmongers, and criminal elements—are familiar to the Red rulers of East Germany; in fact their base attempt to foist on children the idea that these are the badges of identification of the West is not unlikely to succeed with young children—at least until contact with the outside world can, if ever, be made.

The German Dilemma

Professor Arthur Henry Moehlman has characterized the German dilemma as a conflict between Force and Freedom.[21] That this diagnosis is applicable to the Germany of the First and Second Reichs requires no elaboration. In both the Holy Roman Empire of the German Nation and Bismarck's empire such struggle was indeed joined. Hitler rejuvenated this conflict in a Faustian-like renascence, only to fall prey to the diabolical forces that he himself had unleashed. Now the struggle has taken on a different political coloration through the machinations of Moscow. But let Moehlman express the essential fissuring: "A gifted Swiss historian, Jacob Burckhardt, saw this conflict . . . clearly from his ancient university of Basel on the Rhine. . . . He had a historical consciousness of the main points of difference between civilized man and the barbarian. [He] foresaw the twentieth-century political-military juggernauts. He saw the ter-

---

[21] Arthur Henry Moehlman and Joseph S. Roucek, *Comparative Education* (New York: Holt, Rinehart and Winston, Inc., 1952), pp. 301-3.

rible simplifiers of our own century being born of an
enormous will to power. . . . He was particularly concerned
about Germany and visualized it as a country in which
there was warfare between the spirit of freedom in religion, art, and research on the one hand and the spirit
of force typified by bureaucracy, the army, and cartels on
the other."

Obviously, the Nazi interregnum fulfills a part of Dr.
Burckhardt's prediction, as indeed had the conflict between the democratic and the military through other
Reichs. Yet the new Soviet aggression provides an even
more terrible challenge. The brutal efficiency with which
the Marxists have attempted to organize their schools as
an instrument for the perpetuation of their ideology of
force is less than mysterious. Moreover, an irony exists in
their invocation of the name of "democracy" to cloak such
an activity. Nor is this pedagogical aspect of the situation its least.

Stranger than fiction is the source of a new warning
about German militarism—Paris—since General Bethouart, writing in *Figaro*, is not concerned about West Germany, the lineal successor to the former German Reichs.
He indicts East Germany—the Marxist puppet beyond
the Elbe—once again as the modern symbol of Burckhardt's ancient *vis*. Bethouart[22] reported:

Anyone who witnessed the ceremony staged by the Democratic
Republic of East Germany on May 1 believed he saw a Nazi parade all over again. It had everything—the Wehrmacht uniform
and helmets, the goose step, all the survivals of Prussian military
tradition—everything that the Federal Republic of West Germany
had abandoned. All the Nazis, all the S.S. men, all the members of
the Gestapo had been brought together again, because all had
been "converted," giving the police the odious character the French
knew so well.

Young East Germans learn that Russia was always allied with
the Germans in their struggle against French imperialism and
that these "lessons of history" show the way to continue the struggle U.S. imperialism now carries on. . . .

Nevertheless, East German (and Soviet) pedagogical
principles are sound—given such a goal as that to which
they aspire. Their mobilization of youth in extracurricu-

---

[22] "The German Danger," *Figaro* (Paris), May 25, 1961. As
quoted in *Atlas* (New York), II, No. 1 (July, 1961), 4-5.

lar and paramilitary organizations likewise is orthodox—
given their objectives. The soundness of the method has
been proved many times, and Pavlov is a secular saint in
the Marxist pantheon.[23]

However, regardless of the lip service to democracy in
East Germany, their education system is only synthetically a Single Track. As noted above, party considerations and gross indoctrination render the form of organization only another instrument of propaganda!

At the other pole, Western Germany—although class
considerations and tradition have not been abandoned—
offers greater hope for the future. Perhaps with a reunited Germany the Western idea (that to which the
German Federal Republic is attempting to conform) can
prevail, but before that can ever be accomplished the
threat of Soviet Germany to the West must be reduced.
The inclusion of German areas west of the Elbe in the
Soviet sphere is the grave danger which, if the acceptance of this *status quo* in East Germany is unquestioned,
is a large part of the long-range Marxist plan. This is a
circumstance that must be avoided at all costs.

Yet a few commentators profess to see in West German
resurgence the old threat of Force, the reality of which
Europe faced in 1870, 1914, and 1939. One writer says:
". . . it becomes more and more evident that [Adenauer]
is a revered leader without challenge or rival, and the
precedents for that kind of leadership in Germany are far
from happy. Increasingly, for all his allegiance to the
Western alliance, Adenauer is becoming the symbol of a
national Germany. The analogy with Bismarck, with
Kaiser Wilhelm II and briefly with von Hindenberg, inevitably occurs. And, as the world has hardly forgotten,
it was another and demoniac leader who came at the end
of the succession. . . . A revived Germany will no longer
be restrained by reminders of the guilt of the war or the
mass crimes of the Nazis."[24]

---

[23] For a satirical approach to an evaluation of this method see
Kenneth V. Lottich, "Total Organization for Youth," *The Clearing
House*, XXXIII, No. 3 (November, 1958), 173-75.

[24] Marquis Childs, "Nationalism Becoming Increasingly Strong
Force in Western Europe," Syndicated Distribution, June, 1960.

Nonetheless, Dr. Ernst Lemmer, Federal Minister for All-German Affairs, Bonn, has pointed up the basic problem: "The brutal violation of human rights [concerning collectivization and regimentation] in the Soviet occupied Zone of Germany concerns the solidarity of all non-Communist peoples. The deepening of the cleavage between East and West Germany by the violent Bolshevization of additional sectors of Central Germany, makes the demand for German reunification on the basis of the self-determination right of our people all the more urgent."[25]

Perhaps even as pertinent is the German nationalism still existent in the Soviet sector. This, of course, was made manifest in the uprising of 1953 and upon many other occasions. Flight from the Zone continues unabated; in fact, because of the Berlin issue it was greatly stepped up in 1960-61. This spirit is inherent in the following verses said to have been current among the slave workers[26] of the uranium mines of south Saxony:

> Brüder in sächsischen Gruben
> Schürfen verzweifelt Uran
> Dort in Barracken un Stuben.
> Zwingt sie despotischer Wahn.
>
>> Our brothers in Saxon shafts
>> Desperately shovel uranium
>> There into barracks and hovels.
>> They are driven by despotic madness.
>
> Dort liegt die Freiheit in Bänden,
> Dort wird das Recht frech verhöhnt,
> Dort wird der Fortschritt zuschanden,
> Dort ist das Denken verpönt.
>
>> There freedom is in chains,
>> There the right is impudently sneered at,
>> There progress is turned into shame,
>> There thought is derided.
>
> Brothers in the big mines,
> Know that you don't stand alone,
> Even from this crime
> Werden wir Deutschland befreien.
> (We will set our Germany free).

---

[25] "Soviets Capture Another Pawn," *Sudeten Bulletin, A Central European Review*, VIII, No. 6 (June, 1960), 141-44.

[26] "Scorpio," "Singing Slaves," *East Europe and Soviet Russia*, VIII, No. 401 (November 13, 1952), 1-2.

It is further reported that songs with a similar nationalistic import are sung in the forced labor camps. These, however, are impossible of reproduction because of their furious language—directed, of course, at East Germany's Russian overlords.

Stirring rebellions among the very youth trained by the tactics mentioned above are still occurring. On January 23, 1962, two upper school students, seniors at the Anklam High School in Mecklenburg, were sentenced to three and one-half years' imprisonment by the District Court of Neubrandenburg. Their crime was the organization of a demonstration against militarism in the Soviet Occupation Zone following the proclamation of the so-called "Defense Act of the German Democratic Republic" late in 1961. They were said to have been responsible for encouraging their entire class at Anklam to appear in school dressed in mourning clothes. The State Security Service went into action immediately upon the students' announcement: "We are carrying our future to its grave!"[27]

Granted that principles of nationalism and the demand for self-rule are again strongly motivating Germany and West Europe, this is not an isolated phenomenon but an affair of the entire globe—except, perhaps where effectual development of the idea (as behind some sectors of the Iron Curtain lands) is impossible. Nor is this resurgence of nationalism an unqualified evil; much good can come of this new striving of peoples for bread, education, and recognition; such a rise is the direct antithesis of the drab regimentation of the Communist police state.

Certainly such a document as the "Declaration of the Human Rights of the United Nations" of December 10, 1948, is in many ways another statement of an educational principle. The violation of human rights—anywhere in this shrinking world—whether by outright seizure, by coercion, by abrogation of men's right to a free choice of occupation with suitable and satisfactory working conditions is antagonistic to education in its true sense and

---

[27] See Karl Wilhelm Fricke, "Soviet Germany's Skeptical Youth," *The Sudeten Bulletin* (Munich), X, No. 4 (April, 1962), 93-96.

proper interpretation. These are the instances presently being desecrated by the Red regimes in East Central Europe and throughout Asia; they are the concern of educators as well as political statesmen.

Since the foregoing paragraph was written the Soviet overlords and their East German stooges have placed (August 12-13, 1961) a solid wall of metal and concrete between East and West Berlin.[28] Emphasizing the fundamental cleavage between Communism and the Free World, the purpose of such a barrier is obvious. The wall also stands as a confession of cultural defeat on the part of Walter Ulbricht's satellite regime and Soviet Communism as practiced in the Marxist-occupied Zone of Germany.

A further substantiation of East German reluctance to behave in harmony with conventional integrity—and within the "Declaration of Human Rights"—is furnished in the denial by Walter Ulbricht of an appeal submitted by 178 of the world's leading authors and scholars from Britain, Denmark, France, Iceland, Italy, Japan, Norway, Sweden, and West Germany to release the students and intellectuals who exposed themselves politically in 1956 and still remain incarcerated in the jails of the German Democratic Republic. This petition, addressed to Herr Ulbricht on the occasion of his seventieth birthday as written by German television journalist and author Gerd Ruge, requested the act of mercy suggested above as a simple deed of humanity.[29] Gauleiter Ulbricht's intransigence, and deafness, indicate the sheer unwillingness of this Red satrap and his "German Democratic Republic" to comport themselves decently in this matter any more than in the case of the now infamous wall. East German failure—in the words of the Ruge appeal—"to

---

[28] For further details see Hans Speier, *Divided Berlin* (New York: Frederick A. Praeger, 1961), pp. 173-85; for the Communist view of the barrier see *Foreigners Talk about the Wall* (East Berlin: German Democratic Republic, 1962), Code V-5-1/1597/Ag212-84-62-DDR, 16 pp.

[29] "178 Intellectuals of 9 Lands Ask Ulbricht to Relent," *The Bulletin* (Bonn), II, No. 28 (July 30, 1963), 3.

make a contribution towards improving the political climate in the world"—stamps the Pankow regime as one of the most reactionary in the whole galaxy of Soviet satellites.

While there are reports that Nikita S. Khrushchev is no admirer of Ulbricht and this dangerous "Stalinism," the facts are that he has no other German ready to succeed him; hence must preserve Pankow with all its explosive potential for the time being. Ulbricht's political prisoners, estimated at about 10,000 several years ago, may now number twice as many.

Trying incessantly to capture youth, *Mosaic*, a slick magazine depicting "cultural life" in the DDR, heralds the opening and operation of a sports school, the Werner Seelenbinder Kinder- und Jugensportschule in East Berlin. Students are selected on account of their athletic talents but must remain in the good graces of the school to continue. Headmaster Delenschke says "He who excels in athletics and cares little about learning is soon made to realize the folly of such attitude."[30] Of course the KJS program includes history and Marxism-Leninism.

---

[30] *Mosaic* (Dresden), 1962 issue, p. 31; see also Kenneth V. Lottich, "Extracurricular Indoctrination in East Germany," *Comparative Education Review*, 6; No. 28, 209-11.

CHAPTER VI

THE BALTIC STATES: A RUSSIAN "SOLUTION" TO THE BALTIC QUESTION

The Plight of the Baltic States
Historical Background
Short Period of Independence
Satellite Status
"Pacification"
Religious Oppression
Undercurrents of Resentment
Geopolitical Importance
Western Nonrecognition of These Seizures

The Plight of the Baltic States

A QUICK GLIMPSE AT THE MAP shows the dismal predicament of northern East Central Europe.[1] Finland (although presently beyond the Iron Curtain) has been shorn of geographical significance, her borders pulled back from Leningrad and the Barents Sea, and her independent existence placed in grave jeopardy by the reptilian maneuvers of Moscow. Estonia, Latvia, and Lithuania were annexed by the USSR in 1940—their coastline had become a "necessity" for the Russian bear now rapidly learning to swim under water, their perimeter islands a site for the Soviet missile bases that threaten Western Europe. "Most important is the fact that the Baltic fleet has come out of its mouse-trap in the innermost corner of the Gulf of Finland into the drill-ground of the open Baltic Sea."[2]

Kaliningrad (Königsberg), in former German East Prussia which was split between the Kremlin and its Polish satellite, plus Poland and the littoral of the "German Democratic Republic," completed this Soviet advance on the great northern inland sea of Europe. Weishar calls this sweep "the greatest geopolitical trump to be played by Russia in the last century."[3]

Considering only the three Baltic States, Estonia, Latvia, and Lithuania, the territory involved comprises

---

[1] Reprinted by permission of *The Journal of Human Relations*, Central State College, Wilberforce College, Wilberforce, Ohio. See Vol. 9, No. 2 (February, 1961).

[2] Weishar, Richard, "Red Water in the Baltic Sea," *Sudeten Bulletin*, VII, No. 11, (November, 1959), 225-28.

[3] *Ibid.*, p. 225.

67,000 square miles and contained (in 1956) an estimated six million people. Although the seizure has never been recognized by the United States, Britain, France, and the West in general, possession—in this case, at least—represents considerably more than the usual nine points of the law.

If one were callous enough to disregard the lives and fortunes of the six million inhabitants of these three states, it might be remarked that the USSR has, at long last, solved the "Baltic Question." This phrase—an item of history—has been in existence for several millennia, and the problem which it suggests an issue among the empires of Europe for an even longer duration.

Although—properly speaking—Finland and Sweden are likewise "Baltic" countries and the situation in Lithuania is indeed similar, the "Baltic Question" is most frequently discussed in terms of Livonia (that is to say the recently established—yet currently Communist-annexed countries of Estonia and Latvia).

Nevertheless, the Baltic Question is not solely a national question, despite the fact that Baltic nationalisms are involved. It is international and—in many ways—may be considered as significant as that of the land-locked areas in East Central Europe directly to the south. Specifically, the Baltic question "refers rather to the role which the eastern Baltic region played in world affairs. It reflects the influence which this area exercised upon the development of the surrounding great powers."[4] Moreover, Kirchner, a historian of the Baltic, alleges that "during four thousand years of historical knowledge, the Baltic provinces have been equalled in importance by but few regions: Mesopotamia, Egypt, Sicily, the Rhine Valley, and perhaps two or three others—all of them at the junction of great communication lines between East and West or between North and South."[5]

---

[4] Kirchner, Walther, *The Rise of the Baltic Question* (Newark: University of Delaware Press, 1954), p. 2.

[5] *Ibid.*, p. 4.

Historical Background

To put this theme another way, the very land itself—
the geographical, political, and cultural potentialities of
this naturally favored situation—appears to be the controlling factor. There are indications, it is true, that the
Latgalians and Semgalians—Baltic people in the proper
sense—and the Cours, Livs, and Estonians (Finno-
Ugrian), who settled this maritime province beginning
as early as the fourth and fifth centuries,[6] were influential in its social, economic, and political development;
nevertheless—rather curiously—it is the situation, the
land and its potential, that seemingly dominates the historical mission of the Baltic States.

Thus the favored position of their realm has become the
tragedy of the peoples of this eastern Baltic coastland.
Their situation a focus of envy, brief periods of independence have been largely overshadowed by long epochs
of vassalage.

According to Kirchner the *history* (using the word
with the chief accent on its political connotation) of the
section of the Baltic region lying between the Gulf of
Finland and the Frisches Haff (Königsberg) begins with
the Christianization of these "Livonian" peoples in the
twelfth century (regardless of the almost one thousand
years of preliminary cultural progress).

The first epoch comprises the period of rule by the
German Knights of the Sword—a crusading organization
which brought Teutonic conceptions of government and
commerce as well as the Christian faith. Although these
"Balts" apparently occupied an inferior position socially
and in the government structure, this does not seem to
have been overly resented. And the native peoples accepted the feudalism of the Knights, perhaps because they
had wearied of holding their own against one thousand
years' invasion by the eastern Slavs and Mongols, receiving the Roman Catholic religion of the conquerors
as well.

---

[6] Bihlmans, Alfred, *Latvia in the Making* (Riga, 1925), p. 8; Wal-
ters, M., *Le Peuple Letton* (Riga, 1926), pp. 47, 86. As quoted in
Kirchner, *op. cit.*, p. 4.

Much could be said here of the unique characteristics of the "Livonians," the complex of which—it seems—serves to establish these varied—yet similar—peoples as "nationalistic" although of a passive rather than the usual dominant type.[7] Yet, as indicated earlier, it was the land that controlled; the inhabitants played a quiescent role.

A second chapter of Livonian history begins in 1582 with the era of Polish-Swedish rule, terminating in 1721 with the cession of Livonia to Russia. Sporadic revolts there were indeed from time to time, but with defense and trade largely in the hands of the German "Balts," Swedes, or Poles and the indigenous population chiefly an agricultural people; no organized rebellion or "revolution" ever occurred. Furthermore, with the advent of Lutheran Protestantism, the Livonians remained Catholic.

The third section of their history is that of the first Russian domination which continued for approximately two centuries—ending only with the World War I collapse of the Czarist regime in 1917.

"Livonia's" most recent period began with the postwar independence championed by President Wilson at Versailles of Estonia and Latvia and, along with that of Lithuania, continued for two decades up to the second Russian attack on their sovereignty in 1940. Nazi occupation from 1941 to 1944 and "liberation" by Moscow have placed the peoples of these Baltic States in many jeopardies, and the so-called "People's Democracies" set up by the Soviet rest only on Russian bayonets.

Short Period of Independence

Baltic nationalism, in the modern sense of the word, may be said to have flowered in the twentieth century; in the original form (and in the passive assumption of some elements of cultural homogeneity) it may be over one thousand years old. Nevertheless, Estonia, Latvia, and Lithuania (along with Finland and Poland) were the only nationalities subject to Czarist rule that were able

---

[7] See Kirchner, *op. cit.*, "The Livonians," Chapter I, pp. 5-23.

to break away from the Kremlin. In fact, the Marxists' "trouble-shooter," Joseph Stalin, failed dismally in his attempt to gain the Baltic republics for Bolshevism—an episode which he spent a third of a century trying to forget.

Twenty years of freedom, however, came to an end with the beginning of World War II on September 1, 1939. Actually independence had been earmarked for destruction a few days prior to this when Molotov and von Ribbentrop signed the Soviet-Nazi pact of *friendship* and *non-aggression* of August 23. A secret protocol placed Finland, Estonia, Latvia, Lithuania, and Bessarabia in Soviet Russia's sphere of influence. On August 28, plans likewise were made for the "fourth partition" of Poland, an event which was to signal the death knell of small nations in East Central Europe.

September and October saw "mutual assistance" pacts forced upon Estonia, Latvia, and Lithuania. On trumped-up charges the following June 14, Molotov presented the Lithuanian government with an ultimatum demanding free admission of the Soviet army and the establishment of a new government "friendly" to the USSR and willing to execute the mutual assistance treaty "honestly." Within two days Estonia and Latvia also had their turn to "cooperate."

Satellite Status

As military occupation was completed the new "friendly" governments were set up. Under three Russian commissars the puppet regimes quickly came into being. On July 14 and 15, elections of "people's parliaments" were held in each state. The franchise laws having been corrupted, only one slate, that of the so-called "Union of the Working People," was approved. The events of this dreadful day have been reported as follows:

In Estonia and Latvia a group of patriotic citizens had attempted to present to the voters a list of independent candidates . . . such action was immediately suppressed by the government and the initiators were arrested. . . . a great many citizens abstained from voting. . . . [Yet] the day after the elections it was

announced that 92.8 percent of the voters had cast their ballot for
the single pro-Communist slate in Estonia, 97.6 percent in Latvia,
and 99.19 percent in Lithuania.[8]

Of course this result should not have been surprising.
As an actual instance—but highly significant in revealing
the mentality of the Communist masters—the following
conversation between Deputy Prime Minister Professor
V. Kreve-Mickevicius of the Lithuanian People's Government and Molotov in Moscow on July 2, 1940 excels in
frankness: Molotov—"You must take a good look at
reality and understand that in the future small nations
will have to disappear. Your Lithuania along with the
other Baltic nations, including Finland, will have to join
the glorious family of the Soviet Union. . . . Lithuania
cannot remain an exception. . . . You would be doing the
most intelligent thing if you would accept without any
hesitation the leadership of the Communist Party which
is determined to effect the unification of all Europe and
the application of the new order."[9]

"Pacification"

Horrible events in the subjugation of Estonia, Latvia,
and Lithuania are related by Swettenham as, for example,
the terrors of the night of June 14, 1941. In Lithuania a
total of 30,485 persons seized and deported is substan-
tiated by police and railroad documents, including
"freight lists" of human cargoes showing car numbers,
capacity, and destinations. In Latvia and Estonia "the
M.V.D. raided thousands of homes during the night, ordered men, women, and children out of bed, gave them ten
to thirty minutes to pack a few belongings, bundled them
into lorries and took them to railway stations where cattle
trucks with barred windows waited. . . . Hundreds of

---

[8] Schwabe, Arvid, "The Baltic States," in Stephen D. Kertesz
(ed.), *The Fate of East Central Europe*, Chapter 5 (Notre Dame
Indiana: University of Notre Dame Press, 1956), p. 109. See the
entire chapter for other developments including the German occupation and second Soviet seizure.

[9] *Third Interim Report of the Select Committee on Communist
Aggression*, 83rd Congress of the United States, 2nd Session (Washington, 1954), pp. 341-44.

children and old people died even before the trains crossed the frontier on their way to Northern Russia and the wastes of Siberia."[10] The following figures representing executions in one year of Soviet occupation, based upon evidence found in the hundreds of mass graves, shock the sensibilities: Estonia 62,769; Latvia 64,250; Lithuania 65,000.[11]

As late as 1960, in order to cover their own atrocities, the Soviets continued to broadcast claims that "authorities in Communist Estonia have uncovered evidence showing Nazis slaughtered 3,000 Czech and German citizens near Tallinn in 1942-43."[12] Obviously, such communications are of a piece with Stalin's attempt to place the blame for the Katyn forest massacres on German forces—an expedient that was rejected almost universally by the West.

Nor is deportation by the Marxist a forgotten device today. Weishar reports "In its craving for expansion the Kremlin is not satisfied to hold the southern Baltic Coast (in addition to the eastern sector) and place it partially in the hands of satraps. Together with the military occupation and political subjugation went an ethnic change of vast proportions: the German Baltic Coast from Memel to the mouth of the Oder was denationalized. . . . The Baltic peoples constitute an uncommonly high percentage of the inmates in the Siberian slave labor camps. The Finns, too, were expelled from the Karelian Isthmus after the war's end and their land annexed to the Soviet Union, which also swallowed a considerable strip of the north coast of the Gulf of Finland."[13]

---

[10] Kareda, Endel, *Technique of Economic Sovietisation*, as quoted in John Alexander Swettenham, *The Tragedy of the Baltic States, a Report Compiled from Official Documents and Eyewitnesses' Reports* (New York: Frederick A. Praeger, 1954), p. 139 ff.

[11] Swettenham, *op. cit.*, p. 141.

[12] Associated Press (London), September 10, 1960; refer also to "Russ 'Explain' Pact with Nazis," AP (London), July 24, 1960.

[13] Weishar, *op. cit.*, p. 226.

Religious Oppression

Because of the strength of Roman Catholicism in the eastern Baltic States, the Communists from the first have endeavored to wean the population from their religious moorings. Heavy taxation was imposed on all churches in the newly acquired territory and excessive rents charged for the use of dwellings which formerly belonged to the Church and were domiciled by clerics. Education suffered too. It is well known that, in Lithuania, the Catholic Faculties of Theology and Catholic high schools were closed; only one of Lithuania's four seminaries was allowed to function and the number of students eventually reduced; religious services in the army, hospitals, asylums, and prisons were stopped; religious teaching in the schools was forbidden and this portion of instruction replaced by lessons on Marxist materialism."[14]

At the same time eleven of Latvia's 110 Catholic priests were arrested, tortured, and finally either executed or deported. In Lithuania, eighty out of eight hundred suffered a similar fate. Apparently the Soviet overlords believed that the liquidation of 10 percent of the Baltic priests would intimidate the population. It did not and therefore, during the first year of the second occupation, thirty-three Catholic priests in Latvia and 350 in Lithuania were transported or killed raising the proportion to close to one-third.[15]

Yet not all of the clergy in the Baltic were attacked. For example, Archbishop Antonius Springovics remained at Riga, on orders from Rome, during the entire first occupation. While he personally was not molested, he was powerless to prevent either the arrest, torture or execution of his priests or the deportation of the Latvian population, a maneuver by which the Communists expected him to lose prestige and indirectly to denigrate the power of the Church.

---

[14] Listowel, Judith (Countess of), "Luxury Tax on Churches," *East Europe and Soviet Russia*, VII, No. 327 (April 19, 1951), 11-14.

[15] *Ibid.*

When the Russians returned after the German invasion (in May, 1945) he was, at first—in keeping with the much propagandized policy of "religious freedom"— shown proper consideration. Then, toward the end of the year, the Kremlin invited him to move to Moscow, where he—as "Metropolitan of the Roman Catholics in the Soviet Union"—could "wield a larger power." Upon his indignant refusal the Communists showed their other face. Although it is not yet established whether of his own free will or on Marxist orders, in 1947 Archbishop Springovics removed to a tiny domicile well beyond the limits of the city of Riga.[16]

Unquestionably we can assume that the exercise of religious rites in the Baltic, in addition to the spiritual comfort gained, serves also to iterate feelings of common nationality as opposed to folk activity—that fostered by the Red regime—in the political sphere. Nor is religion the only mode of expression available. They can show a common spirit in many ways that are passive rather than active. For example, it is admitted that "on January 18 (1951) the Communist *Rahva Hääl* (Tallinn) reported that the department of the cinematography (which owns all the nationalized cinemas) ended 1950 with a considerable deficit, because of the drop in cinema attendance."[17] Two good reasons for public refusal to go to the pictures are suggested by the fact that all films have Russian sound-tracks and the Estonians do not care to speak Russian; further, that the cinema fare is so heavily loaded with Soviet propaganda that they are boring in the first place.

Undercurrents of Resentment

A little later, February 21, 1952, the Secretary-General of the Latvian Communist party is revealed as wailing that "the people's minds are much influenced by capitalist relics. . . . Bourgeois nationalism makes itself felt in all walks of life; . . . class alien elements

---

[16] Listowel, *op. cit.*, p. 14.

[17] *East Europe and Soviet Russia*, VII, No. 322 (March 8, 1951), 23.

spread rotten, reactionary theories and encourage the inclination to private property in the *kolkhozes*."[18]

Then there is the Estonian youth problem—a phenomenon that has been reported as plaguing Moscow itself.[19] Again it is reported that "On March 26-28 in Tallinn at a plenary session of the Central Committee of the Estonian Communist party, its Secretary, Comrade Lentsman, and the Secretary of the *Komsomol*, Comrade Pomazkin, stated that the political education of the workers and the young people left much to be desired. Local party organizations," he said, "paid no attention to the Communist education of the masses."[20]

The parallel between the expansionist policies of Czarist Russia and those of the current Red regime are too visible to require much comment. Dr. Rudolf Lodgman has recently restated this truth in pertinent fashion: "It is not the first time in history that Eastern peoples have reached out to conquer Europe. Huns, Magyars, Mongols, and Islam have, in turn, been a threat; today Bolshevism, emanating from Moscow, would execute, if possible, the testament of Peter the Great."[21]

As a surface ideology Pan-Slavism is again invoked. This old myth of the "Big Brother to the Little Slavs" (and other small linguistic groups of East Europe) is pretty threadbare, but the Marxists are not above utilizing it. The historical record must be rewritten to make the ism palatable, but the Kremlin's method of writing history easily takes care of this. Yet those of East Central Europe with longer memories can only know that their earlier contacts with Russia, "Mother of the Slavs," were anything but felicitous; the existence of Moscow's "Third Rome" together with the various Pan-Slavic

---

[18] *East Europe and Soviet Russia*, VIII, No. 367 (February 21, 1952), 17-18.

[19] *Soviet Survey, an Analysis of Cultural Trends in the USSR*, No. 12 (February, 1957), "Part I, Conflict Between the Generations," pp. 1-7.

[20] *East Europe and Soviet Russia*, VIII, No. 377 (May 1, 1952), 17.

[21] Lodgman, Rudolf, "Tug of War for Europe," *Sudeten Bulletin*, VII, No. 11 (November, 1959), 217-19.

ideologies contributed to an uneasiness, which the fullness of time has shown to have real reason for being.[22]

Geopolitical Importance

Jean Gottmann, the geographer, calls East Europe "The Tidal Lands." His meaning is clear. "The Central European powers have worked out for themselves an indisputable personality which often benefited by the many contacts it had with a diversity of neighbors. This personality was so linked to some of the surrounding areas that many times it attempted to dominate them, while a power that developed in any part of Europe and expanded over the continent was bound to find the central section in its way. It thus happened that throughout history Central [East Central] Europe was a land of ebb and flow; it has been the most unstable part of the continent, and therefore should be defined as the area between those parts endowed with more stability.[23]

Although Gottmann uses the expression "Central Europe," he defines this as "those tidal spaces between Germany and Russia," in fact the identical area denominated by Halecki as "East Central Europe."[24] When speaking of the "pivotal" nature of this unique living space between the Baltic and the Black and Adriatic, both Gottmann and Halecki offer recognition to the peculiar demands placed on the people of this area: they must "nationalize" or perish. Perhaps this is only the "indisputable personality" referred to by Gottmann who inquires further, "Is Central Europe an axis or a buffer?"[25]

Throughout history the Baltic States have served as a pivot or axis. This is the real meaning of the "Baltic Question." Presently the Soviet masters in playing up

[22] For an excellent expose of this ism see Joseph S. Roucek, "Panslavism, an Ideological Myth," *Prologue*, III, No. 1 (Spring, 1959), 18-25.

[23] Gottmann, Jean, *A Geography of Europe* (New York: Henry Holt, 1954), p. 351.

[24] Halecki, Oscar, *The Limits and Divisions of European History* (New York: Sheed and Ward, 1950), p. 137.

[25] Gottmann, *op. cit.*, pp. 360-61.

their "rimland" characteristic may perchance consider them as buffers. At any rate the inhabitants of these unfortunate countries must suffer expulsion and frequently graver penalties merely for having been born in one of the most strategic and significant spots on earth. Dr. Kurt Rabl, an expert on international law, cites the "legal" basis for such action—in an illustration particularly pertinent to the Baltic region: Expulsion or resettlement has been in recent years, applied (among other circumstances) to "Persons who, within a State of which they are citizens, are also resident there, but by the authority of that State are deported to other localities of the interior for reasons of 'public order and security' or for reasons of economic planning. That applies to the politically or socially 'undesirable' Estonians, Letts, Lithuanians, and Ukrainians; it has been the case of certain Mohammedan Caucasian peoples, and also to the Japanese living on the Pacific Coast of the United States who, under the impact of the outbreak of Japanese-American hostilities at the turn of 1942-43, were deported to barren regions of the Rocky Mountains and interned in guarded camps."[26] It should of course be pointed out that Dr. Rabl sees these events as violations of the spirit of international law.

What steps have the Western democracies taken to remedy the situation in East Europe, especially in the Baltic States? In 1951, the Voice of America enlarged its program to include broadcasts to these Soviet-enslaved peoples of Estonia, Latvia, and Lithuania in their native languages. In 1953, the Congress of the United States created a "Select Congressional Committee on Communist Aggression." This committee compiled a huge quantity of evidence concerning the "annexation" and subsequent Marxist atrocies in the Baltic countries. This was published in 1953-54.

---

[26] Rabl, Kurt, "Mass Expulsions and International Law," *Sudeten Bulletin, A Central European Review*, VIII, Nos. 8/9) August-September, 1960), 207-12.

Western Nonrecognition of These Seizures

George F. Kennan in *Russia and the West Under Lenin and Stalin* speaks of the severity with which Stalin implemented the provisions of the Molotov-Ribbentrop Pact in the Baltic States and of the brutality with which thousands of the Estonians, in particular, were dragged into the interior of the USSR or were caused to perish in the deportation proceedings.[27] This plus the dislocations of the German occupation and the horrors of the second Russian seizure so changed the composition of the population and its opportunity for indigenous development that a consideration of educational practices and policies becomes rather superfluous; the three Baltic States became "republics" within the Soviet Union with the indoctrinatory approach to the work of the schools common throughout the R.S.F.S.R. and the other eleven republics that comprise the USSR. Thus the contemporary educational organization of Estonia, Latvia, and Lithuania is a minor feature of our current survey.

Under Russian occupation the three Baltic States are almost as isolated as Albania. Nevertheless, current evidence through the facilities of the *Daily Telegraph* (London) suggests rough weather for Communism in the former free republics. Evidence that many of the six million inhabitants of Estonia, Latvia, and Lithuanian have not forgotten their yearning for independence and self-government from time to time reaches the Free World via Sweden—often by way of the Baltic Committee in Stockholm.

It is reported that, in Latvia, the Minister of Education, Vilis Kruminsh, was sacked recently for "fostering national sentiments." Valdemar Kalpinsh, Minister of Culture, was dismissed too because of his failure to promote "the comity of the different peoples of the Soviet Union."[28] Translated from the Marxist jargon,

---

[27] Boston: Little, Brown and Company, 1960, pp. 331-33.

[28] As reprinted in *The National Observer* (Washington), I, No. 43 (November 26, 1962), 13.

these phrases indicate that too much Latvian and not enough Russian was taught in the Latvian schools—another case of "bourgeois nationalism," as the Reds view it.

In Lithuania, the report states, that five Roman Catholic clergymen were jailed for "bourgeois nationalism." In Latvia and Estonia, several laymen are said to have been shot or imprisoned. To counteract these "national sentiments" Marxist pressure has been augmented in each country. In Estonia the "Association for the Dissemination of Political and Scientific Knowledge" gave 63,000 lectures in 1962 and (according to plan) will increase this figure to 105,000 by 1964. No less than 11,000 lecturers are said to participate in the program, their listeners being calculated as 2,200,000.[29] These numbers, of course, sound typically Marxist, i.e., well rounded.

On the positive side, the USSR has brought a greater industrialization to the Baltic States and, in Estonia, the output per man is reported as 250 percent more than before World War II. Technical developments have been achieved and, as mentioned earlier, the area has been highly fortified, the islands Saaremaa and Hiiumaa becoming (undoubtedly) rocket bases. But the local inhabitants have not profited thereby and real wages have not risen. There are sharp housing shortages attendant upon the advancing urbanization, and large numbers of these Baltics would willingly migrate except for the fact that the Red regime will not let them.

A great statement of American policy toward the Baltic countries by the late Secretary of State John Foster Dulles is revealing of the attitude of many citizens of the United States regarding the captivity of Estonia, Latvia, and Lithuania: "The United States, for its part, maintains the diplomatic recognition it extended in 1922 to the Baltic nations. We continue to deal with those diplomatic and consular representatives of the Baltic countries who served the last independent governments of

---

[29] *Idem.*

these States. . . . The captive peoples should know that they are not forgotten, that we are not reconciled to their fate and, above all, that we are not prepared to seek illusory safety for ourselves by a bargain with their masters. . . ."[30]

---

[30] As quoted in Kertesz, *op cit.*, p. 128.

CHAPTER VII

CZECHOSLOVAKIA: A BRIDGE BETWEEN EAST AND WEST

Historical and Cultural Position

PERHAPS THE MOST PUZZLING event in the whole Communist take-over of ten countries of East Central Europe was the bloodless *coup d'état* by which the Soviets seized Czechoslovakia. This remarkable country, born of the Peace of Versailles, yet with a history one thousand years long, represented to most Westerners the nearest approach to their own civilization, a flower of Catholic Christianity, and a military bastion against, on the one hand, the aggressiveness of Teutonic central Europe and, on the other, a hedge against the hordes of Marxist Russia. France and Britain had made the country of the Czechs and Slovaks a key *dexter* in their *cordon sanitaire* and signed treaties respecting its independence, and the American President Woodrow Wilson had considered the fortunes of Bohemia and Slovakia one of his most highly cherished responsibilities.

Yet in what appeared to be the twinkling of an eye Marxist machinations so altered the complexion of Czechoslovakia as to render its Western orientation a myth and its democracy a farce. This terrible metamorphosis was accomplished through a little force but a prodigious amount of propaganda.

To the Western idealist, scarcely second to the great political transformation wrought in the USSR and her East European satellites is the rape of history by the Communist mentality. Let this great cultural shift be illustrated by the following report taken from Victor S. Mamatey:[1]

---

[1] *The United States and East Central Europe, 1914-1918* (Princeton, N.J.: Princeton University Press, 1957), pp. vii-xi.

"Before World War II the western traveler arriving by the Orient Express in Prague, Czechoslovakia, would detrain at the Wilson Station. Coming out of the station, he would face Wilson Square and the Wilson Park, with a statue of President Woodrow Wilson in its center. There were innumerable Wilson Avenues, Wilson Squares, and Wilson Statues in Belgrade, Bucharest, Warsaw, Prague, and the other cities of the new national states of East Central Europe, all testifying to the fact that the Yugoslavs, Rumanians, Poles, and Czechoslovaks regarded President Wilson as one of their liberators and heroes."

Yet in 1953—just five years after the Communist coup —the Czech Marxist historian, J. S. Hajek, published in Prague a vitriolic study devoted to dethroning President Wilson and eradicating the above mentioned symbols of the West from Czechoslovakian (and Eastern European) life, literature, and geography. Titled *The Wilson Legend in the History of the Czechoslovak Republic*,[2] Hajek attempts to demonstrate that Czechoslovakia owes nothing to either Wilson or to the Western Allies for her rebirth in 1918.

The Wilson Legend may be described as "an elaborate attempt to 'debunk' Wilson in the esteem of the Czechs and Slovaks, based on published American sources." The collapse of Austria-Hungary and the creation of the Czechoslovak state are interpreted as products of an internal social revolution set into motion by the Bolshevik Revolution. Wilson is denigrated and considered a foe of the Czech and Slovak peoples. He supported their independence movement only as bourgeois counter revolutionary tactic. He feared their newly found social-revolutionary zeal. Mamatey reports that Communist historians in the other satellite countries in East Central Europe employ this same method, and indeed this is well known.

Geographically, Czechoslovakia stands as the westernmost outpost of the Slavic world in East Central Europe,

---

[2] *Wilsonovská legenda v dejinach Ceskoslovenské Republicky* (Prague, 1953).

and together with Poland represents the chief focus of contact between the Communist and non-Communist spheres. A landlocked island, almost completely surrounded, first by threatening Teutons and now by the Communist world, Czechoslovakia's mountain ranges traditionally acted as breakwaters against enemy pressures. Czech history is a record of constant wars against invaders. Moreover, since Czechoslovaks view their history in terms of centuries, there has never been a single one in which the need to defend—either with sword or spirit—their patrimony from foreign aggression was absent. Usually (although temporarily) the Czechs have lost; by the same token, no invader, whether German, Austrian, or Turkish, has ever succeeded in permanently enslaving this little country.

In their efforts to survive, the Czechoslovak people have been able always to present strong cultural arguments to the world. Long before Leipzig and Heidelberg became world-famous university centers—and at a time when there were, in the whole of Europe, only four such havens of learning (Bologna, Avignon, Paris, and Oxford)—the *Alma Mater Pragensis* (1348) was founded by King Charles IV of Bohemia.

That education and learning have been good fountainheads for the Czech national life is demonstrated by the fact that the first novel in Czech—a popular version of the history of the Trojan War—appeared a full quarter of a century antecedent to the landing of Columbus. The famous Sorbonne Press is two years junior to its Bohemian sisters and, in the British Isles, eight years were still to remain before indigenous printed books appeared.

When Charles established his university he made Prague a center of European civilization. The fortunes of John Hus, rector, reformer, and popular preacher in Czech, are well known. Hus preceded Luther by more than one hundred years and set into motion the currents of nationalism and Protestantism which led to the undoing of the Bohemian state. Catholic forces of the Empire defeated the Czechs at the battle of White Mountain (a part of the Thirty Years' War) in 1620, and the freedom of the Bohemian people was so circumscribed that the very life of its letters was to be virtually buried for almost three centuries.

"Extirpate that entire unholy and rebellious Czech nation," advised the Spanish ambassador at the court of Vienna, when the result of *Weissenberg* was made known. This advice was very nearly followed by the avenging Habsburgs. The majority of the rebelling Czech nobles lost life and property or were driven into exile. The Catholic sweep was of such magnitude that the practice of Protestantism was forbidden in Bohemia. The Habsburgs regained control and the "winter king," Frederick, was shunted into ignominious banishment. The Bohemian Brethren (The Moravians) were likewise reduced to wanderers; many made their cultural contributions in foreign lands—even in far-off America.[3] Comenius, the greatest, retired to Poland where—such was the tolerant attitude of seventeenth-century Poles—he gained sanctuary to write that greatest of all educational classics, *Magna Didactica.*

The Slovaks suffered an even worse fate. By 906 the Magyars, having completed their conquest of the Danubian plain, had driven the Slovak inhabitants northward into the confines of the ring of the Carpathians. The Magyars became masters in Hungary and Slovakia. For one thousand years the Czechs and Slovaks were separated; thus difficulty of intercourse produced a divergence in what was originally a common language. Finally, in the nineteenth century, the dominant Magyars attempted to destroy, culturally, the Slovak nation. During a period of only forty years, 739,565 Slovaks emigrated to the United States, where they generally settled in the industrial areas of Pittsburgh, Cleveland, Detroit, and Chicago.

In this manner the cultural reputation of the Czechs continued to live on, although on foreign shores, and the Slovaks added a solid respectability to the North Amer-

---

[3] For further details see "Moravian Brethren in the United States," *The Slavonia Encyclopedia*, Joseph S. Roucek, ed. (New York: The Philosophical Library, 1949), pp. 823-24; also Joseph S. Roucek, "Moravian Brethren in America," *The Social Studies*, XLIII, No. 2 (February, 1952), 58-61.

ican areas to which they had transplanted their lives and customs. Yet had nothing else ever been accomplished in the world by a Czech or a Slovak, the fame of Hus and Komensky (in Latin, Comenius) could have assured Bohemia, Moravia, and Slovakia a place in history.[4]

Now in the homeland the bugles of the French Revolution and the hum of the first industrial mills in Bohemia-Moravia aroused Czech national and cultural life from a sleep of two hundred years. Slovakia too awakened, and the nationalistic rebirth was under way. Slovak as a separate literary language was first established at this time. Father Antonin Bernolak, a Roman Catholic cleric, published in Pressburg (now Bratislavia) his epochal *Dissertation Philologico-Critica de Litoris Slavorus* (1787). In this work Bernolak insisted that the Slovaks—in company with all other Slavic peoples—merited, both nationally and culturally, their own written language.

The Czechs were more favored by the course of history, having had a greater opportunity for contact with the Western world than the Slovaks, whose enslavement by the Magyars had not furthered their political and cultural development. Both were, of course, Roman Catholic, and church contacts had reduced somewhat the isolation enforced by Habsburg and Magyar. In 1867 the two were reunited, although within the famed "Dual Monarchy" and henceforth, until the end of World War I, served the same master.

---

[4] The literature on Comenius is especially extensive. See Jan Jarucec, *Johannes Amos Comenius* (Prague: Orbis, 1928); I. L. Kandel, "John Amos Comenius, Citizen of the World," *School and Society*, LV (April 11, 1942), 401-6; M. W. Keating, *Comenius* (New York: McGraw-Hill, 1931), W. S. Monroe, *Comenius and the Beginnings of Educational Reform* (New York: John Scribner's Sons, 1900); Otakar Olozilik, *Jan Amos Komensky* (Chicago: Czechoslovak National Council of America, 1942), Joseph Needham (ed.), *The Teacher of Nations* (Cambridge: University Press, 1942); M. W. Keating, *The Great Didactic of John Amos Comenius* (London: Adam and Charles Black, 1896); S. S. Laurie, *John Amos Comenius* (Syracuse: C. W. Bardeen, 1892); W. S. Monroe, *Comenius' School of Infancy* (Boston: D. C. Heath, 1896); William W. Brickman, "John Amos Comenius," *School and Society*, LXXXVI, No. 2131 (April 26, 1958), 192-94; Robert Ulich, *A History of Educational Thought* (New York: American Book Co., 1950), pp. 188-99.

Founding the Republic

After Hus and Comenius, Czechoslovakia's most famous son possibly could be identified as Professor Thomas G. Masaryk. Like Comenius, Masaryk's prestige became well known in the United States and indeed in the entire Western world. When in the course of the events of the first World War, the Austro-Hungarian Empire faltered, the Czechs and Slovaks rose in revolution. Woodrow Wilson's principle of self determinism made the American President perhaps the most popular man in East Central Europe. Dr. Masaryk preached national union of the Czechs and Slovaks in the United States, and in fact the arrangement for the new state was concluded in Pittsburgh, U.S.A., and a declaration of the same name ushered Czechoslovakia into the family of nations.

Consequently, the efforts of Dr. Masaryk and Dr. Eduard Benes, a second Czech professor, together with the inspiration and best wishes of Woodrow Wilson (the contention of J. S. Hájek to the contrary notwithstanding) served to reconstitute Bohemia, Moravia, Slovakia, and Ruthenia as an independent democratic republic based on features of the American Constitution and the French cabinet system.

The year 1918—almost an exact three centuries following the catastrophic defeat at the White Mountain—began the existence of a new East Central European government destined to play a role in the world's history at once both consequential and fearful. Czechoslovakia became the Achilles' heel of Europe! Her geopolitical position vis-à-vis West and East predicated this; her political policies and strong national spirit confirmed it. At this situs, World War II was to originate.

Yet war was certainly not the wish of the Czechoslovak state. For twenty years (the long Armistice) she preserved a dignified and influential existence. Ally of France, leader of the *cordon sanitaire,* and culture exponent of East Central Europe, blessed with a strong economic position, Czechoslovakia's future appeared to be secure. Yet her geographical position was such (along with that of Poland and the Baltic States) that her destiny was being shaped by circumstances far beyond her own control.

Unfortunately, the new "nation" was one in some ways synthetic. Her ethnic problem was more pressing than that of Poland. There were the Germans (Sudetens) in the West, Poles at the north, the Ruthenians in the east, and to utterly complicate the picture the frequent lack of common feeling between Czech and Slovak, all of which served to produce a most precarious situation.[5]

But would geography alone have decided her fate? With a peaceful Germany at her front door (West) and a territorially satisfied USSR at her rear (East), could not Czechoslovakia have experienced a hundred years or so of quiet and stability—a bridge between East and West?

It hardly needs to be said that such Arcadian conditions could not and did not obtain. The German Reich fell under the control of a psychopathic adventurer; the Soviet monolith represents a dynamic power complex such has not appeared in the world since the days of Genghis Khan.

Tragedy

In September, 1938, Adolf Hitler demanded of Czechoslovakia the western rim of the Bohemian saucer, inhabited chiefly by the Sudeten (South) Germans. Deserted by her French ally and denied by Britain, with the United States in an isolationist mood, President Benes quickly complied. Nor was this the extent of the damage. The following spring Germany annexed Bohemia and Moravia and made a satellite of Slovakia. The USSR took Ruthenia, as a treaty of nonaggression and "friendship" was negotiated between the Reich and the Soviets. Po-

---

[5] In this connection, see Franz Tiso, "Slovakia's Road to Freedom," *Sudeten Bulletin*, VII, No. 4 (April, 1959), 82-84. Accusing Masaryk (actually a Slovak although a native of Moravia) and Benes of duplicity in regard to Slovakia, thus producing the gradual erosion of Slovakia's position in what originated as the "Czecho-Slovak Republic into the final "Czechoslovakia," as a fruit of Czech intolerance, Tiso goes so far as to consider the chapter of "self-rule" for Slovakia under the Third Reich as an illustration of Slovak political abilities, when uninhibited by the aggressive Czech.

land was invaded from both west and east, and the notorious "Fourth Partition" took place. France and Britain—at last in their senses—declared war; and a little later the United States joined the Grand Alliance; and there were many other contending parties.

Dr. Eduard Benes, exiled President of Czechoslovakia, reports an interview with President Franklin D. Roosevelt, which took place on May 22, 1939, at Hyde Park. Roosevelt asked Benes, "Tell me frankly how you envisage the possible course of the political situation in Europe and how you think events will progessively develop."[6]

Benes replied, "It is necessary to reckon with the fact that after Czechoslovakia and Poland all other Central European states as far as Greece will also fall. Hitler will thus come face to face with the Soviet Union. His real objective is the Ukraine and the definite pushing back of the Soviet Union as far as possible to the East. I am fully confident that Great Britain will oppose this. What will happen to France, I cannot say; but I hope that in the end France, too, will pull itself together for real resistance."[7]

"What do you think the Soviet Union will do?"

"In the end it too will enter the war."

"Of course, on our side. War between the Soviet Union and Germany is sooner or later quite inevitable. This springs necessarily from the Nazi and Communist ideologies, from Hitler's conception of German national interests, from his concrete plans and from the character of the people who are in power in Germany."

---

[6] See *Memoirs of Dr. Eduard Benes* (translated by Godfrey Lias; Boston: Houghton Mifflin Company, 1953), pp. 77-78. This work was originally published in Czech in 1947—one year before Benes' death. Three volumes were projected, of which this, subtitled "From Munich to New Victory," was the only one completed. As will be noted later, Dr. Benes appeared under the illusion that Czechoslovakia could maintain her "independence" even under Russian vassalage. The well prepared *coup d'état* of February 25, 1948, by the Communist party of Czechoslovakia so shattered his will and health that, on February 29, he left the Hradcany (Presidential Palace) never to return. He died September 3—by a grotesque coincidence almost exactly a decade after Hitler's subversive demand on the little nation.

[7] *Idem.*

Quite right! But Benes' excellent discrimination did not extend to a true evaluation of the real purpose of the USSR. Near the close of the war, with Yalta already an item of history and the evidence of Communist double-dealing already available in Greece, Poland, and Romania, Benes still cherished his illusion.[8]

When Czechoslovakia was "liberated" by Soviet (and American)[9] troops, Communist prestige was strong in the first few years that followed 1945. Benes (blissfully unconscious of the forces rapidly bearing down upon him and the little country) once again served as President, and seemingly Czechs and Slovaks sought once more to operate a democratic government. However, there still

---

[8] Of course Dr. Benes was not alone in his confusion. The exceedingly complex situation was aggravated by the necessity of winning the war against Hitler; neither the suddenness of its end, nor the significance of the atom bomb, could then be known. Russian assistance must have appeared to be vital. This is the only straightforward explanation possible of the "sell-out" of Czechoslovakia, Poland, and East Central Europe generally. The cries of "conspiracy" are vague, although sometimes nagging, reminders of the most peculiar climate of opinion prevalent in the United States and in parts of Europe in the thirties and forties. See Oscar J. Hammen, "The 'Ashes' of Yalta," *South Atlantic Quarterly*, LIII (October, 1954), 477-84; *The Meaning of Yalta* by John L. Snell, Forrest C. Pogue, Charles F. Delzell, and George A. Lensen (Baton Rouge: Louisiana State University Press, 1956) undertakes a thorough exploration, comes up with approximately the answer suggested above.

[9] For the unusual role played by the American Army in this affair, see Ivo Duchacek, "Czechoslovakia," Chapter 8, Stephen D. Kertesz, *The Fate of East Central Europe* (Notre Dame, Indiana: University of Notre Dame Press, 1956), pp. 179-218 (especially pp. 200-204); Dwight D. Eisenhower, *Crusade in Europe* (Garden City, N.Y.: Doubleday and Co., 1948), has little to say on this very significant matter: "Patton directed the V [Fifth] to push eastward into Czechoslovakia. The corps captured Pilsen May 6 [1945]. In this area the Russian forces were rapidly advancing from the east and careful co-ordination was again necessary. By agreement we directed the American troops to occupy the line Pilsen-Karlsbad, while south of Czechoslovakia the agreed line of junction ran down the Budejovice-Linz railroad and from there along the valley of the Enns River" (pp. 417-18). Regardless of whatever military strategy was involved, this abandonment of Czechoslovakia to the Communists may be ranked as one of the top fatal blunders of the war. In addition to the overt advantage gained by the USSR, the propaganda inherent in the American turning aside (as it later came to be viewed) was of incalculable leverage for the Marxists and unquestionably enabled them to gather strength in Czechoslovakia for the inevitable seizure.

was friction between the two and this, among other things, gave the Communist party a greater freedom—as well as a cloak to hide under.[10]

In fact, Benes somewhat earlier had reported, "I left Moscow with my collaborators on December 23rd, 1943, with feelings of extreme respect and gratitude to the whole Soviet people, to their Army and their leaders. Grateful as I was to the British and Americans for all they had done for us in this war, I was not less grateful to the Soviet Union both for its deeds of prowess in the war and the really friendly and cordial reception given us in Moscow and all over the country; and for the favours and recognition which the Soviet Union bestowed with so much sincerity on our soldiers who fought on its front."[11]

Edward Taborsky, secretary to Dr. Benes, reports that, in his visit with Stalin on December 11, 1943, at the Kremlin, the President felt that everything was satisfactorily settled. "We came to a complete agreement, absolutely, complete," Taborsky repeats. About Stalin the secretary writes: "There was nothing about him to suggest to Benes that he stood face to face with a ruthless oriental despot." Yet, of course, the long history of Russia might have been thrown into the scales, had the President utilized customary alertness and, more than that, Benes' long political experience should have suggested caution. Regardless of all this, Benes himself considered his great decisions in the light of *sub specie aeternitatis,* and this state of mind may at once have proved to be both asset and liability.[12]

Indeed, there may have been in Benes' mind high ques-

---

[10] Franz Tiso, "The Clergy in Czechoslovakia," *Sudeten Bulletin,* Vol. VII, No. 7 (July-August, 1959), accuses the Czechs of cooperation with Marxism through the various levels of the Roman Catholic clergy; it is not nearly so critical of Slovak priests. Disillusionment with the West, especially France and England, is given as a strong reason for Communist success and the apparent resignation of the habitants to a *fait accompli* in both Bohemia and Slovakia.

[11] Benes, *Memoirs,* p. 280.

[12] See Edward Taborsky, "The Triumph and Disaster of Eduard Benes," *Foreign Affairs,* XXXVI, No. 4 (July, 1958), 669-84.

tions of civilization and empire which, disregarding his curious naïvete and lack of prudence, could easily have swayed his better judgment. "The question has been put to us and is again being *put today*: Is our national culture Eastern or Western? And what inferences can be drawn from this? Indeed, our conduct during the war sometimes gave the West the impression that we were preparing to change over from our former Western cultural orientation to a so-called Eastern one . . .[But] the cultural development of a nation is not a value which can be put off and on like a coat . . . The cultural development of a nation consists of centuries-old values which build themselves up in the course of ages and are imperishable, which are continually developing and which adapt themselves to new cultural facts and values only by slow degrees . . . It is simply ignorant and unreasonable to speak of a change in our national cultural orientation . . . In our cultural development one great fact has never ceased to be valid . . . *We have always taken deliberately a general and universal line.* That is to say, a line which includes not only the development and progress of the West, but also the progress and development of the East. Perhaps, therefore, we will in this or that direction deepen our cultural contact with the East after the war to a somewhat greater extent than in the past . . ."[13] Here a brash and forward speculation suggests that Benes saw himself in his dealings (even with Stalin) the great statesman and compromiser, the role he had essayed (and rather creditably) in the pre-Munich era and also saw his country as holding the balance of power—a power which he even then deemed Stalin respectful of. While this is, of course, madness, it must be remembered that both Roosevelt and Churchill, greater figures by far than Eduard Benes, had also been taken in by Stalin's charm.

The ties with the Russian East were strengthened. The possibility of Czechoslovakia's serving as a bridge between East and West became more and more forlorn as the Iron Curtain dropped. That a certain shade of disillusionment may already have been forming in the Benes'

---

[13] Benes, *op. cit.*, pp. 281-82.

mind in 1944 may be inferred from the President's remark on learning of the Patton advance, "Thank God, Thank God," a jubiliation that was quickly to subside with the later information that the Americans were "deliberately halting their drive to the East." Near the end his faithful secretary relates that his "Grand Master of Compromise" had suffered a strong reversal of mind and that "these doubts had never ceased to trouble him in that six-month interval between his final departure . . . and the fatal stroke."[14]

With Benes immobilized through his own processes of thought, the Communist infiltration became more and more pronounced. Klement Gottwald, a Marxist, became Premier and, upon the lethal inability of the President, became chief executive, a post he was to hold until 1953. Many other positions of power were held by Communists and, although free elections were consistently against them, they were able to deal their coup and seize control of the total governmental organization in 1948, backed, of course, by Mother Russia.[15]

The Denouement

Jan Masaryk, son of the first President, Thomas G. Masaryk, and Foreign Minister, was either killed or forced into suicide in a plunge from his window within two weeks after the coup. Yet there was little reaction from the Czech people. Even in 1956, the year of trial for the Communist forces in East Europe, the Czechs remained relatively indifferent. "The Congress of Czech writers met in Prague, and complained about the Party's supervisory committees for literature; later a series of student meetings took place, at which the students denounced the rigidity of the regime and demanded its liberalization; a strike was reported in a factory in Pilsen; however, these relatively limited expressions of dissatis-

---

[14] Taborsky, *op. cit.*, p. 669.

[15] See D. A. Tomasic, *The Communist Leadership and Nationalism in Czechoslovakia* (Washington, D.C.: Institute of Ethnic Studies (Georgetown University, 1960), pp. 1-2.

faction were easily suppressed and passed almost un-
noticed in the outside world."[16]
What had happened to the national spirit of the Czechs
and Slovaks? What had altered their conception of the
democratic processes? The rationalizations of Dr. Benes
mentioned above offer a general explanation; Professor
Tomasic suggests that "religion as a defense against the
materialistic and atheistic doctrines of Marxism and of
Leninism was weak among the Czech"; Professor Ivo
Duchacek lists several specifics which may have been responsible: (1) the shattered hope and disillusionment
with the West after Munich; (2) the rigors of life under Hitler's satraps; (3) liquidation, exile, or deportation
of the more aggressive and perhaps intellectual (many of
these having left voluntarily) of the Czechs and Slovaks,
first by the Nazis, then by the Marxist regime; (4) alien-
ation between Czechs and Slovaks—a deliberately fostered policy of the Nazi *divida et imperia* and an oblique
tactic of the Communists. Bohemia was occupied and its
administration shifted to Hitler's gauleiters, but Slovakia
was endowed with a satellite government; and (5) although this is a highly unpalatable item to the West, the
efficiency of the seeming economic and social planning,
e.g., Czechoslovakia's position of primacy among the
satellites of the USSR in industry and trade.[17]
Yet in a sense the Communists did "restore" Czechoslovakia, although indeed not the country of Hus, Comenius, and the elder Masaryk; nor did the Soviets restore the Czech "nation," although population transfers

---

[16] Tomasic, *op. cit.*, p. 2.
[17] See Stephen A. Kertesz, *The Fate of East Central Europe*
(Notre Dame, Indiana: University of Notre Dame Press, 1956),
pp. 206-18; see also Ivo Duchecek, "The Strategy of Communist
Infiltration: Czechoslovakia, 1944-1948," *World Politics*, II (April,
1950), 345-72; and "The February Coup in Czechoslovakia," *idem*
(July, 1950) 511-32; Howard K. Smith, *The State of Europe*
(New York: Alfred A. Knopf, 1949), pp. 340-47; Sir Robert Bruce
Lockhart, *Jan Masaryk: A Personal Memoir* (New York: Philo-
sophical Library, 1951); Hubert Ripa, *Czechoslovakia Enslaved*
(London, 1950); Edward Taborsky, "Benes and the Soviets,"
Foreign Affairs, XXVII (January, 1949), 302-14; Paul Zinner,
"Marxism in Action: The Seizure of Power in Czechoslovakia,"
idem., XXVIII (July, 1950), 644-58; D. A. Tomasic, *op. cit.*, pp.
1-15 (1960). But Czechoslovakia's position today is not prosperous!

and even the slogans and watchwords of the Communist party in Czechoslovakia were always couched in terms which suggested as a leading goal the unification of nationality.

The key to the circumstances just described (aside from the weakness of Eduard Benes, the ineptness of the Western powers, and the brutal strength of Russian Communism) is, of course, the strength of the Marxist ideology. Quoting an interpretation by Joseph S. Roucek: "Thus ideologies are not only potent political creeds which set the armies of the world to march again in World War II; they are also the hidden forces which penetrate all aspects of social life and form the spiritual basis for the existence of every social struggle. They give logical meaning to all social struggle . . . When integrated, an ideology, as a systematic scheme of ideas, accompanied by a particular mode of interpretation or perspective characteristic . . . [is] an attitude on all problems of life. To put it differently, an ideology is the way that we see the world around us, its past, present and future, through rose-colored glasses . . . Communist . . . Nazi . . . Democrat . . . Socialist—and so on down the line."[18] The compulsive nature of the philosophy of Marxism-Leninism to certain groups and under given conditions is well known. That these conditions obtained in Czechoslovakia between 1944 and 1948 offers a partial, although emotionalized and irrational, explanation for the Communist coup.

That such a catastrophe could have occurred, indeed that it could have been accomplished by a minority group, whose election strength varied from 10 to 20 percent, still appears incredible to Western eyes. And perhaps likewise to those Czechoslovak émigrés out of touch with the real, internal conditions in their native land. And herein lies the potential danger—both for the West as well as for the "uncommitted areas" of the world. The fact that Czechoslovakia was not taken by the Marxists as were the Baltic States—or Poland either, for that mat-

---

[18] Joseph S. Roucek, "Ideology as an Aspect of the Sociology of Knowledge," *Sociologia (Saõ Paulo)*, XXII, No. 4 (December, 1960), 386-87.

ter—indicates the supreme necessity for alertness and realism in domestic and world politics. Czechoslovakia (as we know it) fell because of complacency, a weakened will, the seductive power of an irrational idea, and surrender to a few acts of violence.

One may well argue that the Red Army had in its power the means to pulverize the Czechs and Slovaks, yet it did not do so; nor was such a blunt recourse necessary. Perhaps the peoples of Bohemia and Slovakia did not correctly apprehend (nor do they yet) the creeping danger until their democratic leadership was shaken into suicide or death by Communist success. Even then there was no expression, at least on anything more than an individual level, of resentment or the fury of the Pole or Hungarian. This is not to say that Communism became acceptable to all (it is impossible to substantiate this one way or the other) in the land of the Czechs and the Slovaks. It did, however, become moderately respectable, and here Western minds are tempted to dwell on the old rationalization re Mussolini, "He made the trains run on time." Even so, one hesitates to agree completely.

Post-Mortems

Serious question has been raised as to Czechoslovakia's true acceptance of Communism[19]; however, Czech apathy and current timidity suggest more than a mere unwillingness to essay the role of East German, Pole, or Hungarian. Dr. Richard Weishar, Munich, claims that the true orientation of Czechoslovakia is Russian; he alleges that President Benes looked East rather than Westward and accuses the war President of grave duplicity.[20] Roucek emphasizes the "cracks in the Communist structure," and considers the Czech-Slovak antagonisms, from the Marxist point of view, a dangerous manifestation, perhaps one which eventually may result in the creation of a schism in the Communist party, Czech-

---

[19] See Theodore M. Herrmann, "Is Prague a Reliable Satellite?" *Sudeten Bulletin* (Munich), VI, No. 2 (February, 1958), 71-82.

[20] *Idem*, VI, No. 4 (April, 1958), 79-81.

oslovakia, and an ensuing liberation struggle. He says: "This difficulty has been mirrored in the relations of the regime with the masses as well as in the Party organization itself . . . Czechoslovakia's brand of 'national communism' has been most evident in the case of Slovak autonomist survivals, and some leading Slovak Communists have objected to the selection of the comparative newcomer Novotny for the Presidency of the Republic instead of Premier Sircky, a Communist veteran—and a Slovak. . . ."[21]

On the other hand, President Norman P. Auburn, the University of Akron, who returned from an extensive tour of Czechoslovakia, Poland, East Germany, Hungary, Romania, and Bulgaria four years ago, views Czechoslovakia as the sixteenth Republic of the USSR. Dr. Auburn comments that: "Fifteen years have elapsed since the U.S.S.R. took over its European satellites. During those 15 years the Kremlin has concentrated on twisting and molding the minds of the young people in the schools and universities . . . [and] the Czech regime now wants full acceptance as an autonomous republic of the U.S.S.R. If Czechoslovakia acquires U.S.S.R. status it will be following the inevitable pattern of Russian imperialism."[22]

Moreover, Czechoslovakia's Red masters are by far the most subservient puppets to Moscow of all the Communist leaders behind the Iron Curtain. They are compelled to insist on Soviet superiority in everything. Nevertheless, when international honors are at stake—the Brussels World Fair is a case in point—non-Communist artists, architects, engineers, etc., were taken from their third- and fourth-rate jobs to which they had been assigned because of their "political unreliability" to compete with the cream of the world's artists. Consequently, Czechoslovakia won first prize for the pavilion and carried off many awards in the Belgian capital. However, when the

---

[21] Joseph S. Roucek, "Stresses and Tensions in Satellite Czechoslovakia," *Prologue* (New York), III, Nos. 2-4 (Winter, 1959), 21-29.

[22] Norman P. Auburn, "How Russia Is Sovietizing Her European Satellites," *The Cross and Crescent*, XLVII, No. 4 (November, 1960), 27-30.

fair was over, these same prize-winners were promptly criticized by the stooges at home "for failing to show the Socialist aims of the country as set by the Soviets"; they are now—it is reported—for the most part, "back in the dog-house."[23]

It is indeed clear, and Czechoslovakia offers the prime example, that the masters of the Kremlin are still intent upon implementing the testament of Peter the Great.

Czechoslovakian Education

Independent Bohemia boasts of a rich educational history. Czech historians stress that the greatest historical figures of their country were professional educators (John Hus, Comenius, Masaryk, Stepanik, and Benes).

The Czech documentary history begins in the seventh century. While under their kings, the Czech people often struggled for their very existence. Under Charles IV (1347-78), "the father of his country," the nation fully reestablished its independence, except for the honorable connection with the Holy Roman Empire. Charles, reared in France, was a Czech patriot and showed great understanding of the importance of education and spiritual development of Bohemia by promoting the works of native writers. As noted previously, he founded the Charles University[24] in 1348; the Foundation Charter read:

Among the desires of his heart stood first the care that his Bohemian kingdom, which before all other countries he cherished, should abound in learned men as much as in worldly riches, that the faithful subjects of this Kingdom who ever hunger for the fruits of beautiful arts should not in foreign lands beg for alms, but that they themselves always have a table set for all, that they should not be forced to seek enlightenment in foreign parts of the world, but themselves enjoy the honor of inviting others to participate in such happiness.

---

[23] See *The American Bulletin* (Chicago 23, Illinois), No. 50 (April, 1961), p. 3.

[24] It is important to note that, with the absorption of the remnants of Bohemia-Moravia by Germany in 1939, the German Protector proclaimed this university a German institution on the theory that it was founded by Charles IV in his capacity as Holy Roman Emperor, although the university was chartered in 1348 and Charles did not become Holy Roman Emperor until seven years later, in 1355.

The highest distinction was bestowed upon the university by Magister John Hus (1369-1415), both as its Rector and as a popular preacher at the Bethlehem Chapel, where the sermons were preached in Czech (although the German language was predominant both in public offices and in the churches and schools throughout the country). Hus's efforts at a reform of religious life led to the Czech Reformation.

A sturdy peasant from southern Bohemia, Hus studied in Prague at the intermediate school and at the university. In 1396, he became Master of Arts and began to lecture at the university. In 1402, he was elected not only Rector (president) but also preacher in the Bethlehem Chapel (built by a Prague merchant and a country squire with the stipulation that the word of God be preached there exclusively in Czech). Hus taught the young Czech intelligentsia at the university, and in the Bethlehem Chapel he preached to burghers and nobles, to artisans and laborers, in rich, picturesque, and vivacious Czech. This led to serious conflicts between him and the German priests who were also bitterly opposed to the moral principles urged by Hus. The Czech "nation" became a factor at the university, and the Czechs bore with impatience their unjust representation there, which gave three votes to the foreign "nations"[25] (allowing the Germans to dominate) while the Czechs had only one. On the surface these quarrels seemed to be merely secular, but the real dividing factor between Czech and German was the movement for religious reform. Hus started as a religious reformer and gradually developed into the spokesman of the nationalists. He introduced a simplified spelling of the Czech language, giving the Roman letters newly devised accents to carry the soft sound of the Slavonic tongue. But controversy ranged around him which darkened all Europe and with which we are not concerned here. Sufficient to state that this great reformer and educator was burned at the stake in 1415, and the Hussite wars followed. The subsequent protracted wars between the

---

[25] The "nations" at universities in that day were corporate bodies representing students and teachers, with various rights and privileges.

Hussites and the Catholics strengthened the antagonism between Czechs and Germans and made the Czechs aware of their affinity with other peoples speaking a similar Slavonic language. From that time, Hussitism has signified for the Czechs the backbone of nationalistic ideology. To the Czech nationalist, the Czech nation took up as an inheritance from Hus the fight for truth, respect for personal conviction, loyalty to freedom, and a love of fraternity and democracy (exemplified by Hus's teaching the lower classes and using the native language). His followers believe that Hus's ideas traveled to Luther, from Luther to the era of Enlightenment, and finally to the Declaration of Human Rights on both shores of the Atlantic Ocean (in Virginia in 1776 and in Paris in 1793).

Educationally, we must also note that Hus's followers formed the Czech Brotherhood, whose members agreed to accept the Bible as their only standard of faith and practice and to establish a strict discipline which would keep their lives in the simplicity, purity, and brotherly love of the Apostolic Church. The formal organization of the *Unitas Fratrum* ("The Unity of Brethren") followed, and its preaching, theological publications, and educational work soon raised it to a great influence in Bohemia, Moravia, and Poland.

In 1620, the battle of White Mountain ended the independence of the Bohemian (Czech) people. At the beginning of this Thirty Year's War, there were 3,000,000 people in Bohemia, nearly all Protestants. At the end, there were only 800,000 all (nominally) Catholics. One Jesuit priest boasted that he alone had burned 60,000 Czech books; the very possession of a Bible or hymnal was punishable by death.

Under the Habsburgs the Czech language nearly ceased to exist. The Jesuits suppressed all literature, science, and the schools. Actually, after 1627, the Bohemian nation lived spiritually only in exile (in Germany, Poland, and the Netherlands). The most famous of these exiles was John Amos Comenius (Komensky, 1592-1670), the last bishop of the Czech (Bohemian) Brotherhood, who wandered for more than forty years in exile and died in

Amsterdam. He was welcomed and honored in courts and universities, where he introduced new educational principles that revolutionized teaching methods. He advocated a free and universal system of education; education for both sexes; preschool home training; instruction in the native tongue; graded subject matter adjusted to the psychological development of the pupils; dramatization of the subject; close correlation of thought with things; incorporation of history and geography; of drawing and manual training, in the curriculum.[26]

Not only the educational theories of Comenius have contributed to what is known today as "progressive education," but the theories and educational experiments of his followers are still with us. By way of Saxony, these refugees (known as Herrnhuters) eventually settled in Georgia, and sent missions to the West Indies and Greenland; they also made Bethlehem (Pennsylvania) the center of influence in America for the Moravian Church, which considered education of primary importance to the community. The Moravian Seminary and College for Women was the second girls' boarding school in the United States, and became important as the training institution for women teachers.[27]

While the educational accomplishments of the Czech peoples survived, in an acculturated form, abroad, the Czechs under Austria could hardly speak of any educa-

[26] Matthew Spinka, *John Amos Comenius, That Incomparable Moravian* (Chicago: University of Chicago Press, 1934), and Bibliography, pp. 156-77; W. S. Monroe, *Comenius and the Beginnings of Educational Reform* (New York: Charles Scribner's Sons, 1900); Robert F. Young, *Comenius in England* (London: Oxford, 1932). It is little known that Comenius is also the spiritual founder of modern Masonry; see: Joseph C. Roucek, "Freemasonry in Czechoslovakia," *The Builder*, XV (February, 1929), 45ff.

[27] For the many references about the educational heritage of the Moravians, see: Joseph S. Roucek, "The Moravian Brethren in America," *Social Studies*, XLIII (February, 1952), 58-61; A. L. Fries, *The Road to Salem* (Chapel Hill, North Carolina: University of North Carolina Press, 1944); J. T. Hamilton, *A History of the Unitas Fratrum or Moravian Church in the United States of America*, (New York: The Christian Literature Co., 1894); Thomas Woody, *A History of Women's Education in the United States* (Harrisburg, Pennsylvania: The Science Press, 1929), I, 179, 216, 331-33, 380; Mabel Haller, *Early Moravian Education in Pennsylvania* (Philadelphia: The Author, 1953).

tion. Whatever educational reforms undertaken, they were steps taken by the Austrian authorities, and directed from Vienna, a truly imperial and Germanized city. The Habsburgs were the true Catholic rulers.

At the end of the Thirty Years' War, higher education was entrusted to the Jesuits. During the eighteenth century, the period of "Enlightened Absolutism"—the centralization process, within a framework of a modern bureaucracy—efforts were made by Empress Maria Theresa (1740-80) and her two sons, Joseph II (1780-90) and Leopold II (1790-92) to improve the lot of the masses. But the results were meager, and the liberal and revolutionary ideas of the French Revolution began to agitate Bohemia. The Czechs, like other minorities in the Empires (the Poles, Italians, Romanians, Yugoslavs), began to make their nationalistic demands heard. The Germans, who made up only about one-fourth of the total population, were the dominant nationality in Austria (together with the Hungarians after 1867).

By the *Ausgleich* ("Compromise") of 1867, the Hungarians were handed over the eastern part of the Austro-Hungarian Empire to rule, and the Austrian Emperor became Emperor in Austria and King in Hungary. But the bitter rivalry between Hungarians and German Austrians continued; the picture was complicated by the bitterness of other groups against both the Hungarians and the Austrian Germans, whose minor national concessions mollified nobody.[28]

All through the nineteenth and twentieth centuries, the Czechs fought for national rights, schools, and national equality in public life—in short, for more democratic privileges and rights. Better education always stood in the forefront of Czech efforts. Czech educational hopes received a great opportunity for further development by the formation of a separate Czech University in Prague in 1882. Led by such leaders as Dr. Thomas G. Masaryk, the nationalistic agitation continued. The *Sokol*

---

[28] A good survey of this period is: Arthur J. May, *The Hapsburg Monarchy*, 1867-1914 (Cambridge, Mass.: Harvard University Press, 1951); see also, Oscar Jaszi, *The Dissolution of the Hapsburg Monarchy* (Chicago: University of Chicago Press, 1929).

gymnastic and educational movement did a great deal to raise the self-confidence of the Czech people. Under Masaryk's leadership, his followers stood for nationalization of science and philosophy, for better education, intellectual, moral, artistic, and political advancement, and for a realistic outlook on life through taking things as they really were and not as they appeared to be; this realism fought against shallow patriotism and liberalism, fantastic romanticism and historicism (such as Pan-Slavism).

Under this nationalistic reawakening, by the end of the nineteenth century, education was widespread and the passion for learning was great among all classes of Czech society. Students of statistics will recall that, among the various ethnic groups from the Habsburg Empire that came to America, Bohemia-Moravia furnished the lowest percentage of illiteracy and the highest percentage of skilled laborers. The Czechs erected excellent school buildings and formed a fine system of education, notwithstanding innumerable obstacles and the resistance of the pro-German government.

The system that the Czechoslovakia of 1918 inherited from Bohemia-Moravia dated from 1848. After many decades of struggle, the Czechs succeeded in building up the compulsory period of school attendance from the sixth to the fourteenth year of a child's life, with the required studies in the Bohemian (and also German) language (reading and composition, with spelling and penmanship), arithmetic and elementary geometry, history, drawing. geography, natural history, religion, and gymnastics, with domestic science added for the girls. There were two divisions of the elementary school period—the first (people's school) included the five early school years, and the second (citizens' school), the sixth, seventh, and eighth school years. The Czechs succeeded in switching the local control to the hands of the municipalities; hence they had less trouble in this field than in secondary education, where the control still remained largely in the hands of the Vienna government. But both the cost of erecting and of maintaining these schools fell chiefly on the municipalities.[29]

The Schools

In the elementary schools, the children in the first and second grades attended school in the morning from 8:00 to 10:00; in the third, fourth, and fifth grades, from 8:00 to 11:00 A.M.; and in the sixth, seventh, and eighth grades from 8:00 to 12:00 noon. In the afternoon all the grades were in school from 2:00 to 4:00 P.M. There were brief rest pauses at the end of each hour. There was also a brief session on Sunday morning for religious instruction and attendance at mass, the teachers supervising the children. Teachers in the elementary schools were trained in normal schools. The sexes in all schools were separated.

Higher education was offered at secondary schools, of which there existed various types. They comprised either seven or eight grades. Pupils were admitted upon successful completion of the first five grades of a lower elementary school; but completion of the first four years sufficed in cases of exceptional talents. Specialization in these various types of secondary schools was according to the type of college and study which the student intended to choose after having graduated from the secondary school. In addition to these seventh-to-eighth-grade secondary schools, there existed various kinds of first-to-fourth-grade professional (vocational) schools for technical, agricultural, commercial, pedagogical, and various other types of studies. Graduates from upper elementary schools, usually of exceptional talents, and pupils of secondary schools who had successfully completed the first four grades of those schools were admitted to the professional schools.

On the whole, the secondary school system, controlled mostly by the central government, discriminated against

---

[29] Will S. Monroe, *The Spell of Bohemia* (Boston: L. C. Page & Co., 1919 and 1929), chap. XII, "Education in Bohemia," 233-39, is a convenient survey of prewar education, in Bohemia and Moravia.

the Czech peoples. For instance, in Prague, there was one gymnasium for 62,000 Czechs, while the Germans had one for 6,700 inhabitants. The education of girls was entrusted mostly to monastic institutions.

There were also numerous kinds of technical schools, which received, when German, the lion's share of appropriations for education from the state. There remained numerous industrial schools maintained by the municipalities and private associations. There were two Institutes of Technology in Prague (one for Bohemians and one for Germans), coordinated with the university in rank, several art schools and conservatories. There were two universities, with complete faculties of theology, law, medicine, and philosophy for the Czechs and for the Germans.

Thus Slovakia, separated from Bohemia for ten centuries, suffered more under the Magyar nationalistic regimes than the Czechs under the Austrians. Although there had been "proportional education" in the lower schools of old Hungary, a new policy of Magyarization was started in 1867. By 1876, the three middle schools (high schools for the ages of twelve to nineteen) in which the language of instruction had been Slovak, were closed. All Czech and Slovak elements were removed, even from technical schools and from teacher-training schools, for few Slovak teachers were to be required in the future. *Slovenska Matica* (the "Slovak Academy") was dissolved; it was the last means the Slovaks possessed of influencing their own education and cultural life.

So large a proportion of elementary schools were Magyarized that, according to official Hungarian statistics of 1914, 214,267 Slovak children were attending purely Magyar elementary schools and only 42,186 had the opportunity to attend Slovak schools: 265 schools with 539 Slovak teachers. After the law of 1907, none of these schools was purely Slovak but taught many subjects in Hungarian. By 1918, the numbers had been reduced to 30,118 children in 276 Slovak schools with 390 teachers. Only 390 Slovak teachers for a population of some two million Slovaks. At the end only four to six hours of instruction in Slovak a week were allowed—to twenty-two hours in Hungarian, even in the so-called Slovak schools.[30]

The Educational Concepts of Masaryk and Benes

The most definite influence permeating Czechoslovak education during the three decades of its independence were the ideas of President Thomas G. Masaryk (1850-1937), who wrote no special studies in pedagogy but paid attention to it in his various writings as a former university professor and as a practical statesman.[31] He considered pedagogy a practical science, having its theoretical foundation in psychology, and especially in educational and abnormal psychology. Criticizing the school for its excessive intellectualism, he demanded the training of emotions and aesthetic and moral education by work. He believed that religious education is not a subject for public schools and should be left to the family. He favored a free and democratic school for all, with individualized training but socializing aims. The nationalistic aspects of education were to be integrated with humanitarianism and democratic ideals. The teaching of economics and politics should be a regular part of the school curriculum. But education ought not be left to the schools alone, since preschool and post-school education are quite indispensable in a democracy. Women ought to receive more education and training as future mothers and as the first educators of their children. Morality and ethical self-control are the ultimate goals of all educational endeavors.

Dr. Eduard Benes (1884-1948), Masaryk's successor as Czechoslovakia's President, also exerted his influence on education, but more in the practical than in the theo-

---

[30] The Czechoslovak Information Service, "*Democracy in Czechoslovakia* (New York, June, 1943), pp. 37-38. See also: C. J. Street, *Slovakia Past and Present* (London: P. S. King & Son, 1928); R. W. Seton-Watson, *Racial Problems in Hungary* (London: Constable, 1914); and *The New Slovakia* (Prague: Borovy, 1924).

[31] Joseph S. Roucek, "Concepts of Education in Czechoslovakia," pp. 377-80, in "History of Education and Comparative Education," *Review of Educational Research*, LX, 4 (October, 1939), and Bibliography, pp. 432-33.

retical aspects. As a sociologist, supporting the so-called "critical realism," he elaborated Masaryk's general ideas on education, cultivating the democratic bases of the educational system and the integration of enlightened nationalism with internationalism and humanitarianism.

Education Under Masaryk and Benes

A basic principle of the new Republic, founded in 1918, was to make education and training accessible to every child. Education was compulsory for a period of eight years, from the ages of six to fourteen, and an extension to the age of fifteen was in preparation. All the children had to attend the public primary school for the first five years[32]—rich and poor receiving the same program. There was a total of 15,257 public primary schools, with a school population of 1,799,004. A three-year course at a senior elementary school followed; this too was open to every child and was free. There were 1,973 of these senior elementary schools, attended by 449,601 children. The secondary schools were of two kinds: the humanistic "gymnasium," with an eight-year course, and the more practical "real gymnasium," with a seven-year course. These secondary schools numbered 292, with 133,050 pupils, while 10,095 teachers were being trained at 63

---

[32] For the changes in Czechoslovakia's educational system under Masaryk and Benes, see: R. J. Kerner (ed.), *Czechoslovakia* (Berkeley, Calif.: University of California Press, 1940), especially chaps. IX and XVI; Joseph S. Roucek, "Recent Reforms and Progress in the Czechoslovak Educational System," *School and Society*, XXXVIII (December 23, 1933), 837-39; and "Problem of Maturity Examinations in Europe," *Ibid.*, XXXVI (November 19, 1932), 664-65; and "Some Phases of Development of the Czechoslovak Educational System," *Ibid.*, XXXIII, 100 (January 25, 1936), pp. 125-27; and "The Education of Gypsies in Czechoslovakia," *Ibid.*, XXXXV, 1164 (April 17, 1937), pp. 548-49; and "Militarization of Czechoslovak Education," *Ibid.*, XXXXVII, 1210 (March 5, 1938), pp. 413-15; and "The Oversupply of Education for Defense in Czechoslovakia," *Ibid.*, XXXXVIII, 1244 (October 29, 1938), pp. 562-64; "The Extension of Education for Defense in Czechoslovakia," *Ibid.*, XXXXVIII, 1260 (February 18, 1939), pp. 214-15; and "Educational Trends in the 'Second' Czechoslovakia," *Ibid.*, IL, 1264 (March 18, 1939), pp. 349-50; and "Educational Changes in Slovakia," *Ibid.*, L, 1286 (August 19, 1939), pp. 249-50; and "Educational Reforms of the Protectorate of Bohemia-Moravia," *Ibid.*, L, 1294 (October 14, 1939), pp. 503-4.

teachers' training colleges. Specialized training was given to 97,452 students at 722 commercial, technical, agricultural colleges, and theoretical training to 177,233 industrial, commercial, and agricultural apprentices at 3,038 continuation schools. There were fifteen universities or institutions of higher learning with 29,327 students.

The primary, senior elementary, and continuation schools were all entirely free, all expenses being covered out of public funds. In the secondary schools, vocational training colleges, and universities, fees were paid, but these were very low and were remitted in the case of promising scholars too poor to pay them. This democratic educational system made higher education accessible to all talented children, and higher education ceased to be the privilege of certain classes. There was a total of 24,134 schools of all kinds, attended by 2,818,866 pupils and students (or approximately one-fifth of the entire population).[33]

Minorities and Schools

The right to use their own language in schools, courts, newspapers, theaters is a bone of contention with all peoples subject to foreign domination. The language law of February, 1920, of Czechoslovakia allowed great liberties to minority languages. The law provided that wherever any language was the mother tongue of at least 20 percent of the population, that language had to be permitted in the courts, state and municipal offices. Schools were conducted in the minority language in every town and village where there were forty school-age children of the minority. In very small settlements a proportional amount of educational budget was used to transport children to the nearest school where their mother tongue was

[33] For more details on Czechoslovakia's formal educational system under Masaryk and Benes, see: Bracket Lewis, *Democracy in Czechoslovakia* (New York: American Friends of Czechoslovakia, 1941), XI, "Democracy in Education," pp. 34-42, and XIII, "Adult Education," pp. 46-47; S. K. Turosienski, *Education in Czechoslovakia* (Washington, D.C.: Government Printing Office, 1936); F. H. Stuerm, *Training for Democracy* (New York: Inor Publication Company, 1937).

the language of instruction. All children had to learn the national tongue of the country—Czech or Slovak.

That none of the minorities was deprived of educational opportunity was proven by the fact than 96.2 percent of all German school children, 94 percent of all Hungarian, and 92.5 percent of all Polish school children attended purely German, Hungarian, or Polish schools, taught in their own languages by teachers of their own nationality. The small number of Jewish schools was due to the fact that Hebrew parents preferred that their children attend Czech or Slovak schools in order to master the national language thoroughly. Hebrew was studied at home.

There were eleven institutions of university rank in the country before 1918, including the Czech and German universities, both related to that founded in 1348 by Charles IV, and the Czech and German polytechnicals founded in 1806. There were no higher institutions of learning in Slovakia before 1918. It was against the law in Hungary for a Slovak to attend Prague institutions with the intention of studying his own language—Slovak or Czech—and many students were arrested for such offenses.

On the formation of the Republic, Masaryk University in Brno and Comenius University in Bratislava were founded and the Czech and German polytechnicals in Brno reorganized. The German university and polytechnicals were supported in Prague at the expense of the state, and a German polytechnical in Brno. The Hungarian minority had a theological faculty in Comenius University in Bratislava, and Masaryk gave the endowment for the newly founded Hungarian Academy of Science and Art.

Education Under Communism

Following World War II, for three years (1945-48), Czechoslovakia was ruled by coalition governments in which the Communist was already the strongest party, but did not have a majority. No far-reaching changes were introduced in education. Additional exemptions from fees were granted to secondary school pupils. Formerly, teachers of lower and upper elementary schools were graduates from special four-grade teachers' institutes; in 1945, it was decreed that "the teachers of the schools of all degrees and types shall acquire their education at pedagogic and other university faculties"; in 1946, pedagogic faculties were created at all universities. The length of studies varied, being four semesters (two years) for kindergarten teachers, six semesters (three years) for teachers of lower and upper elementary schools, and eight to ten semesters for teachers of secondary and professional schools. But, for a provisional period of study, these terms were reduced to two semesters in the case of the kindergarten teachers, and to four semesters for teachers of the lower elementary schools.

However, this idea that the status of the elementary school teachers could be raised by extending to them university education, motivated by the efforts to satisfy the class aspirations of this large population group, backfired. The slow process of university education did not produce the desired results, especially in the field of pro-Communist indoctrination. The faculties of pedagogy were abolished and replaced by the former teachers' training colleges, now named pedagogical seminaries, whose level is again that of the other secondary schools. But their candidates are carefully chosen from the boys and girls from the workers' families or the children of small peasants, and the members of the Union of the Czechoslovak Youth; in the last year, female applicants are more favored than boys.

In the Cabinet, formed on February 25, 1948, as the result of the Communist coup, Professor Zdenek Nejedly, a well-known Communist who had spent several years in Moscow, became Minister of Education. Less than two months after the coup, the purged National Assembly in "an act concerning the basic organization of uniform education" (cited as "School Act"),[34] compulsory attend-

---

[34] A good survey is: P. Korbel, *Some Basic Information on the Czechoslovak School System* (New York: National Committee for a Free Europe, September, 1952); and *Czechoslovak Universities* (New York: National Committee for a Free Europe, November, 1952); Free Europe Press, Research and Analysis Department,

ance was extended to nine years, achievement of which the new Minister and the whole Communist regime were extremely proud. The lower four grades of existing eight-grade secondary schools (the seven-grade secondary schools had been discontinued) were abolished. A new uniform four-grade type of upper elementary or lower secondary school was established, covering the sixth and ninth grades of compulsory school attendance. The lower five-grade elementary schools remained unchanged. The so-called schools of the first degree were known as "national schools," the new four-grade upper elementary schools represented the "schools of the second degree" and were called "middle schools." (They may perhaps be compared to the junior high schools in the United States.)

Furthermore, the new act created various types of "schools of the third degree." They were either compulsory (the so-called basic professional schools to be attended by young people who were already gainfully employed) or optional (selective). The latter schools were either vocational (professional) schools with less than four grades or the so-called upper middle schools, which were a kind of higher secondary school (roughly equivalent to the American senior high schools).

The second Communist school reform came in 1953. The speeches accompanying the presentation of the bill in Parliament and a programmatic preamble state the reasons for this innovation:

(1) For the Socialist society which we are building, our school must train fully developed and thoroughly prepared new Socialist citizens —workers, farmers, and intelligentsia.

(2) This mission can be accomplished only by a school which is linked with the great tasks of Socialist building and the political, economico-technical and cultural development of the motherland and her defense.

(3) To the great mission of the Socialist school there must correspond such a preparation and erudition of the teachers, those main factors in the school education of youth, as insures a high ideological and professional standard of their pedagogical work.

Research Report: *Sovietization of the Czechoslovak School System* (New York, July 2, 1954).

Speaking on the bill in the National Assembly, Ernest Sykora, then Minister of Education, admitted quite candidly the changes were cause by a shortage of medium and highly qualified cadres as well as by their poor training. Then the graduates of secondary schools preparing for study at colleges did not cover even half of the requirements of the colleges for their first academic year —and such difficulties would continue until 1956. A similar situation existed in the fourth grades of the middle schools. The only solution appeared to be the shortening of general school education to such an extent that students fourteen years of age could be admitted to optional schools and students of seventeen years to colleges where their "more thorough specialization, particularly in technical subjects, would be insured by more profound study. . . ."[35]

A sharp criticism of the old system, voiced by Nejedly, pointed out:

Our school was still insufficiently linked with practical life, it lagged behind it and badly prepared our youth for it. The uniform school act [of 1948] represented a great step ahead because it eliminated the bourgeois system of several tracks which implied discrimination against the youth of the workers' class and the small farmers. However, not all relics and shortcomings of the bourgeois school have been eliminated. The curricula of the individual degrees were not organically linked with each other, overlapped on the other, repeated themselves, so that in reality there was no uniform school. . . . At the same time all degrees were permanently burdened with a wealth of superfluous matters which are quite unnecessary for the life of Socialist man, and on the other hand they did not supply the pupils with sufficient knowledge and erudition for their future task of builders of Socialism. . . . For the time being our school lags badly behind these foremost requirements of our building efforts (incessant increase of the political and professional standard of the economic organs) exactly in the most important subjects— mathematics, physics, chemistry, natural science.

It frequently teaches formalistically, superficially, and insufficiently. How else could we explain the fact that most pupils still fail at school in mathematics, and many of those who complete school do not master the subject well. . . . A similar situation has developed in the teaching of the mother tongue. . . . To give a deeply political basis to all . . . knowledge and erudition [of the pupils] is another great task of our school. . . . The failing of pupils, this unpleasant phenomenon, which resulted from defective methods of instruction on the one hand, and from underestimation

---

[35] *Rude Pravo* ("Red Justice"), April 25, 1953, No. C.

of the child and indifference towards his proficiency on the other, must disappear from our schools. . . . The Soviet school has shown us that it is possible and we too must learn it. . . . The Communists must concentrate their efforts so that the new school shall educate a generation capable of building Communism in our country.[36]

The new act made basic general education compulsory and free of charge; it is provided by the eighth-grade middle school or by the first eight grades of the eleven-grade middle school. The obligation to attend school lasts eight years, and begins at the sixth year of age. The eighth-grade middle school provides basic general education and prepares for a profession, a vocational (professional) school, or for higher general education. The eleven-grade middle schools offer the pupils general education during the first eight grades, and higher general education during the last three grades; it prepares, above all, for study at a college. The last three grades are optional; pupils may be admitted to them who have successfully completed an eighth-grade middle school or the first eight grades of an eleven-grade middle school.

In localities where middle schools are lacking, the first five grades are called a "national school"; pupils who have completed the fifth grade of a national school continue school attendance at the sixth grade of the nearest middle school.

The first grades of all types of general educational school are preparatory grades; their task is to prepare the children for systematic school education.

Vocational (professional) schools are optional and provide "professional education for the various branches of the economy, state administration and cultural life." They admit graduates from eighth-grade middle schools or from the eighth grades of eleven-grade middle schools.

Professional qualified workers for the important branches of the national economy are trained by the formation of the State Labor Reserves. These establishments are not part of the school system under the Ministry of Education but are controlled by the Ministry of

---

[36] *Rude Pravo*, April 26, 1953.

Manpower.[37] They admit pupils who have "finished compulsory school attendance and attained the necessary general education." This means that successful completion of the first eight grades of a school of general education is not necessary. The "pedagogical schools for the education of kindergarten women-teachers" are three-grade schools to which graduates from eighth-grade middle schools or from the eighth grades of eleven-grade middle schools are admitted; graduates complete a one-year "guided practice" at kindergarten. Then four-year pedagogical schools for the education of teachers of the first up to the eighth grade of middle schools and of five-year national schools were set up; the admission requirements are the same here. Two-year higher pedagogical schools admit graduates from eleven-grade middle schools, from pedagogical schools or from optional vocational (professional) schools and train teachers of the sixth-eighth grades of eleven-grade middle schools; all teachers of pedagogical and vocational schools are trained in pedagogical colleges; they are open to graduates of eleven-grade middle schools, pedagogical schools, and optional vocational schools.

Youth groups, pioneer homes, children's homes, and other extra scholastic educational establishments were set up for "the completion of school education and in the interest of health and social care for the school population," together with associations of parents and friends with the task of "insuring cooperation of the school and the family and of helping the school in its educational mission."

The 1953 School Act is briefer and more "flexible" than the first act of 1948, with two exceptions: legislative powers for its implementation are vested in the Ministries and not in the Cabinet. In addition to the changes we have already noted, we might notice several additional distinctive features: While in 1948 the schools cared for the "universal rational, emotional, moral and physical development of the pupils" in "the spirit of progressive

---

[37] For more details, see: P. Korbel and V. Vagassky, *Population Transfers and Deportation in Czechoslovakia* (Second Supplement, Free Europe Press, September, 1952).

national traditions and the ideals of humanity" and led youth "to active participation in the life of the school and the constructive achievements of the Republic," the stress is now on the education of "Socialist citizens,"— that is, on economic aspects. The 1948 provisions that instruction would be in Czech and Slovak, and that exceptions would have to be determined by the government, now disappeared. The same applies to the 1948 provisions for maximum numbers of pupils in the classes of the individual types of schools. Formerly, the school was bound to provide for the religious education of the pupils according to their religious faith (with the exception of those cases where the parents had withdrawn the child from such education) ; religious education and its supervision were vested in the organs of the churches and religious communities without prejudicing the supreme supervisory rights of the Ministry of Education. But now these religious provisions have been left out—with the sad result that all religious aspects are at the discretion of the Ministry of Education. The new act reduced primary legislation (by governmental ordinance) to a minimum and shifted the bulk of legislative activities to the Ministries, other central and similar more easily manageable and more "elastic" bureaucratic and quasi-bureaucratic organs. In the case of Slovakia, in 1948 there were provisions restricting the jurisdiction of the central organs, which were obligated to insure the cooperation of the corresponding Slovak national organs—the Slovak Commissioners and the Slovak Commissariats concerned. The new act does not mention this cooperation at all, although the 1948 Constitution insures such cooperation; this omission indicates the ever-increasing centralizing tendencies of the Prague Communist leadership.[38]

Minorities Schools

The Constitution of May 9, 1948, describes the Czechoslovak Republic as a "uniform State of two equal Slav

[38] See: Eduard Taborsky, "Slovakia Under Communist Rule, 'Democratic Centralism vs. National Autonomy,' " *Journal of Central European Affairs*, XIV, 3 (October, 1954), pp. 255-63.

nations, the Czechs and the Slovaks." According to Fundamental Article VIII, the state power in Slovakia is vested in the Slovak National Organs, which "shall in the spirit of the People's Democracy, ensure the equality of Czechs and Slovaks. All organs of the Republic shall endeavor, in harmony with the Slovak National Organs, to ensure that equally favorable conditions be created for the economic, cultural and social life of both nations." Section 96 of the Constitution, which deals with the aforementioned Slovak National Council as the Slovak Legislative National Organ, states that its legislative power covers, among others, the care for national, middle (secondary), vocational, and artistic schools "within the framework of the laws"; the care of kindergartens, and nurseries. This indicates that basic regulations by law remain within the jurisdiction of the central government and Parliament. This assumption is certified by the second Communist School Act of 1953.

Whatever reports are available, it is evident that, numerically, the Slovak school network has been considerably developed and the increase of classes and numbers of pupils in Slovakia is greatest in the case of kindergartens and industrial schools, the consequence of the rapid industrialization of Slovakia.

As a reprisal to Nazi terror after the seizure of Czechoslovakia by Hitler in 1938 and 1939, to which an overwhelming part of the Germans in Czechoslovakia had supported, about nine-tenths of this population, exceeding three million, either fled the country at the final stage of the war or were expelled after cessation of hostilities. Most of the remaining Germans—from two to three hundred thousand—were assigned to new working places, frequently in the areas which are populated only by Czechs; their children attend Czech or Slovak schools.

The Hungarian minority in Slovakia (about 650,000 formerly and now about 550,000 to 600,000) was to be exchanged or expelled, but only a small portion was affected. In the Ostrava-Karvina Tesin (Teschen) region of Moravia and Silesia exists a Polish minority of about 100,000. Some 120,000 Russians and Ukrainians lived in the eastern portions of Slovakia; about 80,000 to

100,000 are left. Before the Communist coup, a definite anti-minorities policy was followed. But the first School Act of 1948 already provided that exception could be made in the rule that instruction would be given in the Czech language in the provinces of Bohemia-Moravia-Silesia, and in the Slovak language in Slovakia. In the fall of 1948, the Communists ordered a change of policy with regard to the Hungarians; an "improvement" of the Czechoslovak-Polish relations had already been prescribed by the Kremlin earlier in that year. A more lenient policy in the case of the German minority was introduced in 1950 after the "German Democratic Republic" was established in 1949. More attention was also given to the Ukrainian and Polish minorities.

According to the Prague report, in 1952, there were in Slovakia 215 Hungarian kindergartens, 553 national schools with 44,033 pupils, and numerous senior pedagogical, industrial, health, and agricultural schools for students of Hungarian nationality.[39] In 1951, the Commissariat of Education, Sciences and Arts set up a section with Hungarian as the language of instruction at the Pedagogical Department of the Slovak University in Bratislava. The following branches of study were introduced: Hungarian and Russian, Hungarian, history and citizenship, Russian and musical instruction, history, citizenship and instruction in fine arts, mathematics and physics, natural history, chemistry and geography, and Slovak and Hungarian. In regard to the Ukrainian minority, settled around Presov and Kosice, it was reported in 1953 that there were: 2,120 children in 67 kindergartens, 135 national schools, 54 middle schools with 6,069 Ukrainian students, and several other gymnasia. No data on the total number of Polish schools are available. But a supplementary protocol to the Treaty of Alliance and Cooperation between Prague and Warsaw was signed for a twenty-year period on March 27, 1947, providing for protection of minority rights in both states. In the region of Cesky Tesin, where there is the greatest concentration of the Polish minority, there are thirty-

---

[39] Prague *News Letter*, October 24, 1953.

nine kindergartens and fifty-six eight-year schools. As far as the Germans are concerned, since the summer of 1952, teachers have been trained for German-language classes and the instruction of German children in the German language began in 1953 in sixty-five places.

Universities

We have already shown that Charles University was founded in 1348 and has the distinction of being the oldest institution of its kind in Central Europe. When founded, the university was merely called the *"studium generale Pragense."*[40] But from the sixteenth century, under the influence of the "New Learning," it began to be called the Caroline Academy, which, from the end of the fourteenth century, was the center of all university life and identified with the University of Prague. When Ferdinand of Habsburg, King of Bohemia and Holy Roman Emperor, called the Jesuits into Bohemia in 1592 as an instrument of Counter-Reformation, he founded a Faculty of Philosophy and Theology for them and called it the Academie Ferdinandea. Thus the Hussite (Protestant) Caroline Academy existed side by side with the Catholic Ferdinand Academy until the fateful defeat of the Czech Protestants at the White Mountain (1620). As a result, the Czech Protestants were deprived of the Caroline Academy, and in 1654 it was united with the Jesuits' Academy and given the name of Universitas Carolo-Ferdinandea; this name was retained until the liberation of the Czech nation in 1918, after which it was called Universitas Carolina.

The Latin language was originally used in Charles University—as in all medieval educational institutions. After the Hussite revolution at the beginning of the fifteenth century, Czech was also employed. In the Carolo-Ferdinandea University, Latin again prevailed.

---

[40] Vaclav Cahloupecky, *The Caroline University of Prague* (Prague: Orbis, 1948), contains also numerous documents on the history of the university; Otakar Odlozilik, *The Caroline University, 1348-1948* (Prague: Orbis, 1948), is a scholarly survey of the university's history by a specialist now serving as T. G. Masaryk Professor in History at Columbia University.

During the reign of Empress Maria Theresa and her son Joseph II, German was introduced in 1784 as the language of instruction instead of Latin (except in pastoral theology and obstetrics, which used both Czech and German). In 1791, a concession was made to Czech demands for the formation of a special chair of Czech language and literature. In 1848, new concessions were made, and lectures thereafter were given in Czech or German or another language. But the number of Czech students and professors was growing, and the Edict of 1882 divided the Carolo-Ferdinandea University into a German and Czech University, both having the same rights and both continuing the heritage of the old University of Prague, although the German University was favored in the division. Both Czechs and Germans found a source of pride and inspiration in the university, with its almost six centuries of uninterrupted existence. It was not surprising that, in the past (as we noted, during the Hussite period), as well as by the end of the nineteenth century, violent controversies did break out as to the respective rights of the two nations and concerning the relationship of the two universities after the partition of 1882. The strife mirrored the national conflict as a whole. To the Germans, the Czech claim to equality meant the ultimate pre-eminence of the Czechs in the institution, and accepted the division only as a counterweapon.

Both nationalities held diametrically opposing views regarding the historic mission of the university. The Czechs wanted it to promote the intellectual needs of the Kingdom of Bohemia—arguing that Charles IV had founded it for that purpose. But the Germans viewed the university as an institution founded to meet the requirements of the whole Austrian half of the Monarchy and to serve the intellectual and academic needs of all Europe. Charles IV, Emperor of the Holy Roman Empire as well as King of Bohemia, had in their view founded the institution as an intellectual center for scholars of all nationalities in order to promote the same intellectual aims in Central-North-Eastern Europe as did Paris and Bologna in the west and south. Hence, the use of Czech was only of secondary importance; German, the international language of the Austrian peoples, was to remain its language of instruction and examinations. The Imperial Decree of April 10, 1881, affecting the partition of the university represented a turning point in the university arguments. But the Czechs were dissatisfied with the assignment to the German University of the bulk of the existing institutes. The Czech University began its life poorly equipped and had to experience a long period of slow development. It had to start with two faculties only—of philosophy and law—while the German University contained four faculties, including the as yet undivided faculties of medicine and theology. At any rate, one of the first appointments to the faculty of philosophy was that of Dr. Thomas G. Masaryk in 1882;[41] this Chair, under the impact of Masaryk's teaching and actions, became a fertile source of political ideas which eventually led to the independence of Czechoslovakia in 1918.

Universities Under the Republic

Both Czech and German universities continued to function in the new Republic, except that a parliamentary act of February, 1920, proclaimed the Czech University the successor to the old Charles University. The German University continued functioning as the Czech University —theology, law, medicine, and philosophy; in June 1920, the philosophy faculties of both institutions were each divided into a philosophy faculty and a natural science faculty.

In 1919, two new universities were founded: Masaryk University in Brno (the capital of the province of Moravia) and Komensky (Comenius) University in Bratislava (the capital of Slovakia). Masaryk University had four faculties—law, medicine, natural science, and philosophy; Komensky University had no natural science faculty. In addition to the four universities, the Republic supported four independent theological faculties (Cy-

---

[41] H. Godon Skilling, "The Partition of the University of Prague," *The Slavonic Review*, XXVII (May, 1949), pp. 436-40.

rillus-Methodius Catholic Theological College at Olomouc, to which status the original Moravian Olomouc University had been reduced in 1854; the Catholic Theology Faculty in Bratislava; the Hus Czechoslovak Evangelical College in Prague; and the Czechoslovak State Evangelical Theological College at Bratislava). There were also seven technical schools of university rank; two of these technical schools—one Czech and one German—date back to the first engineering school in Europe, established by Christian Joseph Willenberg at Charles University in 1717; this school was separated from the university in 1815, and in 1868 was divided into Czech and German institution. The former was designated in 1920 as the Czech Institute of Technology in Prague; the latter was known as the German Technical University *(Deutsche Technische Hochschule)*.

Altogether, Czchoslovakia had twenty-one institutions of university rank (mining and engineering, agriculture, forestry, veterinary medicine, creative arts, music, dramatic arts, library archives, war college, military college of technology, and military academy). The universities were administered by the state; but their academic freedom was insured by law. The chief governing body was the Academic Senate, elected for one year and presided over by the *Rector Magnificus;* the latter was selected each year from each of the faculties in rotation and by vote of the regular professors.

The faculties elected their deans for one year in similar fashion. The teaching staff consisted of professors, ordinary and extraordinary professors (full and associate), docents (assistant professors who held no official appointment at the university but were allowed to lecture— *venia docendi*—with the approval of the Ministry of Education, and *lectors* (lecturers), who were paid assistants. The Senate handled all administrative, educational, and disciplinary matters, and acted as court of appeal in disputes between professors and their deans. The professors were named for life by the President of the Republic on the recommendation of the Professors' Council and upon the proposal of the Cabinet). Professors were pensioned at seventy.[42]

In practice, there was hardly any limit to freedom of academic opinion and of scientific research—guaranteed by the Constitutional Charter of February 29, 1920; the universities also enjoyed complete autonomy. Although much foreign criticism was voiced about the conditions of minorities, there were three Czech and Slovak universities, one German, three Czech and Slovak technical universities, and two German. According to the 1930 census, of all the Czechoslovak citizens (14,729,536), 22.32 percent were of German nationality. This shows that the proportion of six principal Czech and Slovak universities to three German principal universities really favored the Teutons.

The number of university students in the First Republic was steadily increasing—creating a serious problem of the "intellectual proletariat," although not as serious as in Germany or in the Balkans. In 1920, there were 28,155 students (91.1 percent men and 8.9 percent women), while in 1935 the total number had risen to 31,640, of which 4,558 were women (more than 14 percent).[43]

The Nazi occupation nearly extinguished Czechoslo-

---

[43] For the comparison between the system prevailing in Central Europe and the United States, see: Joseph S. Roucek, "The European and the American Professor: A Study in Contrasts," The *Bulletin* of the American Association of University Professors, XXX, 3 (Autumn, 1944), pp. 393-99.

[43] For this period of Czechoslovakia's higher institutions of learning, see: M. M. Chambers (ed.), *Universities of the World Outside U.S.A.* (Washington, D.C.: American Council on Education, 1950), pp. 308-19; J. G. F. Druce, "Chemical Sciences in Czechoslovakia," *Central European Observer*, XXIV (November 28, 1947), 349; H. M. Knox, "The University of Prague," *Universities Review*, XXI (September, 1948), 39-42; Otakar Odlozilik, *The Caroline University, 1348-1948* (Prague: Orbis, 1948); V. Prihoda, "Czechoslovakia," pp. 470-89, in *The Yearbook of Education*, 1948 (London: Evans Brothers, 1948); Vaclav Vojtisek and Dobroslav Lebal, *The Carolinum: Pride of the Caroline University* (Prague: Orbis, 1948); Francis H. Sturm, "Education in a Democracy," Chapter XVI, pp. 302-15, in Robert J. Kerner (ed.), *Czechoslovakia, Twenty Years of Independence* (Berkeley, Calif.: University of California Press, 1940); S. Harrison Thomson, *Czechoslovakia in European History* (Princeton University Press, 1953), pp. 193, 223-24, 343ff., 409, 413.

vakia's university life,[44] aimed at depriving the young
Czech generation of the possibility of educational advantages. All Czech universities were closed. The situation
was different in Slovakia, where the Nazis were obviously
not interested in the immediate elimination of the young
Czech intelligentsia. The Komensky University was renamed Slovak University and the faculty of natural sciences added; a Slovak Technical University in Bratislava
with six facultes was also added. On July 3, 1940, the
Slovak University was allowed to have six faculties, its
official language being Slovak or Latin. The "President
of the Republic" was made honorary Rector (president)
of the University ex officio with the title *Rector Magnifi-
centissimus,* and the Minister of Education and National
Enlightenment named honorary University Chancellor
ex officio with the title *Supremus Cancellarius.* The right
of the professors to elect the Rector and deans was abolished, the appointments to be made by the President of
the Republic. When the Soviet armies were already approaching Slovakia, on December 21, 1944, the Slovak
University of Commerce in Bratislava was transformed
into a full-fledged university and allowed to award a
higher academic degree—*"doctor rerum commercialium"*
(RCDr.).

At the end of 1943, an underground Slovak National
Council, composed of the representatives of the important
resistance groups, began to assume full governmental and
legislative powers over the liberated territory. It retained its limited power also after the reconstitution of
the central Czechoslovak governmental machinery in
April, 1945—and still exists as the national organ of legislative power in Slovakia under the Communist-enacted
new Constitution of May 9, 1948. This body decreed in
1945 that the name of Bratislava University was to be
changed again to Universitas Slovaca Bratislavensis and
the prewar democratic regulations were reintroduced; it
also decreed that the existing independent Catholic Theological Faculty in Bratislava (renamed Slovak Roman

---

[44] For details, see: P. Korbel, *Czechoslovak Universities, op. cit.,*
pp. 3-7.

Catholic Faculty in Bratislava) and the Slovak Evangelical Theological Faculty in Bratislava to be independent universities; the private Slovak Commercial University (formed a state university in 1944) was converted into a state university.

When the government of Benes (which included Communist representatives forced on Benes) returned to Prague on May 10, 1945, one of its first steps was to restore the Czech universities closed by the Nazis. Then, in order to ease the great shortage of doctors, a branch of the medical faculty of Charles University was set up at Hradec Kralove (an industrial city in eastern Bohemia). Then the German University, it was decreed, "ceased to exist on May 5, 1945, the first day of the uprising of the people of Prague" forever as an "institution hostile to the Czech nation"; Charles University acquired its property and equipment; the German technical universities in Prague and in Brno were also abolished. By the end of the year, an Academy of Arts was established in Prague with the departments of music, drama, dancing (ballet), and motion pictures (and it was reorganized again on October 2, 1951). Another branch of the Medical Faculty was set up in Plzen (Pilsen), and later a Political and Social University in Prague (with the departments of political, journalistic, and social sciences). Another somewhat chaotic social faculty was set up in Brno mainly for diplomatic and consular studies within the political faculty (consisting of university professors, private docents, and "outstanding personalities who had distinguished themselves in the political, social, or journalistic field")—called "internal university professors," to which were added the "contractual internal professors" appointed by the President of the Republic upon the proposal of the Cabinet and the Academic Senate of the University. The regular university professors were lecturing as "auxiliary teachers," and were called "external university professors." In 1949, this "university" was replaced by the University of Political and Economic Sciences in Prague.

The fervor of promoting all levels of education was also reflected in the Communist insistence on restoring the University of Olomouc by adding to the still existing Cyrillus-Methodius Catholic College the faculties of law, medicine, and philosophy (in 1946). The same urge produced the foundation of the "Artistico-Industrial University in Prague" (which transformed the senior high school into a university). Then pedagogical faculties were established at all universities in Czechoslovakia in 1946.

Slovakia was already supplied with the higher institutions during the Nazi regime; yet, a new University of Agricultural and Forestry Engineering was set up in Kosice in 1946.[45]

The Sovietization Process

For the Imposition of Soviet Ideology a pro-Russian tendency in the Czechoslovak government circles was more than obvious already in 1945 when the Benes government returned to Prague by way of Moscow, with Clement Gottwald included in the Cabinet with several other Communists. The pro-Russian and Pan-Slavic tendencies were already the appeals of the day, and it took some months before the general populace of Czechoslovakia realized the price they were to pay for their "liberation" by the Russian armies.[46]

The most systematic step to reorient the pro-Western tendencies of the Czechoslovak people began to be enforced, however, only with the inauguration of the Communist regime in 1948. In 1949, it was announced that:

Throughout the 20 years' duration of the pre-Munich Czechoslovak Republic, the ruling bourgeoisie endeavored to force upon the Czechs and Slovaks the consciousness of their being a "small nation." Being a small nation, they were to submit to the role

---

[45] For the way the Communist regime has treated "autonomous" Slovakia, see: Eduard Taborsky, "Slovakia under Communist Rule, 'Democratic Centralism' vs. National Autonomy," *Journal of Central European Affairs,* XIV (October, 1954), 255-63.

[46] That Prague was not liberated by Patton's army, which was ordered to return to Plzen by Eisenhower, was one of history's greatest mistakes, never fully explained. But see page 195.

allotted them by the bourgeois ruling class, that of an obedient instrument of Western Imperialism. . . ."[47]

Furthermore, it was propounded that (prior to 1918) :

the two leading personalities of the bourgeois left wing, Professor T. G. Masaryk and Dr. E. Benes, went abroad during the war and undertook many political and diplomatic steps to interest the imperialist Entente Powers in the idea of Czechoslovak independence. . . . In the years after 1920 the bourgeoisie endeavoured to strengthen and stabilize its ruling position in the country. This consolidation of the bourgeois position, of course, took place entirely and exclusively at the expense of the working people. . . . Czechoslovakia's liberation by the Red Army was a tremendous triumph of that conception of the Communist Party which had always maintained that our liberty would come from the East, and that our national destiny was inseparably tied to the Soviet Union. . . . [The Communist coup of 1948] was a "reactionary attempt at a putsch. . . . The reaction wanted to foil the full realization of the Programme of Action, wanted to disrupt the real National Front, wanted to create conflict between our country and our Slav allies. . . .[48]

While the Communist shadow was spreading over all aspects of Czechoslovakia's life, many representatives of several American universities, who had arrived in Prague in April, 1948, for the sixth hundredth anniversary ceremonies of Charles University, shocked by the complete abolition of academic freedom and the expulsion of many professors and hundreds of students because of their opposition to Marxist pressure,[49] withdrew their acceptances. As a result, the purge of the university's faculties was temporarily halted, when authorities suddenly realized what the effect would be on the foreign institutions invited to participate. But the hope of the Czechoslovak professors that the visit of foreign professors would

---

[47] Ministry of Information and Public Culture, *Czechoslovakia on the Road to Socialism* (Prague: Orbis, 1949), p. 5.

[48] *Ibid.*, pp. 14-20.

[49] Many of these expelled professors and students established a Free Czechoslovak College abroad; it was founded on October 28, 1948, in a refugee camp in Ludwissburg in the Allied Zone in Germany, with the name "The Masaryk University College"; its staff consisted of twelve professors, with some three hundred students. The institution received generous aid from the American Women's Club in Stuttgart.

strengthen the importance of academic freedom and liberty was soon dashed by the subsequent steps of the Action Committee's political dictatorship.

Czechoslovakia's celebration of the thirty-first anniversary of the founding of the Republic, October 28, 1949, was already characterized by the absence of the portraits of the nation's two founders, former President Masaryk and Benes. As of November 1, 1949, pictures of the two founders were no longer to appear on the country's postage stamps. The pictures displayed in the nationwide celebration were those of Stalin and Gottwald. Flags along the streets were those of the USSR and Czechoslovakia. The country's workers went to their jobs as usual, as the government decreed that they should "celebrate by work."

On the educational fronts, by the end of that year, the Communist regime was censoring, barring, and burning Western literature to eradicate traces of "cosmopolitanism." The Communists thus copied the Nazi burners of books in their eagerness to comply with Moscow's order that "cosmopolitanism" had to be rooted out wherever the Red Flag flies. Not content with making it compulsory for children, students, workers, and collective farmers to read Marx and Stalin, they started to censor, segregate, and even destroy Western literature in all its forms. The Czechoslovak government decreed the nationalization of the publication of books, controlling their distribution, and even envisaged the taking over of secondhand bookshops.

Control of Colleges and Universities

The problem of intellectuals and professionals in Czechoslovakia, and the high rate of literacy, induced the Communist masters to pay special attention to the control over its frantic university building drive. The Communists tightened their grip over the system by its June 3, 1950, Soviet-patterned University Act, doing away with academic freedom and the administrative, educational, and disciplinary autonomy of the universities. A State Committee on Universities in the Ministry of Education,

Sciences, and Arts was set up as a "consultative, initiatory, and coordinating body," all members appointed by the Minister; a special Slovak branch also appeared, with two sections, one for scientific universities and one for artistic universities. The Rector, with the assistance of the university secretary and the Rector's office, "directs and administers the university, is responsible for its ideological and educational activity and represents it in relationships with the public. He is appointed by the President of the Republic upon the proposal of the Cabinet for a period of three years, as a rule among the number of university professors by the above-mentioned State Committee which acts after previous consultation with the University Council." The Rector became responsible to the Minister, with two pro-Rectors also appointed by the Minister in the same way. The Council of a university, the Minister determining its selection, "decides upon the basic pedagogical, scientific, administrative and economic matters of the university. The faculty deans and pro-deans are likewise appointed by the Minister for two-year terms. The Minister also determines the method of selecting a faculty Council and a Dean's office and the heads of the *cathedrae* (the teachers of the same or of closely related scientific or artistic branches). Students are admitted to the universities according to their qualifications and with regard to the planned economic, social, and cultural requirements of the state. Graduate students, and in exceptional cases "workers," selected according to their ability for creative scientific or artistic work, may do graduate work as "aspirants" of a certain scientific or artistic sphere (branch).

The following categories of university staff were established: professors, docents (assistant professors), lecturers, qualified assistants, assistants, and qualified instructors. The professorial appointments are made now by the President of the Republic upon the proposal of the Cabinet—without any participation by the university authorities; the rest are appointed by the Minister.

A special regime was set up for the theological faculties of Charles University and of Palacky University at

Olomouc by subordinating them to the Minister in charge of the State Office for Ecclesiastical Affairs. In 1950, all Roman Catholic theological educational establishments in Bohemia, Moravia, and Silesia were fused into an independent Roman Catholic theological faculty in Prague and named, "Cyrillus and Methodium Roman Catholic Theological Faculty in Prague"; a similar "Cyrillus and Methodius Roman Catholic Theological Faculty in Bratislava" was founded in Slovakia. The Hus Czechoslovak Evangelical Theological Faculty in Prague was replaced by two independent faculties—the Hus Czechoslovak Theological Faculty in Prague and Komensky Evangelical Theological Faculty in Prague. All other evangelical theological teaching faculties were abolished; the Slovak Evangelical Theological Faculty in Bratislava concentrated all evangelical studies in Slovakia. An Orthodox Theological Faculty in Prague concentrated all theological studies in the entire state. (The Greek Catholic Church had been suppressed, and some priests joined the newly founded Orthodox Eparchy).

The administration of the theological faculties rests in the deans and faculty councils, appointed by the Minister in charge of the State Office for Ecclesiastical Affairs; otherwise the organization resembles that of the university faculties.

Several additional reorganizations took place in the engineering, law, and medical faculties.[50] Of interest, in this respect, was the change in the philosophical faculty of Charles University, which was subdivided into a philosophical-historical faculty and a philological faculty. In 1951, the Minister was authorized to determine, in accord with the Cabinet members concerned, for the individual university (college) and faculties such a specialization of studies as would train the various types of experts who are required "for the economic, political and cultural construction of the state." These and other changes were designed to show the Czechoslovak people that the new regime was trying to do much more for the development of the highest levels of education than any

---

[50] For more details, see: Korbel, *op. cit.*, pp. 15-16.

other former regime. While the steps of 1950 were under the pressure of Moscow to have Czechoslovakia pattern its universities after Soviet Russia, the innovations were also the result of the pressing needs, especially in the fields of chemistry, railroads, and new diplomats with proletarian background who would be trained in Marxist-Leninist doctrines.

Changes in regard to the admissions and handling of university students came also. Up to 1949, graduation from a selective school of the third degree (especially from a gymnasium) was a prerequisite for admission to university studies. Early in 1949, "State courses for the preparation of workers for university studies" were set up, the selection entrusted to the plant groups of the uniform trade union organization, and village groups of the Czechoslovak Youth League. Those between the ages of eighteen and twenty-eight were recruited for eight-to-ten-month courses. A Special Workers' Law School was founded under the auspices of the Minister of Justice. In 1951, the University of Political and Economic Sciences started to admit students without graduation examinations, "descent from the rank of the working population" being an essential qualification. In 1952, evening and correspondence courses were started by the Mining University of Ostrava, with correspondence study centers set up in Kladno (a mining locale), Most, and other mining and industrial towns. Examinations are held in these centers, study is directed by correspondence, and broadcasts are supplemented by short courses at the university.

As in all satellite states, Czechoslovakia's Communist regime has claimed enormous increases in the number of students, due to the frantic efforts of the regime to put on an impressive show. This has been partly achieved by the lowering of admission standards for university students. The state budgets show lavish appropriations for the universities, their equipment, and the subsidizing of students. For the politically acceptable and conforming applicants, liberal scholarships, including accommodations in students' hostels and maintenance allowances for members of the student's family, were made available.

Revised Textbooks

By March, 1950, Czechoslovakia's school children were studying brand-new books written in the spirit of the "People's Democracy." Texts for the first five grades no longer contain "dull articles about balloons and ships' screws, but humorous articles, Czech national tales, verses, etc." In the second grade, children begin to spell out stories about the "construction of the people's democratic republic and the fight for peace." Third graders are taught in their readers to be "patriots" . . . conscious members of the working class . . . to love the Soviet Union and to honor labor." In the fourth and fifth grades, ten- and eleven-year-olds read about "the stupefying teachings of the bourgeois schools concerning justice in our democratic republic," the stories of the "shock worker Jindra," and Marek's stories of "courageous work."[51] The books extol the virtues of the Soviet state. The part played by the Western armies in the liberation of Czechoslovakia is ignored. The books describe in great detail the "evils" of Czech life before the Communists came to power in February, 1948.

A typical question and answer from the science and history books for the third grade is: "Who invented the first electric light?" Answer: "The Russian Ladygin." (The time given is four years before Thomas A. Edison's first incandescent lamp.) In the fourth-grade textbook, *Pictures from History,* the pupils are told that Thomas G. Masaryk, founder of the Czechoslovak Republic, and Eduard Benes, its second President, "went to the U.S. to set up a state with the help of the capitalists." It states that Masaryk founded the Czech Legion in World War I, "misleading the people into thinking that they were fighting for freedom, whereas they actually fought the Russian worker." Charles IV, commonly known as the Father of Charles University of Prague, is described as a "tool of the Catholics." The priests of this time are described as "drunkards, living in luxury."

---

[51] "Prague Government Revises School Books," *New York Times,* March 29, 1950.

Russian Is the Password

The extent of Russian infiltration into Czechoslovakia is apparent in numerous ways: Compulsory Russian language courses, the large "circulation" in satellite libraries and bookstores of books on all subjects in the Russian language, the large number of works published on Russian and Soviet pedagogy, and the preponderance of Russian material in textbooks. Stalin's photograph, together with that of Gottwald, at the front of every textbook was (until the eclipse of Stalin), of course, standard in every edition.[52]

The Marxist-Leninist principles governing Soviet teaching methods are embodied in the "Soviet science of pedagogy" which, like other Soviet "sciences," serves political ends. "We must not forget for a moment," wrote the official Soviet Pedagogic journal, *Sovietskaia Pedagogia* (Moscow) in the fall issue of 1946, that "Every science is Party Science." Nor are satellite educators allowed to forget. Soviet pedagogy is faithfully followed by the teachers who are to play the role of "Socialist builders."

A growing number of Soviet guest professors in Czechoslovakia every year has insured forced coordination among Czechoslovak teachers and professors. The benefit of studies in Soviet universities "enjoyed" by hundreds of Czechoslovak students every year also has become a regular and permanent feature of the Czechoslovak university study picture.

Communist Methods of Control

The constitutional decree organizing the postwar Czechoslovak cabinet of April 2, 1945, provided for a Ministry of Education and Enlightenment; at the same time, a Ministry of Information was set up. In a Communist regime "information" and "enlightenment" overlap, and indeed are frequently identical. For a while,

---

[52] For a description of some Czechoslovak textbooks of this kind, see: "From Discipline to Diversion," *News from Behind the Iron Curtain*, II, 3 (March, 1953), p. 46.

even before the Communist coup, a strong rivalry developed between the two Ministries in the field of "enlightenment." Soon after the coup, it was clear that the aging Minister of Education and Enlightenment, Professor Zdenek Nejedly, was losing out to his considerably younger and more energetic colleague, Information Minister Vaclav Kopecky. An act of October 7, 1948, which, though referring only to a "change of names," represented in fact a legalization of the true state of affairs. The Ministry of Information was renamed "Ministry of Information and Enlightenment," and the Ministry of Education and Enlightenment became the "Ministry of Education, Sciences and Arts." As we have pointed out, in 1953, this latter Ministry was subdivided into two ministries: the Ministry of Education and Enlightenment and the Ministry of Universities. At the same time, the Ministry of Information and Enlightenment was abolished and a State Committee for Arts and a Committee for Foreign Cultural Relations were created.

At Gottwald's death (March, 1953), the Ministries were merged into one, but no longer concerned with "enlightenment" and with the "arts." A special Ministry of Culture was set up in accordance with the new Soviet pattern, and the two State Committees for Arts and for Cultural Relations with Foreign Countries again abolished. Today, the new Ministry is in fact a Ministry of Education and Sciences. It need not be stressed that the governmental machinery is but the executive branch of the Communist party which operates in Czechoslovakia as in Soviet Russia and the satellites. As in these states, a remarkable character of the Czechoslovak institutional education is its standardization, completely under the control of the government or its organs. Here the state actually holds the monopoly of all education and determines who will teach what, whom, and how.

The educational control is geared into the thought control on all levels carried on by the state, whose organs are controlled and prodded by the Communist party.

The Party does not trust the old family institution in a matter as important as education of the second generation—which should be the first Communist generation.

In order to make education conform to the standard political pattern, the Party has limited the educational function of the family and the children educated directly in the state institutions from the very prime of their lives; and the pattern of the family itself has been molded by Communist pressure. A number of women, for instance, were forced to join the large army of the "toiling masses." The Communist regime has been especially interested in the education of the children of preschool age. The regime figures that every new infant-home enables twenty-five to thirty women to take full-time jobs and help "in this way with the reconstruction of the state." Before World War II, Czech lands had 921 kindergartens; at the beginning of 1950, there were 3,775 kindergartens with 161,067 children, and 72,845 in Slovakia.[53]

The personnel of these homes and kindergartens receive special instruction for educating the children in a collective, political spirit. The songs which the nurses sing, the fairy tales which they tell—these all reflect the spirit of the time and aim at indoctrination. The place of old "witches," "dragons," "evildoers" is taken by the "capitalists," "rich peasants," "saboteurs," whom a young "Pioneer" (the member of the early youth organization) has to struggle with and whom he defeats in the long run, to be celebrated by the thankful "toiling masses" afterward.

The second way of molding the family pattern is by exposing the family to all means of pressure from outside—films, literature, radio, as well as existing Communist organizations. The direction of this pressure is "towards the class-hatred and towards the hatred of the enemies of the people—at home or abroad."[54]

The National School is controlled by means of the political selection and training of the teachers, as well as by the direct supervision exercised over them. In addition to the control through the selection of personnel, there exists a constant supervision by the school inspectors, by

---

[53] I. Gadourek, *The Political Control of Czechoslovakia* (Leiden: H. E. Stenfert Krose, 1953), p. 109.

[54] *Ibid.*, p. 110.

the Communist fellow teachers, and by the parents of the children. The latter exercise their control through a special organization: the School Friends Association. The control through the fellow teachers runs either through the organs of the Revolutionary Trade Union, to which every teacher must belong, or through the "teachers' conferences" arranged several times a year. Ideas originate with the Commissariat of Education, which issues instructions through school inspectors, transmitted to school principals. The principal holds a "work meeting" twice a week with teachers and outlines instructions to them. These are then incorporated by the teacher into a highly detailed daily "plan of operation," which is submitted for the principal's signature at the following meeting. The plan, which is posted in the classroom, must adhere to the following formula: (1) subject of instruction for each class hour; (2) tie-in on topic with contemporary political events in the village or district; (3) description of visual aids to be used; (4) any special occasion (such as birthday anniversaries of Communist leaders or heroes) to be observed and discussed during class sessions.

Discussion must be held in prescribed terms. A mathematics problem, for example, would be phrased as follows: Thirty members of a JZD (Uniform Agricultural Cooperative) pledged themselves on the occasion of the Party Congress to work voluntarily without pay for 2,100 hours as a brigade; how many hours did each member of the JZD work?"

The most distasteful disciplinary device for teachers is the "observation visit" required of each member of the teaching staff. Instructions are to enter classrooms without warning and "listen" for teacher's "mistakes." Each teacher must report his findings "critically" at the next work meeting.

Not only all teachers but every university professor or lecturer must be a member of the Communist-controlled Trade Union section, and must take part in special courses organized by the Ministry of Education. But above all each professor is controlled daily by the Communist students who register every "suspicious" word of their instructors and report it to the functionaries of the faculty cell of the Party.

Control of the Student Body

To tighten its hold on the pupils in the higher-grade schools, the Pioneers' Organization was established according to the Soviet pattern. Its members come from young school children who attend the national and middle school. The minimum age of admission is nine years; the maximum age was fifteen until the summer of 1953, but then reduced to fourteen (following the school reform which curtailed compulsory school attendance). Older children and young people up to twenty-six years of age are members of the Czechoslovak Youth League proper, to which the Pioneers are attached as a preparatory stage. The Youth League was set up shortly after the end of World War II, while the Pioneer Organization was founded in April, 1949, after the Communist coup. At the end of 1953, there existed 11,213 Pioneer groups with 518,869 members. At that time, members of the fourteen-to-fifteen-year age groups had not yet been transferred to the Youth League; this transfer was carried out in January, and resulted in a reduction of the membership to 437,595 by February 1, 1954. The *Mlada Fronta* ("Youthful Front") is an example of youth control. The Prague daily central organ of the Youth League, published the "curriculum of the basic political circle of the Czechoslovak Youth League" for the annual course running from October 15, 1953, to June, 1954, on October 6, 1953. The curriculum is composed of six themes: (1) The "Czechoslovak Youth League, the Loyal Helpmate of the Party in the Building of Socialism"; (2) "The Soviet Union, the Country of Victorious Socialism"; (3) "How Czechoslovakia Became a People's Democratic Country and a Strong Component of the Camp of Socialism and Peace"; (4) "The Communist Party of Czechoslovakia, the Leading and Directing Force of Our Country"; (5) "Following the Example of the Soviet Union, Under the Leadership of the Party We Will Build Socialism in Our Country"; (6) "In the Friendship and Alliance with the USSR Lies the Guarantee of the Happy Future of Our Nation."

Examinations as Party Weapons

The political character of advanced and secondary education is reflected also in the examinations. The directive of June, 1951, established that the final examination (the last examination a pupil has to pass before matriculating in a university—except the admission examination, which is a mere screening procedure) should be revised in such a way that no pupil loyal to the regime should be afraid of it. The themes on which the pupils are examined are mostly pieces of Communist propaganda—the pupils simply have to show their propaganda skill. For instance, the pupils of the seventh and eighth secondary schools in Prague passed the written examination by writing an essay on "How Shall I Help to Build Our Socialist Country?"[55] University students are granted scholarships only if their party record is good. Their control runs through the following channels: (1) through selection; (2) through faculty organs; and (3) through youth organizations. Those who have succeeded in passing a final examination must sign the application forms at a certain faculty; they are then invited to present themselves before the Admission Board, composed of elder Communist students and assistants; the Chairman asks the local Party for the information about the candidates or the party cell of the secondary schools where the candidate studied or the corresponding unit of the Union of the Czechoslovak Youth. On a fixed day, the Admission Board cross-examines all candidates in order to ascertain their true attitude toward the present regime. Those who are admitted are divided by the Dean's office into groups of about twenty members, with a chairman, a political instructor, and an organization functionary. The chairman is responsible for the regular meetings (every week at least six hours) in the course of which

---

[55] Gadourek, *op. cit.*, p. 118.

the lectures of the professors are discussed under the supervision of the political instructor. The organization functionary organizes the public activities of the group: work brigades and participation in political manifestations. Every student must carry a special booklet (the original *index lectionum*) in which every lecturer checks the presence of the student at his lecture; since 1950, the professors have been instructed not to sign the booklets of the students not members of the Union of Czechoslovak Youth.

According to Communist leaders, Czechoslovakia's universities are "democratic" today. No one, they say, whatever his means or station in life, is barred from taking a degree in a People's Democracy. This sounds well, but unfortunately, for the teaching staff and the students, the word "democratic" has a meaning under Communism which differs from that accepted in the Western world. For instance, at the Slovak University at Bratislava, the dean, professors, and lecturers are hailed as "comrades" and everything is "democratic." Part of every lecture is devoted to "discussion and criticism"—which means that the students are obliged to criticize the unhappy professor for ten minutes, not on the substance of his lecture, but on his ability to teach; the accused is not allowed to defend his methods.[56]

If a student falls behind because of his "negligence," he is forced to submit a detailed schedule of his private study time in triplicate (one copy for the group instructor, another for the political secretary, and the third remains with the lazy student). He is then "shadowed" by a professional informer—usually a Communist undergraduate—who reports on his movements. Members of the Party are exempt from this "democratic guidance," for they are a race apart.

It scarcely matters what one may wish to study, for the most important part of any "democratic degree" is the study of Marxism-Leninism, and the Russian language (grammar and conversation), and the so-called social

---

[56] "Life Is Restricted in Slovak College," *New York Times*, September 4, 1953.

doctrines (history of the workers' movement throughout the world and the history of the Soviet Communist party) ; no less than twelve lessons a week are devoted to these subjects.

Outside study hours of the "democratic" student are bound by unwritten "democratic laws." A few of them in force in Bratislava are: No student may participate in any entertainment other than that organized by the Socialist Youth, Communist party, or factories; such entertainments must be visited collectively. On such occasions, students must be dressed in blue Youth Movement shirts and long trousers cut in "Eastern" fashion. Students may indulge only in Czech, Hungarian, Slovak, and Russian dancing. Students are not allowed to consume alcohol; only 4 percent beer is allowed. Students are forbidden to visit Socialist entertainments individually with a girl, or to meet girls other than those dressed in the blue uniform blouses of the Youth Movement. To go to church, listen to Western broadcasts, or to learn Western languages—particularly English—is frowned upon.

Military Training

Up to the fall of 1951, the regime paid little attention to premilitary training because it had to concentrate its attention on the sovietization of the army proper. In 1951, defense training was established in the schools, in the working youth centers, and in voluntary organizations. This training is controlled by the Ministry of Education in cooperation with the Ministry of National Defense. Such control is exercised directly through district inspectors of physical training, who cooperate with the army. Each inspector visits the schools of his area three times monthly. In 1953, defense training in the schools, institutions of the Labor Reserves, working youth centers, and other institutions performing similar tasks were to remain compulsory until August 31, 1953. The training consists of studying topography, the course of projectiles, correct and practical shooting, and other subjects. School outings are also used for "defense" training. In August, 1953, the Ministry of Education made compulsory premilitary training of boys attending the ninth, tenth, and eleventh grades of schools of general education and the first, second and third grades of pedagogical and vocational schools a special subject of instruction; special marks are awarded for premilitary training. In the fourth and fifth grades, boys and girls participate in the work of school circles of special interests guided by instructors of the Czechoslovak Red Cross; girls attending the sixth, seventh, and eighth grades are trained in similar circles. Boys of the latter grades work mostly in aviation modeling courses controlled by the headmaster in cooperation with the district committee of the Cooperation of the Army Union. Pupils over fourteen are expected to volunteer for membership in the basic organizations of the Union. The activities of these organizations are directed by their committees, which consist of five to nine members, at least half of whom should be pupils. On the organizational side, headmasters, teachers, Pioneer and Youth League groups at the schools, committees of the CPCS and of the Revolutionary Trade Union Movement are expected to cooperate.

Physical training was set up in all universities as of the beginning of the academic year 1952-53. It was the logical consequence of the ever-increasing militarization of civilian and educational life of Czechoslovakia. Special curricula have been worked out "with due regard to Soviet experiences," and, unlike other subjects (classes), physical training was entered in the students' indices (registers of selected classes) with graded marks "which will be a decisive factor for advancement to higher courses." The *cathedrae* are also expected to "care for ideologico-political education and the popularization of physical training, sport and Soviet experiences."

Science and Arts

Communist control aims to extend itself into the areas of human activities which are often described as individual: the process of scientific thinking and aesthetic creative work. In order to achieve such control, the Party has transferred the intellectual activities from the individual to the collective sphere, acting on the principle that only the manifestations which take place in groups can be kept in line; thus, they can be checked by fellow members and manipulated by stimulation, support, or suppressions of arguments. Acting on these guidelines, the intellectual life of Czechoslovakia is crisscrossed by numerous organizations of intellectual experts—the Union of Czechoslovak Writers, the Union of Employees of the Cultural Service, the Union of the Czechoslovak Componists, the Union of the Workers in Science, etc.; they are formally subsumed under the huge mass organization—the Revolutionary Trade Unions. Most of them are split into two national groups. For instance, the National Union of the Slovak Newspapermen exists side by side with the Union of Czechoslovak Newspapermen.

Only those recognized by the government as "experts" are admitted to the membership of such organizations. The members have to pay regular contributions, participate in the activities, and follow the instructions of the appointed leaders. Exclusion from membership means the end of scientific or artistic career. Thus the Party maintains the ideological control of intellectual leadership.

The most important methods of exerting persistent pressure to have the organizations conform to the "General Line" of the Party's cultural policy are: (1) the meetings, lectures, and courses organized by the Unions; (2) the system of collective obligations; (3) the system of Socialist competition; (4) the property control; and (5) the legal methods.[57] During the special holidays, for instance, the Party runs holiday courses for the elder writers to teach them how to follow the party line in their writings. There are daily meetings of the local branches of the Unions, presided over by Communist boards. Every writer and scientist is expected to make solemn announcement of a plan for his work for the coming year, and the pledges are published in the daily press. The government periodically announces public competitions

---

[57] Gadourek, op. cit., p. 134.

in the areas of culture or science which are to be filled; accepted products are featured by the government, the author given a financial reward and sometimes special honorary titles—as "The Artist of the People," which means a great honor for his lifetime and a state funeral after his death. Every May, distinguished "People's Artists and Scientists" are given special decorations by the President of the Republic. The Socialist competition is organized by the Union of Czechoslovak Youth, which asks boys and girls to write poems on Lenin or model busts of the Workingman—or similar subjects; the awards consist of special badges, small busts of Lenin and Commissars, and the winners are selected for the Academy of Art and pushed along so that they may become Socialist artists of the future.

We have already discussed how the members of the faculties of the higher institutions of learning have been sovietized. Interestingly enough, the new Communist regime draws a sharp line between the scientific and educational professions, and those who teach cannot work in science or vice versa. Parallel to the universities, new research institutes have been established where no lectures are given. This system allows a better party control of the teachers and prevents the interference of scientists with educational theories. All research is centralized, and the planning of all research is related to the various national economic plans.

Since the arts and science in the People's Democracy serve the propaganda goals of Soviet policy, the tasks of the intellectuals are always adjusted to the goals of the Communist party; the artists and scientists merely help the Party in its struggle for the masses (that is, propaganda through art) and for technological and military supremacy over the world (that is, through science).

The basic approach to one aspect of social control is, for instance, stated by Malenkov:

In creating artistic images, our artists, writers and art workers must always remember that the typical is not only that which is most frequently encountered but that which most fully and pointedly expresses the essence of the particular social force. . . . The typical is the basic sphere of the particular social form. . . . The

typical is the basic sphere of manifestation of the Party approach
in realistic art. The problem of typicalness is always a political
problem. . . .[58]

In regard to science, we hear that: "Only Socialism
can free science of its bourgeois shackles, of its enslavement by capital, of its service to the interests of dirty
capitalistic greed."[59]

In Czechoslovakia, the present cultural life has had to
be attuned more than in any other state (with the possible exception of Poland) to the nationalistic slant. At
the same time, Czechoslovak artists and scientists have
found it difficult to accept uncritically and without their
nationalistic ideology the culture of the Russian people.
In order to counteract nationalistic tendencies, the party
line in Czechoslovakia has persistently stressed that the
USSR is the source of all positive cultural influence, the
land of all important discoveries, while the Western
world is the source of all negative, perversive influences.

Only in the field of folklore, folksongs, and folk dances
has Czech and Slovak nationalism been allowed to operate rather freely (although we have pointed out how even
the fairy tales of the Czechoslovak people have had to
change their heroes and villains along the Communist
line). The Czech literary classics (such as the famed historical novels by Jirasek) are allowed, but with the understanding that they feature the cause of the People's
Democracy. In general, the worship of past folklore and
classics (Smetana in music, Jirasek in literature, and Mi-
kulas Ales in art) are allowed as a compensatory gift for
the lack of cultural independence. Folklore is strongly
stimulated; collectives of People's Creativeness have been
formed throughout the country, consisting of boys and
girls who form a band playing national songs, or groups
of dancers or choirs; but many of them are merely bands

---

[58] Georgi Malenkov, "Report of the Central Committee to the
19th Congress of the All Union Communist Party," *Pravda*, October 6, 1952, and in *Soviet News* (English text), October 18, 21,
22, 23, 1952.

[59] Lenin, quoted in talk by Academician I. I. Artobelevsky, "Successes of Soviet Technical Science," *Radio Moscow*, Soviet Home
Service (April 29, 1953).

of wind instruments playing the Russian songs, the popular dance music, or the music of Communist composers (marches or other lighter pieces).[80]

Above all, Marxism-Leninism and even Stalinism were forced upon all forms of the present Czechoslovak arts and science. The rigid canons of this doctrine are applied even to empirical science. Following this formula, in 1949, a well-known Czech biologist, Dr. F. Hercik, proclaimed:

> In the first place we shall require from our scientists that they would and could deduce their specific science from the social economic basis. They must realize that every scientific fact which they ascertain and which they ascribe a place in their theory and hypothesis has, in the long run, its social and class consequences . . . We want to have class-conscious scientists, partial scientists who know what is their part in the struggle and who will play their part with all skill and enthusiasm.[61]

This ideological trend is also related to the militarization of literature, art, and science since 1950. Czech papers and periodicals feature poems, entitled "Songs of Peace," which exhort the workers to raise their output (much of which is armament), warn the "reactionaries" and "imperialists" by stressing the decision of the "People" to fight against them, and glorifying the "final victory of Socialism"; the same themes have been featured in the novels, paintings, or sculptures. Jirasek has been widely promoted because of his anti-Catholic tendencies and his glorification of the war heroes of Czech history.

The Control of Cultural Media of Communications

Presentation through cultural media is rigidly controlled in Czechoslovakia. Every National Committee has a special officer in charge of cultural matters; he can prohibit any cultural affairs (concerts, theatrical performances, lectures, debates). All cultural activities must

---

[60] Gadourek, *op. cit.*, p. 139. We have treated in another chapter of this book on how the Soviets have been Russianizing minorities cultures.

[61] Quoted by Gadourek, *op. cit.*, p. 139.

be reported weeks ahead and permits granted to hold them.

The promotional activities are carried on under numerous auspices. Above all, the Communist party has numerous branches engaged in such work. The Union of Czechoslovak Youth has already been described. The army has its bands of musicians, dancers, its choirs and actors. Then there are numerous organizations of the cultural workers, which we have described. The local government also controls education, libraries, and community buildings.

These community buildings, called Houses, Homes, or Clubs of Culture, in all communities disseminate art and refinement on a local scale and keep close watch on the citizens' spare time. They are the centers for the Russian Friendship Societies and also the local Peace Campaign headquarters. They are usually lodged in fine town houses, country chateaux, and ex-noblemen's castles. The average club is open from 9:00 A.M. until 10:00 P.M. Every club has an auditorium, well-stocked Communist library, radio, movie facilities, dance hall, and busts, photographs of the Kremlin and scenic shorts of the Soviet Union. Russian classes, lectures, folk singing, amateur theatricals, and carefully planned "spontaneous" dances take place in these centers, where the absence of a community resident is noted with displeasure.

The pro-Soviet regime took a great deal of pains to absorb a powerful *Sokol* organization which, by its very nationalistic spirit and traditions, could threaten the Communist goals of formal and community education. The *Sokols* ("falcons") were a nonmilitary, or semi-military gymnastic organization. Founded in Bohemia in 1862 when the Czechs were Habsburg Empire subjects, the movement was inspired by Italy's (Garibaldi's) struggle for freedom. The *Sokol* idea was to develop traditions of voluntary discipline, self-reliance, strength, culture, and independence. *Sokol* signifies "falcon," a bird that symbolizes heroic manhood to Slav peoples.

The organization promoted adult education activities, which soon became intertwined with the nationalistic, social, educational, and physical background of prewar

Bohemia and postwar Czechoslovakia. The core of its activities were *Sokol* centers, where the members met two or three times a week, exercised in their well-equipped gymnasia and open-air stadia. Gymnastic exercises, practiced in groups, alternated with training on a series of apparatus, and both supplemented with education stimulating the mind. Of Czechoslovakia's 12,000,000 postwar population, nearly a million were devotees of *Sokol* gymnastics; they held frequent local and regional (as well as international) displays of their calisthenics perfection; every six years, normally, they held an All-*Sokol* Congress in Prague. How important this national organization was, was evident from the fact that it was dissolved by direct orders by Hitler in 1939 and all its property confiscated by the Nazis in 1940.[62]

The Communist regime alleges that "before 1939, little attention had been paid to physical culture and sports at the universities"[63]—disregarding entirely that all this form of training was actually practiced by the *Sokols,* together with the University Sports Clubs, which existed in all university centers and which cooperated with physical training institutions. The main centers were at Prague (the so-called Straka Academy), at Brno, and at Bratislava. The Communists also underplay the fact that, after the reopening of the universities in 1945, physical training institutes were started at the universities, which were responsible for the physical training of undergraduates, which was compulsory for first- to third-year students at all faculties. In addition, special groups in these institutes cultivated various sports on a voluntary basis—especially soccer, light athletics, basketball, handball, various water sports, and table tennis. In fact, the

---

[62] The *Sokols* have branches throughout the world, and the American *Sokols* are powerful elements among the descendants of American Czechoslovaks. They were also important in furthering Masaryk's and Benes' activities during both wars, and are now active in formulating anti-Communist groups among American Slavs. See: "Sokol," pp. 1240-42, in Joseph S. Roucek, *Slavonic Encyclopedia* (New York: Philosophical Library, 1949).

[63] National Union of Czechoslovak Students, *Students in Czechoslovakia* (Prague: Orbis, 1949), p. 143.

physical culture festival of Czechoslovak schools, featuring university sports, was held in 1947.

In February, 1948, the Marxist government unified all physical culture unions sports associations in the Czechoslovak *Sokol* Community under Communist leadership: the *Junak* (named for the Czechoslovak Scouts' Movement after World War II, with 186,089 members) ; *Orel* (a Roman Catholic version of the *Sokol*, with 168,555 members) ; *D.U.J.* (Workers' Gymnastic Union, 110,000 members) ; and all sports organizations (the Union of Skiers, the Union of Boxers, etc., and especially the Czechoslovak Football Association, with 655,800 members). But such totalitarian unification had hard going, especially because of the uncompromising attitude of some *Sokol* leaders. Purges were turned on, and the *Sokol* movement was fused with all organizations of physical instruction and a close relationship with the Union of Czechoslovak Youth established. The new instructors and officers of *Sokol* have been recruited from the cadres of the Union. Then a drive began to get new members for the *Sokol* ranks. Today, the *Sokol* organization resembles that of the Communist party. It is headed by the State Office of Physical Instruction and Sports and the Committee for Physical Education and Sport. While the office is theoretically only an advisory body, it actually determines all activities of *Sokols* in detail; it is headed by a member of the Cabinet, a "Minister charged with the Office of Physical Education and Sport." The Minister controls the *Sokol* organization through the organs of the local government (the National Committees) and through the Action Committees and other organs of leadership in the *Sokol* organization.

Every National Committee (County, District or Local National Committees) has a functionary who is in charge of the care of education and of physical instruction; he is also responsible for the development of the *Sokol* activities and for their governmental support. The *Sokol* movement is split into geographical units as is the local government or the Party: the county, district, and local committees and Action Committees of the *Sokols*. The members of various committees and the delegates to the General

Meeting of the whole *Sokol* organization are "elected" according to a fixed precept—so many delegates must be "workers" (51.9 percent), white-collar workers (19.28 percent), teachers (10.07 percent), pupils (2.26 percent), peasants (0.55 percent), members of the army and police (0.39 percent), employees (0.31 percent), "without professions" (housewives, 1.25 percent), etc.

In Marxist Czechoslovakia, everything printed is a monoply of the party government. Before the Communists even seized power, all typographers were controlled by their Trade Unions and refused to print anything criticizing the Communists or the articles favoring the non-Communist parties, always threatening a strike if forced to do so; this control played an important role during the coup against Benes. Today, all editors of all periodicals are Communists, or the press is controlled by the so-called "technical editors." While the editors are party members, the others are former editors now supervised in their writing and functions. In order to tighten the control over the "technical editors," the principle of "collective writing" has been used: every article is discussed by a group of editors and then rewritten as a product of the whole group.

In 1949, the Central Council of Editors was founded at the Ministry of Information; this body works out yearly plans for the publishing of nonperiodical literature; the plan must be approved by the Minister. Only books suggested and approved by the Council are allowed to appear. In the spring of that year, all secondhand bookstores were closed and the selling or circulation of "non-approved" books prohibited. In 1950, special schools were established for libraries, and a special Council of Librarians established at the Ministry of Information with an advisory function. The new libraries report on those requesting the books of Masaryk, Benes, or other "reactionary," "bourgeois," "Fascist," or "imperialistic" literature.

All newspapers of the Czechoslovak nationalized press are produced by political or cultural organizations. Of twenty dailies, thirteen are published in Bohemia and Moravia, and seven in Slovakia; their circulation totals

2,400,000 copies daily.[64] The two news agencies are also owned and subsidized by the state: CETEKA (Ceska Tiskova Kancelar) covers Bohemia and Moravia, and maintains news contacts abroad through a dozen foreign correspondents, and by exchange agreements with Tass, Reuters, New China News Agency, and others. The Slovak News Agency (ZAS) serves the Slovak papers, has exchange agreements with several foreign agencies and also receives information through CETEKA.

It was easier to establish direct control over broadcasts, since the radio has been under governmental control from the very beginning. But the programs of the broadcasts have been changed, since radio is entirely a branch of political and cultural propaganda. Especially the hours from 6:00 to 9:00 P.M. are jammed with all kinds of programs serving the AGITPROP (the party sections dealing with propaganda—"agitation through propaganda.") There are popular broadcast courses in Russian; there is a "broadcast university," whose program explains the new reinterpretation of Czechoslovakia's history; the "broadcast newsreel" (from 8:00 to 9:00 P.M. comments on daily affairs. Symphonic music or opera performances are often interrupted by political appeals or short slogans. Listening to foreign broadcasts is associated with criminal behavior.

Programs are produced by the state-owned Czechoslovak Broadcasting Company, with the Postal Department providing technical facilities. A special staff prepares twenty-eight educational broadcasts per week; listening is compulsory in primary and secondary schools. Considerable attention is given to programs broadcast to neighboring countries, and to shortwave programs to distant countries.

The control of the motion picture has proved rather difficult, since home production, at the introduction of the Communist regime, was not sufficient to supplant the imports and popularity of the films from the West, and especially from Hollywood. Hence, the Communist re-

---

[64] UNESCO, *World Communications* (Paris: UNESCO, 1951), pp. 106-7.

gime has concentrated on short films (especially news-reels), and on featuring imports from the USSR and from other People's Democracies. At the beginning, films from England and Hollywood were allowed to run, especially if featuring unfavorable aspects of Western ways; Steinbeck's *Grapes of Wrath* and such plays as *Tobacco Road* have been given many showings in Czechoslovakia. Since Soviet films proved mostly unpopular, party members received special tickets on which the attendance of Soviet films was registered; competitions for the highest number of visits to the Russian films were started; compulsory attendance was provided in the army, in the Union of Czechoslovak Youth, and other organizations.

Conducive to Communist control is the fact that all cinemas have been expropriated and are run by the local organs charged with cultural service.

The whole film industry, Czechoslovak State Film, is under the Ministry of Information and a Film Council. Film production in Czechoslovakia has been rising, but has not reached the prewar level of thirty to fifty feature films annually. Each week three newsreels appear, and twice monthly a news review, *New Times*, is released. Attention is paid to educational films, and to providing schools with projectors. At present about one in eight of the primary schools is equipped with a 16-mm. projector. The film faculty of the Academy of Arts and Letters and the Czechoslovak Film Institute between them provide professional and technical training to Czechs and to students from neighboring satellite countries. As far as distribution and censorship of films are concerned, Slovakia is treated as a unit, and a small proportion of production is devoted to Slovak films.

The Church and Communism

According to the 1930 census, Czechoslovakia's population was 76.85 percent Roman Catholic. The regime has not dared to annihilate the churches, but it has not spared any effort to bring them under the complete control of the government, proving the Kremlin's thesis that the religious issue had to be handled the Communist way. The steps taken showed that the Communist masters wanted to nationalize Heaven, but had no objections to letting God stay on as general manager, provided He would take orders from the Communist government.

As early as in 1948, articles were published and speeches made by Communist leaders criticizing the Catholic hierarchy for opposing Communist policies. In the spring of 1949, the negotiations between the government and the Roman Catholic bishops became deadlocked, and the government developed a plan to create a split in the ranks of the Catholics. On June 10, 1949, an organization of Catholic clergymen and laymen, called Catholic Action, was founded as an instrument for bringing the Roman Catholic Church under the complete control of the atheistic government. Archbishop Josef Beran ordered the clergy to boycott this government-sponsored organization. But the government reacted fast. On June 15, 1949, Beran's palace was placed under guard, the consistory searched, and the Chancellor arrested; when another pastoral letter of his was read in the churches, the Archbishop was confined to his palace and reduced to silence. (In March, 1951, he was committed to the "concentration monastery" of Nova Rise in Moravia.)

The Church Bill, enacted on October 14, 1949, which became law on November 1, 1949, made the Roman Catholic Church a legal adjunct of the Communist state. The protests of the Catholic bishops were of no avail, and their attempts to authorize a "conditional pledge" of loyalty to the government appeared to conflict with the determination of the Communists to allow no reservations. On November 10, 1949, the government placed all religious publications, educational, financial, and charitable activities under the thumb of the new Ministry of Church Affairs. In addition, the Ministry began to decide what could be taught in the seminaries and theological schools, what textbooks could be used, and how much was to be spent for the upkeep or restoration of religious institutions.

According to the new church law, all archbishops, bishops, and apostolic administrators are required to give their oath to the Premier. They are classified as "Grade Four Clergy." The rest of the clergy are divided into three other grades. Grade Three, including auxiliary bishops, abbots, and heads of orders, took the oath from Alexei Cepicka, Minister of Justice, who headed the new Office for Church Affairs. Grade Two, including heads of seminaries, consistory chancellors, seminary faculty, and canons, read the oath to the chairmen of Czechoslovakia's nineteen regional committees. Grade One, the ordinary priests, went before the chairmen of the district national committees, Czechoslovakia's government bodies.

From Archbishop Beran down, all were forced to take the following oath:

I promise on my honor and conscience that I will be faithful to the Czechoslovak Republic and its people's democratic order and that I shall not do anything which would be against its interests, security, or integrity. I will, as a citizen of the people's democratic state, fulfill honestly the duties which result from my position and I will try with all my power to support the building [constructive] efforts aimed at the welfare of the people.

A memorandum from the bishops, October 21, 1949, told priests to take the oath with this qualification, either orally or in writing: . . . "unless it is in contradiction to the laws of God and the Church and the rights of man." On November 1, the qualification was modified to: "Since I am convinced that the government would never ask anything which would be contrary to the laws of God or human rights."

The decree also provided these new details of the law: (1) Priests will be paid just as other civil servants, receiving a basic salary plus an additional sum for rank and efficiency; the basic salary is 36,000 crowns ($720) with 3,600 crowns ($72) increases every three years for a maximum of twelve years. (2) The four grades receive the following extra payments: Grade One, 12,000 crowns ($240) ; Grade Two, 24,000 crowns ($480) ; Grade Three, 36,000 crowns ($720) ; and Grade Four, 48,000 crowns ($960). (3) The clergy receives pensions. (4) Priests are required to teach religion in schools without pay if there is no special religious teacher in the school. (5) If any priest is appointed to a church post without prior state approval, the post is considered vacant until it is filled by a state-approved man. (6) Priests unacceptable to the government have their salaries retained and successors are named to take over their pulpits.

In 1950, the theological faculties were transferred from the competence of the Minister of Education to that of the State Office of Church Affairs, as we have already pointed out.

At first, the non-Roman Catholic Churches were not exposed to such direct attack. But today, they are subject to the same Communist controls. The Protestant and Jewish churches are subordinated to the State Office for Church Affairs; their priests are sworn into their offices by the state authorities from whom they receive their salaries, together with the regular orders and directions. The Protestant churches have been especially exploited by the organs of the "Peace Movement," and Professor Hromadka, who lived for a while in the United States, is now officially recognized in the regime as the spiritual leader of the Protestant churches and frequently speaks at the "Peace Conferences" at home and abroad. In addition to the organized pressure, the government has also employed special "ideological weapons" against Protestant organizations. A very suitable tool in this respect has been the Barthian theological teaching (which, reinterpreted in Czechoslovakia, propounds that, since there is no contact between God and the world, we cannot refuse Communism on ethical or religious grounds, since nothing is absolutely right or absolutely wrong). The position of the Orthodox Church has been given precedence; its masses are broadcast at solemn occasions by all stations in Czechoslovakia; a special law "securing" the position of the Orthodox Church has been passed. Specifically prohibited are the bodies outside the Communist sphere of direct influence—the Salvation Army, the Mormons especially, together with the Society of Friends and the various evangelical sects.

Ideological Factors

In spite of claims of the Czechoslovak propaganda agencies that the Czechoslovak people are more than well off, that the United States is "cursed with unemployment, the 'slump,' corruption and lynching," that the Marshall Plan countries are suffering from the infringement of sovereignty and with markets flooded with American goods (and consequently with idle factories), and that Czechoslovakia is cursed with "imperialist agents," the "remnants of capitalism," and "misguided Czechoslovaks living abroad," the country has provided a certain resistance to the Soviet imperialistic processes. There have been countless arrests and merciless persecutions and public trials; in some cases there have been open revolts.[65] Some 50,000 refugees have been carrying on a rather well-organized opposition to the Soviet yoke from all parts of the globe, including the United States. The propaganda against the ideals of Masaryk and Benes has been rather unsuccessful, and even some of the Communists themselves cherish the memory of their great leaders. "Masaryk and Benes remain the symbol of true democracy, the symbol of freedom from Communist oppression, and the effort of party and government leadership to destroy their memory and the people's attachment to them adds fuel to the general discontent."[66]

The Czechoslovakian general public appears to be more reluctant to express opinions than the neighboring Poles or Hungarians. The memory of police terror seems to be as effective in inhibiting free communication as its reality. There is no easy access to foreign newspapers and indiscriminate radio listening is a crime.

Within this general framework, the three main sources of resistance to the Communist regime are: (1) the Catholic Church; (2) the peasants, upset by the Communist measures against the Church and collectivization; and (3) the ruined intellectual and middle class. Czecho-

---

[65] For more details, see: Committee on Foreign Relations, *Tensions Within the Soviet Captive Countries: Czechoslovakia* (Washington, D.C.: Government Printing Office, 1954).

[66] *Ibid.*, p. 87.

slovakia's young people often show no enthusiasm for the so-called proletarian way of life, and Communist leaders complain about bourgeois individualism, religious prejudices, and "political apathy" of the young functionaries of the Party.

Then the worker is not happy with growing demands imposed upon each Czechoslovakian, not because of national needs, but Russian demands. Mobilization of manpower, first carried out on a voluntary basis and now simply carried out, has been met with hatred—especially the government forced labor camps. (One of the chief factors here has been the fact that, although the government has increased wages, especially of miners and workers in heavy industry, the workers have received no benefits either because of former rationing, or because of the system of a double market—rationed and free goods, but the later costing so much more).

The peasant resistance on all levels has resulted in a shortage of food so serious that the government, unable to meet its obligations under the rationing system, was finally forced to abolish it. As the agricultural cooperatives have become a trap for the independent farmers, the communal enterprises have become a trap for the independent artisans. The rationing system has become another tool in the hands of the Communist government in its effort to destroy the vocal and rebellious independent middle class. By confiscation, nationalization, and various other Communist devices, not only wealthy people but also members of the middle class were deprived of their property, business, and possibilities of earning their living independently. Homes, pensions, and even savings accumulated as the fruit of their lifelong efforts were taken away from these people who became victims of the policies of a hostile regime.

It is true that "years of systematic intimidation and police terror have been unable to break the spirit of resistance of the people."[67] But the fact remains that the older generations will pass on, and that the younger generations, knowing only the Communistic way of life

---

[67] *Ibid.*, p. 114.

and reasoning, are occupying every year the replacement sectors of the pre-Communist generations. The answer can be nothing but pessimistic if measured only within the terms of two or three decades.

It is significant that in Czechoslovakia, the last country to become a Soviet satellite, the progress of anti-religious activity has been very successful. This may be explained by the fact that nowhere in Europe was the number of officially recognized agnostics so high as in that country, and that already after World War I, the Catholic Church was shaken by the more political than religious secession from it of the "national" Czechoslovak Church, which as early as 1920-25 had attempted to unite the progressive and patriotic factions within the Catholic Church. This progressive and patriotic formation within the Church became the strongest weapon of Communism after World War II. In Czechoslovakia (as well as in Hungary, Yugoslavia, and Poland), the Communists were able to find among both Catholics and Protestants— not numerous, but nevertheless active and resourceful— groups which assisted in dynamiting the organized religious bodies. Under the pressure of these "patriots," even Catholic bishops were obliged to proclaim that, while preserving their canonic fidelity to the Vatican, they nevertheless repudiated all interference by the Holy See in secular matters and organizational problems of the Church. A similar trend can be observed among the Protestants.[68]

It is true that the religious forces of Czechoslovakia are but one of the resistance forces in the country. The strongest elements, in fact, are provided by the exiled Czechoslovak intellectuals and professionals scattered throughout the world, who are continuing the work of their great historical predecessors—also exiles—Komensky (Comenius), Masaryk, Benes, and others.

"There is no post-Stalin thaw in Czechoslovakia and writers are not permitted to criticize the government. However, the urge sometimes is irresistible. For in-

---

[68] George N. Shuster, *Religion Behind the Iron Curtain* (New York: The Macmillan Company, 1954).

stance, in a literary magazine (we are not divulging the name) a writer made fun of the ties forced upon the oppressed Czechoslovaks by the Big Brother:

> The stork and the nightingale decided to swap experiences: the nightingales were to visit the storks and catch fish for them, and the storks were to visit the nightingales and sing for them. The nightingales, being polite and cultured, applauded the idea. They tried to catch fish, but the stork nation began to die out from starvation. Those that remained sang out of revenge, above the call of "agreement," so that the nightingales, unable to bear it any longer, also began to dwindle away. One day a nightingale, out of sheer desperation, opened his mouth to sing and discovered that the tones flowed beautifully. Other nightingales joined in the singing. The storks were insulted and flew home and, having no one to sing to, they began to catch fish again. The moral: It is good to know how to catch fish and sing at the same time, but it just isn't possible.

"It is clear that the oppressed Czechoslovaks are the nightingales who yearn to be able to speak out and sing again in freedom, and that they are looking to the day when the Soviet storks will fly away and leave them alone."[69]

The Contemporary Scene

Rude Pravo ("Red Justice"), Prague—the official Communist party organ in Czechoslovakia—has revealed that almost one-third of the university students in Czech and Slovak institutions of higher learning have had to withdraw.[70] The most astonishing feature of this situation is the fact that, following the Communist seizure of 1948, the entire school system of Czechoslovakia was radically reorganized to conform to the basic Soviet pattern and to provide education on all levels for children of every class, especially those of worker and peasant origins. The new measures abolished the former system of the five-year primary school, eight-year secondary school, and four or five years of college or university.

---

[69] Quoted in *The American Bulletin* (Chicago), No. 50 (April, 1961), p. 3.

[70] Eberhard Mahnert, "The Failure of Communist Schools," *Sudeten Bulletin, A Central European Review* (Munich), IX, No. 1 (January, 1961), 11-12.

The new plan introduced a system with an eight-year primary and a three-year high school—a program approved as an adequate basis for entrance into higher education. For example, courses in several subjects were cut in half, making it possible for students to obtain degrees in engineering at the age of nineteen or twenty (the previous level providing for graduation at twenty-two or twenty-three). Courses that formerly were granted preferred status were replaced by an intensive routine of political propaganda which, of course, stressed Communist Party dialectics.

Moreover, "in selecting aspirants for college preparatory schools and universities, the authorities show preference for children from proletarian homes, a tactic that envisages the complete annihilation of the Czech middle class with its (traditional) high standards of education."[71]

Between 1952 and 1953, quite a few schools of technology—*ad hoc* supplements to the "higher education" program being innovated—were established. Many of these are reported as little better than the crudest types of technical institutions, with inadequate laboratory facilities and scanty libraries. There is even a textbook shortage, and frequently students are forced to work from scripts which they—in medieval fashion—have compiled from lectures, manuals and whatever library materials they may have found available. There are approximately twenty of these "technical schools."

In addition to the weakness of this type of training, stands also the fact that much of the student's time is taken up with the paramilitary training, Communist Youth Association duties, and the regular Communist party of Czechoslovakia activities. Several weeks out of the year are taken up with "polytechnical" experience at unpaid jobs in industrial installations. As though this were not enough, in 1959, following the example of the Russian school reform (Khrushchev Reform) of 1959, the new work plan was also introduced, set to begin intensively in the fall of 1961. To buttress the educational

---

[71] *Ibid.*, p. 12.

level of the general public, the lower school is extended from eight to nine years. Polytechnicalization will become obligatory as will a strengthened paramilitary training program.

Dr. Mahnert insists that this revision of the school system to fit the aims of Moscow "will certainly not raise the over-all educational level. . . . If unchanged, such conditions will reduce a population with a higher-than-average educational potential to a generation of robots."[72] Indeed, one recalls that only a few years ago Czechoslovakian Karel Capek, in *R.U.R.*, envisaged such a state. In Capek's famous drama, however, the robots learned to defy their masters, but perhaps this is too much to hope for in the situation just described.

A New Polytechnicalization

The so-called "Khrushchev Reform" in the USSR by which polytechnical—a euphemism for work experience —training became an integral part of the elementary and secondary school program following 1958 soon became the mode in the satellites.

In order to justify this departure, the Marxist leadership in Czechoslovakia quickly developed a rationale or rationalization for this fundamental shift in educational policy. As usual, a justification was found on historical and "moral" grounds. The announced reforms were headed with the usual Communist polemic: "All affairs of public education and the school system of the Czechoslovak Republic have undergone profound changes during the years the democratic regime (that is, since 1948, the date of the Marxist coup) has existed. From a school of the *bourgeoisie*, based on social and property inequality, from a servile weapon of the ruling clique of exploiter-capitalists, the Czech schools have been transformed into a really public school which educates conscious builders of socialism."[73]

---

[72] *Ibid.*, p. 12.

[73] G. A. Kasvin and A. A. Shibanov, "The Reform of the Schools in the Czechoslovak Republic," *Soviet Education* (New York, a translation of the Soviet Pedagogical Journal), I, No. 4 (February, 1959), 64-70.

Then these "extenuating circumstances" leading to the
change are enumerated: "Although certain reforms were
established in Czechoslovakia on the basis of 'The Law
of the Unified School' by the National Assembly in May,
1948, and the April, 1953, Act reducing the term of compulsory instruction from nine to eight years and the term
of instruction in the complete secondary school from
thirteen to eleven years, some dissatisfaction with the
program still existed. Among the chief reasons appended
for change were (1) overloading and extended homework; (2) failure of the school to enroll sufficient numbers
of children from the worker and peasant background;
and (3) the adolescent was found, at age fourteen, in
many cases incapable of correctly choosing a future
vocation (in this the school could not help him, since
almost no kind of work in vocational guidance was conducted).[74] As a reason for change this is indeed a familiar refrain.

To continue the report and to detail the expedient
chosen:

[Thus] the Central Committee of the Communist Party of Czechoslovakia at the 11th Congress proposed a series of measures which
will contribute to the further development of public education in the
country and to the regulation of the school system with the object
of bringing it closer to the needs of socialist construction. . . . In
his speech to the Congress, Comrade A. Novotny said, "The chief
task of our school must become the training of thoroughly developed people, who possess the basic facts of knowledge in the field
of science and technology and at the same time are trained for
skilled physical labor and conscious participation in the construction of Communist society. To create such a truly socialist school
means, by all possible methods, to join teaching in school increasingly more tightly with the productive labor of pupils so that they
acquire not only working habits, but in the senior classes of the
secondary schools, also gain a basic skill in the field on some kind
of working occupation. . . ."[75]

In order to interpret this new move, and because of the
current significance of polytechnicalization, tables elab-

[74] *Ibid.*, p. 66.

[75] *Ibid.*, p. 67. See also E. P. Gusarov, "Labor as a Factor in the
Pupils' Upbringing," *Soviet Education*, Vol. I, No. 5 (March, 1959).
Contains anecdotes and anthropometrical studies.

orating the program (from the Kasvin-Shibanov report mentioned above) are appended. The revised system of education in Czechoslovakia, which includes Khrushchev's plan of training pupils for labor, contains three levels, as follows in Tables I-IV:

TABLE I (Classes 1 to 5)   Handiwork, the First Level

Kinds of work	Number of lessons by years of study					
	I	II	III	IV	V-1	V-2
Work with small objects used, for example, in teaching safety, to clear up the workplace, etc.	6	0	0	0	0	0
Work with paper and cardboard	10	10	10	10	0	10
Work with plastics and clay	6	6	4	4	0	4
Work with fabrics	0	6	12	12	0	12
Work with wood and metal (soft tin, wire, etc.)	0	0	6	6	26	6
Work in nature corner and on garden plot	7	7	18	18	24	18
Socially useful labor	4	4	10	10	10	10
Excursions connected with handiwork lessons	0	0	6	6	6	6
Total	33x	33x	66	66	66	66

x lessons per week, all others 2 lessons per week.

Table II represents a combination of two indices: the agricultural and the industrial. Where paired figures are shown, the first refers to the emphasis granted in agricultural regions; the second figure that in industrial areas—otherwise the program is similar. (It will be noted that two basic plans have been set up for use (1) in predominantly agricultural regions, or (2) in industrial areas; nevertheless, every student is given contact with each field at some time during his study in classes VI-IX. Futhermore, annual totals progress from 89 hours per year of instruction in grade VI to a total of 165 hours in grade IX.)

TABLE II:

The Second Level, "Bases of Production" (Classes VI-IX)

Sections of "Bases of Production"	Number of hours by years of instruction, by semesters						
	VI	VII		VIII		IX	
Bases of technology, ind. ..11	0/0	0/0	0/8	0/15	15/15	23	23
Work in craftshops, ind. 29	0/0	0/0	0/30	0/26	33/26	33	33

The Second Level, "Bases of Production" (Classes VI-IX)

Sections of "Bases of Production"	VI	VII	VIII		IX	
Socially useful labor, ind... 4	0/0	0/0	0/6	0/4	10/4	3	3
Talks, industrial emphasis 2	0/0	0/0	0/2	0/2	4/2	2	2
Trips, industrial 4	0/0	0/0	0/3	0/3	4/3	5	5
Bases of technology, ag. 0	7/7	7/7	7/0	15/0	0/0	0	0
Work in craftshops, ag. 0	30/30	25/25	25/0	33/8	0/8	0	0
Socially useful labor, ag. .. 0	6/5	10/10	10/0	10/5	0/5	17	16
Talks, agricultural 0	2/3	3/4	3/0	2/1	0/1	0	0
Trips, agricultural 0	4/4	5/4	4/0	6/2	0/2	0	0
Total 50	49/49	50/50	49/49	66/66	66/66	83	82

In the third level, Classes X through XII, the general polytechnical education is combined with production training in many specialties. Training in urban areas is in the bases of machine-building, of the leading branches of heavy industry, in the bases of textile production, and in the bases of the construction industry. In agricultural regions, the program is as indicated in the tabulation below. This new program was planned to be in complete operation by September 1, 1961.

TABLE III General Polytechnical (Classes X-XII), Cities

Component parts of production training	X	XI	XII	Yearly total
Technology	2	2	3	222
Mechanical Engineering	2	2	0	132
Production practice and productive labor	6	7	9	700

(Heading: Number of hours per week by years of study)

TABLE IV: General Polytechnical (Classes X-XII), Rural

Component parts of production training	By years X	XI	By semesters XII		Yearly total
Crop raising	2	1	1 or 2	0	132
Livestock raising	2	1	2 or 1	0	132
Mechanical engineering	0	2	0	3	156
Production practice and labor	6	7	9	9	700

As one expedient for deemphasizing the distinction between members of the Communist society and as a device for reducing the number of higher trained proto-professional or white-collar workers, it would seem that the new polytechnicalization shift could easily produce the desired results. Yet Dr. Oskar Anweiler, Hamburg, sees an apparently unanticipated problem in this resort to "polytechnic emphasis" in the schools, from primary through university, in the Communist-oriented bloc including the USSR, mainland China, and the "People's Democracies" (satellites) of East Central Europe: Czechoslovakia, East Germany, Hungary, Romania, and Bulgaria (but with the exception of Poland and Albania—and, of course, Yugoslavia).

In addition to specific objections raised by factory managers bent on efficiency and the necessary provision of school buildings with special space for workshops and technical equipment—to say nothing of the retraining required to develop adequate school staffs—Anweiler maintains that:[76]

> Here the aim is to preserve the scientific structure of the various disciplines, whilst at the same time paying special attention to their practical applications. . . . the children's age, their attitude to work and their participation in "workers' collectives" also present various problems with respect to the methods of teaching and giving work experience.
>
> Seen as a whole, the main educational problem consists in the conflict between, on the one hand, the forms of life and teaching suited to children and young people and, on the other, the early adaptation to and preparation for the adult working world which it is sought to achieve.

Thus it remains to be seen whether in Czechoslovakia (or in any other of the East European satellites of the Kremlin) the Marxist myth is adequate—or satisfactory—for the stabilizing of the new 1958 system.[77] Yet, given the conditioning which has already occurred and is being perpetuated by the various youth organizations and paramilitary fronts, the transformation (except perhaps in East Germany) will not be found to be an impossible one.

---

[76] Oskar Anweiler, "School Reform Problems in Eastern Europe," *International Review of Education* (The Hague), VI, No. 1 (1960), 34-35.

[77] For an interpretation of the possible success of the 1958 reforms, see Elmer H. Wilds and Kenneth V. Lottich, *The Foundations of Modern Education* (New York: Holt, Rinehart and Winston, Inc., 1961), pp. 449-59.

This conclusion, however, discounts, of course, all possible recourses to the local nationalisms of the individual countries and the possibility of outside or even subterranean intervention.

On the other hand, a remark by ex-President Eduard Benes, made at a time of earlier travail of the Czechoslovak nation, may indeed eventually prove to be pertinent to the current situation. Benes wrote: "Washington, Jefferson and Lincoln, as well as all the leaders of the democracy before, during, and after the World War, were also our leaders and teachers. . . . The Czechoslovak people . . . have not deserted these ideals, and will not desert them. They only await the moment when they will be able again to express and cultivate them fully and freely."[78] Obviously, this is a standard to which all well-wishers of East European democracy can repair.

Of all the satellites, Czechoslovakia is cherishing most its cultural traditions, tied inseparably to the West and the United States. Such "deviationists" as Dr. Vlado Clementis and Rudolf Slansky paid with the hangman's noose for their notions that Communism could be combined with their nationalistic heritage.

Such sentiments, by a leading Czech professor now situated in the United States, are hopeful, if not helpful. Certainly the overseas Czechs subscribe to them. Yet the verdict of history has not appeared; a rising and reorientation (toward the West) of the currently downtrodden Czech and Slovak nation will fulfill the expectations of both Benes and Woodrow Wilson.

---

[78] Eduard Benes, *Democracy, Today and Tomorrow* (New York: The Macmillan Company, 1939), pp. v-vi.

CHAPTER VIII

HUNGARY
CHALLENGER OF THE KREMLIN

Two Bitter Fruits
An Early Nation-State
Unrest Under Habsburg Rule
Hungary's Reign of Terror
The Horthy Regime
The Communist Take-Over
The Hungarian Uprising of 1956
Education in Hungary
Education Between Two World Wars
World War II Fortunes
The Pro-Communist Reorganization of Education
Sovietization
The Formal Structure
Education as a Branch of Politics
Auxiliary Organizations
Control of Mass Communications
Adult Education
Higher Institutions of Learning
Employment and Assignments
Education of Minorities
Religious Problems
Russification
Resistance
Education Under the "New Courses"
Continuing Tensions

Two Bitter Fruits

AMONG THE BITTER FRUITS of World War II are two expressions which produce a shudder each time they are heard. The first, "mass expulsions," offers a threat to international law; the second, "genocide," which frequently is coupled with expulsion, offends common decency. Perhaps nowhere in the modern world have these disturbing manifestations of materialist philosophy occurred as violently as in Central Eastern Europe during the past three decades. Every nation from the Rhine to the Volga has suffered frightfully, and the end is not yet in sight. While only a sadist could relish the calculation of who has suffered the gravest iniquity, it is common knowledge that Hungary has borne her share of these woes.

Because of a long history, but more particularly because of significant events related to colorful leaders and democratic principles, the West—and especially the United States—has long considered Hungary (with the possible exception of Poland) as the outstanding nation of Eastern Europe. Moreover, although such a comparison does injustice to other freedom-oriented peoples presently behind the Iron Curtain, it is Hungary that has provided the USSR with her greatest challenge to date. Thus, it may be well to review the development of Hungarian nationalism and its will to survive the Red tide of Communism.

An Early Nation-State

Early recognizing the political advantages of European Christianity—Roman Catholic, that is—the Hungarians (a Finno-Ugrian stock from the heart of Asia) hastened to adopt this faith. Stephen (St. Stephen, 907-1037), the most prominent figure in their dawning history, took as a gift from Pope Sylvester II in the year 1000 the Holy Apostolic Crown—the most puissant symbol of the continuity and prestige of the Hungarian state. Consequently, in company with Poland and Bohemia, the Magyars have continued to reiterate their belief that —landlocked between Slav and German and belonging to neither—they stood as representatives of Latin Christianity in the East of Europe; they continually strove to identify themselves with the Western World via religion and culture.[1]

Under Louis the Great (1342-82) Hungary reached the zenith of her territorial expansion and constitutional independence. Hungarians dwell much on the "Golden Bull," promulgated in 1222; comparing this with Magna Carta, they consider it the origin of Magyar parliamentarianism and chartered liberties. Nevertheless, in 1526 the Ottoman Turks invaded Hungary from the direction of the Balkans, and the terrible battle of Mohacs led to the subjugation of the greater part of the country. Defeated at Vienna in 1683, the Turks withdrew while as potent a danger now threatened from the west. The Habsburg forces of German Austria seized Hungary and initiated a control that was to last for several hundred years.

Unrest Under Habsburg Rule

Early in the nineteenth century Hungary was swept by the rising demands of the national minorities—Slovaks in the northwest, Serbs in the Banat and the Backe, and the Swabians (peasants from southern Germany) in the west. In 1848, revolution broke out in Austria, and the

---

[1] See Joseph S. Roucek, "Hungary, 1918-1945," chap. XVI, pp. 323-37, and Hans Kohn, "Austria-Hungary," chap. II, pp. 31-59, in Joseph S. Roucek (ed.), *Central-Eastern Europe* (New York: Prentice-Hall, 1946); C. Revy, *Policy of Hungarian Culture* (Budapest: Athenaeum, Ltd., 1946), pp. 5-6; G. C. Paiker, "Hungarian Foreign Policy in Intercultural Relations, 1919-44," *American Slavic and East European Review*, XI (February, 1952), 42-43.

Hungarian liberals, chafed by Habsburg rule and galling restrictions on any but the highest magnates, rebelled. Many feudal privileges and the exemption of nobles from taxation were abolished. A national flag was chosen, and a revolutionary government under the leadership of Lajos Kossuth originated.

Embittered by his contacts with the Austrian monarchy, Kossuth had become an extreme nationalist. Liberal tendencies in his government were counterbalanced by his chauvinism, and the Slavic, Romanian, and German groups were inclined to intrigue against him. Non-Magyars within the Austrian Empire stirred Vienna to action, and Jellacic, a Croatian general in the imperial service, marched against the Hungarians. From Bohemia the Emperor called General Windischgratz and even relayed to St. Petersburg his plea for aid. Now it was German and Slav against Magyar, and Kossuth—who by this time had declared Hungary an independent republic, himself becoming President—succeeded in stirring the masses to a fierce patriotic resistance. Yet defeat against these odds was inevitable, and Kossuth fled to Turkey. In his visits to England and the United States he was hailed as a champion of liberty. Although the Republic had failed to survive, the Magyars had demonstrated their hypernationalism to the whole world. When, in 1894, Kossuth died in Italy, his remains were returned to Budapest and were buried in state.

Yet defeat had not stifled Hungarian patriotism, and Francis Deak, treading softly where Kossuth had threatened and roared, at last persuaded Emperor Franz Joseph to grant Hungary coordinate status in the realm. The *Ausgleich* of 1867 established the Dual Monarchy called Austria-Hungary. Austria ruled the Bohemians, the Poles, and the Tyrolese; Hungary the Banat, Croatia, and Transylvania. By this stroke both German and Magyar precedence were confirmed.

World War I brought Habsburg ruin and deprived Hungary of 75 percent of its territory and 60 percent of its people. Slovakia was joined with the Czechs; Transylvania went to Romania; Croatia and other southern areas became parts of Yugoslavia; and Burgenland shifted to Austria.[2] Otherwise the first World War brought little change in Magyar minority relations. While the King (the Emperor in his role in Hungary) was not permitted to return, Stephen Horthy de Nagybanya (vice-admiral in command of the imperial fleet at the war's end in 1918) served as "Regent."

Hungary's Reign of Terror

Horthy, an unbending member of the old Magyar aristocracy, represented his class well, but beyond that he thought in terms of the Hungarian nationalism of an earlier day; there was a reality about his severity which may explain without condoning. For, between the defeat of the Triple Alliance and Horthy's election on March 1, 1920, by the National Assembly,[3] the country had experienced a reign of terror almost unparalleled.

For, at the close of 1918, constituted government in Hungary had virtually collapsed, and a "National Council" was formed composed of Count Michael Karolyi, his friends, and a group of left-wing radicals. As one of his final acts, the Emperor appointed Karolyi Prime Minister. Immediately offering a formal resignation, the Count, in

---

[2] Burgenland, a medieval area of castles and rich estates, lay on Hungary's western border reaching from the Danube to the Drave. In the rural sections, the German population predominated; the home of Josef Haydn, Franz Liszt, and Josef Semmelweiss, Burgenland was also the domain of the Princes of Esterhazy—the most wealthy lords of Hungary. Today, following the latest Communist seizure of the Magyar state, Burgenland is the "border of the curtain"; "new mines have been laid and wire entanglements connected to signal rockets have been set in front of the barbed-wire fence" of this "last bastion of freedom." A Hungarian land, populated by Germans, this odd enclave stands emblematic of the conflict now raging on a global scale. See Leopold Rainalter, "Burgenland, Austria's Eastern Province" *Sudeten Bulletin* (Munich), VII, No. 3 (March, 1959), 61-62.

[3] See Nicholas Horthy, *Memoirs*, (New York: Robert Speller and Sons, 1957). The admiral writes: "The National Assembly, being the guardian of national sovereignty, solved the problem [the selection of a head of State] by taking a decision that accorded with the facts; that the Union with Austria and the 1867 Compromise should be dissolved and that the King's rule should be considered to have been dormant since November, 1918. Until such time as it could once more be openly exercised, a Regent of the State was to be appointed," p. 110.

order to further his revolutionary designs, persuaded the monarch to release the Hungarian troops from their oath of loyalty. Organizing them into semi-guerrilla bands, Karolyi (perhaps inadvertently) accomplished the death of former premier Count Tisza, and sought to conclude a separate peace, in which he was most unsuccessful.

Under the terms of the armistice, the dismemberment of the state was begun. In order to gain popular favor, Karolyi now dissolved the Hungarian Army and instituted a radical agrarian reform policy—a move which remained only a gesture. On January 11, 1919, Karolyi was named provisional president of the "Hungarian People's Republic," doubtless calculated to negate his influence and to make way for an even more radical regime. The final blow fell quickly. Upon Romania's occupation of Transylvania—although this was sanctioned by the Paris Peace Conference—Count Karolyi's position became untenable and, after turning the government over to the extremists, he resigned.

Karolyi's Social Democratic supporters had already turned far to the left. Upon the news of the loss of Transylvania, they combined with the Communists, the leader of whom was a Moscow-trained Hungarian Jew, Bela Kun by name. Karolyi's resignation proclaimed that he was turning "to the world proletariat for justice and help" and releasing his power "to the proletariat of the Hungarian peoples."[4]

It was indeed relinquished to the proletariat—although it may well be questioned whether there was any power left in his possession by March 21, 1919—so swift had been the leftist infiltration. Bela Kun already had incited the peasants and proletariat, and through his revolutionary organ *Voros Usjag* ("Red Sheet") was at the very moment threatening their rising against the other classes. Now that the government was his, he proceeded to set up what to all intents and purposes was a Communist dictatorship, although he styled the regime the "Hungarian Soviet Republic,"—*Magyar Tanacskoztarsasag*.

---

[4] As quoted in Horthy, *op. cit.*, p. 97.

A series of Communist "reforms" was promulgated: nationalization of banks and industries, expropriation of the land, secularization of the schools, public control of the press. Raising a Red Army, Kun went to war against Slovakia. Called by some a "cruel, fat, spiderlike monster," who tried by unspeakable methods to erase all the old traditional ways of thinking and living, Kun excited the greatest admiration among his associates and fellow travelers. With Kun at the front, a campaign of terror at home was conducted by Tibor Szamuelly, who is said to have boasted, "Terror is the principal weapon of our regime." The capital faced starvation as the Bolsheviks went about the countryside holding "courts martial" and hanging those unfriendly to the peasant-proletarian class. Budapest became a city of fear, where bodies hung from the lamposts and the stench of death was in the air.[5]

Overreaching himself, Bela Kun directed his Red Army toward Romania. That ended the affair, the Romanians coming all the way to Budapest, seizing trainloads of "damages" en route. Bela Kun fled to Austria, entering a mental hospital there. (He had held power for 143

---

[5] Fantastically, the present Communist government in Hungary, in a "White Book" titled *The Counter-Revolutionary Conspiracy of Imre Nagy and His Accomplices*, compares the activities of the Hungarian patriotic uprising in Budapest on October 23, 1956, with the destruction of Bela Kun's regime of terror in 1919. Replete with photographs, this official document attempts to justify Russian intervention, the treason trials, and the execution of Nagy. For example, "Several references have been made in this book *(Counter-Revolutionary Conspiracy . . .)* to the fact that the occurrences during the counterrevolution of 1956 in Hungary could be compared only to the events of the ghastly White Terror in 1919 . . . After the Great October Socialist Revolution, the Hungarian people were the first to support the cause of Socialism. They established the Republic of Councils, defending it, their homeland, with their lives against the aggressive imperialist powers and their Hungarian lackeys. The imperialists helped Miklos Horthy to power, in order to drown in blood and ruthlessly avenge the struggle for independence and freedom of the Hungarian people, to restore the power of the big capitalists and landlords. Horthy's henchmen tortured and murdered the best sons and daughters of the Hungarian people with indescribable brutality. . . ." See "letters of witnesses" and rotogravure section also. *The Counter-Revolutionary Conspiracy of Imre Nagy and His Accomplices* (Budapest: Published by the Information Bureau of the Council of Ministers of the Hungarian People's Republic [*Miniszterlanacs*], 1959), pp. 158-64.

days.) As to his end, it is believed that Kun was liquidated—no longer important to the Kremlin—in the Russian purges of the 1930's. (Although Hungary demanded his extradition, Vienna refused, but permitted his return to Moscow, where he disappeared from history).

The Horthy Regime

Meanwhile, a group of Hungarian nationalists, members of the old Magyar aristocracy, formed a coalition at Szeged to reclaim the realm. Having raised a "White" Army, the leaders of this new national government reached Budapest two days after the withdrawal of the Romanians, who had been influenced by the Western powers to return to the boundary set at Paris. Count Stephen Bethlen, Count Paul Teleki, and Admiral Horthy were the leading members of the junta. This government's effort to destroy the Communists' remaining power has been labeled the "White Terror," for, while a certain justice was inherent in bringing to earth the followers of Szamuelly and Bela Kun, unfortunately a *pogrom* was initiated. By the government's official reckoning at least three hundred perished.

Nevertheless, the Horthy regime could command respect abroad and secured peace through acceptance of the Treaty of Trianon (1920); with Bethlen as Prime Minister, a new economic stability was achieved, although Hungary's trade position—shorn of three-quarters of her former territory, her markets and raw materials—was indeed perilous. Moreover, deserved or no, Hungary gained the reputation of harboring the first Fascism in Europe. Resentment of Trianon and the shrinkage of her boundaries set into motion a call for revisionism, which with the slogan *"Nem, nem, soha!"* ("No, no, never!") was to crystallize Hungarian patriotism and national spirit into a willingness to enter the second World War in the interest of *revanche* and a hope of the return of her irredenta territory.[6]

---

[6] See Victor S. Mamatey, *The United States and East Central Europe, 1914-1918* (Princeton, N.J.: Princeton University Press, 1957), pp. 351-53; Horthy, *op. cit.*, pp. 99-106. Horthy has this

Horthy always held the Western powers responsible
for the Hungarian dilemma of dismemberment and bar-
barianism. Subscribing to an analysis by Owen Rutter,
he says: "Hungary would never have gone Bolshevik if
the Allies had restrained the Secession States from pre-
empting their rights under the coming peace treaty.
Much of the mischief was caused by the extraordinary
influence secured in Paris by the Czech leaders, who not
only obtained the reversion of Slovakia, but also permission to occupy it before the treaty which was to regulate
the cession was either published or signed, while the Romanians and the Yugoslavs secured similar advantages
at Hungary's expense."[7]

While this judgment must be regarded somewhat sus-
piciously, it is—in a way—right. Its correctness springs
from the existence of the power vacuum obtaining in
Hungary at the cracking of the Habsburg Empire; and
defeat in war constituted the real cause. But to put it
another way, Hungarian nationalism was not, at this
time, adequately organized to control the internal situation—although this soon was remedied by the Horthy-
Bethlen group. Strangely enough, Communist revisionist
Hajek puts his finger on the reality of this event, although
his purpose in writing what follows is diametrically opposed to ours. Hajek argues: "As all other proclamations
of President Wilson . . . so also this Wilsonian note [of
October 19, 1918, to Vienna] was not at all a blow leading
to the complete break-up of Austria-Hungary. *This was
already collapsing under the blows of the waves of the
national movement.* On the contrary, one may see in the
note still a reminder of the efforts of the American imperialists to save the Monarchy, at least in the form of a
broad federation. The President simply referred the
Austro-Hungarian government to negotiations with the
bourgeois leadership of the individual nationalities, of

---

comment on the White Terror: "The Communists in Hungary,
willing disciples of the Russian Bolshevists, had indeed let hell
loose [in Hungary]. It took time for the stormy waves to subside
and for law and order, in keeping with our ancient traditions, once
more to prevail throughout the land."

[7] Owen Rutter, *Regent of Hungary* (London: 1939), p. 160. As
quoted in Horthy, *op. cit.*, p. 97.

which Wilson, no less than Vienna, knew that it was
trembling in fear of a real revolution."[8]

With the typical Communist double-talk, Hajek con-
fuses "nationalist rising," undoubtedly the reality, with
"a real revolution," by which one supposes he means
the rise of the proletariat—a Marxist euphemism for the
seizure of the government by Soviet agents. Aside from
the innuendo directed at President Wilson, one can admit
that he correctly assesses the urge to self-determinism.
That Bela Kun gained the power in Hungary does not
prove that he truly represented the "waves of the national
movement." Hungary's demoralization and the temporary hiatus in responsible organized power are sufficient
to demolish Hajek's contention.

With the expectation of regaining what she considered
her lost territories, Hungary entered the second World
War as a partner of Italy and the German Reich. Her
entrance was not effected, however, until mid-1941, and
there are even grounds for believing that she went to
war unwillingly—although the revisionist tendencies
mentioned above were widely shared.[9] Horthy, in his
memoirs, disclaims territorial aims. "Hungary, for her
participation in Hitler's war, has been called an unwilling
satellite. It would have been truer to say that Hungary
tried, with the relatively small means at her disposal, to
defend herself against two encroaching forces: against
the Soviets with all her available arms; against the Nazi
ideology with all her diplomatic powers. . . ."[10]

At the partial collapse of the Axis, Hungary tried, in
October, 1944, to withdraw from the war. Horthy's proclamation reiterated the pacific intentions he attributed
to himself in the *Memoirs:* "Ever since the will of the nation put me at the country's helm, the most important
aim of Hungarian foreign policy has been, through peace-

---

[8] J. S. Hajek, *Wilsonovska legenda v dejinach Ceskoslovenske
Republicky* (Prague, 1953), p. 112. As quoted in Mamatey, *op. cit.*,
pp. 340-41. (Italics added.)

[9] See William L. Shirer, *The Rise and Fall of the Third Reich*
(New York: Simon and Schuster, 1960), pp. 387-88; 449-50. Shirer
shows that, although at first Hungary held back, she eagerly
reached for the plums as the branches of the tree swept lower.

[10] Horthy, *op. cit.*, p. 255.

ful revision, to repair, at least partly, the injustices of
the Peace Treaty or Trianon. . . . Hungary was forced
into war against the Allies by German pressure, which
weighed upon us owing to our geographic situation . . .
the German Reich has lost the war. . . . [Thus] I informed
a representative of the German Reich that we were about
to conclude a military armistice. . . ."[11]

The Communist Take-Over

It was, however, too late for such a maneuver. The
Russians had entered Hungary on October 6. Although
his Western Allies were as yet unconscious of Stalin's
duplicity, Soviet preparations had been made carefully,
and with the Red Army came reserves of professional revolutionaries, including Matyas Rakosi, Zoltan Vas, and
Mihaly Farkas.[12] The lesson learned in 1919 was still
fresh in Soviet memory; this time they acted much more
subtly. Bela Kun was unmentioned. Lajos Kossuth,
said the Marxists, was the patron and precursor of Communism! His opponents, the bourgeois landlords and the
magnates, were enemies of the people, said the Communists. This time the revolution would not be nationalistic
but proletarian.

The Red Army, of course, provided the chief support
for Rakosi and his Communist henchmen. The armistice
agreement with the Soviet Union compelled Hungary to
deliver reparations amounting to the 1938 equivalent of
$200,000,000. The Reds ruthlessly exploited this ar-
rangement, virtually bankrupting the country, and the
systematic impoverishment of Hungary's economic resources is still continuing. A further gimmick for draining the country's economy dry was the so-called Soviet-
Hungarian joint stock companies under Soviet control

---

[11] Horthy, op. cit., "Proclamation of October 15, 1944," pp. 259-
60; See also Shirer, op. cit., p. 1090ff. for mention of the amazing
feat of German agent Otto Skorzeny, who kidnapped the Hungarian
Regent to forestall his surrender to the advancing Red Army (then
in good standing as an equal partner of the Grand Alliance).

[12] See Committee on Foreign Relations, Tensions Within the
Soviet Captive Countries, Part 7: Hungary (Washington: Government Printing Office, 1954).

and management.[13] These phony organizations, by preserving a semblance of private business, eased the path into Socialism on the Russian model.

It is perhaps not too much to assume that actually the Soviet Union was pursuing a policy, similar in most respects to that later identified as genocide. Thousands of Hungarian prisoners of war are still detained in the USSR or have been murdered; steady deportations have sent large numbers of Hungarians to Soviet penal camps and concentration centers. A recent estimate notes that "together with the prisoners of war, about 60,000 men and women were deported to the USSR, especially to the Siberian prison camps."[14] This was only the beginning. It is not likely that the Hungarian people will ever forget —or forgive—the lawlessness, humiliation, and indignities loaded on them during the early Red Regime.[15]

Yet, regardless of propaganda and pressures, the membership in the Hungarian Communist party in 1945 was embarrassingly small. To "correct" this situation, the Party began a broadening of the base of power through the use of a by now familiar device called the "United People's Front." Agreeing to a parliamentary election, the Marxists apparently accepted the principle of parliamentarianism and majority rule. Nevertheless, in the November elections, with 4,700,000 votes cast, only 17 percent went to the Communists. The Reds held only 70 seats as against 245 gained by the Smallholders.

By every parliamentary prerogative, the Smallholders had the privilege of forming the government. The Com-

---

[13] See Howard J. Hilton, *Hungary, A Case History of Soviet Economic Imperialism* (Washington: Department of State, Office of Public Affairs, 1951), pp. 323-27.

[14] Joseph S. Roucek, "The Forced Labor Camps in the Soviet Orbit," *Prologue*, IV, Nos. 1-2 (Spring-Summer, 1960), 64-65; see also Hungarian National Council, *The Memorandum on Forced Labor and Forced Labor Camps* (New York: Free Europe, 1942). Figures submitted by the HNC indicate that the USSR now holds 60,000 prisoners of war and 120,000 civilians.

[15] See Anton F. Wuschek, "A Policy of Genocide," *Sudeten Bulletin* (Munich), IX, No. 1 (January, 1961), 13-14. Although speaking of deportation in the USSR, editor Wuschek's theme correctly describes the tactics by which Hungary was potentially emasculated.

munists, however, notwithstanding their miserable minority, demanded the posts of Vice-Presidency and the Ministry of the Interior. The significance of controlling this latter Ministry in European countries is tremendous, and the Marxists had laid their plans deliberately. The Red Army came to their assistance and, among others, arrested Bela Kovacs, the secretary-general of the Smallholders' party, and the Communist-controlled police placed other members of Parliament under surveillance, even imprisoning or deporting some. A short while later the first President of the Republic, Zoltan Tildy, and the second, former Social Democrat Arpad Szakosits, were taken into custody and removed from office. Following the neutralization of the Smallholders' party, a new election was staged on August 31, 1947, four new parties now replacing the Smallholders. Even more violently anti-Communist in their views, these groups won almost as many votes as had the original Smallholders' party.

In the face of this lack of popularity, the Hungarian Marxists were reduced to abruptly seizing the country's political and constitutional machinery. Backed by Moscow, the Communists forced liquidation upon opposition parties, arrested and killed their leaders, and such collaborationist Social Democrat leaders who remained were summarily merged into the Marxist ranks. On August 18, 1949, a new constitution proclaimed Hungary a "People's Republic of Workers and Working Peasants," the document itself closely resembling that adopted in the USSR in 1936 and in the other satellite "People's Democracies."

By February 29, 1952, the Communist party leaders were bold and secure enough to reveal the workings of their infiltration tactics. "The time has come," spoke Matyas Rakosi at the Main Party School of the Hungarian Workers' party, "to make our Party and the working people understand that the creation of a People's Democracy, as a variety of the dictatorship of the proletariat became possible because . . . the heroic army of the Soviet Union liberated us from the terrible serfdom of the German Fascists and of their Hungarian satellites. . . . It is obvious that the decisive prerequisite, the starting point in the creation of the People's Democracies, was the struggle and the victory of the Soviet Union. Without them there would have been no People's Democracies."[16] Surely the Western world can appreciate how true a statement this is!

Rakosi arrogantly continues:

> The Hungarian Communist Party worked out as early as during World War II the methods which . . . made it possible to win over gradually the support of a majority of the working people. . . . As early as during the Land Reform, we used the tactics of dividing our enemies or of neutralizing them. . . . First we demanded only Governmental control of the banks, later we demanded the nationalization of the three largest. . . . The Smallholders Party and the Social Democratic leaders fought for the survival and strengthening of the Capitalistic system . . . but they did not dare say this openly to the masses. . . .[17]

Where the blunt truth is not enough to reveal Marxist duplicity, there appears the curious inversion or double-talk of Communism, which always attributes to their opponents the subtlety or double-dealing which their own minds at the moment are conceiving.

The Hungarian Uprising of 1956

The results of the Hungarian revolution of 1956 are well known and have already been mentioned. Here again the "White Book" issued by the Information Bureau of the Council of Ministers of the Hungarian People's Republic in 1959, *The Counter-Revolutionary Conspiracy of Imre Nagy and His Accomplices*[18] reveals the Communist mentality a great deal more than it presents history. And the mass expulsions following the revolt were clearly in violation of the spirit of international law.

Dr. jur. Kurt Rabl, an international law expert, reports on the deportations as follows:

---

[16] Quoted from *Tarsadalmi Szemele* (Communist Hungarian party Organ) in *East Europe and Soviet Russia* (London), VIII, No. 375 (April 17, 1952), 5. Other issues of this international newspaper continue Rakosi's revelations.

[17] *Ibid.*, pp. 5-7.

[18] Refer to citation 5.

As we know, the Red Army deported a large number—just how many we shall never know—of Hungarian freedom-fighters to the Soviet Union. This action was unanimously condemned by international public opinion and especially by the investigating committee of the UN on Hungary; these deportations were cited as a "disregard of human rights and basic freedoms." [Yet] as for Soviet Russia, it never called into question this juridical qualification. The deportations were denied, and it was said that no deportations had taken place and if so, they were "blunders of subordinate officers."[19]

Regardless of all this, there are some indications that many Hungarians, unable to leave their homeland, are losing hope that they can throw off the Soviet yoke, and it is undoubtedly true that this cannot be accomplished without Western aid. This, of course, was not forthcoming in 1956.

An Associated Press dispatch on the third anniversary of the Hungarian rising, based on interviews with Dr. Joseph Kovago, former mayor of Budapest, and General Bela Kiraly, former commander of the Hungarian "Freedom Fighters," accused the Soviets of both savagery and treachery. Placing the responsibility for Russian brutality directly on Nikita S. Khrushchev, they said, "He will kill—if his own interest dictates it." These reports, part of a series of U.S. House of Representatives Committee on Un-American Activities findings, are typical of a section entitled "The Crimes of Khrushchev."[20]

Mayor Kovago testified that "the new wave of terror which took place in Hungary after the 1956 unsuccessful revolution [see the Hungarian "White Book" mentioned above] is increasing, and the complete control by the Soviet Union of the country is so striking and so clear to every Hungarian that the people are gradually losing their hope of [ever] regaining freedom." General Kiraly adds: "It means that Hungary today is a nationwide prison, imprisoned by the army units of Nikita Khrushchev."[21] The Red Army is less evident today.

[19] Kurt Rabl, "Mass Expulsions and International Law," *Sudeten Bulletin* (Munich), VIII, Nos. 8/9 (August-September, 1960), 210.

[20] B. L. Livingstone, "Hungarians Said Losing Hope," Associated Press release, October 23, 1959.

[21] *Ibid.*

That the Marxists are maintaining their stranglehold on Hungary is confirmed by recent "election" reports which allocate 99.6 percent of the ballots to the Party. *Nepszabadsag* (Budapest, November 18, 1958) pretends that 98.4 percent of the eligible voters went to the polls to cast an almost total choice for party chief, Janos Kadar, and his People's Patriotic Front slate. While, of course, this list was unopposed and, although it may readily be assumed that various subtle or overt pressures were mustered to drive Hungarian citizens to the "voting" places, the fact remains that—in this first show of parliamentary balloting since October, 1956, and the brutally efficient supression of the Hungarian revolt—the Leninists have demonstrated what must be considered (if only on the grounds of an effective propaganda machine) a terrible and overpowering display of force.[22]

The Red regime furthermore had the gall to assert that "Six-and-a-half-million yeses" (the controlled vote in the November, 1958, balloting) thus "passed the Last Judgment on UN reluctance" and on the positions taken vis-à-vis Hungary "by British and U.S. delegates and their dependents."[23]

The strengthening of Kadar's power is likewise indicated by a strong attack on the Catholic Church in Hungary. Recent reports state that fifty-eight priests have been arrested as the opening round of a strategy to denigrate the Church and to render it unacceptable to Hungarians. The clerics were accused of homosexuality and child molestation.[24] The same pattern of attack has been used in the other satellites especially in the Baltic States.

George F. Kennan, a few months after the Hungarian elections, stated, in as objective a manner as perhaps is possible to American citizens, the U.S. position in regard to Red imperialism, satellitism, and the cold war.

The road to peaceful coexistence lies, admittedly, through many gates; but one of these is the abandonment by Russian Communists

---

[22] "Elections Bring No Changes," as quoted in *East Europe* (New York), VIII, No. 1 (January, 1959), 51-52.

[23] *Idem.*

[24] *Newsweek*, January 30, 1961, p. 10.

of the absurd contention that theirs is a party which has always had a perfect understanding of the human predicament and has never made a mistake.[25]

In conclusion, unless Hungary is to stand as an example for the world of the impunity with which subversive power can corrupt the morals and institutions of an erstwhile free country, commit ideological and actual genocide in respect to its victim, and indulge in a policy of mass expulsion while great democracies nod or avert their eyes, the Western nations and the American people especially must inform themselves of Hungary's role in the war against world Communism, her present precarious situation, and her hope (if indeed there is any) for another chapter of democratic history.

Otherwise, the fruits of a thousand years, the advent of a true and democratic spirit of nationalism, and the recent sacrifices of the great Hungarian people may become nothing more than a further instance of the Communist consignment of the wastepaper of history to the "Memory Hole"—and oblivion; an inadequately played drama that provides for the Party's rationalization of the existence of the Marxist state and its perversion of objective truth.

Yet a recent traveler from the West considers that he was well received by the rank and file of Hungarians regardless of party watchdogs. "I was almost mobbed by friendly people in Budapest. At one stop I was given 27 bouquets of flowers. . . . I'm convinced that 90 percent of the Hungarian people would, if they had the chance, cut the throats of their Communist leaders."[26]

A dissent to friendliness, however, comes from a subgroup in Hungary—the Gypsies. Radio Budapest (statecontrolled) reports that mail from Ujszask, in central

---

[25] George F. Kennan, "Peaceful Coexistence, A Western View," *Foreign Affairs*, XXXVIII, No. 2 (January, 1960), 190. Actually Mr. Kennan's statement represents an American (and Western) rebuttal to Nikita Khrushchev's contentions under a similar title in the October, 1959, issue of *Foreign Affairs*. Kennan considers that "no term has been used more loosely, and at times unscrupulously, than the word "coexistence."

[26] *The Christian Science Monitor* (Boston), August 17, 1963, p. 2.

Hungary, offers complaints of discrimination regardless of the Soviet's vaunted equality of peoples. Two adolescent Gypsies wrote that, although both are members of the Communist youth organization in their locality, "other young people will not associate with us." The rift had gone so far, they said, that they had been blackballed from the House of Culture and had been "driven out" of the Ujszask dancing school.[27] While, as Radio Budapest said, such exclusion naturally violates the stated Soviet policy of pluralism, it is a fact that Hungary's 200,000 Gypsies are generally unsympathetic to the Communist pattern of life. Perhaps the trouble at Ujszask reflects both national feeling and an aversion to Communism—an instance presenting some small expectation of the eventual resurgence and liberation of Hungary.

Richard Nixon, the traveler mentioned above, corroborates this opinion. He saw "something at work there that is similar to the rising nationalism in Western Europe. . . . The United States must not treat East Europe as a bloc."[28] The emotion aroused by Nixon's statement is indeed gratifying, but we must now turn to the agencies of propaganda and education by which the Communist masters plan to retain Hungary.

Education in Hungary

Hungarian authors delight in pointing to the traces of medieval universities on Hungary's soil as the roots of their educational system. Conditioned by the use of Latin as the Hungarian official language for nine hundred years and the literary form for five hundred years, Western culture early gained a foothold. In the thirteenth century an embryonic university appeared at Veszprem, having fifteen doctors to teach Roman and canonical law, and became known for its faculty of law. In 1367, Louis the Great founded another university at Pecs (which, however, ceased to exist in the sixteenth century); the

---

[27] Monitored by Radio Free Europe, Munich, Germany (via *Chicago Daily News* Service, August 7, 1962).

[28] *Christian Science Monitor, loc. cit.*

same fate overtook several similar institutions. In the seventeenth century, the ardor for founding new universities flourished. Peter Pazmany (1570-1673) founded the theological and philological faculties of the present-day Budapest University at Magyszombat, and provided it with boarding schools, library, colleges, and printing offices; later the faculty of law was added. Empress Maria Theresa instituted the faculty of medicine and removed it to Buda (1747). Under King Franz Joseph I, new higher institutions were founded. Koloszvar (now known as Cluj to the Romanians) received a university in 1872, which moved to Szeged after World War I.[29]

When Hungarian spokesmen discourse on the university developments in their country, they tend to tread softly when dealing with the history of fundamental education. According to the government decree of 1868, Act XLIV, provision was made for the equality of education for all peoples of Hungary (according to the Constitution).[30] Individually, each person had a legal right to such an education regardless of nationality; further stipulation was granted which permitted instruction in national tongues. But, in actual practice, Magyarization was prevalent; and the minorities, as well as lower classes, had hardly any educational opportunities. Some authorities consider that the whole educational system was but an instrument of Magyarization. Starting with the elementary school law of 1879, continuing with the law of secondary education of 1883, and ending with the act in regard to kindergarten education of 1891, all these steps were characterized by ever-growing efforts to Magyarize the teachers, to expand public instruction in the Magyar tongue, and to check the use of non-Magyar languages.[31]

---

[29] For more details and pictures of the various historic Hungarian institutions, see: Central Committee of the Budapest Thermal Baths and Health Resorts, *The Cultural Aspirations of Hungary, from 896 to 1935* (Budapest, 1935), pp. 39-81.

[30] C. Revy, *Policy of Hungarian Culture* (Budapest: Athenaeum Ltd., 1946), p. 33; P. H. Pearson, *Schools of Austro-Hungary* (Washington, D.C.: Bureau of Education, Department of Interior Bulletin, No. 54, 1919).

[31] Oscar Jaszi, *The Dissolution of the Habsburg Monarchy* (Chicago: University of Chicago Press, 1928), p. 328.

The denominational schools of the minorities were persistently persecuted, and the state supported exclusively state schools in the Magyar language in the regions inhabited by minorities to counterbalance the schools of the nationalities which, under the circumstances, had insufficient resources and were not too efficient. The resulting high rates of illiteracy were further promoted by the fact that even the agricultural proletariat of a pure Magyar stock did not have even the most elementary instruction. A similar policy was developed in regard to the secondary schools, considered the most important weapons of Magyarization because the leading intellectuals of Hungary were recruited from them. "The chief care of public instruction was not so much the imparting of useful knowledge as a sentimental education according to the ideology of the ruling class."[32] The Slovak high schools, under the pretext of Pan-Slavic intrigues, were closed, and the only non-Magyar college in the country, the German Law School of Magyszeben, was similarly closed. In general, the Magyar population, compared with the non-Magyar population of an almost equal size, had at its disposal in its mother tongue four times as many schools and five times as many teachers; the participation of the Magyar students in secondary and higher education varied between 79.9 percent and 88.8 percent, and that of the Magyar professors was 75.5 percent.[33]

Yet in spite of the numerical differences, the assimilation results were poor, especially on the elementary level, since the pupils went back to their peasant huts, where the old nationalistic pattern was thoroughly efficient in its appeals to all generations. Better Magyarization results were secured in the secondary schools, as instruction there was far more intense and the educational institutions in larger towns and cities were helped by the attractiveness of Magyar social life. In this respect, the ruling group succeeded in recruiting members from every minority, though principally from among the Germans and the Jews. The Germans, although deserted by Vienna

---

[32] *Ibid.*, p. 329.
[33] *Ibid.*, p. 329-30.

and by Germany, retained their dominant position in commerce and industry and often acquired Magyar cultural characteristics in the process; the Jews, after emerging from the Ghetto, became vocal advocates of "assimilation," and helped Magyar culture with their brilliance in literature and the arts.

At the same time, however, many graduates from the secondary schools, and some university graduates, became the most persistent supporters of the claims of their nationalities. Others had studied abroad, and their contacts with the minority leaders helped to kindle their irredentism. The Slovak youth went to Prague to study under Masaryk; the Romanians visited Bucharest or France; and the South Slavs often attended the Belgrade institutions (although even more frequently they went to Prague, France, and to a lesser extent to Germany). The resistance process was strengthened by the administrative policy of the government which favored appointments of the members of the Magyar ruling classes, who usually could not speak the language of the minority groups. The resulting administrative grievances became but another expression of Magyar oppression and of the general conviction that the government had not the least interest in the real or imaginary grievances of the minorities. This cultural and administrative policy was carried on, furthermore, with the help of the antiquated and corrupt electoral system. Hundreds of thousands of unhappy emigrants left for America. In 1914, three-fourths of the male population in Hungary could not vote.

Education Between Two World Wars

After World War I, the Hungarian educational system again allegedly insured the instruction of minorities in their mother tongue more than any other Danubian country. The nation was divided into eight school districts (which excluded the high schools). Among the ten categorized types, three principal ones were: The *Nepiskola* ("People's School"), an elementary school of eight grades (similar to the typical American grammar school), the *Polgari* ("Citizen") School catering to the *bourgeoisie*, and the *Gimnasium* (a modified high school). Students were allowed to enter the latter after completing only four years of the *Nepiskola*. The *Polgari* consisted of four grades for students between the ages of ten and fourteen; the *Gimnasium* had eight grades and enrolled students between the ages of ten to eighteen; *Polgari* graduates were allowed to enter the fifth grade of the *Gimnasium* after passing an entrance examination.

The educational system reflected the social structure of the country. In 1935, of the 16,326 university and high-school students, 40.3 percent came from the following backgrounds: landowners, independent tradesmen, civil servants, capital investors, military officials, and other intellectual and professional groups; 59.7 percent were from agricultural, small holding, laborer, and commercial origins. These figures are clarifying, as the Communists claim that in the past a "gigantic" percentage of the students were from the upper classes.[34]

World War II Fortunes

Fighting under the Nazi, Hungary lost World War II. From being a Kingdom (without a King), and ruled by an Admiral (without a navy), Hungary, under Russian occupation, changed into a Popular Democracy. The ruling clique was swept aside, this time really in earnest. The magnates who until recently had owned one-half of the soil and national wealth were suddenly outlawed as property owners, together with the home-grown Fascists who had started to share their power since the 1930's.[35] In their ranks were many of Hungary's landed gentry, who had sold their depressed farms and could find no occupations in towns—in spite of their education—especially government jobs; they wanted to move into the professions and business and industry—only to find them al-

[34] Louis Nekam, *Cultural Aspirations of Hungary* (Budapest: Pazmany University, 1935), p. 74.

[35] Howard K. Smith, *The State of Europe* (New York: Alfred A. Knopf, 1949), p. 16; "Hungarian Rhapsody in Red," pp. 296-319. For the changing fortunes of Hungarian politics, see: Joseph S. Roucek, *Governments and Politics Abroad* (New York: Funk and Wagnalls, 1948), chap. 12, "Hungary," pp. 388-406.

ready overcrowded by Jews. This combination of feudal lords and the sons of landed wealth, bitterly anti-Semitic and feudal in outlook, had controlled the government with their anti-Semitic slogans and imperial chauvinism in foreign policy. But the Hungarian Nazis and magnates were not too happy when fighting together in the war. At any rate, Hungary received more territorial favors from Hitler than any other satellite (parts of Slovakia and all of Carpatho-Ukraine from Czechoslovakia, all of Transylvania from Romania, the Banat from Yugoslavia, and was promised colonies in dismembered Russia). When the Stalingrad fiasco came, Admiral Horthy tried to make a separate peace with the Allies. But it was too late. The Russians invaded Hungary and took it in a few weeks. In subsequent months, and for long years, Hungary underwent an all-embracing revolution which changed the country more than the previous nine centuries. Because of the presence of the Red army, the transformation was "the smoothest transition to 'People's Democracy' effected by any of the East European countries."[36] There was no mass upheaval and threats of civil war (as in East Germany), no actual civil war (as in Poland), and only a few arrests. Formerly the most feudal country in Europe, the regime became the most promising of the new Communist dictatorships. Of course, the change was effected with the Russian forces ready to "help" any unwilling "volunteer" in this process. Then Russia started to "harness the satellite to her forever by economic and political measures." Reparations were used to dictate the economic and industrial changes and plans of Hungary; at the same time, according to the Peace Treaties provisions, Russia took over all formerly German-owned industries (5 percent of all Hungarian industry). Long-term trade treaties tied up the economy of Hungary.

All these tasks were accomplished by the native Hungarian Communists, who formerly had had no popular support in the country. The Communists made a special effort to cultivate the mighty, conservative Catholic

---

[36] Smith, op. cit., p. 300; Paul E. Zinner, Revolution in Hungary (New York: Columbia University Press, 1962), pp. 3-23.

Church, by agreeing in the land reform to let the Church keep a large proportion of its land and by retaining compulsory religious education in the schools—for a while; they even sent Communist Youth brigades to help rebuild damaged churches. They were also slow, at first, to purge Fascists and reactionaries, retaining many of them in the bureaucratic setup. Only after the elections of 1945 and the formation of the Cominform, Matyas Rakosi, the chief of the Communists, maneuvered the destruction of the powerful Smallholders' party, with the help of their more pro-Communist allies, the Socialists and the Radical Peasants. Pressure was exerted to purge the Socialists of the "rightists" and have them fuse with the Communists in a big "Working People's party." By 1949, the change to "People's Democracy" was complete, and the usual run of executions and persecutions of the "deviationists" as in other satellites began to feature Hungary's political course, including the persecution of the Catholic Church.[37]

At first the country was bled white by feeding the Russian occupational army and by paying reparations. But, at the end of 1948, when Cardinal Mindszenty was arrested, industrial production was above the prewar level, and the standard of living of the masses was higher than in all of Hungarian history; the budget, for the first time, showed a surplus.

Then came the sovietization measures, aimed to win a majority of the smaller peasants and workers. All factories employing more than one hundred workers were nationalized; the middle classes were hit by the revaluation of prices and wages paralleling the conversion of currency at the end of the inflation. While the land reform had distributed 6,400,000 acres among 600,000 landless peasants, the government started attacking the

---

[37] The case of Cardinal Mindszenty, the Prince Primate of the Hungarian Catholic Church, attracted world-wide attention; but strange to say, the argument was not entirely on the principle of religious freedom. Smith, *op. cit.*, p. 311, reports that, "The Cardinal allowed himself to be maneuvered into the position of fighting to maintain the near monopoly of privilege enjoyed by the Catholic over the Protestant and Jewish churches." There are other views of this, however.

rural middle classes by pushing cooperatives and making them the main channel for distributing town goods. Then the government proceeded to replace the bureaucratic elements with the sons of poor peasants. "Of 7,000,000 students enrolled in the government's new schools to train civil servants in 1948, no less than 6,000,000 were of working-class or peasant origin."[38]

While Hungary showed, in subsequent years, some astounding advances in its economic plans, political repression featured periodically all the news from there; Budapest also has carried on a "cold war" with Washington, and evidently became more and more dependent upon the USSR. By 1952, it had become evident that the grandiose schemes for the industrialization of Hungary and its integration with the Soviet bloc were not going according to schedule. In July, 1953, Matyas Rakosi was dismissed as Premier, and his successor was the former Minister of Agriculture, fifty-seven-year-old Imre Nagy. Impressed by the popular uprising against Communist rule in East Berlin two weeks earlier, Nagy told his countrymen he would follow a policy of less forced industrialization, lower prices, higher wages, more food, and a general amnesty for past offenses. (The implications of his "New Course" policy are treated at the end of this chapter.)

The Pro-Communist Reorganization of Education

A complete transformation of the education of Hungary has been effected by the Hungarian pro-Communist government. The usual claim has been that preliberation Hungary possessed a class-biased system which collided with the best interests of state Socialism. The pro-Communist regime has allegedly abolished this feudal type of organization by permitting the masses to acquire a means of education. The government pronouncements of new policies intended to connote raised standards of education. For instance, nationalization of the schools, it was asserted, was a century-old demand which had

---

[38] Howard K. Smith, *op. cit.*, p. 317; Zinner, *op. cit.*, pp. 123-25.

been ruefully neglected. Theoretically, this state approach to education was the cause of the struggle between the clerical-bourgeois (conservative) groups and the Communists. With the Soviet experiments as its shining model, the Hungarian state's educational program proceeded to meet the goals of Socialist education.

Before World War II, say the Communists, two-thirds of the population was composed of peasants and workers —and yet this group comprised only 5-6 percent of the total school enrollment. The schools of the prewar period and during the war days, according to the Communist claims, had housed the forces of chauvinism, racialism, and Fascism. Furthermore, the regime claims that the Horthy government had inflamed the upper levels of society against the neighboring states. The Church, too, had dominated the educational scene. These claims are forever heard in the Communist drives against the so-called "clerical reactionaries."

The reorganization of the educational system, which commenced in 1945, was to achieve the following goals: (1) to disestablish the class character of education; (2) to break the monopoly of the ruling classes in their hold on the educational future of the country; (3) to elevate the standards of education which had been neglected for the past century; (4) to free the teachers who had been the tools of reactionary regimes and vested interests; (5) to terminate the educational heritage of the Church; (6) to revitalize the spirit of education by the replacement of fascist ideologies with Marxist-Leninist philosophies; and (7) to neutralize nationalistic tendencies through the creation of Socialist patriotism. These were to be attained through the complete, unlimited, and unrestricted power of the state in guiding educational policies.[39]

The new regime was faced with many problems when starting to promote these goals, especially the achievement of equality in education and the attainment of mass

---

[39] The best systematic study of this aspect is: James S. Bodnar, *Education:* "The Communist Weapon in Hungary" (unpublished M. A. thesis, October, 1953, New York University).

cultural participation as part of the educational policy of the state.

According to the Hungarian Constitution of 1949, the workers were assured the right to have access to all educational media. The government further implemented this right through a grant of all educational facilities, by providing a free and compulsory education (through the general school level), state secondary and high schools, and aid to adult students (evening students, those working during the day). An educational "revolution," the Communists believed, was possible only through the combination of the educational program with the economic plan of the state. This meant nationalization of the schools—the Church standing alone as the sole opponent to such a drastic change. (But the new organization of 1948 allowed the maintenance of a number of schools outside the state system by Protestant denominations, and an agreement was signed whereby the Catholic Church held onto several institutions.)

Regarding the gearing of the education program into the economic plan, the broad objectives of the five-year plan (1949) enhanced the allocation of two and a half million *forints* for cultural advancement, which included compulsory eight-year schooling; the training of 100,000 new specialists in the administrative, economic, and cultural fields; construction of educational institutions; improvements of teacher-training courses; new equipment; and industrial apprenticeships.[40]

Operating on the premise that man is constantly changing himself as society changes, the Communists reformed the methods and content of teaching procedures. The broad and general education was designated to emphasize the "bread and butter" subjects—languages, mathematics, gymnastics, social and natural sciences, with opportunities in the fields of music and art. Science curricula have been raised and related to the practical problems of the day (in terms of the Communist changes).

---

[40] Simon Sandor, *The Five-Year Plan of Hungary* (Budapest: Athenaeum Nyomda, 1949), pp. 27-31.

Prior to 1945, Hungarian children could enroll in six-year public schools, or eight-year "civic" schools. Children between ten and eighteen were eligible for eight years of (private) gymnasium, which during the prewar years had evolved into two types: the humanistic gymnasium with emphasis on classical languages, and the real gymnasium stressing science and mathematics. "Civic" schools were attended by graduates of the first four grades of grammar school who either did not wish or could not afford to go through eight years of gymnasium. However, "civic" school graduates could enroll in the fifth grade of gymnasium after passing a special examination.

Sovietization

With the advent of the Communist regime, an eight-grade public school and the general school, sometimes referred to as the "united school," replaced the schools of the prewar period. The major differences between the Communist public school curriculum and that of the prewar period, and that of the transitional period of 1945-48, were the omission of religious instruction, Latin, and modern languages, and the insertion of such courses as "Life of Man" and "Free Conversation." Furthermore, greater emphasis was placed on natural history, science, and technical training. Russian was introduced as the main foreign language. The prewar humanistic gymnasium became the classical or modern language school, and the real gymnasium evolved into the scientific gymnasium. Instead of being an eight-year school, it is now comparable to a four-year high school. Set up by the Ministry of Education's decrees of 1947-48, the curriculum of the scientific gymnasium, the most prevalent type of high school (secondary school in American terminology) (approximately 80 percent of the total) includes among its courses the fifteen which are noted below in order of their importance. (The hours indicated refer to the aggregate class hours of all four grades of the school per week): Russian—nineteen hours per week; Hungarian language and literature—thirteen hours;

history, physics, arithmetic—twelve hours for each; physical culture—two hours; Everyday Problems, music, natural history, art—four hours for each; economic and social sciences, hygiene—three hours for each; Marxism-Leninism, geography, and ethnography—two hours for each.

Communist ideology is taught in the classes of economic and social sciences, Marxism-Leninism and Everyday Problems; every class is conducted according to the principles of Communist dogma, particularly those in history, Hungarian literature, geography, and Russian. Science is given priority in the scientific high school as well as in the united school.

Latin is taught as the second language in the classical gymnasium for a relatively large number of hours per week. But the significance of including this otherwise taboo subject in the curriculum is lessened because of the small percentage of such gymnasia in the country as a whole. The classical school represents only 3 percent of all high schools and only 10 percent of the gymnasium system. The modern language gymnasium offers a choice between French and German. English is optional, theoretically, but does not appear on the official listings of school programs.

The Formal Structure

The educational system is rigidly controlled by the state through the Ministry of Religion and Public Education, with an advisory body, the National Council for Public Education. The Educational Ministry ranks eighth among a total of twenty-four Ministries existing within the Council of Ministers, the highest organ of state authority. Local administration in education simply enforces the decrees and laws of the central authority.

A unified school system has been established for all children between the ages of six to fourteen, up to and including the eighth grade. The *Polgari* and the first four grades of the gymnasium have been abolished. The gymnasium starts with its former fifth grade.

The following divisions show that Hungary has a com-

prehensive educational framework, state style, from
"birth to death."

Nursery schools fell in line with the educational goal
set forth by the government in 1952-53. This was a policy
of molding "new soldiers" for the "New Order." The
nursery schools provided the beginning of Socialist training (from three to six) ; these institutions are also helpful
to the regime, since they permit the parents to work
longer hours in factories.

General schools, compulsory and comprehensive in
nature, enroll children within the age bracket of six to
fourteen. In 1949-50 there were more than 1,214,000 out
of 8,000,000 students of compulsory school age who attended general schools in which the children of six
through ten were taught by general instructors; and the
ten- to fourteen-year-olds taught by specialized teachers.
But the problem of how to maintain a complete system
of educational quality within the rural framework has
not been solved. In order to relieve the situation, the
government has tried to maintain schools for the students
of ages six to ten in the villages, transporting the older
students to cities and neighboring towns which possess
more adequate facilities.

Secondary schools train children between the ages of
fourteen and eighteen; they are arranged in four divisions: General, technical (thirteen of them), agricultural, and economic. (The agricultural branch is directly
under the control of the Ministry of Agriculture.) The
economic schools indoctrinate students with the ideas of
planned economy of a Socialistic state. The Communists
claim that 60 to 65 percent of the students in secondary
education are from peasant and worker origins.

Those passing on to the high schools (universities) are
selected on the basis of report cards and parental status,
as well as "state selection" by the school principal; the
former I.Q. examinations have been abolished. One agricultural, one economic, and two technical universities
are located at Budapest, Pecs, Szeged, and Debrecen
The most important demand on the universities is that
of producing specialists' schools for the training of students in the fields of arts and sciences.

Religious and ethical studies have been discouraged and have nearly disappeared. In order to enroll in religious courses, the students must provide statements of intention from their parents and submit them to local councils. School reports do not include marks for religious subjects. Religious teachers are under constant surveillance of state authorities. More emphasis has been placed upon natural history, science, and technical training. Dialectical propaganda is the chief form of Communist education in high schools. Latin and some modern languages have been eliminated and Russian has been substituted.

Education as a Branch of Politics

To the Hungarian Communists, education is a branch of politics. The February, 1950, issue of Budapest's *Kozneveles* ("Public Education") outlined an elementary school curriculum produced by the Hungarian Ministry of Education, running true to the pre-Khrushchev doctrine:

First Grade: Lectures on Stalin's military life. Poems and songs about Stalin learned by heart. Pupils to be shown pictures from various stages of the Soviet Generalissimo's career.

Second Grade: "Stalin, the best disciple of Lenin." Soviet military campaigns in World War II. The liberation of Hungary by the Red Army. How Russia aided Hungary's postwar reconstruction.

Fifth Grade: Comparison of current Hungarian Five-Year Plan with the Soviet plan. Machinations of the Standard Oil Company's imperialistic saboteurs.

Sixth Grade: Stalin's peace policy. How the USSR in World War II crushed Fascism in Europe.

Seventh Grade: The United States, bulwark of imperialism. While Soviet science moves mountains and diverts rivers for the good of the people, in the United States science and industry prepare for war. Wheat is burned, workers exploited, and the Communist party persecuted. Even courses apparently unrelated to Communism are taught in terms of Soviet propaganda.

Kozneveles instructs teachers to draw their arithmetic and geometry problems from figures relating to Russian industrial production, culture, and farming.

The methods of teaching have been revised and are based upon Russian terms: Stalin's linguistic principles, Mongolin's theories of reading; Golubkov's methods in teaching literature, Bregyes' procedures in mathematics; and Feldt's principles of chemistry. Historical styles have been introduced by Korcev, as well as Makarenko's pedagogical principles. The traditional and formal approaches to education have been dubbed "reactionary."

In July, 1948, a committee with the Hungarian Working People's (Communist) party was formed to serve as a vigilant outpost for Narodniklike deviations, appearing as bourgeois liberalism in education. Rejecting the bourgeois liberal trends as well as the psychoanalytical works of the aforementioned Soviet scholars like Kalanin and Makarenko.

Teaching in Hungary is among the lowest paid professions. Hungarian teachers can earn on the average of 600 to 670 *forints* a month ($54-$60), the amount a Stakhanovite worker can earn in a week. His first promotion comes only after five years, then his salary is increaed by 65 *forints*. This contrasts sharply with the salaries of instructors in charge of party indoctrination courses organized for teachers. Such instructors are paid $1,100 *forints* a month and enjoy additional privileges.

Auxiliary Organizations

The Ministry of Education has stressed the operation of Parent Organizations, whose aim is: (1) to enlist support of parents for the program being carried out by the state schools; (2) to enable the parents to understand Socialist pedagogy in the discharge of their educational duties; and (3) to establish close relations between the school and community. According to the authorities, at least 60 percent of the parents have been active in such groups, meeting fortnightly.

The teachers' Union has been hailed by the Communists as the most powerful weapon in the educational field; the membership is more than fifty thousand (including all grade levels). The Unions help in the administration of social insurance (marriage, sickness, death, etc.) and a half-dozen "holiday homes." Supposedly teachers receive a three-month vacation period per year; but four of these weeks are spent in summer camps helping children to improve their regular course of education. Receiving extra pay for these additional jobs, the teachers have allegedly, also obtained steady increments.

There are numerous school clubs and youth organizations; the school clubs, on all grade levels, have their organizations named after famous Russians who, in most cases, had been up to now unknown to the Hungarians. The chief objective of these organizations is Russification and education according to the Communist spirit.

In 1950 the Communist party decreed the foundation of a Hungarian youth organization, called DISZ, a group similar to the Russian *Komsomol*.[41] Like similar organizations in all satellite states, it is a direct auxiliary to the pro-Communist regime. It amalgamates all youth between the ages of thirteen and twenty-one. Before forming the DISZ, such organizations as the MINSZ (Popular Federation of Hungarian Youth) directed the work of its affiliated groups—the SZIT (Trade Union Youth), MEFESZ (University Students), and EPOSZ (Peasant Youth).

Control of Mass Communications

Budapest is in complete control of all mass media of communications. The press is concentrated in the capital; Budapest's six largest dailies have national circulation. First and foremost among the dailies is *Szabad Nep* ("Free People"), run by the Ministry of Public Information; it is the central organ of the Hungarian Working People's party. (The only foreign-language newspaper is a weekly, published in Slovak.)

----

[41] For more details see William Juhasz, *Blueprint for a Red Generation* (New York: Mid-European Studies Center, 1952).

The government has boasted of a tremendous increase in the number of radio licenses granted (some six thousand). Like the news agencies, the Hungarian Broadcasting Company is owned by the government and by the Central Council of Trade Unions; programs are controlled by the Central Office of Information. Short-wave programs, lasting eleven hours daily, are broadcast to other European countries in six languages. Educational broadcasts are transmitted daily to more than five hundred listening schools, and one hour per day is devoted to adult education. There is a radio distribution system for hospitals and many of the rural villages are provided with public loudspeakers.[42]

Of special interest is the use of "wired radio" in Hungary (and this is found in Romania as well); this represents a system of radio broadcasting in which the broadcasts are transmitted by means of a wire connected to all receivers. It is based on one centrally directed program, which is the sole fare allowed to listeners. The loudspeaker does not pick up radio waves from the air, but only amplifies the program transmitted by wire. In this way it resembles a large telephone network, where one person is capable of speaking to many at the same time. (This same system was used extensively by the Germans during World War II and is called *Drahtfunk;* it is also utilized in the Soviet Union, where the wire is conventionally connected to the local "House of Culture," where the population has been assembled to listen to the broadcast.)

Hungary has been the center of the satellite radio propaganda network. Programs are beamed to Great Britain and the United States. Programs to France include the Trade Union Program and the Youth Program; both of these appear on most of the language schedules. The German programs are beamed to Austria and Germany, West as well as East. The DISZ (the Hungarian Federation of Democratic Youth) arranges special radio broadcasts to "acquaint the youth of the world" with Marxist-

---

[42] UNESCO, *World Communications, Press, Radio, Film, Television* (Paris: UNESCO, 1951), p. 114.

Leninist teachings. The World Federation of Democratic Youth broadcasts from Peking and Prague, as well as Budapest, with special programs in ten languages.

The film industry has also played a considerable role in the formation of Communist goals in education. There are three main production systems united in one state company. Some twenty documentaries have been produced since the war, and the state newsreel company, UNFI, issues one weekly and one monthly newsreel. Showing of domestic newsreels and documentaries is compulsory. The majority of the imported films are from the USSR. The Educational Film Institute, under the Film Office, produced five educational films in the 1945-49 period. Most characteristic of the film themes is the intense aim of the regime to overcome and eradicate public reverence for the past traditions which might be contrary to the Communist ideology; there have been three basic sources of film plots: (1) the incessant hatred for the Habsburg monarchy; (2) the corruption of the Church; and (3) capitalistic exploitation of the masses in preliberated Hungary and the West.

The first model of a television receiving set was to have been completed in Hungary by Stalin's birthday on December 21, 1951, but the birthday passed without any statement on television. Somewhat later, however, a press item noted that "only one sample will be completed and it will take a long, long time until a series of sets can be made."

According to the reports of refugees, research proceeded along English lines until the introduction of Soviet equipment. The primary work in this field has been the imitation of foreign, chiefly Western instruments. Because these no longer reach Hungary legally, several officials have been commissioned to cannibalize parts from old material and instruments obtained by dismantling shot-down American planes. Other components were obtained from the London Radio Exhibition in 1948, and these are still used as the basis for research, But the lack of vital parts prevented the construction of even a primitive TV station by the Orion factory in Budapest. The Technical Research Institute was founded in

Budapest and ordered by the government to produce the missing parts. Research Institute III, as it was called, studied Western technical publications and worked on available equipment but was unable to complete the project; the imported Russian specialists returned home advising the twenty or more Hungarian engineers employed on the project to do their best and make use of local products. These Hungarian technicians continued their research under the aegis of the Communications Research Institute, which controls all developments in the communications sphere; in its laboratories, located in Budapest's Tungram factory, Hungarian experts have been experimenting on magnetrons and klystrons (the klystron, used in TV transmitters, is an ultra-high device and although long used in the West was demonstrated to Hungarian technicians as new).

Adult Education

All adult "workers" in Hungary are expected and compelled to become militant students within the framework outlined by the Communist masters. They are constantly subject to ideological teaching, to molding and remolding —even those who are considered to be reliable Communists, so that they would not be subject to the danger of deviation. Party education is compulsory for all, even for those in the jails and concentration camps. "Adult ideological 'education' is probably more intense in a Communist Hungary, and the other satellite countries, than it is even in the Soviet Union. This is because, after thirty-five years, the average Soviet citizen has no personal experience of any but Communist life and is considered politically safer."[43] Since Hungary has a predominance of people who had hated Russia and who remember that their country had been independent, they have to be subjected to a constant and intense ideological barrage. This is done not only by persistent repetition of simple slogans and catch phrases in the press, the radio, in the schools, and by speakers at every compulsory

---

[43] Juhasz, *op. cit.*, p. 75.

meeting, but also by all other means of communication reaching places of employment and the home. All apartment houses have house commissars who control the tenants; each city block has a "public educator," and more recently a separate "fight for peace" Commissar. All cities are subdivided into districts over which local Soviets have authority, and each district has its own party secretariat and cultural committee. The public educator visits each family in his block at least twice a week and conducts a brief ideological examination of its members. He is also responsible for the appointment of house cultural commissars for the large apartment buildings, and with their help holds weekly discussions of suggested materials and books. The "fight for peace" Commissar indoctrinates the worker and his family with the Communist approach to world politics—all of it but the exposition of various world Communist plans created by the Cominform. The eternal theme is a fight against the bloodthirsty imperialists, headed by the United States, for a fuller, happier life; all Soviet achievements and "peace steps" are glorified. Special women's meetings are held by the "fight for peace" Commissars in each large apartment house or at a *designated location for those living in a block of smaller buildings.* Attendance is compulsory, and women are encouraged to bring their children.

Since Hungary is in desperate need of a whole new stratum of Communist "educators," twenty-five new schools of culture were opened in Budapest in different districts. They are of five types and serve the special training of culture wardens, public organizers, librarians for factories and mass organizations, organizers of "Homes of Culture," and those for training actors and producers among the gifted members of "cultural groups." These courses last for eight weeks.

Equal or greater importance is attached to adult education in rural districts, where cultural committees are organized to embrace the less populated farm districts and smaller villages. Special adult discussion groups take up the "scientific problems of agriculture." Rural adult education is primarily carried out on Sundays, with the local schoolteachers, the librarian, and the cultural Commissar bearing the load.

Special Workers' Schools have been founded to give higher education to adults with four to six years of elementary schooling. Two-year condensed courses have been inaugurated and award a technological high school diploma.

The National Committee of People's Culture runs the endless rounds of National Cultural Competitions in various dramatic and choral groups in villages, towns, and cities. Folk dancing and singing are especially featured. Numerous intercultural and sports visits are carried on with other satellite countries (including Communist China), or at least were before 1960.

Higher Institutions of Learning

It is in the field of higher education that Communism has achieved its greatest expansion in Hungary.[44]

There are twenty-one universities and high schools in Hungary, compared to only twelve in 1938 under Admiral Horthy's regime. The number of students in these institutions has more than doubled from about 12,000 in 1938 to nearly 30,000 in 1950. Applicants are carefully screened as regards both their politics and their parentage and those of bourgeois or kulak (wealthy farmer) origin are excluded as far as possible.

Hungary, with a population of 9.50 million people, maintains, in addition to a long list of old and new junior colleges, several technological universities (Technological University of Budapest, Heavy Industrial Technological University in Veszprem, Heavy Industrial Technological University in Miskolc, etc.) which have assumed paramount importance. Hungarian industrialization and the growing industrial requirements of Eastern Germany, Czechoslovakia, and Hungary have created a tre-

---

[44] William Juhasz, *Blueprint for a Red Generation* (New York: Mid-European Studies Center, 1952, "Higher Education," pp. 53-60; M. M. Chambers (ed.), *Universities of the World Outside U.S.A.* (Washington: American Council on Education, 1950), "Hungary," pp. 499-507.

mendous demand for new engineers. The relative change in importance of different majors in universities is shown in the following table comparing the distribution of university students according to colleges today with prewar distribution:

College	Precentage of university students Prewar	Today
Engineering, chemistry	9.0	34.0
Philosophy	18.3	24.8
Medicine	12.4	8.8
Economics	6.6	9.8
Law	39.0	3.8
Art	2.7	3.9

But we must view these figures critically, especially in the field of philosophy; this field, according to the present masters of Hungary, means the study of Marxist and Leninist philosophy and the various branches of Communist dogma and dialectics.

In 1953, it was decided that the Budapest Polytechnic University was to be decentralized; the faculty of architecture was to become a separate university; and near the Polytechnic a new university was to be built.

According to the Soviet pattern, universities maintain departments of Marxism-Leninism, sociology and economics, literature and history, medicine and natural sciences. For technological studies there are separate universities such as the University of Transportation and Traffic, the University of Industrial Chemistry (which deals largely in explosives), and that of Heavy (machine) Industry. Although Western subjects are excluded in the university as well as in the schools, university students receive a short course in Western philosophy entitled "Reactionary Philosophy." This course includes such philosophers as Aristotle, Plato, Descartes, Leibnitz, and Kant, and deprecates their works in favor of Karl Marx and his contemporaries (Engels, David Strauss, and Feuerbach). Hegel is the one exception to this rule, in recognition of the fact that Marxian philosophy is based on Hegel's dialectics. Each university has a Russian institute for the study of the Russian language, literature, philosophy and constitution, and history. In order to be in good standing, each student must register with this Institute.[45]

Employment and Assignments

Academic specialization under the pro-Soviet plan is the prelude to professional specialization for the fulfillment of the state's requirements. In 1952, according to a decree, it became compulsory after March 23 for university, high-school, and trade-school students to acquire practical professional experience. (The decree did not apply to members of the Armed Forces or graduates of universities, high schools, or technical secondary schools maintained by the Armed Forces, graduates of the academy for diplomatic service, or for those attending evening or correspondence courses.) The period of compulsory professional practice is two years for university and high-school graduates and eighteen months for the graduates of technical secondary schools. The pupils are assigned to their places of work by the Minister under whose jurisdiction their particular school belongs. The graduate must receive the ministerial decision in writing simultaneously with his or her degree, diploma, or graduation certificate. The new graduate enters his assigned place of employment under contract for a fixed term. If he wishes to continue to work for the same firm after the expiration of that term, the labor relationship may be prolonged indefinitely, and in that case the start of the compulsory practice period counts as the start of employment only by permission of the competent Minister. If, however, the assigned job is not in accordance with the graduate's professional training, his complaint is heard personally, and, if justified, remedied by the head of the immediate supervisory organ. Completion of the compulsory period must be registered in the employment book.[46]

Under the new university statutes issued in 1951, the

---

[45] " 'Patriotic' Re-Education," *News Behind the Iron Curtain*, I, 4 (April, 1952), 33.

[46] *Ibid.*, p. 34.

traditional right of the universities there to appoint their own deans and professors was transferred to the government.

Within the framework of their present cultural isolation, the satellites have been trying to give Communist culture a worldwide significance. Cultural contacts with the Communist Far East have been especially promoted. Hungary, Romania, and Poland have cultural agreements among each other and with China. In compliance with Moscow's orders, Hungary became host to Chinese, Korean, and Vietnamese students who were put to work in the Stalinvares Iron Works (on the Danube near Budapest). A delegation of Hungarian Pioneers visited the schools of North Korean children on the occasion of Liberation Day (Liberation of Hungary from German occupation). Hungary has also imported North Korean children and "educated" them.

Education of Minorities

Communist spokesmen have made a great deal of fuss over the endowment of cultural rights of minorities in Hungary. The 1949 Constitution provides that the minorities may be educated in their own national tongues and possess the right to foster their own culture. This has been applied in particular to the South Slav communities in the region of the Tisza River (southwestern Hungary), representing settlements of some 60,000. They have their own general, secondary, and teacher-training institutions and textbooks. University students can hear lectures in Croat and Serbian.

Religious Problems

The Marxist regime has made every effort to destroy Hungary's religious spirit. (Hungary had 65.6 percent Catholics, 26.8 percent Calvinists and Lutherans, 2.5 percent Greek Catholics, 1.4 percent Jewish, and 0.4 percent Greek Orthodox followers.) During 1944-47, a comparatively tolerant attitude toward religion was taken by the rulers. But in January, 1948, the most

violent phase of the anti-religious campaign opened. Denominational schools were nationalized; by 1950 all religious instruction was controlled and regimented; religious orders abolished; convents and monasteries closed,
and priests, monks, and nuns deported. The trial of
Cardinal Jozef Mindszenty, Prince Primate of the Roman
Catholic Church in Hungary, shocked the Western world.

After 1948, under duress, agreements were concluded
between the regime and the regimented Church. But the
government has continued in transforming church organizations and the religious press into instruments of
Communist-led propaganda. Yet all reports indicate that
faith and religion persist in Hungary. Significantly
enough, the Party was forced to warn the machinery
against establishing adherence to religious beliefs as an
obstacle to party membership.

We can readily accept the conclusions of a special report on 1954 conditions in Hungary:

> The Communist regime in Hungary is confronted with the inexor-
> able alternative of either maintaining its minority dictatorship
> which is bound to generate an ever-increasing opposition among
> the people, or of loosening its total grip on the country by making
> real concessions—a course which would be incompatible with Com-
> munism's fundamental tenets and purposes. Neither alternative
> augurs well for the future of Communism in Hungary.[47]

Russification

The task of building a "new Socialist man" begins at
the cradle in Hungary. The child grows up ignorant of
Western "bourgeois" culture, and in the classroom is
taught to hate the West and love the Soviet Union. The
"love of the fatherland" implies the child's willingness to
defend it against "imperialist attacks," and therefore
paramilitary training has an important place in the
school curriculum. But nowhere is Marxist direction so
apparent as in the rewritten textbooks used by the satellites. The Communist aim is to present a revision of

---

[47] Committee on Foreign Relations, *Tensions Within the Soviet
Captive Countries*; Part 7: *Hungary* (Washington, D.C.: Government Printing Office, 1954), p. 206.

history and life in the Western world which glorifies the Soviet Union and Socialism, which makes the United States appear to be a nation of slave drivers, capitalists bent upon war, oppressed Negroes, hungry children, and unemployed workers.[48]

This ideological conditioning is but one aspect of the basic goal of pro-Soviet education: the complete destruction of the cultural heritage of Hungary, which has always been anti-Russian and pro-Western. This process is aimed directly at youth and intended to bear fruit in ten to fifteen years. A campaign to substitute "mass songs" for the famed old Hungarian folk songs has been undertaken; the nature of these mass songs is indicated by the Moscow radio, which declared them the "songs of Soviet celebrations in Hungary."

Before 1953, children as well as grown-ups learned the proper way to say "Josef Stalin." The intonation and inflection must be just so. Moreover, it was never just plain Stalin; he must be referred to as "The Great Stalin"; likewise, it is always the "glorious" or "liberating" Red Army. Russia is always referred to as "the world's leading power." Although Stalin has been pulled off his pedestal, the principle remains.

Annually, the Russian-Hungarian "Month of Friendship" celebrations are held. For instance, in 1950, when the second such celebration was held in Budapest, in its honor a large Soviet delegation, including representatives of Russian science, literature, music, painting, sculpture, and industry, visited Hungary's capital. Their hosts spared no efforts to impress them with the sincerity and extent of their veneration of the motherland of Communism. Erik Molnar, former Minister, even proclaimed to an audience of students that studious application of Lenin-Stalin theory had convinced him that the Magyars originally had been a pastoral Slav nation. He reported that this ethological fact had been denied and minimized by bourgeois science, but the fact remained that the Hungarians had no connection with Finno-

---

[48] For excerpts from such textbooks, see "From Discipline to Diversion," *News From Behind the Iron Curtain*, II, 3 (March, 1953), pp. 45-57.

Ugrian people to whom conventional ethnology had linked them.

In this "Slavic" aspect, however, Soviet Russia's appeal to the Hungarian masses had to be different from that used in Slavonic lands (Czechoslovakia, Bulgaria, Poland, and Yugoslavia). Pan-Slavism has been one of the most hated terms in the history of Hungary; the help extended to the Austrian Emperor by the Russians during the 1848 revolution has remained just as bitterly imbedded in the minds of the Hungarians as the short Bolshevik terrorist regime in 1919. But the Soviets still turned the trick, to a certain point, by their policy of Russification. The regime has led the Hungarian people to believe that understanding Soviet Russia and its people could only be made possible through the instruction in the Russian language as a part of the regular school curricula.

Aside from the strictly institutional standpoint, other means of promulgating Russification have been used—government measures (a government led by pseudo-Hungarians who are really Soviet citizens and speak the Russian language fluently), monopoly of the press, and control of all media of communications. The Russian language has been adopted as a regular curriculum study in elementary schools (including kindergartens), high schools, and colleges. In Hungarian universities, Russian is the main language taught; in order to receive a degree an individual must pass state examinations which show a command of the Russian language.

Many students receive scholarships and other forms of financial aid which permit them to travel to the USSR and study at Russian universities (and frequently they are compelled to remain in the Soviet Union to work). Instrumental in pressing this Russification policy have been the school clubs and youth organizations, particularly the latter. In all schools, literature, history, and geography are taught with a strong Russian emphasis. For instance, literature is concerned mainly with Russian authors, characters, and events.

Every effort has been made to bring Hungarian literature and art in line with what Moscow would expect. *Szabad Nep*, organ of the Hungarian Communist party, pointed out that "incredible heights are reached by those artists who accepted the hand which the Party reached out to them and turned their eyes to the capital of supreme culture—Moscow." Beza Losonczy, Undersecretary of the Ministry of Culture, declared that "we must dismiss the reactionary foreign slogan of art for art's sake," and that the "Ministry of Culture will support the creation of Socialist Art." Joszef Kolb, General Secretary of the Musicians' Union, complained that Hungarian musicians are misinterpreting Soviet dance music on the lines of American jazz, although "Soviet music is pure and perfect which needs no alterations." Yet, despite these efforts, the visiting artists from Russia have been critical of Hungarian art and literature. Professor A. I. Zamushkin, director of the Moscow Tretyiakov Gallery, found Hungarian artists still "too individual" and stressed "the program made by fine arts in the Soviet Union on the basis of party directives."[49]

After 1949, Communists in Hungary were censoring, barring, and burning Western literature to eradicate traces of "cosmopolitanism," complying with Moscow's orders that "cosmopolitanism" must be rooted out wherever the Red flag flies. Not content with making it compulsory for children, students, workers, and collective farmers to read Marx and Stalin, they started to censor, segregate, and even destroy Western literature in all its forms. Compulsory "literary movements" were launched. Underlying the drive was the "relentless hatred of the enemy." "We must foster hatred for the enemy in our children by pointing out its destructive activities, by unmasking the beastly face of the imperialists and by unveiling the anti-social activity of the right-wing Social Democrats and clerical reactionaries," was the editorial comment of a Hungarian newspaper on a report of Joseph Darvas, Minister of Education. "School principals and educators must take firm and determined steps to eradicate the cynical and undisciplined manifestations of

---

[49] John MacCormac, "Hungarians Extol Soviet Art Today," New York *Times*, (March 19, 1950).

cosmopolitanism and nationalism which have recently cropped up in our schools."[50]

In the hope of preventing the younger generation from being "infested by the poison of cosmopolitanism," the Hungarian educational authorities have been trying to insure that the tiny tots in the kindergartens and day nurseries, established at factories to enable mothers to take industrial jobs, are taught "political knowledge" and "self-assurance." "In Korea," a little boy was made to say, "there is war. Children cannot be taken to day nurseries and not even into hospitals because the Fascists have destroyed everything." Or, six-year-olds are reciting a poem, the girls rendering the first half and the boys the second, which runs: "People will not shed their blood for capitalists but safeguard peace with united forces."

Resistance

In spite of periodic proclamations of the great accomplishments in educational advancement, the authorities also periodically allow reports showing their disappointments. In 1952, for instance, *Kozneveles* (Public Education) complained that "the number of insolent pupils who neglect their studies, speak disrespectfully to their teachers, avoid schools and are 'flashy' in their outward appearance has increased a great deal."[51] According to this report, the rebels "mock the wonderful achievements of our work of production, deprecate the victories of our Five Year Plan and spread the destructive, hostile atmosphere of cosmopolitanism." Some of them "demonstratively and regularly shirk the Russian language class"; they spread imperialistic propaganda, literature, American thrillers, and "the wicked pamphlets of the Voice of America in the schools." Their final iniquity is to "teach American dances in the corridors to the other pupils."[52]

---

[50] "The Collective Life," *News From Behind the Iron Curtain*, I, 10 (October, 1952), p. 32.

[51] Godfrey Lias, "Glimpses of Two Hungarian Schools: How Pupils View American Ideals," *Christian Science Monitor*, March 1, 1952.

[52] The reference to the "wicked voice of American pamphlets"

The year 1956 was a year of rebellion against the Soviet masters in Poland and Hungary. While in Poland, as has been indicated, the Kremlin agreed to the "Gomulka compromise" that, although giving more fancied than real concessions to Polish nationalism and autonomy, did serve, at least temporarily, to lessen the overt police pressure of the Marxists. As a result of this, in some quarters Gomulka was hailed as a Polish hero. That the change was more apparent than real was soon shown in Marxist abrogation of freedom of the press and in both oblique and direct attacks on the Roman Catholic Church. The pressure to augment industrial production was likewise a concomitant as was the minatory presence of the Red Army.

In Hungary, as is well known, the revolutionists were ruthlessly suppressed. Since Hungary thus became a symbol, both to East Central Europe and to the non-Marxist world in general, the revolt has had much vital significance to nationalist movements and to educational policies as well.

Two items, however, do stand out as a result of Hungarian repression. First, although the event allowed Nikita Khrushchev to consolidate his power in the USSR, this was not done without peril to his future position and the whole status of the Soviet Empire. He did, indeed, remove Marshal Zhukov and President Bulganin, and seemed impervious to attack domestically; however, he was forced to justify his actions to the world in the Hungarian crisis, and in this he did not succeed. He accepted full responsibility for the decision to send his counter-revolutionary forces into the state (although there are grounds for believing that this move was not unanimously agreed to and that, at least initially, Khrushchev was in the dissenting group) and blatantly "justified" the action of sending the Red Army—the hope of the world proletariat—against that very proletariat that was seeking liberty in Hungary, as an instrument of "protection"

---

was probably intended to describe the Free Europe literature, distributed by balloons from Munich, in the languages of the satellite countries.

against what he called "the counterrevolutionary conspiracy of Imre Nagy and his accomplices." Indeed he
proclaimed this dogma from the very capital of the Hungarian state—Budapest itself—in the winter of 1959.[53]

To defend itself, the Hungarian People's Republic was
forced to issue a "White Book" in which it reported the
trial of Imre Nagy and his associates together with a
great deal of "documentary" material purporting to establish the fact that the revolution was unpopular, West-
inspired, and indiscriminately brutal to the mass of Hungarians themselves. Photographs were used and cap-
tioned in such a way as to provoke horror and disgust
toward the revolution, which was compared to Horthy's
suppression of the Bela Kun regime of post-Trianon
days.[54] That the whole volume is anti-historical, illogical,
and deliberately provocative is of no moment to Communist historians, who write history as a matter of course
in the Orwellian fashion.

All in all, the Hungarian crisis of 1956 (regardless of
the "failure" of the Western democracies to provide
positive assistance of any kind) may well go down in history as one of the turning points in the Soviet expansion
program.

This brings us to the second consideration springing
from the Hungarian setback. Brutal as the suggestion
is, there are grounds for believing that the martyred
Hungarians served the cause of peace in their unsuccessful rising to a greater extent than had such a limited
achievement as that in Poland been consummated. Moreover, had Western intervention been a fact, it would
have been exceedingly difficult to convince the governments and nationals of the so-called neutralist bloc of the
basic insincerity of the Kremlin, which in their interven-

---

[53] See press releases for November and December, 1959, especially
AP, December 16, under byline J. M. Roberts, "Move May Have
Altered History."

[54] *The Counter-Revolutionary Conspiracy of Imre Nagy and His
Accomplices* (Budapest: The Information Bureau of the Council
of Ministers of the Hungarian People's Republic, 1959), 172 pp.
and rotogravure section composed of numerous "photographs" of
revolutionary activity and reproductions of much "documentary"
material of questionable merit.

tion became crystal clear to even the most ardent of the non-committed. Moreover, had the event resulted in the creation of another Gomulka-type Poland or even a Tito-type Yugoslavia (that is, suggesting non-intervention on the part of the Russians), given time, it is quite possible that Moscow could in the long run have consolidated its position much more successfully than can now ever be the case.

Regardless of Soviet success in holding the satellites of East Central Europe in subjection for a decade and a half, several outstanding failures may be noted.[55]

(1) Marshal Tito's refusal to acknowledge Russian hegemony over Yugoslavia constituted, indeed, the first defection from Moscow;

(2) The Soviet plan to make the satellite states a *cordon sanitaire* between the USSR and the West has not yet been achieved. Two curtains are necessary; one between the satellites and the West to shield the colonies from Western ideology; the other between the satellites and the USSR to shield the motherland from the satellites' discontent.

(3) The Soviets planned to create a dependable military force of Poles, Czechs, and Hungarians. The men are in uniform, but neither the USSR nor anyone else believes them to be dependable.

(4) The Kremlin hoped to establish in the satellite states sources of cheap raw material and heavy industrial goods that would bolster the Russian economy. Although Poland and Czechoslovakia stand as partial exceptions, generally speaking the results anticipated have not materialized. The Soviet continues to explore this plan, however.

(5) Russian propaganda—Marxist-Leninist line—was to teach the younger generation Soviet dogma so that it would develop docilely and enthusiastically support the Soviet rule. While a certain success with the very young has been achieved, university students have generally provided a center of opposition to Marxist rule.

---

[55] See *President's Report*, The Free Europe Committee, Inc. (New York, 1959). 32 pp. especially pp. 1-2.

Education Under the "New Course"

In his announcement of the New Course on July 4, 1953, Premier Imre Nagy made several observations pertaining to educational difficulties in Hungary:[56]

As far as training the new intelligentsia is concerned, our educational program has become unbalanced. We have pressed the development of college education at great sacrifice. Now we must be more conservative in this field. . . . We must devote far more attention to our public schools. . . . It must be admitted that . . . we have grievously neglected elementary education.

More details on these shortcomings were revealed on February 1, 1954:[57]

In drawing up our plans for education, we overlooked the principle of "proportionate progress." We failed to improve our general schools and over-expanded and over-specialized secondary and higher education. . . .

What had happened was that, during the first years of the new regime, thousands of new experts were needed, and the facilities for higher education were improved at the expense of the general schools. This resulted in the neglect of the broadest forms of public education and weakened the backbone of higher education provided in the elementary and secondary schools. Higher education, like industry, was overexpanded. For a short period, the "New Course" tried to shift from quantity to quality.

It was apparent that even university students did not command a minimum mastery of basic educational tools such as spelling and grammar or of the most elementary techniques of how to study. In this respect, the shortage of teachers, especially of specialized teachers, has been one of the major causes of the low level of education in the general school. Now that the general schools of Hungary have been expanded to include the lower four grades of high school, there is a shortage of specialized teachers. In village schools, not only are the subjects taught by one

---

[56] "Education in Hungary under the New Course," *News From Behind the Iron Curtain*, III, 10 (October, 1954), pp. 23-31.
[57] *Ibid.*, pp. 23-24.

teacher, but several grades study simultaneously in one classroom. Although many new schools have been built, the increase in classrooms has not kept pace with the increase in the number of pupils. The New Course admitted that specialization has been overdone especially in the case of colleges and universities. There were complaints that "far too many students" took chemical and electrical engineering; students were to be encouraged to enroll for mathematics and physics, law, teaching, and philosophy (thus reverting to the trend dominating Hungary's education between the two World Wars).

As far as the methods (though not the substance) of university teaching is concerned, the New Course Communists returned to pre-1945 practice. Prior to that year, university courses were based on professors' lectures and individual research work rather than "cramming" from textbooks, as was the method in subsequent years. The party resolution on education called for the elimination of the "failing high-school methods in university teaching. University studies should be based on lectures. The professors, instead of touching superficially on all the aspects of a subject and going into minute detail, should rather review the basic facts and essence of the subject. . . ." The students must be taught how to take initiative, to become familiar with scientific methods and follow new developments in the field. The "overworking" of both pupils and teachers was criticized. The textbooks were charged with being "maximalistic," containing the maximum amount of information on the subject concerned and the teachers insisting that the children learn it all.

Prior to the New Course, competitions were continually being conducted in schools to force the children to study harder. Under the New Course, these competitions were regarded as "unrealistic." Pledges for extra performance —analogous to overfulfilling the "norms" in production —are to be eliminated.

For years, under the slogan of discarding the "old bourgeois morality," the Communists encouraged "freedom" both in and outside the school. But recently the administrators started complaining about lack of discipline among the pupils. Unruly behavior was a glaring problem in the universities, too, and more discipline was to be imposed.

It seems too that Pavlov's teachings in pedagogy started to lose their significance, although the remnants of Pavlov's experimental psychology are still found in educational literature, often in connection with the teachings of Makarenko, who has remained a great educational authority.

At the same time, the teaching of so-called "political economics"—Marxism-Leninism—was being intensified. But there was much criticism of "empty slogans that have taken the place of scientific facts." (A night school in Marxism-Leninism was opened in 1954.)

That the regime can no longer finance its former heavy educational program was given final proof by the announcement over Radio Budapest on September 10, 1954, to the effect that education in Hungarian schools must be partly paid for in the future by the parents. There will also be special examination fees for students at secondary schools and universities, and the number of scholarships is reduced.

The educational policies of the New Course reflected the political and economic policies of the time. In general, there was to be a scaling down in quantity and a scaling up in quality in the "educational plans." There was also a clear recognition that education is a process basically different from industrial production and agriculture, and that neither norms nor "socialist competition" could be successfully applied to it. Furthermore, the Communists were also more interested in the educational competence of the teachers and the academic competence of the students than in their political pasts or class origin. Greater emphasis was to be placed on the national traditions of Hungary. In the background was the Communist need for a better-educated intelligentsia and bureaucracy to implement its New Course policies.

Continuing Tensions

The New Course was soon to be abandoned; but even

the New Course improvements have not helped to quiet the deep discontent in Hungary—manifested in such ways as: increased church attendance; aiding "enemies" of the regime; carrying on sabotage through absenteeism; slowing down production and delaying crop deliveries; disseminating anti-Communist material and spreading information received from foreign radio news; and, finally, many escapes to the West.[58]

Today, the worker, as well as the farmer, is faced with life fraught with oppression, frustration, and protracted anxiety. Forced labor and slavery used to combat high labor turnover have no attraction whatever for the aged and infirm.

In Hungary all secondary-school pupils of thirteen have to fill out an elaborate questionnaire to determine whether or not they may proceed to a university, and if so, whether they be given a grant. "They have to answer detailed queries about their parents' social background and profession (past and present), about the part they have played in the Communist Youth Organization, and so on. In assessing the chances of a pupil for futher education the School Committee must take into consideration: social conditions, the results obtained at school, political attitude, and knowledge." (These instructions are printed at the bottom of page two of the questionnaire; the Committee's decision is to be written on page 3 of this form.)[59]

Regardless of a so-called liberalization under Janos Kadar, victor in the recent Hungarian revolt, a contemporary journalist, Ladislaus Szeberenyi, considers that "Hungarian youth today is no less critical than the youth of the 1956 uprising. Its skepticism of state management is just as keen as it was a few years ago. . . ."[60] In educational matters perhaps more subtlety is employed;

---

[58] Committee on Foreign Relations, *Tensions Within the Soviet Captive Countries*, Part 7: *Hungary* (Washington, D.C.: Government Printing Office, 1954), p. 180.

[59] Judith, Countess Listowel, "Class War on Children," *East Europe and Soviet Russia*, VIII, No. 389 (August 21, 1952), 9-11.

[60] "Hungarian Youth Under Communism," *Sudeten Bulletin* (Munich), XI, No. 9 (September, 1963), 277-82.

new educational objectives, too, are demanded—as in mainland China, the accent is on the training of Red experts. Although political reliability is still the chief prerequisite, it is maintained that there is no longer any discrimination against applicants for college and university entrance because they come from the intelligentsia or from a former bourgeois stratum.[61]

As usual, the youth movement is highly utilized as psychology is brought to bear. To the "Young Guard" are assigned duties similar to those of the police. Various flattering titles are distributed, viz., "District Brigade Leader," "Young Champion in his Field," and various political awards for high school and university students are granted. In the movement, "Youth for Socialism," a compulsory work program, Communist sources report as many as 800,000 young people participating.[62]

New boarding schools, on the Soviet model, have been introduced for high school and university students while more are being planned for elementary school pupils. The advantage to the state of such schools is obvious. They are administered by reliable Communists whose clear task is the production of the "Socialist man." A recent Hungarian law (No. III/61) on school reform does not permit teachers to remain lukewarm to state policy. In the future, no one can pass the teaching exams who has not completed the training course for *KISZ* (*Kommunista Ifjusagi Szovetseg*, the state-controlled Hungarian youth organization).

While Hungarian youth is skeptical, it is reported as cooperating generally with Communism, because this mode of conduct offers the only road to advancement. Perhaps there is some thought of a change, and in this Magyar young people would be only too glad to acquiesce. Nevertheless, the intellectuals and white-collar workers, educated in the European way of life and in Western science, literature, and arts, are particularly resentful of the pro-Communist system and ideological emphasis.

---

[61] *Magyar Nemzet,* May 12, 1963. As quoted in Szeberenyi, *op. cit.*

[62] *Vas Nepe,* February 26, 1963. As quoted in Szeberenyi, *op. cit.*

Especially harrassed by the imposition of the so-called cultural revolutionary principles have been the teaching staffs—compelled to accept Communist ideas contradicting both their backgrounds and experience. Obviously, Communism's recipe for success lies only in the destruction of the old cultural traditions of Hungary or in bending the nationalistic urge of all Hungarians— pro or con—in its Kremlin-oriented direction.

So the Hungarians do not enjoy as much freedom of access to Western newspapers as do the Poles, for instance. Yet like the Poles they have virtually abandoned "socialist realism" except in the motion picture industry; writers are becoming more prone to criticize the gross inequities of the Communist system. The influence of the Catholic Church appears to show progress; however, Cardinal Mindzenty retains his asylum at the American legation. While Hungarian agriculturalists have not been permitted to decollectivize, they are given more freedom to produce on private plots; more initiative has been allowed the building industry which is, in Budapest, at least, booming.

Hungary's masters hope for a *detente* between East and West in the cold war and now actually foster tourism. By such means they expect to recover from the Western world some part of the respectability lost in 1956.

CHAPTER IX

ROMANIA
GATEWAY TO MIDDLE EUROPE

Historical Antecedents

THE ROMANIANS—and thus also the Kremlin—rule one of the most rewarding pieces of real estate in the world. The long journey of the Danube from the Schwarzwald of southern Germany, passing through the plains of Walachia into the Black Sea, ends here; the rich valleys of Transylvania reach down to the Hungarian plainland from the Carpathians and the Transylvanian Alps. Constanta, the oil port on the Black Sea, is here, as well as Ploesti—the oil capital of the Balkans.

Although of ancient origin and roughly synonymous with the Roman province of Dacia, modern Romania dates from the days of the American Civil War; indeed, her first complete sovereignty did not begin until 1881 under King Carol I—a Hohenzollern. Nevertheless, Romanians pride themselves on their descent from ancient Rome and, in fact, speak a Romance language in many ways closer than modern Italian to classical Latin.

Although not, strictly speaking, a Balkan country, Romania has sometimes served as an example of the reputed instability of this area of Europe. Several circumstances combine to account for her—and for the riverine states in general—susceptibility to political change, economic imbalance, racial agitation, and an oftimes unreasoning chauvinism quite difficult for Western mentalities to comprehend.

The most significant of these factors is the Danube itself. This great river is not a good political boundary —not a natural frontier; it invites rather than discourages invasion (and so it has been for the past three thousand years). The Danubian region is one of the three main avenues of access through and across East Central Europe—the north Baltic littoral and the Polish plainland representing the other corridors. Each has been—and still is—of the utmost significance to the creation of (and the understanding of) European history.

Perhaps the fiercest nationalisms of the civilized world have arisen in the Balkan-Danubian setting. This fact, plus the ever-present minorities problem, the colonial enclaves, and *irredentas,* make the southern half of East Central Europe a strong contender as the world's most difficult political perplexity. Economically, too, and socially, these dilemmas demand a regional solution, and yet there is an equity due East Central Europe's multiplex nationalities that cannot—especially in the light of today's ideological schism—be disregarded.

Another ingredient in this strange collation stems from the proximity of much of Danubia to that old center of political discord: Byzantium. In addition to religious orientations must be mentioned the scars of Byzantine imperialism, the autocracy of the Second Rome, its famed intrigue, and the East-West schism of almost a thousand years' standing. And then the Turks—their conquests and subjugations with the resulting glorious (sometimes, unfortunately, inglorious) chapters of vigorous Danubian nationalisms.

Thirdly, one must mention the diversity of peoples. This, of course, devolves from the geography and from three thousand years of history with subordinate and superordinate "races" sometimes changing positions with confusing rapidity; then, too, the minorities whose name is legion; religious complexions likewise, again due to geography and history sit beside each other in unique fashion.

Fourth in this series of complications is the general absence of a middle class (regardless of the Soviet slanders concerning the bourgeois tendencies to be uprooted, and so forth). There were always only a few great families, lords, boyars, magnates, at the top, and a pitifully large majority of peasants and unskilled workers far below them. The lack of common educational opportunities was a natural concomitant and served to maintain the gap established in medieval and feudal times.

Theory suggests abridgment of nationality in terms of confederation or union; practice demands the security nationalism frequently offers. The Marxist-Leninist "solution" for East Central Europe is little more advanced than that of Cyrus of Persia, the satellites representing his satrapies, Moscow replacing Susa, while royal roads by rail and air radiate like spokes in a wheel from Soviet nerve centers. Nationality problems wrecked the old Persian Empire. One is not loath to invoke this analogy as the antidote for Russian imperialism.

Violent nationalism—based on the native soil as well as the natural desire for solidarity against foreign invasion—can be felt in the folk music and especially in the patriotic anthems or devotional hymns of these peoples. The Romanians[1] voice their national and cultural aspirations (as Professor Roucek noted in Chapter III) so:

> Awaken, Romanian, from thy deadly sleep
> Into which thou wert forced by barbarous tyrants!
> Now or never: create another fate for thyself
> To which even thy cruel enemies should bow!

As in each of the East Central European countries, and particularly in Danubia, the prime weapon against indigenous nationalism has always been physical division of the peoples—and nations—through a reshuffling of the lands. Byzantine, Habsburg, and Czarist Russia, each in turn followed this stratagem. Therefore it should not be unexpected that the Soviets—inheritor of the Czarist expansion policies—would employ this device (already so clearly indicated in the case of Poland) in Romania,

---

[1] Although this rendition of Romanian desire is of pre-Communist origin, it is easily seen that its words fit well the present crisis. For an excellent treatment of national and dynastic patriotism see Oscar Jászi, *The Dissolution of the Habsburg Monarchy* (Chicago: University of Chicago Press, 1929), pp. 447-50. Dr. Jászi, who served as Minister of Racial Minorities in the Habsburg Empire, construes the royal dilemma just prior to the breakup of the Dual Monarchy as follows: "The dynastic patriotism of the Habsburgs became more and more pale, losing its real driving force . . . [while] the various national hymns too, this real emanation of the popular souls, symbolized even more strikingly that Habsburg was incapable of checking the national patriotism."

Bulgaria, and the other East European satellites. Indeed, a Central European writer points up the fact that "Romania is an example to the world that Soviet Russia even abuses Communist ideology in its own imperialistic and colonial interest. . . . Marxism-Leninism is important only when it helps Soviet ambitions."[2] The identical point was made earlier in this chapter; here it refers specifically to Soviet juggling of the Romanian lands along the Black Sea and in the Pontic Plain: Bessarabia, Moldavia, the controversial Dobrudja, and, of course, landlocked Transylvania.

As a result of the mixed fortunes of war, Romania emerged in 1919 with a territory virtually doubled in extent. In fact, her frontiers very nearly attained those of the ancient Roman province of Dacia, which Romanian legend represents as the foundation of the modern state. From Hungary was taken Transylvania (which actually contained an extensive Romanian population), Crisana-Maramures, and a portion of the Banat of Temesvar; from the USSR she received that part of Bessarabia between the Dniester and the Pruth (including a population mixture of Romanian-German-Jewish peoples). A recent census indicated approximately four million non-nationals out of a total of eighteen millions. Represented were 1,500,000 Magyars (in Transylvania), 1,000,000 Ukrainians, 750,000 Germans, 750,000 Jews, and 250,000 Bulgarians (in the Dobrudja and elsewhere along the Black Sea littoral).

As will readily be inferred from their history, the Romanians themselves represent a somewhat mixed ethnic strain. Although one may begin with the classic Dacians and carry the history up to the establishment of the Romanian Kingdom under Carol I in 1881, the story of this "Roman" land includes only a precious few—very brief—periods of independence. Moldavia, Walachia (from the Vlachs, an early people), and Transylvania appear as separate entities from time to time. Emerging after her Latin days for a short-lived moment of free-

---

[2] Rudolf Wagner, "Partition—A Soviet Weapon," *Sudeten Bulletin* (Munich), VII, No. 7-8 (July-August, 1959), 151-55.

dom from the Hungarians and the Turks under Radu Negru—Rudolf, the "Black Prince," a Vlach chieftain of the mountain fastnesses of Bagaras—soon the darkness of oppression fell heavily again.

Another interlude of liberty appeared in 1601, when Michael the Brave of Walachia united the "Romanians" on both sides of the Transylvania Alps. After the early seventeenth century, as the Turkish juggernaut swept over the Balkans toward Vienna, the Romanian "nation" disappeared under the cloak of the Ottoman Sultans. Reconstituted in 1861 as a by-product of the Crimean War under the rule of a Moldavian colonel, Alexander John Cusa, the country remained under Turkish suzerainty until 1881 when, at Bismarck's Congress of Berlin, full sovereignty was guaranteed to the Romanians under the German Princes of Hohenzollern-Sigmaringen.

The inhabitants themselves are said to be a mixture of Sythians, Sarmatians, Dacians, Cumans, Thracians, Magyars, Szekely, Greeks, Romans, Goths, Huns, Bulgars, Slavs, Tatars, Alsatians, Jews, Gypsies, and Ukranians. Their Latinate speech is somewhat similar to modern Italian. Romanians, moreover, pride themselves on their Roman "descent," and Romanian, naturally, is classified as a Romance tongue.

With a population beset by minority problems and four-fifths peasant, with the centuries of Turkish rule everywhere in evidence, and a precarious position geopolitically speaking, the future of Romania did not appear any too bright even after her remarkable land gains following World War I. However, she had somehow chosen the "right side," the Western (Entente) powers, and Romanian prestige abroad was promoted so cleverly by Queen Marie—a granddaughter of England's Victoria —that in the world view Romania had already arrived. She joined the Little Entente, a French alliance, and attempted—and succeeded to a large extent—to play a decisive role in the political affairs of East Central Europe.[3]

Although Romanian post-World War I governments

---

[3] For details see Joseph S. Roucek, *Contemporary Romania and Her Problems* (Palo Alto: Stanford University Press, 1932), *passim*.

were typical "Balkan" regimes, the large landowners lost much of their holdings as the result of major agrarian reform. As the Romanians own a most fertile acreage, this redistribution created new political forces. Great parcels of land were wrested from Magyar and Czarist aristocrats and from the Roman Catholic Church, whose properties Romania gained in the peace settlements. Consequently, nearly 90 percent of the country's tillable land fell into the hands of small peasant proprietors. Nevertheless, redistribution was in large part a political move, which may be seen from the circumstance that the maximum size of estates depended upon their location in the various parts of the country.

"In the 'Old Kingdom' it was placed at 1,250 acres; in Bukovina, it was 625 acres; in Transylvania, 300 acres, and in Bessarabia only 250 acres. The expropriated lands were distributed among the peasants in farms varying from 12 to 62 acres at 65 percent of their expropriation price. By 1924 the legislation had been carried out so far that even the largest farm in the 'Old Kingdom' was 1,235 acres, and the average size of the estates remaining in the hands of the former large landowners was only 500 acres."[4]

Furthermore—as might have been anticipated—the Western civilization of the farther slopes of the Transylvanian mountains provided a leavening and "de-Balkanizing" influence on the remainder of the state. Romanian wheat began to bring, in return, machinery from abroad. Romanian oil attracted capital and technicians from Britain, France, Italy, and the United States. Westernization made rapid strides.[5]

Romania's resources, too—in an industrial age—enhanced her importance. Oil, coal, iron, lead, zinc, copper, gold, silver, mercury, bauxite, aluminum, antimony, graphite, and salt, together with newly located uranium, made Romania a treasure trove.

Before 1914 the two principal parties were identified

---

[4] F. Lee Benns, *Europe Since 1914* (New York: Appleton-Century-Crofts, 1943), see Note, p. 644; see also Eugene Horvath, *Transylvania and the History of the Rumanians* (Budapest: Sárkány, 1935), pp. 5-24.

[5] See Roucek, *Contemporary Romania, passim.*

as Liberal and Conservative. The first was concerned
with banking, commerce, and industry and, directly following 1919, controlled the state; they passed an expropriation act against foreign oil holdings; it was they who
directed the land redistribution mentioned above. However, soon the Conservatives enjoyed a renaissance under the leadership of Iuliu Maniu, a former Romanian deputy in the Hungarian national Parliament. The new
party, known as the National Peasant party, founded in
1926, adopted a progressive foreign and domestic policy. In 1928, Iuliu Maniu became Premier.

While economic conditions were definitely improved,
outside capital again was welcomed, and peasant circumstances further improved, a problem now arose in
connection with the reigning family. Carol II, barred
from the throne because of marital difficulties (and apparently quite happy in Paris exile), suddenly reappeared
in Romania in June, 1930, and was quickly proclaimed
King. Carol was aided in this maneuver by the National
Peasant party out of enmity toward the Liberals, especially the Bratianu family, that had long existed as
the power behind the government in Romania and that
(along with the Queen Mother, Marie) had opposed
Carol's candidacy.

As a result of this coup—as usually is the case of those
who "ride the tiger"—the Peasant party was now forced
out, King Carol undertook a dictatorship, the Liberals
were reinstated, then forced out, and Carol assumed
again what to all intents and purposes was another dictatorship. Contributory to all these kaleidoscopic events
were the formation and influence of the "Iron Guard."
This organization, Fascist, anti-Semitic, and hyperna-
tionalist, was not connected with its counterparts in Germany or Italy, but built on much the same ground as the
Italian Fascists and the Nazis. Moreover, this front was
extremely popular, and, although King Carol ostensibly
fought the Guards, he was inclined, as time went on, to
adopt more and more of their extralegal tactics.[6]

---

[6] For a more extensive account of post-World War I Romania,
see Robert Lee Wolff, "Rumania," chap. 10, in Stephen D. Kertesz,
The Fate of East Central Europe (Notre Dame, Indiana: The

Nevertheless, in 1939, Romanian foreign policy, which had stood the state so successfully for twenty-five years, became a house of cards. Caught between the millstones of the Ribbentrop-Molotov Pact, Romania's vast territorial gains melted like snow in the sun. In June, 1940, the Soviets demanded both Bessarabia and northern Bukovina. The Bulgarians asked for and got the southern Dobrudja. The Hungarians repatriated much of Transylvania.

Unable to withstand such blows, Carol fled into exile once more. Although young Michael became the nominal successor, the real power belonged to Marshal Ion Antonescu and his Iron Guard. This situation was one made to order for the Rome-Berlin Axis.

With the German attack on the Soviet Union in June, 1941, Romania entered the second World War and repossessed the Black Sea lands as far as Odessa. That Transylvania likewise should be returned seems to have been in the mind of Romanian strategists. Nevertheless, the Romanians had, this time, chosen the wrong side—a realization made more strong by American bombing of Ploesti and the rout of the Germans at Stalingrad.

Consequently the Romanians changed sides. Dropping Antonescu, King Michael assumed control. On September 12, 1944, an armistice was signed restoring Transylvania but indemnifying the USSR to the tune of $300,000,000 plus the "entire cost" of the liberation.

That the stage had been cleverly set for the Communist absorption of this ancient land may not have been apparent in 1944, but an unfortunate political development had already occurred that was, in the long run, to have the effect of dropping the Iron Curtain in East Central Europe.

Romania and the Soviet Thrust

In October, 1944—in the final year of the war—Winston Churchill and Marshal Stalin had reached their in-

University of Notre Dame Press, 1956), pp. 249-73; also Walter C. Langsam, *The World Since 1914* (New York: The Macmillan Company, 1943), pp. 598-607.

famous understanding relating to "influence" in these borderlands of Europe. For a 90-10 sphere in Greece, Churchill had allowed Stalin the same ratio in Romania; Bulgaria was slated 75-25 for the Soviet Union, while Hungary and Yugoslavia were to be allocated at 50-50.[7] Although such an arrangement may have saved Greece for the Western Allies, and consequently the Straits, the result in the Balkans was nothing less than catastrophic; indeed much of the remainder of this chapter must be devoted to the documentation of this gloomy event.

Thanks to this doubly opportune situation (1) the presence in Romania of the Red Army; and (2) the 90-10 agreement with the West, the Communization of Romania followed an almost "ideal" blueprint. Wolff reports: "Between the surrender of August 23, 1944, and the spring of 1948, the tiny Romanian Communist Party, relying on Soviet backing, ousted, destroyed and replaced all opposition, transformed the monarchy into a republic, and made itself ruler of Romania, in the face of ineffectual opposition from the Western powers."[8]

In order to bypass the recital of these dreary events, it may be necessary only to say that the usual tactics were employed: the creation of a "Union of Patriots" and the "Ploughman's Front," founding of the clandestine press, utilization of the local "Commies" Patrascanu and Groza, and the reimportation of the exiles, Ana Pauker, Vasile Luca, and Emil Bodnares—an unsavory trio if there ever was one. Next, of course, the "Society for Friendship with the Soviet Union," together with the semi-Fascist guard, "Patriotic Defense," the youth "Ready for Defense and Work," and the "Artistic Agitation Brigades" ought not to go unmentioned.

There were, however, from the local standpoint, at least two sore spots. Regardless of the raw materials, or possibly because of the rape of them, economic conditions

---

[7] See Winston Churchill, *Triumph and Tragedy* (Boston: Houghton-Mifflin Co., 1953), pp. 226-28; for a picture of Churchill's disillusionment with these "gentlemen's agreements," see Kenneth V. Lottich, "Berlin, Stalin's Greatest Blunder," *Sudeten Bulletin* (Munich), VIII, No. 3 (March, 1960), 63-69.

[8] Wolff, *op. cit.*, p. 254.

were far from rosy. The so-called Sov-Rom "cooperatives" milked the economy, while the shift to heavy industry presented much peril to the Soviets and to the
balance of trade in Romania as well. SovRomPetrol and
SovRomQuartz, the last two coops organized by the
Marxists, were not relinquished until 1955. Meanwhile,
the country had undergone inflation and "currency reform" several times.

From the standpoint of Western hopes, Romanian
opposition to Soviet agricultural policies probably offers
the best example of the power of local patriotism and nationalism to survive in the face of monolithic planning.
To understate it, collectivization, machine-tractor centers, even TOZ-type cooperatives (in which the peasants
do not have to surrender their property rights) and the
"labor brigade" system remained highly unpopular.

Evidence of foot-dragging by agricultural and other
non-factory workers in Romania continues to develop.
The weekly newspaper, *East Europe and Soviet Russia*
(London), finds frequent occasion to note such inade-
quacies. For example:

> On September 28, the Communist *Scânteia* (the Spark) com-
> plained that in several collective farms the statutes governing
> them were still being infringed. Cluj, Arges, Sibiu, Buzau, Galati,
> and other regions were particularly at fault in this respect. At
> some collective farms there was "not even a single copy of the
> Collective Farm Statute." The farmers were not [being] called
> to assemblies; the quality of the work was bad; the *norms* were
> not observed; [and] organization was in a pitiful state.[9]

A year later the song is somewhat the same: "On
August 7 the Communist *Scânteia* said that there was
'an urgent need to give new impetus to the organization
of agricultural associations. The Right wing deviation-
ist group has slowed down or altogether stopped collecti-
visation'!"[10] The reference here to deviationists means
that Ana Pauker, Vasile Luca, and Teohari Georgescu,
former ministers under the early Communist regime,

---

[9] *East Europe and Soviet Russia*, VII, No. 351 (October 11, 1951),
21.

[10] *East Europe and Soviet Russia*, VIII, No. 389 (August 21,
1952), 22.

had failed to inspire the proper enthusiasm among farmers in the interests of "cooperation." For this fault—and on charges that they conferred together (as well they might at this juncture)—the three were pronounced deviationists, stripped of their positions, and, it is rumored, executed without trial.

Another and more recent report indicates that collectivization is still running into difficulties. The American publication *Newsweek* suggests that: "Romanian (i.e., Marxist) officials are keeping it under wraps but their much-heralded collectivization speed-up resulted in complete disaster in the land-rich Transylvania region. Independent-minded farmers literally adopted a scorched-earth policy, burned thousands of acres."[11]

Nor were these troubles in Soviet Romania related solely to farming. Items dealing with other occupations, too, continue to arrive. Thus: "On June 17 a delegation of miners was received by Premier Gheorghiu Dej. The miners complained about food shortages, shortages of living space, of badly built new houses, and so on. There were no restaurants for miners. Moreover, there was a lack of coal trucks, lack of timber for galleries, and so on."[12]

And: "On January 15 the Communist *Scânteia* said that in industry strict economic stringency must be observed. There was too much waste, such as leaving the light on overnight, indenting unnecessary stationery, long personal telephone conversations, unnecessary travelling, and so on. It often occurred that four or five representatives of one Ministry visited a factory on the same day. One cloth factory in Bucharest had had seventy-six visits from one Ministry within two months."[13] Grievous faults these, and especially in a planned society!

Romania, the perfect satellite in resources and geographic position, refuses to be completely sublimated under the Red wave. Contemporary dispatches hint of

---

[11] *Newsweek* (New York), LIV, No. 21 (November 23, 1959), 26.

[12] *East Europe and Soviet Russia*, VIII, No. 386 (July 3, 1952), 22.

[13] *East Europe and Soviet Russia*, VIII, No. 364 (January 31, 1952), 22.

even graver defections, although credible news from behind the Iron Curtain is becoming more and more difficult to come by—or evaluate.[14] Perhaps these independent-minded people may yet survive as they already have against the despotisms of imperialistic invaders for the past two thousand years.

Education in Romania

The educational history of Romania reflects perfectly the development of the Romanian statehood of modern times. The system—in its pre-Soviet period—bears the influence of twenty-five centuries of accumulated culture, in addition to the Latin, the impress of which was somewhat annulled during the long Slavonic period when the authority of the Church of the Middle Ages was predominant. (The old Slavic language was the medium of instruction in the church schools of this period.)

At the end of the seventeenth century, the use of the Slav tongue, however, began to be replaced by Greek—popularized especially by former pupils of the Byzantine schools. In the nineteenth century the influence of France became established (especially that of the Second Empire) ; next German pedagogical theory was superimposed on all of this.[15]

When, in 1826, Romania and Walachia became Russian provinces, they were administered by bureaucrats from Moscow; General Pavel Kiseleff, a supporter of the French enlightened ideas and of Pestalozzian methodology, endeavored to introduce their concepts in the re-

---

[14] See various issues of *Newsweek* (New York) for the calendar years 1960/1963.

[15] See Donation Carnegie (ed.), *Enquête sur l'ésprit public en Roumanie* (Paris, 1927) ; P. Éliade, *De l'influence Francaise sur l'esprit public en Roumanie* (Paris, 1898) ; Christine Galitzi, "Education in Romania," Society of Friends of Roumania, *Bulletin* (October 18, 1926), pp. 89-95; Nicholae Iorga, *A History of Roumania* (London, 1925) ; R. J. Kerner, *Social Sciences in the Balkans and Turkey* (Berkeley, California: University of California Press, 1930) ; I. Nistor, *Zur Geshichte des Schulwesens in der Bukowina* (Czernowitz, 1912) ; A. Vizanti, *La Réforme de l'enseignement public en Roumanie* (Bucharest, 1887) ; Joseph S. Roucek, *Contemporary Roumania* (Palo Alto, Calif.: Stanford University Press, 1932), pp. 373-81.

gion. Nevertheless, after 1848 and the Russian and Austrian occupations of 1858-64, the educational situation again became more than depressing. The vast majority of children simply did not attend school; whatever teachers there were could hardly write their names; most of these "schools" were only huts without wooden floors. For example, in all Moldavia, up to 1859, only twenty-five grammar schools were to be found in the villages and only thirty in its cities.

The Educational Act of 1864 in Romania created the principle of free and compulsory education, "where schools are available" under state supervision. These same motives were revealed in the Romanian Constitution of 1866. Yet because of financial and organizational deficiencies this basic law was never effectively applied. Efforts to strengthen the system were made in 1896—supplemented by the Decrees of 1901, 1903, and 1908, but little progress was made. The requirement of four years' attendance was introduced, and the state imposed upon itself an obligation to support and extend educational means and to provide for the training of teachers—important and necessary way stations on the road to the development of a viable system of education.

Nonetheless, the educational situation faced by "Greater Romania" in 1918 was most distressing. Nearly 70 percent of the population was illiterate, due to accretions of undeveloped territories and to the historical development of the Romanian Kingdom itself.[16]

The Romanians who had lived in the former Austro-Hungarian provinces of Transylvania, Bukovina, and the Banat (which became part of Greater Romania in 1918) had never benefited from the general advantages of the Habsburg educational system. The Hungarians had been suspicious of educating their minority groups on the theory that education might render submission to the policies of the ruling classes less effective. As a consequence, only members of the landed aristocracy and urban *bourgeoisie* (about 20 percent of the total popu-

---

[16] See Stephen A. Fischer-Galati, "Communist Indoctrination in Romanian Elementary Schools," *Harvard Educational Review*, XXII, No. 3 (Summer, 1952), 191-202.

lation) were permitted to attend the few public (and private) elementary schools, available usually in the chief urban centers—with perhaps none being found in villages or outlying areas. Only about 25 percent of the peasantry, which actually constituted almost 80 percent of the total population, had an opportunity to attend one or two years in an elementary school which functioned irregularly and, when found, was usually conducted by the local priest. Similar conditions prevailed in the "Old Romanian Kingdom" (the provinces of Moldavia and Walachia), where the landlords or boyars considered popular education a waste of valuable working time. Education was, consequently, almost exclusively the privilege of the *bourgeoisie* and the landed aristocracy (about 15 percent of Romania's people) and was provided prior to 1918 by less than two hundred urban elementary schools.[17]

Conditions were even worse in Bessarabia and the Dobrogea. Just a handful of elementary schools were available for the urban Jewry of Kishinev and Çetatea Alba. In the Dobrogea there were no schools whatever, as far as is known, and even the Bulgarian statistics indicate that 90 percent of the population (which included a great number of Gypsies among other minority groups) there was illiterate at the beginning of World War I.[18]

Following 1918, the new Romanian government honestly attempted to improve this difficult situation. In June, 1924, the elementary and normal education laws were enacted. The former extended and intensified elementary education, the duration of which was set at seven years to be divided into two parts: the first, or primary, of four years, for the teaching of basic elementary education, and the second, of three years, completing the general education and offering certain directives affecting practical subjects. The attendance period of the normal school was raised from six to seven years; admission was granted to holders of certificates from the first stage of elementary education; and the first three years of normal school corresponded to Stage II in the new elementary

[17] *Ibid.*, p. 191.
[18] For details see Joseph S. Roucek, *op. cit.*

schools. The final four years in the normal school were devoted to preparation for actual teaching, with pedagogical and other methods courses as well as other elements of professional education. Normal school graduates were than appointed to the primary schools as three-year probationers, and were required to pass an examination prior to definite appointment. A special pedagogical faculty was set up at Bucharest University, to which teachers only were admitted, for post-normal school work.

On the secondary school level, high schools became uniform (the division among classic, modern, and vocational was abolished in 1924) and the duration of courses was set at seven years; the point of view was that of inculcating general knowledge rather than that of providing specialized instruction. Graduates, in order to enter the higher branches, such as university or higher technical schools, were required to pass a baccalaureate examination and to complete the preparatory year which was compulsory for all universities. Secondary school teachers were recruited from university graduates and were obliged to pass a stiff examination in their special fields. Permanent appointments were had only after a successful three-year probationary period.

Romania maintained four universities: Bucharest, Iasi, Cluj, and Cernauti. Bucharest University was composed of six faculties: philosophy and literature, law, theology, science, medicine, and pharmacy and veterinary medicine. In addition to these, postwar Romania had two schools of plastic arts, at Bucharest and Iasi; two dramatic schools (Iasi and Bucharest), a Law Academy (Orădea), an agricultural academy (Bucharest), two polytechnical institutions, at Bucharest and Timisoara; a commercial academy (Bucharest), and thirteen orthodox theological seminaries plus a single Mohammedan seminary.

After the 1930's the Romanian government (under the spur of the new supernationalistic movement) promoted various youth movements, the most significant of which was the *Străjeri* ("Guardians of the Country"), essentially a patriotic, highly nationalistic scout movement.[19] Children between the ages of seven and fourteen were encouraged to become *Străjeri*. Young members were doubtless attracted by the ceremonies and parades of *Străjeri* and furthermore were guaranteed "A" in physical education and music.[20]

Romania Under the Soviet Heel

Historically, lying athwart the road to Constantinople from Russia, Romanian territory has always been the short cut of Russian armies bent on reaching the Bosporus. And on the twelve occasions, when Russian troops occupied or crossed the country, they were only "a little less welcome to the population than the Turks themselves."[21] The annexation by the Muscovites in 1812 and 1878 of the eastern half of Moldavia (renamed Bessarabia), and their persistent attempts to annex all or other parts of the principalities, left little doubt in the mind of Romanians as to the real aims of Russia. As a result, Romanians always were willing to accept help extended to them by the powers (or the groups of powers) resisting Russian aggression; first the Triple Alliance, later the Rome-Berlin Axis. After World War I, two whole decades were dominated by arguments regarding the legal allegiance of Bessarabia to Romania, which, as mentioned above, had acquired this territory in 1918.

In short, the Romanians have never enjoyed anything Russian. Fascinated by the idea that their survival depends on their remaining a Latin island in the Slavic

---

[19] For details see Joseph S. Roucek, "Romania and Bulgaria," *The Phi Delta Kappan* (November, 1939), pp. 83-86; *Străja Tarii* (Bucharest, 1936).

[20] For a further description of Romania's educational policies between two World Wars, see Joseph S. Roucek, "The People's University—Professor Torga's Experiment at Valeni-de-Munte," *School and Society*, XXXI, No. 867 (August 8, 1931), 199-200; "Recent Tendencies of the Romanian Educational System," *ibid.*, XXXIV, No. 872 (September 12, 1931), 373-75; "Secondary Schools of Romania," *ibid.*," XXXIV, No. 1134 (September 10, 1936), 377-79; and "The New Educational System of Romania," *ibid.*, XXXXVI, No. 1191 (October 23, 1937), 537-38.

[21] Committee on Foreign Relations, *Tensions Within the Soviet Captive Countries: Rumania* (Washington, D.C.: Government Printing Office, 1954), p. 27.

sea surrounding them, they developed a will to survive. Culturally, they always considered Muscovy as being less Westernized than themselves.[22] That the fear of the Romanians was not unjustified can easily be demonstrated by Russian reannexation of Bessarabia, the ruthless plundering of the country after the armistice of 1944, and the continued exploitation by the Soviet under the guise of joint Soviet-Romanian companies (the SOVROMS, dissolved in 1954, but Romania was obligated to pay the USSR for Romanian property, for example).

Although perhaps the most reluctant of all the Soviet satellites, the Romanians have also been the most thoroughly "Communized." Since Romania played the role of Germany's outstanding ally against the Soviet in providing more combat troops and conquering more territory than Italy, the Russians, when invading Romania, repaid the Latins in kind. General Radescu's government, which had made peace with Moscow, was pushed aside by force and intimidation; power was assumed by the National Democratic Front—a Communist façade in which fourteen out of eighteen Ministerial seats were held by the Communists—with the poker-playing big businessman, Dr. Petru Groza, as Premier. As King Michael attempted to stem Communist inroads by dismissing the government, Russia's Vishinsky commanded Groza to remain at the helm and to proclaim decrees with the force of law although minus the King's signature.

This tested pattern of Marxist aggression defeated King Michael. Opposition cabinet members were forced out, "plots" discovered, and all dissent removed. Michael was forced to abdicate and the small Socialist party was intregrated with the dominant Communists. Romania became a tight pro-Soviet country, nominally led by Dr. Petru Groza, but actually by his masters in the Kremlin. Their orders were executed by such inner clique members as the infamous Ana Pauker (of Bessarabian Jewish extraction) as Foreign Minister, Emil Bodnaras, born a Ukrainian, as War Minister, and an old-line Commu-

---

[22] Robert Strausz-Hupe, "Rumanian Nationalism," in "A Challenge to Peacemakers," *Annals of the American Academy of Political and Social Science*, CCLII (March, 1944), 86-93.

nist, Vasile Luca, born in Hungary, as the Minister of Finance. All of these eventually were purged, but their places were quickly filled by other Communists of the same stripe.[23] As to legality the government confirmed itself through "elections" held under Communist duress —with all opposition elements extirpated and the secret police working at their diabolical best.

Romania, moreover, is of greater importance to Moscow's plans—thanks to its resources, grain, petroleum, minerals, and agricultural products—than its neighbor Bulgaria. Shortly after occupation the Russians took over all German-owned property and began to expand industrial and agricultural production; the various "cooperatives" mentioned earlier were set up. Much was made of Soviet success in Romania and the country was considered for a time as a showpiece.

Yet, needless to say, life is not easy for the Romanians. A Marxist "Festival of Youth for Peace and Friendship," attended by persons from many countries, was held in Bucharest in mid-August, 1953. Great efforts were made to impress foreign correspondents and thousands of other visitors with the usual Communist claims of prosperity, contentment, and freedom that are said to obtain in the so-called "People's Democracies." The shops were full of food and clothing retailing (momentarily) at low prices. But, after the visitors had departed, goods disappeared, prices were advanced, and life again became drab. Socialism was encountering difficulties. The government was, in 1953-54, forced to adopt the "New Course" policy, slowing up deliveries of grain and modifying the rhythm of industrialization and allowing a greater annual investment in consumer goods, industry, and agriculture. With the exception of "perhaps a few thousand convinced Communists, all Romanians naturally resent the domination of a foreign nation and ideology and suffer from the resultant moral and material privations."[24]

---

[23] For details concerning the spectacular and erratic career of Madame Pauker and others of this inner set, see John Gunther, *Behind the Curtain* (New York: Harper, 1949), pp. 123ff.

[24] Committee on Foreign Relations, *op. cit.*, p. 31.

The Sovietized Educational System

Romania has long been one of the most difficult countries behind the Iron Curtain from which to secure information on educational matters.[25] It appears that the
census of 1948 showed a rather high rate of illiteracy—
23 percent for the age levels of seven and over. The Educational Reform Law of August 3, 1948, is the basis for
all Romanian education. It presumably made attendance
at elementary school free and compulsory, and provided
three levels of training: I. elementary—seven years; II,
medium—four years; and superior (through institutes,
universities, and faculties)—three to five years. Almost
all schooling is segregated according to sex, save in the
smallest villages possessing but one school. Attendance
in 1950-51 was: 209,000 children in preschool institutions; 1,800,000 pupils in the 15,337 elementary schools;
166,767 in 721 secondary schools; and 54,000 students in
153 universities and/or faculties.[26]

The basic law of 1948 loudly proclaimed that the fundamental aim of elementary education in a People's Democracy such as Romania is "to educate our children
in the spirit of popular democracy." The new curriculum
was announced in the sixth Article of the law; religious
teachings, "harmful and useless because they bewilder
the tender minds of children with great confusion and
prevent them from acquiring a knowledge of all that science has produced to our day," were to be replaced by
the Russian language (obligatory beginning with the
fourth grade), which, it is said, is to help acquaint
pupils with the benefits of "the great scientific conquests
of the Soviet Union."[27]

Following the enactment of the law of 1948, the Min-

---

[25] UNESCO, *World Handbook of Educational Organization and
Statistics* (Paris: UNESCO, 1952), for example, contains no information whatever on Romania!

[26] See Joseph S. Roucek, "Rumania," in *The New International
Year Book*, 1952 (New York: Funk & Wagnalls Co., 1953), pp.
471-73.

[27] For details of this new program, see Stephen A. Fischer-Galati,
"Communist Indoctrination in Romanian Elementary Schools,"
Harvard Educational Review, XXII, No. 3 (Summer, 1952), 191-202.

istry of Education issued educational "ukases" for textbook authors and the state schoolteachers entitled *The
Guide for Elementary Schools* and *The Teacher's Guide*
respectively. According to these directives, the Romanian teacher must satisfy the following minimum requirements in order to qualify as a teacher of children in the
spirit of "popular democracy":

(1) To be profoundly devoted to the cause of the people, to the
     working masses, and to the Romanian Worker's Party;
(2) To have a thorough knowledge of Marxist-Leninist science;
     and
(3) To be familiar with events in the U.S.S.R., Soviet progressive
     literature, and the great Soviet pedagogical experience.[28]

In addition to constantly explaining and interpreting
textbook materials and delivering addresses on related
classroom subjects the pedagogue must act also as master
of ceremonies at the various celebrations organized by the
local Communist party in honor of "important events."
These occur at the rate of about two per month and are
carefully organized by the Ministry of Education. Appropriate and detailed instructions are issued to each elementary school principal as to how these indoctrinatory
affairs are to be conducted. The teacher thus, in effect,
becomes a popular priest—although his religion is that of
the reigning state ideology rather than of God.

In 1949, the Red regime began the publication of new
textbooks. A few of the old texts were edited in 1948 and
placed in use, but, "in order to improve them and to remove any mistakes which might still exist," four hundred teachers were engaged in revising thirty-one textbooks up to September, 1949, and in the publication of
two million copies of the same. Additionally, another
thirty-nine new textbooks were ordered printed in September, 1949. These were offered a circulation of
4,500,000 copies. At the same time, the Ministry of Education initiated the production of texts in fourteen languages (Hungarian, German, Greek, Bulgarian, Serbian,
Yiddish, Russian, etc.), and these were issued in edi-
tions of one million copies each.

---

[28] *Ibid.*, p. 197.

In 1952, substantial changes were introduced in the system of higher education. Following the precedent of the Soviet system, the Great National Assembly founded a Committee on Higher Education to supervise all advanced training. The Mecano-Naval Institute, the Bucharest Institute for Village Administration, the Juridical Institute of Cluj, and the Faculty of Philosophy's Journalism Section (Bucharest) were established. To properly identify this advanced training, the title "aspirant" was adopted (in the Russian manner) as an intermediate step between university graduation and the conferring of the Doctorate.

The Romanian Academy of Sciences, following the Soviet pattern, was completely reorganized and thus became a centralizing agency in charge of all higher institutions and laboratories and, of course, quite responsive to the Moscow line. Professor Traian Savulescu was named as the first president of this Academy of Sciences.

Again following the lead of the Soviet Union, Romania has numerous minorities schools and special courses for minorities in the higher institutions of learning. For example, at the Bolyai University at Cluj and at the Targu Mures Medical and Pharmaceutical Institute, instruction is in Hungarian. Hungarian language departments have also been formed in the I. Andreescu Fine Arts Institute, the Gheorghe Dima Conservatory, and the Cluj Drama Institute; sixteen faculties where instruction is conducted in Hungarian are said to be functioning in the universities of Cluj and Targu Mures.

On May 9, 1949, the National Assembly discontinued all teachers' seminaries previously operated by the universities. Under party guidance the Ministry of Education began the organization of special schools for teachers. The purpose of this move hardly needs elaboration.

The Sovietization Process

Today the task of building the "new Socialist man" begins at the cradle. In this captive nation, the Romanian child grows up in ignorance of Western "bourgeois" culture; in the classroom this ignorance is exploited through teaching him to hate the West and to love the Soviet Union, all the while giving a completely distorted picture of the nature of each. Beginning with kindergarten, children are obliged to learn songs glorifying Lenin and the current Russian leader, the principles of Marxist doctrine, and the Russian language—introduced, as mentioned above, in the fourth grade of each elementary school. Naturally, English has been eliminated, and French, formerly taught to all children beginning at the age of ten because of Romania's close rapport with the West and, of course, because of her Latinate origins, is now limited to the upper grades of the secondary schools. On April 15, 1959, the Marxist regime ordered the closing of all private foreign language and secretarial schools.

Bereft of home influences at an early age and placed in summer camps for indoctrination in Communism, children are increasingly estranged from the "old order." The patent objective of this new system is the thorough suppression of all individualistic tendencies, of all normal curiosity, of anything which may be labeled "philosophic doubt," objectivity or creative speculation. It is the severance of all ties with Western thought and culture. Its ultimate goal is, in short, to turn out vast hordes of standardized, docile robots that will move solely at the command of whatever levers are manipulated in Moscow.

In company with all of satellite East Central Europe, on May 1 endless cohorts of school children, wearing red scarves or neckties and waving Communist slogans, march in orderly ranks to the rhythm of their voices, singing in unison the same mesmerizing chant (or its contemporary version), "Sta-lin, Sta-lin, Sta-lin!"

The standard Marxist-Leninist ideological approach to everything is used; pro-Communist and anti-"imperialist" propaganda is even included in the arithmetic, natural science, and music textbooks. To educate Romanians in the proper Soviet spirit, the pro-Communist regime closed Romania's frontiers to all Western intellectual penetration. No book, magazine, or newspaper from France, Britain, or the United States could enter the country. The same restriction applied to film offerings; the only foreign

films are Russian. The masses have been forced to prefer Ivan Ivanovici to the late Clark Gable and Vera Po-
pova to Marlene Dietrich. At the beginning the public,
in droves, avoided the cinema; now, since there is nothing else to do, people go in increasing numbers. At the
theater it is much the same. Only plays by Romanian
Communists or those translated from the Russian are
permitted to be produced. And, of course, the only foreign reading matter of any kind must be Russian.

How hatred of the United States (and the West in
general) is promoted can easily be seen from the following review of an address to an International Students' Union conference in Bucharest on September 5,
1952, during which Chairman Bernard Bereanu com-
mented on a contemporary item in an American student
association newspaper. According to Bereanu, this newspaper insisted that education in the United States of
America was characterized by "ineffectual student leadership, discontent in student organizations, absence of a
real opinion, lack of international consciousness, super-
accentuation and commercialization of sports, whipped-
up hysteria, paralysis of student freedom, relaxation of
morality, spiritual decay, lack of interest, apathy, fear
and prejudices. . . ."

The chairman then added that "as a result of war preparations a new tide of racism, Fascism, and other ob-
scurantist theories have broken out in the universities
of the West, especially in the United States. There is an
interesting trend toward recruiting heads of higher institutions from among military men. Scientific research
in certain universities is now devoted primarily to detecting new methods of mass extermination."[29] When one
learns to read Communist double-talk backward, as it
should be understood, the implications of Bereanu's
speech are fairly obvious—both in terms of Romania and
the Communist Empire generally.

To enable good and true Communists to attend universities, the regime has short-circuited higher education

---

[29] "From Discipline to Diversion," *News from Behind the Iron
Curtain*, II, No. 3 (March, 1953), 44.

requirements and geared them into the Communist plans
to provide university education for those who have not
secured the traditional preparatory training. Complaining that formerly "the Universities were a privilege of
the exploiting classes," in 1949, special two-year courses
were introduced.[30] They were designed to "give to workers from the factories and fields desirous of instruction,
the opportunity of acquiring in two years the necessary
instruction to permit them to continue their studies in the
Institutes of higher learning."[31] In such schools, the
workers receive the equivalent of a high school education—although the instruction is carried on by a faculty
of the university. Pupils receive monthly allowances of
between 50 and 100 percent of the salary they formerly
had been receiving in the establishment where they were
employed before entering these "Workers' and Peasants'" courses.

The Training of Communists

Only a few schools in all the world have a regimen to
compare with that of the Andreei A. Jdanov "Advanced
School of Social Sciences" of Bucharest. Prospective
students are ferreted out by a special committee of the
Communist party; they must come from a semi-literate,
non-political, working-class family and must be able to
account for their every action since the age of ten. Once
approved, they undergo a two-year course calculated to
confiscate their minds; to prepare them to become the
professional and political elite of the nation. The methods
of the Advanced School overlook nothing. The two-year
course covers the history of the Communist party in the
USSR, political economy based on *Das Kapital*, dialectics
and historical materialism, structure of the Socialist
state and the Communist Party, "world history," the

---

[30] For the contrary argument, see *The Perversion of Education in
Romania* (Washington, D.C.: Romanian National Committee, 1950).
This pamphlet describes Romania's educational system in the four
stages of infant supervision, elementary schools, secondary schools,
and higher education and universities and is documented from publications of the Communist government.

[31] *The Romanian News* (Bucharest), No. 85 (July 2, 1950), p. 3.

Russian language, and contemporary international politics—at least from the Kremlin's angle.

Attempts to analyze the party line are considered heretical. The one irrefutable argument is always a quotation from a party resolution or a Politburo's decision (formerly Stalin's pronouncements were invoked). The student's day begins at 6:00 A.M. and ends at midnight, with every second utilized. "Free time" is utilized for supervising agitation groups or propaganda activities and organizing labor competitions at various plants. The heavy and time-consuming schedule is designed to deny students opportunity for reflection and the development of outside interests. Friendships are taboo. Rivalry and suspicion are fostered through student informers set in the school's ranks.

Paramilitary Education

Integrally related to the education system as a whole, Romania has created four major organizations for paramilitary training: (1) The Union of Working Youth; (2) The Ready for Work and Defense Complex; (3) The General Direction of People's Security; and (4) the Paza ("The Watch").

The Union of Working Youth (UTM) has the task of organizing the military training of youth. It is composed of five sections: the Pioneer section for children up to fourteen years of age, an organization for teen-agers, an order for college students, a group of young workers, and a military section.

On April 30, 1949, the first detachments of Pioneers, consisting of those between the ages of nine and fourteen, were formed. The role of this body was to train a new generation, devoted to the country, to Socialism, and to the Party—"faithful militants of Lenin's and Stalin's Cause." On the same day, in the Dudesti Hall, Bucharest —in the presence of the local representatives of the Communist party and the Youth Union, as well as their parents—the Pioneers received their crimson Communist insignia, "tiny bits of the red flag of the working class."

Pioneers greet their comrades with "Forward in the

Struggle for the Cause of Lenin and Stalin!" The proper reply to this salutation is "Forward All!" They wear a special uniform, including the three-cornered necktie—the symbol of labor. The Pioneers, some 150,000 strong, are organized by school units under the leadership of instructors who are qualified members of the Young Workers' Union—their parent organization.

Pioneer members spend the greater part of their out-of-school time at such special tasks as cleaning city streets or marching in ritualistic parades. In the school, as the "vanguard of those who will enter the ranks of the Young Workers' Union, and later the Party," these carefully indoctrinated Pioneers "assist their teachers in inspiring their fellow classmates with a glowing love "for the most advanced country of Socialism, the Soviet Union, and a deadly hatred for the enemies of the country and the working people, the Anglo-American Imperialists and their Romanian lackeys, the *Kulacks,* and former members of the *bourgeoisie* and landlord classes." They also edit youth newspapers, decorate the school and classroom with red flags, portraits of Lenin, Khrushchev, and other Soviet and Romanian Communist leaders, and are, at all times, ready to publicly denounce the "non-Socialist" activities of their teachers and fellow students. They are also required to read and to interpret to their classmates the contents of the Pioneer magazine, *Iicurici,* during recreation periods of the school day.

In addition to regional UTM organizations, there is a UTM group in each university, secondary school, military school, training center, factory, collective farm, and tractor station. The UTM works in close collaboration with the army and some of its members hold the rank of major. In the plants and factories, UTM organizations train young workers in pistol and rifle practice and a few even have their own aviation and parachute training stations.

The Ready for Work and Defense Complex (GMA) was founded on June 26, 1949, to "stimulate and develop physical culture and sports." The GMA, together with the Committee for Physical Culture and Sports, organizes premilitary activities and holds the so-called GMA tests;

its mass sport competition took place for the first time in January, 1951. The General Direction of the People's Security was formed in 1948, as part of the Ministry of the Interior—its chief purpose being espionage. Some of the People's Security members wear light-blue uniforms as do the militia but with a changed insignia; all members hold military rank.

Paza was instituted at the end of 1950 by the Ministry of the Interior for the purpose of guarding industrial plants, bridges, prisons, etc., against "saboteurs" and hooligans, and of supervising factory workers. Within a year the organization had attracted approximately 60,000 members. Not the least of *Paza's* contribution to the Communist state is its propaganda value; Marxists are eternally alert to the dangers, potential and real, from dissenters or minority groups—and they should not be judged inconsistent here, for this is the very role played by themselves in power seizures and the identical task set for their agents beyond the confines of the Iron Curtain.

Local Public and Adult Education

The "People's Athenaeums" in the towns and "Houses of Culture" in the villages are heralded as an important means of spreading Marxist culture and education throughout the body of the people. In Bucharest alone there were, as early as 1949, at least eighty-four of them. These centers sponsor all sorts of cultural and artistic activities. The Ministry of Arts gives guidance and assistance throughout Romania; publications such as *Albina* ("The Bee"), a weekly with a circulation of 130,000, are influential. Another organ of the Ministry of Arts, *The Cultural Guide*, a monthly, has a circulation of 35,000 in Romania, 5,000 in Hungary, and 500 in Serbia (all in the respective languages of the country). It contains poems, music for choirs, scenarios for one-act plays, correspondence and reports on activities in the various Houses, advice on dramatic production, with directions as to scenery, costumes, and make-up. A third publication, *The Guide for Libraries,* is issued also. Since Socialism claims to be scientific, the spreading of scientific knowledge in agriculture, hygiene, the prevention and cure of illness, constitute an important role of the culture organization.

Nevertheless, quite an interesting "thought-control" system is the "wired-radio" installed about 1950 in many Romanian communities. This *radio-ficare*, as it is called in Romania, refers to a system of radio broadcasting where the "broadcasts" are transmitted by means of a telephone wire hooked to all receivers. It consists of one centrally directed program which is the only one that can be listened to. The loudspeaker does not pick up radio waves from the air, but only programs transmitted by wire. In this fashion, *radio-ficare* resembles a huge telephone network where one person speaks to many.[32]

More than one hundred centers have already been created in Romania; they serve industrial units, working sites, machine and tractor stations, state and collective farms, and so forth. At Husi (Moldavia) a *radio-ficare* installation was constructed having 864 loudspeakers. In the Bucharest region alone five times more loudspeakers were in operation in 1952 than there were in 1949.[33]

New Institutes of Higher Education

The pro-Soviet Romanian regime offered as its first compliant in the direction of higher education that formerly "the universities were a privilege of the exploiting classes," and that in 1943-44, out of 20,742 students, a mere "58 came from the working class."[34] Yet, they allege, "during the people's democratic rule, higher education has been made available to all the people." Today more than 62,000 students are in attendance at institutions of higher learning, says the regime, and it is further

---

[32] This system was used extensively by the Nazis during the course of World War II and called by the Germans, *Drahtfunk*. It is also used extensively in the USSR, particularly in rural areas where the wire is usually terminated at the local "House of Culture." Here the population is asked to assemble to hear the "broadcasts."

[33] See "The Pragmatic Approach to Culture," *News from Behind the Iron Curtain*, I, No. 2 (February, 1952), 40.

[34] *The Romanian News*, No. 227 (March 25, 1953), p. 2.

pointed out that "the sons of the working people account for 95 percent of them."[35]

On May 9, 1949, the National Assembly, as noted above, discontinued all teachers' seminaries operated in connection with the universities. The Communist party in Romanîa and the Ministry of Education proceeded to reorganize teacher training through the establishment of special (indoctrinatory) schools for teachers. The Education Directorate of the Ministry of Education and Culture has drawn up syllabi for application in general culture secondary schools. Method inspectors, drawn in the case of each subject from teachers judged to be, from the technical and educational standpoints, the best equipped, work under the Education Directorate in the preparation and revision of these syllabi. Such courses, it is maintained, prescribe a general cultural knowledge "which ensures the sound training necessary to young people for pursuing their studies in any higher education establishment."[36]

Control of Religion

As elsewhere in the satellite countries behind the Iron Curtain, persecution of religious groups proceeded with dispatch immediately on the inauguration of the pro-Soviet regime; moreover, after the Communists had consolidated their control of the governmental apparatus in 1946, it moved ahead with remarkable efficiency. Since then the regime has brought all the regularly organized churches and religious bodies under state control—although it has been utterly unable to root religion out of the lives of the people. The 1948 census gave the following estimates of the strength of the various religious denominations[37] then existent in Romania:

---

[35] For an opposing statement, see *The Perversion of Education in Romania* (Washington, D.C.: Romanian National Committee, 1950). The figures cited above are highly dubious.

[36] See "Rumania," *Preparation of General Secondary School Curricula* (Geneva: International Bureau of Education, 1960), No. 216, pp. 266-70.

[37] As in most areas of East Central Europe, religion generally

Denomination	National Origin	Adherents	Percent
Eastern Orthodox	Romanian	11,500,000	72
Greek Catholic (Uniate)	Romanian	1,600,000	10
Roman Catholic	Hungarian, German	1,050,000	7
Calvinist	Hungarian	730,000	4.6
Evangelical Lutheran	German	250,000	1.6
Unitarian	Hungarian	75,000	.4
Baptist	Romanian	120,000	.7
Adventist	Romanian	60,000	.3
Lipovan	Russian	30,000	.1
Jewish	Hebrew	372,000	2.3
Moslem	Turks, Tartars	10,000	
Totals		15,797,000	100.

The Red regime attempts to control the clergy through a "Union of Democratic Priests," led formerly by Minister of Cults, Father Burdecea; in 1947, the National Assembly enacted two laws relating to the religious situation: (1) for the pensioning of priests, thus bringing them under the secular control of the state; and (2) for the redistributing of Sees and the promulgation of new rules for episcopal assemblies (and containing a clause permitting the government to replace recalcitrant clergy with its own Communist followers).[38] Over 30 percent of the steadfast parish priests in towns and villages were thus dismissed from their charges. The new rules for episcopal assemblies paved the way for the election of three new "People's Metropolitans" and, in 1948, after the death of Patriarch Nicodemus, his replacement with a Marxist partisan, Patriarch Justinian Marina.[39]

Periodical Literature Under the Soviet Regime

In order to promote the pro-Communist ideology, soon after the new regime came to power, the Red government

coincides with national origin. For example, in Romania, Lutherans are generally German-speaking, Calvinists, Hungarian-speaking, and so forth.

[38] In this connection see Judith, Countess of Listowel, "The Birth of a Heretical Church," *East Europe and Soviet Russia*, VII, No. 331 (May 17, 1951), 10-13; also for an exposition of similar tactics in Poland, Joseph S. Roucek and Kenneth V. Lottich, "Church and State Relationships in Poland," *Il Politico (Pavia)*, XXV, No. 3 (September, 1960), 517-18.

[39] For details, see *News from Behind the Iron Curtain*, Vol. II, No. 2 (February, 1953).

initiated or promoted a host of scientific and/or cultural periodicals.[40] *Contemporal* ("The Contemporary") is a weekly that prints articles on all aspects of current life, "propagating the Marxist-Leninist theory and the progressive point of view on the problems of political, social, and cultural life." *Flacara* ("The Flame"), another weekly—the organ of the Union of Writers, Composers and Artists of the Romanian People's Republic—deals with the "ideological problems of art and literature." *Viata Romaneasca* ("Romanian Life") is the monthly review of the Society of Writers; it claims to contain and continue the traditions of the earlier *Viata Romaneasca*, suppressed in 1940. Its editors insist that this periodical has published "studies with an ample documentation evincing the decline of Western bourgeois literature." *Problems de Literatura si Arta* ("The Problems of Literature and Art") represents a fourth magazine sponsored by the regime and devoted to its concept of culture. This is underwritten by the Institute for Romanian-Soviet Studies and features "the great movement of ideas, initiatives, and innovations characteristic of Soviet thought in general."

The Central Committee of the Romanian Worker's party sponsors *Lupta de Clasa* ("The Class Struggle"), as its theoretical and political journal; *Lupta de Clasa* traces its origins to July, 1920, when the Communist party began operations in Romania. *Studii* ("Basic Studies") aims to review science and philosophy from the Marxist-Stalinist point of view; it is a "cultural guide for the new type intellectual, the intellectual who has ceased to be a 'specialist' with a one-sided vision, a narrow-minded and minor professional, and has become an active fighter in all walks of ideology." The Institute for Romanian-Soviet Studies publishes a bi-monthly, *Analele Romano-Sovietice* ("The Romanian-Soviet Annals"), whose basic objective is to "make known to Romanian people of science and to Romanian intellectuals in general, problems of Soviet science and working methods of

---

[40] N. Tertulian, "Periodicals of Science and Culture in the Romanian People's Republic," *Romanian Review*, Fourth Series, No. 1 (1949), (Bucharest: 5-7 Bis. Amzel), pp. 87-95.

Soviet savants, and to place at their disposal a rich information material on Soviet scientific research work in all walks of life." The educational nature of Romania's series of cultural and scientific publications is readily apparent, although, of course, their propaganda influence is the aspect most noted in the West.

Stresses and Strains Under Communist Rule

In spite of the perennial claims of Communist spokesmen in Romania, the new regime has had glaring difficulties confronting its educational experiment. There has been a serious shortage of pro-Communist pedagogues and scholars; the regime has been forced to employ a great many "whose views are to say the least hardly compatible with Marxism. Every now and then they are violently taken to task, but the great majority seems to get away with a public apology and a promise which does not always seem to be kept—to do better in the future."[41]

A survey of the Communist press shows that Romanian intellectuals resist sovietization, and this tendency is even discernible among the younger scientists. For example, the Institutes of Biochemistry, Mathematics, and History of Art of Bucharest and likewise of Cluj—as well as the Romanian Academy—have been accused of not "helping the builders of Socialism in their hard struggle." The Academy's Philosophical Institute has not published during recent years a single work "attacking vigorously the reactionary theories of the Rumanian bourgeois philosophers." It is a further cause for complaint that the Institute of History has failed to "unmask aggressively the reactionary theories of the bourgeois historians."[42]

A few years ago the Romanian Legation in Bern, Switzerland, was the scene of a bizarre clash between the Communist regime's representatives and other Romanians who had already made the trip to freedom in safety. Charging that the legation harbored espionage activities

---

[41] See Committee on Foreign Relations, *Tensions Within the Soviet Captive Countries: Rumania*, Part 2 (Washington, D.C.: Government Printing Office, 1954), pp. 33-34.

[42] *Ibid.*, p. 35.

and distributed Communist books and other propaganda, seven Romanians seized the legation and barred chargé d'affaires Emeric Stoffel and his staff. Persuaded by a priest's plea to relinquish control of the building, after destroying quantities of propaganda materials and smashing files, the invaders marched out, surrendering to the police their rather formidable arsenal of submachine guns, rifles, Browning revolvers, ammunition, and axes.[43] Such attempts clearly show the schism within Romania and suggest that, given half a chance, many of these Latins would gladly rise against their Slavic masters.

Regardless of the reported "endless efforts of the Soviet regime to eradicate illiteracy," Romania's problem in this respect is still grievous. According to the official statistics of 1948, there were 23 percent of illiterates over seven years of age within the total population (14 percent males and 31 percent females).[44]

That this illiteracy problem has greatly annoyed the Marxist regime (if for no other reason than that of propaganda difficulties) was admitted by Minister of Education Vasilichi, on September 23, 1949: "Millions of illiterates and semi-illiterates are an enormous hindrance in the way of building up Socialism in Romania. . . . There are whole districts, especially in the north, without schools. . . . Several teachers have moved from rural areas to urban districts, and in the villages there are up to 120 children for each teacher."

The government has also faced difficulties on the high administrative levels since—with few exceptions in the higher ranks—the vast body of educated officials are the bitter enemies of a small group of Communists provided by Moscow and presently in the saddle. In spite of the claims of having developed large numbers of university-trained people, Romania has frequently lacked educated and indoctrinated personnel on all administrative and professional levels.

The Marxist-Leninist evening universities in Bucha-

---

[43] Associated Press release, July 14, 1955.

[44] In 1950, Romania's population was 16,094,000 living in an area of 237,000 square miles, with an average of 68 inhabitants per sq. km.

rest, Cluj, Arad, Stalintown, and other cities have been criticized for their distortions of Marxism-Leninism. Romanians of the Orthodox faith (as well as the Protestant, Moslem, and Jewish communities) resent the treatment that their churches have received—and are still receiving. Above all, not only is the Red regime attacking everything that the Romanian peasant has always aspired to—individualism and private property—but all Romanians conceive Muscovites as the traditional enemy —the most hated, and indeed in this respect close to the Turk. Romanians, despite the official machinery promoting this "traditional Romanian-Russian friendship," cannot forget how Russian troops occupied or traversed their country on many occasions, how they annexed Bessarabia in 1812 and 1878—and again during World War II—and how they have been plundering the country systematically since the armistice of 1944, and that Russification attempts by the Soviet just simply do not have any attraction for these proud Latins set down in a Slavic sea.

Polytechnicalization

Both Romania and Bulgaria felt the impact of the new Soviet policy in education when, in June and July, 1957, respectively, the Communist Party Central Committees demanded the introduction of "polytechnicalization" in all institutions of higher learning. To accomplish this, lecture hours and examinations were to be reduced, laboratory, shop, and factory practice were to be increased; and, because of this shrinkage, many specialized facilities and institutes were merged. In order to improve material standards—chiefly equipment and furnishings—all factories were ordered to supply gratis one article or unit of their manufacture to each of the institutions of higher education.

As opposed to Poland, new, more "class-conscious" admissions requirements were laid down in both Pontic countries. For instance, in Romania the Central Committee decreed that 40 percent of university students must be of "working class" origin and from 30 to 35 percent of peasant birth. Thus, of all ten satellites, Romania insisted upon the largest proletarian representation in higher education. The same decree also provided for an increased number of, and a higher stipend for, scholarships available to the above-mentioned groups.

The objective in Romania and Bulgaria, it appears, is the creation of a "people's intelligentsia." While it is true that in both countries a prewar middle class (although proportionately small) did exist, much of this has already been liquidated; moreover, the remaining members are thought to be either insignificant or (from the Communist point of view) unconvertible. Furthermore, university students have proved to be a thorn in the flesh of the Romanian Communist authorities. These new regulations, both in work regulations and in the new selection practices, offer a better opportunity for pupil control. There is likewise the thought that—just as soon as it is possible—both Romania and Bulgaria may be absorbed outright as constituent republics of the USSR (the same recourse has been suggested for Czechoslovakia, as has been mentioned). Their resources, maritime position, and geopolitical significance as the avenue of approach along the Pontic plain to the straits and the Near East especially suggest this maneuver. However, a prodigious amount of "missionary" work will have to be done, particularly in Romania, where the huge Hungarian minority must first be sublimated.

Gazeta Invatamintului (Bucharest) on January 11, 1957, reported that the chairman of the Bucharest Party Committee had accused university instructors of having "misconstrued" the resolutions of the Soviet's 20th Party Congress and the Second Congress of the Romanian Party regarding the struggle against "dogmatism" charging that "under the guise of criticism, some instructors have belittled the achievements of the People's Democracy and have slipped on the path of liberalism."[45] Duplicating the complaints in Czechoslovakia, the Romanian press has reprimanded professors for shirking ideological instruction on grounds that "politics" has no place in their pro-

---

[45] As quoted in *East Europe* (New York), IX, No. 6 (June, 1959), 15.

fessional tasks. Although it is believed that unrest in Romanian universities has been considerable, the strictly controlled press has barely hinted at this and there is no documentation of any overt anti-Red regime activity.

Nevertheless, the repercussion of the Hungarian Revolt of 1956 on students in Romania was generally conceded, but was concealed by the Romanian press. However, *Gazeta Invatamintului* (January 4, 1957) did print an article by the Rector of the Bolyai University (Cluj), a university for the Transylvanian Hungarian minority, praising the way in which students and faculty had "stood up to the political-ideological test" of the 1956 revolt.[46] Although he was complimentary of the way party and youth organizations had "succeeded in preserving order," the Rector admitted that there was need for a more thorough political-ideological work to combat "wavering" students when the first news of the Hungarian uprising was known. He called for an intensification of this labor in the light of the fact that the present generation "never knew the intensity of the suppressive activities of the past regime."

Scinteia Tineretuliu (Bucharest) on March 29, 1957, likewise criticized the "low level of Marxist-Leninist instruction" at V. Babes University and the Medical Pharmaceutical Institute, also in Cluj, saying that "the need for improvement of these courses, which are an integral part of the Party's propaganda machine, is accentuated by the prevalence of imperialist views regarding people's capitalism, the vacuum in the Middle East, and the insistent cries of those who demand a reform and revision of Marxist views."[47]

On June 6, this same paper attacked the Marxist-Leninist instruction in the faculties of legal sciences and philosophy at Bucharest University. A special target of criticism was the "parrot-like knowledge" of Marxist-Leninist principles and the high rate of failure (20 percent) among the fourth-year journalism students. Their "factual confusion" was said to be great and—particu-

---

[46] *Loc. cit.*
[47] As quoted in *East Europe, op. cit.*, p. 16.

larly to be deplored—their knowledge of social science
was sketchy indeed; many of them were unable to identify the leading philosophers of the past (we are told)
and even "confused the Utopian Socialists with the En-
cyclopedists"; they did not know the name of a single
contemporary bourgeois philosophical movement.[48]

Educational Content

A favorite topic of Communistic propaganda is the
"criminal militaristic education of American youth." Yet
this same propaganda mill is enthusiastic about the mili-
tarist spirit which shapes the education of youth behind
the Iron Curtain. The infamous treason trial (concerning
Rudolf Slansky and others) in Prague provided a terrible
example of the moral depths to which youth is driven in
the Soviet orbit; the Soviet press never stops inveighing
against children in the United States who play with toy
soldiers, tanks, and guns, read comics devoted to mayhem
and murderous gangster stories; listen to "warmongering
broadcasts"—in such manner being already prepared to
wage war on the peace-loving Soviet Union and the People's Democracies.

It is perhaps true that in Red Russia and her satellite
countries youth is educated much more seriously than in
the West. Instead of playing with toy rifles and tin air
pistols, boys and girls are trained with small-calibre regular rifles; and from the age of ten upward they are
taught sharpshooting and military drill. There is a
great pressure for all youngsters to affiliate with the
young Pioneers; next comes one of a number of auxiliary
organizations in which they undergo paramilitary instruction and compete for the Ready for Defense badges.
So by the time they are called up, they already have a
first-class military grounding.

Simultaneously youth are indoctrinated to hate "all
internal and external enemies of the Soviet regime and
of Communism"—the capitalist imperialists, the Vatican,
the Anglo-American warmongers, and so on to absurdity.

---

[48] *Idem.*

They are taught to inform on their friends, neighbors, parents, and peers, and to report them to the Security Police.[49]

In fact, many times, in Romania, Bulgaria, Hungary, and Czechoslovakia, it has been announced over the government radio, "Thanks to the help of the Red Pioneers, the ———— Security Police have arrested bandits" (or terrorist, kulaks, illegal frontier crossers, class alien elements, hooligans, and so on). Such achievements are held up as examples for youth: "Red Pioneer Morozov, who denounced his *kulak* father (subsequently executed, while his mother and the remainder of the family were deported to Siberia) is venerated as a hero, to be imitated by young people in the Soviet Union and in the captive countries."[50]

During the first half of July (1952), both in Bucharest and in the provinces, many children of both sexes between the ages of nine and seventeen years were arrested. These arrests were carried out after the customary Communist midnight raids and searches. In Bucharest, three hundred young people were arrested; there are no reliable figures for the provinces. Some correspondents believe that these children are being held as hostages for the good behavior of their parents; others that they will be influenced into denouncing their families. Others assert that the young people had distributed "seditious pamphlets." All parents were strictly warned not to divulge the facts of the seizures. During the weekend of July 19-21 a reliable source indicates that fifty teen-agers were seized in Bucharest alone. They, too, had handed out "seditious literature."[51]

With diabolical cunning the Romanian Communists spirited these youngsters away during the summer holidays when their disappearance was "least likely to excite comment." In Siberia or Central Asia, there perhaps was little comment either—for there could be none, nor any-

---

[49] See B. P. Yesipov, *I Want To Be Like Stalin* (New York: John Day, 1947), pp. 42-52.

[50] "Confused Morality," *East Europe and Soviet Russia*, VIII, No. 404 (December 4, 1952), 10-11.

[51] *Ibid.*

one to hear it anyway. Unfortunately, the rumors excited little comment in the West either. This persecution of children is the lowest form of class war. Unless the Free World protests loudly against it, it will sow seeds of hatred difficult to uproot when—at last—Communist domination of East Europe comes to an end.

Contemporary Scenes

Her territorial losses notwithstanding, Romania is just as important to Soviet Russia as she had been to Nazi Germany. Her geopolitical position is one asset. To the Russians she provides a pathway to the straits; to Germany she provided a buffer against the Slavs. Her agricultural products and minerals are almost without parallel, given a land of Romania's area. With one-sixth the population of former Germany, she produces as much wheat, both on the fertile upland of Transylvania and on the black soil of the Old Kingdom. She produces more oil and gas than all of the rest of non-Soviet Europe combined—though approximately three-fourths of it is wasted through poor management. Indeed the oil bubbles out of the ground east and west of Ploesti, just opposite the Predeal Pass, on the southwestern slope of the Transylvanian Alps. The Romanians also possess coal, iron, lead, zinc, copper, mercury, bauxite, antimony, gold, silver, salt, and graphite. Yet it is only lately that she has begun the long process of learning how to extract and utilize such assets. Needless to say, the Russians have grasped as much of this natural wealth as possible through one device or another. Moreover, the Soviet masters today are trying desperately to transform this formerly overwhelmingly backward agricultural country into a thoroughly industrialized state—a resource bastion of their slave empire.[52] The mechanics of this drive have already been described. Halasz presents the story of the rape of East Central Europe as follows: "The Soviet sys-

---

[52] See Nicholas Halasz, *In the Shadow of Russia, Eastern Europe in the Postwar World* (New York: The Ronald Press Company, 1959), chap. 2, pp. 54-89.

tem itself may be regarded as the Russian form of industrializing nationalism with a messianic bent."[53]

Yet actually there has been considerable progress—at least in the diversification of industry. A local guidebook indicates the following aspects of production: oil extraction and processing, the processing and distribution of natural gas (Romania is reported as second in all Europe in these branches), extraction of ferrous and non-ferrous ore and coal, steel metallurgy, machine building and the processing of metals, production of electric power and electric equipment, farm tractor production, building material industry, exploitation and industrialization of timber resources, chemicals and pharmaceuticals, textiles, footwear and leather industry, food processing and distribution.[54] The degree to which Romania's economic position has improved may be illustrated by the fact that the 1938 production of cast iron reached only 133,000 tons—in 1960 over 1,000,000 tons were produced. In 1938, the production of 284,000 tons of steel showed only promise—in 1960, 1,806,000 tons were forged. The 1938 mark of half a million tons of cement was bettered sixfold by 1960.[55] Industry by 1960 had become the determining factor in the formation of the national income.

Romania is served by six railway communications agencies; three originate in the West: the Arlberg-Orient-Express and the Orient Express, from Paris, and the Baltorient Express from Stockholm; three connect Bucharest with the Communist bloc: the Carpati Express from Warsaw, the Belgrade-Bucharest from Yugoslavia, and the Danibus Express from Moscow. Seven airlines land (or have their termini) at Bucharest.

Educational Recapitulation

The country actually has begun increasingly to show a greater independence from the USSR. In 1963 she re-established diplomatic relations with Albania and also

---

[53] *Ibid.*, p. vii.
[54] *Romania* (Bucharest: Carpati, 1962), p. 2.
[55] *Ibid.*

began to ship oil to Red China. Romania, furthermore, recently signed a convention with Yugoslavia's Tito abolishing visas for mutual travel. Her educational practice has, however, shown only a slight variation from that of Marxist Russia.

Since the Romanian educational system is but a phase of the Soviet model, it is difficult to view it dispassionately. That progress has been made in combating illiteracy is granted—yet there is still a long road to travel. On the other hand, the substitution of ideology for conventional learning raises deep and serious problems— which the Western world will eventually have to face. Nevertheless, education in Romania is perhaps more of a "going concern" than many Westerners would like to admit.

In 1956-57, there were 81,206 full-time students in Romanian institutions of higher education. This, allegedly, is more than three times the number reported in 1958.[56] It is also reported that, in 1957, Romanian university administration was "liberalized" in that a greater degree of self-government is permitted than is usually the case in Soviet circles. Although such a statement must be considered in the framework in which it exists, the election rather than state appointment of university officials such as the Rector and Dean, is followed. Likewise that scholastic requirements for obtaining degrees, titles, and teaching posts were raised. On the other hand, the effect of the new polytechnicalization most certainly will be felt—and perhaps will influence scholarly work as well; the same is true in regard to the percentage basis for admission to university work; if class quotas continue as announced, it is quite possible again that science will suffer. Yet, however all this may be, it remains to be seen just how the changes described in the foregoing chapter will fit the political situation or with what degree of seriousness they should be accepted; since self-government in Communist terminology means Soviet control, it may well be argued that the situation rather than having been liberalized has actually been tightened.

---

[56] *Anuarul Statistic* (Bucharest: 1957).

CHAPTER X

BULGARIA
SOFIA UNDER THE RED STAR

An Ancient Balkan Empire

THE REVISION OF HISTORY at the hands of Soviet historians has taken some strange forms. Yet one of the grossest distortions of all is the fable they presently attempt to foist on the Bulgarian people. According to Moscow, the Bulgarians are "in reality" an offshoot from the Russians. Indeed, they have easily prevailed upon their stooges at Sofia to announce this "fact" over the Bulgarian radio.[1]

In direct contradiction to this assertion, the Bulgarians are actually descended from the Turan tribes who arrived in the Balkan peninsula during the seventh century—coming from the Volga region on the north shore of the Black Sea. The Slavic peoples who eventually constituted the bulk of the Bulgarian population reached the area a century or less earlier; however, they had effected no well-defined political or military organization until the arrival of the Turanic tribesmen brought an urge to united political action. Under Isperich, the Bulgar chieftain, the foundations of the new state were laid on January 5, 681. Moreover, with the passage of time the Bulgars and Slavs became inextricably intermingled.

In the days of Charlemagne, the Bulgar khan had become strong enough to seize Sofia (809) from the Byzantine emperor; he laid seige to Constantinople itself and withdrew only upon receiving the Emperor's promise of a yearly tribute, a promise that Nicephorus I dared not abrogate. Christianity was introduced by the Khan

---

[1] "The New 'Socialist' Man," *News from Behind the Iron Curtain,* I, No. 7 (June, 1952), 36.

Boris I in 865 and the title of Czar was assumed by Boris' son and successor, Simeon I.

As though this were not enough, Bulgarians claim that their history began in earnest when, in the ninth century, they adopted and transmitted to the remaining Slavonic nations the original Slavonia alphabet. Under Simeon a Bulgarian literature was created, and in the tenth century the famed and controversial heresy of the Bogomils emanated from this center of early Balkan culture.[2]

Nevertheless, in the eleventh century, Byzantium rose again, asserted her strength, and Bulgaria lost, although temporarily, the independence and prestige of the first epoch. By 1186, however, a new empire was in the making. This greatest Bulgarian realm of all time controlled the entire Balkan peninsula (with the exception of Greece) even humiliating the armies of Constantinople. The memory of this glorious period did much to fix the self-esteem of the Bulgar people; soon, sad to say, their empire was to enter another dark period of subjugation and satrapy.

The newest conquerors were the Ottoman Turks and at Kossovo (1389) and Nikopol (1396), Bulgaria's heart-rending defeats, began the captivity which they were to endure until the Turkish eclipse in 1878. The hardships of her yoke are too numerous to recount here; it is enough to say that Bulgarian nationalism persisted just as it is persisting under Soviet rule today—although, in many ways, Bulgaria has become one of the most tractable of Red Russia's satellites.

---

[2] For the history of the "Old Slavonic Script," and the religious tendencies accompanying its spread, see various titles in Joseph S. Roucek (ed.), *Slavonia Encyclopaedia* (New York: Philosophical Library, 1949), especially "Orthodoxy and the Slavs," pp. 910-11; "Patriarchates," pp. 927-28; "Bulgarian Orthodox Church," pp. 119-21; "Bogomilism," p. 105; and "Cyril and Methodius," pp. 205-7. See also Dimitry Obolensky, *The Bogomils: A Study in Neo-Manichaeism* (New York: Cambridge University Press, 1948), for a valuable account of this unique movement which spread from the East into Europe between the ninth and fourteenth centuries, flourishing especially in Bulgaria.

World War and Aftermath

Yet these persistent memories of her long-dead empire may have induced her to enter two World Wars; however, Bulgaria chose the wrong partners and has suffered accordingly.[3]

Priority given to attack from the south in the last two years of the second World War coupled with Bulgaria's geographical position rendered both Bulgaria and Romania vulnerable to Allied Air strafing, and Bulgaria became a target of the United States Air Force in 1943. By this time the Nazi fortunes of war were at low ebb and it was becoming increasingly clear that Hitler had lost the war. Bulgaria, having failed militarily twice in twenty-five years, now sought a negotiated peace through the formation of a new government. This was done with the hope that she might be allowed to retain territory seized during the progress of the war from her neighbors Greece and Yugoslavia. Consequently, on August 30, 1944, emissaries of the moderate Bulgarian regime appeared in Cairo at the British and American headquarters. They got nowhere, and furthermore the Western Allies saw fit to inform Stalin of the event. The Georgian made his own plans.

According to Churchill, "I never felt that our relations with Romania and Bulgaria in the past called for any special sacrifices from us." Yet he already had perceived (and admitted) that "Communism raised its head behind the thundering Russian battlefront. Russia was the De-

---

[3] For further details, see Joseph S. Roucek, *Balkan Politics* (Stanford University: Stanford University Press, 1948), chap. III, "Bulgaria," pp. 42-77; Ygael Gluckstein, *Stalin's Satellites in Europe* (Boston: Beacon Press, 1952), *passim;* Michael Padev, *Dimitrov Wastes No Bullets* (London: Eyre, 1948); Elizabeth Barker, *Truce in the Balkans* (London: Percival Marshall, 1948), chap. 3, "Bulgaria's Fatherland Front," pp. 38-48, chap. 6, "Portrait of Bulgaria," pp. 88-101; Christo Tronkov, "Bulgarian Bibliography," *Slavonic Review*, XXVII, No. 68 (December, 1948), 259-77; R. H. Markham, *Tito's Imperial Communism* (Chapel Hill: University of North Carolina Press, 1947). For excellent accounts of the social process in pre-Communist Bulgaria, see R. H. Markham, *Meet Bulgaria* (Sofia: The Author, 1931) and I. T. Sanders, *Balkan Village* (Lexington, Kentucky: University of Kentucky Press, 1949).

liverer, and Communism the gospel she brought."[4] To
save Greece he had already agreed to a 90-10 power ra-
tion in Romania and 75-25 in Bulgaria (in favor of Stalin, that is).

The Communist Thrust

Communism was, indeed, rearing its head. Bulgaria
was not to be permitted to withdraw from the war. Suddenly, on September 5, 1944, with no other provocation
than that the Bulgarians had organized a government in
which Communism was not represented, Stalin declared
war. The Soviet armies entered Bulgaria without resistance three days later.

On September 9, under the wings of the Red Army, another change in government was effected. The Communists now held four ministries and were thus prepared
to dominate the country. Next ensued a reign of terror
with old scores, right and left, being settled. Within
three months, over two thousand people had been executed (these are the official figures; the actual number
no doubt surpassed this number). By 1947—a little
over two years—a new constitution, modeled on the
Soviet Constitution of 1936, had been adopted.[5] This
form is familiar and need not be discussed here.

Bulgaria's history for the past twelve years represents
a mournful chapter in the saga of this once-glorious nation. Her economic woes have been growing steadily.
One terrifying feature in this grim situation has been
the freezing of wages and salaries; the worker's "take
home" pay falls short of the bare subsistence level even
by Bulgarian standards. Recent price reductions on a few
staples had little effect—if any—on the purchasing power
of the money earned. Worst off is the peasant—followed
by the industrial worker and the white-collar man. These

---

[4] Winston S. Churchill, *Triumph and Tragedy* (New York:
Houghton Mifflin Company, 1953), p. 208.

[5] For a complete review of the Communist seizure of the govern-
ment in Bulgaria in 1944-47, see R. Wolff, "Bulgaria," chap. 11, in
Stephen D. Kertesz, *The Fate of East Central Europe* (Notre Dame,
Ind.: University of Notre Dame Press, 1956), pp. 274-96.

three categories constitute 90 percent of the total population.[6]

Bulgarians suffer not only from high prices but in terms of the quality of the goods—for much that is produced defies description. This is especially true in relation to the shoddy consumers' goods offered for sale. High-quality products are chiefly for export to the USSR. For more than a decade exports to the USSR have been sold at prices well under the world market. For example, a pair of top-quality men's shoes are sold at 40 *leva* to the Soviets, whereas footwear of a much lower grade is offered locally at 200 to 240 *leva*. Since the signing of the so-called Soviet-Bulgarian Trade Agreement in February, 1957, textile plants have been producing large quantities of clothing for the USSR. *Ad hoc* "tailoring cooperatives" have been set up for the purpose and they have "full employment"—working on a three-shifts-a-day schedule.

In addition to direct purchases, the Soviets often act as middlemen between Bulgarian industry and prospective buyers in the Eastern bloc satellite countries, with the terms of the sale being fixed in Moscow. In like manner Bulgaria has been supplying Syria with cement and Red China with electric motors, telephones, and X-ray equipment. The net result has been a gradual pauperization of the people, and strong resentment has been expressed throughout the entire country.

Forcible collectivization in agriculture has been carried out more intensively in Bulgaria than in any other East Central European satellite, although East Germany in the past few years feels much the same sting. By the close of 1937, around 90 percent of the tillable soil (compared with approximately 20 percent in Romania) had been collectivized. Recently, however, the veil over "unconstrained" collectivization practices was lifted by Ellie Able, a special correspondent for the *New York Times*. While the use of force had long been suspected, incidents on the outskirts of Sofia in the relatively prosperous villages of Dragalevtzi and Semyonovo on January 22, 23,

---

[6] Joseph S. Roucek, "The Plight of Bulgaria," *American Bulgarian Review*, IX, No. 2 (Spring, 1959), 25-29.

1958, provided substantial proof of these Marxist tactics. During the night both villages were surrounded by squads of Communist party volunteers and policemen armed with machine pistols. When the industrial section of these villagers—employed in Sofia factories—attempted to board, as usual, buses for the city, they were informed by the police that they would be allowed to leave only if they produced documents indicating their enrollment at a collective farm. Similar cases of "persuasion-by-siege" have been reported from the rural centers of Bistritsa and Zhelezhnitsa.[7]

Persistent troubles with students, too, have been reported. After two consecutive students' demonstrations in the capital during January, 1958, over a thousand were seized and shipped to slave-labor camps, although the existence of such camps is currently denied by the Kremlin. In order to forestall a popular uprising spearheaded by youth, the government recently has deported thousands of young men and women to Siberia and Khazakstan on so-called "voluntary" contracts. On arrival, these Bulgarian young people are to participate (or so the official communiqué reads) "with the U.S.S.R.'s youth in Communist construction."

Reliable information reveals further that the police have been instructed to rid the cities—Sofia, Plovdiv, Burgas, and Varna especially—of "hooligans." A new wave of arrests has included aged people too—on charges of "hooliganism"—and most of these have been transported to the notorious forced labor camp of Belene, on the Danube, where a ten-hour day at hard labor is complemented with compulsory daily Communist ideological indoctrination.[8]

Life in Sofia, called by the Bulgarians "the Most Beautiful Fruit of Europe," as described by a recent visitor, pictures "the average citizen, the average Bulgarian, as an extremely charming person, who, despite his hard life,

---

[7] As quoted in Roucek, "Plight of Bulgaria," p. 27.

[8] See Joseph S. Roucek, "Forced Labor Camps in the Soviet Orbit," *Prologue*, IV, Nos. 1-2 (Spring-Summer, 1960), 52-70.

has not lost his happy disposition, whose hospitality, as before, knows no bounds."[9]

In fact, the changes which have—since 1944—come to Bulgaria are not entirely unwelcome in themselves—especially the concentration of industrialization and trade; only the unfree condition of the Bulgarian people, the economic ups and downs, and the "tiresome official propaganda against the so-called capitalist-imperialist West," which force Bulgarians to wear a mask, are resented.

Although Bulgaria's position geographically speaking is much less conducive to dissent at Communist practice than that of East Germany or Poland, there is a strong anti-Soviet feeling in the universities. A former Bulgarian student, now resident in the United States, cites mass disapproval of Bulgarian university students toward Soviet handling of their fellow students during the 1956 Hungarian revolt. He reports that every university student is required to be a Communist party member and that studies of Marxism and the Russian language are basic requirements—as indeed they are unique throughout the Soviet slave empire.[10] He deplores the subjectivity of the system which stacks the cards in examinations and progress in favor of dedicated Marxists, and declares that his native land will at last "join forces with other Communist-oppressed nations and throw out the Red Army."

The long isolation from the thinking and activity of the West which the average Bulgar has experienced has developed in him a certain provinciality and unreality. Bulgarian agriculture—which is now almost completely collectivized—in former times represented the mode and best recognized pattern of livelihood. Now it shares this prestige with industry. Yet, while the Bulgarian's thoughts turn toward the past, he still appreciates the

---

[9] Karl Rau, " 'The Most Beautiful Fruit of Europe' Under the Red Star," *American Bulgarian Review*, IX, No. 2 (Spring, 1959), 30-31.

[10] G. A. Burden, "Entrance in Bulgarian Colleges More Difficult Than American," an interview with Andrei Yakamov. *Montana Kaimin*, Missoula, Montana, March 4, 1960.

potential of industrialization as a new hope for his country, for it is rich in mineral resources. Nonetheless, this rapid leap forward into mechanization has been—like the kolkhozy—forced upon him, and he resents bitterly the chains of his Soviet "protector," who stands by to pocket the profit from his own toil and the severance of his natural resources.

In the postwar years, Bulgaria's population has increased from five to eight millions; completely new cities have been constructed—from the ground up, for example, Madan, Rudosem, and Dimitrovgrad; a third of the country's population now lives in the cities; Sofia's public buildings are indeed impressive; the national library is most popular; and the new University (at Sofia) has more than five thousand students, who—as mentioned above—do not willingly follow the Party line. In fact, although their yoke is even heavier than that pressed upon them by the Ottoman Turk, Bulgarians still have a strong sense of pride and nationality. Without doubt, the USSR will some day have to reckon with this.

A further expression of Balkan nationalism is found in the fervor with which these southern Slavs enter into the "Macedonian Question." This question refers to the ownership of a strip of land with a historic name, a domain that has been a football for almost a hundred years. For in 1878 the Congress of Berlin, alarmed at the "Big Bulgaria" created at San Stefano, restored the sector to Turkey. A later solution saw the area divided among Bulgaria, Serbia, and Greece—to the satisfaction of none.

During the summer of 1958, the Bulgarian-Yugoslav border was opened briefly, ancient rivalries flared anew, and the feud was immediately resumed. In the same autumn the most strident aggressors in the campaign against Yugoslavia's Tito were the orthodox Communist regimes in Bulgaria and Albania. Reviving the old Macedonian specter, Yugoslav newspapers charged that Bulgaria—as a part of the Kremlin's deep-laid campaign against Tito—has revived her claim to the Serbian part of classical Macedonia. Bulgarian leaders, on the other hand, quickly asserted that Macedonia is "Bulgarian"—

that there is no such thing as a "Macedonian" people—
only Bulgars *irredenta*.

It has been reported that a "kind of hysteria has been
whipped up over the issue, an easy thing to do in Bulgaria, where the bitterness over the "Macedonian Question" has been utilized as a political device and policy-
making factor ever since Bismarck as the "honest broker"
called the Congress of Berlin.[11]

It is clear that the nationalist spirit still exists along
the Maritza. Would that the fervor which surrounds
"Macedonia" could be transferred (or transformed) into
a campaign against the greater enemy—Soviet Russia
—that took *all* of Bulgaria, not merely an interior county.[12]

Most ironical of all—in the face of current hostilities
and recriminations—is the fact that, even prior to the
first World War, the Turks and Bulgarians had signed, in
the peace treaty of September 29, 1913, a covenant that
expressly guaranteed (Art. 9, par. 2) that the nationals
of either party, although residing on alien soil, should "in
no way be molested" as to their property and human
rights.[13] Specifically the document referred to the Turks
in Macedonia and western Thrace, to the Bulgarians in
eastern Thrace and western Asia Minor. It is considered
by Dr. Kurt Rabl, an expert in international law, as one
of the prominent instances of the existence of "human
rights" in the law of nations.[14]

Current Significance of Bulgaria

Historians are shocked—and rightly—at Clio's status
in George Orwell's *Nineteen Eighty-Four*.[15] Here, as may

---

[11] See a review of these events in Carlton J. H. Hayes, *Political
and Cultural History of Modern Europe*, II (New York: The Macmillan Company, 1939), 190-97. Hayes judges that "the main result . . . was an intense quickening of Bulgarian nationalism."

[12] See Joseph S. Roucek, "The Plight of Bulgaria," p. 29.

[13] Kurt Rabl, "Mass Expulsions and International Law," *Sudeten
Bulletin, A Central European Review* (Munich), VIII, Nos. 8-9
August-September, 1960), 207-12.

[14] *Ibid.*, p. 208.

[15] George Orwell, *Nineteen Eighty-Four* (New York: Harcourt,
Brace and Co., Inc., 1949).

be remembered, Winston, our "hero," was engaged (at the dictates of "the Party,") in a daily revision of the official records to suit the contemporary motives of his masters. At the conclusion of each day's work the remains of the "old" history were unceremoniously tossed into an adjacent incinerator, the "memory hole." The "new history" was carried to the waiting archives.

When "history" is rewritten (as in Bulgaria) to justify the oscillations of politics, as a camouflage for part expediency, it is difficult to view the product as more than the vilest propaganda, for, in addition to being false in itself, it tends to vitiate the entire validity of history.

The Kremlin's tactics in Bulgaria represent an example of the viciousness of this type of falsehood. Respect for history, and especially the German concept of the objectivity and impartiality of history as written from its basic sources, has been a convention of Western civilization for many centuries. We have been taught to consider history as a special variety of reality; viz, "the lessons of history," "history tells us," "those who will not learn from history are compelled to relive it." To the Western world, then, events in Bulgaria (and indeed *ubique* throughout the Soviet slave empire) should offer a lesson; otherwise such a rape of truth and seizures of people and property will be repeated again and again.

Education in Bulgaria

The formal educational history of Bulgaria actually began only at the end of the five centuries of slavery under the Turkish conquerors. The Turkish domination lasted for 480 years, from 1393 to 1878. Because of its geographical proximity and topography, Bulgaria was more rapidly and completely dominated by the Turks than Serbia, and was slower to free itself. National life was practically exterminated.

Those who survived under Turkish rule could do so only as serfs or by embracing the Moslem religion; the rebels had to choose the careers of outlaws in the mountainous districts. The situation was complicated by the Greek control of the Bulgarian church, vested in the

Greco-Bulgarian Patriarchate of Okhrida, in Macedonia, from 1393 to 1767. Positions in this system were bought from the Turkish authorities at high prices and went only to the Greeks who had made money as officials of the Turkish bureaucracy; hence, the Bulgarian Christians were spiritually ruled from Constantinople.

When independent Patriarchates were abolished in 1767, Greek dominance became absolute, attempting to do away with the last vestiges of Bulgarian national spirit in the Church, promoting among the Bulgarians a bitter hatred which has lasted well until today. For instance, the Patriarchate ordered the destruction of the library of the ancient Bulgarian patriarchs, opened in 1825, as it was afraid of its influence on the independent Bulgarian nationalistic spirit; the Greek priests prohibited the use of national songs and excommunicated from their churches national bards.

These steps were, however, fighting the rising tide of national rejuvenation. A nationalist renaissance began in the eighteenth century with the study of historical and cultural backgrounds by such monks as Paissi (1722-98), who was born in Macedonia and went to the Greek Academy of Mount Athos and in 1762 wrote his famous *History of the Slavic-Bulgarian People, Czars and Saints*, which subsequently set the spark for the educational movement and spiritual awakening of the Bulgarian nation.

About and after that time, there existed a very few schools in some monasteries and villages giving instructions in Slavonic. Though these schools, called "cells" or cloister schools, were poorly equipped, they were of great significance for that dark age. At any rate, Father Paissi was a monk of the Chilender Monastery in the days when Mount Athos was a Greek center of intellectual activity, and the birthplace of the famous Greek Academy founded at the Monaster of Vatoped. Here, Eugene Bulgaris, a Hellenized Bulgar, a man of great erudition and liberal ideas, gave his lectures on the philosophy of Locke and Leibnitz. He also introduced the ideas of the Encyclopaedists, and Paissi then popularized them in Bulgaria. He was helped by another monk, Sofronii, and by historians such as Venelin—some of whom also began the development of the Bulgarain dialect as a literary idiom.

Yurii Venelin, a Slav from the Ukraine, wrote, in 1824, *The Ancient and Modern Bulgarians*. Vasili Aprilov, "born anew" after reading Venelin's book, decided to open a school for higher learning in his native town of Gabrove. This higher institution was founded in 1835 under the leadership of Neophitus of Rilo, who wrote a Bulgarian grammar and introduced the Bell-Lancaster method of instruction in this and other schools. The influence which the school of Gabrove exercised was very great, not only because it was an example of educational possibilities in Bulgaria, but it also served as a teachers' training institution. In a short time many schools of this kind were formed in such towns as Kalofer, Svistov, Kazanlik, Kotel, Koprivshtitsa, Plovdiv, and elsewhere. It was remarkable that, at the same time, ten girls' schools were opened, thanks to the philanthropy of Peter Beron, who himself was for the time being the most noted educator and scientist in Bulgaria.

The struggle for national emancipation was also helped —in contrast to the overwhelming of the Serbs—by agrarian and peasant society; by the Bulgarian gentry *(chorbaji)* and the commercial and artisan groups, which, though small, gained experience in administration and a leadership of great importance in the struggle for liberation. In addition, the Bulgarian merchants and refugees in Constantinople, Odessa, Bucharest, and other cities came in contact with the ideas of the French Revolution and with the extreme ideologies of the nationalistic and radical circles in Russia. American colleges and missions also helped in speeding up the Bulgarian movement toward self-determination.

But the public educational system was miserable indeed. There were no public schools, only church schools, directed by monks, and some private schools *(kilie)* ; both taught only reading, writing, church songs, and some arithmetic. Up to 1835, Greek was the language of the schools of the country; it was only in the early sixties that the Bulgarian language usage began to spread. When the Bulgarian church broke away from ancient Constantinople, the priests started to limit their activities to religious functions, and the communities began to support their schools (together with rich individuals) and assigned teaching to secular teachers. For a time there was a feverish competition among the communities for the founding of their own schools; since there was a marked shortage of trained teachers, they engaged practically anyone who indicated a desire to instruct. At the same time, the communities competing in the introduction of new subjects in some places introduced even law and philosophy into the elementary school curricula. Gradually some improvements took place, especially thanks to periodic conferences of teachers which tried to find an agreement on the foundations of the rising Bulgarian school system. The Bell-Lancaster system (the essential idea here was that the actual teaching could be done by the older pupils) began to be given up gradually, and replaced by Stephen's method introduced into Bulgaria by Kovachec and Blagoev; the number of schools was growing so rapidly that the system of twenty-seven schools at the beginning of the century had grown to 488 in 1950; but the attendance was poor and the status of the teaching profession miserable. Yet, even today, the Bulgarians look with appreciation and respect at the old *kiljni* and *vzaimna* teaching places, as they were, at the time, the only source of support for the resistance of the oppressed peoples and the only source of national culture.

Independent Bulgaria's Schools

In 1878 Bulgaria became independent, and its first Constitution included a provision that elementary education should be without fees and obligatory (while for the instruction in the colleges and university, a small fee was charged). Every village that had forty houses or more was to have a school, while smaller units were grouped together with a common school.

But the evolution of Bulgaria's educational system was sporadic. Between 1879 and 1911, Bulgaria had thirty-two Cabinet Ministers, and forty Ministers of Education (so that each Minister was in office only three-fourths of a year, and sometimes only twenty days), all of whom tried to put into effect new laws and edicts. There were the educational laws of 1880, 1886, 1892, and 1907; but it was only the law of 1909 which became of some consequence. Changes were continually made in the length of school attendance, the curriculum, the status of teachers, examinations, and the relation of the schools to the communities (at the time the whole system was nationalized). In most cases, none of these legal provisions was ever executed. If anything is to be surveyed or generalized from these frantic efforts, it might be stated that these steps were but imitations of the German examples which, salutary, could not be adopted to the primitive conditions of the newly formed state.

According to the Constitution of 1909, school attendance was made compulsory and feeless, although parents could send their children to private schools, if these took yearly examinations. In the primary and in high schools, as well as in the university, coeducation existed. Both the boys' and the girls' colleges or gymnasia were full to overflowing. In some of the larger towns, the government was obliged to support more than one high school and college in order to meet the ever-increasing demand for education. Illiteracy was diminishing, however, year by year, and after World War I, Bulgaria was one of the few states in the Balkans, or in the world, with three faculties of law, philosophy, and mathematics, which provided for one of the lowest percentages of illiterates in that area.

At the beginning of the reform, school attendance was three years, but was extended, just before the war, to four years; graduates had to attend another two-year continuation course (if not entering a secondary school). Although the school year ran from September 1 to June 29, it was often shortened. Originally, the curriculum included only the old *trivia*; but it was persistently extended until it also included religion and morals, civics, drawing, hygiene, physical education, and manual work. The Bulgarian language was taught according to texts approved by the Ministry. Physical punishment was specifically prohibited. Especially stressed were the excursions and the physical education and plays in the *Junak* organizations, and the work in school gardens. The support of the school building and care of school tools were the task of the individual communities, helped with state grants; the communities elected commissions of three to five members. A new teacher was not to have more than fifty children. Private schools could not be formed without the approval of the Ministry.

But the system had no time to absorb the feverish publication of new decrees and laws; additional handicaps were frequent economic, political, and financial crises, not to speak of wars, the poor hygienic level of the schools, the low level of the teachers, and lack of educational goals, not to speak of the communities' misunderstanding of the teachers and commissions.

More successful were the few kindergartens (fifty-five before World War I), for children between four and seven. The continuation schools were obligatory between the fall and February, and taught the Bulgarian language, mathematics and accounting, drawing, civics, and hygiene, but most of them were only projects on paper due to the lack of buildings and teachers.

There were provisions for commercial and professional schools; under the Turkish regime no such schools existed, nor were there any agricultural institutes. The new regime eventually founded two such schools, specializing in improved methods of agriculture, dairy farming, and stock breeding. During the summer vacations, the students were sent out among the villagers to instruct them in these various methods.

School Organization

Normal and pedagogical schools were planned, although only a few of them came into existence. The decree of 1878 demanded only the graduation from the upper elementary school or from some vocational courses. In 1891, it was decreed that all teachers had to be graduated from a state normal school of four years, with pupils from fourteen to eighteen, which gave instruction in the usual general and specialized subjects and also

Russian, German, and French, civics, stenography, accounting, writing, piano-playing, and violin-playing. The 1909 law extended the courses to five years, but in such a way that the first three years were identical with the classes in the gymnasium; only the last two classes were to determine whether the pupils really wanted to become teachers. Before World War I, Bulgaria had five male and four female teacher-training institutions. The teachers were appointed by the school committees and certified by the district inspector.[16]

The seven-year elementary schools, which had in their curriculum civics, French, hygiene, and manual work, became popular in the cities. From the very beginning they tried to imitate the secondary institutions and so ceased to be popular and were severely criticized. The law of 1909 tried to solve their problem by calling them progymnasia, and by making a break between the three years of the elementary school and the secondary school; they taught French as well as German; the civic attitude was promoted in geography and history, and the natural science course stressed commerce, economics, and industry. The weekly hours of instruction were not to exceed twenty-four for the compulsory subjects. Most of the gymnasia were coeducational, and graduates with a good record received a final examination. The classes were limited to forty pupils.

The number of these institutions was growing by leaps and bounds before World War I; they existed in nearly every community, and those unable to get them established in their communities formed central progymnasia for the neighboring communities. In a way, it was an anarchical system; the teachers, appointed by the Ministry, were to be university graduates or at least graduates from the continuation education courses and with a special state examination. But, in actual practice, even the elementary schoolteachers taught here.

---

[16] Bulgaria had some interesting disciplinary provisions: a female teacher was deprived, for three years, of her appointment if she punished her pupils physically, left her position without permission, or invited a man to spend a night with her. Another speciality was that the Bulgarian teachers had no voting rights before World War I.

The gymnasia started their careers with an initial opening in Plovdiv in 1850, and enjoyed the support of the government as well as the communities. But their structure was frequently changed. In 1915, the five-year gymnasium course was added to the four-year elementary school and to the three-year progymnasium, so that the course of instruction lasted twelve years. The strengthening of the curriculum consisted of adding civics, economics, hygiene, and music. Three types of gymnasia were introduced: (1) real gymnasia (without ancient languages, but with drawing); (2) semi-classical gymnasia (with Latin and drawing); and (3) classical gymnasia (with Latin and Greek). The girls' gymnasia had no classical divisions. In addition to Bulgarian and French (or German), all three types taught Russian, geography, history, civics, economics, mathematics, physics, chemistry, natural sciences, philosophy, singing, music, and physical education; the girls' institutes had manual work and pedagogy. The maturity examination covered only the subjects of the last year. The teachers were to have academic training. Many had studied in Germany—hence favored the German educational theory and method; they were appointed by the Ministry of Education; their state examinations were on a written theme selected by the Ministry and on practice teaching under supervision (there were no oral examinations). Before World War I, Bulgaria had thirty-one gymnasia (eighteen for boys and thirteen for girls), with more than seventeen thousand pupils, eighteen incomplete ones (six for boys and eight for girls), and four coeducational ones, with eight thousand students. The prevalence of girls in these institutions was remarkable.

But in general educational condtions before the World War remained poor; the pupils frequently went on strike, especially since about one-fourth failed; the Ministry changed its mind periodically about the rules and regulations and interfered with the pupils' grades; often the whole faculty of an institution on whom an unpopular director had been forced resigned as a body.

Among professional institutions, the leadership was taken by the Theological Seminary in Sofia under the Holy

Synod, accepting graduates from the progymnasia for six and one-half years of study. Sofia also had an art school. The music conservatory was, before the war, a private institution but receiving state support; it was organized in 1912. The technical school, as a secondary industrial institution, was opened in 1909; it accepted progymnasia students. The military school in Sofia trained officers; there were also institutions for naval reserve officers. On the secondary level, there were two three-year agricultural schools, one three-year vine and fruit school; and several lower schools for the education of the peasantry. Also on the secondary level were the commercial schools (two state and two private), imitating foreign examples. Professional standing was also granted to those who completed the three two-year pedagogical courses on the university level, one for the historic-philological group, one for the physics-mathematics group, and one for the study of languages, in which graduates of the secondary schools and of pedagogy received training for teaching in the progymnasia.

Sofia's university was founded in 1880 and originally had only pedagogical courses; it was changed into a university of three faculties: historico-philological, physico-mathematical and legal, and later the technico-agricultural faculty—which never functioned because of war. The administration of the school consisted of the Rector and the Deans, an academic senate of fifteen members, elected from among the professors, and representatives from each faculty. The organization was that of all Central European universities. But a special provision was that the graduates of normal schools were allowed to attend the school for two years for a probationary period, and if, during this time, they passed the maturity examination in the gymnasia, then the period of attendance was counted as having been the same as for regular students. The first examination took place after four semesters, and the second (final) examination after eight semesters. Women were allowed to enter the university after 1901 in any field; their number increased from 705, in 1913-14, to 2,210 in 1923-24. Interesting also was that numerous Bulgarians studied abroad rather than at home —in 1909, for instance Sofia had only 1,500 students.

Before World War I, the educational system was headed by the Ministry of three sections with five general inspectors (a mathematician, physician, philologist, historian, natural scientist, and a pedagogist); they supervised twelve district inspectors selected from gymnasia directors and professors, and sixty-four regional inspectors of the elementary teachers. Each community had a school council, usually consisting of three members, and of five to seven members in the cities, elected by the citizens.

The Bulgarians also had numerous schools abroad, especially in Turkey and Romania, including theological seminaries. After the unhappy results of the Balkan War of 1913, numerous Bulgarian schools in Macedonia were destroyed, with many teachers fleeing to Bulgaria; but only those who had passed examinations in Bulgarian institutions were appointed. On the other hand, there were numerous foreign institutions on Bulgaria's territory, Mohammedan, Tartar, Gypsy, Greek, Armenian, Jewish, Romanian, German, and French; and American schools (one for boys and one for girls); after World War I, they were officially recognized by the government and granted the privilege of giving diplomas equivalent to those given by the state schools.

On the whole, and when comparing Bulgaria's education to that in neighboring states, prewar Bulgarian education stood very high, especially when considering its agricultural background, its lack of resources, poor communications, and war's destruction. Yet most of the leading Bulgarians had received their education abroad, especially in Germany, England, and America.

Bulgaria Between Two World Wars

Between the two World Wars, Bulgaria, as all Balkan states, had no end of difficulty keeping out of domestic and international troubles. Defeated in the second Balkan War, and again in World War I, the country was saddled with the "Treaty of Neuilly," with all its reparations and losses of territory. Unredeemed Bulgarian populations were given to Romania in the Dobrogea and to Greece and Yugoslavia in western Thrace and Macedonia. Furthermore, Bulgarian spokesmen always stressed the loss of access to the Aegean Sea, the fact which made Bulgaria a landlocked state. Thus, defeated Bulgaria went through several domestic crises, unable to solve any basic problems. Stambuliski, the "Peasant Dictator," ruled the country as the spokesman of the Agrarian party immediately after World War I and initiated many radical reforms; he also envisaged a sort of South Slav federation ruled by democratic, peasant governments. But his conciliatory foreign policy antagonized the IMRO (The Macedonian Revolutionary Organization), which united with the bourgeois and army groups against him; he was murdered in June, 1923, and thereafter, for some years, a violent anti-Communist and anti-agrarian government ruled the country, antagonizing, at the same time, Yugoslavia and Greece with its pro-Macedonian demands. Boris III, who succeeded his exiled father, Czar Ferdinand, in 1918, eventually had to become a royal dictator in 1935. He also sponsored the revisionist ambitions of the Macedonians, who wanted to change the territorial settlements of 1919. His irredentism also induced Boris to join the Nazis in World War II and so become a base of Nazi efforts in the Balkans—although Sofia did not declare war on Russia.

Education Between Two World Wars

At the end of World War I, Bulgaria was a desperately poor country. Yet, interestingly enough, this difficult general economic situation increased the concern of the Bulgarian people in education; this, in turn, produced substantial educational reforms during the first postwar years. In 1921, under Minister Omarchevsky, the four-year elementary school for children, starting at the age of seven, was extended by three years of compulsory attendance at the progymnasia for children from eleven to twelve. The elementary school taught religion, Bulgarian (with the Old Slavonic methods), mathematics, geometry,

Bulgaria's history, natural sciences, economics, and hygiene, drawing with manual work, singing, and physical education. The progymnasium was put on a permanent basis for the first time, and a foreign language was made compulsory (French, German, or English).

School supervision was exercised by school inspectors, formerly selected from among teachers, but later only from secondary school professors on a competitive basis. Since the school committees were greatly influenced politically, after 1934 teacher appointments went to special committees and inspectors, so that the school committees remained only advisory and economic organs.

Since most of the progymnasia existed only in the cities, in 1931 the Ministry opened new progymnasia in 154 smaller communities. The communities having twenty children of compulsory school age had to form elementary schools; progymnasia had to be opened anywhere that there were twenty pupils in the fourth class. The school administrator was appointed from the teaching staff by the inspector (the election having been abolished). A special attention was paid to physical education.

The outstanding characteristic of the Bulgarian school system was its uniformity. Bulgaria has never had different school systems for different classes. Inequalities of educational opportunities were due rather to financial or economic difficulties. For instance, in 1924-25, there were in Bulgaria 605,102 children of elementary school age, of whom only 13,060 boys and 34,202 girls failed to attend school.

In spite of numerous discussions, the normal schools remained essentially the same, so that the five-year institutions had their first three years corresponding to the secondary schools, and only the last two years were specialized, giving eight hours weekly to pedagogy, and the rest to languages and the usual historical subjects. There were seventeen normal schools, while the progymnasia teachers were trained in the two-year teachers' academies. The gymnasia teachers, after their university studies, taught for a year under supervision (following the German example), and then had to pass a state examination. The teachers in the secondary agrarian school studied five years. The teachers of home economics had their two-year course extended to three years.

The kindergartens were not too extensive. They were obligatory only in cities with more than twenty thousand inhabitants for children from five to seven, after 1934. An example here was served by the American Kindergarten School in Sofia, which organized a course for training kindergarten teachers under the direction of Miss E. Clark.

Secondary education underwent some changes under Stambuliski in 1921, but in 1925, the Tsankov government returned to the old system, which had a five-year course after seven years of elementary school. There were general (gymnasia) schools and professional (pedagogical) schools. The gymnasia comprised three kinds (previously described). There was no flexibility in the organization of pupils' curricula, because all subjects (with a few exceptions) were required of all students. The apparent lack of provision for vocational education accounted for the constant rush of graduates to state or clerical positions.

There was only one university in Bulgaria (Sofia), having seven faculties: philosophico-historical, mathematical, legal, medical, theological, agronomical, and veterinary. Sofia also had the Free School of Political and Social Sciences, the Musical Academy, and the Art Academy.

After the disaster of World War I, the need for industrial and economic rehabilitation was glaring. An intensive but inadequate vocational policy was started. Many lower vocational schools were added to those already existing. The term of all these vocational schools was two years' schooling and one year of practice in the field. In nearly all these institutions, students were given a small allowance sufficient to cover their living expenses by half.

Bulgaria Under the Soviet Yoke

When the Comintern was officially dissolved in 1943, Dimitrov, a Bulgarian, the central figure in the Reichstag fire trial in 1933 and secretary general of the Comintern thereafter, slipped into the Moscow shadows. But he remained Stalin's adviser and the Kremlin's chief expert on Bulgaria—just as Ana Pauker was on Romania. Bulgaria had fought on the Nazi side during World War II. Although King Boris had shown himself a dexterous statesman in the previous successive crises at home, his alignment of Bulgaria with Hitler's Germany in 1941 was one of the most unfortunate steps in Bulgaria's diplomatic history, since the strong traditional and sentimental attachment of the Bulgarians to the Russians had been one of the main pillars of Bulgaria's nationalism. There was no Communist sympathy, it is true; but there was a very strong link between Russian Slavs and Balkan Bulgarians.[17] If anything, the Bulgarian people were not behind their King in his pro-Germany policy. But Germany was able to satisfy Bulgaria's territorial longings—actually an empty gift.

When the collapse of Nazi Germany was approaching, Russia, aware that it was not at war with Bulgaria and thus would have no voice at the peace conference regarding Bulgaria's fate, suddenly declared war on Bulgaria on September 5, 1944. With the Red Army on Bulgaria's frontier, the Bulgarian government went to the Soviet Legation in Sofia and asked to surrender (although the Soviet ambassador did not even know that the countries were at war). Eventually, the Russians offered terms which disposed of the old government and, under the underground coalition, the Fatherland Front, led by the Communists, took over power. Dimitrov returned to his native land, resumed his original citizenship, and as leader of the Bulgarian Communist party was named Prime Minister in November, 1946.

Thereafter, the pro-Soviet changes were ruthless and in no way resembled the rather cautious course taken by the Communists in Czechoslovakia, Poland, or Hungary. The Russians were afraid of the fate of the ELAS move-

---

[17] Christ Anastasoff, "Bulgaria's National Struggles," pp. 101-6, in "A Challenge to Peacemakers," *The Annals of the American Academy of Political and Social Science*, Vol. CCXXXII (March, 1944).

ment in Greece (conquered by the British Army and the Greek officers), and the parties representing the urban middle classes and the conservative better-off peasants, led by G. M. Dimitrov (not to be confused with the Communist Georgi Dimitrov). Brutal purges took place almost immediately. The People's Courts dealt rapidly with the crimes covering "statements that might impede economic life . . . creating mistrust in the government . . . spreading opinions that harm relations with a friendly state."[18] War crimes trials assumed epic proportions, and took care of all the three Regents, and most of the former Prime Ministers and Cabinet Ministers. The officers' caste "was cut down as with a scythe." Conformist leaders of the Agrarian party and of the Socialist party were also disposed of very quickly. By January, 1945, Bulgaria was directly in the Kremlin's orbit, ruled by a new Politburo run by Georgi Dimitrov, as Prime Minister of Bulgaria, together with four other men who had been for the past decade citizens of the USSR.[19]

The government proceeded rapidly, and more basically than any other Balkan government, to break down the barriers between town and country. The unemployed and half-employed intellectuals (doctors, lawyers, teachers, students) were mobilized and sent to the country over the weekends, working for the peasants, nursing the sick, teaching, and the like; medical students were given their degrees only after spending their first two years' practice outside the towns. New industries began to be constructed and helped, somewhat, to absorb the surplus farming population. A Two-Year Plan for industrialization (1947-48) was put into motion (and supplemented by other plans ever since), aimed at a practically complete nationalization of the state's economy.

When Dimitrov died (July 2, 1949, "while on a leave of absence in the USSR"), his successors carried on his ruthless pro-Kremlin policies, characterized by frequent purges, executions, and brutalities. Meanwhile, the Soviet

---

[18] Quoted by Howard K. Smith, *The State of Europe* (New York: Alfred A. Knopf, 1949), p. 357.

[19] *Ibid.*, p. 358.

Russian government has been bleeding Bulgaria white by exacting reparations from the country and through the *Komekon* system which had geared all the economic planning into the Kremlin's long-range goals for Russia and its satellites.

As far as the world's public opinion is concerned, whatever might have been Bulgaria's constructive achievements, they were erased by the headlines of the trial of Nikola Petkov in 1947 (the son of a former Bulgarian Prime Minister, educated in Paris and who had moved in urban intellectual circles), as the leader of the left wing in the Agrarian party. One of the founders of the Fatherland Front, who had cooperated loyally with the Communists in the wartime resistance movement, this "Titoist," like others in the satellite states favoring national Communism rather than international Communism, was tried in 1946 under flimsy accusations and hanged on September 23, 1947. After his execution, the final destruction of all non-Communist elements followed quickly.

With the change from the so-called "Fascist" regime to the "democratic" regime on September 9, 1944, Bulgaria soon began to shape its educational system according to the example provided by its Soviet masters. The Constitution of December 4, 1947, modeled after that of the Soviet Union, notes the educational ideology in Article 69:

Every citizen has a right to education. Education is lay and infused with a democratic, progressive spirit. Ethnic minorities have a right to instruction in their mother tongue; they also have a right to develop their own national culture, although the study of the Bulgarian language is compulsory. Primary education is compulsory and free. Schools belong to the State. The passage of a law is necessary when the private schools are established; such schools are placed under State control. The right to education is assured by the schools, the institutions of teaching and of education, the universities; by scholarships, boarding faculties, financial and special assistance to particularly gifted pupils.

The subsequent changes created a "general secondary school" with a course extending over all school years. The dominant types of Bulgaria's schools are: (1) the

primary school (four years) and the elementary school
(seven years), or (2) the secondary school (eleven
years).[20]

Organization of the Communist School System

Theoretically, all Bulgarian children have a chance to
complete their studies by attending a network of kindergarten, primary, secondary, and technical schools and
universities.

For children up to three years of age, there are, in
some places, crèches for orphans, for children without
parents, and weekly crèches for children whose parents
are employed at productive work. The kindergartens take
care of children up to the age of seven years; they are
daily, half-daily, weekly, and seasonal types. Seasonal
kindergartens are open only during the summer; the day
kindergartens are usually used by the children with
working parents.

According to the law of 1948, the school-leaving age
was extended by one year, from seven to fifteen, applying to all children of school age; according to Article 79
of the Constitution, compulsory education is free of
charge. In 1954, Bulgaria boasted of 6,611 general educational schools—elementary, grade, and secondary. If
we add the kindergartens and the special schools for mentally deficient and crippled children, the total number of
schools was (in 1954) 8,635, with an enrollment of
1,092,042, and a staff of 44,207. Special hostels have
been set up for the children living far from the school.
"As a result of these measures and the improved living
standards of the population, 99.5 percent of the children
of school age attended school in recent years."[21]

Beginning with 1945, the course of general education

---

[20] UNESCO, *World Handbook of Educational Organization and
Statistics* (Paris: UNESCO, 1951), pp. 72-77. Since this valuable
global survey of education has articles on other countries with
bibliographic references, but none on Bulgaria, we might assume
that there is no other available reference in English, except those
cited subsequently in the present study.

[21] Marin Geshkov, "Development in Secondary Education," *Bulgaria Today*, III, 16-17 (September 1, 1954), pp. 24-25.

was cut down from twelve to eleven years. The classical and semi-classical high schools (where stress was laid on classical languages) were closed and a unified high school course was established—a high school of general education. In 1950, the first secondary unified schools (from the first to the eleventh class) were set up; they united the three stages of education (elementary from the first to the fourth class), intermediate (from the fifth to the seventh class), and high school (from the eighth to the eleventh class). The director and the instructor in charge of tuition constitute the unified administrative and methodological executive board of the general educational school.

Institutions of higher learning are open to all students who have successfully completed the general secondary or the vocational schools. The general secondary school leads to all academies and faculties of the university; the vocational school gives access only to faculties that are related to their curricula. But the students from the vocational schools may enter the university by passing an examination.

Under the Communist regimes, higher education has been greatly expanded. Twenty institutions of higher learning ("as against three under the Fascist regime") were opened between 1944-54, with an enrollment of 30,000, four times greater than that before September 9, 1944. According to the official statistics, 21 percent of the students in the higher educational institutions are "workers directly engaged in production, or boys and girls of workers' origin. The rest are mainly sons and daughters of working peasants, employees or intellectuals."[22]

For the training of teachers, twenty-three pedagogical colleges and ten teachers' institutes had been opened by 1954. Teachers for the higher classes of the unified schools are also trained in the various pedagogical departments of the university. Teachers in physical culture, singing, and drawing are trained at the Higher Institute for Physical Culture, the Academies of Music

---

[22] Marin Geshkov, *op. cit.*, p. 24.

and Art respectively. An Institute for the Specialization
and Improvement of Teachers has been created in Sofia.[23]

Administration

According to official claims, the whole educational administrative system is based on a principle of democratic "centralization" with line-and-staff direction. But
when describing this system, we must remember that
Bulgaria is controlled by the Communist regime, which
penetrates all aspects of social, political, and thus also
of the bureaucratic operation.

The system is headed by the Minister of Public Instruction, assisted by the Deputy Ministers. The Ministry has the following sections: vocational, primary, secondary education, institutes and part-time education for
teachers; preschool and accounting; "work and salaries";
equipment; complaints; and administrative services. The
democratic control is exercised by the popular local and
provincial councils. The local (including urban) councils
have sections or bureaus of public education with a chief
officer, to whom are attached local school inspectors who
supervise schools in helping with the Ministry's instructions. The councils are also educational commissions,
which assist and direct the work of the education sections or departments. Above them are the provincial
Popular Councils, which have a board of public education, headed by a chief officer. Two or more inspectors
are attached to each board; they control the school sys-

---

[23] For the formal outline of Bulgaria's higher institutions, see:
M. M. Chambers (ed.), *Universities of the World Outside U.S.A.*
(Washington, D.C.: American Council on Education, 1950), pp.
163-66; "Bulgaria's New Educational System," *Times Educational
Supplement* (London), Nos. 1676 and 1677 (June 14 and 21, 1947),
pp. 292, 309; Kiril Dramallev, "The New Law on Education," *Free
Bulgaria*, III (September 15, 1948), 268; Dmitre Katzaroff, "Bul-
garia," pp. 502-9, in *The Yearbook of Education, 1948* (London:
Evans Brothers, 1948); Dentche Mintchev, "Report from Bulgaria," p. 31, in *XI International Conference on Public Education*,
convened by UNESCO and the International Bureau of Education
(Geneva, 1947); Petko Spirkov, "Svishtov," *Free Bulgaria*, III
(July 15, 1948), 223-24, description of the city and its University
for Economic and Social Studies.

tem in conformity with the regulations and instructions
of the Ministry.

It appears that the main task of the Popular Councils
is to provide for the material upkeep of schools.

Teacher Education

Primary schoolteachers must graduate from the pedagogical secondary schools. Prospective teachers of the
middle course in the unitary school (with a course of
eleven years) are required to spend two years in a preparatory institute after finishing their secondary school
studies. Teachers in the highest classes of the unitary
schools have to possess a university degree from the
faculties of arts and science. All teachers are appointed
by the board of education of the provincial or local councils. Promotion is offered to teachers who pursue higher
education by councils. Promotion is offered to teachers
who pursue higher education by part-time or full-time
teaching. Teachers may retire after a minimum of twenty-five years of service, and at the age of fifty-five. All
teachers belong to a social insurance scheme, and their
families are offered free medical services.

The idea of an education of an intercultural nature is
an experiment carried on by the pro-Soviet regime on
behalf of the Turkish minority. The Turks are being
taught the Turkish language, and their Turkish origin
has been emphasized. In 1952, a new Turkish boarding
school for teachers was opened in Sofia and accommodated eighty youths. At the University of Sofia three departments were opened to train teachers in history, the
Turkish language, literature, physics, and mathematics,
all subjects which are needed for Turkish secondary
school. Up to September 9, 1944, there had been only a
few Turkish schools in Bulgaria. In 1952, the government
was supporting seventy Turkish grammar schools, two
junior high schools, 176 primary schools, and two schools
for teachers. Furthermore, ninety-one students had

scholarships to study at universities. The total number of Turkish students reached around 80,000.[24]

Mass Communication

Learning from the experience of the Soviet Union, after September, 1944, the Bulgarian radio achieved considerable success. Since then the content of the radio programs has changed entirely. The power of the radio transmitters has increased twenty-six times. In 1951, Bulgaria already had over three hundred villages using radio receivers, totaling 40,000 loudspeakers. There are radio receivers in many factories, plants, and industrial establishments, which use broadcasts to indoctrinate the Bulgarian people along Communist lines and in accordance with the resolution of the Fifth Congress of the Communist party. Efforts have been to promote radio listening by scheduling assemblies where the most important broadcasts from the central station are discussed, such as "Help to Propagandists," "Hours of the Workers," "Review of the Central Soviet Press."

The majority of the Bulgarian people have small sets capable of receiving only medium-wave broadcasts, which means that only Bulgarian domestic programs can be heard. Larger sets are distributed only to party and public organizations and to some top Communists. Every citizen, department, organization, cooperative farm, school, and enterprise—and all those using radio sets—must possess a permit from the Ministry of Posts, Telegraphs, and Telephones, and pay a subscription tax.

As with all means of communication, radio is a state monopoly. The Bulgarian state radio operates five transmitters with a total power of 128 kw. Programs for schools are put on the air one hour daily. Numerous cultural programs are broadcast for the public at large. A radio redistribution system serves 5,090 loudspeakers in clubhouses and homes, and ninety are located in public squares.

---

[24] "The Collective Life," *News from Behind the Iron Curtain,* I, 10 (October, 1952), p. 36.

Bulgaraska Kinematographia, a public corporation, controls production and distribution of films. There are only a few educational films used in schools. Public showings for various organizations are provided by 16-mm. projectors. In 1948, seventy-five new 16-mm. theaters opened their doors. Bulgaraska Kinematographia is controlled by the Committee of Science, Arts, and Culture. Technicians are trained in the film schools of Moscow and Prague.

The Soviets have also adopted a program of social control by music and folk dance. In order to achieve complete thought control over the regime which the Communists dominate, the party has endeavored to transfer artistic activities from the individual to the collective sphere, acting on the principle that only the manifestations which take place in groups or crowds can be kept in check; one can take notice of them (while asking some members of the group to report on their fellow members) and one can manipulate them (while making the loyal members stimulate, support, or suppress the arguments going on regarding their merits). Music and dance—especially folk dances—are important weapons in this armory of Communist control. How this propaganda is manipulated in Bulgaria can be evaluated from the official reports of the Bulgarian leaders.[25] The Song and Dance Ensemble was set up at the Ministry of the Interior, as well as the Labor Corps. These developed into large art groups, which give "hundreds of concerts annually in towns, villages and enterprises. They have a great share in popularizing the new mass songs." A state choir was organized at Radio Sofia. "The State Folk Song and Dance Ensemble, staffed with folk singers, instrument players and dancers, is the youngest and most original music collective." The Bulgarian trade unions are "the main levers, the most efficacious disseminators of musical culture and important organizers of musical groups. There is not an enterprise or office in [Bulgaria] without a choir or a dance group organized by the local trade

---

[25] Venelin Krustev, "The Art of Music," *Bulgaria Today*, III, 22 (November 15, 1954), p. 13.

union. The 11,000 amateur art groups enjoy generous material support and qualified artistic assistance. Their activity is reviewed at numerous festivals on a nation-wide or local scale."

The government has been giving generous subsidies to musical institutions and activities. There are twelve state symphony orchestras, five state and three amateur operas. The old small National Opera of Sofia is today "a big operatic institute. With the aid of Soviet producers and choreographers, it has produced quite a number of classical Russian operas with imposing mass scenes." There is a considerable number of semi-professional ensembles, two state string quartets, and a growing number of soloists at the Directorate of Musical Creative and Interpretative Art. New music high schools were opened in Sofia, Plovdiv, and Stalin. The Sofia State Academy of Music has added a boarding school for boys and girls. The Bulgarian Academy of Sciences was enlarged by the addition of the Research Institute in Music.

Sovietization and Russification

The repatriates who run Bulgaria today are pushing a tremendous campaign of sovietization and Russification. (Premier Vulko Chervenkov fled to the USSR in 1923 at the age of twenty-three and lived his adult life there [until 1944], marrying the late Dimitrov's sister; others of the repatriates' clique are General Ivan Mihailov, Deputy Prime Minister, and Peter Pauchevski, Defense Minister; Raiko Damianov and Karlo Lukanov, Deputy Prime Ministers; Dimo Dichev, head of the State Control Commission; Ferdinand Kozovski, president of the National Assembly, Georgi Damianov, chairman of the Presidium; and Kiril Lazarov, Finance Minister.) A countrywide program of popularizing Soviet "achievements" in the arts, science, and productions, and promoting the study of the Russian language is pushed through the Union of Bulgarian-Soviet Societies—one of the "transmission belts"—which claims 4,800 chapters and one and a half million members.

Educationally, the regime has tried to sovietize the

youth through Marxist-trained teachers and professors. Elementary school lessons are divided into principal and secondary school subjects, the Bulgarian language and mathematics comprising the principal ones. Communism and its theories are not taught as separate subjects, but all teachers are expected to make daily reference in all courses to such topics as Marx, Lenin, the Red Army, the "liberation" of Bulgaria by the Soviets (September 9, the date on which the Communist regime took over), the Fatherland Front, and other themes pertaining to the history of Communism in Bulgaria and in the satellite states. History as it is taught to elementary school children stresses the traditional nationalistic approach up to the year 1879, the year in which the Bulgarian people regained their national independence from the Ottoman Empire; but from that date to the present it has been altered to become a defamation of the Bulgarian kings' reigns; their German origin is stressed and they are depicted as iniquitous enemies of the "people," hostile to Bulgarian freedom and interests. The history of the Fatherland Front (a Communist-dominated parliamentary bloc which includes non-Communists and maintains the fiction of an independent political unit) is taught as a continuation of regular history.

Youth Organizations

The control and indoctrination of youth in Bulgaria are affected by two "transmission belts" of the Central Committee of the Party, the Dimitrov Union of People's Youth and its subsidiary, the children's organization Septemvriiche. All youth from seven years of age to twenty-five is included by the program. The Union (UPY) united in 1947 with the Workers' Union Youth, the Union of Social Democratic Youth, the Agrarian Youth Union, and the youth organizations of the political circle of *Zveno* and of the Radical party. The cornerstone of the Union was the Workers' Youth Union—the most disciplined youth organization in the country. After the death of Georgi Dimitrov, the Union was renamed the Dimitrov Union of People's Youth, with more than one

million members, and the following goal: "Following
Georgi Dimitrov's behests to safeguard Bulgarian-Soviet
friendship as the apple of our eye, the DUPY educates the
youth in a spirit of boundless love and loyalty to the great
Soviet Union."[26] The DUPY has study circles in all
schools and universities and "helps the students make
progress and contributes to the stiffening of school discipline." The organization is a member of the World Federation of Democratic Youth and of the International
Union of Students. It has also organized youth camps and
sport gatherings. Its branches are in all the industrial
enterprises, larger Socialist and construction sites; and a
great many large projects, the Communist spokesmen
claim (such as the road through the Hainboas Pass, the
Stalin Chemical Plant, the Georgi Dimitrov Dam, the
Lovech-Troyan and Pernik-Voluyak railroad, and thousands of kilometers of highways), "are the the fruits of
youth labor."

Another organization related to the youth program is
the Volunteers' Organization to Assist the Defense
(DOSO), where the youngsters receive, next to political
indoctrination, premilitary training in firearms, parachute jumping, wireless communications, flying engined
planes and gliders, driving, air defense, chemical defense,
and other military skills. A few years ago the Bulgarian
Communist party passed a resolution to the effect that
state enterprises and party and mass organizations must
take over the leadership of the "Pioneers," the Communist children's organization. This support was to be given
mainly by building new Pioneer Homes where boys and
girls between the ages of five and fourteen would receive
Marxist indoctrination.

The Curtailment of Religion

The Bulgarian Communists have displayed tactical
flexibility in regard to religious groups whenever they
have estimated them to be potential instruments in

---

[26] "The Power of Organized Youth," *Bulgaria Today*, II, 17
(September 15, 1953), pp. 4-5.

carrying out their policies. Ideologically, the regime is committed to a complete negation and destruction of all religion, but, in practice, the religious bodies were allowed to survive to a certain extent.

According to the 1934 census, Bulgaria had 5,218,890 Orthodox, 821,298 Moslem, 48,398 Jewish, 45,704 Roman Catholic, and 8,371 Protestants.

In 1945, in order to support a Soviet design to extend Soviet political influence in the Middle East by means of the Orthodox Church,[27] the Bulgarian Orthodox Church was allowed to elect an Exarch on January 21, 1945, and effect a reconciliation with the Patriarchate of Constantinople on February 22. On May 10, 1953, the Bulgarian Church was elevated to the status of Patriarchate (which it had not been since 1933), in order to make the Bulgarian Church a full-fledged member of the community of Orthodox Churches on the side of the Russian Patriarchate. At the same time, the Church was also eviscerated. In September, 1948, the independent-minded Exarch Stefan, elected in 1945, was deposed and banished to a monastery. The hierarchy was intimidated through the medium of the so-called Union of Orthodox Priests— another "transmission belt"—led by Red priests who had sided with the Communist government. The modern printing press plant belonging to the Holy Synod in Sofia was nationalized, and the Committee for Science, Art, and Culture was entrusted with censoring all publications of a religious nature. Religious textbooks were banned in 1948 when all religious instruction was banned in the schools. The few religious publications which still appear in Bulgaria are written by Communist agents and not by members of the clergy. All religious publications must be prepared in accordance with the "true Socialist ideal. . . ."[28]

By virtue of the general law on religious denominations

---

[27] The plan was to make the Russian Patriarch, supported by loyal heads of the Serbian, Romanian, and Bulgarian churches, the spiritual leader of Orthodoxy and thus a useful vehicle of influence in the Middle Eastern Orthodox areas.

[28] "Ideological Weapons," *News from Behind the Iron Curtain*, I, 5 (May, 1952), 34.

of 1949, the Church was prohibited all contact with the youth or conduct of charitable activities. Under Section 12 of the law, the government is further entitled to remove any clergyman whom it should find objectionable for one reason or another. Church affairs are handled by a department under the Ministry of Foreign Affairs. The higher clergy is closely supervised by this office and forced to cooperate with their Soviet peers. Religious services have been reduced to reading scriptures, though even this is considered subversive. People are forced to attend Communist-sponsored meetings during the time religious services are held.[29]

The new statute of the Church decreed in 1951 formed other methods of government control. The government passes on the candidates before a patriarchal election is held or bishops are consecrated. No celebration of religious holidays is allowed.

The other religious groups in Bulgaria have faced gradual extermination. The Protestant community (comprising Methodist, Baptist, Congregational, and Pentecostal churches) was attacked first. After closing the foreign schools (French Catholic and American Protestant) in 1948, the government proceeded to destroy the churches themselves. On February 25, 1949, a trial of the leading fifteen Protestant pastors on charges of espionage for the United States and Great Britain opened. The 1949 religious law prohibits foreign churches to establish missions or charitable institutions in Bulgaria; the existing ones were closed and their properties confiscated by the state. Financial aid and gifts from foreign sources may be received only with the government's permission. All contacts must be channeled through the government Office of Denominations. All messages, epistles, correspondence, and publications must be passed by the government. Religious and educational work among the youth is especially prohibited, since education and organization of youth "are conducted under the care of the state and are outside the purview of the denomina-

---

[29] *Ibid.*, pp. 34-35.

tions and their clergy." Likewise, all religious charity is prohibited.

The Roman Catholic community, both Catholics proper and the Uniates, was violently suppressed. The first step to cut its ties with the Vatican was taken on February 17, 1949, when the government ended the mission of the Apostolic Delegate in Bulgaria. In September, 1952, a trial of forty leading Catholic priests and laymen on charges of espionage was held. The trial ended with the conviction of the Bishop of Nikopol, Evgeni Bosilkov, and three priests (death), and the rest to prison terms.

The second largest religious group in Bulgaria, the Moslem, is composed mostly of the descendants of Turkish settlers living in rather isolated ethnic enclaves. While expanding the educational facilities to win the support of these Moslems, the government also deported to Turkey others who proved indifferent or antagonistic to their regime. In August, Sofia suddenly announced its intention to deport 250,000 Moslems to Turkey within three months. The Turkish protests induced the abandonment of the deadline, but a considerable portion of this number was actually sent to Turkey. The "wholesale expulsion of Moslems clearly demonstrates that among them, as among other groups, the Communists have met with resistance and have written them off as a source of insoluble difficulties and tension."[30]

Appeals to Pan-Slavism

Next to Czechoslovakia, Bulgaria has been the most receptive ground for the Pan-Slav propaganda since the Bulgars, defeated in World War II by their "Slavic Brothers," have had to make the best of their alleged ties with the conquering Slavs. In the instruction in history, no efforts have been spared to remind Bulgarians that "the first great figures in the history of Slav letters were Constantine [later called Cyril] and Methodius, the renowned brothers of Salonika who lived and worked in

---

[30] Committee on Foreign Relations, *Tensions Within the Soviet Captive Countries: Bulgaria* (Washington, D.C.: Government Printing Office, 1954), p. 21.

the ninth century. Their day, May 24, is celebrated by the whole Bulgarian people as the Day of Slav letters, books, and culture. Cyril and Methodius created the Slav alphabet *glagolitsa* and laid the foundations of the Slav literature," rhapsodizes a Bulgarian spokesman.[31] After extolling the Pan-Slavic aspects of Bulgaria's history, Professor Georgiev tells us: "However, Slav culture has marked the greatest of all achievements in our day when the Slav peoples set out along the road to Socialism."[32]

The historical facts have been twisted for the propaganda purposes of Russia, as well as Bulgaria. As a matter of fact, Constantine and Methodius were not Slavs, but two sons of a Greek *drungarios* (battalion commander of noble birth) by the name of Leo. Constantine became a professor of philosophy, but later gave up a brilliant scholarly career for monastic orders. Likewise well-educated, Methodius held the post of district governor in a Slavic-speaking area not far from Salonica; i.e., today's Macedonia, but eventually became a monk on Mount Athos. Both brothers spoke the Bulgarian dialect which prevailed in the environs of their native city. Recalled from their retirement by Byzantine Emperor Michael III when a mission asked for Slavic-speaking priests, Constantine invented a Slavic alphabet and translated into the Slavic dialect a selection of passages from the Gospels. This translation is the beginning of all Slav literature, but there are two Slavic alphabets. The so-called Glagolitic, "somewhat enigmatic in origin," and the Cyrillic, a combination of the Greek and Latin alphabet with Slavic sounds; the latter is "the ancestor of the modern Russian, Serbian, and Bulgarian scripts. On account of the difficulty of the Glagolitic, it was later supplanted in Bulgaria by the Cyrillic, which is relatively close to the Greeks," reports Samuel H. Cross.[33]

Then we must remind ourselves again that, periodi-

---

[31] Prof. Emil Georgiev, "The Day of Slav Culture," *Bulgaria Today*, III, 11 (June 1, 1954), 5.

[32] *Ibid.*

[33] Samuel R. Cross, *Slavic Civilization Through the Ages* (Cambridge, Mass.: Harvard University Press, 1948), p. 58. See also: "Cyril and Methodius," pp. 205-7, in Joseph S. Roucek (ed.), *Slavonic Encyclopaedia* (New York: Philosophical Library, 1949).

cally, the Bulgarians claim to be really Slavs. It is true that the Bulgars belong linguistically to the eastern branch of the Slavs, but are Finnic in origin, although now European in physical type. But for the Pan-Slav claims, it is important to note that the Old Bulgarian was the earliest of the Slavic languages to be written and that it persists even to this day in the liturgy of the Orthodox Church under the name of Church Slavonic; the Cyrillic is the oldest form of all modern Slav alphabets, and Bulgaria possesses the oldest Slavic literature. But this Slavonic affinity did not prevent Bulgaria from importing a German as its ruler and from fighting several times with its Slav neighbors the Serbs (Yugoslavia) over Macedonia, and from joining the anti-Russian camp in both World Wars.

Strains and Stresses

In spite of the persistent propaganda (carried on in the United States especially by sending here the Marxist indoctrinatory organ, *Free Bulgaria*), from the Red regime of Bulgaria, controlled by the repatriates from Moscow, in this country of spirited peasantry and industrious middle class, collectivization, return to medieval serfdom, dispossession, and denial of free enterprise have antagonized the vast bulk of the people.[34] The frequent subversion trials certify to the general unrest, not to speak of the antagonism between the Bulgarian repatriates enforcing Soviet control and exploitation and the local Communists striving for some degree of independence (which erupted in the Traicho Kostov affair).[35]

Especially tragic have been the execution and destruction of the upper strata of the old Bulgarian society— politicians, intellectuals, businessmen, civil servants, members of the independent professions, and army officers. Those who have been spared make up most of the

---

[34] *Tensions Within the Soviet Captive Countries: Bulgaria, op. cit.*, is a documented survey of this problem.

[35] See Adam B. Ulam, *Titoism and the Cominform* (Cambridge Mass: Harvard University Press, 1952), pp. 200ff.

population of the forced labor camps. Economically, they have been depressed to a level of bare existence.

Although the Communist party allowed the opportunists to join the Party's bandwagon, yet the official reports indicate that the surviving experts, and especially the university professors, Academy and Science members, researchers and writers, have been giving the regime much trouble as "reactionary, counter-revolutionary, and subservient to imperialist Anglo-American science."[36]

The difficulties confronting the repatriates are also evidenced in the fact that no literary works were found in Bulgaria worthy of awards for 1952—a certification of cultural stagnation. This was admitted by Premier Chervenkov in the following polemic:

What should we do on the ideological front and the field of culture, noticing that there is a lag and in some respects serious short-comings and even fiascos?

The deduction is (1) that we must further strengthen the alliance of workers and peasants with the intelligentsia; (2) that we must not slow down, on the contrary, step up the educative self-enlightening program among the intelligentsia; we must help that part of it which has been for a long period under bourgeois idealistic influences to shake off these influences for good; we must help the entire intelligentsia to accept, not because of fear, but because of conviction, the Marxist-Leninist teaching—the only correct science of the laws of social development; (3) that we must boldly raise a new intelligentsia from among the workers and the peasants.[37]

Not only have the repatriates been battling the "old" intellectuals, but also the younger generation. The 1953 graduates of the universities were fourteen and fifteen when the Soviet Army moved in and seventeen and eighteen when the overt opposition was crushed in 1947. Recollections of conditions existing prior to the Soviet seizure still form the basis for the thinking of the generations now coming into positions of responsibility. For instance, the Bulgarian Minister of Education, Dimiter Yaneff, censured in 1952 "a lack of political intensity" which had become manifested in a number of Bulgarian schools and cautioned teachers on certain shortages.

---

[36] *Novo Vreme* (Sofia), No. 7, 1952.

[37] *Rabotnichesko Delo* (February 1, 1953).

The scholarship standing of our schools is still unsatisfactory. Especially poor results have been observed in the basic school subjects, Bulgarian, mathematics, and Russian. Instruction on scientific subjects is at a very low ideological and theoretical level. Many shortcomings have permeated the field of Communist education . . . the depraved habits of the bourgeois school have not been completely eliminated, many subjects are not taught with sufficient political intensity; we must find the main reasons for the drawbacks of our school system and for the unsatisfactory work of many teachers who lack the necessary ideological, political, scientific, and pedagogical training. The Ministry of Public Education and the nation's teachers must do their utmost to instruct and explain their subjects according to the doctrines of Stalin, Michurin, and Pavlov. It is of paramount importance that the Soviet pedagogical experience be regulated and systematically studied.[38]

Even the work of the Pioneers appears unsatisfactory. For instance, on March 24, 1953, *Rabotnichesko Delo* (Sofia) complained that many party organizations had shown no interest in the "Socialist education" of the younger generation; sports activities, in particular, had been neglected; the Communist youth organization (DUPY) had failed to provide Pioneers with competent leaders; and Communist teachers showed a lack of interest in Pioneer work regardless of DUPY prodding.

A recent bobble in education and international relations placed Sofia very much in the news at the onset of 1963. A group of education-hungry Kenyans, who claimed that they had been "hijacked" into transit to Sofia on the pretext of later entrance into Western universities, found themselves gravely discriminated against there because of their color. Wilfred Nganga, twenty-five, having finally left the Bulgarian capital, testified as follows: "We were unable to leave until we could get enough foreign currency to pay our fare. . . . People used to follow us in the streets continually, calling after us, in English, 'black monkeys.' The atmosphere was intolerable."[39] Obviously, such publicity for a "worker's and peasant's state" proved shattering indeed when reported in the world press.

Robert Kotey, twenty-five, Ghana, after arrival home

[38] "The Collective Life," *News from Behind the Iron Curtain*, I, 10 (October, 1952), 32.

[39] The *Hindustan Times* (New Delhi), April 2, 1963.

in Accra spoke in similar fashion: "Whoever among us had leftist leanings has been cured. . . . We have been called black monkeys and jungle people and we were treated like dirt."[40] The immediate cause of the Africans' humiliation and departure is said to have been the arrest of seven leaders of the executive committee of the All-African Students' Union in Sofia. The Communist regime first banned the union, then police and militia beat up the African students when they attempted to stage a protest parade. Yet the union was not the basic cause, said Kotey. "There was more racial discrimination in Bulgaria than there could be in any so-called capitalist country. We are absolutely certain that this discrimination was not incidental but backed from above—by the Communist authorities."[41]

Trends

The Communist party of Bulgaria came to power in 1944. Although composed of only some eight thousand members, it was able to control the state because of Soviet Army backing. Charged with the task of reshaping Bulgaria to the benefit of the USSR, it has found considerable difficulty in gaining loyal supporters among the seven and one-half million Bulgarians, who, as mentioned elsewhere, are among the world's most pleasant and extroverted people, given normal conditions. The interminable civil war has been necessary to sustain the regime as the upper strata, religious groups, peasants, workers, and any dissenters have been subjected to repression, exploitation, dispossession, and execution. Frequent desertions, a tight internal security system, liquidations, and institutionalized slave labor testify to the grave difficulties facing the pro-Soviet government.

In prewar days often called the vegetable garden of Europe, Bulgaria has not reached the economic level of its sister satellites of the Eastern bloc—much less that of West European nations. Continual shortages of basic

---

[40] Associated Press dispatch, Vienna, Austria, February 15, 1963.
[41] Ibid.

food items have led to rationing. Scarcities of consumer goods have placed Bulgaria's living standard next to Albania's—the lowest in Europe. In 1962, butter was priced at $1.80 per pound, beef from $4.00-$6.00, with men's suits at approximately $100.[42] Of course, little can be bought by the Bulgarians at these prices.

Sofia's *Semedelsko Sname*, early in 1963, announced that the government, seriously concerned with Bulgaria's low birthrate, has devised measures to combat its leveling population. The Communist hope is for a 2.2 percent increase with a total population for the country by 1980 of 9,300,000.[43] A logical explanation for the failure of family formation and for the falling birthrate is the shortage of housing. Press reports maintain that the majority of Sofia families, for instance, are squeezed into one-room flats, with sometimes as many as four or five to a room. Officials are quoted to the extent that Sofia alone has a need for no less than 80,000 family units. An unidentified spokesman says: "The most important reason for our falling marriage and birthrates is that young people simply don't want to marry when they must wait up to five years for a home."[44]

One may well ask how long the Bulgarian people will be able to continue their spirit of resistance in the face of such odds as pitiful living standards and the repressive state apparatus. As Bulgaria tends more and more to resemble an Orwellian nightmare state, the conclusions of Milovan Djilas[45] likewise become more and more pertinent:

"As I became increasingly estranged from the reality of contemporary Communism . . . and am now struggling for a better world . . . I am one of its critics."

---

[42] Associated Press, Sofia, December 16, 1962.

[43] Via Associated Press, Vienna, January 15, 1963.

[44] Sofia, December 16, 1962.

[45] Milovan Djilas, *The New Class* (New York: Frederick A. Praeger, 1957). See his Preface, pp. v-vii et *passim*.

CHAPTER XI

YUGOSLAVIA
A SATELLITE IN REVOLT?

Geopolitical Setting

SITUATED, SO TO SPEAK, in the heart of the Balkan region, Yugoslavia dominates, geopolitically, one of the most strategically important areas in the world. In the first place, the Balkan region is a strategic region where the Russian landmass is nearest to coveted warm seas. The Balkan peninsula did not emerge as a crossroads of world forces only recently; it has been in the mainstream of world events since the beginning of recorded Western history; it is a key area to three landmasses of the world: Europe, Asia, and Africa. Only the narrow straits of the Bosporus and the Dardanelles separate it from Asia, and through Asia Minor the Suez Canal is easily accessible. (Unlike the Italian and Iberian peninsulas, the Balkan Peninsula has no definite boundaries; it is easily penetrable from the east through the Russian steppes and the door of Forcani, from the north along the Danube, and from the south by sea.) Historymaking events have originated or culminated in this area.

Alexander the Great started his ill-fated world conquest from Macedonia (a territory bitterly contested among Yugoslavia, Greece, and Bulgaria, part of which now is one of the "republics" of Yugoslavia). The Eastern Roman Empire centered on Constantinople, survived the barbarian onslaught for a thousand years longer than Rome, and remained a center of civilization while Europe was engulfed in medieval darkness; later the Osmanli Turks annihilated the power of Byzantium and approached the heart of Europe through the rugged Balkan valleys and along the Danube. In the eighteenth and nineteenth centuries. Russian troops repeatedly marched through the Balkans with the Sea of Marmora as their goal. It was the Serbs and Montenegrins who during this period transformed their guerrilla warfare (conducted by *Haijduks*) into a national uprising against the Turkish rule in 1804, gaining a semi-autonomous status which was transformed into independent Serbia in 1878. Although the Congress of Berlin (1878) prevented Russian predominance in the Balkans, it left the door open for German ambitions; the famous *Drang nach Osten* ("Advance to the East") sought to make the Balkans a steppingstone toward the Middle East. German expansionist policies through the Balkans antagonized Russia, and the Berlin-Baghdad railway plan threatened British control in India. Thus forces conflicting in the Balkans contributed to an odd British-Russian detente and to setting the stage for World War I. This was triggered in Sarajevo (1914) with the assassination of Archduke Franz Ferdinand of Austria-Hungary by a Serbian patriotic student. The Kaiser's hope of conquering the Transversal Eurasian Axis *(Mittel-europa)* was defeated in World War I, but rose again at the will of Hitler during World War II. Since the last chapter of World War I had started with the invasion of the Balkans by way of Salonica, more recently it has been debated whether a major landing in the Balkans during World War II would have been feasible and, if so, how far it could have influenced the postwar situation in regard to Soviet Russia's contemporary domination of the satellites there.

The Ideological Rift

Yugoslavia, under Tito, was the original Communist nation at least ostensibly to oppose the Soviet Union. In 1948, Marshal Tito, Yugoslavia's ruler, broke with Stalin and set out on his own. Since that time, he has been straddling the fence, unwilling or unable to move to either side—although he has not hesitated to accept American dollars.

Why has Tito—an ideological opponent of American capitalism—been granted this aid, although he has been running Yugoslavia as a Communist country and has been walking a tightrope between the West and the Kremlin, carefully striving for an independent middle position in the "cold war"? Because Yugoslavia clings to its Communist ideals and form of government, it is unwilling to side definitely with the Western nations; and, since Tito defied the Soviet's Stalin, he can't completely rejoin the camp without facing the possibility of suffering the "bear's hug." The need to keep Yugoslavia more on the side of the West than of the Kremlin has been glaringly clear to Washington—and hence this investment in "aid" to Tito costing the American people more than a billion dollars.

Yet, far from indigent, Yugoslavia occupies one-third of the Balkan Peninsula; covers an area of 98,826 square miles (a little more than the area of United Kingdom); and has a population of about sixteen million, which is a little larger than that of Canada. Its soil is more fertile than that of England and it has more mineral wealth in raw materials than Britain (except coal) and is richer in nearly all raw materials than Italy, although its resources have yet to be developed. The mountain regions are heavily wooded, making the country one of Europe's leading timber producers (beech, fir, and oak); mountain streams provide a high potential hydroelectric power, used frequently in the development of mining. In known deposits of bauxite, lead, and antimony, Yugoslavia leads Europe; it is second in quicksilver, copper, and zinc; it is third in the world as a producer of mercury. Oil reserves, in the Landova oil fields, adjacent to the Hungarian border, could make the country independent of oil imports. And, above all, Tito's Yugoslavia represents a broken link in the chain of satellites stretching from the Baltic to Albania, the latter thus being separated geographically from the USSR—and now ideologically!

This Balkan and Slav state, which is Communist but not a satellite state of the USSR, has common borders with Romania, Bulgaria, Greece, Albania, Austria, Hungary, Italy, and Trieste; it also controls the Adriatic Sea (which borders the country on the south and forms one-third its frontiers). From an overview standpoint, it is a bridge between the Moscow Empire, stretching from the Baltic to the Adriatic Sea and the West.

On the ideological level, Tito's Yugoslavia is the exponent of national Communism ("Titoism"), a good example that the Western world would like other satellites to follow. Tito's defiance of Moscow and continued outspoken independence have constituted a serious—and in retrospect even crucial—threat to Soviet hegemony over Central-Eastern-Balkan Europe. Furthermore, socially and educationally, Yugoslavia represents the classic example of how the initial effort in international Communism can be transformed into a national Communist state, accepting, occasionally, a sort of Western democracy. Also, the Yugoslav experiences in subduing bitter nationalistic tribal differences into a national pattern, by superimposing the nationalistic Communist ideology, is also a worthwhile historical lesson.

The present as well as the historical troubles which have contributed to the rise of Tito can be understood only within the historical framework. The Yugoslav people (16,691,000) occupy the territory which (before World War I) belonged to different states: Serbia, Montenegro, Turkey, Austria-Hungary, and Greece. The division can be appreciated better if related, at the same time, to the percentage of illiteracy[1] (1948):

	Percentage of Total Population:	Percentage of Illiteracy: Both Sexes	Male	Female
Serbs	41.5	27.7	14.1	40.2
Croats	24.0	18.1	11.2	24.0
Slovenes	9.0	2.3	2.3	2.3
Macedonians	5.1	30.2	18.7	42.0
Montenegrins	2.7	24.1	11.0	35.5
Autonomous Moslems	5.1	54.6	36.6	70.6
Bulgars	0.4	19.9	6.8	33.1
Czechs	0.2	3.0	2.4	3.5
Slovaks	0.5	4.8	4.2	5.3
Shiptars	4.8	73.7	55.9	92.5
Hungarians	3.1	8.0	6.0	9.6
Germans	0.4	6.2	5.9	6.4
Rumanians	0.4	17.6	11.2	23.2
Valaques	0.7	38.2	22.7	51.6
Italians	0.5	6.9	4.9	8.7
Turks	0.6	63.9	47.4	80.7
Gypsies	0.5	74.0	61.9	85.7

[1] UNESCO, *Progress of Literacy in Various Countries* (Paris, 1953), p. 166.

Thus, approximately three-fourths of the population is of Slavic origin. But the Slavic background again becomes complex when we note that the Serbs use the old Russian script and are Greek Orthodox in religion (with a strong substratum of Turkish culture), historically Pan-Slavs (but who hated Communism under the Monarchy). The Croats, on the other hand, who lived for centuries under Vienna's rule, are Western-oriented, using the Latin alphabet and for the most part being Catholics (with historical pro-German leanings). Bosnia-Herzegovina shows Turkish and Moslem influences, while Montenegro is peopled by primitive and isolated folks; Macedonia is an ethnological crazy quilt, claimed to be an independent nationality by the irredentist Macedonians but to be a Yugoslav branch by Belgrade, a Bulgarian branch by Sofia, and a "Slavic-speaking Greek minority" by Athens.

When these historical units were brought together in 1918, they presented the problem of political and cultural consolidation which has even today been only partly solved by Tito's regime. There is still a hiatus between the southern republics, Orthodox in religion and Cyrillic in their script, and the northern ones, which are Roman Catholic and write as Latins. The "northerners" still grumble over money invested in the poorer republics (Bosnia, Montenegro, and Macedonia); they still insist that Serbs hold too many key positions in Croatia, and their nostalgia for Vienna still seems alive. Furthermore, the Slovenes are still separated from the others by their language.

History of Separatism

The historical experiences of the various regions of contemporary Yugoslavia offer the explanation of the separatism of the various Yugoslav branches. We must member that Tito's Yugoslavia is a direct descendant of the Kingdom of the Serbs-Croats-Slovenes, founded on December 1, 1918, which, although not an altogether new state, was in effect pasted together from the Kingdom of Serbia, the Kingdom of Montenegro, and the Yugoslav sections of the former Austro-Hungarian Empire. Hence,

Yugoslavia has never been one nation—and the "one nation theory" with three names (Serbs, Croats, and Slovenes) was an old doctrine and stemmed from the great Serbian ruling circles in prewar Servia; in fact, the application of this theory by forming the Kingdom of Yugoslavia (the official name adopted by the royal dictatorship in 1928) caused endless minorities troubles. The present regime feels that all Yugoslav nationalities came from the common fatherlands (southern Russia), but that this is not a good reason to deprive them of their national characteristics.

The Serbs started coming to the Balkan Peninsula in the sixth century; they inhabited the parts east of the Croats and gradually penetrated more and more into the east and south. Stephen Dushan, who ruled from 1331 to 1355, was the founder of a great Balkan Empire, comprising Serbia, Albania, Epirus, Macedonia (and some portions of Thrace and of Thessaly). The Czar hailed from Serbia, it is true, but did not represent a national mission—but a supra-national idea of empire, and called himself "Emperor of Serbs and Romans." At any rate, his empire became a prop to the modern nationalistic ideology of the Serbs who have been trying to create a "Greater Serbia."[2]

In 1389, the Serbs were defeated at Kosovo Polje ("the plain of blackbirds"), a defeat which created a national philosophy among the southern Slavs known as the "Spirit of Kosovo." The national poetry *(Pigjesma)* sung in Serbia, Bosnia, Herzegovina, Dalmatia, and Montenegro conveyed through the centuries this memory of defeat, a sacrifice by a nation of its resurrection through resistance and death.

From 1459 until the beginning of the nineteenth century, the Serbian people, subjugated and enslaved, kept resisting the invaders by *Haijduks* (Balkan Robin Hoods); this guerrilla warfare transformed itself into a national uprising against Turkish rule in 1804. The leader was a peasant from Shumadia (central Serbia),

---

[2] Walter Kolarz, *Myths and Realities in Eastern Europe* (London: Lindsay Drummond, 1946), X, "From Great Serbia to Greater Yugoslavia," pp. 189-212.

named Karadjordje (Black George), who liberated the country for a while; in 1815, the second uprising was led by another peasant—Milosh Obrenovich, who succeeded in securing recognition by the Turks as "Supreme Chief" of Serbia. (He was founder of the dynasty which was exterminated by a *coup d'état* on May 29, 1903.) The Karadjordjevich dynasty then came on the throne (and its last descendant was exiled by Tito at the end of World War II).

The fight of the Serbian people for independence was rooted in the memories of Serbia's greatness during the Middle Ages and the memories of the battle of Kosovo. During the opening years of the nineteenth century, the nationalistic renaissance was guided by a minute body of intellectuals, nearly all of whom were either schoolmasters or priests, inspired by Herder's teachings to study the various peasant dialects and impressed with the richness of the Serb peasant art, folk songs, folk dances, and traditions. They were headed by Dositej Obradovich (1742-1811), who advocated the use of the spoken or "common" Serbian language in place of Church Slavic Serbian, which was used mainly by the clergy and the intelligentsia, but not by the masses; he thus promoted spoken Serbian to the status of a literary language. Furthermore, he was one of the first apostles for Yugoslav unity. Another clerical leader was Jovan Raich (1726-1801), who wrote a history of the Slavs. Later, the Serb Vuk Stefanovich Karadzich (1787-1864) standardized the Serb orthography and despite bitter opposition lived to see his alphabet adopted; in addition, he published a long collection of Serb and Bulgarian folk songs and epic poems of heroic deeds which, passed from mouth to mouth, kept alive a spirit of pride and resistance throughout the Serbian lands under the Turkish yoke. It was this background which became the basis of the "Greater Serbia" idea.

Without delving into the details of Serbia's history during the nineteenth century, sufficient to state here that the feud between the Obrenovich and Karadjordjevich dynasties plagued Serbian politics. It was essential that, in 1830, one of the rulers (Milosh) gained the Sultan's recognition as hereditary Prince, enlarged his territory, and started to rid his principality of Turkish landholders and troops. Also of importance was Serbian emancipation from Greek ecclesiastical domination, achieved by the establishment in 1831 at Belgrade of a Metropolitan of Serb nationality as the head of the Serbian Church. The principality was launched on its course toward independence by the strengthening of the state and by granting certain constitutional guarantees, although political instability and foreign interference handicapped progress.[3] The Treaty of Paris (1856) placed Serbia under the protection of all the great powers, thus removing it from the vague but exclusive tutelage of Russia.

A step of historical consequence was taken in 1878 when Bosnia-Herzegovina was occupied by Austria-Hungary, thus laying the foundations for future conflicts between Serbia and the Dual Monarchy, culminating in the assassination of Austria-Hungary's Archduke and the Duchess Sophie.

In 1912, Serbia and Montenegro joined Bulgaria and Greece in the Balkan Alliance and were victorious in 1913; but then Bulgaria fought over the spoils with Greece and Serbia and lost. In 1914, Gavrilo Princip, a young Serb (native of Bosnia), assassinated the heir to the Austro-Hungarian throne in Sarajevo on June 28 (on St. Vitus's Day—the national holiday of Serbdom, the anniversary of the battle of Kosovo in 1389!).[4] This gave Vienna a chance to declare war on the Serbs, whose leaders had been agitating for the liberation of all southern Slavs, a majority of whom lived under the Austro-Hungarian rule. The retreat of the Serbian Army across the snowy mountains in Albania, known as "Albanian Golgotha," represents one of the great historical memories of the Serbs; those who survived were transported by

---

[3] For details, see Malbone W. Graham, "Constitutional Development to 1914," chap. VII, pp. 107-17, in Robert J. Kerner (ed.), *Yugoslavia* (Berkeley: University of California Press, 1949).

[4] For the detailed account of the background of this assassination and the related international politics, see: Bernadotte E. Schmitt, "Serbia, Yugoslavia, and the Habsburg Empire," chap. IV, pp. 41-65, in Kerner (ed.), *Yugoslavia*.

the Allies to the Greek island of Corfu. The reorganized Serbian Army continued to fight on the Salonica front until the creation of the Kingdom in 1918.

Croat tribes, closely related to the Serbs, settled the areas of the northwestern part of present-day Yugoslavia. The first ruler of great importance was Tomislav who assumed the royal title *(Rex Chroatorum)* in 924; he was recognized by the Pope, and Split became the Archepiscopal seat. The last Croat national King Peter Svachich fell in 1097 in a battle against the Hungarians, and the Hungarian King Koloman was crowned King of Croatia and Dalmatia in 1102. Throughout the subsequent centuries of Hungarian rule, the Croats retained the memories of their independence, mirrored in their claim to the "historic rights" of their Kingdom; in addition, this nationalistic ideology is interlinked with the conception of Croat history as a long process of self-sacrifice for "the cause common to all Christian people."[5]

A deep mistrust existed, however, between the Croats and the Serbs. While the Serbs had been under the influence of Byzantium, used the Cyrillic alphabet, and belonged to the Orthodox Church, the Croats, under Hungary, derived their culture from Rome and Western Europe, used the Latin alphabet, and paid allegiance to the Pope in Rome. Then, in 1867, Budapest granted a certain degree of self-government to the Croats, led by a small group of native nobility, whose few members participated in the revival of the native language. But their particularistic nationalistic revival went so far as to oppress not only the Croat peasants but also the Serbs living in Croatia. This Serbo-Croat rivalry stood in the way of any possible Yugoslav unity, since some Croat leaders wanted only an autonomous principality within the framework of the Habsburg Empire, which would enable it to remain Catholic as well as Croat in character. The Serbs, on the other hand, could conceive no future state dominated by the Habsburgs and wanted a "Greater Serbia," which would be mainly Orthodox in character and dominated by the Serbians.

[5] Kolarz, *op. cit.*, p. 204.

At the same time, a social revolution was on the way during the nineteenth century. After the profound though temporary changes of the Napoleonic period, Croat-Magyar relations were characterized by ever-increasing differences, represented by the feuds of the medieval Croatian and Hungarian Estates and the Croatian and Magyar representatives in the Hungarian *Reichstag*. The argument was mainly over the question of which language, Magyar or Latin, the Croat representatives were to use in the *Reichstag*, the Magyars insisting, in the main, that Magyar instead of Latin was to become the official language of the relations between Magyars and Croats. (The new Hungarian electoral law of 1848 provided that even the name "Croatia" was no longer to be mentioned!) The resentment of the Croats against the pro-Magyarization policies promoted Croatia's very active participation in the military intervention in Hungary and the support of Austria's forces by the Croats during the 1848 revolution.

The Croatian Estates resolved, unanimously, in 1847, to substitute the Croatian for the Latin language in government administration and the schools. The social consequences in the area of national evolution were tremendous. Formerly, only a very limited part of the Croatian (and Magyar) upper classes—aristocracy, gentry, and the higher clergy—spoke Latin. The introduction of the national language widened the range of group interests concerned: the representatives of bourgeois culture (trade, commerce) and a growing professional class. In turn, this change was followed by the rise of a new brand of nationalism on the political stage, the southern Slav union movement, which started to replace Croatian autonomism.

The idea of "Illyrianism" became quite attractive to many southern Slavs. The Kingdom of Illyria was founded by Napoleon in 1809, when Austria had to cede her coastal regions, all her Slovene, and most of her Croatian territory to France. The new Kingdom, set up under a French Viceroy (as a springboard for Napoleon's expanding eastern ambitions), comprised the greater part of Carinthia, Carniola, Gorizia, Istria, Dalmatia, and Croatia. Thus, for the first time, united Slovenes and Croats came under one political rule. Although the rule of Marmont, the Duke of Ragusa (now Dubrovnik), was only brief, its ideological heritage became quite important. New ideas and reforms in governmental administration and in the school system brought on resentment of the backward Habsburg rule after the Congress of Vienna. In the 1840's, an "Illyrian" movement was revived, glorifying it as the brightest and happiest period of Croatia's history. "Illyrismus" was initiated, as a literary and political movement, by Ljudevit Gaj (1809-72), a Slovene poet and journalist, aiming to bring together all the branches of South Slavdom and to have them think and act in unison. The movement excited the South Slav intellectuals so much that the Hungarian authorities prohibited the use of the word "Illyrianism," so the term "Yugoslav" was substituted. Gaj reached the peak of his popularity it 1848, when he was the acknowledged spokesman of South Slavdom.

During this period, the Croatian nationalist renaissance had been on the way. For a long time Croat culture had been dominated by foreign influences, especially German; most of the sons of well-to-do Croats studied in Vienna or Graz, and most Croat intellectuals spoke German. Under Gaj's influence, the national language was modernized, and pride in the country's past was promoted by the publication of historical treatises, romances, folk ballads and songs, and the study of Croat folk customs and traditions.[6]

A unique position was held by Bishop Joseph George Strossmayer (1815-1905) who, with the historian Franko Racki (1828-94), proclaimed "Yugoslavism" as a substitute for "Illyrianism"; both believed that the "Croat Question" and the "Serb Question" could be solved only

---

[6] Of no particular importance to subsequent Croat history was the concept of the "Greater Croatia" idea, connected with the work of the Slovene Bartholomaus Kopitar (1780-1844), who introduced the idea of a tripartite Austrian-Hungarian southern Slav empire organization, known as "Trialism," into the political theory of the Habsburg Monarchy—the idea of a union of the Austrian and Hungarian southern Slavs under the leadership of the Catholic Croats; for more details, see Kann, *op. cit.*, pp. 250-59.

by complete national unity in an independent Yugoslav state, where mutual respect between Croats and Serbs could produce a synthesis of their hopes and aspirations. The Bishop acquired a unique place in the cultural renaissance of Croatia by patronizing Croatian scholars, endowing Slav cultural societies in Zara, Laibach, Prague, and Belgrade, and founding secondary schools, a seminary, and a South Slav learned Academy (1867). "No institution perhaps did more to foster Yugoslav national feeling than Strossmayer's Academy, in which Yugoslavs from all over the Balkan regardless of creed were welcomed."[7] Findings were published in Croat and Latin. The Bishop was also responsible for the establishment of a national Croat University at Agram (Zagreb) (1874), with the faculties of philosophy, theology, and law, staffed at first mostly with professors imported from Prague. One of his pupils, Franko Racki, regarded as the foremost Croat intellectual of the last century, founded and became the first president of the South Slav Academy. He and others helped to build a Croat or a Yugoslav concept of nationalism.[8]

Agram (Zagreb) became the center of Croat cultural activity and was known as "The Athens of the South Slavs"; it was also the headquarters of the *Matica Hrvatska* (founded in 1842), which published the writings of Croatian men of letters. In the surrounding area of Croatia-Slovenia, were more than fourteen hundred elementary schools with Croatian as the language of instruction, and nineteen secondary schools. From this system and the university came the intellectuals who promoted the national movement and provided leadership for it.[9]

These educational advances show that, next to the Poles, the Croats were one of the most privileged minor-

[7] Arthur J. May, *The Habsburg Monarchy, 1867-1914* (Cambridge, Mass.: Harvard University Press, 1951), pp. 76-77.

[8] For details, see Arthur J. May, *The Habsburg Monarchy, 1867-1914* (Cambridge, Mass.: Harvard University Press, 1951), pp. 76-80.

[9] For details, see Joseph S. Roucek, "Pre-War Educational Theory in Yugoslavia," *Educational Theory*, VI, L (January, 1956), pp. 35-46.

ities in Austria-Hungary.[10] This is most important to note, together with the fact that the "Hungarian-Croatian Compromise of 1868" granted a special status to Croatia until 1918.

Slovenia, the northwestern republic of Yugoslavia, is situated in Central Europe where the Alps taper off into the Pannonian plains. In the eighth century, Slovenia was part of a mighty Slovene state ruled by King Samo (623-658); Slovenes in Carinthia, the eastern Alps, and the upper Sava Valley were incorporated into this state. After Samo's death, the broad alliance of Slovene tribes disintegrated. Thereafter, Slovenia's history is that of numerous invasions; eventually Austria conquered Slovenia and ruled it (except for a short period from 1809 to 1813, when it formed a part of the Kingdom of Illyria, created by Napoleon) until 1918.

Wedged between Germans and Italians, and being the smallest Slav nation in the world of Slavdom (except for the Lusatian Sorbs), Slovenia's history had been that of the struggle for mere survival. Even at the time of the national awakening of the Slovenes in the nineteenth century, the young Slovene civilization had difficult times competing with German and Italian cultures; and there are many thousand Germanized Slovenes in southern Austria (but also many thousand Italians of Slovene origin in Istria and Trieste).

Ethnically, the Slovenes are more distant kinsmen of the Croats than are the Serbs. While the Serbs in Austria-Hungary lived mostly in the lands of the Hungarian Crown, the Slovenes were located in Austria proper. The Slovenes, like the Croats, are Roman Catholics, but do not speak the same language, which, "as in many ways, indeed, their entire tradition, forms the connecting link between the southern and the northern Slav languages."[11] (Actually, the Slovene language is mostly closely related to the Slovak language.) But they are culturally close to the Croats, due to the common inheritance of Western

---

[10] Robert A. Kann, *The Multinational Empire*, Vol. I: *Empire and Nationalities* (New York: Columbia University Press, 1950), chap. VII, "The Croats," pp. 233-59.

[11] Kann, *op. cit.*, pp. 235-36.

Latin culture, although they never formed a part of the Croatian Kingdom.[12]

The nationalistic pride of the Slovene people was roused by the writings of Bartholomaus Kopitar (1780-1844), who raised the practical use of the Slovene language from a mere peasant idiom to its rightful place as a newly restored literary language; he also encouraged Karadzich to collect popular ballads and other folklore materials. His enthusiasm led him so far as to claim that the Slovene language was identical with the Old Church language of the Slavs; hence the Slovenes were the base of the whole Slav Christian culture, and (especially) Catholicism—the faith of the Slovene people—paved the way for the Christianization of the eastern Slav world. Hence the Slovenes, godfathers of the redemption and the destiny of all Slav peoples, were the creators of the language of salvation. (These, indeed, were, piously, exaggerations, although the Slovene contributions to the spread of Christian culture in the Slav world were really outstanding.)[13]

At any rate, the Slovene nationalistic renaissance in the late eighteenth and early nineteenth centuries followed the pattern evident in the genesis of the other South Slavs. Slovene cultural nationalism was tolerated by the Austrian authorities, who saw in it a device for fighting the influence of Russian Pan-Slavism. The Catholic Austro-Slav ideology was also upheld by Kopitar's principal Slovene disciples, France Presere (1800-47) and Franz von Miklosich (1821-91). The first promoted Slovene national culture by specializing in the national legend and folklore; the second authored the great comparative grammar of the Slav peoples and compiled the etymological dictionary of the Slav languages. But Illyrianism was not without influence in Slovenia and the Slovenes remembered the jurisdictional, educational, and agricultural reforms (tenant self-emancipation) promoted by the French administration; the chief ideologist here was Stanko Vraz (1810-51), a poet, who, writing in the

---

[12] For details, see Kann, *op. cit.*, I, chap. XI, "The Slovenes," 294-304.
[13] *Ibid.*, p. 295.

Croatian language, cherished the Croat-Slovene cultural union.

On April 1, 1848, a Slovene manifesto to the Austrian Emperor asked—among other things—for a "guarantee of our nationality and general equal rights for the Slovene language as for the German language. . . ." This changed the benevolent tolerance which Austrian centralism had shown for Slovene cultural nationalism to rejection; only after 1879, were Slovene language rights granted recognition in Carniola, "the heartland" of the Slovenes. In 1907, introduction of general equal franchise in Austria gave an increased percentage of representation in Viennia's Parliament; the Slovene People's party was conservative, Catholic, and anti-Liberal, using mostly opportunistic methods. Accordingly, the Slovenes contributed, relatively, very little, when compared to the intensity of the Serbs and Croats, to the Yugoslav union movement during World War II; Slovene lay intellectuals were mostly Germanized, and hence political leadership was assumed by the clergy, whose leadership was motivated by patriotic conviction and social Catholic teachings. They had little, with a few notable exceptions, consciousness of community with their linguistic cousins in the south.

Montenegro (Black Mountain or *Crna Gora* in Serbo-Croatian), developed from one of the earliest Serb states called Zeta (which comprised the area around the Zeta River, with Shkadar, Boka Kotorska, and a part of Herzegovina). In the twelfth century, Zeta became an independent state. While the states of all southern Slavs were subjugated by Turks, Hungarians, Austrians, or Venetians, Montenegro had never been fully conquered. In the seventeenth century, it became a theocratic state ruled by a bishop *("Vladika")*. Vladika Petar Petrovich-Njegos (1813-51) was one of the most important rulers of Montenegro; he was also one of the greatest Serbian poets.

Montenegro is a place of extraordinary contrasts and extraordinary people—place and people as distinct from the rest of the Yugoslavs as geographically the mountains for centuries held them secure and inaccessible to their enemies. Much of it is rocky wilderness, much a mountain paradise of breathtaking loveliness falling steeply into the blue Adriatic. Its people are as proud and independent and as poor as they come, either in the Balkans or elsewhere.

Yet, first to take advantage of Ottoman decline were the Montenegrins, who (under the leadership of their Prince-Bishops of the Petrovich-Njegos family) forced the Sultans, after nearly a century of intermittent warfare, often timed to coincide with attacks upon Turkey by Austria and Russia with whom the Montenegrins were frequently allied, to recognize their independence in 1799. But frequent warfare between them and Ottoman troops continued for another seventy-five years. Nicholas I (1860-1918) won complete independence from Turkey by the Treaty of Berlin (1878) and started to modernize the state slowly. It was Montenegro which opened the First Balkan War (1912). During World War I, the country was overrun by the Austrians, but when the Austrian Empire cracked, and the Habsburg armies disbanded, Serbian troops entered Montenegro. The wave of enthusiasm for Southern Slav unity ran quite high then. A broad autonomy was promised to the Montenegrins. The few oppositional voices were drowned in the joyous chorus of acclamation when the incorporation of Montenegro into the Yugoslav state was proclaimed. The promised autonomy was, however, never granted.

Political and religious ties between Russia and Montenegro date back to long before World War II; hence even today the area has many Communist Russophiles. Cetinje, deposed as capital, is sleeping, pathetic, and steeped in its past; and Titograd, its successor, boasts the biggest, grandest hotel in Yugoslavia today. Otherwise, less has been done in this cattle-raising mountain eyrie than in any other of Yugoslavia's six federated republics. "Here, where even electrification is only beginning, one feels that not even the Communists seriously believe they can make much imprint on its people and a way of life wherein liberty has always meant more than poverty and suffering," wrote Eric Bourne, an American correspondent of the *Christian Science Monitor* (August 24, 1957).[14]

Macedonia, an eternal bone of contention between Yugoslavia, Bulgaria, Greece (and even Albania), has been shuffled back and forth, historically, among these states; its history has been, more recently, that of violent uprising against the Turks, and later against the Serbs and Greeks, and constant internal warfare carried on by bandits and the IMRO (the Internal Macedonian Revolutionary Organization). There is an immense literature about Macedonia, nearly all of it distorted by the hatred of opposing claimants.[15] The long series of murders and executions carried on by the dreaded IMRO at the turn of the present century and up to the second decade after World War I, culminating in the murder of King Alexander in 1934 at Marseilles by the right-hand gunman of Mihailov, the Macedonian master killer, is something which can hardly be comprehended by a Western observer not inclined to favor the Nazi and Communist methods. Open warfare in the streets of Balkan capitals (including Vienna) and the ruthless disposal of persons who dared to question the wishes of Mihailov, leader of the IMRO, were quite extraordinary in the political procedure of leading European countries before the rise of Fascism and Communism. Most of these outrages were carried out because of the cry for the liberation of Macedonia.

Macedonia is located in the very heart of the Balkans, sitting on the Vardar Valley which ends in Salonika. "Whoever dominates the Vardar Valley is master of the Peninsula," is one of those wise axiomatic statements known to the students of the Balkans. This desolate land, without definite frontiers, remained under the Turkish

---

[14] Strangely enough, the rate of illiteracy in Montenegro (1948) is nearly equal to that in Serbia (26.8 percent) and surpassed by Bosnia-Herzegovina (44.9 percent) and Macedonia (40.4 percent). See also Milovan Djilas, *Montenegro* (New York): Harcourt, Brace, 1963).

[15] For a summary of the more recent literature, see Joseph S. Roucek, *The Politics of the Balkans* (New York: McGraw-Hill, 1939), chap. VIII, "Macedonians," pp. 138-50; Leonid I. Strakovsky (ed.), *A Handbook of Slavic Studies* (Cambridge, Mass.: Harvard University Press, 1949), 7, 9, pp. 279-80, 282-84, 605, 610, 615-17, 618-21; R. J. Kerner (ed.), *op. cit.*, 46ff, *et passim*.

rule until the outbreak of the Balkan War I (1912-13).
Historically, the Slavs who entered the Balkans in the
fifth and sixth centuries colonized the Roman province of
Macedonia, taking over the name of the people of the
Emperor Alexander the Great of Macedonia. Macedonia
was then ruled by Byzantium; in the fifteenth century,
Macedonia belonged to the Empire of Czar Dushan (1331-
55). After the disintegration of the Serbian state, Macedonia came under Turkish rule.

The Macedonians are a mixture of peoples, most of
them being Slavs. But Macedonian idioms belong neither
to the Serbian nor to the Bulgarian languages; they form,
so to speak, a link betwen these two branches of the
South Slavic family of languages. The Serbs, however,
classify the Macedonian language as "southern Serbian,"
and use it officially in the present Macedonian state in
Yugoslavia; the Greeks contend that the Macedonians are
only "Slavophones" (Slavic-speaking Greeks) ; the Bulgarian claims are that they are pure Bulgars. The Macedonians themselves claim that they are so different from
everybody that they are a special nationality entitled to
an independent Macedonian state. More than 90 percent
of the Macedonians are peasant, poverty-stricken, illiterate (53.9 percent illiteracy in Yugoslavia's Macedonia, formally, in 1948), producing chiefly tobacco and
emigrants.

During the nineteenth century, the newly formed Balkan states worked assiduously for the incorporation of
their oppressed "fellow nationals" and fellow Christians
in Macedonia into their spheres of influence. The oldest
claim was that of the Greeks, who had for a long time
dominated the Church and the schools there; the greater
number of the Macedonians did not speak Greek, but
the Greek spokesmen were pointing out that their civilization was Greek. The Bulgarians propounded that the
majority were Bulgarian both in speech and in sympathy;
but this was contested by the Serbians, who claimed that
certain features of Macedonian dialects, as well as their
folklore, were more Serbian than Bulgarian. The Albanians maintained that the essential thing was the race,
and that the Macedonians were of the hardy Albanian

race. Romanians were not far behind pointing out that a certain section of the Macedonian population was related to them in language and civilization. Even the Turks, the rulers, were not above mentioning that they had numerous followers and relatives among the population.

Out of this cockpit has arisen not only recurrent friction among the claimants for the prize, with constant threats to peace in Europe but also an excessive Macedonian nationalism, headed by the IMRO, professedly autonomous in purpose, but whose accepted program was revolution, insurrection, reprisals, and extreme violence.

The concept "Macedonia" came into use only about the middle of the nineteenth century, when the Balkan nations were engaged in their struggle for liberation from Turkish rule. European Turkey was divided into vilayets; and the territory now currently understood under the term of Macedonia comprised the vilayets of Kosovo (of the battle of Kosovo legend), Monastir (Bitolia), and Salonika. Today its vague boundaries extend from the region of Salonika (Greece), along the river Vardar to Skoplje (Yugoslavia), westward to the Albanian frontier, and eastward to Strumica (on the Bulgarian border).

Under Turkey, Macedonia's inhabitants were subjects of the Greek Patriarch, the Phanar, who used his power to forward Grecophile policies in Macedonia; this was opposed by the awakening Bulgarians, who agitated for their own independent schismatic Church. On February 28 (March 11), 1870, the Sultan granted, under Russian pressure, the firman forming the Bulgarian Exarchate in Constantinople, which had most of Macedonia under its jurisdiction. This gave a great advantage to Bulgarian claims; these were strengthened when the short-lived Treaty of San Stefano (March 3, 1878) created a vassal principality of Bulgaria, which embraced Macedonia (without the city of Salonika). But the Treaty of Berlin (1878) excluded Bulgaria from Macedonia, returning it to Turkey. Ever since Bulgaria's historical policy has been shaped by the desire to regain Macedonia, unproductive though it is.

After the Second Balkan War (1913), Macedonia was

partitioned between Serbia and Greece (Bulgaria obtaining only a small portion around Strumica). Bulgaria joined both wars, and acquired Macedonia—for a while —each time. Today, Yugoslavia's Macedonia is one of the states. At first Tito started hounding the Greeks for persecuting Macedonians, and the Bulgars, when prodded by Moscow, are now also complaining about the brutal treatment of their Macedonian "Brothers" in Yugoslavia and Greece.

Bosnia-Herzegovina comprises the central districts of Yugoslavia. The first king of Croatia, Tomislav, was crowned on the Duvansko Field in Bosnia. By its cultural heritage, Bosnia-Herzegovina belongs more to the East than to the West. The dominant ethnic element here has been the Mohammedans, who differ both from the Croats and Serbs. If we identify the Catholic faith with Croatian and the Orthodox faith with Serbian nationality, then the Mohammedans turn the scale in this autonomous state of Yugoslavia.

Although Bosnia had its own rulers (twelfth to fifteenth centuries), the country was reduced to a Turkish province until 1878, when, at the Congress of Berlin, Austria-Hungary obtained the right to occupy it; however it remained nominally Turkish until its annexation by Austria-Hungary in 1908 (a move which greatly accelerated the ultimate World War I crisis of 1914). This equilateral triangle, which forms the northwestern section of the Balkan Peninsula, with a short frontage on the Adriatic Sea, has held a unique place in modern European history (just like Macedonia). The region of constant revolts, its uprising in 1875 produced the 1877 war between Russia and Turkey; and it was in Sarajevo that Franz Ferdinand, Austria-Hungary's heir to the throne, was assassinated.

A little more than 18,000 square miles in extent, the region contained a population of about 1,158,000 in 1879; more than half belonged to the Orthodox Church, while almost as many people were Moslems, and the rest belonged to the Roman Catholic Church; there were also some Gypsies and Jews. "Not more than one resident in a hundred could read."[16]

Roughly, the nationalistic tendencies here were at odds. The Orthodox population wanted a union with Serbia, while the Roman Catholics supported the idea of Bishop Strossmayer (in whose seminary some of the clergy had been trained) favoring Yugoslav unity. At any rate, Belgrade's propaganda for rebellion against the Sultan helped to bring on the resurrection of 1875; and even more effective were the similar propaganda appeals issued from Montenegro.

When the Austrian troops occupied Bosnia-Herzegovina, both the Moslem and Orthodox Bosniaks resented the exchange of the Ottoman domination for Habsburg. The Orthodox leaders wanted a union with Serbia or Montenegro, while the others joined Albanian mountaineers in their guerrilla tactics. It took some 150,000 Habsburg soldiers to put down the rebellion of 1878 headed by 90,000 insurgent troops; the memories of the "holy and heroic rising" against the Turks in 1875 and against the Austrians in 1878 were elevated to the dignity of popular Serb ballads and folk legends.

Under the jurisdiction of the common Habsburg Ministry of Finance, the regime soon replaced the Turks adminstrators with Habsburg officials (mostly Croats), thoroughly detested by the native Orthodox population. Later, discontent increased when merchants from the monarchy began operating here, the Moslem landowners remained powerful, and military conscription was applied to the province. Yet the region experienced phenomenal economic and cultural improvements. Under Austria, the population doubled, the roads and railroads were built, and Bosnian industry (carpetmaking and the working of metals) was growing. Primary education was provided by the government, and the government also helped schools conducted by religious bodies (but attendance was not compulsory). Specially talented students were sent to Vienna on scholarships (on condition that

[16] Arthur J. May, *The Habsburg Monarchy 1867-1914* (Cambridge, Mass.: Harvard University Press, 1951), p. 118.

they would not engage in political activities) ; but many students preferred Belgrade to Vienna, where they also spent their time on political scheming. Vienna also founded a few specialized agricultural schools, model farms, and breeding studs.[17] But the Austrian administration failed to solve the land problem, one of the deep grievances of the Orthodox (mainly Serb) population. Their opposition was joined by Orthodox Serb intellectuals, who objected to limitations on civil freedoms, and claimed that their churches and schools were given less financial assistance than Roman Catholic institutions and resented having commercial concessions and government contracts given only to Roman Catholics and to foreigners. Outright annexation in 1908 of Bosnia-Herzegovina to Austria-Hungary immediately created great fury and popular commotion in Serbia, and Austria's Bosnian adventure set rolling a new wave of irredentism which led directly to the assassination of Franz Ferdinand in Sarajevo on June 28, 1914.[18]

Yugoslavia Between World War I and II

The Kingdom of the Serbs-Croats-Slovenes was founded on December 1, 1918, at a Belgrade gathering of delegates from all Yugoslav provinces. But, from the very beginning, the crux of overheated and eventually murderous Yugoslav politics lay in the arguments over the alternative of centralization and federalism—the Serbs fos-

---

[17] For more details, see May, op. cit., pp. 406-7.

[18] We shall not discuss here the rich but complicated history of Dalmatia, since, in contemporary Yugoslavia, Dalmatia is not a separate autonomous state. For details about Dalmatia's history, see R. J. Kerner (ed.), op. cit., pp. 95, 99-101, 136-39, 304, 340, 356; May, op. cit., 9ff. et passim, especially pp. 119-20, 170-73; Strakovsky, op. cit., pp. 7, 192, 193, 608; Kann, op. cit., I, 97, 236ff., 242, 266, 324, II: 10, 264. Dalmatia, part of the old Croatian Empire, was occupied by the Turks in the interior, while the Venetians occupied the coast, with the exception of the City of Dubrovnik (Ragusa), which was an independent republic. Napoleon gave Dalmatia to Austria in 1797; then, in 1805, to the Vice-Kingdom of Italy; finally, in 1809, to the short-lived Illyrian Kingdom. In 1814, after the fall of Napoleon, Austria took over Dalmatia and kept it until 1918.

tering the notion of a "Greater Serbia" and the Croats advocating regionalism.

With the historical diversity of varied interests and cultural experiences, this patchwork of sudden enthusiasm at independence could not hide the course of contradictions: How to integrate the claims of the Serbs, with headquarters in Belgrade, using the old Russian script and Greek Orthodox in religion, to run Yugoslavia, against the opposition of the dissident Croats, hating the Pan-Slav Serbs, and not sympathetic to the Orthodox claims as good Roman Catholics (with their neighboring Slovenes), and with usually strong pro-German leanings. The complex picture was also complicated by additional differences in the constituent parts of the Kingdom; Montenegro, inhabited by isolated and primitive peoples; Bosnia-Herzegovina, with its Turkish and Moslem influences; and Macedonia, an ethnological Joseph's coat of many colors.

This tangle of regional nationalism, antagonistic creeds, and contrasting cultures, faced simultaneously with exasperating economic and international problems, reached a climax in 1928 when several Croat leaders were shot by a Montenegrin deputy in the National Assembly; it was this incident and the alarming domestic situation that led to the inauguration of King Alexander's dictatorship—a dictatorship which survived until the opening of World War II. For, despite their geographic and cultural affinity, their original enthusiasm for the ideology of "Illyrianism," the various branches of the Yugoslav peoples were cursed with a heritage of separatism. The new state was unable to create spiritual unity among its constituent parts, because its Slavic (as well as non-Slavic) population had lived too long under different sovereignties—Austria, Hungary, Serbia, Montenegro, and Turkey. During this era of separation, the Yugoslavs had been unable to participate in the same political, cultural, and economic development. The geopolitical conditions of the Balkans, furthermore, intensified centrifugal tendencies, stressing differentiation and diffusion rather than integration. When the old dream of national unity had finally come true, tribal tendencies had already been too deeply rooted to give way to broader allegiances. The Croats did not want the new state to become an extension of Serbia; Zagreb, strongly Catholic, seemed farther apart than ever from Belgrade, the new capital, "modern" in many things and proud of its record in war and victory. The heavy hand of Serbians' administration, centralistic and overstaffed, soon released the full force of tribal enmity. Religious differences helped to make the contest deeper. The Croat distrusted his Serb cousin in "Oriental" Belgrade as an "infidel." The inequality of economic standards also contributed its share. Industrialized Croatia and Slovenia, having received for their development financial support from Vienna and Budapest, were embittered by the thought that their economic interests and their tax revenues were being sacrificed to the support of almost entirely agricultural regions— Serbia, Bosnia, Herzegovina, Montenegro, and Macedonia. Zagreb and Ljubljana complained that their own region, "Sava Banovina," was treated as a second-rate and remote periphery of Belgrade, although the numerical proportion of Croats to Serbs was roughly four to five. Zagreb agitated for increased representation of the Croat element in the administration of Yugoslavia, asking for more career opportunities for Croat intelligentsia in the foreign service, the army, and the *gendarmeries*, since all of the services were reserved mostly for the Serbs. And then there were numerous other minorities who had their own bitter objections to the treatment given to them in the new state—the Macedonians, Magyars, Albanians, Moslems, Romanians, Germans, Jews, Mohammedans, and Protestants of several varieties.

The situation was complicated further by the differences in cultural experiences of the main subdivisions of the Old Kingdom which are now the constituent republics of Yugoslavia: Montenegro, Bosnia-Herzegovina, Macedonia, and Voivodina.

At any rate, while Serbia's Pashich wanted a "Greater Serbia" and the Croats and Slovenes wanted a federation with equal rights for each member, the end of World War I enabled the Crown Prince Regent Alexander to proclaim the South Slav Union under Serbian leadership. The initial enthusiasm for the new state soon evaporated. The Croat opposition was headed by Stefan Radich (1871-1928), who had studied in Prague, Moscow, Budapest, and Paris, and founded the Peasant party of Croatia with the slogan, "peasant government, peasant administration, peasant parliament." In 1914 he preached the idea of triune Habsburg Monarchy, and in 1918 was for a "nationalist, Slavic revolt" against Austria-Hungary and for federal union with the Serbs. After 1919, he spent most of his time in jail or abroad—and for a short period also as Minister in Belgrade. His bitterest enemy, Pashich, died in 1926, but the regime continued its pro-Serb policies. On June 20, 1928, Radich was shot by Deputy Punisha Ratchich, a member of the Pashich party. The Croat deputies left the Parliament.

Meanwhile, government changes had been and were endless, and Serbia's "Radical party" ruled the country through terror and bribery. To save the country and his throne, on January 6, 1929, King Alexander proclaimed his personal dictatorship. A new constitution was another façade, and the government naturally won the elections. All efforts to appease the Croats failed.

We must note here the organization of the terrorist society—USTASHI—which, using the pattern of the Macedonian IMRO, cooperated with the Macedonians against the regime, under the leadership of Ante Pavelich, Croat deputy and lawyer (a pro-Nazi quisling in the war, now living in Argentina). Pavelich trained his terrorists in Borgotar (Italy) and in Yanka Puszta (Hungary). In October, 1934, Alexander "the Unifier" was murdered in Marseilles by a Macedonian IMRO man, Vlada Thernozemiski, "The Chauffeur." Alexander's brother, Paul, became Regent. Educated at the court of the Czar in Russia, Paul was reactionary and, in addition, a weak character. The Serbian Radical party continued providing its politicians as Prime Ministers.[19]

During this terrible time, the Nazi storm had been gathering on Europe's horizon. After 1934, Nazi eco-

---

[19] For more details, see Joseph S. Roucek (ed.), *Governments & Politics Abroad* (New York: Funk & Wagnalls, 1948), chap. 14, "Yugoslavia," pp. 426-57, and Bibliography.

nomic imperialism started expanding its net over Yugoslavia's economic life. The Berlin-Rome Axis of 1936
ended Belgrade's efforts to play off Italy against Germany
and vice versa. Belgrade switched its allegiance from the
French alliance, the Little Entente, and the League of
Nations to the pacification of Hitler. Radich's successor,
Dr. Machek (now living in the United States), signed a
temporary agreement with the government (in the summer of 1939) to cooperate. But the pro-Fascist policies
of the government continued—on the domestic as well
as the foreign front. Finally, in March, 1941, the Cvetko-
vich government signed a pact with the Axis. The horrified nationalistic opposition staged a revolt under General Dushan Shimovich. But this was a "kiss of death."
At 5:15 A.M. on Sunday, April 6, 1941, the full fury of the
German blitzkrieg struck at Yugoslavia. In a few days,
the Yugoslav Army, defeated by the Nazi hordes, was
divided by Shimovich into guerrilla parties—the kind of
fighting carried on by the Serbian *Comitajis* for centuries
against the Turkish rulers, one of them being under the
control of Colonel Mikhailovich.

The Italian and Nazi occupation is a tale of horrors.
Ante Pavelich became Croatia's Prime Minister, while
the Bulgarians, Hungarians, and Italians took the rest
under benevolent Nazi supervision. A virtual civil war
was promoted by the Nazis, who fostered the enmity between the Serbs and Croats.

What is important to note is that Colonel Mikhailovich
led the Chetniks under the blessing of the United States
and England, taking his orders as Minister of War in the
cabinet of the government-in-exile in London (and later
as General). But, to simplify the very complicated story,
he, as the representative of the old regime, and taking his
directives from London, did not suit the policies of Stalin,
who needed a "second front." This task was assigned to
the then mysterious figure, Josip Broz, nicknamed "Tito,"
who soon became known not only as the fighter of the
Nazi forces but also of the guerrillas of Mikhailovich.
Tito's Partisans were accusing the Chetniks of supporting
the prewar cause of a greater Serbia and of trying to
reorganize the country at the expense of the other racial

groups. (On numerous occasions, the Chetniks had been charged with actually helping the enemy; at any rate, this was the reason given for the execution of Mikhailovich at the end of World War II.) The Chetniks on the other hand, accused the Partisans of trying to weaken the country by fomenting dissension and starting civil war; they claimed that the Partisans were nothing but Communist rabble and bandits, as shown by the support given to them by the USSR.

Communism in Yugoslavia

Contrary to a widely held notion, Tito's rise to power was no sudden wartime incident, nor was Communism a novelty to the country. It is true that, up to 1914, Serbia had not had a large enough industrial proletariat to form a basis for any important growth of the Socialist movement. There were few great estates, and not many landless laborers in Serbia or the other regions now in Yugoslavia—and even then the very conditions in Croatia and Bosnia-Herzegovina were against any attractive Socialist ideology, since these lands were Catholic and Mohammedan in their social make-up. Roughly speaking, the area was dominated by small-scale peasant farms of a very primitive sort. It is true that conditions differed from place to place, but, generally speaking, the peasants held onto their small holdings even if they were on the subsistence level. The urban centers were dominated by artisans—handicrafts carried on in small workshops— with a factory here and here, mostly financed by foreign capital and mostly producing textiles. The absence of a landed aristocracy, especially in Serbia, helped the evil lot of the peasants after the driving out of the Turkish overlords. Hence in all the Balkan countries Socialism was of minor influence before the war of 1914.

What influenced the Serbians more than anything else had been really the pro-Russian sentiment; the ideas of the Russian *Narodniks* had their impact on Serb Radicalism especially during the 1870's and 1880's. In 1872 the Radical leader (the Radicals, at that time, were extreme, and after World War I, the most reactionary party of

Serbia), Svetozar Markovich (1846-75) tried to apply Marxist principles to the peculiar problems of the Balkans. (Tito's regime hails him as a spiritual forerunner of the Yugoslav Partisan movement and has republished his works.) Markovich studied in Belgrade and St. Petersburg, where he came under the influence of the Russian radicals; in Switzerland he came into contact with a group of Serbian revolutionists, among them Nikola Pashich (the pro-Serb leader, who turned out to be the most conservative of all postwar Serbian leaders); he diagnosed the fundamental problem of Serbia not as the evil of capitalism but as that of stupid bureaucracy, and hoped for democratic self-government expressed through the *odbor* ("local committee") responsible for economic and cultural affairs. He was moved by the ideas of the Russian thinkers who put their faith in the virtues of the *mir* (a concept derived from the Old Church Slavic—an association of several families under one head), while he expected great things from a revival of the *zadruga* (the basic social, economic and familial institution living in a common household);[20] through it, private property should be brought into public ownership and the state should be transformed into one great *zadruga*. (He held that a primitive society might leapfrog from the capitalistic phase and achieve collective economy through the development of traditional cooperative forms.)

After the suppression of the peasant rising in 1883 in Serbia under the leadership of the Radical party, the Party developed into a peasant party, with intellectuals providing the leadership, and Socialism died away. It revived a little at Belgrade around the turn of the century, and a few trade unions were formed. A Serbian Social Democratic party was founded in 1903, and won a single seat in the Serbian Parliament, and a second in 1905. By 1912, the party had two thousand members.

---

[20] For details, see Dinko Tomasic, *Personality and Culture in Eastern European Politics* (New York: G. W. Stewart, 1948), especially, chap. IV, "Power Indifference in Zadruga Society," pp. 149-205.

"It had no intellectual theorist and no considerable body of intellectual support."[21]

In the regions under Austria-Hungary, Socialism had even more handicaps to face. The Austrian state was committed to uphold Catholic principles. Freemasonry, for instance, was not even allowed to take root[22] and anybody criticizing the established order was severely prosecuted. As in Austria, in Hungary the Socialist party was divided by factionalism. Above all, the Socialist thinkers (like Otto Bauer and Karl Renner, the latter to become Chancellor of the Austrian Republic in 1919 and 1945) were more interested in the application of Marxism to the party doctrine of cultural autonomy for nationalities than in Communism.[23] In fact, Marx and Engels devoted considerable portions of their writings to the experiences to be derived from the Austrian national revolution. Basically, the leftist tendencies were represented by a small group of leftist liberal intellectuals, seriously divided among themselves, without too adequate political organization.

Then, suddenly, there appeared a home-grown Communism after World War I in Yugoslavia; the Constituent Assembly, elected in 1919, already had fifty-eight Communist deputies—the largest representation in any parliament outside Russia. Even the peasant and backward regions—Macedonia and Montenegro—voted for Communism. And, strangely enough, the great Croat Peasant party of Croatia, a Roman Catholic region, favored Communism, and Radich visited Lenin in Moscow. When the Communist movement was made illegal, its following continued growing among the students and professors of the universities. But this home-grown movement of Communism, having its main strength in rural areas, although sponsored from the urban areas, had to be fre-

---

[21] G. D. H. Cole, *The Second International 1889-1914* (London: Macmillan & Co., 1956), II, 603.

[22] For details, see A. B. T., "Masonry: Yugoslavia," pp. 757, in Joseph S. Roucek (ed.), *Slavonia Encyclopaedia* (New York: Philosophical Library, 1956).

[23] Robert A. Kann, *The Multinational Empire* (New York: Columbia University Press, 1950), I, 103-8, 276ff., 291; II: 154-78, 345-50, 365, and *passim*.

quently purged from Moscow—usually by a special emis-
sary, a certain Comrade Walter—alias Tomanek, alias
—"Tito."

Tito could not have won, during World War II, without
American and British help. "Ironic as it may seem today,
Tito was, in a way, a creation of Winston Churchill's. For
a time the British Prime Minister, enraptured by the
Partisans, even got into the habit of calling Yugoslavia
'Titoland.' "24

According to the Anglo-Soviet agreement of October,
1944, Yugoslavia and Britain agreed to share their influence on a fifty-fifty basis in Yugoslavia.25 Meanwhile,
the Germans, plus the Italians, the Croatian Ustachi, the
quisling troops of Serbia and of Bulgaria, and Mikhailovich's Chetniks had been unable to liquidate Tito's Army
of Liberation—the largest native Allied force after the
Russian Army on Europe's continent. When the war
was nearing its end, Yugoslavia's situation was unique—
it was the only satellite which liberated itself. The Russian armies came in at the end of the war, but, although
welcomed as "liberators," they had played only a minor
role in the creation of the new Yugoslavia—although Tito
would have never been able to form his state without
Stalin's help.

Tito had set up his National Committee of Liberation
as a provisional government in November, 1943. After
the occupation of Belgrade, Tito's government held a
national election in November, 1945, and, in the Balkan
manner, won it with 88.7 percent of the total vote. The

24 John Gunther, *Behind the Curtain* (New York: Harper, 1949),
p. 60. The literature on Tito and "Titoism" has been growing
rapidly in recent years. Among the more important works, see:
Slobodan M. Draskovich, *Tito, Moscow's Trojan Horse* (Chicago:
Henry Regnery, 1957); Harry N. Howard, "Foreign Policy in the
Second World War (1939-1946)," pp. 338-52, and Wayne S. Wu-
cinich, "The Second World War and Beyond," XX, pp. 353-86, in
R. J. Kerner, *op. cit.*, and Bibliography, pp. 542-43; Vaso Trivano-
vitch, *The Case of Drazha Mikhailovich* (New York: United Committee of South-Slavic Americans); R. H. Markham, *Tito's Imperial Communism* (Chapel Hill, N. C.: University of North Carolina Press, 1947); David Martin, *Ally Betrayed* (New York: Prentice-Hall, 1946).

25 See Winston S. Churchill, *Triumph and Tragedy* (Boston:
Houghton Mifflin Co., 1953), pp. 226-28.

Monarchy was abolished and the pro- or really Communist regime, which has been ruling ever since, came into being.

When compared to the other satellites, the pro-Communist regimes in Poland, Hungary and Romania started as coalitions; but Yugoslavia was the only country where the left-wing Socialists were left out. Thus the pattern of Yugoslavia's government was the same as in the USSR (while the other satellites followed, for a while, the pattern of the Western states). The six Yugoslav Constituent Republics (Serbia, Croatia, Slovenia, Montenegro, Bosnia-Herzegovina, and Macedonia) were (and are) in theory autonomous in certain respects (as are the Ukraine and Byelorussia in the USSR). But, in spite of the fictional autonomous provisions, and the changes in the formal structure of the country, the Communist party has dominated the political life of the country (the official membership in 1952, 779,382). The trade unions, youth, women's groups, and affiliated organizations, comprising a membership of about 8,000,000, are completely controlled by Communist leadership.

Tito's control over the CPY has been such that few divergencies of significance have come to light in the controversy with the Cominform which broke out publicly in June, 1948. (The party name was changed to Union of Communists of Yugoslavia at the Sixth Congress of the CPY in November, 1952.)

A Brief History of Titoism

Before the expulsion from the Cominform, in June, 1948, Tito's Yugoslavia was the prototype of "People's Democracies." Overnight that exemplary pupil, Tito, standing first in the class and quoted everywhere as a model, was thrown out of the Cominform for insubordination. This is a strange story, bizarre and full of contradictions.

When Tito's victorious army joined the Red Army upon its entry into Belgrade, October 20, 1944, the Yugoslav campaign was virtually over. Tito immediately signed a treaty of mutual aid with the USSR on April 11, 1945.

This was a significant step, since Yugoslavia had no diplomatic relations with Russia. But soon the domestic policy of the new state made Tito's regime unpopular with the West. Unrelenting religious persecution, the trial of Archbisop Stepinac of Zagreb, and Mikhailovich's execution, drew upon Tito Western aversion, especially so since Tito's foreign policy was openly favorable to the USSR and hostile to the Western countries. The shooting down of unarmed United States planes in August, 1946, which resulted in the deaths of five United States airmen, provoked bitter indignation; it was, moreover, intertwined with the intransigeant attitude of Tito toward a possible solution of the Trieste question.

Then, suddenly, at the end of June, 1948, the Cominform condemned Tito—and Tito refused, publicly, to accept the condemnation. Scorching rebuttals were issued and counter accusations made. Basically, Tito refused to kowtow to the dictates of Moscow, insisting that he, himself, was the sole and faithful guardian of Marxism-Leninism. Moscow then proclaimed Tito as belonging to the capitalist and imperialist camp. The sequence of events showed that the Kremlin had underestimated the internal cohesion of the Yugoslav Communist party and the strength of Tito; Tito remained strong because his Communism never denationalized him; as the acknowledged leader of the guerrilla warfare against the Axis, he fought and nearly lost his life; he and his army were the first to liberate Yugoslavia, and the Russian Army came in only later. (Most of this complex situation has to be contrasted to that of neighboring satellites, whose leaders came or went to Moscow during World War II.)

To the West, Yugoslavia represented the first break in the Iron Curtain—and created hopes that other satellites may follow as they come more slowly to realize that they are serving as mere cat's-paws in the general scheme of Soviet imperialism. In short, the West has looked upon Yugoslavia as an element in a political struggle rather than an ideological one. The West knows that Tito and his some thirty divisions stand between Moscow and the Mediterranean, and that these divisions can be counted on, so intense is their love of their country, to defend their independence against an invader. For seven years, the Soviet press, as well as all organs of World Communism, had been referring to Tito as a "traitor," "Fascist dog," "capitalist spy," and by similar epithets. Then, at the end of December, 1954, one Sunday night in Moscow, the highest Soviet leaders, not handicapped by the late Stalin, raised their glasses to toast "Comrade Tito." When Khrushchev and Bulganin made their "Canossa" to Belgrade, Yugoslavia was no longer outside the Cominform bloc.

In and out of the Kremlin's good graces thereafter, Yugoslavia's renewed "friendship" with Soviet Russia's bloc has been viewed with many misgivings in Western quarters. The showdown between Stalin and Tito in 1948 was the culmination of a struggle for power. Who was to control Yugoslavia? Stalin was determined to keep Yugoslavia a subservient satellite; he wanted to force the pace of peasant collectivization there and retard industrialization; to regulate her trade with the other satellites and with the USSR in such a way as to suck her riches into the veins of the Soviet economy; to control the new Yugoslav Army through Soviet political agents. Rather than submit, Tito risked Stalin's punishment—and got it. But he survived. He survived economic blockade, political isolation, propaganda onslaughts, and threats of military attack across the satellite borders.

Above all, Tito outlived Stalin. And in May, 1955, he stood at Belgrade airport and watched Stalin's successors arrive to apologize and explain that it had all been a mistake. Stalin's successors decided to remedy Stalin's miscalculation. Tito had shown he could stand up to Russian threats and deal with Russian hostility successfully; Stalin's successors realized that the response by the rest of the world to this threat of war—a response both physical and psychological—had been so powerful that it could not be challenged. If war was impossible, a new policy was necessary. No effort to relax world tensions could succeed so long as the quarrel with Yugoslavia continued. It had to be ended if a policy of non-interference in the affairs of foreign states was to be believed. At home, blame for international tension could be laid on

Western leaders—frightened capitalists, greedy war-mongers, imperialists seeing their favored positions slipping from their grasp. Then there was also the need to restore some logic and coherence to the position of the Soviet Communist party in the eyes of Communist parties abroad.

Of greatest importance was that Soviet Communist leaders admitted the claim of the Yugoslav Communists that there are various paths to Socialism. (Stalin shot Bukharin and dozens of other leading colleagues for arguing just that; it was one of the charges trumped up against Rajk and Petrov and the other so-called "Titoists" shot or hanged in Hungary and Bulgaria and Albania.) Stalin's successors now accepted Tito's heresy as good Communist dogma.

It is true that Tito has survived only because of American aid. But it is also important to note that Tito's regime must be given credit for worthwhile achievements. Not merely the physical ones of doubling steel and coal production and erecting huge hydroelectric dams, laying thousands of miles of new roads, establishing new schools, and improving health standards. Nor even the purely Socialist yet quite admirable system of social insurance. Without doubt, however, the greatest of the Yugoslav leader's triumphs is the victory of his own personality over the Communist catechisms on which he and his associates fed (although Djilas views it otherwise).

A part of the dynamic atmosphere of Communism in Yugoslavia stems from the character of the people. In this country of 17 million, there are a multitude of different national, cultural, religious, and economic influences—not to mention substantial national minorities from neighboring Hungary, Romania, Bulgaria, and Albania. There are three major religions (Roman Catholic, Serbian Orthodox, and Moslem). Most of the country is agricultural, although an industrial working class, a managerial class, and a bureaucratic class are rapidly growing. All this is held together by Tito's personality and his brand of Communism. He and his associates have changed their minds about the efficacy of certain

Stalinist methods. They have even adopted ideas they caught in their contacts with thc Western democracies.[26]

Learning from the disastrous history of the Monarchy, Tito has decentralized his state and, by making Yugoslavia a federation and by enforcing racial and religious equality, he "has brought not only internal unity but greater efficiency to centralized government.[27] This has been accomplished by the federative principle and a series of formal and informal equalization policies. Tito had laid the ground during the war years when his Partisans played down the Communist aspects of the movement and instead stressed the struggle for liberation from the foreign enemy and for a wide scale of social reforms which appealed to all nationalities.[28] The Presidium, the central organ of the National Liberation Movement, was granted the power of nominating the Committee of National Liberation, which in turn was entrusted with the functions of a government. It was headed by Tito, with six Serbs, five Croats, four Slovenes, one Montenegrin, and one Bosnian Moslem. The Constitution of 1946 recognized the sovereignty of the six Republics (Serbia, Croatia, Slovenia, Macedonia, Montenegro, and Bosnia-Herzegovina) and granted a more limited form of sovereignty to the autonomous province of the Voivodina and the autonomous region of Kosovo-Metohija; each republic, province, and region has its own constitution (or basic statute, in the case of the two autonomous areas), and its own government. (The principle of autonomy was, however, not noted in the 1953 Constitution.)

These principles toned down, if not eliminated, the reasons for the Serb-Croat antagonism. Tito used clever tactics here. Instead of dividing Bosnia-Herzegovina between Serbia and Croatia, Tito formed a separate republic of Bosnia-Herzegovina—although the area is peopled

---

[26] For the ideology of Titoism, see Edvard Kardelj, "Evolution in Yugoslavia," *Foreign Affairs*, XXXIV, 4 (July, 1956, pp. 580-602.

[27] Charles P. McVicker, *Titoism* (New York: St. Martin's Press, 1957), p. 37.

[28] For details, see: *Ibid.*, chap. IV, "International Dissension Checked," pp. 37-52.

mostly by Serbs and Croats. (Around 31 percent of Bosnia-Herzegovina's population are Moslems, originally Serbs and Croats, who were converted to Islam under the Turkish rule, and are more interested in religion than nationality.) While formerly the Serbs wanted to absorb Macedonians as "South Serbs," Tito's Macedonia is a republic which acknowledges the difference between Macedonians and Serbs, while chopping down the former territorial sovereignity of Serbia. The idea of a "Greater Serbia" is further weakened by the autonomous province of the Voivodina (where only a little over one-third of the population is not Serbian), and of the autonomous region of Kosovo-Metohija where Albanians dominate. But since the Serbs were the core of Tito's experiments in creating a Serb-Croat equilibrium, both districts have been placed under the guidance of Serbia, which was granted the responsibility of approving their basic statutes and of enforcing certain specific supervisory prerogatives. The Croats were also weakened in Bosnia-Herzegovina. Here the Catholic Croats form about 23 percent of the total population but not proportionate representation in the top ranks of the Republic's leadership. In addition, "the prewar orientation of the cultural relations of the Moslems of this area toward Zagreb was shifted to Belgrade. The large mosque built in the center of Zagreb in the interwar years as a symbol of this orientation has since the installation of the Titoist regime been converted to a Croatian folk museum."[29]

An additional safety valve was the Council of Nationalities created by the 1946 Constitution. It had an equal number of deputies from each of the six republics, and a proportionately smaller number from each of the two autonomous districts. In power, the Council was equal to the other chamber of the Parliament. In 1953 this Council was merged with the Federal Council (made the upper house of the newly constituted National Assembly), but allowed the Council of Nationalities to re-emerge as a separate body under certain specified conditions; its pur-

---

[29] McVicker, *op. cit.*, p. 43.

pose is to guarantee each national group that the federal policy will not disregard its interests.[30]

All this, however, has to be viewed on the pragmatic level, since the "real protection of nationality group interests rests more in the representation each has within the leading party and government circles, and in the honest desire of the men who make up these circles to do away with all vestiges of international rivalry."[31]

These "facts of life" also apply to Tito's policy giving the appearance of economic equality among the six republics. Tito's group has been deliberately favoring the three poorer and most underdeveloped republics of Bosnia-Herzegovina, Macedonia, and Montenegro, although the reaction, known as "localism," has been felt in the more privileged areas against paying for the poorer areas.

Efforts of Tito to alleviate Serb-Croat antagonism have also benefited the non-Yugoslav minorities (who, in 1953, formed 2,038,000 out of the total population of 16,927,000, and, officially, were divided into more than seventeen groups, ranging from 752,000 Albanians to one thousand Greeks). On coming to power, the Law on the Prohibition or Provocation of National and Racial Hatred and Discord was passed by Tito's regime. The Constitution of 1946 strengthened it, guaranteeing equal treatment and opportunity for all national minorities and granting them the right to their own cultural development and the free use of their mother tongue:[32] "National minorities in the Federal People's Republic of Yugoslavia enjoy the right to and protection of their own cultural development and the free use of their own language." And "all citizens . . . are equal before the law and enjoy equal rights regardless of nationality, race and creed." The mother language of the larger minority groups are official languages of the republics and autonomous districts; such larger minority clusters are rep-

---

[30] For more details, see McVicker, *op. cit.*, VII, "Major Political-Administrative Reforms," pp. 135-78.

[31] *Ibid.*, p. 44.

[32] For the 1946 Yugoslav Constitution, see Joseph S. Roucek (ed.), *Slavonic Encyclopaedia* (New York: Philosophical Library, 1949), pp. 1431-45.

resented in proportion to their number in all the federal, republican, and autonomous district organs of the government, and also in the local governmental organs ("People's Committees").

The 1953 Constitution refers to national minorities only once—Article 9, which enumerates the specific rights and duties of the federal government, and includes the protection of the unity and equality of all Yugoslav people, the duty to protect the freedoms and democratic rights of citizens, and their equality of rights regardless of nationality, race or religion.[33]

More specifically, the largest minorities are located in the Republic of Serbia and are organized in two autonomous units—the Hungarians, Romanians, and others in the autonomous province of the Voivodina, and the Albanians (as the Shkipetars are now called) in the autonomous district of Kosovo and Metohija (Kosmet). Their treatment has paid dividends to Tito since 1948, when the Cominform failed to foment national discord in Yugoslavia. Instead of forming opposition groups, these minorities are now the base for the activities of political refugees from behind the Iron Curtain. The Albanians in particular, one of the most backward and illiterate national groups in Europe, have been enjoying a great educational and cultural uplift and a degree of autonomy under their own rulers. Although their economic development is far behind that of Macedonia or Bosnia, they seem to be satisfied with their position.

In conclusion, "the national problem of Yugoslavia is by no means finally solved and . . . one cannot speak of one Yugoslav nation," reports Frankel.[34] Realistically, in official terminology the reference is most frequently made to the "Peoples" of Yugoslavia not to the "People"

---

[33] The 1953 Constitution was published in: *New Fundamental Law of Yugoslavia* (Belgrade: Jurists' Association of Yugoslavia, 1953). See also Joseph Frankel, "Federalism in Yugoslavia," *American Political Science Review*, XLIX, 2 (June, 1955), pp. 416-30; Frankel, "Communism and the National Question in Yugoslavia," *Journal of Central European Affairs*, XV, 1 (April, 1955), pp. 49-65.

[34] Frankel, "Communism and the National Question in Yugoslavia," *op. cit.*, p. 64.

of Yugoslavia. Whatever difficulties there are—and there are many—the official policy has been to ignore such divergencies, with the hope that a regime of tolerance and growing economic integration will eventually eliminate them. The fact remains that the New Yugoslavia is much more firmly established than First Yugoslavia.

The recently rumored *detente* between Nikita S. Khrushchev and Yugoslavia's Josip Broz "Tito" has much the sound of a phonograph needle playing over and over again the same broken record. Their strange meeting in Moscow in the autumn of 1962 suggests another period of tranquillity vis-à-vis the Soviet Union. However, such events have occurred before, and it would perhaps be best to wait and see what permanent results spring from the encounter.

Heterogeneous Educational History

The educational history of the areas now composing Yugoslavia, before 1918, resembled, closely, the difficult nationalistic and general political and social conditions faced by the various Yugoslav peoples under different rulers.

Serbia. The Serb historians trace the history of education to the times of St. Sava (who even today is worshiped among Serbs as the Patron Saint of Learning).[35] He was the first Archbishop of Serbia (1171-1236) ; thanks to him the Serbian Church became autonomous and was raised to the dignity of a Patriarchate. The Archbishop formed nine Bishoprics in the Kingdom and supported schools and education. (It is worthwhile to note also that he had joined the monks at Mount Athos, which at that time was not only a republic composed entirely of monastries and monks, but also the highest divinity school of the Eastern Orthodox Church; he became a monk *(sava)* and a few years later induced his father, the king, to resign the throne and finish his days as a monk in the "Holy Mount" *(Svata Gora)*. At Mount

---

[35] Paul R. Radosavljevich, *Who Are the Slavs?* (Boston: Richard G. Badger, 1919), II, 30.

Athos, St. Sava and his father built up a Serbian monastery which, during the twelfth and thirteenth centuries became the high divinity institution for the Serbian theologians and ecclesiastics and the metropolis of Serbian learning and literature.[36]

From these times on, the monasteries became centers of education of whatever form of instruction they offered to Serbia's youth. In some places (as in the Mount Athos monastry, or in *studenica*) was offered the highest educational forms of instruction of the times. The monks also ran city and private schools. The laws of Serbia in the fourteenth century provided that all villages should have schools. Yet the children of wealthy parents could receive all forms of higher education in Constantinople and Dubrovnik (Ragusa). After the subjugation of Serbia by the Turks, all public schools were closed and only church schools remained.

During this period of national subjection, the portions of Serbia under Austria fared better than those under Turkey. In fact, the "Black George" "The Liberator," the first ruler of Serbia, was an illiterate who could sign official documents only by making a rude cross with his hand.[37] Conditions were even worse in the southern regions of Serbia. Although compulsory education between the ages of seven and thirteen was decreed in 1904 in Serbia, there was a general lack of schools; some pupils had to travel fifteen kilometers to attend a school, and had to be fed in communal kitchens with food they themselves supplied. Continuation schools, although provided for by the law, did not exist. The attendance in all schools was apathetic, and poor students were generally excused from attendance; hence conditions were appalling. There was a glaring lack of qualified teachers; they were miserably paid, had no right to vote, no vacations, and their health leave of absence was limited to two months. By

---

[36] We have summarized here: Joseph S. Roucek, "Pre-War Educational Theory in Yugoslavia," *Educational Theory*, VI, 1 (January, 1956), pp. 35-46.

[37] For the educational theories of Obradovich, the first Serb Minister of Education, and of Vuk Karadzich, whose construction of the alphabet in Cyrillic characters on strictly phonetic lines helped the educational development of Serbia, see Roucek, *op. cit.*

comparison, conditions in the northern sections were better than in the southern districts. But only 54.8 percent of the national populace as a whole could read and write in 1918.

There was hardly any secondary education in Serbia before World War I. The first so-called "high school" was opened in Serbia in 1808, but was closed again in 1813 with the fall of Serbia's independence. In independent Serbia, another secondary school opened its doors in Belgrade in 1830, was transferred to Kragujevac in 1838 with the title of "gymnasium"; it taught philosophy, history, mathematics, statistics, the German language, and drawing. In 1841, a law department was opened and the school returned to Belgrade. (Several other secondary institutions sprang up in the 1830's.)

The gymnasium in Belgrade was to evolve into a university; by the turn of the century, its faculties started to produce governmental officials. The university was formally inaugurated on October 2, 1905. Although most Serbian students continued getting their degrees abroad, the university was developing rapidly before 1914. On August 19, 1914, fourteen Austrian shells struck the university building and wrought havoc. The work of the institution was suspended for the next five years.

Meanwhile, Serbia's secondary schools continued springing up in increasing numbers after 1886; especially the "real schools" (not requiring Latin) were popular. Admission examinations were introduced in 1873, and maturity examinations in 1876. The reorganization of the secondary schools in 1898 provided, in theory, for three kinds of secondary schools, but in actual practice, classical gymnasia were mostly transformed into "real gymnasia." (The last classical gymnasium, attached to a small branch of the Belgrade gymnasium, was closed in 1902 for the lack of pupils.) In addition, there were eight secondary schools for girls (the oldest being that of Belgrade, opened in 1863, with three and later six years' training). But the professional and technical training was of poor character. The church institutions accepted pupils from the fourth year of elementary school and gave them nine years of training in their "internats." There was a private music training school, a private industrial training school, and a commercial academy in Belgrade, three state trade schools, and a few agricultural and wine schools. Serbia's specialty was a school for the training of physical education teachers in secondary schools as well as elementary and university students. There were also a military academy in Belgrade and a state military school at Kragujevac.

Croatia-Slovenia. Here the Catholics were ahead of the state in setting up schools in the villages. Especially in Slovenia, these village schools were fairly numerous and widespread; they helped the foundation of a large network of village education after the introduction of state schooling in 1869. In Croatia, efforts to found church village schools were less successful; but the initiative taken by Archbishop Strossmayer (1815-1905) helped. Even the girls were finally induced to attend village schools, and after 1860 there remained a few village schools for girls under the direction of nuns. In the Viovodina, the German-speaking Protestant communities had their own village schools from the very beginning of their settlement there by Empress Maria Theresa (who promised religious toleration). Hence, when the government took over elementary education, these communities reached a level of literacy which was higher than that of either their Hungarian or Slav neighbors.[38]

In addition to these institutions, there were also a few schools supported by Croatian nobles on their estates, inaugurated more as a hobby than because of any interest in promoting the education of the "barbarous Slavs." The Hungarians, in general, refused to recognize the existence of Slav nationalities. When the Dual Monarchy materialized in 1867, the Magyar nobles tried to save their dying feudalism. The peasants resented the revival of the practice of compulsory labor after 1890 and the reintroduction of the flogging of peasants in 1907; they reacted by listening eagerly to bourgeois leaders of Croat nationalism.

---

[38] For more details, see Ruth Trouton, *Peasant Renaissance in Yugoslavia 1900-1950* (London: Routledge & Kegan Paul, 1952).

Nationalistic tensions were growing, just at the time when the Austro-Hungarian Empire was trying to set up its school system. The Germanizers, representing the dynasty, were willing to have the Slovenian and Croat peasant taught in his language, but wanted German to be the second language; they were mainly interested in teaching loyalty to the Emperor and in emphasizing the superiority of German culture. But the Hungarians wanted to "re-educate" Croat peasants into 100 percent Hungarians, without helping them to promote themselves economically, socially, or educationally. Hence they decided that, wherever there was a Hungarian majority or a minority, the language of instruction was to be Hungarian for all, and deliberately pitted the Hungarian schools against the weakened Slav institutions.

Austria-Hungary established the universal free elementary educational system in 1869. (The Kingdom of Serbia did the same in 1888.) In Croatia, in 1894, a skeleton system of elementary schools was founded. Slovenia, in spite of the difficulties offered by the mountainous character of the area, became the most literate region of the entire Balkan Peninsula; of the million or so Slovenes, about three-quarters were literate at the turn of the century.

In summary, before World War I, all Yugoslav areas (Macedonia coming under Serbian law in 1912) had elementary schooling free and compulsory—by law. But, in application, schooling was not universal—except in Slovenia, parts of Croatia and Dalmatia, and to some extent in the Voivodina. Elsewhere, only about a quarter of the peasant children had elementary schooling.[39]

As far as post-primary education is concerned, some higher elementary schools were supported in Croatia and Dalmatia—and a good number in Slovenia. In addition, there were the excellent civic *(Gradjanske)* schools (especially popular in Slovenia), modeled on the German *Gurgerschule*, stressing agricultural subjects (farm bookkeeping, simple surveying, farm technology, study of the

---

[39] Trouton, *op. cit.,* p. 100; for the character of peasant elementary education, see pp. 100-105.

imperial agricultural law) ; since they also trained students from the urban lower middle classes, they supported the rise of the native middle class.

Actually, only a few Yugoslav peasant children had a chance to advance their schooling beyond the age of twelve in either continuation or civic schools. As a matter of fact, the peasant wanted his sons to go to the gymnasium (imitating the German models before scientific subjects started to play an important role in schooling) which emphasized literary subjects. Their full course lasted from ten to eighteen years, but there were also numerous "incomplete" gymnasia with three to four junior classes. The main purpose of these institutions was to prepare students for the university.

While elementary school was free and compulsory by law in Slovenia, parts of Croatia and Dalmatia, and in some parts of the Voivodina, Islam in Bosnia-Herzegovina was not interested in peasant education. The few Moslem schools there taught only town pupils, and instructed only in the Koran. The same applied to the areas were Albanian Moslems were located (the borders of Montenegro, the west of Macedonia, and the districts to the south of Serbia, known as the Sandzak, or Old Serbia, and now called Kosmet, or Kosovo and Metohija). On the other hand, several Catholic orders were running several schools of a relatively high standard in Bosnia, with the hope of enticing into the Catholic fold the more intelligent and ambitious youth from the Moslem as well as the Orthodox circles. At the same time, Bosnia-Herzegovina, occupied by Austria-Hungary in 1878 (and annexed in 1908), was covered by the imperial law of 1869; some village and town schools were set up; about one-third of the peasants went to school, but the Moslem influence prevented the girls from attending.

Montenegro established its Ministry of Education in the 1880's but the government made hardly any efforts to build up an elementary school system. Only a few elementary schools existed in the few towns of the Kingdom, with some two or three thousand children attending (out of a total child population of about 30,000).

Macedonia, up to 1912, had only a few private schools

but a larger number of schools promoted by the nationalistic ambitions of the Serbs, Bulgars, and Greeks (while
most Albanians as Moslems learned the Koran and a few
Albanians went to Catholic schools). The governments
of Serbia, Bulgaria, and Greece sent a number of teachers to Macedonian villages between 1900 and 1914,
where, remarks Trouton, they "mixed education with in-
transigent politics." In fact, the Macedonian teachers
were the founders and promoters of the underground
movement, the IMRO, which started with the aim of
driving out the Turks, and eventually saw teachers participating in the fights between the IMRO, the Serbs, and
Bulgars. When Serbia acquired the greater part of Macedonia in 1913, the Serbian law of compulsory education
of 1912 was extended to the region.

Dalmatian Ragusa had a general system of free schools
for the urban population, with elementary schools for the
peasants in the hinterland in the sixteenth to the eighteenth centuries; with the collapse of the Republic, these
educational institutions ceased to exist. Austria-Hungary's administration of the Dalmatian territory benefited the area educationally; there were also some higher
elementary schools introduced here.

The Problem of the Intelligentsia

The striving for university diplomas was nearly a disease in prewar Yugoslavia, for it offered the prestige of
being employed by the state, the certification of possible
appointment to the all-powerful bureaucracy; the medical
and legal professions were somewhat less popular. The
results were astounding in their social implications, for
as Yugoslavia's urban society developed, "it became strat-
ified according to educational attainments; at the top
were well-trained individuals, but with little direct knowledge of practical affairs; clinging to them were less
successful students, who still wanted to belong to the
intellectual elite and who had acquired some tastes and
habits of that class; then came the traders and craftsmen with a poor general education; finally, there was the

floating population of the unskilled workers, largely illiterate.[40]

At the same time, the Balkan intellectuals were pain-
fully aware that the standard of living in their country
was far below that of Western and Central Europe; they
tried to make up for the loss of time by resenting the
term "Balkans." Most of them, after a sojourn abroad,
returned with a definite inferiority complex, which translated itself into a furious eagerness to glorify, by imitation, some forms of the native culture. In general, Balkan
nationalism found expression in a literary and linguistic
renaissance and in the development of national Churches.
Western concepts of liberalism, constitutionalism, and democracy had a strong appeal for them, although their
efforts to transplant them to their native country failed,
since they were not home-grown products, only foreign
importations. In fact, national independence spelled the
doom of liberalism, while the emerging ruling class nimbly
combined lip service to such ideals with the straight forward pursuit of its self-interest.[41]

At the same time, the whole evolution of the state promoted the ever-widening abyss between the masses and
the intellectuals. When the Serb state was organized,
anybody with any kind of education was needed and draft-
ed into the state service. Such appointments also meant
higher incomes, an easier life attained by emancipation
from hard manual labor, a better social position. Since
the state was, at the beginning of its existence, short of
such servants, it was at first easy to secure to such appointments. But as the decades went by, a prevalent
atmosphere of public opinion stressed that "men of education" were entitled to state jobs; a fetish of diplomas,
the "academization" of occupational preparation became
a definite disease. And as the road of approach to governmental positions was being steadily narrowed, only
those who had passed through the higher institutions
could expect such career opportunities. Hence, the grow-

---

[40] Trouton, *op. cit.*, p. 121.

[41] For more details, see Joseph S. Roucek, *Balkan Politics* (Stanford University Press, 1948), pp. 10-25.

ing body of unemployed intellectuals began to curse Yugoslavia's political life as early as 1918.

Education Between the Two World Wars

With the formation of the Kingdom of the Serbs-Croats-Slovenes in 1918, the government had to cope with numberless educational problems of the greatest magnitude.[42]

The new state, young in its political form, tried to arrange modern methods of instructing its youth from infancy to early manhood and womanhood in an orderly series of schools of general education. Specifically, this began with the infant school for children from the ages of four to seven. Compulsory education came into effect when the child was seven and continued for eight years. The first four years of that time were spent in a primary school, the Yugoslav form of the common foundation of education. Once out of this four-year primary school, the child, as far as general education was concerned, had a range of three choices. He could continue elementary education in an advanced elementary school and in four years complete compulsory schooling; in that case, his formal full-time attendance ended then. Or he could enter a civic school and study for four years, and in doing so the assumption was that at its completion he would

---

[42] The best systematic formal survey of postwar Yugoslav Education is: S. K. Turosienski, *Education in Yugoslavia* (Washington, D.C.: Government Printing Office, 1939, U.S. Department of the Interior, Office of Education, Bulletin 1939, No. 6), and Bibliography, 134-35; S. K. Turosienski, "Education," chap. XIII, 230-43, in R. J. Kerner (ed.), *Yugoslavia* (Berkeley, Cal.: University of California Press, 1949) ; League of Nations, *European Conference on Rural Life, Yugoslavia* (Geneva, August, 1939), 48-54. Details can also be found in: Ruth Trouton, *Peasant Renaissance in Yugoslavia 1900-1950* (London: Routledge & Kegan Paul, 1952), 122-269; Joseph S. Roucek, "Recent Changes in the Organization of the Yugoslav Universities," *School and Society*, XXXVII (March 11, 1933), 331-32; "Educational Work of Yugoslav Sokols," *Ibid.*, XXXVI (July 30, 1932), 150-53; "The New Reforms of Yugoslavia," *Ibid.*, XXXVI, 927 (October 1, 1932), 431-32; "The Development of the Educational Structure of Yugoslavia," *Ibid.*, XXXX (August 25, 1934), 250-53; "The Higher Institutions of Learning and Professional Schools of Yugoslavia," *Ibid.*, XXXXI, 1063 (May 11, 1935), 650-52; "The Secondary Schools of Yugoslavia," *Education*, LVI, 10 (June, 1936), 583-86.

continue as a student for a few years longer. Third, he could go into any one of the three types of eight-year secondary schools; this third choice presupposed later studies in some one of the universities or other institutions of higher education.

The advanced elementary school, the civic schools, and the first four years of the secondary schools were parallel and intended to cover the period of early adolescence, eleven to fifteen years of age, but each had a different purpose. The final four years of the three types of secondary schools of general education were nonterminal; they were preparatory to studies in the traditional university faculties of theology, philosophy, law, and medicine.

In general, Yugoslavia's secondary schools followed the system long current in Austria-Hungary. Most of them were of the type of "real gymnasium," either complete (eight years), or incomplete (first four years). The first four years were called the junior court (roughly corresponding to the American junior high school), and taught religion, the national language, literature, French, mathematics, natural sciences, history, geography, singing, drawing, and gymnastics. Girls were taught religion, domestic science, and embroidery. The school year was divided into three parts of three months each. At the end of each year, those completing their term with at least "good" marks (i.e., 33 percent) passed into the upper division. At the end of the fourth year, there was an examination, known as the "little *matura*," a sort of synthesis of the knowledge acquired during the first four years in the school; those who passed the examination could join the upper division of the institution where the following subjects were taught: religion, national language (with literature), French and a second modern language (German or English), Latin, history, geography, mathematics, natural sciences, and philosophical subjects. (Of the fine arts, only drawing was taught.) At the end of the final year, the pupils had to pass the dreaded "maturity examination," partly oral and partly written in all the most important subjects taught in secondary schools. The passing of this "great *matura*" entitled the candidate to enter universities and high schools.

A distinction was drawn between general and specialized education in the secondary schools. The civic schools (tuition-free) paralleled advanced elementary instruction and overlapped and paralleled the first four years of the eight-year secondary school; they resembled the civic schools of Hungary, the *mellemskolen* of Denmark, and the middle schools of Germany. The curriculum was the same for all in the first two years; in the last two years, the student chose one of the three fields: trade and industrial, commercial, or agricultural.

In fact, Yugoslavia built up an unusually wide variety of schools for the students between the ages of fifteen to nineteen years. In addition to the classical gymnasia, real gymnasia, and real school types of general education, there were normal schools to prepare teachers for elementary schools, normal schools for domestic science, and vocational normal schools for girls; secondary technical schools, some of them giving highly specialized instruction; commercial academies and naval commercial academies; secondary schools of agriculture; secondary schools of religion; and schools for nurses and hospital attendants.

Overlapping the junior and secondary schools (and not of senior standing) were trade schools for boys and for girls, army and navy trade schools, lower and special agricultural schools, schools of rural housekeeping, and schools of forestry. Mostly in the junior secondary stage were vocational continuation schools, railway craft schools, and vocational courses for maritime workers.

Most of the teacher-training institutions were state-owned; only a few were primary schools. Their pupils were the beginners who had completed their fourth year in a secondary or public school. The instruction here lasted four years; after the fourth year the pupils had to pass their "teachers' maturity examination," which entitled them to become teachers in the elementary schools. All the teachers' training schools, both state and private, had in the main the same organization; yet, till 1929, they had been developing under different laws which were valid in the various provinces after World War I. A new law, unifying all the systems, was promulgated on September 27, 1929; the instruction was raised from four to five years and enlarged with the addition of new general and professional studies. Greater attention was given to the choice of schoolmasters, and plans were made for domitories for all pupils and a hall for practice teaching. At the end of the fifth year, the candidates had to take their examination for the teacher's diploma in elementary schools. After two years of successful teaching in the elementary school, the apprentice teachers had to take an examination which was in essence a test of their skill and ability to teach.

There were five universities, headed by the University of Belgrade and then by the University of Zagreb. Their curriculum also showed the conflict agitating the differences between the Serbs and Croats. Belgrade's institution aimed to restore the Serbian culture lost under Turkish rule, while Zagreb represented the Croat cultural traditions rooted in Austria-Hungary; the religious differences were also shown in the faculties of theology—the one at Zagreb being Roman Catholic and that a Belgrade being Serbian Orthodox. Each of the five universities had eight faculties (departments): philosophy (corresponding to an American college of arts and sciences); law (which included economics); medicine; pharmacology; theology; agriculture and forestry; technical sciences (architecture, civil and electrical engineering); and veterinary medicine.

The university students passed a comprehensive examination at the end of the fourth year; a doctor's degree was granted on the basis of an original dissertation publicly defended; the medical training took five years and carried with it the degree of Doctor of General Medicine; an additional year was required to receive the degree of Doctor of Medical Sciences.

The university appointments were made by the practices resembling those of Central Europe. Professors were selected from university "docents" (which would correspond to "lecturers" or "assistant professors" at most in the United States), having Ph.D.'s, and by a faculty council from candidates who had passed a competitive public examination; they were appointed by the Minister of Education, without terms of tenure. Private docents (instructors) had to hold, like all candidates for university positions, a doctor's degree and submit a thesis; they did not take a competitive examination but were elected by a faculty council and approved by the university Senate. All docents were appointed for five years, but could be reappointed. Professors were chosen by a faculty council from docents who had passed their competitive public examination; in exceptional cases a well-known scholar or scientist could be appointed without taking an examination. The university assembly approved the selection of a professor, who then could be appointed for life by the King on the recommendation of the Minister of Education.

Social Implications of the
Educational System Under the Monarchy

In spite of the ambitious claims and real advances of the education system under the Monarchy, the educational system had some rather weak aspects. In 1921, the percentage of illiteracy (of twelve years and over) was 50.5 percent (40.3 percent for males and 60 percent for females) ; ten years later, the percentage was (for eleven years and over) 44.6 percent (32.3 percent for males and 56.4 percent for females).[43] The new nationalistic ideology of the educational system was confronted with serious difficulties because of the persistent demands made by the Serbian Orthodox, Roman Catholic, and Moslem religions; in fact, religious education was compulsory in all elementary, secondary, civic, and vocational schools, and the curricula were prepared by the respective denominations (and approved by the Ministry of Education). Furthermore, the principle of inculcating a spirit

---

[43] The percentage of illiteracy was the highest in Macedonia (67.5 percent), where the heritage of Turkish rule was still evident, and the lowest in the Slovene districts (5.5 percent), where the more enlightened rule of Austria-Hungary had permitted education at a much earlier date.

of national unity was made more difficult by the efforts to satisfy the rights of national minorities (protected by the Minorities Treaties). For instance, in spite of the existence of compulsory education after 1911, Moslems continued clinging to their own *Mekteb*, confessional schools for Moslems, where the emphasis was on Arabic and Turkish languages, literature, and history, the Koranic exegesis, and jurisprudence (while the graduates of secondary schools could register in either the Moslem colleges of jurisprudence and religion or the regular universities). It was only in 1928, at the Moslem Congress at Sarajevo, that an agreement was reached between the spiritual and the secular intelligentsia to extend religious education among Moslems; the state was asked to establish as many schools as possible in Moslem regions, to extend compulsory public education to Moslem girls, and to increase social work among Moslems through cooperation of the state with cultural and educational societies.[44] Supplementary cares were created by numerous multilingual schools in Serbo-Croatian, Slovenian, Czech, Russian, Ruthenian, German, Magyar, Romanian, Italian, and French; in addition, Germans, Magyars, and Czechs supported their own schools.

An additional problem was presented by the divergence between the school attendance laws in different regions. The new state had seven cultural centers (Belgrade, Zagreb, Ljubljana, Cetinje, Split, Sarajevo, and Novi Sad), and seven different educational laws. Most of the country required an attendance of four years, but in certain regions (and especially in towns) from six to seven years; the village children usually completed their education at the age of ten, simply because there was no definite provision for continuing it in the villages; most girls stayed home anyhow. While urban conditions were more favorable to school attendance, the diversity of educational laws produced regional differences. Some efforts were made to improve the short period of elementary school attendance and the high percentage of illiteracy by the

---

[44] Wayne S. Vucinich, "Yugoslavs of the Moslem Faith," chap. XV, 261-78, in R. J. Kerner (ed.), *op. cit.* (Turkish was also used in the Higher Islamic School at Sarajevo.)

People's Universities. While they operated in nearly all towns, their activities were generally confined to lectures without any special plan. (Probably the most successful of these activities were lectures accompanied by films, the most popular ones having been produced by the School of Social Hygiene at Zagreb.) Attempting to imitate similar institutions in Denmark, the first peasant university in Yugoslavia was formed under the auspices of the Social Hygiene School. Peasants, from eighteen to thirty years of age, went into residence for five months, where they received instruction in general as well as in practical subjects, but mainly in the subjects connected with agriculture and health. The objects of the peasant universities were: (1) to improve the peasant's own health and that of his family; (2) to train him in agricultural pursuits; and (3) to teach him his duties as a member of the family and as a state citizen.[45]

Efforts were also made to extend the work of the elementary schoolteachers into the villages, but most of the peasants had no time or interest in attending such courses (especially when conducted in towns). Attempts were then made to promote courses lasting four months, with lectures twice a month from 6:00 to 8:00 P.M., for both sexes, offered in the mother tongue and covering geography, arithmetic, agriculture, rural economy, hygiene, history, civics, and manual work.

Related to these educational activities were the People's Libraries (2,136 in 1939). Just before World War II, the broadcasting stations at Belgrade, Zagreb, and Ljubljana tried to reach the rural populace (which represented only 10 percent of the subscribers).

Peasant-Urban Conflicts

World War I resulted in a virtual social uprising; the former upper classes practically disappeared after 1919, and the rest were deprived of their wealth as a result of the agrarian reform. The resulting social vacuum was filled by the *Bourgeoisie*, already differentiated from the

---

[45] League of Nations, *European Conference on Rural Life, Yugoslavia* (Geneva: August, 1939), pp. 51-52.

peasant masses, and by the rapidly growing bureaucracy, most of which was "hardly emancipated from the traditional peasantry loyalty to family and group, and were often influenced in their decisions by these interests." In fact, "the civil service had members appointed more because of their personal relations with the higher authorities than because of an effective system of competitive examinations, entrance and promotion and educational qualifications."[46]

The insistence of the "educated" Yugoslavs on taking up professional and clerical occupations was hardly satisfied by 1930, when already nearly 5 percent of the population was absorbed in these occupations; nearly two-thirds of them were in some form of government service, as teachers, engineers, lawyers, administrators, clerical workers, and various lower grade civil servants. This class formulated its requirements for admittance, and these educational qualifications divided its members from the lower grade commercial and industrial workers. "To have some link with government service gave prestige which was sometimes held to be more important than the question of salary. Their clothing, homes, social habits aped those of similar classes in Western Europe, but their income averaged out at considerably less. The scarcity of outside employment made the professional and intellectual class cling closely to their government jobs."[47]

This general social pressure to get settled in government appointments was the result of the attendance figures at the universities. The universities of Belgrade and Zagreb were already established before 1918; a New University was established at Ljubljana, and university faculties opened in Subotica and Skoplje. Right after World War I, there were only about 2,000 university students—and in 1940 there were 20,000. In 1940, more than half were registered in the faculties of law (7,400) and philosophy (3,900) ; engineering and medicine came next

---

[46] Ruth Trouton, *Peasant Renaissance in Yugoslavia 1900-1950* (London: Routledge & Kegan Paul, 1952), p. 138.
[47] *Ibid.*

(about 2,300), while agriculture and veterinary medicine attracted only about 10 percent; economic students numbered 600.[48]

The relationships in Yugoslavia's society reflected the growing peasant-bourgeois tensions, already aggravated by the rapidly growing problem of overpopulation. In spite of the terrible death toll among the Serbs during World War I, the postwar birth rate soon produced overpopulation, only partly relieved by the remittances of the overseas emigrants (around 10,000,000 *dinars* in 1930). The population pressure, plus the depression of the 1930's, more than ever before induced the peasants to make sacrifices on behalf of their sons attending the secondary and higher institutions, in the hope that they would ascend from the miserable lot of the peasantry.

In turn, these ambitious but more often than not inadequately trained "intellectuals" proved to be a problem to themselves and to their families. Before World War I, the Yugoslav cultural life had its indirect contacts with the West, mostly through the medium of Austria-Hungary and Germany. After the great conflict, numerous students who revolted against German and Austrian influences went to universities in France, England, and Italy. But they now came under the influence of foreign ideas which opposed the old-established trends of Slav peasant society and stressed the already existing dividing line between the masses of the peasantry and the educated, urbanized minority. "Everywhere, in Kafanas, in the universities, in schools, there was the typically lively Slav discussion of the borrowed intellectual material."[49] The tendency to imitate the Western political intellectual crosscurrents was especially seen in the use of the language of Western liberalism and constitutionalism. But since these prophets of liberalism soon found that their abstract principles, although freely preached to the masses, were nullified by political practices, many became bitter critics and Socialists (and Communists). These urban-rural tensions found expression in numerous ramifications, even

---

[48] *Ibid.*, p. 176. For the educational problem of the minorities, see pp. 180-88.

[49] *Ibid.*, p. 131.

in the clearly defined Serbo-Croat split, which had its Western-Eastern aspects, a rural-urban aspect, Catholic versus Orthodox, the Croat peasant versus nascent capitalism, and local autonomy versus administrative centralization.[50]

Contributions to Scholarship

In spite of the difficulties presented by the growing numbers of the intelligentsia in prewar Yugoslavia, who were insistent on getting state appointments, since they conceived of themselves, especially in the field of politics, as the elite discharging their function of national leadership even at the expense of the peasant masses, the Yugoslav universities did make definite contributions to scholarship, especially in the field of social science.[51] The best graduate work was done in history and political science.[52] Little attention was paid to psychology, and, although anthropology and sociology were not taught as such, Yugoslav scholars were (and still are) especially active in the field of ethnography, folklore, and social anthropology, following the groundwork laid by Baltazar Sogischich, F. Demelich, Tihormir Gjorgjevich, and especially Jovan Cvijich, whose *La Péninsule balkanique* (1918) is a gold mine of information on the forms of settlement, migrations, psychical and cultural differentiation, and economic life of the Balkan peoples. (Today, the most active of this group of specialists is Bozo Skerlj of the University of Ljubljana.)[53] The former Professor of Sociology at Zagreb, Dinko Tomasic, had an interna-

---

[50] See also Roucek, "Trends in Yugoslavia's Higher Education," *Journal of Education* (Karaikudi, South India), IV, No. 1 (March, 1960), 19-30.

[51] Alexander Hertz, "The Case of an Eastern European Intelligentsia," *Journal of Central European Affairs*, XI, 1 (January-April, 1951), pp. 10-26, is a definite contribution to this problem, especially as it developed in Poland.

[52] Robert J. Kerner, *Social Sciences in the Balkans and Turkey* (Berkeley, Cal.: University of California Press, 1930), chap. II, "Jugoslavia," pp. 14-42.

[53] See Bozo Skerlj, "Yugoslavia: Anthropological Review for 1952-1954," *Yearbook of Anthropology 1955* (New York: Wenner-Gren Foundation for Anthropological Research, 1955), pp. 651-70.

tional reputation even before his arrival in the United States in 1939 when he settled at Indiana University.[54]

Education Under Tito

Tito and his followers had the typical Communist faith in education even when busy with guerrilla warfare. Thus most units of the National Liberation Army carried schools with them, and the Partisan movement had already proclaimed its three immediate educational aims: (1) the completion of the network of elementary schools throughout the country; (2) the liquidation of adult illiteracy; and (3) the raising of the level of the backward areas, with special attention to the language problem in relation to the minority schools. On coming to power, Tito's system of education was assigned this basic aim: to confirm the social and economic changes brought about through the National Liberation movement and to make possible the further alterations in the social situation which appeared desirable.

The Constitution of 1945[55] provides in Article 38 that

[54] Among his numerous works, see Dinko Tomasic, *Personality and Culture in Eastern European Politics* (New York: G. W. Stewart, 1948). For other Yugoslav sociologists of note, see: Joseph S. Roucek, "Sociology in Yugoslavia," pp. 740-54, in Georges Gurvitch and Wilbert E. Moore (eds.), *Twentieth Century Sociology* (New York: The Philosophical Library, 1945).

[55] *UNESCO, World Survey of Education* (Paris, 1955), pp. 875-83; Bozidar Kicovic, *Schools and Education in Yugoslavia* (Beograd: Edition "Jugoslavija," 1955); Jugoslavia, Savet za Nauku i Kulturu, *Education in the Federal People's Republic of Yugoslavia, 1945-46 to 1950-51* (Beograd, 1952); Mitra Mitrovic, "Women and Education in Yugoslavia," *Women and Education* (Paris: UNESCO, *Problems in Education*, No. V, pp. 183-255, 1953); New Education Fellowship, *Yugoslavia* (The People's Revolution and Education) (New York, 1947); Ruth Trouton, *Peasant Renaissance in Yugoslavia 1900-1950* (London: Routledge and Kegan Paul, 1952), especially 202ff.; "Yugoslavia," pp. 490-501, in *The Yearbook of Education, 1948* (London: Evans Brothers, 1948); M. M. Chambers (ed.), *Universities of the World Outside the USA* (Washington, D.C.: American Council on Education, 1950), pp. 897-990; "Yugoslav University Training," pp. 4-6, in *Youth Life* (a quarterly published by the People's Youth of Yugoslavia, Decanska 35, Belgrade), 4 (December, 1951); "General Law on Universities" (June 30, 1954), can be secured from the Yugoslav Information Services, 816 Fifth Ave., New York City; Roucek, "Tito's Educational Experiences and Experiments," *The Educational Forum*, January, 1957, pp. 193-201.

"with a view to raising the general cultural level of the people, the State shall guarantee to all citizens access to schools and cultural institutions." Furthermore, "Schools shall be public. Opening of private schools shall be subject to special legislation, and their activities shall be supervised by the State. Primary education shall be free and compulsory. Schools shall be separated from the Church." The constitutions of the constituent republics reproduced all these provisions in their documents.

A new constitution was promulgated in January, 1953, following "decentralization" and "democratization" of public and social life of the country. All these provisions remain in force, while the constituent republics amended their constitutions in January, 1953. Basically, the federal authorities now enact only the basic legislation, which lays down the principles on the basis of which the legislatures of the republics can prepare their own laws.

The federal decrees promulgated in 1952, which have replaced the 1945 law, now make compulsory the eight-year (formerly seven-year) education period introduced in 1951; today education in Yugoslavia is compulsory for all children between seven and fifteen. Regarding vocational schools, the 1952 decree on apprentices and on vocational schools laid down the basic principles for vocational education. On June 30, 1954, the General Law on Universities provided a uniform type of self-management to Yugoslavia's five universities, making each university a "community" of semi-autonomous constituent faculties.[56]

Administration and Organization

According to the federal constitutional law of January 13, 1953, as well as the state constitutions (which made such subsequent changes), steps have been taken to "democratize" and "decentralize" public education and culture. The Council for Science and Culture of the Federal People's Republic of Yugoslavia has been abol-

---

[56] Charles P. McVicker, *Titoism* (New York: St. Martin's Press, 1957), pp. 196-201, is a convenient summary of this measure.

ished, and replaced by a Committee for Public Education attached to the Executive Council of the Federal People's Republic of Yugoslavia which discusses the general lines of educational policy in Yugoslavia and submits to the Executive Council draft laws covering the whole of the country; offers measures intended to promote the development of educational and cultural life and coordinate the activities of the various republics; proposes measures aimed to improve the material situation of education, science, and culture. The republics, after reorganization, control education through the republics' executive councils, with their committees for public education (of five to eight council members). Their duties resemble those of the Federal Executive Council, except that their jurisdiction is limited to their republics. In addition, the republics have their councils for education, science, and culture, consisting of ten to twenty members (chosen by associations of primary and secondary teachers, the teaching staff of universities and higher professional schools, and of cultural and scientific workers, and those selected by the executive councils of the republics from educational, scientific, and cultural personnel), the chairman of this council is appointed by the executive council of the republic. (In Croatia, the chairman is also a member of the executive council.)

Each council has a secretariat, which executes the directives of the council and controls education, supervises the work of administrative bodies and independent units, applies resolutions of the council, and studies the problems with which the latter is dealing. Each secretariat employs research experts, inspectors, and an administrative and technical staff.

District and municipal people's committees have their own councils; their first concern is the material needs of the school and other cultural and educational institutions; they also arrange for supervision by inspectors of the appropriate districts or municipal people's committee, or by distinguished teachers. The district and municipal councils are also state organizations, consisting of representatives of associations of educators and of citizens concerned with cultural problems.

The first grade of the Yugoslav school system is provided by preschool education and is carried on in children's nurseries, children's homes, and kindergartens. Children's nurseries are the most numerous institutions of this kind (248, with over 13,000 children in 1953). Children's nurseries take in children from three to seven years of age, where, if their parents are employed, they spend eight to ten hours a day. The children are divided into several social-educational work groups, each group having its nurse. Their education is carried out through individual and collective work. Children's homes for preschool children (three to seven years of age) are state institutions for children who have no one to look after them (sixteen of them, in 1953, with 1,024 children). Kindergartens educate children from four to seven (251 in 1950). In addition, there are also children's playgrounds usually within the blocks of different city streets for play and entertainment; Pioneer (children) Cities and summer resorts have the same purpose. In 1948, special schools were opened for the preschool institutions, offering a four-year course; women holding certificates from these training institutions can complete their education by a supplementary course and become regular teachers.

Primary and Secondary Schools

In 1945, the period of compulsory education was lengthened from four to seven years, and in 1950 to eight years *(Osmoletke)*. These schools for general education have four primary classes and four lower secondary classes; after completing four grades, the pupil may enroll in the higher grades of the eight-year elementary school or in the lower grades of secondary school; both have the same plans and programs of instruction, and the pupil who completes the eight-year elementary school, or four grades of the secondary school, acquires the same qualifications allowing him to resume his studies in the higher grades of secondary school of four years; similarly, upon completing the eight-year elementary school or lower secondary school, the pupil may continue his studies in secondary technical or other similar schools. In places where no eight-year school exists, higher primary schools or complementary schools with at least two classes (fifth and sixth) have been opened (on a temporary basis). Roughly, general education schools are organized on different lines in each republic, but efforts are made to form a single type.[57]

At the end of their eighth year of compulsory education, pupils start working in agriculture or industry, or enter the higher type of general secondary education or a primary or secondary vocational school.

Secondary education has lower and higher stages. The lower types have two forms: the lower classes of the *gimnazija* (from the first to the fourth class), and the higher classes of the eight-year school (from the fifth to the eighth class). The "little baccalaureate," taken at the end of the higher stage, admits students to the universities, the higher professional schools, and the academies of art. Yugoslavia has classical secondary schools in which Latin is taught from the first grade and Greek from the third grade. Three languages are compulsory in all the secondary schools, of which one is the mother tongue and the two others selected from English, Russian, French, German, and Italian). The other subjects are: history, geography, biology, physics, chemistry, mathematics, philosophy, ethics, drawing, and physical culture. In 1953, the country had 606 secondary schools, with 239,220 pupils (compared to 409 schools and 222,800 pupils in 1945). The increases had taken place especially in Macedonia and Bosnia-Herzegovina.

Schools for Minorities

Tito's regime always stresses that "one of the significant aspects of Yugoslavia's educational policy is the opening of new schools in the languages of the national minorities."[58] Officially, there are eleven national ethnical groups. Primary schools have been opened in all

---

[57] For details, see *UNESCO, op. cit.*, p. 373.

[58] Kicovic, *op. cit.*, p. 22.

the areas where these minorities live, and lower and higher secondary schools in the bigger towns. Where there are only a few minorities' children, special sections have been opened in the regular schools. The medium of instruction is the language of the minority, while the language of the republic in which the school is located is taught as a separate subject. The curricula are the same as those of corresponding Yugoslav schools, the only difference being the medium of instruction. In general, the development of the minority schools has been comparatively more rapid than the general development of school network in the country:[59]

NUMBER OF PUPILS IN SCHOOL—MEMBERS OF NATIONAL MINORITIES
In 1938-39 and 1952-53:

National Minority	Number of Pupils in elementary schools		Number of Pupils in secondary schools	
	1938-39	1952-53	1938-39	1952-53
Bulgarians		4,954		3,034
Czechs	7,480	8,805	516	3,122
Slovaks	1,415	2,034		1,001
Ruthenians Shiptars		96,978		13,689
Hungarians	27,915	40,885	419	14,695
Germans	38,458	3,828	750	1,990
Romanians	4,742	3,526	161	1,395
Italians	422	2,609		1,506
Turks		18,180		2,700
Others		1,800		1,272

For instance, the Shiptar (Albanian) minority, which numbered (according to the census of 1948) about 750,000 persons, and which had no single school before World War II, now has 821 elementary schools, 126 secondary schools, and two teachers' vocational schools. The picture presented by the literacy figures of the Yugoslav minorities is also quite interesting:[60]

---

[59] Ibid., p. 23; 1960-61 total enrollment figures indicate 2,764,369 elementary school pupils and 79,676 secondary. Educational Trends (Geneva: International Bureau, 1962), 38.

[60] UNESCO, Progress of Literacy in Various Countries (Paris, 1953), pp. 165-66.

Percentage of illiteracy in the population of Yugoslavia,
10 years old and over by national groups and by sex: 1948:

National group	Percentage of total population	Percentage of Illiteracy Both sexes	Male	Female
All groups	100.0	25.4	15.4	34.4
Serbs	41.5	27.7	14.1	40.2
Croats	24.0	18.1	11.2	24.0
Slovenes	9.0	2.3	2.3	2.3
Macedonians	5.1	30.2	18.7	42.0
Autonomous Moslems	5.1	54.6	36.6	70.6
Montenegrins	2.7	24.1	11.0	35.5
Bulgars	0.4	19.9	6.8	33.1
Czechs	0.2	3.0	2.4	3.5
Slovaks	0.5	4.8	4.2	5.3
Shiptars	4.8	73.7	55.9	92.5
Hungarians	3.1	8.0	6.0	9.6
Germans	0.4	6.2	5.9	6.4
Rumanians	0.4	17.6	11.2	23.2
Valaques	0.7	38.2	22.7	51.6
Italians	0.5	6.9	4.9	8.7
Turks	0.6	63.9	47.4	80.7
Gypsies	0.5	74.0	61.9	85.7

Technical Schools

Lower Technical Schools. The aim of these schools is to train pupils, in addition to general education, in technical and theoretical subjects. According to the method of practical work, these schools are divided into: (1) schools where pupils acquire practical knowledge in workshops especially organized for this purpose; (2) schools in which pupils acquire practical knowledge while working in enterprises and receive theoretical instruction in the school; these are called schools for apprentices in the economy. Lower technical schools admit pupils of at least fourteen years of age, who have completed elementary school. Schooling in these lower technical schools lasts as a rule for two or three years, and, for certain trades, for four years.

There are several types of these lower technical schools: industrial, boys' and girls' artisan schools, agricultural, forestry, and veterinary schools; in addition, there are also commercial catering schools, as well as medical schools, which are divided into: schools for hospital nurses, schools for midwives, schools for children's nurses, schools for disinfection personnel, etc. In 1952, there were 101,577 pupils registered in 869 schools (with 7,919 teachers). Industrial and artisan schools rank second in number after the schools for apprentices, and a considerable influx of girls to these schools has been noticeable.

Secondary Technical Schools. Along with general education these schools also provide technical theoretical education and practical training required for work in different branches of the economy; they are divided into (1) regular technical schools and (2) workers' technical schools *(technicums)*. Regular secondary technical schools admit pupils who have completed lower secondary schools and passed for four years; instruction here is mostly theoretical; all subjects taught in secondary schools are also taught here (only in a somewhat more concise form). Practical instruction is carried on in special school workshops, laboratories, and the like. In addition, pupils during their summer vacation must spend some time doing practical work in different enterprises. The main types of secondary technical schools are: engineering, building, mining, transport, economic, agricultural, and medical schools; some of these schools have separate sections (such as: electrotechnical, geodetic, chemical-technological, etc., or general agricultural sections, land-tilling, livestock raising, fruit growing, and viticulture sections, etc.); secondary medical schools also have their sections (for doctor's assistants, dentists, etc.).

Workers' technical schools are a new type of secondary technical school, founded during the 1947-48 school year; they offer skilled workers an opportunity of acquiring higher training and the necessary general education. They admit workers of the corresponding trade if they have previously completed lower secondary school or school for the general education of workers; they also register skilled workers who have completed the corresponding lower technical school after passing the entrance examination. Instruction is mainly theoretical and lasts four years. There are sections for specialization. The workers attending these schools keep their regular jobs but have shorter working hours. The pupils, after completion of the regular secondary technical

schools or the workers' technical schools, may continue
their studies at the corresponding high schools of learning
or faculties. The number of secondary technical schools
and pupils has been increasing steadily; especially marked
has been the increase in the number of technical agricultural, economic, and medical schools.

Art Schools. There are two kinds of art schools in
Yugoslavia: lower and higher. The lower art schools
are divided into music and ballet schools. These institutions offer the pupils the necessary basis for further
musical education and training. Anyone who has passed
the entrance examination, and has completed at least one
form of elementary school, may enroll in these schools;
instruction in the lower music schools lasts six years.
Lower ballet schools are located in those places where
there are music schools; they admit pupils of eleven years
of age and instruction lasts for three years. There are
several types (music, ballet, schools for applied art and
dramatics) of secondary art schools; they take pupils
who have completed the lower music school, or a two-
year preparatory course, or who pass the entrance examination regardless of their qualifications. Instruction
takes four years and they also train teaching staffs for
music, for practical and organizational music work,
and prepare the future students of the music academies. Secondary ballet schools, where instructions lasts
for six years, also admit pupils of eleven years of age, but
pupils must also attend secondary schools for general
education. Dramatic schools admit pupils who have completed lower secondary schools and are at least seventeen
years of age; they train pupils who, owing to insufficient
general education, lack the necessary conditions for admission to the academies for dramatic art. Dramatic
schools have two sections: (1) for acting (four years)
and (2) for theatrical technical personnel (two years).
Schools for applied art train cadres for artistic crafts,
for teachers of drawing for the secondary schools for
general education and lower technical schools; they also
provide the necessary pretraining for "high artistic education" in the academies for applied and plastic art.
Pupils who have completed elementary eight-year school,

lower secondary school, lower technical school, or school for apprentices, may enroll here (for five years) in various sections (decorative painting, applied graphic art, decorative sculpture, scenography, decorative architecture, ceramics, etc.).

The state has given every support to these art schools, granting help to special scholars, lodging them in boarding schools and hostels, as is customary in the USSR.

The art academies have the rank of university faculties (music academies, academies for plastic arts, for applied arts, and academies for dramatic art) ; instruction in these institutions (all having their sections) lasts four years. There are at least eleven academies, with 1,500 students (of which three are academies for plastic arts, two academies for applied arts, three music academies, and three academies for dramatic art) in Yugoslavia.

Teacher Education

Teacher-training schools (normal schools) train primary-school teachers, the students who have completed their lower secondary education. Pupils must attend four primary classes, four lower secondary classes, and five classes at the teacher-training school; a primary school, where trainees gain practical experience, is annexed to each school. The course has been extended from four to five years in Serbia, Croatia, Slovenia, and Montenegro. Generally speaking, the following subjects are studied: the principles and history of education, psychology, methods and practical work, philosophy, mother tongue, a foreign language, geography, history, natural history, hygiene, civics and ethnics, mathematics, physics, chemistry, handicrafts, music, calligraphy, physical training, preparation for military service. (In Serbia, courses in educational science, history and geography, had been started in the fifth class.) The minorities have their teacher-training schools, where their mother tongue is the language used.

Lower secondary-school teachers are trained in higher teacher-training institutions, where the trainees study a group of two or three subjects (since in many villages the schools have a very small attendance and the teacher has to teach several subjects). Teachers for the higher classes of secondary schools and teacher-training schools, and teachers of general subjects in secondary vocational schools are trained in the faculties of letters or those of natural sciences and mathematics.

Status of Teachers

The criteria for the salaries are length of service, qualifications, and professional performance. Members of the profession are classified in the twenty categories of the salary scale for civil servants. Primary schoolteachers range from grades XV to VIII, secondary schoolteachers and university "demonstrators" from XIV to VI, assistant university lecturers from VI to IV, university lecturers from IV to III, and full professors from II to I. Promotion from one category to another is automatic at the end of three years, except in the case of primary teachers' promotion to category VII; in these two cases, the approval of the Personnel Commission of the Republic's Council for Education, Science, and Culture is needed. Male members of the teaching profession can retire after thirty-five years of service, women after thirty years of service, from the age of fifty upward.

The war reduced the number of teachers in the whole country drastically, and there was a serious shortage of this personnel after World War II. Immediately after the war, there was on an average one schoolteacher to over sixty pupils, while in Bosnia-Herzegovina the teachers had to handle even from 150 to 200 pupils. A corresponding situation existed in other schools—especially secondary schools, technical schools, and university faculties. To ease this difficult situation, new teachers' vocational schools were established, as well as several pedagogical schools, faculties of philosophy, natural science, and mathematics. (In some republics, the schooling period in teachers' vocational and other schools was temporarily shortened to three years, while courses for the training of teaching staffs were simultaneously formed.)

School Welfare Services

A considerable social contribution has been provided by school meals, which are provided by the parents' associations (together with the Red Cross, the Mothers' Union, etc.) in towns and industrial centers; in rural districts such contributions are organized by the schools with the help of the parents and the grants of public institutions. While school meals are available to all school children, certain categories are entitled to priority. Secondary vocation schools and teacher-training colleges also offer boarding facilities. While the parents pay for the boarding expenses, the public authorities meet the initial costs and the salaries of the staff. (Every university town has students' centers and canteens, each under independent management.)

School health is promoted by school clinics and special sections of the outpatients' departments of hospitals and ambulances (which are specifically assigned to general public). Health institutes are organized in each republic. Special courses are given for doctors practicing in school outpatients' department. All children are given a medical examination at the beginning and end of each school year. Medical treatment is free. University students are especially favored; the University of Belgrade has a special clinic, with ten ambulances and three sanatoria.

Physical Training and Sports

Special attention has been given to physical training for the people in general and for school children in particular. In all secondary schools, two hours of physical training per week are compulsory. But, thanks to the shortage of teachers, it has been found necessary to set aside one afternoon each week for sports, compulsory for all pupils. In order to raise the professional standards for teachers in this field, a series of courses has been introduced for physical training instructors, and higher teacher-training schools have been provided with physical training sections. Unfortunately, this shortage of teachers, both primary and secondary, still persists as recently as 1962 or 1963.

Adult Education

Work for the eradication of illiteracy had already been started during World War II; after the formation of Tito's republic, the work was systematized. Anti-illiteracy courses were introduced in villages and towns, as well as in industrial enterprises, the army—in short, wherever possible. While in 1931 the number of illiterates was over 4,400,000 (45.2 percent over ten years of age), between then and 1952, over 2,300,000 persons had learned to read and write (of whom over 600,000 were in the Serbian republic). The workers flowing from the countryside into the newly built industries presented a specific problem. Special courses were worked out for them; beginners' educational courses have been formed for illiterate workers, and after they learned to read and write, they were taught the rudiments of mathematics, history, and geography (in courses lasting from three to six months). In addition, schools for the general education of workers and employees have also been founded (with the rank of lower secondary schools), lasting two years. Workers completing a school for general education are entitled to continue their studies either in lower secondary technical schools (if they have not exceeded their age limit), or in workers' technical schools (from which they may go onto higher schools of learning or universities).

The Workers' University is another institution introduced by the Marxists to enable the workers to gain and extend their general and technical knowledge. It organizes lectures covering the most varied fields of human endeavor: mathematics, technical and economic sciences, foreign languages, and others. In 1953, there were fifteen workers' Universities attended by 115,000 workers. The courses organize public discussions, especially on questions which pertain to the workers' management and the organization of work.

The regime has also developed special courses for women, one-year courses in housekeeping and agricultural work, usually conducted in the district centers or bigger towns and villages; they are open to young girls and women from seventeen to thirty years of age. Another type is the four-month course, usually held during a winter period, attended by women over eighteen. In addition, there is a one-month course adapted to specific regional conditions.

Communists feel that a significant role has been played in the need to raise the general educational level by People's Universities, which are founded in villages and towns, in settlements and municipalities. (In 1953, there were 838 such universities offering 17,000 lectures, performances, and discussions, attended by 2,064,000 persons.)

Next to the radio facilities, libraries and reading rooms have been favored by the regime. In addition to the regular school libraries, reading rooms are usually attached to the "Homes of Culture" in most settlements.

Universities and Faculties

Higher education in Yugoslavia is classified as that offered in the universities, higher professional schools (some of which rank as universities and others as faculties, advanced schools, and academies of art). All these institutions are providing theoretical instruction as well as training students for scientific research. "Their aim is to turn out highly qualified specialists for all branches of science and art."

The institutions admit pupils who have completed secondary school and have taken their matriculation examination—as well as pupils who have completed secondary technical school. (At certain faculties, such as the faculties of philosophy, law, and economy, "external studies," in addition to regular studies, may also be carried on by those students who are employed and cannot attend lectures.) Studies at all the faculties are free. Regular studies last four years (with the exception of the veterinary and engineering faculties, where they last five years, and the medical faculty where they extend to six years).

Higher education has been developing in each republic; today Yugoslavia has five universities with thirty-four faculties, four higher professional schools ranking as universities (with eighteen faculties), and five higher professional schools (ranking as faculties).

Belgrade has a university with faculties of letters, natural science and mathematics, law, economics, agriculture, forestry, and veterinary medicine; a higher technical school (the result of a separation of the faculty of technology from the university), which has the following faculties: architecture, building, mechanics, electrotechnics, technology, mining and geology; a high school of medicine (formed by the faculties of medicine and pharmacy, separated from the university, together with the recently founded faculty of stomatology) ; and a national institute for physical education. The university of Zagreb has the faculties of: letters, natural science and mathematics, economics, agronomy and forestry, veterinary medicine, technology, medicine and pharmacy. Ljubljana has the faculties of: letters, law, and economics, a higher technical school (with faculties of architecture, building, mechanics, electrotechnics, chemistry, metallurgy and mining) ; a high school of medicine (formed as a result of the separation of the faculty of medicine from the university itself and composed of the faculty of medicine and the recently founded faculty of stomatology) ; a faculty of agronomy and forestry. Skoplje's university was only founded after the Liberation; it has faculties of letters, agronomy and forestry, medicine, technology, economics, and law. Sarajevo, also founded after Communism came, has the faculties of letters, law, agronomy and forestry, medicine, veterinary medicine, and technology.

The various types of advanced schools are primarily concerned with professional training; they offer two to three courses of study (although they do not rank as faculties) ; the graduates can go on to the corresponding faculties, and the equivalence of a certain number of examinations and half-year terms is recognized. There are advanced schools: teacher-training schools, the Naval College of Rijeka, the Advanced School of the Ministry of Home Affairs, and the Higher School of Journalism (Zagreb).

The normal course in faculties (attached to a university) is four years (except in the faculties of veterinary medicine or technology—five years). Faculties of advanced technical schools offer a five-year course (nine half-terms taken up by lectures and practical work, and a tenth-year term reserved for the preparation of a thesis for a diploma). Studies at the faculty of medicine last six years, at the faculty of stomatology five years, and at the faculty of pharmacy four years. The National Institute of Physical Education provides a four-year course. (The various faculties and advanced schools have institutions annexed to them—institutes, laboratories, workshops, clinics, estates, and agricultural research establishments, training centers, etc.)

University and advanced schools register students who have obtained their secondary school-leaving certificate and have passed the entrance examination, and the students who have obtained their diploma at a secondary vocational school and have followed a two-year course of practical vocational training; for these students the entrance examination is compulsory. In certain faculties and advanced schools (letters, law, and economics) there are (in addition to the ordinary students) a number of "extraordinary students" who are not obliged to attend lectures but may take all the examinations. Otherwise, all students must attend lectures for the requisite number of terms, pass examinations, do all the compulsory practical work, and then receive diplomas. Students at the faculties of engineering, forestry, and agriculture have to submit a thesis at the end of their studies and receive the academic degree of engineer, and at the medical faculty the degree of "Doctor." The students of the other faculties are given no special academic title but after graduating receive the calling of their respective profession: "economist," "veterinarian," "jurist," and so on. In order to promote scientific work, the scientific degree of Doctor of Science is granted after spending at least two years after graduation in study and research work of a definite scientific branch, and writing a dissertation which must be an original contribution to science. This, too, is in line with Russian practice.

Education on this level is free of charge. The state provides financial assistance along these lines: it allows grants to students under twenty-four whose parents are employees; bursaries to those whose studies were interrupted by the war and to orphans without resources; subventions to various funds for students' welfare.

The colleges and universities in Yugoslavia have been growing by leaps and bounds. Between 1945 and 1955, a total of 31,720 students graduated (6,959 in 1953 alone); of this number 2,243 were women. The trend in specialization can be seen from the following table:[61]

Faculty of Agriculture and Forestry	3,094
Veterinary Faculty	914
Engineering Faculty	5,040
Faculty of Economy	2,874
Faculty of Law	2,874
Medical Faculty	4,274
Faculty of Stomatology	29
Pharmaceutical Faculty	1,138

Educational Problems

Considering the heterogeneous educational heritage of Tito's Yugoslavia, and the terrible destruction suffered by the country during World War II, the regime has scored some remarkable successes in its educational reconstruction. More specifically, when the work was begun on the enlargement of the system of schools in 1945, there still remained the problem of the generations which had passed the age for regular education and which had had no opportunity to acquire it under the royal regime, or which had missed their education because of the war. Many varieties of courses and short-term classes were immediately organized, especially the courses for illiterates; courses of general education which in a short-term period taught the subject matter of primary schools; and preparatory courses for various middle schools and vocational training courses giving special knowledge and qualifications for various professions and activities.

[61] Kicovic, op. cit., p. 28. The table covers the period 1945-53. See also "Yugoslavia's Higher Institutions of Learning" by Joseph S. Roucek, Journal of Higher Education (Columbus, Ohio), XXV, No. 9 (December, 1954), 478-81.

These short courses were later shaped into permanent schools—such as schools for workers, where the students received education equal to that of the lower stage of secondary schools; others became eight-year compulsory schools, and workers' technical schools which are of some utility as middle vocational schools.

The problem of the teaching staff was—and still is—serious. Many teachers were killed during the war, while others joined the Partisans and Chetniks or went into other occupations. Shortened school terms and various short training courses for teachers contributed considerably to the solution; today most teachers in Yugoslavia are going through regular training.

Adult education, on all levels, is another aspect of the revolutionary changes in Yugoslavia. "Everywhere and at every moment—in their daily work, at classes, lectures, discussions, in school and out of school, through books and through newspapers—workers in the People's Federated Republic of Yugoslavia are acquiring the knowledge for which they have always thirsted and of which they have for centuries been intentionally deprived," reports an enthusiastic Yugoslav team of educators.[62] Special attention has been paid to women's education, and with good results. "In country districts, where women were most backward . . . these successes have been most striking. In fact, women's education is an integral part of the work of every political and social organization."[63] This, of course, is the Marxist viewpoint.

In comparison with the royalist regime, Tito's program of educational planning has refused to allow teachers, and especially professors, to live in ivory towers. All studies are designed mainly to link educational process with national economic and social changes. The relationship between the universities and other educational institutions has been altered. Formerly, the gymnasium monopolized university preparation; today, various sec-

---

[62] Mitra Mitrovich and Vida Tomsich, "Women and Education in Yugoslavia," 183-256, in *UNESCO, WOMEN AND EDUCATION* (Paris: UNESCO, 1953), pp. 185-86.

[63] *Ibid.*, p. 220.

ondary, vocational, commercial, and technical schools
send their graduates to related faculties.

Efforts at Autonomy and Decentralization

The regime's spokesmen make much of the recent
changes made in the relationship between the central
government and the universities. The former system
vested the ultimate responsibility in the Ministry of Education. Since 1954, autonomous privileges were again
regained. Each university is formally administered by
three separate but interlocking agencies: the University
Council, the University Administration, and the Rector.[64]
The Council is elected by the State National Assembly
from specialist groups outside the university; it also
includes the Rector, plus one member of each constituent
faculty elected by each Faculty Administration from its
members, plus one member from the ranks of its educational councilors by the People's Committee of the city
where the university is located, and plus a delegate from
the student body. The Council formulates the statute of
the university, gives its opinion on the statutes of the faculties, and submits them to the Republican People's Assembly; confirms the election of university staff; formulates the estimate of revenues and expenditures; regu-
lates disciplinary responsibility of students; etc. The
Administration is composed of the Rector and the Vice-
Rector (elected every two years by the University Assembly), and the Deans of each constituent faculty, and
discharges the functions considered to be purely university business. Each faculty is administered by a Faculty
Council, Faculty Administration, and a Dean. The
Council is composed of a fixed number of outside specialists named by the Republican People's Assembly, a fixed
number of faculty members named by the Faculty Administration, one student elected by the student body,
and the faculty Dean and Assistant Dean.

---

[64] A copy of the "General Law on Universities" (June 30, 1954)
can be secured from the Yugoslav Information Services, 816 Fifth
Avenue, New York City. A good survey is Charles P. McVicker,
Titoism (New York: St. Martin's Press, 1957), pp. 196-201.

This complicated system is a clever device to have the regime's spokesmen claim that their universities are running their own affairs. Yet these institutions are controlled by Marxism, since Tito's hierarchy decides on the appointments to the Council, while the Administration, composed of teaching staff members and their collaborators, represents the autonomy of the faculties.

The decision to apply a similar system of decentralization to lower educational efforts has resulted, however, in considerable confusion and disunity throughout the country. Formally, the system is headed by the Council for Science and Culture of the central government; it sets up educational plans and curricula and coordinates the work of the Council for Science and Culture in the republics. According to official claims, this provides for decentralization and public control, since the system is tied up with commissions for education and culture attached to the popular committees at several levels—regional, district, and urban. In application, it has happened that various educational concepts have been applied differently by local organs. The confusion led to the creation of the Federal Bureau for the Study of Educational and School Problems (February, 1955), assigned the task of coordinating the entire educational system. In practice, however, it has simply replaced the old Federal Council of Science and Culture abolished in 1953. Another step in "decentralization" was taken in March, 1955, with the passing of the "Law on Social Management of Schools," which created a system of school management modeled on the "General Law on Universities"; each school now has a School Council of representatives from the local People's Committee, important local citizens appointed by the Committee, and, in the secondary and higher schools, a representative of the student body. Each institution has also a Teachers' Council elected by the teaching staff. While the School Council handles the problems involving the social community, the Teachers' Council is involved in scholastic matters.

The educational system of Tito is obviously in a state of flux, and this has been shown by the appointment of a federal commission at the beginning of 1956, whose task is to examine the whole problem of reform of the elementary and secondary schools and formulate uniform standards and requirements for elementary and secondary education throughout Yugoslavia. It is also concerned with the rigidity of school organization, the outmoded methods of teaching, and the remoteness of the syllabus and curriculum from everyday life. It also appears that the teaching of modern languages needs improvement, and teacher training is inadequate.[65]

The rapid development of Yugoslavia's educational system has intensified the problems associated everywhere with overcrowding and the lack of facilities. There are still numerous villages with only the four-year primary schools. Although considerable progress in vocational training has been achieved through industrial schools formed after World War II (and before then such schools did not exist in Yugoslavia; only very backward schools for apprentices), there is simply not enough of them or of teachers. In general, Yugoslavia's educational deficiencies are more than obvious in insufficiently elaborated curricula and programs; too much concern with details in subject matter; some obsolete methods of elaborating sciences; shortage of textbooks, equipment, and modern means of instruction and—partly as a result of all this—unnecessary and much useless verbalism.

Yet it is true that the change between the prewar and postwar situation is marked in regard to the opportunities for adults and for less formal education. An increasing number of villages have built a *Dom Kultura* (House of Culture), where all forms of adult education are offered by means of lectures, films, discussions, and classes. The chief instrument in this respect has been the People's University, which functions in most small towns and even in larger villages; the offerings are concerned with the propagation of general cultural and scientific knowledge in these cultural centers. But the expenses involved are one of the handicaps, since the lecturers are seldom paid (and their expenses have to be

---

[65] See Ludvik Gabrovsek, "School Reform in Yugoslavia— UNESCO's Contribution," Institute of International Education, *News Bulletin*, XXXI, 2 (November, 1955), pp. 9-49.

covered, usually by charging a very small entrance fee or from grants from one or other of the mass organizations). It is true that the Central People's University circulates outlines or provides complete lectures for the republics. But these "lectures" are purely political in character, since the aim is to link "enlightenment" directly with political change. When politics is left out, and entertainment is linked with educational advance—music, acting, dancing, visits and performances by outstanding artists—then adult education is quite popular.

There is also too much faith by the Marxist regime that all problems can be solved by political education; this over-rapid expansion in education has also shown sacrifices in quality to quantity. In the present incessant clash between new and old, Yugoslavia's educational pioneers are endeavoring to create a new kind of school "that will turn to account progressive experiments already made; this is a difficult task because it means both training staff and surmounting all kinds of obstacles to educate social youth in a country that is still underdeveloped despite its gigantic efforts."[66]

The difficult situation created by overexpansion is also complicated by the resistance of many teachers to Communism. Not all prewar teachers are Communistically minded. But many of them have had to be kept on the payrolls in order to keep the school system functioning. Even special ideological courses have not always made them "good Communists."

Party Control

In Yugoslavia, schools, along with youth organizations, are the main instruments for shaping new generations for the Socialist order that the regime is trying to produce.[67] The Communist party not only runs its own

[66] Mitra Mitrovich and Vida Tomsich, "Women and Education in Yugoslavia," pp. 183-256, in *UNESCO, WOMEN AND EDUCATION* (Paris: UNESCO, 1953), 233.

[67] For a bitter attack on the educational system, see Dragnich, *op. cit.*, chap. 15, "Schools in a Strait Jacket," pp. 138-57; less critical and also less penetrating survey is: Charles P. McVicker, *Titoism* (New York: St. Martin's Press, 1957), pp. 190-201.

schools but also exerts its influence on all levels of education as well as all the media of mass communications. But it is hard to discover the relationship between the control machinery by the Communist party and the educational system. Although most leading educators, and especially the administrators, are Communists, Dr. Roucek in his lengthy talks with them, was unable to discover one who would acknowledge that the Party was the dynamo of educational planning. The general tone of the answers to the pertinent questions was that the Communist party (formally, the Union of Communists of Yugoslavia) is one thing and the educational process something else, both being, somehow separate spheres of Yugoslav life. Yet one of the largest buildings in Belgrade is the headquarters of the Party—with the most expensive automobiles parked around it—which, according to "unofficial" reports, is the heart and the brains of Yugoslavia.

In reality, the Party is the most important piece of machinery of the regime; it penetrates the depths of the population and enters the home at any and all times. It has the right of access everywhere and busies itself with everything. All organizations on all levels are completely controlled by Communist leadership, that is, by Tito and his hierarchy.[68] Yet the considerable literature on Yugoslavia pays little attention to the state of affairs within the Party (CPY) of Yugoslavia and its ability to survive under the attacks of Stalinism and internal troubles. But, under Khrushchev, there is less external friction.

The present hierachy still has in its ranks several founders of the present Party. The prewar organization was composed mostly of young intellectuals (rather than of skilled workers), which alone of all the sections of the Third International organized Partisan detachments

---

[68] For details, see McVicker, *op. cit.*, *passim*, and especially chap. XII, "The Role of the Party and of the Popular Front Organization," pp. 266-95; Fred W. Neal, "The Communist Party of Yugoslavia," *American Political Science Review*, LI, 1 (March, 1957), pp. 88-114; Joseph Frankel, "Federalism in Yugoslavia," *American Political Science Review*, XLIX, 2 (June, 1955), pp. 416-30; Ivan Avakumovic, "The Communist Party of Yugoslavia," *Occidente* (Milan), XII, 3 (1956), pp. 197-213.

in the summer of 1941; the loss of three-quarters of these militants was the price paid for their devotion to the "cause." When the Communists came to power, thousands of new members joined for altruistic motives. It produced a new type of Communist, as Tito himself pointed out (1952) : "I am sorry that the type of Communist we have today is not the same as before the war . . . Today a Communist is no longer a militant who has to carry a heavier burden and be an example to others."

These new members, of whom almost half a million have joined since the end of the war, are now showing an increasing aversion to the party organization and its teaching. "Most of them have long ago abandoned the pretense of being militants, fighters for some lofty ideal. They belong to the party, not to fight for Tito's brand of socialism but to get a better job, an extra room, more firewood and similar privileges."[69]

The leadership has tried to remedy the situation by the familiar Communist tactics: a party purge coupled with a campaign to raise the ideological enthusiasm of its members. The purge led to the expulsion of 180,844 members (half of whom were peasants) between 1950 and the end of 1954. By then the party membership had declined from 779,382 in June, 1952, to 654,392; officials, white-collar workers, and the group described as "others" provided almost half of the members. (The percentage of workers within the Party remained stationary—29.5 percent in 1948 and 28.3 percent in 1954—in spite of determined efforts to increase the proletarian element and the industrialization which has increased the number of workers to over a million.)

The Tito-Cominform dispute was basically a conflict over who should hold power in Belgrade. The ideological justification which Tito and his colleagues constructed for their struggle came much later; it proved to be "a rather dreary exegesis of Marxism and Leninism," interspersed with attacks on Stalin's house and foreign policy.[70] Its chief exponent was Milovan Djilas (now one of

---

[69] Avakumovic, *op. cit.*, p. 209.

[70] A. B. Ulam, *Titoism and the Cominform* (Cambridge, Mass.: Harvard University Press, 1952), p. 138.

the bitterest critics of Communism).[71] The leadership was aware, however, that purges and a refurbished ideology were not sufficient in themselves. Hence Tito's group has allowed several reforms which, in fact, have induced many Westerners to believe—mistakenly—that Yugoslavia has started to develop into a sort of Western democracy on a Socialist base. But what actually has happened is that the government has cleverly allowed decentralization in government, has given greater autonomy to the People's Committees, "nearly" handed over a large part of industry and commerce to the Workers' Councils, has decentralized economic planning, and has allowed several features of the competitive market; the Table of Organization of the government rests on a parliamentary system in which committees possess great powers of debate; and of monumental importance is the abandonment of forced collectivization of agriculture (a necessary step in a country still largely agricultural despite intensive efforts at industrialization)—a resounding reversal of Communist doctrine. But, at the same time, the Communists have also retained their power. For instance, in the early postwar years, Tito was secretary-general of the Party, Prime Minister, and Commander in Chief of the armed forces; today he holds not only these three vital posts (becoming, instead of Prime Minister, President of the Republic) but has assumed three more (the Presidency of the Socialist Alliance of the Working People, as the People's Front has been renamed, and the Chairmanship of the Federal Executive Council and of the National Defense Committee). He is the only leader in a Communist country who, after Stalin's death, could say, *"L'Etat, c'est moi!"*

The elections in November, 1953, saw again a single government list with Communists and fellow-travelers returned unopposed and gaining the familiar 95 percent of votes. Yet, Djilas, who received 99.8 percent of votes in his constituency, was deprived of his post two weeks after he had been unanimously elected President of the National Assembly. Tito's supremacy was threatened!

---

[61] Milovan Djilas, *The New Class* (New York: Frederick A. Praeger, 1957), pp. 1-14.

Roughly speaking, Yugoslavia is not a totalitarian police state, but it is still a one-party state; it has democratic features, but all these features are under the thumb of the Party. Above all, there are no available means in Yugoslavia to displace the present leaders and have them renounce having their final say in all key decisions, in spite of the reforms and the decentralization efforts. The only way that these leaders can be challenged publicly is through the political party hierarchy and then only at the instigation of the top Communists. Real authority rests not in the decentralized government but in the centralized Party.

This has been illustrated by the case of Milovan Djilas, who had been considered a potential successor to Tito, and had been elected to Parliament by an announced majority of 99.8 percent in his constituency in Montenegro. But Djilas ran afoul of party doctrine in a series of ill-received articles he published to the accompaniment of great and sycophantic praise in the Yugoslav press; he also embittered his most intimate colleagues in the Party with an ill-mannered commentary on the social life of the leading Communists in his party. But it was only after Djilas had been condemned and expelled by the Central Committee that any word of criticism of him was uttered in the Marxist organs. Only after action by the party leadership—not the rank and file—was Djilas dismissed from Parliament. Furthermore, what later happened to him also illustrates Yugoslav practice. A year after Djilas' dismissal, he granted an interview to Jack Raymond[72] of the *New York Times*, in which he criticized the lack of democracy in Yugoslavia; another leading Communist, Vladimir Dedijer, was at this time being called to account for having defended Djilas a year earlier. The two men were swiftly tried as hostile propagandists and charged with participating in an attempt to undermine the government. Both were given suspended sentences and released. Djilas, unable to obtain employment, lived in Belgrade. In 1956 he was arrested for an article of his published in *New Leader* (New York) which

---

[72] Jack Raymond, "Tito: Different, But Still Communist," (*New York Times Magazine*, December 18, 1955).

he had smuggled out and in which he hailed the Hungarian Revolution as the "beginning of the end of Communism." He is now serving a three-year hard-labor sentence in the Mitrovica prison. The thesis of Djilas was expanded in Djilas' *The New Class,* also smuggled out of Yugoslavia, as publication is prohibited in Yugoslavia.

It is also true that there is only occasional censorship on the reporting out of the country, but the reporters not favoring the "new class" are subject to insults and official displeasures. Furthermore, pressure is used by having police call on private citizens associating with such reporters, and the continued harassment of alleged "bouregois" remnants is carried on. "Students are said to report on each other, so that after graduation allegedly dissident young men and women find it hard to get jobs. In the villages, away from the big cities, there are reports of outright brutality by hoodlums who have not been infected by the atmosphere of freedom and relaxation," reports Jack Raymond. Those who complain too much against the government are still appearing in jail.

Today a gulf separates the upper ranks of Yugoslavia's "new ruling class" from the mass of the people. The Yugoslav Communists want to create a Marxist society based on Socialist ownership, economic planning, and materialist thought; but the majority of the Yugoslav people prefer private ownership (and above all, the peasant, the core of Yugoslavia's whole structure!), free enterprise, and freedom of thought. Hence the Party granted some concessions which give the illusion of "self-government." The leaders propound, ideologically, that this is only a transitional period (which will not last too long) and hence the people should, "voluntarily," support the government program. But, as Djilas points out, the very process further and indefinitely postpones the day when democracy can be permitted.

Tito's group, having been expelled from the Cominform, has changed its mind about the efficacy of certain Marxist methods, and it has even adopted ideas learned in contacts with the Western democracies. Hence Yugoslav Communists have remained Communists—except that they have adopted the doctrine to Yugoslavia's peculiar character and conditions.

The Yugoslav Communist party, then, still acts according to the Stalinist concept of the Party as a "gendarme
for the government." In the field of public opinion, its
primary task is to prod, to indoctrinate, to check, to supervise, to lay down the directives for action. Like capil-
lary veins carrying a living organism's blood, the Party
diffuses its thinking everywhere, and spreads it among
the masses, into every home and every heart, the "correct"
thinking of the rulers throughout the whole of Yugoslavia. "Study sessions," meetings for "self-criticism,"
"conferences," patiently the ant heap spreads its orders
disguised as advice, and "whispers" to the multitude of
ants what it wants them to know.

As far as the educational system is concerned, all educational work is controlled—indirectly and directly—and
when necessary directly by the government, the same way
as all means of communications. The techniques are
rather complicated, but most interesting.

Party Schooling

Following the example set by the USSR, the Yugoslav
Communist party maintains its own Party schools, training the young party elite for positions of responsibility.
Secret police functionaries and members of the Yugoslav foreign service have to attend these institutions also.

These schools are organized into several levels:[73] Evening schools run courses of varied length, but the aim is
to have the same standards as the elementary schools;
they are under the direct supervision of the Central Committees of the Federated Republics and under direct
guidance of the district and local committees. The same
applies to the Elementary Party schools, which offer
training of six months. The Secondary Correspondence
Schools try to follow the standards of the secondary
schools, and are directed by the Central Committees,
which also supervise the Party High Schools, offering
one-year courses. The Party High School in Belgrade
offers a two-year course at the headquarters of the

---

[73] Summarized from *Komunist* (Belgrade), a monthly of the
Central Committee of the Yugoslav Communist party, No. 4-5,
1950, in *News From Behind the Iron Curtain*, April, 1951, pp. 32-33.

Central Committee and has the character of an educational institution on a secondary level. The standard subjects offered in and by all these institutions are: historic dialectics; basic principles of Marxism-Leninism; history of the Russian Communist party and the Communist party of Yugoslavia (the former now being called a History of the International Workers' Movement); the educational program of the Communist party—theoretical and practical; and the economic life of Yugoslavia. After American aid was granted to Yugoslavia, the adult education courses of the Party included in their discussions such topics as The Hoover Dam, Transportation in the United States, and "Canada, A New Capitalist Power."

The Youth Movement

In addition to the official organs dominating the educational system, Communist party control is centralized in the People's Youth Movement, with which are affiliated the Pioneers and the Yugoslav Students' Union. The aim is "to imbue the young socialist citizen with a love of his motherland and respect for other nations, and aims at training him to develop an abundant social life and at making him strong and healthy physically and spiritually."

Historically, the start of youth organizations was provided by the rejuvenation of the prewar underground youth organization. The spokesmen of the People's Youth trace the history of the movement to the Communist Youth League which arose in 1937 under the leadership of Ivo Lola Ribar.[74] The movement had then only a few members, chiefly town students. The outbreak of World War II, the claim is, doubled the strength of the movement; soon armed battalions were formed by the members. The various Communist and "anti-Fascist" groups held the first Congress of the Anti-Fascist Youth at Bihac on December 26, 1942, which formed the United League of Anti-Fascist Youth of Yugoslavia (USAOJ), a union of militant brotherhood and unity of Serbia, Croatia,

---

[74] "Sketches for a Youth History," 22ff. in *Youth Life*, VII (1953), and "First Congress of USAOJ," *Ibid.*, V (March, 1952), 26ff.

Slovenia, Montenegro, Macedonia, Bosnia and Herzegovina." The Constituent Assembly, at its 1945 meeting, decorated the USAOJ with the Order of National Liberation; it had a million members then, who once helped to gather the harvest in the abandoned fields of Yugoslavia, cut fuel wood for the Belgraders, and helped to construct the 90-kilometer railway from Brcko to Banovici, "which 62,000 young people built in seven months." Following the Cominform break, the organization merged with the League of Communist Youth. Today, it has some one and a half million members, with branches in children's organizations, the Union of Students, as well as other cultural, recreational, scientific, and technical organizations. It is primarily a political organization, which "resolutely combats everything obsolescent and fights for new social relationships." It aims to "educate all those most humane and noble traits which should be innate in the citizens of a socialist society."

The lowest organizational unit is the *aktiv*, with five to five hundred members (but most of them have fifteen to thirty-five members), in schools, government enterprises, factories, or peasant communities. Above them, hierarchically, rank the youth committees, covering towns, counties, and regions; then come committees for each of the republics; the top is headed by the People's Youth, governed by the Central Committee. A National Congress, held once every four years, chooses the Central Committee.

The members do not limit their activities to the work of their organization, but are assigned to exert their influence in all educational and social organizations (cultural clubs, sports associations, and other groups). The *Youth Life* is the official organ, but other periodicals are sponsored by the branches and subsidiary organizations. The directives are published in the weekly *Omladina* ("Youth"). Associations of students at Yugoslav universities, component parts of the People's Youth, have their own weeklies—*Studentski List* (Zagreb), *Narodni Student* (Belgrade), a monthly, *Za Otodjbinu ("For the Fatherland")* is edited by the Yugoslav Army for university students as part of their obligatory premilitary training. The *Narodna Omladina* is another monthly devoted to ideological questions.

Furthermore, the People's Youth sponsors lectures, speeches, film showings, and study seminars. Social life is promoted by means of outings, comradely suppers, dances. But quite an important task is to recruit young people for "voluntary projects," especially during the spring, summer, and early autumn months.

Between the end of the war and 1952, hundreds of thousands of young men and women were, in fact, persuaded to leave farms and schools to serve an average of one month each in brigades that built highways, railroads, and numerous other public projects. Then the system was halted by Tito, who felt that the country's economy was strong enough to do without this kind of labor; it was not always economical labor, but ideology more than economy was involved in the decision in 1956 to resume the system. The government houses and feeds members of the work brigades, but they draw no wages. The important thing for the Party, in addition to hardly any cost for labor, is that brigades afford a chance to mix the children of the peasant and intellectual families. Thus a ready-made audience is created for the lectures and ideological entertainment that go with the brigade worker's life.

All Communist youth associations are linked with other youth organizations, including such religious societies as *Kriazri, Drustvo Srca Isusov, Marijina Kongregaci ja,* and form the United Alliance of Anti-Fascist Youth (USAO). After the expulsion of the People's Youth from the Cominform, and from the World Federation of Democratic Youth as well as the International Union of Students, the Yugoslavs established contacts with the Union of Students (independent in relation to the People's Youth in its relations with foreign students' organizations) and with the Socialist youth of England, Belgium, Norway, and the International Union of Socialist Youth.

Premilitary Training

From one point of view, the Yugoslav Army is one huge, integrated educational machine which processes all young men of the country not only for military but also for Communist purposes. Premilitary drill had already been introduced in 1948; it gives young men some elements of military knowledge before they are recruited, and fits them for defending the country in case of emergency after a short term of training. The drill embraces all men from seventeen to twenty years of age—up to the age of recruitment. There are four thousand rural instruction centers divided according to drill years into platoons and parties in the charge of reserve officers and NCOs. The rallies, and camping especially, in which about 400,000 men take part, twice a year, are chiefly promoted. About 150,000 working youth are enrolled in workers' instruction centers, organized in enterprises, drill being carried on under the direct charge and supervision of the enterprise management, in conjunction with army and government authorities. Model studies and classrooms, weapons and military equipment, instructional appliances and textbooks, uniforms and other equipment insure that the premilitary drill is adequate.

In the secondary schools and universities, premilitary training is a regular school subject for about 170,000 boys and girls. While the boys prepare directly for military service, the girls of the secondary schools and universities are trained for medical, anti-gas, postal, and other services, in order to replace the men who might be needed for the front. The importance of this whole setup is shown by the fact that each year, on Army Day, the Supreme Commander of the Yugoslav Armed Forces, Marshal Tito, confers several thousand "decorations for premilitary drill."

Controlled Communications Media

All mass media of communication are carefully supervised and controlled by the governmental and party machinery. As all educational and cultural activities have one focus—that of promoting the goals of the regime—the press, radio, and the film have been brought under government ownership and control and are always mobilized in the service of Communism. The following survey, provided by UNESCO, only hints about the extended firm grasp of the regime over all public opinion media. In general, the press, all periodicals, and book publishing are controlled directly either through outright ownership by the Party, the government, or other instrumentality; the government operates radio, the theater, and the movie houses directly.

Yugoslavia, whose population of 16,991,000 shows a rate of illiteracy between 25 and 30 percent, supports two daily newspapers in Belgrade, which account for more than half of Yugoslavia's total daily circulation. There are some eighteen dailies in all, with a total circulation of 811,000; three dailies appear in Belgrade, three in Zagreb, and three in Ljubljana. Two foreign-language newspapers, one in Italian and one in Hungarian, are published. There are approximately forty-one copies of dailies per thousand inhabitants; weeklies number 101, the largest having a circulation of some 70,000.[75]

The principal source of domestic and foreign news is the national agency, *Telegrafska Agencija Nova Jugoslavija* (TANJUG), founded in 1943 and independently financed. It has headquarters in Belgrade and twelve branch offices throughout the country; it also maintains three offices abroad and a number of regular foreign correspondents.

The state-owned Yugoslav Radio had seventeen medium-wave transmitters with a combined power of 634 kw. and two short-wave transmitters totaling 110 kw. in 1956; the Radio instituted a Second Program in its Home Service for Serb listeners; it carries entertainment and news, as well as school broadcasts and language lessons. The Second Program is beamed from a low-power transmitter in Belgrade and is on the air during the day; it serves Belgrade and its vicinity, which contains about one-third of the total Serb audience. Commercial advertising is prohibited. Broadcasts for abroad are transmitted daily from Belgrade, in French, English, and other European languages, on powerful medium-wave and short-wave transmitters. The number of licensed re-

---

[75] *UNESCO, World Communications: Press, Radio, Film, Television* (Paris: UNESCO, 1956), pp. 225-26.

ceivers is 418,000, and there are numerous loudspeakers in mining centers, factories, and schools.

In 1953, Yugoslav studios produced 11 feature films (including 2 co-productions), 66 documentaries, and 52 newsreels. Some 14 educational films were also made; the 6 local production companies were to complete 13 features, 60 newsreels, and 110 shorts and documentaries in 1955. Of the 89 imported films, 30 percent came from the U.S. There were 1,313 cinemas, including a number of itinerant 35-mm. cinemas and non-commercial 16-mm. cinemas. Total seating capacity is 392,000. Annual attendance was 59 million in 1952, compared with 70 million in 1950 and 1951. Each federal republic has its own distributing agency for all films; these agencies made requests to Jugoslavija Film for the importation of foreign products. Some 79 mobile units operate and are widely used to exhibit documentary and educational films in outlying areas.

The development of television in Yugoslavia is only in the realm of technological possibilities. The basic plan for Yugoslavia's future TV network was laid down by the Commission on TV at the Education Committee of the Federal Executive Council. Under the Stockholm Convention, Yugoslavia adopted the Central European TV system, providing for 625 lines and 7EO9/C channel width; construction of the network is to rely on an integrated domestic program with centers in Belgrade, Zagreb, Ljubljana, and eventually in Skoplje, Titograd, and Sarajevo. (The realization of these plans is to take, the official report states, from seven to ten years.)[76]

The first station to be built is in Beograd (Belgrade), with a transmitter on nearby Avala Hill; on Fruska Gora Mountain, some fifty kilometers from Beograd, a complete TV relay station of lesser capacity will be erected. Operating with these two transmitters, the station is to cover an area with over 3,000,000 inhabitants (the whole Voivodina area, North Serbia with Beograd, and Eastern Slavonia). Zagreb's station is to transmit to about 800,000 people; the Ljubljana station is to reach some

---

[76] "Television for Yugoslavia," *Yugoslav Review*, VII, 4-5 (April-May, 1957), p. 22.

300,000 inhabitants. The subsequent stages of construction would be erection of TV stations in Sarajevo, Skoplje, and Titograd, and, ultimately, relay transmitters in the towns of Subotica, Nis, Kragujevac, Osijek, Rijeka, Maribor, Banja Luka, and Mostar.

The Yugoslavs are planning to produce their own TV sets, and arrangements were made for this production by Radio Manufacturing Establishment of Zagreb, "Telecommunications" of Ljubljana, "Nikola Tesla" of Beograd, "Rudi Cajevac" of Banja Luka, and other local enterprises in cooperation with foreign firms. The Radio and X-ray Apparatus Factory at Nis is also to join this manufacturing pool. TV sets are to be priced about 120,000 *dinars* and to be bought on the installment system. An initial appropriation of one million dollars has been made for purchasing of foreign-made equipment. In Zagreb and Ljubljana, TV programs are already operating and facilities are provided to watch foreign programs as relayed via Graz in Austria.

Strains and Stresses

While the Communist party has been able to handle the lower levels of the educational machinery rather efficiently, its control of higher educational levels has encountered considerable difficulty. The problem had become so serious by 1956 that the admitted estrangement between the Party and the country's youth was discussed at considerable length at a conference of the Party's Central Committee. In opening the conference, Tito said: "We somehow have let our youth slip out of our hands. We allowed it to develop by itself and it ceased to be a political organization, a political sector in social life." It was admitted that political apathy is widespread among youth. While an "overwhelming majority" accepted the country's Communist development, youth was accused of giving the regime no active support.

Basically, the difficulties have been due to an intriguing battle of ideas, the prim and austere ideas of the more strait-laced members of the Party, who feel that Yugoslav youth is "going to the dogs" and lagging in its devotion to Socialism, and the disillusionment of the youth with the vague promises of the system and their liking for the popular forms of amusement and entertainment which are continually filtering in from the West.[77]

The disillusionment has been coupled with a flood of students overcrowding Yugoslavia's higher institutions and creating the same problem as had the "just too many" intelligentsia before World War I (and again before World War II).

Especially troublesome have been the "extraordinary" students, who are employed by civil service, and who started to study before or during World War II, interrupted their education to join the Partisans, and were unable to graduate. The government tried to find a chance for them to continue their studies after the war by granting them a special status in the universities, but many of them have used dilatory tactics when confronted with the necessity of giving up their privileges when their studies are completed.[78]

An even more difficult problem has been that of placing university graduates in provinces and small localities. An important step was taken by the Economic Council of Serbia on October 15, 1952, when it decided to suspend its power to force university graduates to take assignments in the provinces, where special skills were required in industries, local government, and social welfare. (Doctors and veterinarians were still subject to the Manpower Act, known as the "Regulation of Civil Mobilization" in Yugoslavia.) The Council alleged that manpower under the economic decentralization program, which had suffered from a shortage of qualified personnel, would be increased by this step. From then on, jobs for skilled personnel were to be awarded on the basis of public competition.

In reality, this step represented a defeat for the Serbian as well as the federal government at the hands of thou-

---

[77] Joseph S. Roucek, "Tito's Educational Experiences and Experiments," *The Educational Forum*, XXI, 2 (January, 1957), 193-291; Roucek, "A Visit to Titoland," *Contemporary Review*, 1093 (January, 1957), pp. 15-19.

[78] Joseph S. Roucek, "Yugoslavia's Higher Institutions of Learning," *Journal of Higher Education*, XXV, 9 (December, 1954), pp. 478-81.

sands of educated spivs who roam the streets and infest the coffeehouses of all the major cities. The struggle between the authorities and the educated idlers has actually been going on since the end of World War II. The authorities took the positive stand that students who had been educated at the expense of the people had a debt to repay with the skills they had acquired in public institutions. The slackers took the attitude that only "peasants" and fools work in the provinces, and that young people who receive university training should not be made to suffer the hardships of rural life. They further claim that their university education entitles them to comfortable, well-paid jobs in the big cities. They have outmaneuvered the authorities by becoming perennial students, never quite terminating their formal studies, never taking the final examination for a degree, but insisting on the necessity of specialized study. They frequently find easy government jobs in city institutions through the influence of Communist party officials. If necessary, they take positions as clerks which require none of the skills they have spent years to master.

This floating population of permanent students in the cities had become such a problem by the end of 1951 that drastic steps were taken by the governments of the republics, harassed by a lack of skilled personnel in their territories. For example, the government of Serbia issued a regulation forbidding Serbian institutions to give employment in Belgrade to students from the other republics who had taken their degrees, so as to force such students to return home. But this regulation did not help much, and the perpetual student remains in Belgrade.

The authorities hope that the economic forces now operating in Yugoslavia will defeat the educated "proletariat." The loss of state subsidies and the compulsion to operate state enterprises on traditional principles of profit and loss has forced factory managers and their workers' councils to reduce their payrolls, which had been overloaded with white-collar employees—thus promoting, in turn, unemployment in larger cities.

The resistance of the students to the authorities has been expressed by several strikes, something unique to behold in any country ruled according to Marxist principles. Remembering the traditions of persistent opposition to the monarchical government, even today there are students, in spite of the strictest Titoist control, who promote riots and strikes. There were two demonstrations of students at Zagreb University in 1951 (first, against one of the professors) ; another demonstration took place in 1954 in Belgrade University dormitories when it was announced that there would be increases for fees for student mess halls, lodgings, and transport facilities. The resulting riot had to be put down by the militia.[79]

The scene of the clash was in the students' dormitories building area, outside Belgrade, known as New Belgrade; this is a large site on which efforts to build a huge civic center with administration buildings, a hotel, and railway station had been interrupted. The students live here in some of the uncompleted structures.

The disclosure of such fighting between students and civil authorities, common enough before the war, is said to be unusual under the present regime yet no note of the riots appeared in the regular Yugoslav press. In confirming the essential facts of the demonstration, the government spokesmen said that the press did not report it because it had no special significance. The trouble was caused, according to the official version, by the restiveness of the students over their poor financial situation, the incorrect manner in which the increased fees had been announced, and the invasion of the school grounds by the police.

In January, 1955, Belgrade University students demonstrated again against a rise in the price of their rooms and board in the Belgrade suburb of Zemun, and police had to be called out again.[80] Again, no news of the incident was published, and police refused to give information. But to the foreign observers in Belgrade the demonstration served as an indication that the Communists had not been able to establish a complete hold over university students, who were not afraid to react against

---

[79] Jack Raymond, "Belgrade Bares Student Rioting," *New York Times*, November 16, 1954.

[80] "Curbs Vex Belgrade Students," *Christian Science Monitor*, January 11, 1955.

an unpopular decree. Government supporters could argue that this showed a degree of freedom in student life, while critics could argue that it was evidence of the government's lack of support among youth. But a report from the correspondent of the *Christian Science Monitor* claimed that out of the university's 44,666 students, only about five thousand were members of the Communist party—and "party officials consider many of them to be inactive and apathetic."

An example of the inactivity of some student party members was afforded by a recent conference of party members in the mathematics faculty. Out of 427 party members in the faculty, 117 did not attend. Speakers at the meeting criticized students for religious and pro-western sentiments. Two girl chemistry students before taking an examination even went to a church to pray, they said, while others had gone to the examination wearing crosses around their necks, thinking that they would make a good impression on the examiner.

There have been troubles on all educational levels. The regime has produced a generation of "reconditioned" primary and secondary schoolteachers, but the press has been complaining that many of them are "undesirable." Many of them are, furthermore, "competent politically" but not professionally. This weakness was expressed by Tito speaking at the Party's Sixth Congress: "There are among them [teachers] men who are total strangers to our reality, and who harm society more than they help it." (When discussing universities, Tito reported: "But I must, unfortunately, state that in the universities the situation in this respect—textbooks and teachers—is still worse," since the older generation of professors has been "disinclined to write textbooks which would conform to the true science—the science of Marxism-Leninism.") [81]

In fact, the students on all educational levels show their independent attitude toward the Communist authorities. Many fail to report for government-sponsored "voluntary" projects, political conferences, and propaganda demonstrations; many imitate American mannerisms (as seen in the few selected American movies shown in Yugo-

[81] *Borba*, November 4, 1952, quote by Alexander N. Dragnich, *Tito's Promised Land* (New Brunswick, N.J.: Rutgers University Press, 1954), p. 141.

slavia) ; there are even "zoot-suiters," the jazz enthusiasts and "jitter-buggers."[82] And, interestingly enough, reports Salisbury, from Belgrade, in the *New York Times,* that "In Yugoslavia, Mickey Mouse Waves the Red Flag. So do Donald Duck, Felix the Cat and Maggie and Jiggs. Yugoslavia seems to be the only place where comics and Communism have joined forces. . . . Before the war Yugoslavs were great comic fans. Donald Duck and Mickey Mouse had long been features of *Politika,* then the biggest Belgrade newspaper. With the coming of the Communist regime, *Politika* survived as an organ supporting the Government, but the comics were banished. . . . After the break with Moscow, Yugoslav communism made a good many pragmatic decisions. One that was arrived at gingerly concerned comic strips. First, Donald Duck was permitted to quack once more. (He is Paul Duck in the Serbian version.) But the team of Paul Duck and Mickey Mouse proceeded to pull *Politika's* circulation powerfully ahead of *Borba's.* Not long ago the Marxist directors of *Borba* made a serious decision. They agreed to start publishing Felix the Cat and Ripley's 'Believe It or Not,' the specters of Marx, Engels and Stalin notwithstanding. *Borba's* circulation has begun to creep forward for the first time. Once the ice was broken, comics blossomed all over Yugoslavia. . . . There is no strip treatment of the life of Karl Marx or a translation of *Das Kapital* into ideograms. At least not yet."

Since Tito's 1948 break with Stalin, his Communist rule has been considerably less strict and much more tolerant of outside ideas and contacts. But this has led to frequent difficulties. For instance, the weekly jazz performances of the U.S. Information Services in Yugoslavia often led to near-riots because of the demands of enthusiastic Yugoslavian teen-agers for admission tickets, which are limited because of the lack of space. Or, when the first American jazz ensemble (led by Dizzie Gillespie) visited

---

[82] Dragnich, *op. cit.,* pp. 326-28; "Communists in Yugoslavia Take Down the Barriers, and Comic Characters Romp Back," *New York Times,* August 24, 1957; Joseph S. Roucek, "Tito's Educational Experiences and Experiments," *The Educational Forum,* XXI, 2 (January, 1957), pp. 193-201; Harrison E. Salisbury, "U. S. Comics (Zowie!) Captivate Yugoslav Newspaper Readers," *New York Times,* August 24, 1957.

Yugoslavia in 1956, soldiers had to stand guard in Belgrade at the doors to prevent wildly enthusiastic crowds from storming the theater; at the same time, the regime's spokesmen were stumping the country and blasting at "exaggerated, uncultured music, shallow literature, oversensationalized movies" and other Western importations, which supposedly are corrupting the nation's youth. Educated Yugoslav youth today is understandably enough largely apolitical; its sympathies are with the West because it appears to them to spell out opportunities of freedom and taste denied them under Communism.[83]

In March, 1956, the Party's Central Committee decided on an intensive ideological campaign to end the admitted estrangement between the Party and the country's youth. TANJUG, official news agency, issued a summary of a report by Peter Stambolic, a member of the Executive Committee of the Politburo to the conference on the youth problem.[84] He described a political and disinterested attitude of "some" young persons toward current social events. The implication of Stambolic's report was that the "some" represented a minority of the youth. But Yugoslav Communists concede privately that political apathy is widespread among the youth; they maintain that an "overwhelming majority" have accepted the country's Socialist development, but, having accepted this, youth gives it no active support.

Apparently, Yugoslavia's leaders are not so much worried about the immediate future, as they are of the period of ten years ahead when the youth of today will move into responsible managerial, professional, civil service, and government positions. (A recent poll of 212 young factory workers in Montenegro indicated what was confronting the Party; one base question was "Who was Marx?"! 65 percent of those questioned said they had never heard of him.)

Stambolic laid down three lines of action. Most important is to overcome the "conservatism" of many Communists against bringing young persons into positions

---

[83] See Roucek, *op. cit.*, p. 196.

[84] Sydney Gruson, "Red Leaders Woo Yugoslav Youth," *New York Times*, March 15, 1956.

of leadership in the Party and self-government organizations. The Party must also work harder in existing social organizations, and future school instruction must be more closely connected with social and political development and with the development of a Socialist society. Stambolic summarized what had happened as follows:

> Misunderstanding the real meaning of democracy and personal freedom, some young persons, particularly among the intellectual youth, gave vent to unruliness, imitation of outragious foreign models, coarse and swaggering conduct and even anarchic inclinations.
> There is a petty-bourgeois trivial spirit that exercises its influences on inexperienced and unenlightened young men with bad books, inferior printed material, worthless films and foreign customs and manners in behavior and entertainment of young people.

Religion and the State

The Yugoslav regime guarantees, on paper, full freedom of conscience; all churches are equal but have to conform to the Constitution and the laws of the republic. Religious instruction can be given only in churches or buildings belonging to religious denominations. From the very beginning of the Communist rule, however, the Yugoslav Communists have shown their dislike for religion, as all good Communists abhor it; in addition, Tito's hierarchy feels that religious differences have enlarged the Serb-Croat problem. Catholicism was the official religion of the wartime Croatian Kingdom, and "the Ustasha massacres of Croatian Serbs were as often as not carried out in the name of Catholicism."[85] Furthermore, the Serbian Orthodox Church was given, unofficially, a privileged position by the Monarchy, and the favor granted to it by the Karageorgevich dynasty was resented by the Catholic Croats.

---

[85] Charles P. McVicker, *Titoism* (New York: St. Martin's Press, 1957), p. 48. See also Alexander N. Dragnich, *Tito's Promised Land* (New Brunswick, N.J.: Rutgers University Press, 1954), chap. 16, "The War on Religion," pp. 146-57; "The Technique of the Godless," *Newsweek*, November 15, 1954, pp. 104-8; George N. Shuster, *Religion Behind the Iron Curtain* (New York: The Macmillan Company, 1954), p. 4, "In Tito's Land," pp. 98-129; Edvard Kardelj, "The Policy of the Vatican Against Yugoslavia," *Yugoslav Review* (New York), III (January, 1953), 9.

In prewar Yugoslavia, churches had their income from grants from the state treasury and from church-owned property. The regime replaced these by state support and by confiscating almost all church-owned property. The rest is closely supervised by the state. Priests' residences and monastery buildings were often confiscated for state purposes. Some priests, accused of wartime collaboration with the enemy (symbolized by Archibishop Stepinac— named Cardinal in 1952), were purged and imprisoned; others have been mistreated (as Archbishop Arsenije of Montenegro).[86]

Genetically, Tito's government brought Archbishop Stepinac to trial, before promulating the constitution of the Federal People's Republic of Yugoslavia (on January 31, 1946). There "private property and private incentive in economic matters are guaranteed," and "citizens are guaranteed freedom of the press, of speech, of association, of meeting, of public assembly and manifestations"; the Constitution also provided that all matrimonial disputes fall within the jurisdiction of the civil courts. At any rate, these were just mere words as far as religion was concerned, and the trial of Archbishop Stepinac caught world-wide attention, and little was said about the other persecutions. (For instance, who has heard of the trial of Bishop Gregor Rozman of Ljubljana, Slovenia, sentenced to prison *in absentia* on charges of collaboration with the Italians?) Everything possible was done to handicap the limited amount of religious instruction, by terrorizing the priests or the parents sending their children to religious schools. Catholic schools were simply taken over by the government. The new textbooks described Christ as a myth and the Church as an outmoded institution defying the onward march of science. Old Catholic boarding schools were used for the training of a party elite. Youth organizations were used to handicap anything connected with religion, while censorship stopped religious publications and Catholic charities evaporated.

While the Catholic Church suffered materially and

---

[86] For a very fair account of the case of Archbishop Stepinac, see Shuster, *op. cit.*, 107ff.

otherwise, somewhat better treatment was granted to the Orthodox Church thanks to the resistance of Patriarch Gabriel fully to subordinate the Church to the policy of Belgrade.

On June 28, 1948, Stalin and Tito came to a parting of the ways. Tito's need to secure Western help also induced him to tone down his anti-religious campaign. This led to the agreements reached by the Moslem, Protestant, and Jewish religious groups and the government; the Orthodox Church joined this procession soon thereafter. But the census of 1953 was a shock to Tito's group, since it showed that about 85 percent of the population described themselves as belonging to some kind of religion.[87] A strong campaign was inaugurated in 1951 to get priests to join the government-sponsored association formed for the purpose of weakening the influence of the Catholic and Orthodox churches. These priests' associations are of the same type as those formed by artists, physicans, and the like, and offer social security for members; they were immediately banned by the Vatican. An official claim was made in 1954 by the regime that these associations had enrolled about 90 percent of the officials and clergy of both the Orthodox and Moslem communities.[88] But only 60 percent of Slovenia's Catholic clergy joined these organizations (1952), while only 10 percent of Croatia's priests "went the Tito way" (1954).

The "Law on the Legal Status of Religious Communities" was passed in May, 1953. Again it used the standard Communist formula, guaranteeing freedom of conscience and confession to every citizen and prohibiting the reorganization of religious communities as political organizations. Equal status was legally guaranteed to all religions in Yugoslavia.

Today, the authorities tolerate religious practices as long as they keep out of what the Communists define as "politics." A visit to any church clearly shows that only older people and the very young tend to make up the

---

[87] Most of the Orthodox (47 percent) are found among the Serbs, Macedonians, and Montenegrins, while the Roman Catholics (36 percent) are concentrated primarily in Croatia and Slovenia, and the Mohammedans (11 percent) live largely in Bosnia-Herzegovina.

[88] McVicker, *op. cit.*, p. 50.

congregation. These ordinary churchgoers are usually under Communist pressure and surveillance. Communist party members are prohibited from going to church. Official youth groups usually hold meetings on Sundays, at exactly the same time when the children would otherwise go to church. Catholic high schools are not recognized and, to enter a university, a student, after leaving the Catholic high school, must take an examination; thus only a few students from Catholic schools are allowed to enter the university. The state schools are militantly anti-religious at worst and materialistic at best. Teachers going to church are likely to lose their jobs, the Communists claiming that a "man with religious beliefs" cannot possibly be "neutral" as a teacher should. Thus, many Catholics are afraid to marry in the Church or to have their children baptized. Another anti-religious pressure takes the form of not recognizing church holidays (Christmas, Easter), forcing workers, students, and teachers to carry on as usual; none of these is allowed to be away from work or school even on the *Slava* (patron saint) Day, which ranks, in the Serbian Orthodox Church, on a par with Christmas and Easter. The traditional shooting of guns during these holidays is no longer permitted.[89]

The Prospects of National Communism

What will happen at the death of Tito is something one does not even dare to predict. The Yugoslavs speak mostly of Kardelj as Tito's successor; although the chief theoretician of Titoism today, he cannot compare in strength, popularity, or influence with Tito. Yet there is no going back to the Monarchy, as far as the masses feel, in Yugoslavia (and Djilas has read himself out of the Party).

Despite the lack of national unity, New Yugoslavia is much more firmly established than First Yugoslavia. Not only is there a longer tradition of common statehood,

---

[89] For a propaganda report on "religious freedom" of Yugoslavia, see *Religion in Yugoslavia*, "a report on conferences with Roman Catholic, Orthodox, Moslem, Jewish, and Protestant leaders, and investigations through the medium of religious institutions and documents, by Seven American Protestant Clergymen and Editors of Religious Journals who Visited Yugoslavia in the Summer of 1947" (Washington, D.C.: Yugoslav Embassy, 1947).

but there is also the memory of the War of National Liberation in which members of all nationalities fought together against the invader. The history of this war, coupled also with its myths, is now taught to all Yugoslav children, forming a sentiment of unity in the growing generation.

Yet, even education of this type has been unable to eradicate the tribal differences. It is true that the present regime has removed Great-Serbian oppression and allows no tribal antagonism to break into the open. But the conflict between the Serbs and Croats is still smoldering under the surface. The Croats still mumble over state grants to Bosnia, Montenegro, and Macedonia, the poorest sections of the country, and still insist that Serbs hold too many key posts in Croatia. The Slovenes, separated from the other tribes by their language, tended to dominate, as in "good old days," the Ministry of the Interior through Father Korosec; they are also influential through the heir-apparent, Edvard Kardelj.

Another important factor is the group of ex-Partisans, generally individuals in the prime of their life, who occupy the leading positions in the country and maintain strong links among themselves through the Communist party and through the association of veterans and invalids. Another powerful cementing factor is the army, where the Serbs no longer monopolize the highest posts as they did before World War II; but while almost everything has been decentralized (at least in theory), the army is organized as a Yugoslav whole—and the officers' cadres are devoted to Tito.

Economically, Yugoslavia has been in trouble for years, and Tito's regime has been saved by American "capitalism." But Tito's hierarchy has been pragmatic enough about changing its policies to suit the exigencies of the moment, and even letting Communist doctrines go by the board, when necessary, to save the regime. Thus the attempt to collectivize agriculture has been abandoned. The Yugoslav Workers' Councils constitute an important part of Tito's effort to decentralize industry—perhaps his most valuable experiment in practical Socialism. But Yugoslavia's industrial development is critically handicapped by the lack of technicians. While many students

go for medicine, few devote themselves to technical training. This is partly accounted for by a lack of instructors,
and partly by the lack of incentives in industry; an unskilled worker generally earns a minimum of 15,000
dinars a month, but a skilled man is paid at almost 30
percent more than this.[90]

Although the peasant is relatively free today, and is
certainly better off than a few years ago, he remains
suspicious and hostile toward the Communist regime;
but the industrial worker, as a group, stands stanchly
back of Tito. The Yugoslav student sometimes engages
in rioting—following the traditions of previous decades—
but the present generation, more than anything else, tends
toward political indifference, being primarily concerned
with the prospects of earning a living.

Where Titoism will go ideologically is hard to predict.
We must remember that Tito's Communism and his influence on the satellites have played a significant role in
the development of Soviet foreign policy and the general
political setup of world Communism. But it must be recalled also that the first impulse toward Tito's deviation
was caused not by any revisionistic aspirations, but solely by the opposition shown by the Belgrade Communists
to Stalin's intention of degrading Tito to a mere agent of
the Kremlin. The Yugoslav hierarchy, moreover, did not
have to thank the entry of the Red Army into their country for their position, as was the case with the other
satellites, for they had managed to effect a Communist
revolution while waging a war of liberation against the
Nazi occupiers. Thus, Tito had his own apparatus of
authority, which prevented the Soviets from gaining full
military and political control of Yugoslavia (as they had
in Bulgaria, Hungary, Romania, and Poland).

The New Orientation

Before the official break with Stalin, the Yugoslavs had
no intention whatsoever of going their own way. On the
contrary, their policies and their ultimate goal were more

---

[90] "Yugoslavia Revisited: Change and Tradition in the Federal
Republic," *The World Today*, XIII, 5 (May, 1957), pp. 200-207.

radical than those of the other satellites or of the Soviets themselves. Tito's Yugoslavia was the first Communist state to break with the West, and the first People's Democracy to model its economy on the Soviet pattern. In the years 1946 and 1948, decrees were issued nationalizing industry, banking, and other important branches of the economy, while in 1947 the first five-year plan, again on the Soviet pattern, was inaugurated, and agriculture forcibly collectivized at a rapid rate. Indeed, the rate at which the Yugoslav economy was Sovietized was so rapid in this period that even the Kremlin expressed its misgivings at the ambitious Yugoslav industrialization program.

The direct cause of the break between Stalin and Tito was the Yugoslav plan for a Balkan federation of Yugoslavia, Bulgaria, Greece, and Albania, under Yugoslav leadership. Stalin immediately opposed this plan (since it could have led to the formation of a second Communist center in the Balkans, independent of Moscow). After Tito's refusal to beg for forgiveness, he and his followers were accused at a Cominform conference (June 28, 1948) of turning back on the USSR and the People's Democracies, and of being nationalists, not internationalists; Tito and his group were excommunicated, on the grounds of the worse error an orthodox Communist can commit: ideological deviationism and betrayal of Marxism-Leninism-Stalinism.

Tito, at first, defended himself against what he considered monstrous and false accusations and stressed his "unshakable devotion" to the teachings of Marx-Lenin-Stalin. Later he began to correct not only Stalin but also Lenin and Marx—as a result of the grim reality confronting him. He was faced with the alternative of either breaking with this reality and the Russian ideological ballast, or being crushed. Since the Titoists, like all Communists, are doctrinarians, Tito's group had to build an ideological foundation criticizing Stalin. Thus, in March, 1950, Milovan Djilas coined the concept of "Socialist democracy," the Yugoslav answer to Leninist "dictatorship of the proletariat," the intermediary stage between capitalism and Communism. According to Djilas, the state apparatus in the USSR had not weakened, as Marx's theory of the withering away of the state during the dictatorship of the proletariat had laid down, but become stronger. Bureaucratic centralism has become a force outside society. It followed, therefore, that it was not the Yugoslav Communists who were revisionists, but the Soviets, who had departed from the teachings of Marx and set up a state capitalism.[91]

Tito now set out to correct Stalin's errors and to put Marx's theory of the withering away of the state into practice; this started two reforms: the decentralization of state administration, and the transfer of enterprises to the management of workers' collectives. But Djilas went too far to suit Tito and the Party Central Committee decided in July, 1953, to put a halt to inner-party liberalization; thus Yugoslavia's politics are still rigidly controlled from the center.

After the passing of Stalin, Khrushchev's reconciliation with Tito was intended to prove the firmness of the new friendship in the Soviet bloc; the Soviet leaders were striving to restore the solidarity of the Communist bloc, and to increase their authority in the Communist world. But the concessions made to Tito resulted in a loss of Soviet influence in Balkan Europe.

Where is the "independent road" to Socialism likely to lead? The Kremlin recently declared war on all forms of national Communism in view of the warning signals from East Germany, Poland, and Hungary. The equality of the Socialist countries continues to be a myth while "proletarian internationalism," proclaimed now with even more fervor than ever, is in fact designed to establish the USSR's position as the sole model of a Socialist country, a position that Red China challenges!

The conclusions which can be derived from this background indicate that a settlement of these problems might be carried out between Tito's hierarchy and the Kremlin's rulers, with the West looking on—hopefully.

Meanwhile, from behind the prison bars, the deposed Vice-President of Yugoslavia, has defied the Party and branded Communism as a false ideal that corrupts both

---

[91] Stefan Yowev, "National Communism," *Bulletin*, Institute for the Study of the USSR (Munich), IV, 5 (May, 1957), pp. 3-18.

the ruler and the ruled. Milovan Djilas has charged Communism with betrayal of the people, denial of human rights, corruption, demoralization, inefficiency, and endangering peace. Assuming the double role of prosecuting attorney and judge, this former theoretician of Tito's ideology has placed before the world massive evidence to substantiate his charges, and he has pronounced a verdict of "guilty on all counts!" Indeed, Djilas' prediction—that the world will eventually move in the direction of greater unity, progress, and freedom—is a tribute to those intangible realities which the Communist mind shuns. This is a force, avers Djilas, that is more real and thus stronger than any theory or act of brute force.[92]

As to the economic growth and prosperity of the New Yugoslavia, comparative figures testify to its relative success as rated against most other post-World War II governments in Eastern Europe.[93] Indeed, this advance is mentioned as the prime reason for N. S. Khrushchev's about-face in respect to Tito. Both of the writers of *Behind the Iron Curtain* have visited Yugoslavia, the junior member as recently as the spring of 1963. While there is considerable disparity between areas and sections of the country, the south central area especially appears prosperous. Although the comment should not be taken as an endorsement of Titoism, nowhere else visited in East Europe was the political apparatus as inconspicuous as in Yugoslavia.

---

[92] See Djilas, *op. cit.*, pp. 124-46, 191-214; *Conversations With Stalin* (New York: Harcourt, Brace and World, Inc., 1963). Released from his previous incarceration in 1961, Djilas was arrested again on April 7, 1962—putatively as a result of the publication of *Conversations*.

[93] See Vera Tomich, *Education in Yugoslavia and the New Reform* (Washington: U.S. Department of Health, Education and Welfare, 1963) for a later picture of social and educational progress, pp. 97-103.

CHAPTER XII

ALBANIA
THE COMMUNIST WORLD'S
LITTLE-KNOWN SATRAPY

A Balkan Outpost

THE SITUATION IN ALBANIA—the Marxist World's most isolated outpost—has remained obscure in recent years. Yugoslav sources have continued to report growing internal disorders, especially in the mountain areas, and the fact of rigid security measures along the frontiers is well understood by Western observers.

A short historical outline displays the varied fortunes of Albanian history. After the fall of the Roman Empire in the West (476), Albania became part of the Eastern or Byzantine Empire and was successively invaded by the Goths, Serbs, and Bulgarians, who obtained the rule for brief periods; from 1014-1204, Albania again fell under Byzantine authority, which was to give way to the Turkish invasions of the fifteenth century. Albania's misfortune—over the centuries—has been that it lies at the crossroads of the Balkans and Europe, and that it has had to suffer periodic invasion, either from the Middle East (the Turks) or from the nations of Central and East Central Europe (Germans, Hungarians, Austrians, Slavs) and the Italians (or other early peoples from the Italian peninsula).

With few important resources, the Albanians have attempted—for two thousand years—to preserve their cultural heritage, their folkways, their institutions, and their language. Brief periods of independence there have been, but such epochs can be counted in terms of a few decades only.[1]

---

[1] For details, see Joseph S. Roucek, *Balkan Politics* (Stanford, Calif.: Stanford University Press, 1948), chap. V, "Albania," pp. 125-246; also Roucek, "Albania as a Nation," *The Annals*, "A

Albania's modern nationalism has its roots in memories of the historic epic of Scanderbeg (1040-68), a local military genius whose remarkable exploits furnished legends for such romantic poets as Longfellow *(Tales of a Wayside Inn)*. George Castriota *(Turkish: Scanderbeg)* is revered as the foremost of those intrepid Christian warriors of the fifteenth century who checked—at least for the moment—the seemingly forever-victorious march of the Ottoman Turks. Although a literature in the Albanian language existed well before the Turkish invasion, it is only in the latter half of the nineteenth century that Albanian letters with bona fide nationalistic tendencies developed.[2]

Following the Scanderbeg era, Turkish hegemony in the Balkans placed Albania under foreign rule for almost four hundred years. Nevertheless, thanks to the good will of the European great powers (and the course of the First Balkan War), the little country was able to proclaim her independence once more—on November 28, 1912.

Yet, during World War I, Albania was occupied by Italian, Greek, French, Serb, and Austro-Hungarian forces. Somewhat after the general conclusion of peace, Italy recognized Albanian freedom and evacuated her troops. Ahmed Zogu, Premier in 1922-23 and an example of Albania's well-nigh legendary feudal chieftains, ousted the government of Msgr. Fan Noli (afterward Bishop Fan Noli, of Boston) in 1924. A newly constituted republic having been achieved, Zogu became President.

The Zog Regime

By 1928, however, Zogu had concluded pacts with Italy insuring its "protection" of Albania, and forthwith proclaimed himself "King Zog I." In 1938, he married a Hungarian-American countess, much to the delight of certain sections of society and the readers of the tabloids.

Challenge to Peacemakers," Vol. 232 (March, 1944), pp. 107-9, Bibliography, p. 181.

[2] For the role played in this rejuvenation of the spirit by the American-Albanians, see Roucek, "Albanian Americans," in Francis J. Brown and Joseph S. Roucek (eds.), *Our Racial and National Minorities* (New York: Prentice-Hall, 1937), pp. 331-39.

Law and order of a sort were imposed on the country, a civil code modeled upon that of France was instituted, and a penal code, based upon Italian precedent, superseded Ottoman practice.

National consciousness was augmented by the use of a common language in which all school books, newspapers, and literary works were caused to appear—this medium overriding the many local dialects. Another national aim was achieved by the official recognition of the indigenous Christian Albanian Church, which utilized the Albanian language in ceremony and ritual. Agrarian reform laid the foundation for the institution of a class of peasant proprietors whose allegiance was firmly attached to the national authority. In his foreign policy King Zog fondly hinted at Albania's complete freedom of action vis-à-vis Italy, but his desire to show himself no mere puppet of Mussolini turned out to be mere bluster when the Italian took occasion to force his hand.[3]

As a warning against Zog's bombastic conduct, the Italian fleet suddenly appeared in Durazzo harbor (near Tirana, the capital) in 1934. Omitting the customary salute, the Italians caused grave concern for Albanian dominion. Although the usual protestations were made concerning this grave breach of etiquette, the meaning was clear enough—and actually was but a foretaste of things to come.

Indeed, events now moved quickly. On April 8, 1939, Italian troops seized Tirana. Zog with his queen and two-day-old son fled, as Count Ciano, Mussolini's son-in-law, arrived to set up an administrative committee favorable to Italy. Xhafer Ypi, a former Prime Minister, was placed in charge while a speedily convened Assembly asked Shefquet Verlaci, a Zog opponent, to form a new government. The Albanian crown was offered to Victor Emmanuel III in personal union with Italy.

---

[3] For details, see Roucek, *The Politics of the Balkans* (New York: McGraw-Hill, 1939), chap. V, "Albania," pp. 84-98; also William L. Shirer, *The Rise and Fall of the Third Reich* (New York: Simon and Schuster, 1959), p. 469ff.; Walter Consuelo Langsam, *The World Since 1914* (New York: The Macmillan Company, 1943), 369-71; F. Lee Benns, *Europe Since 1914* (New York: F. S. Crofts & Company, 1943), 681-83.

Communist Intervention

Albania's army and diplomatic service were absorbed, and legislation was placed under a local Superior Fascist Corporation—Italy retaining both the initiative and veto. A spirited people like the Albanians were not in the habit of accepting such extreme alterations with contentment, and thus the situation was ready-made for Communist intervention. Within a short space, their legates arrived —Miladin Popovic and Dusan Mugosa from Yugoslavia —and by November 8 an Albanian Communist party was organized. Enver Hoxha was chosen local leader, and he cleverly proclaimed that the Communists had united with Albanian nationalists to form a "National Liberation Front."[4]

Meanwhile, the long-standing dispute between Albania and Greece offered a pretext for an Italian attack; Verlaci's puppet government declared war on the Allies, while the Albanian nationalists stepped up their guerrilla tactics against the invaders; when the Italians were repulsed by the Greeks and driven backward from the Albanian frontier, a three-way civil war took place. The nationalist, Midhat Frasheri, now organized a National Front *(Balli Kombetar)* to combat both Italians and Communists.

But Hitler intervened to protect his axis partner from glaring defeat through his attack on Yugoslavia and Greece in April, 1941; the Greek armies were withdrawn from Albania and the Axis occupation was secured. Yet civil war between the Communists and the Nationalists continued until Hitler's defeat. At this juncture, partly because of the Churchill agreement with Stalin[5] and partly because the United States misguidedly essayed a neutral role, the Nationalists were crushed. On Novem-

---

[4] For an unusually complete description of Communist tactics in Albania at this time and later, see Stavro Skendi, "Albania," chap. 12 in Stephen D. Kertesz, *The Fate of East Central Europe* (Notre Dame, Ind.: University of Notre Dame Press, 1956), pp. 297-318.

[5] Winston S. Churchill, *Triumph and Tragedy* (New York: Houghton Mifflin Company, 1953), pp. 226-28. Although Albania was not included in the Stalin-Churchill division, the effects of this partition affected the entire Balkans.

ber 28, 1944, Hoxha's Communists announced themselves
the "Democratic Government" of Albania.

The usual purges followed, but in order to satisfy the
scruples of the United States an election was staged.
That in the official returns the Democratic Front (Communists) received 93 percent, was nothing more than a
confirmation that another one-party regime had been imposed in the borderlands of Europe.[6] The formality of an
Albanian "People's Democratic Republic" was proclaimed
on January 11, 1946.

Since the original Communist colonization had come
from Yugoslavia, it was only natural that a split should
develop in the Marxist ranks. The pro-Yugoslav group,
under Koci Xoxe, won out temporarily. Hoxha, however,
bided his time and when, in 1948, Yugoslavia defected
from the Kremlin camp, Xoxe was arrested and executed.
For an interim, Hoxha resumed control but Moscow's
chosen instrument, Mehed Shehu, soon arrived on the
scene. As Minister of the Interior and head of the secret
police, Shehu instigated the purging and execution of
Manol Konomi, Minister of Justice. In this affair he was
assisted by the Minister of the USSR to Albania, Dimitri
Chuvakhin, who did not scruple to interfere in—and direct—Albania's sovereign government. Then in July,
1954, Shehu became Premier.

The usual double-barreled propaganda barrage that
emanates from all Communist-controlled countries is not
lacking in Albania. As a sample: "On May 10 [1951] a
verbal note was handed to the Italian Legation in Tirana,
protesting against ten violations of Albanian air space
by Italian aircraft. On May 9 a note was handed to the
Yugoslav Legation, protesting against nine violations of
Albania's frontiers, territorial waters and air space during April. On the same day a note was handed to the
Greek Legation protesting against nineteen violations
of Albania's frontier and air space by Greek armed forces.
. . ." Other areas of complaint dealt with Italy's "considering the revision of Article 29 of the Peace Treaty"

---

[6] Oscar Halecki in *The Limits and Divisions of European History*
(New York: Sheed and Ward, 1950) defines East Central Europe as
the borderlands of Europe; see Skendi, *op. cit.*, pp. 306-7, for a further description of the Communist sweep.

in which Italy had renounced all interest in Albania. All of the aforementioned anti-Albanian activities were alleged by the Communist *Zeri i Popullit* to have been sponsored by the "Anglo-Americans," and Trygve Lie (then Secretary General of United Nations) was identified as a "hireling and warmonger."[7]

Resistance to Communism

Regardless of rigid control, some news from Albania succeeds in filtering out. The Athens radio is reported as suggesting that "although the regime was in control of Tirana, there was trouble in the rural regions." Arrests were said to be frequent, "plots" against the government had been discovered, and the People's Courts in Durazzo and Elbasan had been forced to pass many death sentences. Food was held to be in very short supply; in many regions the population had dared to criticize its quality. The nationalist underground was said to be quite active; many serious clashes had occurred between the Marxists and resistance fighters in the Elbasan and Tirana sectors.[8]

That conditions probably were as described is pointed up by a decree issued by the Minister of the Interior two weeks earlier. This ordered "the surrender of all weapons by April 13"; the implements specifically requested were: machine guns, automatic rifles, revolvers, hand grenades, ammunition, explosives, bayonets, swords and "all close combat weapons."[9] Little imagination is needed to infer the existence of a fairly formidable opposition.

Later reports reveal the zeal with which the Kremlin was engaged in the subjugation of Albania. On February 26, "The Tirana Radio said that a new method of learning Russian suitable for the Albanians had been invented, and that 50,000 copies of a pamphlet on this subject had just been published in Moscow." The same source indicated that "the number of collective farms had grown

---

[7] *East Europe and Soviet Russia* (London), VII, No. 322 (May 24, 1951), 23.
[8] *Ibid.*
[9] *Idem*, VII, No. 322 (March 8, 1951), 31.

from 7 in 1946 to 94 in 1951 and that collectivization would be extended until it had covered the entire country."[10]

Since the inhabitants of Albania are chiefly hill people and because the terrain is unsuitable for collective farming, it hardly seems probable that the Russians can meet their goal in this respect. Indeed, as in Bulgaria, these rugged regions are not conducive to the development of cooperatives. Perhaps the spirit of these people from the non-urban and mountain regions of the Balkans will eventually give Communism its biggest headache. If their nationalism and local spirit are completely crushed, it will be the first time in almost two thousands years of history. (And recent events confirm this judgment.)

Religion, too, has been brought to the aid of the Communist state by a device, which while simple, has grave implications for the remainder of Europe and the Free World. Under usual circumstances, people in the Western world can correctly count on the Christian and Moslem religions to set up bulwarks against atheistic Marxist materialism. In Albania, the churches have become subservient, however, and thus act practically as agencies of the Red regime. On November 26, 1949, legislation was enacted forcing all religious communities "to develop among their members the feeling of loyalty toward 'the people's power' and the People's Republic of Albania."[11] The Communist government has vested itself by law with the power of controlling the selection of church officials. This blow has fallen on the Orthodox Church, the Roman Catholic Church, and the Mohammedan community as well. While the Orthodox group was secured by usurpation of the bishopric plus new ties with the Moscow pa-

---

[10] *Idem*, VIII, No. 370 (March 13, 1952), 23. This report closely parallels a similar item from Bulgaria of just six months previously. "On September 29, Sofia Radio and all newspapers reported the 'solemn opening of the scholastic year for the nation-wide learning of the Russian language.' The communiqué estimated that over 100,000 workers would learn the language and 'more than 5,000 would attend three monthly courses in three grades—beginners, advanced, and Russian speaking grades.' Their aim was to teach 'the tongue of Lenin and Stalin.' " According to Sofia, over 3,200 lecturers were to direct this effort. (*East Europe and Soviet Russia*, VII, No. 351 [October 11, 1951], 22).

[11] Skendi, *op. cit.*, pp. 314-15.

triarchate, it became necessary to pack a "general assembly" of Roman Catholic clergymen, then declare its decision to become a national (Communist) organ. Obviously, there can be no tie between the "Catholic Church of Albania" and the Vatican.

Consequently, any assessment of the part Albania can play in its own liberation must be in part excessively visionary. Coupled with the natural vitality of the people is the dismal fact that the intelligentsia, religious leaders, and natural opponents of Communism have been exiled or executed. The remaining group has strong support abroad but—one may well ask—is this sufficient for the dispossession of the Marxist overlords?

Education in Albania

As noted above, it was only in the latter half of the nineteenth century that modern nationalism as expressed in an indigenous literature appeared.[12] Educationally, Albania was in the worst possible shape even in the period when it was on the way toward becoming an independent nation. Here and there were a few Turkish schools for the education of migratory "writers," who visited the rural villages and, for a fee, transacted business by preparing documents or writing letters for the generally nonliterate Albanians. Southern Albania, however, and especially the region around Elbasan, had numerous Greek schools but they were operated and utilized in the interests of Greek nationalistic agitators. In the larger cities there were Italian schools for the upper classes, but this was not particularly significant in assessing the possibilities for development of the Albanian people themselves.

During the occupation of northern Albania by the Austrian forces, the Vienna government began the founding of schools—especially in Shkodra—utilizing the German language. All of these institutions were on the lowest elementary level; only Elbasan saw attempts to teach beginning Latin. The great majority of them opposed the Albanian national spirit; at the same time, they lacked

---

[12] See Stavro Skendi, "Beginnings of Albanian Nationalistic Trends in Culture and Education, 1878-1912," *Journal of Central European Affairs*, XII, No. 4 (January, 1953), 356-67.

good and well-trained teachers, the usual instruction being given by overloaded priests or half-educated individuals of shady backgrounds. No wonder, then, that most people revolted against schooling, and children in some places had to be forced to attend under the supervision of gendarmes. This was certainly a poor way to create national fervor through the agency of education.

There was even the problem of what constituted the Albanian alphabet. This question was debated as late as 1908, when a Congress of representatives from all parts of Albania was called at Monastir (Bitolje) in December of that year in order to settle upon a common style of letters. Up until this time, writers in the Catholic north had used the Latin alphabet with the addition of some special signs; the southern region had used the Greek letters since they were known to the Orthodox Christians; and the Moslems had used Arabic. This twentieth-century decision to employ the Latin alphabet was represented as a great step toward Albanian national consciousness.[13]

Through the efforts of the Turkish constitutional government, twenty-four night schools with 1,753 pupils and thirty-four day schools with 1,850 students were opened in 1909. A normal school was opened at Elbasan under Tuigj Gurakuqi, a Catholic instructor from Shkodra. Likewise, schools were opened also in Ushkub (Skoplje), Salonica, Monastir, Janina, and Constantinople for the Albanians in their own language.[14]

On the eve of World War I, when Albania became independent (1912), Albanian children who attended Mohammedan schools benefited only to the extent of learning a few verses of the Koran; the Albanian language was tolerated only in the foreign schools, e.g., the Greek and Austro-Hungarian institutions, which by this time permitted the use of the native tongue in the Italian schools in Shkodra, Vlera, and Janina, and in the American school at Kercha.

On April 28, 1912, the numerous Albanian societies in the United States amalgamated into the Pan-Albanian Federation *Vatra* ("The Hearth"), whose activities

---

[13] Skendi, "Beginnings . . ." p. 364.
[14] *Ibid.*, p. 365.

helped considerably to create an independent Albania after the war. Already in 1908 a convention of Albanian Orthodox Christians had determined to leave the Greek Church and to create an Albanian Independent Church; translations of Greek liturgical books into Albanian were made, although little nationalistic progress was achieved due to the antagonism of the Turkish government. In fact, prior to 1912, the only major nationalistic and educational efforts were those originating in the United States.[15]

The independent Albanian government was presented with a staggering problem in the education of its people which, at the same time, was integrated with a variety of other national necessities—especially the lack of an adequate communications system. The inaccessibility of some regions and the distances of most communities from their schools aggravated the general situation. Moreover, the government's efforts to introduce a national system was handicapped by the competition offered by the several institutions of learning supported by international bodies of Italians (who tried strenuously to retain a cultural foothold in the country).[16]

Early Developments

Let us note first the educational system established after World War I, and then we shall deal with the changes introduced in 1933—the later postwar period.

---

[15] Roucek, "Albanian Americans," in Francis J. Brown and Joseph S. Roucek, One America (New York: Prentice-Hall, 1952), pp. 232-39; Roucek, "The Social Character of Albanian Politics," Social Science, X, No. 1 (January, 1935), 71-79; "The Albanian and Yugoslav Immigrants in America," Revue Internationale des Etudes Balkaniques, 1938, III annee, II, No. 6 (1938), pp. 499-519; "Albanian Battle," World Digest, III (August, 1936), 78-80; and "Economic Conditions in Albania," Economic Geography, IX (July, 1933), 256-64.

[16] For a few surveys of Albania's educational efforts between World Wars I and II, see: J. Swire, The New East Year Book, 1931-32, edited by H. T. Montague Bell, (London, 1931), p. 89; A. Mousset, L'Albania devant L'Europe, 1921-1929 (Paris, 1930); Roucek, "Recent Albanian Nationalist Educational Policy," School and Society, XXXVIII (July, 1933), 467-68; Idem, The Albanian Educational Progress, XXXVIII (February 4, 1933), 149-51; Roucek, Balkan Politics (Stanford, Calif.: Stanford University Press, 1948), chap. V, pp. 125-46.

In 1925, there were only a few kindergartens in Albania—around ten. They imitated the methods of Froebel and Montessori; the plans of the government to make them compulsory for children between the ages of four and six were never realized.

Primary education was obligatory for both sexes between the ages of six and thirteen years. But in actual practice, because of inadequate transportation facilities, the authorities did not enforce the law very seriously in some regions. Furthermore, most children of the Mussulman families quit their schools even before they were thirteen years of age, because most of them were married at that age. Often parents kept their children at home, needing them for domestic and agricultural work. But it must be emphasized that the law of June 22, 1928, was one of the very few which excited the least opposition among the vast illiterate masses of Albania.

The teachers in the primary schools were required to be graduates of a gymnasium or normal school. A normal school existed at Elbasan, which admitted students from the sixth or seventh grades of a primary school, and there were the state gymnasium at Shkodra and the technical school at Tirana with normal classes. Most of the instructors were trained abroad. Many young people studied in Italy, where they were offered special privileges. Numerous French teachers were also employed. According to the official statistics of 1928-29, Albania had: 495 state and 39 private primary schools; 12 state and 6 private secondary schools; 20 state and 6 private boarding schools; 22,967 boys in state and 3,703 in private primary schools; and 1,153 pupils in state secondary and 240 in private secondary schools; 94 girls in state secondary and 142 in girls' private secondary schools; 807 teachers in state primary schools and 99 teachers in private primary schools; and 106 teachers in state secondary schools. All expenses of the state schools (with the exception of the support the communes gave toward the maintenance of the schools and school material) were paid by the state, which spent yearly about two and a half million francs.[17]

---

[17] The budget estimates (expenditures) for the Ministry of Edu-

Reorganization

After 1928 the Albanian school system underwent a reorganization in several directions. More attention was given to physical education, an area introduced by an Italian physical culturist. It was planned to make secondary education more practical. Some lycées were abolished in order to provide a place for technical schools.

The teaching of Albanian was obligatory in all state and private schools; this applied especially to southern Albania, where there were located both private and state schools for the Greek minority, their teaching language being Greek.

The French government also aimed at making its influence felt. French instructors were attached to the secondary schools at Tirana, Shkodra, Elbasan, and Korcha. The National Lycée at Korcha was transformed into a technical school; while it had an Albanian administrative director, there was a foreign director of French studies and other French faculty members although the Albanian language was obligatory. Paris recognized its certificate and permitted such holders to enter French universities.

There were many other private schools in pre-Communist Albania. The following may be mentioned: Dr. and Mrs. Kennedy's Primary Missionary School at Korcha supported by Christian friends abroad. Shkodra boasted two gymnasia and a primary school for girls, maintained respectively by the Jesuits, Franciscans, and Stigmatine sisters. Most of these were located at Tirana as was the Naim Frasheri and Vasse Pasha Boarding School, founded by the American Junior Red Cross and subsidized by the state. The Agricultural Secondary School and the Domestic Science School near Kavaya were operated by the Near East Foundation, an organization interested in a broad program of education (including elementary teacher training) and a concern for the needs of backward peoples.

The wave of nationalism which swept Albania in 1933 had a great influence on education. Prior to this time the educational policy of the government had been most tol-

---

cation were (in thousands of *franka-ari*—gold francs) 3,241 in 1928-29, 3,443 in 1929-30, and 3,533 in 1930-31.

erant toward the various Albanian minorities and private educational institutions. But on April 10, 1933, forty-four deputies of the Albanian Parliament proposed an amendment to Articles 206 and 207 of the Constitution; on the following day the motion to completely nationalize Albanian schools was passed. Education of Albanians was made a state prerogative and could be obtained, in the future, in state institutions only.[18]

This measure was specifically directed against such schools as the American Technical School at Tirana, the Italian technical schools, the missionary schools at Korcha, the Albanian Catholic Day Schools in Shkodra, and the Girls' Boarding School at Tirana (which was headed by Miss Kyrias and Mr. and Mrs. Dako—Albanians educated in the United States).

King Zog's government lost no time in enforcing the new law. The American institutions, it is interesting to note, were allowed to continue because they agreed to accept the presence of Albanian supervisors; actually the Technical School was already being supervised. Yet American schools were criticized for their policy—the missionaries excepted—of requiring that Albanian authorities furnish a portion of the expenses and personnel for each school operated. The standard Albanian objection was that the official subventions of the Albanian government could be utilized more effectively by opening or supporting their own schools.

Other privately owned schools suffered more drastically. The authorities closed the Romanian school at Korcha, the Yugoslav schools in the Greek-speaking villages around Argyrocastro—although the Yugoslav institution at Vraka (near Shkodra) and other Greek schools remained open on the assumption that the Albanian government supported them. The Italian Minister at Tirana closed all Italian schools and returned their staffs to Italy. At first the heads of the schools at Berat, Valena, and Shkodra refused to accept Albanian supervision, claiming that authority over them could be exercised only by the Italian Minister; the Albanians retaliated by closing the

---

[18] See *Albanian Educational Progress*, loc. cit.

institution at Berat, whereupon the Italian representative showed his official displeasure.

It is not implied, however, that these measures emanating from Tirana were based on a chauvinistic policy, although it is true that there was much in the Albanian private minority schools to criticize. The chief objection hinged on the fact that most of the funds came from abroad and therefore developed foreign influence; these schools competed with Albanian schools, and the staffs of such establishments were frequently animated by a hostile spirit toward Albania—being at the same time subject only to a foreign and non-Albanian authority.

From the international viewpoint, two main causes for these measures are discernible. The excellent support given to the Catholic schools led the government to become increasingly aware of the spread of Roman Catholic authority in Albania.[19] The Albanian Catholics were, of course, under the spiritual jurisdiction of the Roman pontiff, as elsewhere. Article V of the Albanian Constitution provided that there was to be no official religion. A constitutional provision stated that religious liberty was assured, providing that it did not conflict with the laws of the state and was not employed for political purposes. King Zog and his family belonged to the Suani sect of Islam. Disregarding his religious liberality, he guarded carefully against showing what he thought was too much toleration of Catholic ambitions in Albania. For this reason he appointed Hil Mosi, a bitter anti-clerical, as Minister of Education.

Yet the salient factor centralized around the Italian situation. Italian desires to dominate Albania (and Rome actually was already in the saddle) had always been a main source of anxiety to Zog, who was quite determined now to resist constant Italian encroachments upon his sovereignty. Negotiations over the regulation of Albania's debt to Italy had broken down; the closing of the Italian schools coincided in time with inquiries made by the representatives of the Italian-chartered VEA concerning the payment (strictly speaking, the non-pay-

---

[19] According to the census of 1927, there were 563,729 Moslems, 181,051 Orthodox Christians, and only 88,739 Roman Catholics in Albania.

ment) of the interest on a loan of 50 million gold francs
made to Albania by the company. The King was evidently
attempting to prove to the world (and to the Italians especially) that his country possessed the quality of independence—a myth, as was shown by the subsequent invasion of Albania by Mussolini's forces.[20]

During World War II Albania suffered horribly, first
being overrun by the Fascists, then by the Nazis, with
anti-Fascist and anti-Nazi guerrillas contending with pro-
Soviet Partisans.[21] As has already been suggested, the
Marxists were assisted in their power drive both by Tito
and the Greek EAM (Greek guerrillas opposing the royal
regime). After the break between Moscow and Tito, Albania became the most geographically isolated outpost of
the Communist Empire, facing more and more trouble
with the passing years. The only satellite without a pact
of mutual aid with the USSR, she was brutally exploited
by the Kremlin; for example, some eight thousand
workers, directed by a Soviet military mission and supervised by German engineers, in 1954 fortified Saseno—
a rocky island lying in the bottleneck straits separating
the Adriatic from the Ionian Sea.[22]

Isolation

Today, Albania is virtually insulated from the rest of
the world; at swords' points with her continental neighbors, Greece and Yugoslavia, and with her nearest sea
neighbor, Italy, now indifferent, Albania's position, to say
the least, is indeed unique. Her relations with Western
nations are about as poor as they can be, with only France
maintaining a diplomatic mission in the country. Solely
dependent for supplies on Red China via the Near East
by sea and with little air transport, her situation is precarious. While the 1952 Economic Plan made good its

---

[20] Roucek, "Recent Albanian Nationalist Educational Policy,"
School and Society, XXXVIII (July, 1933), 467-68, and The "Albanian Educational Progress," *Ibid.*, (February 4, 1933), pp. 149-
51; Shirer, *op. cit.*, p. 469.

[21] Roucek, "Trouble and More Trouble in Albania," *World Affairs
Interpreter*, XXV, No. 3 (October, 1954), 315-22; Shirer, *op. cit.*,
pp. 813, 818, 820-21, 825, 1006.

[22] Roucek, "Trouble and More Trouble in Albania," *loc. cit.*

boast about fulfilling the overall schedule by 105.8 percent, in 1953 the Economic Ministry also admitted that cereal yields were low, the collection of agricultural produce considerably below plan, and the high economic hopes hampered by a grave shortage of modern equipment and by a lack of trained technicians and skilled workers. The difficulties regarding collectivization were reported in an earlier section.

Marxist Education

Although a government decree in October, 1949, instituted compulsory schooling for all illiterate men under forty, it is estimated that over half of Albania's population, ten years later, still could not read and write. The usual Marxist polemic heads the call to education, specifically political education: "The duty of our schools is to furnish the new generation with Marxist-Leninist learning. To educate pupils ideo-politically means to endow them with the scientific ideology of Communism. Since education is a phenomenon of social life and as such reflects the ideology of the class in power, pedagogy in the schools cannot be treated separately from the political life of the country and from the problems which preoccupy our party today. . . ."[23]

As elsewhere through the Iron Curtain countries, the task of the teacher is to educate youth to hate "colonialism"—strange though this dictate seems coming from Communist lips. Bedri Spahiu, Albanian Minister of Education, recently proclaimed: "The schools now give all of you a Communist education. . . . That is why you have a great love for your fatherland and the Soviet Union and why you hate the American imperialists . . . your enemies."[24]

And from another source: "The system of teaching in American schools is based on chauvinism and hatred of other peoples. The theory of racial superiority, as in Hitler's Germany, is the main theme in American education

---

[23] Quoted from "From Discipline to Diversion," *News from Behind the Iron Curtain*, II, No. 3 (March, 1953), 48.

[24] *Zeri i Popullit* (Tirana), September 2, 1952.

today.... Copying the methods of Hitler, the reactionary Americans are burning the books of scientists, distinguished writers, and papers and magazines showing a progressive spirit. At the beginning of this year all the books of Howard Fast were removed from all school libraries in New York City. ... In the books which American students study, every reference or page which speaks about successes or ideas in the progressive countries is carefully taken out."[25]

Thus the rationalization for the establishment in Albania (as in each of the ten East European satellite states) of Marxism-Leninism runs. This dogma is hailed as scientific, and is the *sine qua non* of the new intelligentsia and the basis for all cultural activity. On the premise that education, the arts and sciences, and politics are Communist weapons in the struggle for world domination, intellectuals who practice these arts are soldiers of Communism—inspired by the militant philosophy of Marx, Lenin, and Stalin. In line with this general policy, Radio Tirana is found lauding the "Science of Sciences," that is, "Marxist-Leninist Science [which is] concerned with society, the laws on the development of the proletariat and on the building of Socialism and Communism."[26]

Following the Soviet example, the Albanian government first extended itself to promote all forms of adult education among its rebellious subjects. In 1952, twelve daily newspapers and fourteen periodicals were published in the country; about 100,000 copies were issued daily, with the leading organ accounting for around 25,000. The Albanian Telegraph Agency (government-owned and -operated, of course) supplies the satellite's newspapers and radio fare. Albanian Radio is a state system, and operates seven transmitters with a total power of 10.4 kw. Nevertheless, foreign propaganda is considered much more important than even this control of the home educational system by means of radio; short-wave programs are broadcast abroad in ten languages by one

---

[25] *Rini* (Tirana), September 13, 1952.
[26] "Patriotic Re-Education," *News from Behind the Iron Curtain*, I, No. 4 (April, 1952), 32.

transmitter, while locally radio listening is not general, with only one set per twenty-nine inhabitants.[27]

Following the pattern of pro-Soviet societies in the other captive nations, Albania has its "Albanian-Soviet Friendship Society." This was organized, according to Red sources, shortly after the "liberation" of the country. It claims to have more than 160,000 members ("or, in other words, 15 percent of the whole population"). Its journal, formerly titled *Shqiperi—B.R.S.S.* (Albania-USSR), is now a monthly known as *Miquesija* ("Friendship"). We are told that: "In issue after issue the journal familiarizes its readers with the achievements of the outstanding workers of the Soviet Union. . . . The journal regularly publishes notes on Soviet films and articles on the Soviet theatre. A series of articles has also been devoted to the creative work of a number of other representatives of Soviet culture. . . ."[28]

Yet, in an effort to raise the level of the new Albanian culture, several hundred Albanian youths—most of them sons of faithful party members—were in 1954 shipped off to the USSR or the other so-called People's Democracies for higher education. Frequently, high party echelons accompany these educational junkets in order to "freshen up on Communist theory and practice, or to take special training."[29]

A Split with Moscow

But, on the whole there are only a few Albanian intellectuals remaining—for there had not been too many to start with. The gallows, prisons, and forced-labor camps have taken their toll. Those who have until now survived live in perpetual terror; yet pro-Marxist sources frequently wail that even the Communist-sponsored novelists ex-

[27] UNESCO, *World Communications, Press, Radio, Film, Television,* (Paris: UNESCO, 1951), p. 103; "Captive Communications," *News from Behind the Iron Curtain,* I, No. 7 (July, 1952), 36.

[28] *Voks,* "Journal of Albanian-Soviet Friendship," No. 77 (November-December, 1952), pp. 115-17.

[29] Committee on Foreign Relations, *Tensions Within the Soviet Captive Countries,* Part 6, *Albania* (Washington: Government Printing Office, 1954), p. 166.

hibit "a lack of Socialist realism"; another complaint maintains that they fail to show proper reverence and regard for the Soviet Union. And several years ago a reviewer in *Zeri i Popullit* found grievous fault with Albanian writers for failing to note that when Albanian heroes fell in battle, "the name of Stalin was on their lips."[30]

Within the past decade, moreover, a split has been developing between the Soviet Union and her Albanian satellite. Isolated geographically, the Tirana Reds have increasingly sought an orientation other than that of Moscow. This new direction is toward the "purer" Communism of Peking and party leader Enver Hoxha, miffed at Khrushchev's de-Stalinization policy and Nikita's recent willingness toward a new *rapprochement* with Marshal Tito, has engineered a rift in family relations that has all the earmarks of a permanent separation.[31] What the Communist party in Albania's approach to education—if indeed the events just described represent the true state of affairs—will be, has not yet been revealed. Yet, politically, any doubt that still exists regarding the schism appears to evaporate more and more each day as Albania flirts outrageously with Mao Tse-tung and champions Red China at the United Nations and elsewhere.[32]

This independence toward the "Big Brother" in the Kremlin was shown in 1963 when Albania seized the Soviet Embassy buildings in Tirana and accused the Russians of failing to pay their bills.[33] In the United Nations Albania has tried incessantly to secure the admission of Mao's China.

---

[30] K. Trebeshina, *Zeri i Popullit*, January 26, 1952.

[31] See Wolfgang Leonhard, "Moscow's Albanian Headache," *Atlas*, I, No. 3 (May, 1961), 20-23, particularly the translation of Enver Hoxha's speech (from *Zeri i Popullit*, February 14, 1961) to the Albanian party.

[32] See also Harry Hamm, "Albania Under the Police Yoke," *Frankfurter Allgemeine* (Frankfurt), October 7, 1961 (as translated in *Atlas*, II, No. 6 [December, 1961], 461-63); Moscow's reaction as presented in the *Moscow News*, November 4, 1961, in translation and under the heading, "Hell on the Adriatic," appears also in *Atlas*, issue cited, p. 460.

[33] AP, Vienna, February 29, 1964, "Tirana Needles Big Brother."

CHAPTER XIII

MAINLAND CHINA, THE RED STORM OVER ASIA

China, A Short History

THE EARLY HISTORY of the Chinese people,[1] like that of the other countries of fluvial Asia, is masked by obscurity. Claims for a civilization extending as remotely as five thousand years—to 4000 or 3000 B.C. perhaps—have been made, and recent archaeological discoveries appear to place the prehistoric period of China as even earlier. Yet the first dynastic era has been dated as recently as 1994 B.C. (although there is some authority for claiming 2205 B.C. as the earliest chronicled event). Goodrich[2] reports that the people of this genetic epoch, the Hsia, knew agriculture and sericulture, used bronze weapons and chariots, and had developed a system of writing. Their use of the wheel suggests the existence of a culture equivalent perhaps to that of the Mesopotamia of *ca.* 2100 B.C. and one little inferior to that of Mohenjo-Daro in India or of the Cretan sea-kings.

There is no doubt that a true historic period began about 1500 B.C. with the creation of the Shang dynasty (1523-1027 B.C.). Here one finds evidence of a high degree, by any standard, of Chinese civilization. Authority was centralized, common religious rites had been established, a granary system had been devised, and skilled work in metals and ceramics was being accomplished. The antecedent era of city-states had been ended and the peasantry brought under the control of the reigning Shang princes.

---

[1] The educational section of this chapter was contributed by Professor Theodore H. E. Chen, Director, Soviet-Asian Studies Center, University of Southern California.

[2] See L. Carrington Goodrich, *A Short History of the Chinese People* (New York: Harper & Brothers, 1943), pp. 6-8.

The Chou epoch began in 1027 and continued until 256 B.C. It was within this splendid cycle that the great philosophers appeared (Lao-tzu, 604-517 (?) B.C., Confucius, 551-478 B.C., Chuang-tzu, fourth century B.C., and Mencius (371-288? B.C.) Following the Chou, the Ch'in dynasty ruled for a brief period; then, from 202 B.C. until A.D. 220, occurred the rule of the glorious Han. This Han succession touched Rome, both in its chronology and—it is sometimes alleged—commercial and diplomatic relations. Indeed, a revealing parallel exists in the fall of the Han and the interregnum of the Western Roman Empire: a period of political disunion shattered Chinese unity while the barbarian onslaught demoralized those wonderful powers of government possessed by the early Roman Empire.

With Sui (590-618) and T'ang (618-906), imperial China once more asserted herself with further magnificent achievements in the arts and letters. And it was during this fruitful epoch that China's famous civil service examination flourished. China's seventh dynasty, the Sung, now fell to the Mongol invader, who brought an era of Yuan ascendency stretching from 1260-1368. It was, of course, during this great reign that Marco Polo brought Europe again into contact with China, and through his marvelous tales conveyed a renewed knowledge of the East to the West.

However, no foreign invader has ever succeeded in monopolizing the supreme authority of China for long, and a Chinese house, the Ming, succeeded Kublai Khan's empire, ruling until 1644 when another invader from the north, the Manchu, or Ch'ing, gained the peacock throne. Throughout the sequence of conquest and revival, the succession of foreign and native dynasties, Chinese life, while not uninterrupted, moved along more or less peacefully. It has been well said that "China is a great sea that salts every river that enters its confines."

During the Ch'ing, the Western powers sought and obtained trade ports and other concessions in China.[3] The "Boxer" Rebellion took place, ending in further ag-

---

[3] Harold M. Vinacke, *A History of the Far East in Modern Times* (New York: Appleton-Century-Crofts, 1945), chap. II, pp. 29-53.

THE AUTHORS

Dr. Joseph S. Roucek, Professor and Chairman of the Departments of Sociology and Political Science at the University of Bridgeport (Connecticut), is the author, co-author, editor and co-editor of almost one hundred books, and he has written articles and book reviews for leading American and overseas periodicals and journals. He was awarded the Order of Knighthood (with the rank of Commander) and the Star of Romania and a similar title from the pre-Communist government of Yugoslavia. Professor Roucek has lectured in universities in Spain, Italy, Yugoslavia, Austria, Germany, France, and the Netherlands, and is a member of the editorial staff of *Il Politico* (University of Pavia, Italy), *Indian Journal of Social Research* (Baraut, India), and the *Journal of Human Relations*. He is a native of Czechoslovakia.

Dr. Kenneth V. Lottich has taught in several American institutions of higher learning and is the author of many articles, monographs, and book reviews which have appeared in American and overseas social science and education journals. He is co-author of *Foundations of Modern Education* and contributed to *Heritage of American Education*. Among other honors he was granted an Associateship at the Institute of Ethnic Studies, Georgetown University, a Fellowship in the International Institute of Arts and Sciences, and the Award of Merit, Delta Tau Kappa, international social science honor society. Dr. Lottich currently serves as professor, History and Philosophy of Education, Montana State University. In the spring of 1963 he revisited Europe, spending some time in several of the East European satellite states.

grandizement. And it was, of course, the grave dissatisfaction aroused by the policies of the Manchu emperors that stimulated liberal Chinese, especially Dr. Sun Yat-sen, to demand political and economic reform: to initiate the successful Chinese Revolution of 1912. Yet it was one thing to make revolution and to accomplish the overthrow of an old, decaying, and corrupt order; quite another to establish those reforms, including agrarian revision, that the times demanded in its place.

Thus, although a political change had been effected, the newborn Chinese Republic was not entirely prospering. As Goodrich says: "Provincial disunity was strong; vested interests were huge; there were [further] entanglements with foreign powers."[4] Four-fifths of the Chinese people were illiterate and the treasury was virtually empty. Bankruptcy appeared inevitable. His confidence shattered by events seemingly uncontrollable, Dr. Sun died a sorely disappointed leader. More than this, the Chinese Wall had been breached once more at the north as hundreds of Russian "advisers" and "experts" had been summoned to assist in the rejuvenation of the dying state. The unwisdom of this—not apparent at the time—came into full focus under the period of tutelage superintended by the reorganized Kuomintang, Dr. Sun's old Nationalist party under the guidance of Chiang Kai-shek, the husband of one of Sun's daughters.

At first conditions once again seemed rosy and, except for the fact that the Kuomintang exercised a one-party authority over its people not yet considered ready for full democracy, the Nationalist government appeared to be making a qualified progress both internally and in the respect now vouchsafed China by foreign powers.

Japan, unfortunately, could not be numbered among those nations now favorably inclined toward the Chinese renaissance and, in 1931, seized Manchuria. Shanghai, too, was attacked and partly burned. In 1935-37 Japan's conquest of China began in earnest, and Chiang's regime was forced to retire to Chungking, on the upper Yangtze.[5]

---

[4] Goodrich, *op. cit.*, p. 228.

[5] For an eyewitness account, see John Goette, *Japan Fights for Asia* (New York: Harcourt, Brace and Company, 1943), 248pp.

World War II brought increased misery to the Chinese people, their land being subject to the Japanese in northern and coastal areas, to a newly established "agrarian" group led by Mao Tse-tung in the northwest (Yenan Province), and Marxist infiltration throughout. As Mao developed his forces to seize the initiative and became frankly Communistic rather than simply "agrarian," Chiang Kai-shek was driven further and further into a secondary position. By October, 1949, the Communist power was such that Mao Tse-tung was enabled to reorganize the Chinese government as a "People's Republic," and Chiang was pushed off the mainland to the island of Taiwan (Formosa). Here the Nationalists have maintained themselves for a decade and a half, considering their regime as the "true China," with Mao's organization regarded as an interim affair. Periodically Chiang Kai-shek has announced plans to drive the Red regime out of China.[6]

The Communist Approach to Education

China has a long history of absolutist control, broken, nevertheless, with short periods of democracy. Chinese dynastic annals retreat into the era of *ca.* 2000 B.C. But only in the past century has China actually entered the mainstream of world history (in the Western sense, that is)—a forced marriage, as it were. Following World War II, Communist rule under Mao Tse-tung was achieved with resultant shifts of great significance to the rest of the world—Marxist and non-Marxist alike—in the areas of politics, political indoctrination, social order, formal and informal education.

Whatever misapprehension may be current regarding education and its value to the state in Western circles, there is no confusion on this matter in totalitarian minds. The intimate relation between education and the state is clearly recognized in Red China under Mao Tse-tung and his Marxist bureaucracy. Since Communist education is at all times an aspect of politics and economics, any

[6] For a good review of these later as well as earlier events in Chinese history, see "History and Culture," pp. 19-37, the *China Yearbook*, 1961-62 (Tapei: China Publishing Co., 1962).

changes in political and economic goals are reflected in education.

The New Socialist Man

The adoption of a constitution in 1954 signified a shift from the temporary stage of the "New Democracy" to a sustained drive toward Socialism. Just as Socialism became the keynote of the "general line of the state," so Socialist education became the new guiding principle of education not only in the schools and universities, but also in the "remolding" of intellectuals and of business people. Then came the inauguration of the second Five-Year Plan in 1958 and a demand for accelerated production and construction under the slogan of the "Big Leap Forward." There was the Big Leap in industry, the Big Leap in agriculture, and, of course, the Big Leap in education.

To spell out the new tasks of education in the age of Socialism and the Big Leap Forward, the Chinese Communist party convened an important educational conference in 1958. The decisions of this conference were subsequently incorporated in a directive of the Ministry of Education, which laid down three basic principles of education, viz.: (1) education must serve politics; (2) it must promote production; and (3) it must be under the direction of the Communist party in order to insure that it serves the correct ends of a proletarian society.[7]

Ever since the issuance of this directive, all education in Red China has been characterized by these three central emphases. The three "P's"—politics, production, and party—are as important in informal education as in formal schooling, in the literacy classes as in the universities, in the polytechnical schools and scientific institutes as well as in normal schools. Indeed, no education is considered adequate unless it meets these three basic criteria.

---

[7] Professor Chen's comments on the education and political regulation in contemporary mainland China are drawn from papers previously published by him in *The China Quarterly, Current History*, and by the American Association for the Advancement of Science, and are used with their permission.

The Chinese Communists firmly declare that education has no meaning apart from politics. By political education, they mean not only the teaching of patriotism and loyalty to the state, but also the indoctrination of the Marxist-Leninist ideology and specific instruction in the current policies and ongoing programs of the state, in order to produce active supporters for whatever the state or the Communist party proposes to do at any given time. In other words, they aim, through education—and indoctrination—to be able to produce a "new, Socialist man," subservient to the state and dedicated to the permanent revolution.

Education and Politics

Political education is in large part ideological education. Chinese Communists, considering themselves the true interpreters of Marxism-Leninism, have unbounded confidence in their ideology as a "guide to revolutionary action." They hate and shun the "revisionism" currently motivating the Russian sector of the Communist world. They believe that correct ideology produces correct action and that wrong action of any kind can be remedied by ideological indoctrination. When at one time the Five-Year Plan was not advancing according to schedule, Mao ordered that all workers, foremen, and technical personnel be organized for a few weeks of intensive study of Marxist-Leninist ideas.

When graduates of secondary schools were found to be inadequately prepared for higher education, the blame was laid on the inadequate ideological understanding of the teachers, and the remedy proposed was to give the teachers a stronger dose of ideological indoctrination as their summer "refresher course." When doctors, engineers, architects, and other professional personnel did not measure up to Communist standards of work, they were also required to take up further ideological study. More recently when complaint was heard that food in the public mess halls was not popular with the people, the Communists, again guided by their superstitious belief in the efficacy of their ideology, decided that what the cooks needed was a more systematic indoctrination in proletarian ideology!

With such an unbounded faith in ideology, it is no wonder that ideological indoctrination is given a central place in every educational program. Even in literacy classes and the primary schools, reading and writing are considered secondary to the inculcation of the "proletarian viewpoint." Political or ideological education may begin with the study of current events or of government reports or the speeches of prominent Marxist leaders. From the beginning, the concept of the class struggle is emphasized and pupils are taught to analyze the class differentiations in Chinese society and the rest of the world today—especially the United States and Western Europe.

In the secondary and higher schools, more formal studies of Marxism-Leninism are introduced and such subjects as "Dialectical Materialism," "Foundations of Marxism-Leninism," "Socialism and Communism," and so on, are designed to raise ideological education to higher levels of theoretical understanding.

Political education, however, does not stop with classroom study; it is not satisfied with knowledge or verbal understanding alone. It demands that ideological conversion must be tested and proven in what the Communists call "revolutionary action." Important as it is for people to know that all history is the story of the class struggle and that proletarian revolution is a bitter class struggle against the bourgeois and feudal elements, their "class consciousness" must still be considered inadequate until they have plunged themselves into the ongoing struggle and learned to be "valiant warriors" in fighting against all forms of feudalism and "bureaucratic capitalism" at home and abroad.

Consequently, participation in various "mass campaigns" is deemed an essential part of political education. Among such mass campaigns are the land reform, which is essentially a class struggle against the landlords, and the anti-*bourgeoisie* campaigns in the cities. The anti-American campaign is, in a way, an extension of the same kind of conflict beyond the national borders—in other words, class struggle on an international scale. Students and their teachers are required to take part in these campaigns; the more vigorous their participation, the more they are considered and accepted as "activists" or "progressive elements" within the Communist society.

Classes in schools frequently are dismissed to encourage participation in mass campaigns. At any given time, the Communist party may issue to the schools a list of political activities considered to be of value to students in their political education. Such political activities may range from participation in mass demonstrations to shouting slogans in parades; from digging canals or laboring on dam construction to a concerted mass attack on flies and mosquitoes. Or they may consist of aiding the state and Party to ferret out "counterrevolutionary elements" and "anti-Party ideas" in the schools, in their homes, and in society.

This means, of course, frequent interruptions—and a good deal of instability in the formal education program. But the Marxists are proud of the fact that their school is an integral part of social life, and there is no gap between school and society. Furthermore, they maintain that any advance in ideological conversion or in the "political consciousness" of the students must be considered as an educational gain just as important (if not even more so) as progress in academic subjects. For the schools, as well as for the factories, the farms, the government offices, and the various independent professions, the constantly repeated slogan is that "politics must take command."

In other words, the political consideration must take precedence over all other considerations. For this reason, pupils who are judged academically inferior by their teachers have been promoted and awarded honors by virtue of their political qualifications and "revolutionary fervor." On the other hand, academic reliability does not always win recognition in Red China.

One of the major methods of political education is what the Communists term "criticism and self-criticism." It is a method of using group pressure to accomplish political uniformity. It attempts to obtain conformity without the employment of any physical force or direct coercion. In small groups in which the individual comes into contact with his fellows, he is asked to express his views

in regard to various matters, to bring out into the open
his inner thoughts in regard to the Communist party and
the policies of the new state; to criticize the views and
ideological shortcomings of other members of his group,
and to pinpoint his own past and present shortcomings.
The process is repeated day in and day out; any discrep-
ancy between earlier and later statements is immediately taken up for further questioning and clarification.
This is the inquisitional process known as "thought reform" or "ideological remolding," or what writers in the
United States popularly refer to as "brainwashing."
Confessions and vigorous declarations of absolute obedience to the Communist party and the proletarian cause
are expected as indications that ideological remolding
have actually taken place.[8]

Education and Production

The twins, labor and production, have always been
stressed in Communist education, but since 1958 the combination of education with productive labor has been
given a fresh emphasis. (Perhaps this initiated the so-
called Khrushchev Reform, tending toward polytechnicalization in the USSR or, *on the other hand*, it may well
be that Khrushchev was—at that time—influenced by
experience and attitudes from Peking.) Chinese Communists frequently quote Mao's statement that all human
knowledge falls into two categories, viz., knowledge pertaining to the class struggle and knowledge pertaining
to the production struggle. The systematization of the
former has produced the social sciences, and the latter
has given rise to the natural sciences—while philosophy
represents the summation of these two areas of knowledge. Inasmuch as the study of the class struggle comes
under political education, the remaining task of education must, therefore, be the teaching of knowledge and

---

[8] A fictitious account, the basis for a motion picture titled *The
Manchurian Candidate*, shown recently in the mainland United
States—and presumably elsewhere in the Western world—pur-
ports to depict such a remolding of personality, and ideological
set, although perhaps in too extreme an instance. The psychological
foundation for this picture must be considered as sound, although
it is not endorsed otherwise. (Ed.)

skills that have to do with production. Any teaching or learning not directly related to politics or production is to be condemned as "bourgeois" bookishness or an obscurantism designed to mislead the working class and others as to what constitutes their real interests. What is known in the West as liberal education has no place in Communist education.

Just as political education must provide for "revolutionary action" to go with theoretical study, so education for production must provide for actual experience in production along with the acquisition of knowledge. To facilitate the integration of actual production with study, the government has ordered that all schools and universities should establish farms, factories, and numerous other forms of productive enterprises so that students can work in them and contribute directly to the production program of the state. The number and variety of these productive enterprises are truly amazing. There are workshops of various kinds, engineering firms, architectural offices, department stores, machine shops, paper mills, and plants for the manufacture of electrical appliances, medical apparatuses, precision instruments, drugs, chemicals, and many others.

These productive enterprises are not merely laboratories or student workshops. They are regular production units taking and fulfilling orders on a business basis just like regular factories and farms. One group of college students contracted for the construction of a small railway; another built an airplane for commercial use. A large university would have hundreds of various production enterprises carried on by its students. Even elementary schools have their own farms and factories.

From the Communist point of view, this combination of education with productive labor not only has brought about a vast increase in the productive force of the land, but also holds important implications for educational theory. Education is no longer divorced from the practical affairs of life. "Education for its own sake"—the ivory-tower concept of education—has been replaced by education for politics and for production. Theory is held to be useless unless it is directly applicable to practice.

Three major types of schools exist in Red China today: the spare-time school, the part-time school, and the full-time school. Spare-time education is, in essence, adult education. Peasants attend schools in their off season and workers attend after their day's work. Spare-time education, therefore, does not interfere with production activities. There are also spare-time normal schools to engage teachers in study without interruption of their teaching. Spare-time study is continued on the secondary school level, and there are "spare-time colleges and universities" as well as spare-time literacy classes and elementary schools.

While, of course, spare-time education is subordinate to production, part-time education attempts to pay equal attention to production and study. Students divide their time between work and study. There are many different patterns of work-study programs: in some cases, a half day is given to study and a half day to work; in other cases, work and study are scheduled for alternate days or alternate periods of time ranging from days to weeks.

In the full-time schools, the major concern of the student is study. Even here, however, knowledge is supposed to be closely integrated with the actual problems of production and of contemporary politics. The establishment of farms, factories, and other production enterprises is as important for the full-time schools as for the part-time schools. In all cases, work is an integral part of education.

This establishment of production enterprises by educational institutions is only a part of the story. While schools and universities are being turned into "centers of production" as well as "centers of learning," farms and factories and large business enterprises have been ordered to establish schools on ascending levels for peasants, workers, and their families. The most elaborate systems of such schools have been established by the communes, some of which have set up complete programs from the elementary schools through higher institutions. Many of them are spare-time schools, according to the Communist claim, where farms and factories accept responsibility for the establishment of schools. Centers of production have also become centers of learning.

Party Direction

Education in Red China is directly controlled by the Communist party. The Ministry of Education and other government agencies of educational administration carry out the policies set forth by the Communist party. Whenever big plans or changes in education are contemplated, the first announcement usually comes from the propaganda chief of the Party rather than from the Minister of Education or even the Prime Minister. This is an indication not only of the Party's control of education, but also the frank identification of education with propaganda. Explaining the indivisibility of the three cardinal principles of education promulgated in 1958, the party propaganda chief (Lu Ting-yi, by name) said, "Education must serve politics, must be combined with productive labor, and must be led by the Party—these are three interrelated things." (See page 553).

Actually, control by the Party is the key to the entire educational program. The Party, it is maintained, knows best what is good for China and the Chinese people. The Party alone has full knowledge of the political objectives, the economic plans, and the general goals of the proletarian revolution. The Party, therefore, has the responsibility not only of determining the objectives of education but also of supervising the work of the schools, the teachers, and the students to make sure that education serves the best interests of the proletarian revolution.

Every form of education, be it the program of a regular school, or of spare-time education for, say, the crew of a Yangtze steamer, is directly supervised and controlled by a person appointed by the Party and representing the authority of the Party. In every school or university, the real authority is not the principal or the titular head, but the resident party commissioner who represents the "party leadership." His word is law, and any teacher, student, or administrator who happens to incur his displeasure may be accused of "disobeying the leadership," —in Red China, a most serious offense.

The party commissioner controls the appointment and promotion of teachers. He supervises the program of political education; he masterminds the process of thought reform. He reports to the party organization whether teachers are making satisfactory progress in "ideological remolding." In awarding scholarships to students or even recommending them for graduation, his views carry so much weight that they may overrule the decisions of the faculty. He examines the syllabi and lesson plans of teachers. When he discovers that a teacher uses American teaching materials instead of Soviet teaching aids, he promptly exercises the authority of the "leadership" and demands a change; if necessary, a confession of addiction to "bourgeois ideology." Party commissioners have been known to interfere actively even in fields in which they have no competence whatsoever. Nevertheless, they are the symbol of the party leadership which is considered absolutely essential to the conduct of education in China, and they must be obeyed.

The party commissioner directs the life of the whole school. He coordinates the activities of the Communist youth organizations, which play a leading role in school life. He sees to it that the students and teachers alike take part faithfully in the approved "political tasks." Such tasks may be in the form of mass campaigns mentioned earlier in this chapter, or they may even be personal errands for the commissioner.

Much stress is laid on "Communist morality." The essence of Communist morality, it is said, is that the individual must always put the interests of the whole above the interests of the part; the interests of the group above those of the individual; and the interests of the proletarian revolution as the supreme loyalty that supersedes all else. It demands that the individual must at all times be ready to sacrifice his personal advantages for the good of the revolution or "the people." Since the Communist party is the standard-bearer of the proletarian revolution and the symbol of "the people," the essence of Communist morality is to be absolutely loyal and obedient to the Party.

Communism and Youth

Students of all ages are taught that obedience to the Party is the highest virtue. It is constantly preached to young people that the primary purpose of their study is not to pursue personal interests or to seek personal advancement, but to be enabled better to serve the Party and the state.

Young people who have shown "progressive" tendencies and who have taken an active part in "revolutionary activities" are selected for membership in the Communist Youth League; those of a younger age enlisted in the Young Pioneers. Within these youth organizations the process of "remolding" the character of young people is intensified. A special journal called *Chinese Youth* takes up the problems of the young and instructs how youth should behave in various situations. Young people are told that they should seek the counsel of the Party in all matters, personal or social, vocational or political. Even in such matters of family relations, love and romance, young people are told that the interests of the revolution must be given primary consideration and the viewpoint of the Party must be the guide. Every year a campaign is launched among graduates of the schools to get every person to sign a pledge to accept any position—no matter how distant from home or from personal desires—assigned to him. Many a young man or woman has been persuaded either to defer marriage or to give up a lover in deference to the views of the "organization," another term used to describe the Party as the acme of "collective living."

Elementary Education in Red China

Elementary education presents a variety of agencies in Communist China. Besides the regular elementary schools for children, there are adult schools of elementary grade and spare-time elementary schools for youth as well as for older people. There are winter schools for youth and adults in the rural areas, worker-peasant schools, and various kinds of literacy classes.

In elementary education—as in all education in Red China—the aim is stated to be the production of many-sided individuals who can take their part in Socialist construction and will valiantly defend Socialism and its achievements. Writers on education are fond of quoting Mao's words contained in his famous February, 1957, speech titled "The Correct Handling of Contradictions Among the People." "Our educational policy," said Mao, "must enable everyone who gets an education to develop morally, physically, and intellectually, and become a cultured, Socialist-minded worker." Three points of emphasis in elementary education grow out of this central aim: (1) all-round, many-sided development; (2) political and ideological education; and (3) a correct attitude to, and a proficiency in, labor.

The complete elementary school consists of six grades, usually divided into the lower elementary of four years, and a higher elementary of two years. In 1951, a revised school system was adopted and it was announced that the elementary school would be reduced to five years. It was then contended that the six-year elementary was unsuitable for the new China, because the long course was a deliberate scheme of bourgeois society to prevent the broad masses from getting the benefit of universal education. This reduction to five years, it was argued, would make it easier for rural areas to establish schools, and a unitary school without division would encourage more people to complete an elementary education. This alteration of policy was one of the reforms recommended by Soviet advisors who then were active in promoting educational reform in China.[9]

The change to a five-year unitary school proved to be more difficult than expected. Here and there the experiment was tried and much success was claimed, but there was no widespread adoption of the new plan. In December, 1953, the government decided to postpone the change indefinitely on account of "inadequate preparation of teachers and teaching materials."[10]

It was alleged that teachers did not know how to compress the six years' work into five years; further, all available textbooks had been prepared for the conventional six grades of elementary schooling. Besides, the

---

[9] For details, see a report on the five-year unitary school by Wu Yen-yin in *Jen-min Chiao-yü* (The People's Education), December 1, 1952.

[10] This decision by the Government Administration Council was published in *Jen-min Jih-pao* (The People's Daily), December 14, 1953.

condensation of schedule, together with an increase of political education, had resulted in an extremely heavy burden on pupils as well as teachers. At any rate, a return was made to the four-year primary followed by the two-year higher elementary, and this is still current practice in Red China.[11]

Elementary education is not free, although attempts have been made—especially in the schools established by the communes and some industries—to operate some lower schools without tuition fees. The principle of free universal education is accepted, but the current financial situation makes it necessary to charge tuition. Practices vary in different parts of the country. Sometimes, the families of the pupils are asked to contribute to the teacher's board either by taking turns to prepare the meals or by donations of food.[12] It is not uncommon to assess tuition according to the financial status of each family.

The Ministry of Education has published what it considers the standard elementary school curriculum, but, except in larger cities, few schools are able to meet this standard. There are numerous "incomplete" schools with abbreviated courses of study. The table on page 565 shows the program as promulgated in 1957.

The Chinese language is a basic subject of the elementary curriculum. Great emphasis is laid on the teaching of a uniform spoken language throughout all China. A directive of the Ministry of Education ordering redoubled efforts to popularize the national spoken tongue points out that "language is a tool for communicating thought and also a tool of social struggle and social development" and all pupils must learn to be able to communicate in the national tongue.[13] Schools of all grades

---

[11] Yet in 1960, discussion regarding the shortening of the elementary course of study was revived and proposals were made to introduce ten-year schools, which would encompass the entire range of both elementary and secondary education. (This plan was, indeed, the standard for Soviet Russia up to the Khrushchev Reform of 1958 and still obtains to a certain degree.)

[12] See report on such practices in *Jen-min Chiao-yü* (February 1, 1952, p. 47).

[13] The complete text of this directive appears in *Chung-hua Jen-min Fa Kuei Hui Pien* ("Collection of Laws and Regulations of

TABLE I. Time Utilization in the Elementary Schools*
of the Chinese People's Republic, 1957-58.

Subjects	Hours Weekly by Year of School					
	I	II	III	IV	V	VI
Language	12	12	12	12	10	10
Arithmetic	6	6	6	6	6	6
Nature Study					2	2
Geography					2	2
History					2	2
Agricultural Knowledge					1	1†
Manual Labor	1	1	1	1		
Physical Education	2	2	2	2	2	2
Singing	1	1	1	1	1	1
Drawing	1	1	1	1	1	1
Weekly Assembly	1	1	1	1	1	1
Total Hours	24	24	24	24	28	28

* Revised for 1957-58 and promulgated by the Ministry of Education in July, 1957. (*Chiao-shih Pao* ["The Teacher's Journal"], July 12, 1957).

† In 1957, as part of a campaign to encourage youth to favor agricultural production, the Ministry of Education ordered the teaching of agricultural knowledge in all fifth and sixth grades of rural elementary schools.

are ordered to use the national spoken language—*p'u t'ung hua*—as the medium of instruction, first in language classes and gradually in the teaching of all subjects. The phonetic alphabet is taught as an aid to the standardization of pronunciation, and the Peking pronunciation (commonly called Mandarin outside China) has been adopted for the entire country. Special training is given to teachers to enable them to teach this standard pronunciation, and lessons in the phonetic alphabet and pronunciation are broadcast over the radio to familiarize millions of listeners with the national tongue.[14]

The distinguishing characteristics of the elementary curriculum are manual labor and the weekly assembly for political and civic education. Compared with the American elementary curriculum, that of Red China is much more rigidly prescribed and the subjects are narrower

the Chinese People's Republic"), Peking: Fa Lu Ch'u Pan She, 1955, II, 811-18.

[14] Schools have been ordered to teach the newly adopted Latin alphabet as an aid to learning the Chinese language. The question of latinization, nevertheless, is still an unsettled issue; scholars and linguists have expressed skepticism. So far, the only successful changes of the language reform movement consist of the standardization of pronunciation and the adoption of abbreviated written characters.

in scope. As an illustration, the social studies program in the United States is broader and, beginning in the first grade, consists of more than geography and history. Moreover, it must always be realized that few elementary schools actually meet the standard laid down by the Ministry of Education, so that, in actual practice, the three R's, manual labor, and political education constitute the substance of the elementary curriculum. A further problem, to be discussed later, is the difficulty in securing trained teachers for even the three R's—such has been the interest shown toward popularization of learning.

The Chinese people have always valued education, and parents dream and toil to give their children the educational opportunity that they themselves perhaps have not had. With the increase of facilities under the Communist regime, the popular demand for education was greatly stimulated; the results, before party action to curb this tendency in the early 1950's, showed the elementary school ballooning nearly twofold, both in numbers of schools and the pupil population. Around 1953, as indicated by Table II, (p. 567), an arrested growth appeared. This was due to a definite policy of the Party-state. It had been found impossible (and perhaps inexpedient) to try to satisfy the surging demand for general education.

The government directive (mentioned earlier) by which a return to the six-year elementary school, divided into two levels, was mandated, stated categorically that the available supply of teachers and school buildings was inadequate to meet the current demand and made impossible any further expansion of elementary education. Besides recommending such relief measures as double sessions, night schools, incomplete schools, and non-state schools to be established by private groups or individuals, the directive emphasized the importance of encouraging more young people to take up productive labor instead of further education. Supporting this government action, the *People's Daily* cautioned against the contemporary overemphasis on the growth of elementary education or an expectation of early realization of universal elementary education. It further stated that China should keep in mind the example of the Soviet Union, which in its earlier years once had adopted a policy of educational re-

TABLE II. The Enrollment in Elementary Schools
in the Chinese People's Republic, 1949-60*

Year	Number of Schools	Number of Pupils
1949	346,789	24,391,033
1950	383,647	28,923,988
1951	502,189	43,154,440
1952	551,942	49,999,944
1953		51,664,000
1954		51,218,000
1955		53,126,000
1956		63,000,000
1957		65,810,000
1958		86,000,000
1959		90,000,000
1960		100,000,000†

* These data procured from the following sources: figures for 1949-52 from Kuo Lin's report "Three Years of Elementary Education," *Jen-min Chiao-yü*, January 5, 1953; for 1953-55, from the 1957 *Jen-min Shou-ts'e* (People's Handbook"), published by Ta Kung Pao; for 1956, from the report of the Minister of Education, Chang Hsi-jo (in *Jen-min Chiao-yü*, April 9, 1957); for 1957, from Shih Mein-san's article in *The People's China*, Dec. 1, 1957; for 1958, from a report of the State Statistical Bureau (in *The People's Daily*, April 15, 1959); for 1959, from the report of the Minister of Education, Yang Hsiu-feng (in *The People's Daily*, April 9, 1960); for 1960, estimated from data in *The China Yearbook, 1961-62* (Taipei: China Publishing Company, 1962), pp. 700-1, and the *New York World-Telegram World Almanac*, 1963.

It must be borne in mind, of course, that these figures, from different sources and frequently showing a divergence in reporting methods, are not exact, although a correspondence between the numbers for a given year as found in separate records does appear to exist.

† Estimated

trenchment in order to better concentrate on industrial growth.[15]

It is possible that the temporary abandonment of the five-year unitary school was—in part, at least—motivated by a desire to slow down the popular demand for education. A campaign was launched to discourage elementary school pupils from seeking entrance into junior middle schools. It was emphasized that the chief purpose of the elementary school was to produce enlightened workers and that most pupils should consider it normal to take up productive labor when they leave the elementary school. Indeed, the government ordered intensified propaganda to curtail the prevalent desire for more and more study.

[15] Editorial, *Jen-min Jih-pao*, December 14, 1953.

The government spokesmen argued that national construction and industrialization were basic to national life and that to put educational growth (a capitalistic subterfuge) above industrial growth was as unwise as to think only of further study at the expense of immediate contributions to the production program of the state. The Central Committee of the Communist party took a leading role in this campaign by issuing a "propaganda outline" setting forth the reasons why graduates of the elementary and junior middle schools should begin productive labor rather than go on for further study. The Ministry of Education ordered all educational authorities to become familiar with this outline and to publicize it widely. Some of the salient points of this draft may be summarized as follows:[16]

Summary of Reasons for New Work Emphasis

1. The young people who become pessimistic or blame the government because they cannot enter higher schools need educational and ideological guidance to change their thinking so that they may consider it a glorious duty to participate in productive labor.
2. The central purpose of education, in the Marxist-Leninist view, is to increase the productive capacity of the individual.
3. Without the development of production, there would be no real foundation on which educational enterprises could be built. Production, therefore, must come first.
4. The Soviet Union had no plan for universal elementary education until after 1930, when the great advance had already been made in agriculture and industrial production. Even then, effort was confined to the four-year elementary school. The seven-year school and the ten-year school were later developments.[17]

---

[16] The complete texts of this outline and Ministry directive may be found in *Jen-min Chiao-yü*, June 9, 1954. A later official statement on the problem is also contained in Chou En-Lai's report to the National People's Congress in June, 1957; in this connection, see *People's China*, July 16, 1957, *Supplement*, p. 16.

[17] This statement—and argument—conveniently bypasses educational arrangements in Czarist Russia—although, naturally, it is

5. It is wrong for too many young people to consider further (higher) study as their first choice. Their unfavorable attitude toward labor must be changed by education and propaganda.

Following the instructions of the Party and the government, educational authorities carried out a propaganda campaign not only among pupils, but also among their parents and families. It was discovered that parents often felt that their children should have the best opportunity in life and that this opportunity lay in more study. Effort, therefore, had to be made to change the thinking of parents as well as that of their offspring.[18]

Nevertheless, as a result of the officially directed propaganda campaign, it was soon reported that the attitudes of pupils and teachers had undergone significant changes. Investigation in one area revealed that, before the campaign, 90 percent of the pupils were bent on further study but, after the campaign, 80-90 percent had been brought to see the "correct viewpoint." Propaganda among parents in another locality is said to have changed their attitudes from 9 to 93 percent favorable to labor.[19]

In mainland China, as in Eastern Europe (and indeed many areas of the world where elite or party systems flourish) entrance examinations are another way of controlling the advance from elementary schools to junior middle schools (or to higher education in general). In 1954, it was stated that no more than one-third of the graduates of elementary schools could be accommodated in the post-elementary schools of various kinds. Even after 1956, when the rise of non-state schools greatly increased the facilities available, the government continued to pursue a fairly restrictive policy. One reason for this may be the hope of the government to correct the confusion and deterioration of standards which have resulted from the huge expansion of enrollment and the appearance of numerous schools with inadequate facilities

---

not being alleged that universal elementary education was the goal of the pre-Communist Russian state. (Ed.)

[18] For example, see a report concerning parental attitudes in Hupeh Province as published in *Jen-min Chiao-yü*, July 9, 1954.

[19] As reported by Fang Chun-fu in *Jen-min Chiao-yü*, May 9, 1955.

and incompetent teachers. On the other hand, it may well be the policy of the Communist state to permit post-elementary and higher education only for those who are definitely needed for jobs requiring additional training.

Yet it is self-evident that, in the Communist philosophy of education, some education of elementary grade is needed so that people may be more receptive to indoctrination and propaganda, but that schooling beyond the elementary school be reserved only for those whom the state wishes to train for specific tasks or positions. These may be either in agricultural or industrial production or for Red leadership. (Education for the enlightenment or personal advancement of individuals indiscriminately is considered, in Red China, a bourgeois concept that has no place in the Communist scheme of education.)

This campaign to discourage continued schooling for the masses coincided with the new emphasis on labor in the rectification campaign of 1957, and later with the drive to send large numbers of youth to the countryside to stimulate China's lagging agricultural program. Young people who had gone from elementary schools to production were asked to return to the schools to testify to their joy in aiding the production program of the state. These were honored as successful citizens to show the pupils that further study was not the only means of advancement. Students were taken from school to collective farms and factories with the hope that their visits would stir up interest in production. At the same time, "ideological education" was stepped up to rectify any "incorrect" thinking on the pupils' part.[20]

Ideological education to teach the love of labor, patriotism, and Socialist construction was prescribed by the Ministry of Education in order to develop the *right* attitudes toward employment or further study; also a directive on this subject stipulated that such education must be under the sole control of local party authorities.[21]

---

[20] See the report on measures for educating school graduates in *Jen-min Chiao-yü*, September 9, 1957, pp. 13-17; an editorial in the *People's Daily*, pointed out, furthermore, that this problem was especially important for elementary school seniors.

[21] *Chiao-shih Pao*, March 5, 1957.

New Non-State Schools

The aim of the Communists is to put all education in the hands of the state. In 1952, the Ministry of Education announced a policy of taking over all private schools. The enrollment in private elementary schools dropped almost overnight from 34.1 percent of the total enrollment to 5.5 percent in 1952 and to 3.8 percent in 1953.[22] It was soon realized, however, that the state could not possibly provide enough schools to meet the increasing need. Faced by practical necessity, the government reversed its policy and decided to encourage the establishment of educational institutions by the "masses" and by private organizations such as factories, collectives, business concerns, and, later on, the communes. A campaign was initiated to launch large numbers of *min-pan*, or non-state schools.[23] A swift mushroom growth of *min-pan* schools resulted in a big jump in the elementary school enrollment after 1955. (See Table II, page 567.)

In 1957, the Red Regime issued, through the Ministry of Education, a special directive on these *min-pan* ("established by the people") schools. Declaring that it was impossible for the state to provide sufficient educational facilities, it urged the adopting of "many ways and means of establishing schools." The directive continued: "It is therefore necessary to encourage vigorously the establishment of schools by the masses, and to mobilize the inhabitants of cities and villages as well as factories, enterprises, offices, organizations, secondary schools, and higher institutions, the cooperatives, and other units" to provide funds for new schools.[24]

It further laid down the principle that "those who go to school should pay for schooling" and that the parents of the pupils should accept a reasonable share of the cost. In 1958, the Party's Central Committee and the State Council issued a joint "decision" to lay the responsibility for elementary and secondary schools on the local au-

---

[22] See article in *Jen-min Chiao-yü*, June 9, 1957.

[23] These "private schools," although not established by the state, do not escape its control; moreover, the "private organizations" that finance these schools are controlled by the Party and the state.

[24] For text of this directive, see *Collection of Laws*, V, 316-17.

thorities, but emphasizing that "political education and social activities" in such schools must be under the direct supervision of the Party.[25] This, of course, meant that the state was evading its financial responsibility for education without relinquishing its control, since political instruction, considered the heart and soul of any educational program, remained firmly under the strict control of the Communist party.

Unfortunately, many of the *min-pan* schools are poor makeshifts. Classes are held in private homes or in former temples, warehouses, or other unused public buildings, and pupils are often asked to provide their own desks and chairs. Teachers frequently are untrained and, in too many cases, not far removed from illiteracy themselves. Some are only "spare-time" schools; others are "half school, half farm." In the inland province of Kiangsi alone, 19,000 elementary schools were reported as having been established within the short span of two months during the spring of 1958.[26] Schools of this sort could not be expected to be anything but improvisations. They do not teach all subjects of the standard curriculum; the only teaching that is considered indispensable is political and ideological indoctrination. As a matter of fact, such abridgments of the teaching program are officially encouraged and local authorities are told that they should feel free to depart from general regulations and adapt to local conditions.

Political Education

The slogan, "Let politics take command," applies to all aspects of social, political, and economic life in the Com-

---

[25] The text of this Decision may be found in *Collection of Laws*, VIII, 250-52.

[26] See "Educational Leap Forward in Kiangsi Province," *Survey of the China Mainland Press* (SCMP). Hong Kong: U.S. Consulate General, No. 1778 (May 23, 1958), p. 42. George Feng, a third-generation Chinese-American news correspondent, who traveled extensively in Communist China in 1958, reports that "the institution of educational programs throughout the country are not for the benefit of the people but for the Communist State. Teaching is not done to impart knowledge, but to shape an individual to be of greater use as a tool." ("My Three Years Inside Red China," *Stag* [Chicago], XIV, No. 3, [March, 1963], 85. (Ed.)

munist state and is as important in elementary education as in secondary and higher studies. Political education means many things. It means indoctrination in Marxism-Leninism and Maoism as well as the study of current events and government policies. It means "ideological remolding" or thought reform—for teachers as well as pupils. It means the rectification of ideas and attitudes not in harmony with the policies and activities of the state. It means convincing the pupils that productive labor is at times even more important than further study. It means character education and the inculcation of "Communist morality."

The "class viewpoint" and the "labor viewpoint" are considered essential to the development of the "Socialist outlook." From early years, youth must be taught to become "valiant fighters" in both the "class struggle" and the "production struggle." The success of this political education is judged by such practical tests as whether or not teachers as well as pupils change their pro-American and pro-Western attitudes to intense detestation of "capitalistic exploitation," whether they work positively and energetically to carry out the tasks assigned to them by the Party and the state, and whether they learn to appreciate the leadership of the Communist party.[27]

Political education in all schools is carried on under the direct supervision of party authorities. The Party is assisted by the youth organizations—Chinese Young Pioneers and Communist Youth League—and the labor organizations, which exercise an influence not only because the Communist ideology glorifies the working class, but also because labor organizations play an important role in promoting productive labor while pupils are in school

---

[27] See *Jen-min Chiao-yü*, issues of May 1, 1950, p. 63, and January 1, 1951, p. 35. Minister Liu Shao-chi has been quoted as advocating, on June 30, 1961, "re-education" for party learning, to "further understand and command the objective laws of Socialist reconstruction." *The China Yearbook* (Taipei: China Publishing Company, 1962), pp. 692-93. George Feng *(op. cit.)* reports a visit to a vocational school in Kwangnan, where all books except those dealing with woodworking had been removed at the express order of Yang Hsiu-feng (Minister of Education). He asked why this was so. "Students are not permited to read for recreation or enjoyment," the director said. "We regard reading as a means, not an end. . . ." (Ed.)

and in encouraging youth to join the full-time labor force upon leaving school. The Party sees to it that the school bends every effort to turn its pupils into faithful followers of the proletarian-Socialist revolutionary movement.

The content of political education is in part determined by what the Party and state consider the most important issues of the day. During the Korean War, anti-Americanism was a recurrent major theme; during the campaign for the "suppression of counter revolutionaries," the importance of detecting and reporting counter revolutionary activities was stressed; at other times, labor and Communist discipline have been given the central emphasis.

Other topics of study in political education include the "general line of the state," the history of the Chinese (Communist) revolution, Socialist construction, the people's communes, and labor discipline. Reading newspapers, discussing current events, visits to factories, farms, and government offices, and the study of speeches and reports of Communist leaders are regular features of this program. The weekly assembly is an important occasion for political education. The teaching plan promulgated by the Ministry of Education for the years 1957-58 (see time schedule in Table I) stipulates that weekly convocations should be held for each grade in the elementary school "in order to carry on ideological and character education and to report on current events." Needless to say, current events are interpreted from the Marxist-Maoist standpoint. To maintain that young children are not interested in politics, say the Communists, is a fallacy and indeed a bourgeois concept; it is argued that children, properly guided, can become active and effectual supporters of the Party and state.

Youth Organizations

In mainland China, as in other Communist countries, extensive use is made of paramilitary organizations for young children, adolescents, and young men and women as auxiliary organs of the Party and state. Communist morality stresses, above all, the duties of youth to the Party and the motherland. An important role in moral education is played by the Chinese Young Pioneers, the officially sponsored youth organization for elementary school children not old enough to join the Communist Youth League. This youth organization not only molds the characters of its members but also plays a leading role in all branches of school life. The Pioneers set the pace for other children in all kinds of activities, especially those of political significance approved by the Communist party. The emblem of the Young Pioneers is the Red Scarf, which children are taught to regard with respect and honor. Pioneers are not only active promoters of political education in the schools, but leaders in organized activities during the winter and summer vacations. Throughout the entire year they promote a wide range of undertakings approved by the Communist party as excellent vehicles of political education, e.g., the commemoration of revolutionary memorial days and anniversaries, the popularization of the common spoken language, the planting of trees, exposure of anti-revolutionary elements (even among acquaintances and family members), the extermination of pests, and participation in productive labor.

The purposes and functions of Young Pioneers can best be understood by reading the constitution adopted in 1958 by this organization. Among its articles and stated objectives are the following:

3. Our aim: To unite youth and children, to study diligently, to strengthen the body, love labor, love the fatherland, continue the revolutionary traditions of the Chinese Communist party, and resolve to become builders and protectors of Communism.
7. Our slogan: "Be prepared, struggle for the cause of Communism!" Members' reply: "Always be prepared."
9. Our members: Anyone between 9 and 15 years of age who desires to join the Young Pioneers and is willing to abide by the constitution of the corps may apply to the committee of the corps company. He is admitted as a member after his application has been discussed and approved by the committee. When admitted, a member must plant a tree or perform some other public deed. After taking the oath in an initiation ceremony, he is given his emblem to wear.
10. Our organization: Our corps is under the direct guidance of the Chinese Communist Youth League. A headquarters office is established in a city, county, district, or village. A regiment or company is established in a school, street, or agricultural cooperative. Platoons are organized below the level of the company.

Seven to thirteen members may form a platoon, headed by a commander and two deputy commanders. Two to five platoons may form a company. The company is governed by a committee consisting of the company commander, two deputy commanders, and two to four other members. Two or more companies form a regiment. The regiment committee is composed of the regimental commander, two deputy commanders, and four to ten other members. The committee of the company or regiment may, according to the needs of its work, designate its members to take charge of flag raising, labor, study, culture, physical training, organizational activities, wall newspapers, etc.

11. Methods of rewards and punishments: Corps members or corps units which have shown enthusiasm and initiative or achieved outstanding success in their activities are given citations or awards by the corps or the Communist Youth League. If a member violates corps discipline or commits errors in any way, the corps organization should patiently help him to realize and correct them. If after repeated criticism and help he persists in his ways, he should be punished. There are three kinds of punishment: warning, suspension, and expulsion. Warnings should be discussed and approved by the company committee, while suspensions and expulsions should be discussed and approved by the regimental committee. Expulsion of a member is also subject to the approval of the local branch of the Communist Youth League. A suspended or expelled member may be reinstated after he has rectified his errors, upon approval of the regimental committee.

12. Our advisors: The Communist Youth League appoints some of its most prominent members to serve as advisers and intimate friends of the Young Pioneers. They assist in the work and organizational activities of the company and regiment. Corps organizations in junior middle schools or the upper division of elementary schools and those in agricultural cooperatives may carry on without the help of advisers.

Membership in the Young Pioneers was reported to have reached 44,000,000 in 1959 and 50,000,000 in 1960. Every effort is made to establish a corps unit in every elementary school. Directly sponsored by the Party, the Young Pioneers are armed with the prestige and authority of the Party, and consequently their leading role is greatly respected by school children at large and even by their teachers. They organize visits to farms and factories, they help in the work of the communes, they endeavor to study and work as models for other children. At all times they keep in mind their ambition to later become worthy members of the Communist Youth League and, eventually, of the Communist party. Many stories have been publicized which show how these Pioneers make themselves useful workers for various good causes undertaken by the Party and state. For example, the following anecdote[28] appeared recently in the *Peking Review:*

A man, while strolling along the street of a Chinese city, suddenly spat. He was immediately approached by a little girl who politely asked him if he had spat. The man, admitting that he had, was about to walk away when the girl stopped him and gave him a discourse on the evils of spitting. She smiled when she had finished, handed him a slip of paper, apologized for having taken up his time, and wished him good day. The man looked at the slip of paper. It indicated that the girl was a member of a Young Pioneers' Health Inspection Team, which was then doing its part in the campaign against spitting.

The attributes of good citizenship, sponsored by the Young Pioneers and by elementary education in general, may be summarized in the term, "Red expert." It is maintained that education should produce individuals who are both Red and expert. To be "Red" means to be ideologically correct and politically active; to be expert is to be able to contribute to the production program of the state. In 1960 there appeared a new slogan in the elementary schools, namely, "Learn the Yenan Way and become Red children." Children are told that they must recapture that valiant fighting spirit characteristic of life in the Communist base of Yenan prior to the Communist victory in 1949. The "Yenan spirit," said the *Chinese Youth Newspaper,* is the fearless revolutionary spirit that defies hardships and difficulties.[29] Children should be brought up to understand the revolutionary struggle at Yenan so that they might be imbued with the Yenan spirit. Children who complained about the low quality of paper in their exercise books and who did not take good care of their clothes were told how much better off they were than the Chinese children of Yenan days.

---

[28] September 2, 1958, p. 18.

[29] *Chung-kuo Ch'ing-nien Pao,* November 23, 1960. And yet *China Youth* for April, 1961, is found to have remarked rather despairingly of the Communist task in mainland China: "The lack of enthusiasm and courage among the young people is a serious problem. Once confronted with difficulties, they usually become deflated...." *China Yearbook, op cit.,* p. 701. (Ed.)

Communist Moral Education

The Communists make a distinction between their morality and what they call the "bourgeois morality." The Common Program of 1949 listed "five loves," which it said that education should try to develop: (1) love of the fatherland; (2) love of the people; (3) love of labor; (4) love of science; and (5) love of the public property.[30] Since the "fatherland" and the "people" are both symbolized by the Communist party, love and obedience to the Communist party become the highest attributes of Communist morality. Children are taught to sing the praises of the Communist party and to idolize Chairman Mao as a saint who cannot err.

In discussing the teaching of morality, Hsu T'e-li, who is much honored in Red China as an educator because he was the school principal in Mao Tse-tung's home province when this leader was a young student, pointed out that the five loves represented the Communist concept of "public morality," which he contrasted with the bourgeois concept of "personal morality." The Marxist, said Hsu, considers man as inseparable from his social environment and morality as meaningless apart from politics.[31]

A recent editorial in the Ministry of Education's monthly journal, *People's Education*, stated that it was the task of moral education not only to eliminate the influence of bourgeois ideology but, even more important, to foster the steady growth of Communist morality among the masses. It called attention to pupils who were "averse to hard work and indulged in fun-seeking and in quarrels, who disliked learning, and violated discipline." Blaming bourgeois influence for such behavior, it called for a determined effort to remove all evidences of bourgeois ideology. On the positive side, the editorial continued, moral education must be guided by Marxist science and aim to inculcate the Red world outlook and the will to fight for Socialism.[32]

---

[30] A later report adds the following to the basic five loves: love of the party, its leaders, and the army. See report on the Harbin schools, the *People's Daily*, June 1, 1960.

[31] See article by Hsu in *Jen-min Chiao-yü*, July 1, 1950, p. 17.

[32] "How to Strengthen Moral Education," *Jen-min Chiao-yü*, March 9, 1955.

Discipline is an important aspect of moral education. Instances of lack of discipline are frequently reported, and the Marxist diagnosis invariably points to bourgeois influence as a source of corruption and more political education and Marxist indoctrination as the cure.[33] Rewards and punishments are necessary, but corporal punishment is eschewed. It is said that moral education should produce self-discipline, born of a deep political consciousness and a realization of the individual's duty to the proletarian-Socialist cause. An approved code of conduct for elementary school pupils was promulgated by the Ministry of Education in 1955, a code which might profitably be compared with the Soviet Union code as expressed in the volume by P. Yesipov. The Chinese code[34] prescribed the following rules:

Guide for Elementary Pupils

1. Always strive to be a good student; good in health, good in studies, and good in character. Prepare to serve the Fatherland and the people.
2. Respect the National Flag; respect and love the Leader of the People.
3. Obey the instructions of the school principal and the teachers. Protect and promote the reputation of the school and of the class.
4. Be punctual in coming to school and going to classes. Do not arrive late or leave early. Do not be absent without reason.
5. Bring with you to school all the needed textbooks and school supplies. Before the class period begins, get ready all the things needed for the class.
6. Be orderly and quiet and assume a correct posture in class. If it becomes necessary to leave the classroom, first ask the teacher's permission.
7. While in class, study diligently and listen attentively to the teacher's instruction and to the questions and answers of your classmates. Do not talk unless necessary; do not do anything else besides your class work.
8. When you wish to give an answer or to ask a question in class, first raise your hand. Stand up and speak when the teacher permits; sit down when the teacher tells you to.
9. Do all the outside work assigned by the teacher faithfully and punctually.

---

[33] An editorial in the *People's Daily*, June 15, 1955, blames the "corrupt bourgeois ideology" for such school disciplinary problems as neglect of studies and disorder in the classroom.

[34] Entire text published in *Kuang-ming Jih-pao*, June 18, 1955.

10. Perform well the work of a student-on-duty during the day. Participate actively in extracurricular activities.
11. Respect the principal and the teacher. Salute the teacher at the beginning and at the end of the class. Also salute him when you meet outside the school.
12. Be friendly with your schoolmates. Unite with them and help one another.
13. In order to avoid accidents, do not tarry en route to school or in returning home.
14. Respect and love your parents. Love and protect your brothers and sisters. Do what you can to help your parents.
15. Respect the aged. Give way or offer a seat or any other possible help to the aged, to children, to the sick, or to anyone who may have difficulty in movement.
16. Be polite to people. Do not curse, do not fight, do not make unnecessary noise in public places. Do not disturb other people's work, study, or sleep.
17. Do not utter falsehoods or deceive people. Do not gamble. Do not help yourself to things belonging to others. Do not do anything that may be harmful to yourself or to other people.
18. Take good care of public property. Do not damage or soil tables, chairs, doors, windows, walls, floors, or anything else.
19. Eat, rest, and sleep at regular hours. Play and take exercise frequently in order to make your body strong.
20. Keep your body, food, clothes, utensils, bed and living quarters clean and hygienic. Pay strict attention to cleanliness and hygiene at public places.

The Chinese Communists oppose the educational philosophy of John Dewey on both ideological and political grounds. Ideologically, Dewey is attacked as an anti-Marxist. Politically, Dewey symbolizes the extensive American influence on Chinese education in the decades before the Communist conquest. Attack is directed not only against the educational thought of John Dewey, but also against Chinese educators who have been influenced by him. As a matter of fact, Dewey is condemned as an "idealist" and as unscientific, because he is not Marxist. His theory of "education as growth" is opposed on the ground that it aims to divorce education from politics and thus preserve the *status quo* of a capitalistic society. Among his followers in Chinese elementary education, Ch'en Ho-ch'in and T'ae Hsing-chih have been singled out for attack on account of their espousal of "life education." James Y. C. Yen, a well-known leader in mass education, is also a target and he has been called a "faithful servant of American imperialism."[35] In educational circles, many forums have been held to criticize Dewey's philosophy and his "insidious influence" on Chinese education.

Collectivism

The Communist way of life is the collective way. One of the chief tasks of moral education is to train children in collective living. Here again, the Young Pioneers are supposed to set the pace. The collective way is fostered by having children study, labor, and play in groups. The class is organized as a collective with the teacher as head, and with Pioneers and party representatives guiding the activities. Pupils are urged to strive not merely for personal excellence but to raise the level of achievement of the class so that their group might be recognized and honored as a whole. Classes of the same grade engage in emulation contests to see which can get the highest rating. In recent years, the scope of collective activities has been expanded and the slogan of "four collectivizations" has gained increasing popularity. These "four collectivizations" refer to collective study, collective labor, collective residence, and collective boarding. It is contended that the full development of the collective way of life requires having pupils live together in dormitories under the constant supervision of teachers, who in turn are under the constant guidance of the Communist party. The idea of the "four collectivizations" was given great impetus in 1958 by Liu Shao-ch'i, now head of state, who declared that infants should be put in day-and-night nurseries and elementary schools should develop into boarding schools so that the Socialist education of small children might be carried on more effectively. An editorial in the *Kuang-ming Jih-pao* pointed out that education by society was superior to education in the home because the latter was more apt to produce selfish persons averse to labor, and, in the end, the family would be an outworn

---

[35] Much has been written in criticism of Dewey, e.g., article by Chang Chien in *Jen-min Chiao-yü*, June 6, 1955, pp. 23-25. Attack on Yen is found in the June 9, 1957 issue, p. 47.

institution anyway in Communist society.[36] Another writer said that in a Socialist society, children are first of all builders of the new society and only secondly members of the family.[37]

Labor

Productive labor in schools has been given a new emphasis since 1958. As noted earlier, the elementary curriculum has been revised to provide for four to six hours a week of manual work for the senior classes and at least two in the junior classes. Smaller children are assigned duties such as cleaning and sweeping in school and home, and the elimination of insect pests, while pupils in upper classes engage in actual production on farms or in factories. Regular work in agricultural or industrial production or in business enterprises of various kinds has become more and more an integral part of education in elementary as well as higher schools since 1958. In some schools the schedule provides for a half day of study and a half day of productive labor; in others, pupils set aside entire days for work.[38]

Quoting Karl Marx to the effect that any child nine years of age is old enough to be a producer, educational writers and public authorities argue that elementary schools can make substantial contributions to production. A wide range of useful labor activities has been reported by elementary schools: farm work such as sowing, weeding, binding up vegetables, care of chickens and fish, collection of bits of manure for fertilizers, making chemical fertilizers and insecticides; work in carpentry shops and machine shops; and various kinds of work in cooperation with factories.

According to the government regulation on the distribution of time for study, labor, and social activities, participation in labor may be scheduled for a few hours a week only or in concentrated periods devoted entirely

---

[36] October 24, 1958.

[37] *Chung-kuo Ch'ing-nien Pao*, October 25, 1958.

[38] For arguments in favor of school labor, see Tung Shun-ts-ai's essay in *Jen-min Chiao-yü*, April 1, 1958.

to work.[39] Three forms of labor participation are suggested: labor in farms and industries established by the school; sending pupils into the villages and industries for labor; and participation in socially useful labor. The production plans of school industries must be approved by the government and incorporated into the production plans of the state. The regulation further states that the aim of labor by pupils is to form a habit of labor and to impart fundamental knowledge and skills of production, and that remuneration should not be given too much importance. However, many schools with labor programs have proudly pointed out that the income from production has been a vital source of support for them.

The magnitude of the undertaking by elementary schools to establish their own farms, factories, workshops, and such, may be judged by a report from Kirin Province that within a few months in 1958, in response to the call for the establishment of productive enterprises by schools, the elementary schools in that province alone set up as many as 18,048 "factories" producing steel, metal, tools, chemical fertilizers, tiles, cement, textiles, knitting, and stationery; in addition they set up orchards, apiaries, and poultry farms.[40] According to a later report from Hong Kong, elementary schools throughout mainland China were operating in 1959 as many as 490,000 small factories and providing a labor force for 400,000 small farms.[41]

What has been done in the elementary schools is done on an even larger scale in the secondary and higher schools. The productive enterprises established by educational institutes are not merely instructional laboratories. They take orders and turn out products on a business basis. The Communists boast that their schools and universities are centers of production as well as centers of learning.

---

[39] See text for State Council decision in *Collection of Laws*, IX, 263-66.

[40] See report by party organization in Kirin Province, *Hung Ch'i* ("Red Flag"), November 1, 1958, p. 31.

[41] *China News Analysis*, No. 332 (July 15, 1960), p. 5.

Science

Although they put a high premium on science, Communist leaders insist that in science, no less than in other areas, politics must be given prior consideration. The attitude of Chinese Communists toward scientists is essentially the same as their attitude toward all intellectuals. They, of course, need the services of scientists badly, but at the same time they distrust them as products of bourgeois society. Thus in order to be of use to the new Socialist society, scientists, like all other intellectuals, must be reformed. They must rid themselves of every idea and attitude incompatible with the spirit of the new age and they must acquire the viewpoint and ideology of the proletarian-Socialist revolution. In other words, scientists, too, must undergo a thorough "thought reform."

As soon as they came to power (1949), Mao Tse-tung's party heirarchy launched a nationwide program of political indoctrination. Intellectuals were organized to engage in political "study" in order to "reform" themselves. Scientists were told that they needed reform as much as other intellectuals and that they must try to overcome the bourgeois habit of scientific aloofness from politics and to adopt a new and more fruitful philosophy of "serving the people."

One of the important functions of the new Academy of Sciences, established in 1949 in imitation of the Russian body, was to organize a thought reform campaign among intellectuals and scientists. In 1951-52, when college professors, writers, lawyers, physicians, and other intellectuals were gathered in groups for intensive "ideological remolding," the Academy enlisted several hundred research scientists and technicians for four months of "reformative study." According to Academy President Kuo Mo-jo, this "remolding" of scientists meant that they should cast off their old ideological handicaps, paramount among which were liberalism, individualism, and the above-class and above-politics mentality which they had carried over with them from the past.[42] Scientists, it was

---

[42] New China News Agency release, December 29, 1951.

stressed in the reform campaign, must identify themselves with the working class, and in order to do so they must first reform themselves with the ideology of the working class.

An important phase of thought reform is the process of criticism and self-criticism in which individuals are led to examine their own background, to pinpoint their ideological errors and shortcomings, and to make specific confessions and pledges.[43] A person writing a confession usually begins by relating his family and academic background and then goes on to show how such background has saturated him with bourgeois ideas inimical to the working class. He confesses concrete and specific failings, which are obviously the targets the Communists have designated for the "ideological struggle." Many such confessions were made in the thought reform campaign of 1951-52. A quick examination of such confessions and pledges shows that they follow a general pattern. Let us examine some of the most frequently mentioned targets of attack.

Faults Arising from Class Origin

Communists believe that a person born of a bourgeois or petty bourgeois family starts life with an ideological handicap, which he must make a strong, conscious effort to overcome. Awareness of this handicap is one of the first steps in ideological reform. Kao Shang-yin, Dean of the College of Science at Wuhan University, regretfully stated that he began life as a member of a petty bourgeois family; Ch'en Hua-kuei, head of the Department of Agricultural Chemistry in the same university, said he was born in a family which for five or six generations was of the village gentry and landlord class; Ku Teh-jen, of the Department of Electrical Engineering of Sun Yat-sen University, told how he had been influenced in the wrong direction by his father, who was an industrialist, and his

---

[43] Three steps are said to identify this process of remolding: (1) confession of old sins and shortcomings; (2) the resultant feeling of rapport and "brotherhood" with one's fellows and leadership; and (3) a rather severe new attachment or reattachment to the new principles or ideology involved, e.g., Marxism-Leninism.

two uncles, making good livings in the technical field; Lin Cao-tsung, head of the Chemistry Department of Hunan University, confessed that his was a family of landlords engaged in trade, and this class background had conditioned his thinking and blinded him to the fact that his education had been made possible by the exploitation of peasants.[44] One of the most extended denunciations of family background was made by Liang Ssu-cheng, a well-known architect and the son of an eminent scholar and reformer during the closing years of the Manchu dynasty. Liang[45] wrote as follows:

> My class origin, my family background, and my education explain the sources of my erroneous thinking. One major source is my father's conservative reformism and his ardent worship of China's old traditions. The other is the education I received at Tsinghua University and in America.

Pro-Americanism

Second only to bourgeois class origin as a fault is pro-Americanism. One of the major objectives of thought reform is to eradicate all American influence and to stamp out what Communists call the "pro-American mentality" of Chinese intellectuals. To meet this demand, intellectuals in their public statements took pains to denounce the American influence they had received and to pledge determination to overcome this ideological shortcoming. They recalled how they had been dazzled by American materialism and had failed to see how American society was dominated by the exploiter class and how the workers and the Negroes in America were subjected to endless persecution. They confessed that they had been enamored of the American way of life and misled by so-called American democracy. Biologist Hsin-hsuan said that his pro-Americanism had led him to use English names for his botany specimens and to send Chinese flora

---

[44] The complete confessions of these four scientists appeared in *Chiao Shih Ssu Hsiang Kai Tsao Wen Hsuan* (Selected Documents on the Thought Reform of Teachers), Vol. I (Hankow: Chung Nan Jen Min Ch'u Pan She, 1953).

[45] See Liang Ssu-cheng's article in *Jen Min Jih Pao* ("The People's Daily"), Peking, December 27, 1951.

and fauna to the United States for identification and exchange; that he had received grants from Harvard University for collecting specimens in China, and that he had even done some collecting for the United States Department of Agriculture![46]

Other scientists expressed shame at having received fellowships or United States State Department grants while engaged in study in the U.S. Some confessed regretfully that they had taken part in wartime research in America, thus unwittingly aiding the warmongering activities of Imperialist America. Even sending scholarly articles for publication in American scientific journals was deemed an offense serious enough to warrant specific mention in confessions. For example:

> After the war, I was invited to lecture at Yale and I was very happy. . . . [but] I failed to see the true nature of American imperialism.

> This is concrete evidence of my inability to distinguish between friends and enemies. [He published his dissertation in the U.S.].

> I sold out myself; I sold out my nation; I thought that I was achieving fame and status; gleefully and shamelessly I hoped that my expert knowledge was getting me places. [A participator in research under U.S. Army auspices.]

> I received grants from the Rockefeller Foundation for study in England and Germany. . . . What I am most ashamed of is that I accepted the invitation of the U. S. State Department to go to America as an exchange professor in 1943. In two public appearances, I actually served as an accomplice to the reactionaries; in a forum of the New York Chamber of Commerce, instead of exposing the true nature of the Kuomintang policy of opposing the Communists at the expense of effective resistance against the Japanese, I tried to explain away the failures of the Kuomintang armies by saying that their defeat was due to inferior arms.[47]

Individualism

In the Communist view, individualism is the besetting sin of all bourgeois intellectuals. Scholars are charged with bourgeois individualism when they pursue their study according to their personal plans instead of fol-

---

[46] *Chiao Shih Ssu Hsiang Kai Tsao Wen Hsuan*, I. (Hankow: Chung Nan Jen Min Ch'u Pan She, 1953), 49.

[47] Report on thought reform in Yenching University, *Ta Kung Pao* (Hong Kong, April 22, 1952).

lowing state plans, when they prefer to work individually instead of collectively, when they are slow in accepting the guidance and leadership of the Communist party, and when they seek personal or professional advancement instead of putting the interests of the proletarian cause above all else. To absolve themselves, they painstakingly relate how they had been plagued by bourgeois individualism. Biologist Kao Shang-yin, for instance, expressed regret that he had, out of personal interest, wasted precious years in research on the paramecium, which was useless to mankind, while he had neglected the far more important study of Michurin's theories.[48] Another wrote in his confession: "I was not accustomed to the collective way. I feared organization. I feared discipline."[49]

When, in 1951-52, the new government announced its plan to reorganize higher education by the merging of departments or institutions, university professors who raised questions were accused of individualism and "particularism" and putting selfish interests above the collective good. One by one they were brought in line. The head of the Department of Civil Engineering of Peking University wrote a piece titled "My Bourgeois Thinking Was an Obstruction to the Reform of Higher Education."[50] Many scholars confessed that they had not only been motivated in their career by a craving for fame and position, but also had encouraged students to consider advanced study as a means of personal advancement. Those who had submitted articles for publication in foreign journals confessed that they had been seeking fame. Moreover, in their eagerness to attain international recognition, they had allowed themselves to be influenced by "international standards of scholarship" and consequently to become further entrenched in the bourgeois ideology. One said that he had written many textbooks solely for fame and profit. Another said: "My ambition was to be able to solve purely technical or geological problems, to write a few good articles, and to become a famous scholar."[51]

---

[48] Ssu Hsiang Kai Tsao Wen Hsuan, II, 27.
[49] Chiao Shih Ssu Hsiang Kai Tsao Wen Hsuan, I, 32.
[50] Jen Min Jih Pao, March 12, 1952.
[51] Ssu Hsiang Kai Tsao Wen Hsuan, V, 15, 42.

Aloofness from Politics

"Aloofness from politics," "aloofness from class," and a "purely technical viewpoint" all refer to the desire of intellectuals to be allowed to pursue their scholarly work without being involved in politics or the class struggle. The Communists argue that class consciousness is the essence of political consciousness, and that without political consciousness a scholar would not know what goals to work for and could easily become the tool of the exploiting class. In bourgeois society, the argument continues, intellectuals are kept away from politics so that they can unswervingly serve the exploiters, but in the proletarian-Socialist society, professional and technical personnel must take an active interest in politics.

Another name for aloofness from politics is the "suprapolitics mentality." The head of the institution formerly the Peking Union Medical College wrote that he had once thought that it would be best for his faculty to devote themselves to their laboratory work and his students to their studies and to avoid being distracted by politics.[52] An engineering dean also confessed the error of taking pride in being nonpartisan and in belonging to no political party.[53] A hydraulic engineer wrote: "I used to think that belonging to no political party but possessing technical ability, I would always be needed by any government. . . . I had nothing to ask of other people, but other people would always need my services. I was thus haughty and complacent."[54]

The avoidance of politics is also known as the "purely technical viewpoint." A professor of chemistry said that on account of his purely technical viewpoint "he had judged student progress solely in terms of academic achievement without regard to political record or revolutionary fervor."[55] The new regime insists that such an attitude is poisonous to the minds of young people. The

---

[52] *Kuang Ming Jih Pao*, January 13, 1952.
[53] *Nan Fang Jih Pao* ("Southern Daily"), Canton, September 9, 1952.
[54] *Chiao Shih Ssu Hsiang Kai Tsao Wen Hsuan*, I, 83.
[55] *Ibid.*, p. 96.

new viewpoint is that scholarship alone is not enough; it must be guided by correct political ideology.

Ignorance or Suspicion of the USSR

In the pre-Khrushchev-Mao rift thinking of the Chinese Communists, anti-Americanism and pro-Sovietism were but two sides of the same coin and most of China's intellectuals were found wanting in both. Just as intellectuals admitted the mistake of admiring the United States, they as frequently pleaded guilty of harboring unfavorable thoughts about the USSR. In the early fifties much was made of allegiance to Muscovite ideas. For example, Physicist Chou P'ei-yuan, formerly Dean of Tsinghua University and now Vice-President of Peking University, testified that he had consistently opposed the Soviet Union, admired the United States, and distrusted the Communist party. Biologist Kao Shang-yin said his own bourgeois background had prevented him from studying the theories of Michurin. Other biologists hastened to prove their "progressiveness" by declaring readiness to throw Mendel's Law overboard in favor of the Russian's theorizing. Chemist Ch'en Hua-kuei admitted that he had been misled by Anglo-American propaganda to believe the Soviet Union oppressed its people at home and pursued exploitative and expansionist policies abroad. Engineering Dean Ch'en Yung-ling also confessed that his pro-Americanism had made him suspicious of the Soviets and that, "when Chairman Mao asked us to lean to one side, I could not bring myself to do so."[56]

In mainland China whether or not intellectuals should be politically and ideologically sound is not an open question. The unequivocal reply is that no expert is any good unless he is "Red." The question is whether "Redness" is more important than "expertness," and whether in education it is advisable to try first to make a competent expert and then take care of the political and ideological qualifications. The official position in Communist China has been that political qualifications are even more important than technical qualifications, and that "expert-

---

[56] See Ch'en's article in *Ssu Hsiang Kai Tsao Wen Hsuan*, Vol. IV.

ness before Redness" is a bourgeois subterfuge that cannot be tolerated. Scientists who express themselves in public have taken care to conform to the official viewpoint.

A series of forums were held at Tsinghua University to discuss the relative importance of "Redness" and "expertness" with the result that students and faculty alike assailed the tendency of some scholars to take the middle road or to be satisfied with "pinkness" instead of "Redness." In summarizing these discussions, the President of the University, Chiang Nan-hsiang, declared that politics is the soul of scientific work, and the main reason why Soviet scientists beat American scientists in the race to launch the first satellite in space is that Soviet scientists are motivated and guided by Socialist politics.[57] Chiang stressed the class nature of science and said that Communist science must serve the proletarian class.

Similar forums on the relation between "Redness" and "expertness" have been held in other cities and universities.[58] They point out that "expertness without Redness," "expertness before Redness," and "more expertness than Redness" are all dangerous mistakes, and the only really correct course to take is to put "expertness" in the service of "Red" politics.[59]

This demand that educated persons should be "Red experts" is simply another way of saying that they are not allowed to keep aloof from politics. Moreover, in all that they do, they must be guided first and last by political considerations. As noted earlier, their slogan must be, "Let politics take command." In the selection of personnel and in the advancement of students, academic qualifications, often are secondary to the candidate's political qualifications, for the Communists believe that ideological orthodoxy and political dependability can amply compensate for deficiency in technical ability. In the ideological remolding of government office personnel, it was proposed that politics should be assigned 70 percent importance, while professional work should rate only 30

---

[57] *Kuang Ming Jih Pao*, January 5, 1958.
[58] *Ibid.*, January 7, 1958.
[59] *Ibid.*, January 30, 1958.

percent.[60] The true meaning of "Let politics take command," said the President of Tsinghua University, is to let politics guide professional work, to obey the leadership of the Party, to respect Marxist materialism, to study dialectics, and to follow the mass line of the party.[61]

Summary and Prospects

In their revolution for a Socialist-proletarian society, the Chinese Communists are not held back by past traditions. They boldly experiment with new institutional forms and new methods to achieve their objectives. Much publicity has been given to the social and economic experiments summed up under the slogan, "Great Leap Forward." Sometimes it is not quite recognized that revolutionary changes in education are an important part of this attempt to bypass centuries in the urge to create a Socialist utopia and modern economic state.

On September 19, 1958, the State Council and the Central Committee of the Communist party issued a joint directive calling for a speedup of the cultural revolution in order to obliterate illiteracy and to produce "tens of millions of Red and expert intellectuals of the working class."[62]

This directive denounces such "bourgeois ideas" as "education for its own sake" and the "professional management of education by educators." The major defects of education in the past are said to have been its divorce from production and labor, its aloofness from practical affairs, its neglect of politics, and its lack of the leadership of the Communist party. The Communists have tried to reduce illiteracy, to introduce universal primary education gradually, and to make secondary and higher education available to the "masses" and the "proletariat" elements who did not have the opportunity of education in the past. On account of financial stringency, however, most of their plans have been unfulfilled.

According to the government directive, institutions of

---

[60] *Idem*, April 9, 1958.
[61] *Idem*, January 31, 1959.
[62] Text may be found in *Jen Min Jih Pao*, September 20, 1958.

higher learning ought to be administered by committees, instead of presidents or chancellors. The administrative committees function under the guidance of party representatives assigned to each college or university. In the promotion of teachers, political and ideological qualifications must be given more weight than academic qualifications, and in the evaluation of student achievement, primary emphasis must be placed on the level of political consciousness and the ability to solve practical problems.

A central idea of the new program (on all levels) is the integration of learning with production and labor. Communist leadership quotes extensively from Marx and Engels to show that the combination of education with productive labor has always been a key concept of their ideology.[63]

Since productive labor is considered as an integral part of education, the educational program, even in the university, cannot be limited to study. The major universities, such as Tsinghua and Wuhan, are now operated completely on the work-study plan. The work-study pattern is flexible. In one engineering school, classes are held in the winter, with the summer and fall devoted to construction work—supplemented by evening study. In Tsinghua University, some departments set aside one out of the three semesters of the year for production and devote the other two to study; other departments provide for alternate days of work and study or half-day work and half-day study; still others schedule four days of study after two of work.

The Communist regime has decided that to achieve its goals it is not enough merely to increase the number of the regular colleges and universities or to extend the use of the part-work-part-study system in these institutions. It is necessary, in addition, to establish many new institutions different from the conventional type. Indeed, when the Communists talk about the popularization of

---

[63] See, for example, "Education Must Be Combined With Productive Labor," by Lu Ting-yi, originally published in the Chinese Communist Party Central Committee journal, *Hongqi* ("Red Flag"), No. 7 (September 1, 1958), pp. 1-2. An English translation appeared in the *Peking Review* September 9, 1958, pp. 5-12. In 1962 Chang-Tu Hu compiled ten revolutionary articles, *Chinese Education under Communism* (New York: Teachers College, Columbia University), 157pp., including several referenced in this chapter.

higher education, they actually put a new meaning into the concept of "higher education."

Among the unique new schools are the "spare-time colleges and universities" and the "Red and expert universities." These new agencies for the furthering of the Great Leap Forward in education make political indoctrination and technical training their central objectives. Political education is in the hands of Communist cadres and technical training comes from lectures by experienced farmers and craftsmen.

These and other changes introduced in the past few years stem from a concept of education very different from that generally found in Western countries outside the USSR and her satellites. Quite obviously, higher education in terms of a four-year college or university built on a foundation of secondary education of a prescribed number of years is not what the Chinese Communists have in mind when they plan for the popularization of secondary and higher education. In fact, many of the so-called colleges and universities of mainland China seem to be little more than advanced vocational classes tinctured with a heavy dose of political indoctrination, or, at best, *technicums*.

There are no definite standards of admission; the main considerations are the political consciousness and production record of the applicant. Since the teachers are self-educated, the equipment simple and often inadequate, degrees and academic qualifications little regarded, "graduation" from such institutions can, of course, mean little except that the holder of its diploma meets the Communist criteria of a "Red expert." Indeed, with limited formal training, experienced workers and farmers have become "professors." A model peasant has been made the president of one "Red and expert" university, and a cotton grower who had increased his yield in the production drive ordered by the party hierarchy was made the head of a department of grain and cotton cultivation in one of the new-type colleges.

Communist theorists find support in Mao Tse-tung's statement that theory having no relation to action is absolutely worthless. Repeating the Marxist emphasis on the unity of thought and action, they say that institutions of higher learning used to teach much useless knowledge that bore no relation to either the class struggle or production. By weeding out the "useless" bourgeois class-biased cultural impedimenta and self-glorification, it is possible, they say, for the new "universities" to offer more compact courses which students with their rich labor experience can complete in much shorter time. And because theory is enriched by immediate application to practical experience, they further argue, the learning process becomes all the more meaningful, and, consequently, more efficient.

Communist writers reject the idea that only Western-trained academicians or those with university degrees can qualify as professors. They recognize only two kinds of useful knowledge: that of the class struggle and knowledge of the struggle for production.[64] These two fields of knowledge constitute the core of the curricula of Communist China's new universities. As mentioned above, the competency of teachers and students alike is judged largely in terms of these two types of knowledge. The only standards given attention are the degree of political consciousness and proficiency in productive labor. In this view, education is only one aspect of the political and social order. Any change in basic political and economic policies calls for a corresponding change in education. There is no gap between school and society, no line of demarcation between formal and informal education.

Inevitably school work is subject to frequent interruptions and to constant pressures for students and teachers to join the innumerable "mass campaigns." If questions are raised in regard to educational instability and deterioration of scholarship standards, the Communists retort that such worries are expressions of bourgeois thinking. So classes have been suspended for days and weeks to enable students and faculties to take part in propaganda work and in activities ranging from killing flies to dam construction and steel production. Since

---

[64] Refer to Lu Ting-yi's "Education Must Be Combined With Productive Labor," as cited under note 63 supra, page 593. See also T. C. Cheng, "Half-Work and Half-Study in Communist China," *History of Education Journal*, IX, No. 4 (Summer, 1958), 88-92. (Ed.)

these drives and campaigns never come to an end, stability and systematic work in institutions of higher learning have become impossible.

The Chinese Communists proudly proclaim that they are forging a system of education consistent with their ideology. They claim that they are producing a "proletarian intelligentsia" who come from the ranks of workers and peasants and are free from the vices of old-style intellectuals who hold themselves aloof from politics and productive labor. By forcing these old-time intellectuals to engage in labor, by enabling workers and peasants to become new-type intellectuals, by wiping out the distinctions between mental and physical labor, by combining agriculture with industry in the new communes, by integrating education with productive labor, and by developing "all-round persons" versatile enough to be able to shift from one branch of production to another whenever necessary, the Chinese Communists declare that they are moving steadily in the direction of the kind of society that Marx and Engels envisioned in their *Communist Manifesto*.[65]

---

[65] The recent "split" between mainland China and the USSR may be attributed, at least on the surface, to differences in interpretation of Marxism-Leninism. A few commentators, however, consider economic or national factors more significant. But it is of utmost importance for the West to remember that both Red China and Soviet Russia still remain "Communist" regardless of any dissimilarities of an ideological nature. (Ed.)

CHAPTER XIV

THE EDUCATIONAL OUTLOOK IN EAST CENTRAL EUROPE

The Problem of Victory

ANY ASSESSMENT of the results and real significance of World War II—as of its predecessor in 1914-18
—can be made only in terms that are essentially nonmilitary. In such an analysis, three foci immediately present themselves: (1) resurgent nationalisms in both Asia
and Africa; (2) a new and curious satellitism; and (3)
new and stronger recourses to education.

Since it is not the purpose of this chapter to deal with
political processes except to the extent that they *effect*
educational philosophy and/or practice, we shall limit
its scope to only the satellite countries and those new re-
sponses to education having their wellsprings in the newly
changed circumstances so apparent throughout the world.

However, it would be impossible in one section to cover
all of the transformations in satellite areas (including
those oriented to the West and to the USSR) ;[1] consequently, we shall be concerned here only with an interpretation of the altered conditions in education within
the captive nations of East Central Europe.

The expression "East Central Europe" (as used
throughout this book generally) is defined by Oscar
Halecki as the borderlands between Germany and the
eastern Slavic state, the power of which is currently
held by the Union of Soviet Socialist Republics.[2]

We may begin with a little-noticed event that took

---

[1] See J. A. Lukacs, "The American Imperial Disease," *The Amer-
ican Scholar*, XXVIII, No. 2 (Spring, 1959), 141-50; also Nicholas
Halasz, *In the Shadow of Russia; Eastern Europe in the Postwar
World* (New York: The Ronald Press Co., 1959).

[2] Oscar Halecki, *The Limits and Divisions of European History*
(New York: Sheed and Ward, 1950), p. 137.

place in the Polish capital in 1944. The death in be-leaguered Warsaw of Polish Professor Dr. Ferdynand Antoni Ossendowski was completely overshadowed by several occurrences of immediately graver world signi-ficance: (1) the Allied invasion of *Fortress Europa;* (2) a strong reversal of what had appeared to be Japanese good fortune in the western Pacific; and (3) the surge of a great Communist wave in East Europe together with the conversion of China's "agrarian revolt" into a far more sinister evolution than that of earthshaker Genghis Khan.

Perhaps this last was most barometric. For the impact of the Communist East—with its collective and mater-ialistic philosophy—could not be stayed, and even today its bitter fruit twists the stomachs of 100,000,000 East Europeans—to say nothing of the seven times as many Chinese subject to the Red regime in mainland China.

As with the eyes of a prophet, Ossendowski had seen from his window in Warsaw, years before, that "shadow of the gloomy East" which was to become—already by the day of his death—a dynamic force in the history of our time. In November, 1923, as a result of his travels in the Far East and a sojourn in Siberia, Professor Os-sendowski had written:

I hope that the same severe judge will not pass the same sentence [he is speaking of the failure of the Russian intelligentsia to cor-rectly apprehend the Bolshevik danger—and their subsequent downfall] on the Christian civilization, which has [already] been sapped by materialism, and which is passing through its twilight . . . unable to rouse itself with new strength and impulse to loftier ideals. In the face of the danger threatening from Russia, these should be our strength and stay, for in them lies the only salvation from the peril coming up from the East, with its passion for evil and showing its true face, since the mask—which deceived man-kind for so long—is torn off.[3]

Yet the years between 1923 and 1944 had shown little real awareness of this Polish savant's prescience. Totali-tarianism flourished, and recourse to a second World War set the stage for just that peril anticipated by Os-

---

[3] Ferdynand A. Ossendowski, *The Shadow of the Gloomy East;* trans. by F. B. Czarnomski (New York: E. P. Dutton and Co., 1925), pp. vi, 196-98.

sendowski. Indeed, by 1945, it was perhaps already too late for Western apprehension of the fact of Communist penetration deep into the heart of Europe to make much immediate difference.

Sir Winston Churchill reports that, at Potsdam, a gnawing fear of Soviet intentions concerning East Central Europe had begun to seep into his mind. "I drew a line," he says, "from the North Cape to Albania and named the capitals east of that line which were in Russian hands. It looked as if Russia were rolling westward."[4] At this, Marshal Stalin declared that he did not intend to remain; he was (he said) already withdrawing troops from the area.

The Georgian asserted further that "in all of the countries liberated [!] by the Red Army the Russian policy was to see a strong, independent, sovereign State."[5]

It is, of course, futile to comment on Stalin's duplicity. Of the thirteen political entities that, before World War II, comprised the great *cordon sanitaire* lying between Germany and the USSR, only two have maintained their independence (Finland and Greece), one (Austria) has regained her former status, while a fourth (Yugoslavia), although under a Communist regime, apparently is able to defy direct domination by the Kremlin.

When the East German "Democratic Republic"—unrecognized by the West—is added to the unfortunate remainder, a total of ten East European countries are shown to lie within the Soviet orbit. Today the peoples of Estonia, Latvia, Lithuania, Poland, Czechoslovakia, Hungary, Romania, Bulgaria, Albania, and East Germany are experiencing just what prophet Ossendowski had foreseen from his vantage point on the Vistula two decades earlier. Moreover, if the Ukraine, which was subverted in 1920, is allowed to increase the Iron Curtain countries to eleven, 40,000,000 more Eastern Europeans are shown to be affected.[6]

---

[4] Winston S. Churchill, *Triumph and Tragedy* (New York: Houghton Mifflin Company, 1953), p. 636.

[5] *Idem.*

[6] See Kenneth V. Lottich, "Soviet Russia's First Victim," *Sudeten Bulletin, A Central European Review* (Munich), VIII, No. 10 (October, 1960), 243-49.

The Menace of Marxism

The threat of Marxism to objective truth and to democracy (as the West understands the term) must be grasped by students of education as well as politics. Grave though the political aspect of Communism is seen to be, its complementary menace is far greater in that this attacks the sanctuary of the mind. The so-called "brainwashing" tactics so heavily utilized by the Chinese Reds during the Korean conflict of 1950-53 are well known; that this species of thought control is inherent in Marxism-Leninism and is practiced daily in its system of education is less familiar.

In order to visualize the power of the Communist drive via the senses, one must first review the origins of the movement. Although indebted to Marx, the groundwork for a Communist state on Utopian lines had already been conceived by the nineteenth century Russian revolutionary leader. The creator of this Arcadia must be a "new man." Born again in his devotion to the Party, the holiness of his mission allowed neither pity nor patriotism. His only faith to be in the revolution, this individuality must be swallowed up, and—thus expendable—should circumstances demand his life for the cause, he stood ready to surrender it.[7]

For by this route each sacrifice conferred immortality —not to the victim directly but to the state—and so, by curious inversion, to him at last. Fanatic in his zeal (for self-immolation if required) he followed blindly the leader and the party line, and who if need be would lie, cheat, and murder to gain his (that is, the Party's) objective.[8]

It is well known that Lenin added much to the operational structure of Russian Communism and that Marxist-Leninist tactics operate primarily through *reservatio*

---

[7] See Alan Moorhead, *The Russian Revolution* (New York: Harper & Brothers, 1958), p. 33; B. P. Yesipov and N. K. Goncharov, *I Want to Be Like Stalin*; trans. by George S. Counts and Nucia P. Lodge (New York: John Day Co., 1947). Chapter II, "For Bolshevik Character—the Principles of Moral Education," pp. 42-52, stresses the development of the Communist mentality.

[8] Moorhead, *idem;* see also Arthur Koestler, *Darkness at Noon* (New York, Macmillan, 1941), for a purported fictional account of the tactics of the Party, but which reveals quite succinctly the monolithic ruthlessness of Marxist politics.

mentalis. Stalin, whose perfidy vis-à-vis the Western democracies has already been denounced, frequently was asked: "Do you believe that the two divergent, political, economic and social systems can satisfactorily live side by side?" He invariably replied, "I believe it." At no time, however, was the question, "How long will you continue to believe it?" answered.

During the 1956 Hungarian uprising, Premier Nagy (who certainly should have been well aware of this danger) made an agreement with the commander in chief of the Soviet troops, according to which the Red forces were to move out of the state at a designated border point. Yet Nagy failed to have included in the agreement that other Russian troops would not enter Hungary at a different border point.[9] The results of the Magyar revolt are well known. Nagy paid with his life for this mental lapse.

A relationship between political "flexibility" and the program of public education has already been suggested. In the Soviet Union and in the satellites, three doctrinal devices provide for a uniformity which, in its monolithism, is at once both effective and disturbing.

First, Marxism-Leninism provides the core of instruction, and, in the majority of subjects, serves as the basis for selection of curriculum materials; establishes the appropriate emphasis; and dictates the scope of the investigation; *secondly,* extra activities, including the various youth groups and school circles, provide a further base for indoctrination and out-of-school surveillance—significant indeed for the simple reason that the child's further academic progress is largely conditioned by his supervisor's report; a *third* element of great importance (to the state, at least) is the newly imposed work program (the so-called Khrushchev reform), an integral part of each pupil's curriculum responsibilities; frequently coupled with the work experience is the barrack life of the boarding school through which the child is firmly and finally divorced from the conventional family ties.

⁹ See Franz Tiso, "Communist Tactical 'Flexibility,'" *Sudeten Bulletin,* VIII, No. 3 (March, 1960), 71-72.

Educational Revisionism

Yet, even before the 1958 revision, the Soviet school system had, according to George Z. F. Bereday, "significantly re-valued the traditional concept of prestige between liberal arts men and 'engineers.' " Professor Bereday considers further that "Even more telling is the superior social position of Stakhanovites in comparison with the lower white-collar workers. . . ."[10]

The Khrushchev theses called for a drastically foreshortened gap between mental and manual work. Soviet comment on this recent move, which introduces a practical labor program into each phase of Russian education, not only serves to justify this departure but reveals a great deal of the Communist strategy[11] as well:

This is a time of tremendous Soviet progress. The country's economy driving full speed ahead, science and culture are experiencing an unprecedented growth, the working people's living standards are rising steadily. In every field of economic and cultural development, the Soviet people—truly masters of life and makers of history—have won outstanding victories they are justly proud of, which are bringing joy and hope to the hearts of millions of friends of peace and socialism and fear and despair to enemies of the working class.

. . . V. I. Lenin taught that the training and education of the young generation, the preparation of highly qualified cadres for all branches of the national economy, science and culture, must always be a matter of central concern for the Communist Party and the Soviet State.

Thus, speaking at the 13th Congress of the Young Communist League, Nikita S. Khrushchev said in this connection: "Every boy and girl should know that while studying at school, they must prepare themselves for

[10] "Equal Opportunity," *Journal of Education* (London), XC (February, 1958), 47.

[11] "On Strengthening the Bonds of the School with Life, and the Further Development of the Public Education System in the Country. Theses of the Central Committee of the Communist Party in the Soviet Union and the Council of Ministers of the U.S.S.R.," Soviet Education (a translation in English of the U.S.S.R. monthly journal *Sovetskaya Pedagogica*, The Journal of the Russian Academy of Pedagogical Science), I (February, 1959), 3-5; see also George S. Counts, *Khrushchev and the Central Committee Speak on Education* (Pittsburgh: University of Pittsburgh Press, 1959), 66 pp.

working, for the creation of values useful to people, to society. For each one of them, regardless of the position of his or her parents, there should be only one road—to study, then, having learned, to work."

Relative to this—and stripping the above report of its overt propaganda—it will be recalled that, a few years ago, a group of leading Soviet medical authorities published a long letter in the *Literaturnaya Gazeta* charging Soviet educational authorities with "endangering the health of school children" by overloading them with lessons and homework. "Chronic over-exhaustion, frequent headaches, weakened memory and vision, proneness to infectious diseases with various complications, result in a general weakening of the child's organism." The M.D.'s complained further of the "unbelievable over-burdening of school children." Those of eleven to thirteen were averaging, they concluded, including homework, from eight to ten hours a day; and students of fourteen to seventeen from ten to twelve hours.[12]

Since in a planned economy such as the USSR nothing is presumed to happen by chance, this propaganda move may be suggested as the opening gambit to the reduction in the academic portion of the Soviet public school program—which was accomplished in September, 1956. That the current move—unquestionably to counteract a tendency which had been developing in Soviet secondary education (and this is quite comparable to the problem in Britain) of placing prestige on academic attainment in the upper classical and scientific schools—is one way to retreat gracefully from an untenable position is quite rational.

Since it was impossible for all to succeed in the higher level programs and as the prestige factor was seen to be inconsistent with Soviet ideology, this obvious explanation for the proletarian turn is logical indeed. But to return to the rationale of the new work program:

Public education must be reorganized along lines that will allow the secondary and higher schools to play a more active role in all of the creative activity of the Soviet people. . . . One of the major

---

[12] Quoted in Robert J. Havighurst, "Is Russia Really Out-Producing Us in Scientists?" *School and Society*, LXXXVI (April 26, 1958), 190.

defects in the old society was the gulf between physical and mental labor. . . . Marxist teaching has dispelled the bourgeois myth of the inevitable and eternal existence of a grey mass of people on the one side, whose destiny is submission and grinding physical toil, and on the other, a handful supposedly called by nature herself to do the thinking and ruling, to develop science and literature and the arts.

. . . the idea of uniting instruction with productive labor has long attracted progressive thinkers. Such Utopian Socialists as Campanella, Fourier, and Owen, and the great Russian revolutionary democrat, Chernyshevsky, already in this day, picturing the society of the future, spoke of the close bonds of instruction with physical labor under Socialism.

The 20th Congress of the CPSU pointed out, as a serious shortcoming in our schools, the fact that instruction is, in a certain measure, divorced from life, and that graduates are ill-prepared for practical activity. In order to strengthen the bond of the schools with life, it is not only necessary to introduce new subjects into the school curriculum . . . but also to involve them systematically in work at enterprises, collective and state farms, experimental school plots, and school workshops. The curriculum for secondary schools should be revised in the direction of a greater specialization in production so that young people who complete the ten-year (complete secondary school) program have a good general education opening the way to higher education, and at the same time, prepare for practical activity, *since the greater part of the graduates will at once start work in the various branches of the national economy.*[13]

Two stages in providing the new program were envisioned. First, a compulsory eight-year school (to replace the typical seven-year incomplete secondary school) from which "the youth as a whole must become involved in socially useful work at enterprises, or collective farms, etc." The second plateau involves continuation schools, secondary general educational labor polytechnical schools, and technical schools with the complete secondary education program, boarding schools, and a specialized secondary education curriculum for those destined for special service for the state.[14]

The Behaviorist philosophy of this new move stands fairly well revealed in the concluding statement of a directive adopted on November 12, 1958: "In mastering these qualities, the study of the social sciences plays an

---

[13] "On Strengthening the Bonds . . . ," p. 5. Italics added.
[14] *Ibid.*, pp. 6-7.

important role. A knowledge of the fundamentals of Marxism-Leninism is essential for specialists in all fields. ... Our youth must be trained in a spirit of implacability toward bourgeois ideology and any manifestation of revisionism."[15]

Such a monolithic attack on the status problem that badgers England, France, and the United States confirms the views of Dr. George S. Counts, an American interpreter of the Russian educational world for many years. "Teacher and education as such ... are essentially technicians who translate into practice the general and specific directives formulated by the party leadership." For "the goals of Soviet education are to be found in the Bolshevik conception of history, the nature of the social structure, the controlling purposes of the party, the cultural heritage from Old Russia, and the shifting tides of change among the nations."[16]

Indeed the present educational attitude might well be a paraphrase of Lenin himself. "In the field of people's education," said this saint, "the Communist Party sets itself the aim of concluding the task begun by the October Revolution of 1917 of converting the school from a weapon of the class domination of the *bourgeoisie* into a weapon for the destruction of this domination, as well as for the complete destruction of the division of society into classes. *The school must become a weapon of the dictatorship of the proletariat.*"[17]

One would, of course, be naïve to expect that each of the words quoted above should be taken in its literal meaning. At the same time, it must be realized that the problem in the Soviet Union and especially in the satellite states is to devise a working arrangement between Communist ideology and the needs of the Soviet national state. "It seems evident that a growing number of Soviet intellectuals recognize the mythological function of certain elements of the official ideology," surmises Martin

---

[15] *Ibid.*, p. 14.

[16] George S. Counts, *The Challenge of Soviet Education* (New York: McGraw-Hill Book Co., 1957), pp. 32, 50-51.

[17] As quoted in Counts, *op. cit.*, p. 47. Italics added.

Levit in a recent discussion of educational theory in the Soviet Union.[18]

Admittedly, "the influence of the Marxist-Leninist legacy is strong; it colors even the objections of dissenters . . . a reciprocity of influence is discernible between it and other forces—historical Russian traditions, four decades of an embracive Soviet enculturation process, international problems, the development of a giant industrial power, and an increasingly complex social class structure."[19]

Moreover, a higher birth rate than that of the United States before Pearl Harbor, together with a school system geared to higher education requirements, had led to a surplus of academically trained young people which the facilities of the state were unable to assimilate easily. Before 1958, more students were being graduated from the complete secondary school (still largely propaedeutic) than could be enrolled in universities and other higher educational institutions. The paramount need was that of swiftly developing a more extensive, occupationally skilled, and variegated middle class.[20]

"Reform" in Czechoslovakia

This work-study dilemma was likewise one for the Soviet satellites and, since their educational policies are controlled from Moscow, developments in the Iron Curtain countries—and Czechoslovakia offers a prime example—serve to indicate the completeness with which the new move has been formulated. Here announcement of the 1958 reforms begins with the usual Marxist polemic: "All affairs of public education and the school system of the Czechoslovak Republic have undergone profound changes

---

[18] Martin Levit, "Educational Theory in the U.S.S.R. and West Europe," *School and Society*, LXXXVII (January 17, 1959), 22.

[19] *Ibid.*

[20] In 1958, as many as fifty million people were in schools of some sort in the Soviet Union. Ten percent of the appropriate age group was attending higher educational facilities as compared with approximately 35 percent in the U.S.A., yet the number of places and institutions are strictly non-comparable. See George Z. F. Bereday, William W. Brickman, and Gerald Read, *The Changing Soviet School* (Boston: Houghton Mifflin Company, 1960), pp. 7ff.

during the years the democratic [Communist] regime has existed. From a school of the *bourgeoisie*, based on social and property inequality, from a servile weapon of the ruling clique of exploiter-capitalists, the Czech schools have been transformed into a really public school which educates conscious builders of Socialism."[21]

Next, "extenuating circumstances" leading to the change are offered. "Although certain reforms were established in Czechoslovakia on the basis of the 'Law of the Unified School' by the National Assembly in May, 1948, and the April, 1953, Act reducing the term of compulsory instruction from 9 to 8 years and the term of instruction in the complete secondary school from 13 to 11 years, some dissatisfaction with the program still existed. Among the chief reasons appended for change were (1) overloading and extended homework; (2) failure of the school to enroll sufficient numbers of children from the worker and peasant background; and (3) the adolescent was found, at age 14, in many cases incapable of correctly choosing a future vocation (in this the school could not help him, since almost no kind of work in vocational guidance was conducted)."[22] Since we have just considered the same situation in the USSR, this plea has a familiar refrain.

Continuing, the Kasvin-Shibanov report then reveals the expedient chosen. "[Thus] the Central Committee of the Communist Party of Czechoslovakia at the 11th Congress proposed a series of measures which will contribute to the further development of public education in the country and to the regulation of the school system with the object of bringing it closer to the needs of Socialist construction. . . . In his speech to the Congress, Comrade A. [Antonin] Novotny said, 'The chief task of our school must become the training of thoroughly developed people, who possess the basic facts of knowledge in the field of science and technology and at the same time are trained for skilled physical labor and conscious participation in

---

[21] G. A. Kasvin and A. A. Shibanov, "The Reform of the Schools in the Czechoslovak Republic," *Soviet Education*, I, No. 4 (February, 1959), 64-70.

[22] *Ibid.*, p. 66.

the construction of Communist society. To create such a truly Socialist school means, by all possible methods, to join teaching in school increasingly more tightly with the productive labor of pupils so that they acquire not only working habits, but, in the senior classes of the secondary schools, also gain a basic skill in the field on some kind of working occupation. . . ."[23]

Two basic plans have been set up (1) for use in predominantly industrial areas; and (2) for agricultural regions. Notwithstanding this orientation, each student is given some contact with the alternate phase of work at some time during his study in Years VI-IX. Likewise, the yearly totals progress from eighty-nine hours of instruction per annum in Class VI to a total of 165 hours in Class IX. At the primary level, all pupils participate in work with plastics and clay, wood and metal, fabrics, paper and cardboard, and engage in "socially useful labor" appropriate to their sex and grade level.

At the third level, Classes X through XII, the general polytechnical education is combined with production training in specialties of a wide range. Training in cities is in the bases of textile production and in the bases of the construction industry; and in the bases of machine-building and of the leading branches of heavy industry where appropriate. The program in agricultural areas is based on crop raising, livestock production, and mechanical engineering. (See tables on pp. 266-67.)

In deference to their greatest educational prophet—possibly the world's greatest—Jan Amos Comenius (in Czech, Komensky), the Czechoslovakian Academy of Sciences published, in the tercentenary of his epochal work, a photolithic edition of the Amsterdam imprint of *Opera Didactica Omnia*. The introduction (reproduced in the national language, Latin, Russian, English, French, German, and Spanish) runs as follows: "After three centuries in Komensky's native country, there arise the conditions that will make possible the realization of his most daring plans. The Socialist society realizes the unified school system from the primary school up to the

---

[23] *Ibid.*, p. 67; see also E. P. Gusarov, "Labor as a Factor in the Pupil's Upbringing," *Soviet Education*, I, No. 5 (March, 1959), 29-32. Contains anecdotes and anthropometrical studies.

highest school standard, as Komensky has proposed it; in the Socialist society all children are given a general education without any discrimination of sex, social origin, and property as it was Komensky's idea."[24]

Quite obviously, some distortion intrudes here; it hardly seems possible that the great, world-minded Moravian bishop would actually approve the Marxist system; thus we have merely another example of the devices whereby the Communist leadership seizes each possible opportunity to wring propaganda value from every circumstance.

In Czechoslovakia, conditions—on the surface—do appear much brighter, however, for the success of the Communist system than in some others of the satellites. There has been a continued rise in industrial production —yet attributable largely to an increased output per worker (in American terms, speedup). The third Five-Year Plan hopes to extract even more from the exploited working masses. Nevertheless, despite daily notice of production records being shattered, shortages still appear in the domestic market. Whether purchasing razor blades, wire mattresses, notions, kitchen equipment, fresh meat, fruit, or vegetables, one must queue up or (if a member of the privileged group) show a special permit from the Red bureaucracy.

Gradually (it is reported) the populace in even this most successful of the "People's Democracies" are "getting their fill and are beginning to ask some embarrassing questions. Every so often the closely-woven net of the secret police reports that people are getting wise to the real situation."[25] Then from all the agencies of mass

---

[24] Joannes Amos Comenius, *Opera Didactica Omnia* (Editio anni 1657 lucis ope expressa), 3 volumes (Pragae: Academica Scientiarum Bohemoslovanica, MCMLVII). See also Joseph S. Roucek, "Czechoslovakia's Higher Education," *Journal of Higher Education*, Vol. XXVII (January, 1956), and William W. Brickman, "Three Centuries of Comenius' Contributions to Education," *School and Society*, LXXXVI (April 26, 1958), 193-94, for a list of other publications under Czech auspices lauding Comenius' great contributions to the science of education.

[25] *Sudeten Bulletin*, VIII, No. 3 (March, 1960), 76; see also quotations from *Rudé Právo* (Prague) in defense of the Marxist policy, p. 77. Dr. Norman P. Auburn in "How Russia is Sovietizing Her European Satellites," *Cross and Crescent*, XLVII, No. 4 (No-

communication issues a flood of propaganda describing
the excess of all essential goods that the kind Soviet
brothers have just made available to their poor relations
in Czechoslovakia.

Poland's Program Under the Khrushchev Reform

If Czechoslovakia represents Moscow's most tractable
satellite, Poland—along with Hungary before the 1956
hecatomb—is the most troublesome. With this potential
danger in mind, immediately after the seizure in 1944
and under the wings of the Red Army, educational control became one of the first bastions of Marxism. Declaring that its policies in education must be based on
(1) the broadening of the social composition of youth in
schools, and (2) the "democratization" of higher education, a "nationwide" educational conference was held
in Lódz in June, 1945. Here the basic plans for school
revision were elaborated; the changes suggested were
formalized by a decree on November 23, 1945.[26]

So the educational policy of the post-1945 Polish government (Marxist) contemplated a gradual replacement
of the old Polish system by one based on the educational
principles utilized by the Soviet Union. Although the
Red Regime expanded the size of the school system, it—
at the same time—narrowed the range and scope of
studies. Everything was to be controlled by central
ministerial bodies. The stated goal was to (1) indoctrinate along Marxist Socialist lines and (2) to produce
quickly, and endeavor to maintain, a skilled labor force
in order to carry out the government's economic blueprint for a new industrial expansion tied to the USSR.

"On February 25, 1948, a decree was passed on the
'universal duty of preparing the youth in vocational,
physical education, and military fields.' Each boy and
girl between 16 and 21 was obliged to serve for six

---

vember, 1960), pp. 27-30, pictures Czechoslovakia as the sixteenth
Soviet "Republic" of the USSR.

   [26] For a good account of the background of contemporary Polish
education, see Nellie Apanasewicz and William K. Medlin, *Educational Systems in Poland* (Washington: U.S. Department of Health,
Education, and Welfare, March, 1959), No. 12, 32 pp.

months with troops of the 'Service for Poland.' a paramilitary organization. Youth were to work for six hours a day and to spend the remaining time on education, recreation, and ideological indoctrination."[27]

Subsequently new textbooks on biology, history, and geography, rewritten by a special group of Marxist historians, were ready for use. Russian language instruction and Russian literary classics likewise became a part of the revised curricula. The chief purpose of the new Polish educational system was to emphasize industrialization and to build close ties with the Soviet Union.

Currently children between the ages of three and seven may attend nursery schools where special attention is given to play and games so organized that the child may gain a feeling for cooperative living. He learns to count, measure, and help with home duties. Subjects including drawing, music, and the Polish language are taught. Although such schools are maintained by the central government, they are operated by the local school authorities, factories, or other places of employment—not excluding social organizations. If no facilities for regular nursery schools have been provided, centers are established to operate for a few hours' duration, once or twice per week.

The seven-year elementary school (reduced from eight years and initiated in 1948-49) offers the basic education; it is compulsory between the ages of seven and fourteen. However, if a student has not completed the prescribed courses (including the Marxism-Leninism requirement), he must remain in school until he reaches sixteen. This of course is another safeguard in the drive to establish a young and basically educated work force, trained both in the rudiments and in the Communist ideology—especially the latter.

There are in existence two types of secondary schools: the general high school or lyceum, and the vocational or technical school. The lyceum represents a fusion of the former gymnasium (lower secondary) and the original lyceum (upper secondary) ; the former twelve-year course

---

[27] Apanasewicz and Medlin, *op. cit.*, p. 19.

has been reduced to eleven. Entrance is gained through the presentation of the primary school certificate, written and oral examinations in Polish and mathematics, and an oral examination in history and Marxian philosophy; plus (naturally) the proper recommendations from his previous school authorities and youth group leaders.

In the area of higher education the decree of October 28, 1947, abolished traditional forms of academic organization and nationalized all private higher schools—with the exception of the Catholic University at Lublin. In 1950, control passed from the Ministry of Education to the Ministry of Higher Education. In 1951, a new Polish Academy of Sciences—modeled on the Soviet organization—superseded the ancient Polish Academy of Sciences and Letters. The purposes of these controls are perfectly clear; Poles are an individualistic people; they must be taught organization and the Marxist dialectic.

Regardless of all this, the government still was unhappy with the lack of cooperation found and, after the political changes made effective in October, 1956, with the reinstatement of Wladyslaw Gomulka as First Secretary of the Polish United Workers' party, it granted a certain degree of autonomy to universities by allowing them to elect members of the Commission on Higher Education. They have been given some authority also to develop their own courses of study although—in such a situation —this freedom may be reduced as rapidly as it was gained. Moreover, in all these particular matters, Communist motives are not always clear and frequently the granting of new freedoms merely represents squeeze plays in the making.

Prior to 1956, required subjects were Marxism-Leninism, dialectical and historical materialism, political economy, and the Russian language. Since then, these obligations have been somewhat relaxed. Chairs in philosophy have been reestablished, and social science teaching again includes the study of all major points. Nevertheless, speaking of economics only (although this may be considered the epitome of Marxism), the dilemma in Soviet education soon becomes apparent. Scottish economist Ronald L. Meek notes: "It is clear that the student who follows the course . . . will obtain a thorough grounding in the economic ideas of Marx, Engels, and Lenin, together with some knowledge of current Soviet criticisms of "bourgeois" economic theory. It is not clear—although naturally a great deal depends upon the way in which the subject is taught—that he will obtain anything like a really objective view of economic conditions in the contemporary capitalist world."[28]

Summing up the Polish program, it can be said that "it clearly bears the marks of compromise. On the one hand, it reflects a certain revulsion against the dogmatism, apologetics and uniformity which seem to have been characteristic of the teaching of political economy in Poland in the years prior to 1956, and also a feeling (on the part of at least a substantial minority) that the Marxist economists have unduly neglected some of the more positive achievements of 'bourgeois' economics. On the other hand, it reflects the view that a political economy course in a country like Poland should remain basically Marxist in character, and that the freedom of the lecturer to put forth his own views should exist only within this Marxist framework. . . ."[29]

In September, 1958, less than a week after Khrushchev's announcement of educational reforms in the Soviet Union, First Secretary Gomulka declared that Poland should follow the lead of the USSR in measures to tighten the link between education and work. He said that the new program would be a means of integrating university students with the "actualities" of Socialism, politically as well as economically. This, in effect, would serve, too, to diminish possible student leverage as a separate element in society.

Two goals motivate Soviet higher educational planning, both in Poland and the whole of East Central Europe. First, the objective is to replace the old middle-class intelligentsia—too strong in its allegiance to Western culture—with a new "intelligentsia" of workers and peasants, whose support of the Communist system will

---

[28] Ronald L. Meek, "The Teaching of Economics in the USSR and Poland," *Soviet Studies* (Glasgow), X, No. 4 (April, 1959), 347.
[29] *Ibid.*, p. 357.

be insured by its own self-interest as well as by indoctrination in Marxism-Leninsm; secondly, the avowed
function of higher education under Communism is to
train specialists for science, industry, and even professional duties in the expanding Socialist empire. Overall,
its objective is to prepare "not only specialists, not only
class-conscious citizens, but class-conscious fighting Communists who will take an active part in political life after
graduation."[30]

Consequently, admission to the university becomes both
an academic and a political hurdle. The question of prestige in connection with matriculation was discussed in
Zycie Szkoly Wyzszy (Warsaw) in June, 1958: "The
opinion is common that in order to be admitted to a University one has to pay, one has to find somebody who will
fix up the matter for a certain remuneration (bribe). . . .
This creates an unwholesome atmosphere, which threatens the good name of the Universities and of the teaching staff. . . . This kind of intervention no doubt has its
roots in the errors of the past years, when unwritten
privileges or reservations were in force regarding admittance to Universities. It was no secret to anybody that
during those year the pupils of the 11th (final high school)
classes joined the ZMP (Communist Youth League) in
droves in order 'to get into the university.' "[31] Naturally,
the best Communist defense is an offense, and here we
see the admission of a past "error" used as a screen to
suggest purity in the present. The Western world would
do well to learn to understand Marxist double-talk, although indeed no special codebook is necessary.

According to *Polityka* (October 4, 1958), the proportion of worker-peasant students in the universities in
Poland has fallen; during the past academic year 29.7
percent of the students were of working-class origin, 22.9
percent peasant, and 42.4 percent intelligentsia.[32]

Nevertheless, one reads in *Trybuna Ludu* ("The People's Tribune"—Worker's party organ) that the principle

---

[30] *Pravda* (Bratislava), May 19, 1958. As quoted in *East Europe*,
VII, No. 10 (October, 1958), 14.
[31] As quoted in *East Europe*, IX, No. 5 (May, 1959), 19.
[32] *Ibid.*, as quoted on p. 21.

of ability-selection would be maintained and a further suggestion that the decline in peasant class admissions was due to a lack of interest on the part of the worker-peasant parents, plus the inferior showing of worker-peasant students on entrance tests because of the lower academic level of provincial schools.[33] The meaning of this ploy will perhaps be cleared through further administrative regulation.

Yet the problem has not reached a solution of much moment. A November, 1960, report, produced by the Central Office for Sociology in Lódz at the instigation of the Ministry for Higher Education, indicates that of the total number of applicants for university level education, the greatest number, 42.6 percent were offspring of the intelligentsia; 30.3 percent were from the working class; and the children of farmers, 20.5 percent, made up the balance.[34]

Furthermore, 52 percent of the graduates of technical high schools, applying for admission to institutes of technology, did not pass the entrance exam; nor did 35.3 percent of the graduates of general high schools seeking entrance pass. Functionaries of the Communist party in charge of Polish educational policy are quite concerned. They have judged the cause of this unsatisfactory situation to lie in the secondary schools, where a growing lack of interest in higher learning has been noted on the part of senior pupils and where the number of farm and working-class youth is steadily decreasing.

To correct this difficulty, new entrance examination techniques have been devised including the placing of teachers from high schools and other secondary schools on the board of college entrance examiners. Scholarships, likewise, are to be provided for the children of "shortsighted" parents. Dr. Eugenia Kraskowska, Deputy Minister for Higher Education, has promised to improve the social composition of future university student bodies by the admission of more pupils from workers' and farmers' families.[35]

---

[33] *Trybuna Ludu*, May 3, 1958. As quoted in *loc. cit.*
[34] *Sudeten Bulletin*, VIII, No. 11 (November, 1960), 290.
[35] *Ibid.*

In certain contrast to the above, Professor Halasz reports that: "They [the regimes] encouraged adults to attend night courses and shortened the curriculum so that they might be admitted to technical colleges. This class made good, even outstanding specialists, but lacked well-rounded interests, a balanced culture, and a stimulating background upon which to draw."[36] Each of these observations serves to highlight the difficulties inherent in the Soviet educational plan of providing a "worker's and peasant's intelligentsia."

The Political Emphasis in East Germany

On the surface, education in the "German Democratic Republic" bears a strong resemblance to the Single Track 8-4 system of the United States of America, and indeed perhaps it was so designed as to create this impression. The elementary schools (Classes I-VIII) are coeducational, utilize the self-contained classroom idea, and operate on what appears to be "progressive" methodologies; departmentalism, however, does begin, with Class V—a practice usually reserved in the United States for the seventh and eighth grades, or the junior high school.

The secondary schools comprise Classes IX-XII— typical of American practice when the division is not made in terms of Junior-Senior High School organization. Yet there is a "Middle School," a borrowing from the earlier caste-oriented German educational practice. The Middle School technically includes Classes IV through X and is designed to furnish a slightly more advanced program than that of the conventional elementary school, although not as specialized as that of the high school. It leads to a Certificate, however, and thus represents one leaving level of the school system.

In practice, Classes IX and X are sometimes attached to an eight-year elementary school; theoretically, when this expedient has been chosen, the goals of the school are presumed to change likewise. As another alternative, the secondary school itself may provide these upper classes; and of a type which is suitable to the needs of a

---

[36] Halasz, *op. cit.*, p. 302.

terminal ten-year program. Again, the Middle School is sometimes found with its own independent organization—but this is the exception, not the rule.

The regular educational program in East Germany—like that of the Nazi Third Reich—is buttressed by extra-class activities calculated to develop allegiance and loyalty to Communism and also to provide a complete program for adolescent students; such group activity including the work of the "Ernst Thaelmann Organization" (Young Pioneers) and the *Frien Deutschen Jugend* (Free German Youth) is beginning in many localities to supplant the work of home and Church.[37]

In the schools themselves, all textbooks and other materials are closely supervised. Books are published by the state publishing house. No books other than the approved texts are permitted to be used. Teaching aids, including films, charts, etc., are likewise provided by an arm of the Ministry of Public Education. At the beginning of the Soviet "occupation," Russian texts translated into German were utilized in the secondary schools. Although new "German" books have now been provided, their tone is still pro-Soviet and—in the sciences especially—is overladen with records of the accomplishments of the Russian people and with references to the "class struggle."

The similarity between the approach in the satellites and that in the Soviet Union is pronounced indeed. For example, the syllabus of the R.S.F.S.R. (Moscow) lays the following injunction on all teachers: "In the teaching of Russian, emphasis must be laid on the profound patriotism of Russian literature. . . . The teaching of the history of the U.S.S.R. must develop in school-children a love for the heroic past of our people which throughout the whole of its history has displayed unexampled brav-

---

[37] See Paul S. Bodenman, *Education in the Soviet Zone of Germany* (Washington, D.C.: United States Department of Health, Education, and Welfare, 1959); *Die Pionierorganisation "Ernst Thaelmann" in der Sowjetzone* (Bonn: Bundesministerium fuer gesamtdeutsche Fragen, 1957); Gerhard Moebus, *Erziehung zum Hass ("Education for Hate")*, (Berlin: Morus Verlag, 1956); Joseph S. Roucek, "Nazi and Soviet Techniques of Extended Strategy," *Social Science*, XXVIII, No. 3 (June, 1953), 160-70; see also Kenneth V. Lottich, "Extracurricular Indoctrination in East Germany," *Comparative Education Review*, VI, No. 3 (February, 1963), 209-11.

ery. . . . The Russians stopped the Mongols and saved Europe from them. They saved Europe from being enslaved by the French and Napoleon. They have saved the whole world from the most terrible bondage which ever threatened anyone—the bondage of Hitlerite Germany. . . . The teaching of geography [too] must reveal the innumerable resources of our great country."[38]

Further Illustrations

Curricula in the Soviet's East European satellites show a remarkable homogeneity, whether one is dealing with Czechoslovakia, Poland, or East Germany. And as is easily observed, the education system in East Germany is only synthetically a one-track vehicle regardless of the lip service paid to "democracy." It has been noted many times that party considerations and gross indoctrination render every phase of Soviet education—regardless of the form of its organization—anything but a democratic implement.

Further illustrations of the Marxist master plan may be found in a consideration of the plight of education in the Baltic States, Bulgaria, and the Ukraine.

Because of the strength of Roman Catholicism in the eastern Baltic States, the Communists from the first have endeavored to wean the population away from their religious moorings. Heavy taxation was imposed on all churches in this newly acquired territory and exorbitant rents charged for the use of dwellings which formerly were domiciled by the clergy. Education suffered too. It is well known that, in Lithuania, the Catholic Faculties of Theology and Catholic High Schools were suppressed; only one of Lithuania's four seminaries was allowed to function and the number of students was reduced; religious services in the army, hospitals, asylums and prisons were forbidden; religious teaching in the schools was discontinued and this portion of the curriculum replaced by lessons on Marxist-Leninist materialism.[39]

---

[38] Quoted in Eric Ashby, *Scientist in Russia* (London: Penguin Books, 1947), p. 51.

[39] See Judith (Countess) Listowel, "Luxury Tax on Churches," *East Europe and Soviet Russia*, VII, No. 327 (April 19, 1951),

Although Bulgaria's position, geographically speaking, is much less conducive to dissent at Communist practice than either East Germany or Poland, there now is a strong anti-Soviet feeling in the universities. A former Bulgarian student—now resident in the United States— cites mass resentment by Bulgarian student groups during the 1956 Hungarian Revolt. He reports that each candidate for university training is required to join the Communist party and that the study of Marxism and the Russian language are fundamental courses—as indeed they are throughout the Soviet slave empire.[40] "Yakimov" deplores the subjectivity of the Marxist system which stacks the cards in examinations and progress in favor of fellow travelers, declaring that, at long last, his native land will "join forces with other Communist-oppressed nations and throw out the Red Army."

Indeed, persistent troubles with students has been the Bulgarian Workers' government's lot. After two consecutive students' demonstrations in Sofia in January, 1958, over one thousand were seized and shipped to slave-labor camps. In order to forestall a popular revolt spearheaded by youth, the regime has recently deported other thousands of young men and women to Khazakastan on so-called "voluntary" contracts. On arrival they were scheduled to participate—or so the official communiqué read—"with the U.S.S.R.'s youth in Communist construction."[41]

Life in Sofia—called by the Bulgarians "the most beautiful fruit of Europe,"—pictures "the average citizen, the average Bulgar as an extremely charming person, who despite his hard life, has not lost his happy disposi-

---

11-14; also Kenneth V. Lottich, "The Plight of the Baltic States," *Sudeten Bulletin*, Vol. IX, No. 2 (February, 1961), for a review of general conditions in Estonia, Latvia, and Lithuania.

[40] Andrei Yakimov (pseud.?), "Entrance in Bulgarian Colleges More Difficult than American," report of an interview with G. A. Burden, *Montana Kaimin* (Missoula), March 4, 1960, p. 1.

[41] Joseph S. Roucek, "The Plight of Bulgaria," *American Bulgarian Review*, IX, No. 2 (Spring, 1959), 25-29; for a rather thorough discussion of some of the problems faced by the Soviet regime in Moscow itself in relation to a large section of dissenting youth (the "jet set" and the "*stilyagi*"), see "Conflict Between the Generations," *Soviet Survey, An Analysis of Cultural Trends in the U.S.S.R.* (London), No. 12 (February, 1957), Part I, pp. 1-7.

tion, and whose hospitality, as before, knows no bounds." Yet the unfree condition of the Bulgarians, the constant Communist rigging of education, the economic ups and downs, and the "tiresome official propaganda against the so-called capitalist-imperialist West," which forces the habitants to wear a mask, is strongly resented.[42]

The well-publicized shift in the Soviet Union and in the ten East European satellites to "polytechnical education"—basically a work program handled in existing industrial facilities and superimposed on the existing educational situation—has not been completely accepted (as noted in the preceding chapters).[43] Even in the oldest satellite (the Ukraine, not discussed specifically in this book because its seizure occurred prior to World War II), certain repercussions have followed the placing into effect of the work program. Yet this satellite, one which, however, bears the name "republic" of the USSR, indicating a deeper degree of captivity than that of those of the western periphery, raises a fundamental objection to polytechnicalization. A dispatch from Pawlisz, the Ukrainian S.S.R., indicates a measure of dissatisfaction with the Khrushchev Reform. "The Pawlisz educators believe that the incorporation of productive work into the programs of general education fails to give good results. [They say that] most students consider this type of work a necessary evil."[44] This communication goes on to say that an indigenous plan—basically progressive— designed to stimulate student interest and to develop innate abilities, is completely preferable, and leads to better life adjustment—even under collectivization. These Ukrainian educators, however (as is the case in each republic or satellite of the USSR), are bound by the wishes

---

[42] Karl Rau, " 'The Most Beautiful Fruit of Europe' Under the Red Star," *American Bulgarian Review*, IX, No. 2 (Spring, 1959), 30-31.

[43] For a quick summary of contrasts between the new Soviet system including polytechnicalization and the general system of education in the Western world, see Elmer H. Wilds and Kenneth V. Lottich, *Foundations of Modern Education* (New York: Holt, Rinehart, and Winston, 1961), chap. XX, pp. 438-61.

[44] J. Tadeusz Wiloch, "New Models in Soviet Education," *Comparative Education Review*, III, No. 2 (October, 1959), 9-10.

of the Kremlin as exercised through their local party heirarchy.

The unsatisfactory condition under which the university student in the Soviet Union and in its East European satellites fails to receive a balanced education (and this applies to the upper secondary classes as well) may be summed up in the observation of Ronald L. Meek, a Western economist who taught in Russian and Polish universities: "On the one hand, there is a natural desire on the part of teachers of economics to move away from a purely institutional approach to the Soviet economy towards a 'political economy of Socialism,' methodologically similar to the political economy of capitalism. . . . This desire has been reinforced by the political desirability of combating what the course calls 'subjectivist' views on the question of economic laws (particularly in the field of planning), and has a tendency to describe as 'economic laws' a number of basic features of the Soviet economy which appear to have an especially strong air of 'necessity' about them.

"On the other hand, it is fairly clear that some of these so-called 'economic laws' which Soviet economists have propounded . . . have very little except this air of 'necessity' in common with most of the traditional economic laws adduced by the political economy of capitalism. . . . A realization of this fact, whether conscious or unconscious, probably lies at the bottom of the Soviet economists' feeling of dissatisfaction with the 'political economy of Socialism' as it has been developed."[45] This surely represents quite a crack in Soviet higher education and consequently a rather grave defect in Soviet specialized training—especially in the social sciences, the area of their vaunted superiority.

Other Dissatisfactions

Another problem exists in connection with the plight of the creative scholars, writers, and artists in the Soviet orbit (and indeed this dilemma was highlighted by the dilemma of Boris Pasternak in the immediate present).

---

[45] Meek, *op. cit.*, pp. 348-49.

Halasz comments that these "like the aristocracy of the court of an absolute monarch" have been placed at the top of the social hierarchy with only the Stakhanovites equaling them "when they stood on the dais to accept the yearly prizes on the Soviet model." Yet their problem was a most serious one. "The Party expected him [or her] to turn out manuscripts and art work that lived up to their standards, and this became increasingly difficult for an honest intellectual to do." As time went on, "It was difficult to decide whom to envy or pity: the artists and authors whose work had been printed or exhibited and applauded unanimously, or the talented but uncompromising ones whom the regime subsidized but whose works never saw the light of day."[46]

The Educational Outlook

Turning now to conclusions regarding the outlook for education in East Central Europe and to a summation of some of the common and salient principles that characterize Marxist education and its application in the European satellites and Red China, we find:

(1) A constant invocation of "scientific" Marxism-Leninism, which assumes the status of what in many Western lands would be considered a religious faith —complete with prophets, saints, sanctions, and sacrifices;

(2) Recourse in the schools and elsewhere to a Communist system of morality based on Marxist-Leninist materialism; its naturalistic base pronounces necessity, the decision of the party hierarchy, and, in fact, all Soviet law as moral: hence adherence to these is a manifestation of the chief expression of "objective" Communist morality;

(3) The creation of a new "monism"—the relationship between "work" and academic studies. In Marxist theory, these are not entirely supplementary as might be supposed, nor even complementary, but reflect concretely only different phases of the same real existence. (In Western eyes the work program is, of course, nothing but necessity.)

---

[46] Halasz, *op. cit.*, pp. 302-4.

(4) The polytechnicalization of education in the USSR, Red China and in the satellites; new school organization and functions are designed theoretically to implement Marxist dogma related to the work program; the practical effect is to prepare a larger, better trained work force; economize the educational effort; place the satellites in an even more utilitarian position; and provide for a more thorough indoctrination in the state ideology;

(5) The creation, through the university system, of a "People's Intelligentsia," respectful of, and subservient to Marxism-Leninism. Practically, this is secured through quota and admissions policies and through special "guidance" of workers' and peasants' offspring in higher education situations together with a lavish distribution of scholarships;

(6) The organization of Workers' and Peasants' Faculties in the Socialist universities—a device calculated to secure the allegiance as well as the minds of these ideologically favored groups; scholarships and increased stipends are offered as specific incentives. (In practice, the work done under Workers' and Peasants' Faculties is not of university grade.) ;

(7) The reversion, in the Soviet Union itself, to the eight-year school and the generalization of this tendency in the satellites. While a three-year secondary school—exhibiting many forms—does indeed exist, and, in theory, will become universal, the vast majority of students between the ages of fifteen and eighteen will, if they enter it at all, be engaged in what in the West would be considered continuation school or lower technical training. Only an elite is to continue higher education; thus the lower groups will be freed for use in the work force; consequently, these will not be exposed to the possible leisure or potential error which the Soviet has found by experience sometimes accompanies upper academic education, especially under atypical circumstances;

(8) A strong tendency toward the organization of "boarding schools," another by-product and perhaps even a reason for the recent Soviet shift, is now being felt in the republics and is also filtering into

the program of the satellites. The stated purpose of boarding schools is to render the work program more feasible (with the accent on polytechnicalization and advanced training which cannot be provided for in the smaller communities); actually, such schools are designed to promote a longer school day, more rigid supervision, and—most significant of all—direct experience in communal living;

(9) There are two sides to Soviet education: formal school activities and the extracurricular program. From the Marxist standpoint, the second is most significant. Students are urged or pressured into affiliation with the various youth groups, circles, or camps which have been organized for special or general purposes. When pressure is used, it frequently is oblique—but nonetheless compelling; in cases of certain organizations, membership becomes obligatory if progress in secondary or higher education is anticipated. From the standpoint of the state, such groups are the universally indoctrinating agencies;

(10) The final objective, both educational and political (for here it would be impossible to separate these aspects of Socialist life), is the furthering, by every means at hand, of the ideological struggle between Communism and the West—the basic purpose behind the organization of the Bolshevik revolution. As it has already been correctly interpreted, the Red regimes would, consistently and inexorably—when and wherever possible, by sustained attrition or rapacious seizure—"execute the testament of Peter the Great."[47]

Furthermore, as German Chancellor Konrad Adenauer once aptly remarked, "To Nikita S. Khrushchev, Ivan the Terrible and Peter the Great mean more than Karl Marx."[48]

---

[47] For the historical meaning of this phrase and also its restrictions see pp. 38, 178, 203. While Red China can hardly partake of the inclinations attributed to the USSR, Mao Tse-tung, obviously—as shown in Korea, Tibet, India and Indo-China—is not without a certain strategy of his own, to which he brings the aid of education.

[48] Sergius M. Riis, *Karl Marx, Master of Fraud* (New York: Robert Speller & Sons, 1962), p. 39.

INDEX

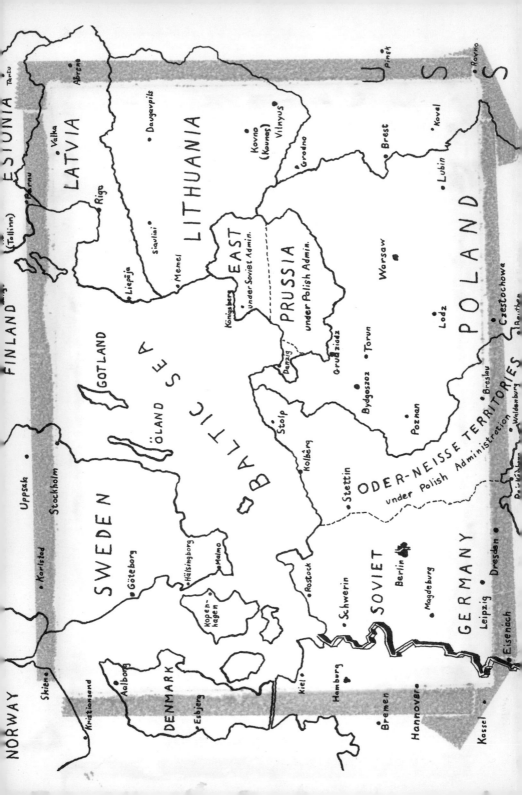